I Spy

I Spy

A History and Episode Guide to the Groundbreaking Television Series

MARC CUSHMAN *and* LINDA J. LAROSA

with a foreword by Robert Culp

McFarland & Company, Inc., Publishers
Jefferson, North Carolina, and London

LIBRARY OF CONGRESS CATALOGUING-IN-PUBLICATION DATA

Cushman, Marc, 1954–
I spy : a history and episode guide to the groundbreaking television series / Marc Cushman and Linda J. LaRosa ; with a foreword by Robert Culp.
p.   cm.
Includes bibliographical references and index.

ISBN 13: 978-0-7864-2750-5
(softcover : 50# alkaline paper) ∞

1. I spy (Television program).   I. LaRosa, Linda J., 1951– .   II. Title.
PN1992.77.I27C87   2007   791.45'72 — dc22   2006038055

British Library cataloguing data are available

©2007 Marc Cushman and Linda J. LaRosa. All rights reserved

No part of this book may be reproduced or transmitted in any form or by any means, electronic or mechanical, including photocopying or recording, or by any information storage and retrieval system, without permission in writing from the publisher.

On the cover: Bill Cosby (as Alexander Scott) and
Robert Culp (as Kelly Robinson) in
I Spy (NBC/Photofest)

Manufactured in the United States of America

*McFarland & Company, Inc., Publishers
Box 611, Jefferson, North Carolina 28640
www.mcfarlandpub.com*

To Robert Culp and Bill Cosby,
for the friendship that changed the face of television
and opened the eyes of a generation

Acknowledgments

A special thank you is extended to Ruth Engelhardt, attorney for the Sheldon Leonard Estate and Three F Productions at the William Morris Agency, for opening the doors.

This book would not have been possible without the help of the following individuals: In alphabetical order, then, with thanks:

Eric Bercovici; Andrea Bershad; Norman Brokaw; Calvin Brown; Ned Comstock, USC Cinema & Television Library; Hillard Elkins; Bernice Fine; David Fine; Ernest Frankel; Anthony Friedkin; Gregory Friedkin; Earle Hagen; Image Entertainment; NBC archives; Ronald Jacobs; Salome Jens; Steven Kandel; Steven Kates; Joy Fielding; Martin Landau; Jerry Ludwig; Barbara McNair; Rick Mittleman; Octavio Olvera, UCLA Library, Department of Special Collections; Alan Oppenheimer; Barry Oringer; The Peter Rogers Organization; Michael Price; Robin Roberts, Screen Actors Guild; Mark Rydel; Richard Sarafian; Warner Brothers Records; John Warren; Michael Zagor

Marc Cushman thanks Michael Zabiegalski, and sisters Dawn and Druanne, for turning the channel to *I Spy* on Wednesday nights in 1965.

Linda J. LaRosa sends a special thank you to Ben Camardi at the Harold Matson Company.

Both authors thank Debbie Lazar for her enthusiasm and research.

And, finally, thank you to Bill Cosby and Robert Culp, for their gift to the fans, first the series, now this book. To Bill, for his example in walking the higher road; and to Robert, for his contribution of time, memories, and photographs, all helping to raise the bar.

Contents

Acknowledgments	vii
Foreword by Robert Culp	1
Prologue	3
1. The History of a Genre	7
2. The Road to Hong Kong	29
3. The First Block of Episodes	48
4. On to Japan	73
5. The Second Block of Episodes	86
6. South of the Border	110
7. The Third Block of Episodes	118
8. Wrapping Season One	143
9. Basking in the Sun	151
10. The Fourth Block of Episodes	160
11. Growth, Genre, Gratitude, and Gondolas	182
12. The Fifth Block of Episodes	192
13. Exposure	224
14. The Sixth Block of Episodes	228
15. Wrapping Season Two	262
16. Tie-Ins	269
17. Morocco to Greece	278
18. The Seventh Block of Episodes	284
19. A Change in Plans	310
20. The Eighth Block of Episodes	315
21. The Grind Continues	334
22. The Ninth Block of Episodes	338
23. Wrapping Season Three	356
24. The Fourth Season	362
25. *I Spy* Stripped	373
26. The First Reunion	379
27. The Second Reunion	388
28. The Third Reunion	402
29. The Fourth Reunion	415
Chapter Notes	419
Bibliography	425
Index	429

Foreword

There was one inexplicable cloud that gathered early in the festivities. Everybody tried to split us up. It seemed to be a national pastime, popular as baseball. Agents, managers, public relations guys, total strangers (male and female), magazine writers, newspaper critics—even my bright, well-informed wife wasn't above it. Only our directors and our producers seemed immune to this effort that was sweeping the countryside—a bizarre, primitive need to drive a wedge between Bill and me.

I thought for a while it was just my own perfectly normal actor paranoia. But Bill noticed it, too. Especially in our friends. Apparently to curry favor, they would suggest malfeasance, repeat things they had "heard" about one of us, trying, or intending to try, to take something away from the other.

He and I talked about it, shrugged and simply dismissed it as people being weird.

In truth, the way our friendship came together made it pretty much bulletproof, given who he was and who I was, at base, long before we met.

Still, even that can't explain how the friendship could last for the next forty years, a bit frayed and tarnished by missed opportunities, bad luck, mischance and vague misunderstanding, yes, but still the same steady belief, surviving all else, the same basic commitment to cover each other's back to the end, rather like the characters we played.

Robert Culp

Prologue

It was May 1966. A 28-year-old man stood in the spotlight before millions.

Bill Cosby was a triple threat before he stepped on stage that night: co-host, nominee, and the result of a great team effort to break television's color barrier. This door had been barred to blacks and their exclusion continued to be tacitly enforced by the industry up to this moment at this Emmy Awards' broadcast.

And now here he was, sharing the stage with Danny Kaye, an acknowledged star of film and television for nearly three decades.

But Cosby had been relatively unknown just one year earlier. At that time, he had two comedy albums out. They sold in respectable numbers. He had been performing in all the usual clubs, gaining attention, bit by bit, joke by joke. And, like any up-and-coming comic with more than ten minutes' worth of good material, he had made a handful of the expected TV appearances. He even managed to get on *The Tonight Show with Johnny Carson* one night, a night when Johnny wasn't there.

That was 1964.

By the end of the year, something fantastic had happened. Cosby had become part of "Sheldon's Folly," as the brass at NBC had referred to it. It was a crazy, new venture—a series that would be the first to film around the world. It would have to invent new technology to achieve a seamless blend of location production and controlled studio photography. It was also going to be the first privately-owned television series.

Sheldon Leonard would borrow heavily to bankroll the entire endeavor. He would take the risks, and, if it hit, reap all the rewards.

This series, by the way, would also invent a new formula: the "buddy genre."

Previously, in the Hope-Crosby "road" pictures, or in comic pairings like Abbott and Costello, one member of the team was superior to the other—meaning, one was always the foil, the butt of the joke to the other. In *I Spy*, both men were equal, working toward a common goal and respecting the other's talents and intelligence. This had not been done before.

Later on, this groundbreaking template would be imitated by *Starsky & Hutch* and *Miami Vice*, and the big screen movies *48 Hours*, *Lethal Weapon*, and even *Butch Cassidy and the Sundance Kid*.

But it started here. Leonard, the high roller, wanted this series to be the first on television to star a white actor with a black partner.

Moreover, these two men, who would live in a world of espionage, would be seen on television traveling together, sharing hotel rooms, sharing bathrooms, and sharing drinking fountains. And the black spy, like the white spy, would carry a gun.

The affiliates in the Northeast might get behind this idea of Sheldon Leonard's, but what about in the South? How many NBC stations in Georgia, Alabama, the Carolinas, and even Florida, would refuse to clear this show about two men of different color, dead equal, judged only by the content of their character?

The network almost buckled.

And now, in that month of May, that year of 1966, this folly was nominated for Outstanding Dramatic Series. Sheldon Leonard had been nominated for Outstanding Direction. The series' writer-producers, Mort Fine and David Friedkin, were nominated for Outstanding Writing. Robert Culp, the recognized star of the series, had been nominated for Outstanding Acting in a Lead Role. And one other thing, this new guy, this comic who had never acted before, was also nominated—as Best Actor—not as a supporting player, but as a lead, against Culp.

Whichever man won, everyone knew that history had already been made.

The winner of the Emmy was announced. The name called was not Richard Crenna, for *Slattery's People*, or David Jansen, for *The Fugitive*, or David McCallum, for *The Man from U.N.C.L.E.*

And it wasn't Robert Culp either, for his role in this history making series, now known as *I Spy*.

It was the new guy. The guy Culp had fought for and had been giving acting lessons to, the guy who was cohosting the Emmys that night—the guy who had barely made a blip on the radar in the world of entertainment one year earlier.

Now Cosby walked back onto the stage. It had been a challenge for him to keep his cool and display humor and confidence to a television audience that could be cheering or hating him.

Cosby had no reason to believe that his cohost was feeling supportive, either. *I Spy*, scheduled opposite *The Danny Kaye Show*, had beaten Kaye every week in the ratings. And now Kaye had to share the spotlight with his rival, with one-half of the acting team that was threatening his very place on prime-time television.

"I wanted Bill to win every goddamn bit as much as *I* wanted to win," Culp recalled. "I thought, 'Hey, it will all sort out, we're here for a while.' And when his name was called, my heart leapt. I felt as pleased as if I had won. Because I did. He and I knew it. Nobody else really did. I wanted the show to win. Sheldon wanted it to win. And, at that moment, when they called Bill's name, I had vindication."[1]

As Cosby made his way to the podium, the world had changed. A door had been kicked opened, which would allow other black actors to get their chance, to be judged only by their talent.

This was history. Not just television history, but the real deal, and millions of people were watching.

Cosby accepted the trophy. He held it. He considered it. Then he looked out at the sea of celebrity faces and the row of cameras.

"I have to thank a man who brought me into his office—that talks out of the side of his mouth—and was talking straight," Cosby began.

A camera in the auditorium focused on Sheldon Leonard, sitting at his table near the front.

Cosby continued: "He looked at me and said, 'I'm going to put you on television.' I said, 'Yeah. Sure. Fine. You call me. I won't call you.'"

There was the expected laughter. The audience fully understood what a crazy notion Leonard's had been. And, yet, here Cosby was, holding the Emmy. The irony of it all deserved a laugh.

"I would also like to thank NBC for having guts," Cosby added.

There was robust applause, much of it from those who worked for NBC, even the ones who had tried to get Cosby kicked off the show twelve months before.

Then Cosby's eyes saw another man, his partner, the man who broke the barrier with him, his "other-self."

"I extend my hand to a man named Robert Culp," he said. "The guy took a comedian who couldn't do anything as far as acting is concerned, and he lost *this*—because he helped me."

Cosby held up the Emmy, then added, "That's the greatest thing a human being can ever do."

The *I Spy* ride had barely begun.

1
The History of a Genre

The Spies Who Came In Out of the Cold

Espionage makes good fiction.

The undercover spy made a significant first appearance in Baroness Orczy's 1905 *The Scarlet Pimpernel.*

Hot on its heels was W. Somerset Maughaum's *Ashenden: The British Agent*, in 1928, recalling the author's acquaintance of spying during World War I. This book would be filmed by Alfred Hitchcock and called *The Secret Agent.*

The character had been established: The Loner.

Into the mix went the innocent bystander in a light thriller written by John Buchan. His name may not ring a bell but the book will: *The 39 Steps.*

The aftermath of World War II brought out Graham Greene with *The Quiet American.* But another man would dominate the '50s.

The Rogue. The Ronin. The Prototype. He is the result of all this character evolution. He would become the standard by which every other spy would be judged for years. His look was tall, dark and handsome. He was daring, witty, had nine lives and lived them all with a cool passion for adventure and sexual conquest. His name was Bond. James Bond.

Ian Fleming, a member of British Naval Intelligence during World War II, a man who saw real life and death tales of espionage, moved to Jamaica where he built a house he named Goldeneye, then ventured into a new career as a writer.

Fleming's first book, *Casino Royale*, went to print in 1953, followed by *Live and Let Die* in 1954, *Moonraker* in 1955, *Diamonds Are Forever* in 1956, *From Russia with Love* in 1957, *Dr. No* in 1958, *Goldfinger* in 1959, *For Your Eyes Only* in 1960, *Thunderball* in 1961, *The Spy Who Loved Me* in 1962, *On Her Majesty's Secret Service* in 1963, *You Only Live Twice* in 1964, *The Man with the Golden Gun* in 1965 and *Octopussy* in 1966.

Exploring the dark corridors of brainwashing, Richard Condon published *The Manchurian Candidate* in 1959.

Still mining the vein of the lone rogue spy was Len Deighton, who wrote the blockbusters *The Ipcress Files* for publication in 1962 and *Funeral in Berlin* in 1964.

John LeCarre would both amplify the prototype—*The Spy Who Came in from the Cold* in 1963—and then destroy it eleven years later with *Tinker, Tailor, Soldier, Spy*, in the guise of a character named George Smiley, looking very much unlike James Bond, with thick glasses, thinning hair, and a body that was short and stocky.

A Genre Comes to Television

In the summer of 1961, as the cold war was raging in Europe between the United States, its allies, and the Soviet Union, a 30-minute espionage thriller was snuck on the air by CBS.

Suave & Deadly, Culp and Cosby, unreleased publicity photograph, 1965 (© 3F Prod.).

The show, the British-made *Danger Man*, starring Patrick McGoohan as secret agent John Drake, an Englishman working for NATO, barely made a stir. It left the air after five months, with half of its 39 filmed episodes left unseen in America. Drake would return later as the "Secret Agent Man." But, for the time being, spies seemed as unwelcome in the black and white world of American TV as Negroes.

It wasn't that TV production companies hadn't tried to interest audiences in a weekly dose of cloak and dagger—they had. Throughout television's 15 years of life, nearly as many series had attempted a foothold.

Pentagon Confidential (1953) was a live summer anthology based on Army intelligence files. *Passport to Danger* (1954–55) presented Cesar Romero as a glib diplomatic courier. *A Man Called X* (1956) had Barry Sullivan playing a U.S. secret agent, code-named X. *Behind Closed Doors* (1958–59) was based on the files of Rear Admiral Ellis Zacharias of Naval Intelligence. *The Invisible Man* (1958–59) was about a scientist who makes himself see-through, then works for British Intelligence. *World of Giants* (1959) had Marshall Thompson, later of *Daktari*, shrunk down to six inches in height for spy work. *Five Fingers* (1959–60) had David Hedison, later of *Voyage to the Bottom of the Sea,* as a Yank posing as a "Red." There would even be a short-lived syndicated series called *I Spy*, which was no relation to the 1960s series of the same title, and then, finally, *Danger Man* in 1961.

Americans were clearly not ready to embrace men of this type on a weekly basis.

In the late 1950s and early '60s cowboys were still the rage on U.S. television. So were panel shows. So were sitcoms. When the family gathered around the TV in the evenings, wholesome American values were the choice of millions. Notorious characters who lurked in the shadows of mystery and intrigue were not yet in vogue.

James Bond opened the door for the popular genre of spy vs. spy in the 1960s, beginning in May of '63 with the U.S. release of *Dr. No*. The film earned $19 million at the box office that summer, a healthy return back in the day of movie tickets for a buck.

In the fall of '63, NBC tried out a spy series entitled *Espionage*, an anthology with no recurring characters. It quickly failed.

Then in April of '64, a second Bond movie was released. *From Russia with Love* would outperform the previous 007 film, pocketing $27 million before the end of the summer.

The brass at NBC was determined. They wanted a spy of Mr. Bond's caliber on their network.

Enter Robert Culp

Born in 1930 in Berkeley, California, Culp's formative years were shaped mostly by his grandfather. "Whatever I know of any value I learned from him. He was a prospector, though he never made much money at it. He taught me how to pan for gold, shoot a gun, and be a carpenter."[1]

More so, he helped to instill a personal sense of right and wrong into Culp, which kept him off the streets and focused on a more productive life and career.

Culp's parents divorced when he was ten, prompting him to later say, "I decided to dedicate my life to being a substitute for my father, by bringing in money and advising my mother on how to run her life."[2]

Culp was an athlete in high school and junior college, excelling in track and pole vaulting, topping all state prep-school records. He was hoping for a berth on a U.S. Olympic team when his interest in drama ignited and, in 1949, led him to the University of Washington in Seattle as a theater major. While studying there, he met Elayne Carroll, a 25-year-old drama student. They married later that year. He was only 19.

In the early 1950s, while attending the university, Culp entered an acting competition. The prize: a role in an episode of *The Philip Morris Playhouse on Broadway*, a radio anthology series that was, essentially, *Star Search*. Culp's score was high enough to merit a return

Enter Robert Culp (Robert Culp Private Collection).

appearance as one of four finalists, all of whom would perform in a 15 minute scene with veteran actor Everett Sloane. Culp was crowned the champ. The prize included a meeting with an agent from the William Morris Agency. That agent was no older than Culp. He had just graduated from the mail room. His name was Hillard Elkins.

Culp immediately began a year of study with the Herbert Berghof Acting Studio in New York. There, he learned "The Method." Berghof's wife, the well-known stage actress Uta Hagen, was a teacher there.

Robert Culp: "Uta and Herbert became surrogate parents. I adored her, but I could never have been in one of her classes. We would have fought. And, if you're an actor, you can't fight with your teacher. Herbert and I finally got into a fight over a girl. I walked away and never went back."[3]

Culp's marriage was also falling apart. After a decade of being a substitute authority figure with his mother, he said, "I alienated my wife and my friends by being bossy."[4]

While holding down night jobs, Culp continued to audition for acting roles.

Ultimately, with "Hilly" Elkins' help, Culp landed the lead in the off-Broadway play *He Who Gets Slapped*. "He" was 25.

Culp: "Hilly came down to see a dress rehearsal. He took me to this little greasy spoon and, on the counter, I signed my first contract with him. He got me above-the-title billing, paid ads, everything. It just wasn't done in those days for off-Broadway; then, he really went to work. He brought down every casting director he knew, and every producer in town to see me. All of a sudden, I just took off—an overnight success—after 14 years."[5]

For his role in *He Who Gets Slapped*, Culp won the very first Obie Award presented. The trophy declared him the "Best Actor of the Year in an Off-Broadway Play."

Culp: "*The Village Voice* manufactured the Obies to sell newspapers. It didn't mean jack shit to me, but if it could get me a job that they pay me for, lead me to it. I was so sick and tired of being poor—constantly poor—forever poor—and just living from hand to mouth."[6]

Suddenly Culp was working. It's one of those things that happens when an actor gets hot.

Culp: "Everybody wanted to give me a job. I said, 'I don't care where it is, I don't care what it is, if they're gonna pay me, I'm gonna go do it.' So I came to Hollywood for the first time.... I got a call from New York, from Hilly. He said, 'Go over and see these people at Four Star.' I said, 'What's Four Star?' He said, 'It's a little company that produces this little TV show called *Zane Grey Theatre*. They want to see you about doing one.'"[7]

After completing the one-week job for television producer Dick Powell, Culp returned to New York and to Broadway. A short while later, he got a another call from Elkins.

Culp: "He said, 'As quick as you're out of this, pack your bags, because you're going to California to do the series.'

'What are you talking about? What series?'

'The series from the pilot that you made on Zane Grey.'

'That wasn't a pilot,' I said.

'Guess again,' he said, 'All the episodes on Zane Grey are pilots.'

"Going to California was the last thing I wanted to do. Broadway was at my beck and call. Jesus, I was hot. All I wanted to do was get on stage and build a career. And I never thought of myself as a movie actor. And I wasn't. But they sold this thing."[8]

The thing they sold was "Badge of Honor," the pilot film for a new Western series.

Trackdown

When Culp returned to Hollywood, his first marriage was over and his second was about to begin. Nancy Ashe, an aspiring dancer and actress, whom Culp had met in New York, made the trip with him.

The instant cowboy had less than two weeks to prepare. Fresh from Broadway, he could neither ride a horse nor fast draw a gun.

Culp: "Fat Jones Stables supplied all the horses for all the shows at Four Star. I went out to Fat Jones and they put me on several different horses. When I came home, my soon-to-be second wife took one look at my backside and said, 'Oh Jesus, honey....'

"She didn't know any better, she put alcohol on it. I jumped ten miles. My ass was raw hamburger."[9]

Culp continued to practice. Next came the gun. He worked for hours at a time at the foot of his bed, allowing the gun to drop on a soft mattress instead of the hard floor. The relentless sessions continued until his hand bled.

Trackdown debuted in October 1957 on CBS. The series introduced Culp as Texas Ranger Hoby Gilman, a loner, traveling the frontier and enforcing the law. Culp was the only recurring character. He was the whole damn show and he knew it, prompting him to often butt heads with series producer Vincent Fennelly.

Culp: "The producer and me hated one another on sight from the moment I walked into his office—and, get this, his feet were up on his desk and the soles of his shoes were pointed at me. I said, 'Okay, doesn't like actors, doesn't like *this* actor, and is very insecure.' And he was. He was an ex-alcoholic, and the worst kind—truly anal retentive. This was going to be his thing. All he'd ever done was a couple of really bad B movies. Westerns. And Dick Powell spotted him as somebody who was focused, which he was, and got him on *Trackdown*."[10]

Trackdown was created by John Robinson, who, along with Jack Webb, developed *Dragnet* several years earlier.

Culp: "This was a Western *Dragnet*, up to and including the cadences of speech. But if there's one thing I will not take, it's the equivalent of 'line reading'—from anybody. I learned that early, long before I went to New York. It has to do with the first adage: 'Don't adopt anyone else's rhythm.'"[11]

Culp tried to do a variant on the Western hero, something a bit darker, but a cowboy lawman that would still be familiar to TV audiences.

Fennelly didn't like Culp's choice.

Culp: "Another thing that will endear an actor to a producer is for the producer to walk up to the actor and say, 'I just came from the dailies. You walk like a fag.'

"I had two choices. I could either punch the bastard or ignore him, which is what I usually did. I simply ignored people."[12]

According to a *TV Guide* article on Culp, Fennelly claimed his star walked more like a "method actor" than a Texas Ranger and, as a result, they didn't speak to one another for a year. *Trackdown* had a bigger problem than a producer who wanted an actor to take a walk.

Culp: "I hated going to the studio every day. Right from the start. The material was puerile. That is what hurt. I'd come from Broadway where people crafted their goddamn words—from a world of real professionals."[13]

Culp went public with his disappointment over scripts. When a magazine article came out printing Culp's uncomplimentary statements, the actor was reprimanded by the grandfatherly Dick Powell.

Culp: "Powell ripped me a new asshole. He said, 'The one thing you never *ever* do is take your problems out of the house.'

"What could I say? He was right. I apologized to him and promised it would never happen again, and it didn't, not then, not ever. Powell accepted that and said, 'Now let's get back to work.' Dick Powell was the best, the wisest producer I ever worked for. I really respected that man."[14]

By the time the series hit the air, Culp had settled into his role as a Texas lawman. True to his word, he kept his mouth shut concerning his problems with producer Fennelly. It was much easier—and, in Culp's mind, more professional—to merely ignore the man.

And then came the perks. One was instant stardom, and through that stardom, Culp would meet a lifelong friend.

It happened in the summer of 1957, while on his way to Hollywood for the second time to do another year of *Trackdown*.

Culp: "It was rubber-band airplanes in those days. We had a layover in Chicago to get another plane.

"My wife and I and our bags were sitting on the tarmac at O'Hare. There was nothing there, man. A bus left you off and you sat.

"There was this Black guy, really nattily dressed, walking back and forth in front of us—just the three of us, going to L.A.

"I said to my wife, 'I think that's Sammy Davis Jr. He just closed in *Mr. Wonderful* on Broadway.'

"All of a sudden, he whirled around and said, 'I know you, I know who you are'—and immediately launched into a description, word for word, scene for scene, line for fucking line, of a *Trackdown*. He even imitated my walk.

"So we were just like instant best friends."[15]

Davis would remain a close friend, practicing fast draw with Culp, having him and his wife over to his home every Friday night to watch movies, and helping the sensitive actor to understand the passion of the civil rights movement.

At this time, Elkins had another client, Steve McQueen, who had met Culp in New York. Using *Trackdown* as a springboard, with two guest star spots, Culp was able to give McQueen a boost into his own series—*Wanted: Dead or Alive*.

Culp would also get acting work on the series for his cousin, Warren Oates, and then for his wife, Nancy.

He would also get additional work for himself—as a writer.

Culp: "One of the few good things to come out of *Trackdown* was that I sold my first teleplay—'Back to Crawford.' And the miracle was Fennelly bought it, without a word. I asked him later, 'Why did you buy this?' And he looked at me with that fishy stare that he had, and said, 'Because it's that good. Is that what you want to hear?' And I said, 'Yeah, sure, any writer wants to hear that, but I was just so surprised.' And he said, 'We're at the end of the line, we're not going to get a pick-up, it's well written, it's a good episode, and so we're doing it.'"[16]

By this point, Fennelly had another troublesome actor to watch over: Steve McQueen in *Wanted: Dead or Alive*. While Fennelly didn't serve as line producer on *Wanted*, he had created the series, produced the pilot, and cast McQueen in the role. Now, with this bigger hit at Four Star, and a bigger problem to contend with, Fennelly's interest in Culp's series began waning, and that allowed Culp to get the episode he had written for his wife produced.

Culp wanted to give the former actress a shot.

Culp: "Somehow it seemed to help her state of mind. She did a perfectly good job. That was the only thing she ever did on film. She never spoke about acting again. It seemed to satisfy a need, so I'm glad I did it."[17]

In Culp's script, the character Nancy played was a former flame of Hoby's, now obsessed with killing him. In the final confrontation, a deputy, played by Warren Oates, blows her away with a double-barreled shotgun. Before Hoby can reach her, she dies, face down in the dirt.

For one year, Culp's career would go the same way.

Culp: "I was *not* relieved when the show went off the air. I was keenly aware that we never had the numbers. *Wanted: Dead or Alive*, which spun off from *Trackdown*, just kicked the shit out of us from the get-go. What I was bringing to the table, which is what they called in *TV Guide*, 'The thinking man's cowboy,' wasn't cutting it. And the thing that *was* cutting it for Steve's show was his persona, the way he shaped the character to fit him. His was newer, fresher, and far more vital and vibrant than mine was."[18]

McQueen, a former street kid, knew how to pick his battles. Halfway through the run of *Wanted*, McQueen had producer Fennelly and his line producer, John Robinson, replaced. The actor, who was not concerned with getting a "bad boy" reputation, won the battle, and the game.

Culp, through his short-lived series, had given McQueen an excellent leg up on his journey to superstardom; however, Culp's journey took a different turn.

Culp was 27 when he started *Trackdown*. He shot the series for two years. He thought he was a star. He had every reason to believe this—here he was, every week, on television. And then, suddenly, the offers for work stopped.

Culp: "I was down to doing fairs and rodeos. I got a guy to teach me to trick ride, so I could add that to my act. I told stupid stories and did gun tricks.

"I finally called Elkins and said, 'Get out here.' I was broke. I had a family coming along, and we were living from hand to mouth. He came out from New York, and I said to him, 'Something's happened.'

"Hilly started poking around town, trying to find out what the hell had happened. I mean, I was hot before the goddamned series.

"What he discovered was that Vincent Fennelly had so poisoned the ground all over this city that nobody wanted to hire me. It was that simple.

"So I went to writing instead."[19]

Culp's professional writing career began at age 15 when he sold his first short story to a magazine. His high school teacher encouraged him to continue writing.

After selling his first script to *Trackdown*, Culp would score again with *The Rifleman*. The producers of that series liked Culp's script so much that they had him expand it into a two-part episode.

"Waste," written in August 1960, was like "Back to Crawford" and pushed TV to its limits.

Lost in a Mexican wasteland, Lucas McCain, son Mark, and Marshal Micah Torrance are taken prisoner by sadistic bandits in a ghost town. After being tortured, Micah is buried up to his neck and left to die in the blistering sun. Lucas is told to dig two more holes, one for him, and the other for Mark. What follows is an examination of humanity at its most primal level—kill or be killed.

Many of the events and characters portrayed and the images seen in "Waste" are truly shocking for a half-hour family Western from this era. Culp's script, and the episode made from it, are both dark and terrifying.

Culp would later be told by the producers that his script was, in their opinion, the best material they had ever bought for *The Rifleman*.

During the production of "Waste," Culp was leaving the studio lot and literally bumped chest to chest into Sam Peckinpah. They recognized each other from *Trackdown*, where Peckinpah had been hired as a writer. He was now producing his own series, *The Westerner*.

After learning that Culp had sold a script to *The Rifleman*, Peckinpah, who had written the pilot for that series, asked to read it.

That night Culp got a call from Peckinpah.

Culp: "He started the conversation by saying, 'You dumb fucking sonofabitch. You absolute asshole. You sold this to *them*?'

"I said, 'Yeah, that was the idea.'

"He said, 'Okay, this is the way it's going to work from now on—You don't ever sell anything to anybody without checking with me first.'

1—The History of a Genre

"That's all you have to say to a writer. I loved him to the day he died."[20]

Next, Culp was hired to write a script for *The Dick Powell Theater* entitled "The Gunfighter." He was also scheduled to return to acting and star in the episode, opposite Tuesday Weld. But, shortly before production could begin, Powell died of a heart attack and the show was scrapped. Peckinpah bought the script from the defunct series, and pursued producing it himself. He failed at that, but not at cementing a friendship between himself and Culp.

In 1962 Culp sold his script "The Swinger" to a short-lived NBC series entitled *Cain's Hundred*. Culp also guest starred in the episode with series regular Mark Richmond.

Cain's Hundred can best be described as *The Untouchables* meets *Dragnet*. The premise dealt with Nick Cain, an agent for the government, assigned the task of tracking down the 100 most elusive mobsters.

In "The Swinger," Culp plays Hank Shannon, a Frank Sinatra-type entertainer with mob connections. Hank is also an old friend of Nick's. The two grew up together. Hank feels he owes a great deal to Nick, and Nick has come to Las Vegas to collect. He wants Hank to wear a wire, allowing him to gather evidence against a mob leader.

Culp's friend, Sammy Davis Jr., sang the music tracks for Culp to lip-synch to throughout the episode.

As with all the scripts written by Culp thus far, the theme of "The Swinger" is dark and deals with the sheer waste of life when anger mixes with greed, lust, and inhumanity.

Culp was proving himself as a writer for the small screen, although his taste in scripts and his take on life could hardly produce consumable material for most televisions shows of the time.

From 1960 to 1964, Culp succeeded in shaking off his bad boy image and elevating himself to being the highest paid "guest star" in television.

He marked over 50 appearances on all the biggest shows of the day, such as *Alfred Hitchcock Presents*, *Rawhide*, *Bonanza*, *Wagon Train*, *Combat!*, and *The Virginian*.

In 1963 and '64, alone, Culp appeared in four feature films, getting top billing in *The Raiders* and *Rhino!*; second billing in *P.T. 109*, the story of John Kennedy's World War II exploits, listed just under Cliff Robertson; and was part of a bright and hip cast including Robertson, Rod Taylor and Jane Fonda, in *Sunday in New York*. During the same two years, he made stand-out guest spots on *Ben Casey*, *Gunsmoke*, and three episodes of *The Outer Limits*, including the classic Harlan Ellison penned, "Demon with a Glass Hand."

In 1964, Culp would also star in the very first made-for-TV movie, *The Hanged Man*.

Acting had again become a means for Culp to support and provide for his wife and children. But the work he was now getting, although plentiful, was primarily a few days at a time.

Culp sought other options.

One option, one of several pilot scripts offered to Culp at this time, came from producer Norman Felton. Culp had worked for Felton in the early days of live TV in New York and the producer had been struck by the talented actor. Now Felton had a script, which had been codeveloped with Ian Fleming, and Culp was the actor Felton had in mind for the lead part. It was a James Bond-inspired comedy-drama called *Solo*. The lead character was Napoleon Solo, an agent with a top secret organization known as U.N.C.L.E.

Culp was attracted to the prospect of portraying a spy, but didn't much care for the handling of the material. He found the writing to be "cheesy," and declined the project.

Culp: "Everybody and his dog had been saying to me, 'You need to do a spy. Spies are everything. Spies are hot. And if anybody was ever perfect to do a spy, it's you.'"[21]

Hilly Elkins suggested Culp write a pilot for himself. Intrigued by the challenge, Culp wrote a 74-page script intended to serve as the basis for a 60-minute "pilot film." The genre was action/adventure; the premise dealt with espionage. The lead character, designed by Culp for Culp, and the title, were one and the same: "Danny Doyle."

Sammy Davis Jr., as he had by singing the tracks for "The Swinger," again offered to lend a hand. He took the script to his friend, Carl Reiner. A week and a half later, Culp met with Reiner in his office at Desilu Studios.

Culp: "Carl said, 'You should have come to me last year. I'm leaving TV and going to make my movie—*The Russians Are Coming*. But I liked it so much I gave it to Sheldon Leonard and he wants to talk to you right now. Just follow that walkway around to the second floor and his office is there.'

"The first words out of Leonard's mouth were, 'I like your idea, kid, but I like mine better.'"[22]

A Mogul Named Leonard

Sheldon Leonard, described by the Museum of Television as "the Brooklyn-toned actor best remembered for his incarnations of quietly menacing gangsters," appeared in scores of films in the 1940s and '50s.

By the end of that second decade, Leonard was well on his way to reinventing himself.

It wasn't the first time he had done so. On the first go-round, he was known as Sheldon Leonard Bershad.

"My dad came out of college planning to be a stock broker," recalled Leonard's daughter, Andrea Bershad. "But it was 1929, the market crashed, and suddenly there was no work."[23]

Leonard had a college friend working on Broadway, who helped him find work on the stage. Dropping his last name for the theater, Leonard saw his acting stint as being merely temporary.

His talent would keep him on Broadway for nine years.

During this time, Leonard met Frances Bober. They were married in 1931, a union that would last for over 60 years. Leonard had found his soul mate, the love of his life, the first time out, with no hesitation.

Eight years later, they had a daughter, Andrea.

Andrea Bershad: "He never planned a thing. It was work. And that work lead to more, on radio, in films, then on television. And he wrote a little bit, then he directed what he wrote. That's how he got into directing for Danny Thomas. He took advantage of opportunities as they were presented."[24]

Norman Brokaw, president and CEO of the William Morris Agency, was an up-and-coming agent in the 1950s. One of his clients was Sheldon Leonard.

Brokaw: "Sheldon wanted to be a director, so he wanted to know if he could look over Bill Asher's shoulder and learn on the *Make Room for Daddy* set. Sheldon was an incredible man. That's why I got him his first job at $100 a week as a director."[25]

That first directing job for Leonard was an episode of the mid–1950s anthology, *General Electric Theater*. It didn't take long for him to get a raise. And, as his rate increased, so did his responsibilities. He became a producer on *Colgate Theater*, another anthology series of the time, as well as producing the pilot film for *Lassie*. A short while later, Leonard was back on the stage at *Make Room for Daddy*, but, this time, sitting in a director's chair.

Once there, Leonard was introduced to music director Earle Hagen. Hagen told him:

"'We're a service, so whatever you need, give a holler.' He asked me, 'Do you know your business?' I said, 'Yes, I do.' His response, 'Great, you'll never hear from me.'

"I worked with him 17 years. He never came to a dubbing, and he never second-guessed me. He did that with everybody. Sheldon's philosophy was, 'I get the best people I can get, stay out of their way, and let them do what they know how to do.'"[26]

At *Make Room for Daddy*, Leonard developed a friendship with Thomas and advanced quickly, soon becoming one of the show's producers.

Thomas and Leonard had much in common. Both were devoted family men, loyal to their wives, attentive to their children.

Andrea Bershad: "Dad adored my mom. They not only talked to each other, but included my brother and I, as well. My father expected intelligent conversation from us at the dinner table, even at the age of five. He encouraged us to speak well, ask questions, and give opinions."[27]

A mogul named Leonard (Sheldon Leonard Collection).

The "family" was also at the core of the Thomas-Leonard partnership. A series of collaborations followed: Thomas provided the financing; Leonard, the ultimate schmoozer, pitched the projects to the networks and finessed the deals.

They called their company "T & L" and it began with *The Real McCoys* (1957–1963), *The Andy Griffith Show* (1960–1968), *The Joey Bishop Show* (1961–1965), *The Dick Van Dyke Show* (1961–1966), *The Bill Dana Show* (1963–1965), *My Favorite Martian* (the pilot 1963), T & L would finish up with a pair of spin-offs from *The Andy Griffith Show: Gomer Pyle, U.S.M.C.* (1964–1970), and *Mayberry R.F.D.* (1968–1971).

Andrea Bershad: "He had a good relationship with Danny. They were friends. Danny had a very brotherly feeling toward my dad. When my dad became Danny's partner, Danny was already a superstar. It wasn't a true partnership. Danny had more money, more power, more of everything. But my dad had something too."[28]

That something was drive. Leonard derived energy from immense work. The pressures of responsibility that might break another man only seemed to fuel him.

Bershad: "Running those shows energized him. He really loved his work. But, as he got more successful, I think he was more critical of Danny than previously. He still cared a great deal for Danny, but it was different."[29]

In September 1963, Leonard was itching to do something on his own, away from the confines of the successful half-hour sitcoms. He took a lunch meeting in a restaurant at the top of the NBC building at Rockefeller Center. Mort Werner and Herb Schlosser, joint heads of programming for the network, were listening to Leonard's idea for shooting a series that could break free of a studio soundstage. He believed that television of the 1960s had barely evolved from the primitive close-up to close-up techniques introduced at the beginning of the previous decade by Jack Webb for *Dragnet*.

Culp: "And he was right. Even Westerns, and there were 36 of them on TV when I was doing *Trackdown*, with all the supposed wide open vistas to define the genre, were largely talking heads."[30]

But, in those early days, talking heads served their purpose. There was a method to Jack Webb's madness. When *Dragnet* premiered in 1951, television screens were seldom larger than 13 inches in diameter. The camera had to fill the screen with a person's head in order for that person to be recognizable.

By 1963, however, most television sets were larger, and the face of TV was beginning to change from black and white to living color. But the industry directors clung to their claustrophobic technique. Most television shows were limited to interior sets, saddled with cameras and lights that were bulky and relatively immobile. And, while more compact and transportable equipment was readily available, television was slow to embrace the new technology.

Leonard, after his experience with T & L, felt trapped on the soundstage. He wanted to bring exotic locations to everyone's living rooms. He promised Schlosser and Werner that, if they would give him a commitment for a full season, he would deliver such a series.

"Done," they said, "subject to casting and premise."

Prior to *I Spy*, location production in the world of television was primarily considered to be "day trips." And, for the most part, those trips were made on horseback.

There had been one TV vehicle, however, not a Western, but a contemporary drama, that had dared to venture off the studio lot. *Route 66* had hit the road in the fall of 1960. The series about two young men traveling the country in a Corvette was undeniably ahead of its time. But *Route 66* never left the United States. For the most part, the Corvette seen in *66* would remain close to the soundstages and back lots and movie ranches of greater Los Angeles, just as *The Fugitive* rarely escaped the confines of Los Angeles during its 1963–67 run.

Leonard, too, had worked well within the illusion of travel. One of the series he produced with Danny Thomas, *The Andy Griffith Show*, put an entire town on the map and into the conscious memory of American TV viewers, a town that never really existed. Mayberry, North Carolina, was the product of someone's imagination, built on a studio back lot and the inside of a Desilu soundstage. Even the opening title sequence, where Andy and Opie carry fishing poles, and Opie takes the time to skip a stone across a lake, was achieved through Hollywood trickery. The lake was actually one of many Los Angeles water reservoirs, this one located in the Hollywood hills.

By the early 1960s, the tricks of the trade, when seen over and over in never ending doses of weekly TV product, were losing their mystique. Cleveland Amory, in an April 1964 *TV Guide* article, gave an enthusiastic review to the World War II series, *Combat!*, with one criticism concerning how all the battle sequences were shot on the back lot of MGM. From one episode, Amory quoted series regular Vic Morrow as saying, "That's Kraut real estate out there,' then made light of the irony, writing, "That wasn't Kraut real estate, Vic—we took it last week, we remember distinctly, Hun by Hun and tree by tree."

Also in *TV Guide*, in an article featuring *McHale's Navy*, it was reported that the series was abandoning its Pacific island for the southern shores of Italy. Series regular Joe Flynn

1—The History of a Genre

dryly commented, "I thought we'd actually go to Europe. But we're not. We're just changing the phony palm trees to phony olive trees."

So Sheldon Leonard had a vision. He didn't know what his show would be about yet. It was still September of 1963. All he had promised was that this show would travel where no other had before. And, for now, that was all the NBC executives needed to hear.

In the months that followed, as 1963 turned into 1964, the entertainment industry was very aware of the popularity of James Bond at the box office.

NBC wanted a piece of the Bond action, but the network was stuck. *Solo*, the series being developed with the help of Ian Fleming, the pilot script that Culp had turned down, had hit a snag when Fleming, now in a legal conflict involving the next Bond movie, had to drop out.

Leonard, knowing the spy genre would yield opportunities for action and adventure and give his show the mobility it needed to honor his development deal with NBC, had the field all to himself.

In the spring of '64, Carl Reiner sent Leonard a script.

"Danny Doyle" is about a former athlete who now travels the world as a spy. He reports to Military Intelligence. The mood of the script is a smooth blend of action-adventure and wit, driven by the lead character.

Leonard liked the tone, he liked the framework, and he liked the potential. But something was missing.

The spies of the recent past had all been loners. Leonard, the family man, decided his spy would have a friend. Only then could true moments of comedy, and personal drama, be interwoven into the series.

"I like your idea, kid, but I like mine better," Leonard had begun when Culp entered his office.

Robert Culp said, "Oh, what's your idea?"

"Two guys," Leonard pitched, "Both spies, working for the United States government, go around the world on cases, one posing as a tennis pro, and the other as his trainer. Period. One of 'em is Black. Period."

Culp: "When Sheldon said 'One of 'em is Black,' it went off in my head like a depth-charge, and I thought, 'Jesus Christ, no one's ever done that.' And I started to go back in history, and it had never happened in the world, it had never happened before in the theater. It had never happened. Period.

"You're right,' I said to him. 'Your idea *is* better."[31]

Leonard's idea to feature a Black man in a lead role on a network dramatic series was not only original, but, if he pulled it off, would be a significant step forward in the civil rights movement. Up to this time, Black males had only been featured in the lead of one series, a CBS comedy called *Amos 'n Andy*, which moved from radio to television in the 1950s and lasted for two seasons. Eventually, the show would be withdrawn from television due to protests from civil rights groups over the way in which the two leads were presented: amiable, shiftless, ill-educated and always looking for the shortcut to the big time.

Not unlike Amos or Andy was the character of Eddie "Rochester" Anderson, a supporting player on *The Jack Benny Show*, seen on CBS from 1950 to 1964. Rochester, the chauffeur and manservant to "Mister Benny," with a bullfrog voice and a bug-eyed expression, was primarily used to provide set-up lines for classic Jack Benny responses. More often played to be the buffoon, Rochester was not viewed kindly by civil rights and Black rights groups.

For three seasons, between 1950 and 1953, ABC carried a situation comedy about a Black maid tending to a White household in *Beulah*. Ten years later, in *East Side/West Side*, a short-lived drama on CBS for the 1963–64 season, George C. Scott played a social worker stationed in the New York slums. A young Black actress named Cicely Tyson was cast to play his secretary. It was a small step in the right direction, but poor ratings and a quick cancellation by CBS kept that step from going forward.

Culp was delighted by Leonard's version of a spy series and committed to the project. This allowed Leonard to use Culp's name in securing his deal with NBC, something Culp hadn't done for Norman Felton.

Culp: "I knew that Norman Felton was probably going to have a hit with *The Man from U.N.C.L.E.*, but I would hate myself in the morning, so I turned him down. I couldn't do camp. To me, if you go to camp, you may succeed, but you fail, also. I wanted to make it real, and I knew it never would be real with Norman and that concept of Napoleon Solo. So it was like I was sitting around waiting for Sheldon to show up in my life, and Sheldon was sitting around waiting for me to show up in his life—because I brought the network with me, and he brought the network with him. He had to get somebody on board that they approved, and I walked in the door. And that was the way *I Spy* was born."[32]

Incredibly, the network signed on without requesting to see a pilot, or even a pilot script.

The contract, dated June 26, 1964, guaranteed payment for 18 episodes of the still untitled, undefined series, whether broadcast or not. This is called a "pay or play" deal, a rarity then, and completely off the negotiating list now.

All NBC knew was that the series would be about a spy; the spy would be played by Robert Culp; it would be an action-adventure-comedy; and it would be filmed abroad.

The idea of the Black partner was not part of the deal—or the contract. But Leonard would prove to be determined.

The first order of business was to have a script written to fine-tune the premise for the series.

Enter Friedkin and Fine

David Friedkin and Mort Fine were writing partners who had also delved into producing. In the 1940s they worked together in radio and wrote the pilot for *Gunsmoke*. It was Friedkin who coined the name Matt, and Fine who came up with Dillon.[33]

A true partnership.

David Friedkin's youngest of two sons, Anthony, remembers: "My dad was born in 1912, and was a *Grapes of Wrath* type of a guy. He was the first son of Russian Jewish immigrants. My grandfather was a tailor, who was the son of a tailor, and lived in Kansas City. He was poor and worked hard, and was extremely religious. It was a dream of my grandfather's that my father become a great violinist. So he made my father practice—and was actually pretty brutal on my Dad—'You're going to get up at 4 A.M., and you're going to practice, and go to school, and deliver the suits I've made.' My grandfather was a very rigid man."[34]

Friedkin was an extraordinary student, who graduated from high school at the age of 15, and at the top of his class. He also won a scholarship to Juilliard to study the violin.

Anthony Friedkin: "So my old man went off on his own to New York. But within a couple of years, while at Juilliard, a 12-year-old kid came in, opened up his violin case, and played so brilliantly, that my father quit."[35]

At the age of 17, Friedkin turned to acting, and became a serious stage actor in New York. His career continued for nearly a decade. In the late 1930s, a Broadway hit was being planned as a major motion picture.

Friedkin (left) and Fine (middle) and an unidentified assistant on the set of *Frontier*, 1950s (Friedkin Family Collection).

Anthony Friedkin: "Dad was up for the lead in *Golden Boy*. They flew him out to Hollywood, did a screen test, and it was either him or William Holden. Well, Holden got it. After that, Dad concentrated on writing and directing."[36]

During World War II, Friedkin enlisted in the army, hoping for combat. After testing him, however, the military brass decided that Friedkin's IQ was too high, and he would better serve his country in Army Intelligence. Disappointed, he soon found satisfaction working with the Signal Corp, and writing radio programs for the GIs.

After the war, Friedkin was stationed in Sacramento. An actress he knew from New York was in Los Angeles. On leave, he traveled down to visit her. She picked him up at the train station.

Anthony Friedkin: "My mother, who was also an actress, was in the backseat of that car. She and my dad looked at each other, and right there, they were madly in love. They would be married for 33 years—for the rest of my dad's life."[37]

After leaving the army, Friedkin turned to full-time writing. Sy Rosenberg, an agent in New York, also represented Mort Fine.

Fine, born in 1916, had something else in common with Friedkin. Fine's father disapproved of his son's interest in a career as a writer, as well. Mort was supposed to become a doctor, like his brother.

Mort's wife, Bernice, recalls: "When I was in college, Mort wrote me a letter every single day. His writing was so beautiful, I showed the letters to my teachers at Carnegie Tech. I could see his talent."[38]

After marriage, and at the end of the war, the Fines drove to California before they even had a plan. They settled in Paradise Cove, a beach community, a short drive north of Los Angeles. At this time, Mort's only credentials were school prizes for writing radio scripts.

Bernice Fine: "When we first got here, we were so naive, we went to the information counter at CBS, and tried to submit a script. They turned us down. We really didn't know anything about anything. And then, the most amazing thing happened. Gypsy Rose Lee and her son moved in next to us, and I became the babysitter. Mort painted her trailer, and she wanted to see what he'd written. Then she immediately sent him to her agent. It was radio days, and it started then, and never stopped. He met David through the agent, after he'd done scripts on his own. The agent thought they would meld, and that was it. 1948."[39]

Friedkin's eldest son, Gregory, continues the story: "Their agent, Sy Rosenberg, brought them in and said, 'I think you guys should collaborate.' And the rest is history. Twelve pages a day is what they would go for. And once they knew where the story was going, they would each write scenes, then exchange them. By the end of the script, both had input into every scene. They were very prolific, and their chemistry was unique. They've probably written more than any other team. If you include radio, that's thousands of scripts."[40]

By the late 1940s, the new partnership of Friedkin and Fine were writing *Bold Venture*, a radio series starring Humphrey Bogart and Lauren Bacall. The pilot for *Gunsmoke* came in the early 1950s, followed by an ABC radio series entitled, *The Adventures of Johnny Fletcher*. A recurring character on the series was played by Sheldon Leonard.

"We had a lot of fun—Sheldon, Dave and I," Mort Fine would say. "We promised each other we'd work together again some day."[41]

In the mid–1950s, Friedkin and Fine made the move to television. One of their first assignments was an espionage script, "Epitaph For A Spy," for the prestigious anthology series, *Climax*. They also wrote an anthology series of their own. *Frontier* was a Western that lasted one year on NBC during the 1955–56 season. Friedkin and Fine received an Emmy nomination for their episode, "Patrol."

Three years later, they wrote a second series, also for one year. This time it was a television version of their earlier success on radio. The TV *Bold Venture* starred Dane Clark and Joan Marshall, both of whom would later appear on *I Spy*.

By the late 1950s, the team found work in motion pictures, writing *Hot Summer Night* and *Handle with Care*, both of which were directed by Friedkin. In 1962, Friedkin directed the pilot film for *The Virginian*. That same year, he won the Directors Guild of America

Award for Best Direction on Television in a Drama, for "The Price of Tomatoes," a presentation of *The Dick Powell Theater*. The star of the one-hour production was a young Peter Falk.

Friedkin and Fine advanced to the producer's chair on *Dick Powell Theater*, and received a nomination from the Producers Guild of America (PGA), in the category of Best Produced Series of 1964. They would be nominated again by the PGA in 1965, for their turn as the show runners on the last season of *Alfred Hitchcock Presents*.

Their most notable achievement, however, was for writing the screenplay for the 1964 motion picture, *The Pawnbroker*. Rod Steiger would earn an Academy Award nomination for his performance. Friedkin and Fine would win the Writers Guild Award for their script.

Despite the accolades, Mort Fine's father continued to disapprove of his son's career.

Bernice Fine: "I don't think his parents ever understood why he wanted to write. It wasn't as good as being a doctor. Mort was used to it — the criticism. When I first met his family, at the train station, his father didn't come to me first. He walked over to Mort and said, 'Your hair is too long. Get a haircut.' No matter what Mort did, it wasn't right."[42]

Director Richard Sarafian recalls Mort Fine as saying, "When I was 18, I told my father that I didn't want to be a doctor, I wanted to go to California and be a writer. My father slapped me. Years later, I had finished going to UCLA to study writing, I had this nice office at MGM, and my father was coming out to see me. To impress him, I had a shoeshine boy stop by the office and do our shoes. I said, 'Pop, this is my office.' Then I took my father in a limo to a soundstage that was across the lot. I said, 'Pop, this is my movie. I wrote this movie.' From there, I took him on a tour of Los Angeles, finally arriving at the impressive UCLA campus. I said, 'Pop, this is where I studied writing.' And my pop looked at the building and said, 'So where's the medical school?'"[43]

Writer Michael Zagor remembers, "Mort had a brother in Baltimore who was a doctor. The family loved him. And doing *I Spy* finally gave Mort some clout. One day we stopped at a sidewalk café, and Mort said, 'The subject for conversation today is fame.' I said, 'Okay.' We sat down and looked at the menu. All the omelets were listed. There was the Gregory Peck, the Tony Curtis, and the Sophia Loren. And they all listed what was in it. And at the very bottom of the menu, it said, 'Mort Fine, Lox.' And he said, 'Wait until I tell my brother in Baltimore.'"[44]

Despite the common ground regarding their fathers, and the mutual respect for each other's talent, David Friedkin and Mort Fine had very different personalities.

Writer Barry Oringer recalls the team: "David Friedkin was a sweet man. A gentle and very supportive person. Mort Fine was very funny, very sharp, very confident in his ideas, and confident without being dogmatic or overbearing. He just knew how to work with writers."[45]

One of those writers, Eric Bercovici, remembers, "Mort was more of a rough and tumble guy. Funny at times, not so funny at other times. And he used to warn me that David was sensitive."[46]

Writer Rick Mittleman agrees. "David was a lovely guy, very refined, compared to Mort, who, like myself, was all East Coast."[47]

Writer Jerry Ludwig shares, "Friedkin and Fine were such an unlikely pair. Whatever the dynamic was, obviously, two guys who could go into a room and what came out was the script for *The Pawnbroker*, that's a working team. Mort was the type who would say, 'Hey, kid, they're showing *Touch of Evil* in Westwood at the midnight show on Friday night, do you want to go?' I just got great affection from him. David was a nice man and a supportive guy. And there was something about them that made them work as a team, and the results were outstanding."[48]

Sarafian adds, "Friedkin was the counterpart to Mort. Between the two of them, they inspired one another. So it was a great team. Mort was a true artist. He was so good with character. And that is one of the things that is a benchmark of all Mort Fine's work, his understanding of character, and getting in deeper to the molecules of who those characters are."[49]

Leonard felt Friedkin and Fine had a knack for balancing comedy and drama in their scripts, essential elements for his Bond-like spy series. He hired them.

And he now had a name for his company: Triple F Productions—FranShel, Friedkin and Fine. FranShel was a combination of Frances and Sheldon Leonard's first names.

There would be no "created by" credit on *I Spy*, and that is a very curious omission. What they had was a financial agreement.

In the June 26, 1964, contract, it was specified, "NBC hereby acknowledges that it has approved a total of 20% of divisible income as profit participation of Messrs. Friedkin and Fine, and 7½% as profit participation of Bob Culp."[50]

The rest went to FranShel.

Culp: "When I found out that Sheldon had made up his mind and hired the two writer/producers, I went to their office. I liked both of them. They seemed very personable, nice fellows. I had slight reservations about Mort, because he lost very little opportunity to diss Sheldon. I thought that was inappropriate to do in front of the star of the show. I kept my mouth shut, I didn't concur, I didn't argue, I didn't do anything. I just listened. David seemed to me to be a soft-spoken man, a gent, a nice fellow in every way. Mort was a little more edgy. I liked that, too. I found that I could relate to Mort's head and his sense of irony in a story, which I perceived was greater than David's. I knew that David had been an actor in New York, he had a lot of stage experience, and that he had directed. And, above all, these two guys had written 'The Pawnbroker.' I remember seeing the picture and being blown away. I am very impressed with good writing."[51]

Friedkin and Fine went to work and wrote the first episode "Affair in T'Sien Cha." It wasn't considered a pilot because NBC had not requested one. They called it a "test film" instead, to test the formula for filming a series that would have one-third of each episode shot overseas, and the remaining two-thirds on a soundstage in Los Angeles.

Leonard chose Desilu, a busy TV factory at the time, and home of all of the Thomas-Leonard collaborations. Formerly RKO Studios, the facility was purchased by Desi Arnaz and Lucille Ball in the mid–1950s during the height of their astounding success with *I Love Lucy*. Dozens of half-hour sitcoms were filmed on the lot, but only two longer format dramatic series, *The Desilu Playhouse* and *The Untouchables*, had seen the green light of production there. After the demise of both shows, the studio was happy to see the development of Leonard's spy show.

The primary problem remained unanswered. The Black partner. Who could fill those shoes?

Culp: "That afternoon (after meeting with Sheldon), I went home and I said to myself, 'Jesus, this is going to be a tough one.'

"By that time in Los Angeles, I had come to know every Black actor that we had working. The Brock Peters, the Greg Morrises, and even Ivan Dixon, who was so marvelous, but he wasn't right for this."[52]

Culp knew that whoever played this part would have to withstand a level of public scrutiny no other Black actor had ever faced before, other than Sidney Poitier.

Enter Bill Cosby

Norman Brokaw was a staunch believer of the "package deal." The William Morris Agency already represented Leonard, Friedkin, Fine, Culp, and the heads of Desilu.

And now, they had a new client.

Brokaw: "I called up Sheldon and said, 'There's a wonderful guy, and my New York office is hot on him. And he's new and he's incredible. And I'd like him to read with you on this.'"[53]

At the same time, Rob Reiner was watching *The Tonight Show* and saw Bill Cosby doing a stand-up routine. He too saw something new and incredible, and he immediately shared his impressions with his father.

Carl Reiner, once again, was in the right place at the right time. He'd first helped Culp to get to Leonard, and now, after being alerted to Bill Cosby's talent, he had the imagination and vision to see the second half of the *I Spy* team. Like Brokaw, Reiner placed a call to Sheldon Leonard.

Enter Bill Cosby (under license from Warner Bros. Records).

Leonard first saw Cosby on a Jack Paar special.

Leonard: "[Cosby] was handsome and animated, with a wonderfully mobile face. He was doing a comedy routine about karate, and he moved like an athlete."[54]

Recalling his first meeting with Leonard, Cosby believed that he was being brought in to audition for a guest shot on *The Dick Van Dyke Show*, even though he had never acted before.

He was not offered a guest star spot on *Van Dyke*. Instead, Leonard was talking about a new series that would costar a Black man and a White man. They would be spies and travel the world. First stop: Hong Kong.

Cosby: "Here I am, first time in California, only the third time I've ever been out of Pennsylvania, and this guy is talking about Hong Kong. That knocked me out of my chair."[55]

With Friedkin and Fine in tow, Leonard journeyed to San Francisco to watch the comedian perform at the Hungry I.

Gregory Friedkin: "My dad called me up. I was at the frat house in Berkeley. 'We're up here to see this Bill Cosby. I'd like you to come and watch him, and bring some of your buddies.' He wanted our feedback about how we felt about him. My Dad was really curious as to how our generation would relate to the show and to Cosby. We watched Cosby's set, and we loved him. He was just so great. Not your typical stand-up. He told stories—the jokes would be in there, with his ambience and the way he works. After, my Dad said, 'What do you think?' And every one of us said, 'Cast that guy now! He's a winner. You'd be crazy not to cast this guy!' All my friends felt the same way. Cosby was part of the '60s, with his comedy, and his improv, which set the table for Pryor, Chris Rock, and so on."[56]

Later that night, Leonard, Friedkin and Fine met with Bill and Camille Cosby.

Cosby went straight into "acting mode," and bluffed television's three self-appointed wisemen about his confidence at being able to perform drama. He also told them he needed assurance that the character he played would be allowed to fight back.

Cosby: "I had to find out that I didn't have to go off into the bushes when a fight started. They said I didn't."[57]

They also told him he would carry and use a gun.

Up to this moment, no Black man on television had ever fired a gun, unless he was shooting at the police.

Cosby was satisfied by their explanation and promise.

A deal was quickly worked out with Roy Silver, Cosby's agent, and the actor-to-be was locked in for the modest price of $1,250 per episode.

Like his character, Alexander Scott, Cosby spent his formative years in the confines of a north Philadelphia ghetto. The oldest of three sons born to navy mess steward William H. Cosby, young Bill had a home which modestly provided food, clothing, and shelter, but rarely a father.

Cosby told director Richard Sarafian, "My dad was a drunk. He only enlisted in the navy to get away from my mother."[58]

Cosby recalled a childhood of hardship. A father whose drinking buddies were more important than his wife and children; a paycheck that never seemed to make it home; a house without a bathtub; and Christmas with no Christmas tree.

The worries over money caused fights. The drinking caused fights. Cosby remembered his father beating his mother on three occasions. He was too small to stop it, prompting him to later say, "These things are very, very painful to think about."[59]

In order to reinforce his belief in his own identity, Cosby turned to sports. And, in order to lighten the mood around the house, he learned to be funny.

"I loved attention," Cosby has said. "To attract it, I turned myself into an athlete and comedian."[60]

Cosby enlisted in the navy, which allowed him to broaden his education. The extent of his travels were to Hawaii, Cuba, and Newfoundland.

When he left the service at age 23, he won a scholarship to Temple University. There, he majored in physical education and played on the school football team.

During his sophomore year, Cosby was offered $5 a night to tend bar and be funny in a pal's small cellar bistro. The amateur comic soon graduated to a larger room, a club called the Underground, where he was paid $25 a night and was no longer required to pour drinks.

At the Underground, Roy Silver, then a booking agent, spotted the comic and began to get him gigs at local clubs. Shortly thereafter, Cosby was traveling to other cities, including Washington, for an engagement at the Shadows Club and the Shoreham Hotel. While there, he met a 19-year-old girl named Camille Hanks. Her father was a research chemist at Walter Reed Hospital. Camille was a psychology major at the University of Maryland.

Like his future boss, Sheldon Leonard, Cosby mined gold at an early age and found his lifelong partner.

It took some convincing to get Camille's parents to see things his way. In their eyes, Cosby, who was leaning toward a show business career and away from his university studies, was moving in the wrong direction.

With Silver's help, Cosby received a booking in New York at the Gaslight in Greenwich Village. It was June 24, 1962, and a critic for the *New York Times* was in attendance.

The following day, Bill Cosby received his first review in print, with the headline, "Comic Turns Quips into Tuition." The *Times* review began, "He is Bill Cosby, a 24-year-old physical education major at Temple University, here for the summer to polish his style, collect new material and save money for the fall semester. Mr. Cosby writes his own material. His view-point is fresh, slightly ironic, and extremely funny."

Cosby's fortunes as a struggling stand-up comic changed dramatically after the appearance of the *Times* review. Something else changed. At the end of his sophomore year, with too few hours in the day for Cosby to be both a full-time student and a working comedian, he chose to leave Temple University.

Next came an appearance on the *Ed Sullivan Show*, and Cosby's income made a dramatic jump. More TV guest spots followed, including the one on *The Tonight Show*. Johnny Carson's guest host that night was comedian Allan Sherman, a big hit at the time with his radio-friendly comedy song, "Hello Muddah, Hello Fadduh, A Letter from Camp Granada." Sherman spotted immense potential in Cosby, and arranged for him to have an audition with Warner Brothers Records. A deal soon followed and Sherman produced Cosby's first album, *Bill Cosby Is a Very Funny Fellow, Right!*

With his first album in the can, Cosby now had the confidence to ask for Camille's hand in marriage. They were married on January 25, 1964.

The debut album was released in the spring of 1964. The record sold well.

Cosby, both personally and professionally, had gone through a life-altering change.

A bigger change was right around the corner.

Kelly and Scott, the First Meeting

With contracts in hand, the partners of Triple F brought Cosby to Los Angeles to read opposite Robert Culp.

It was the first time the two had met. They shook hands and then, before having a chance to even speak, they were given scripts.

Cosby: "It was the moment of truth: All the fears, anxieties and apprehensions were bubbling and boiling, because now I was no good—really no good. I fumbled and mumbled and couldn't concentrate or do anything right."[61]

Culp: "It was so hot it would burn a hole in the sidewalk in that room. So many things were going on for so many people. Bill has said since that it was a really low watermark in his life. He was so angry about making a fool of himself. He felt that he had no business being there. He was being asked to read a script out loud, which he had never done before, in front of some stone pros who were *judging him mortally*. There was just no way around that one. But he was giving me signals without knowing it. That day, that moment, everything that followed came out of those three hours."[62]

Despite Cosby's belief that he had "fumbled and mumbled," Culp knew he had found Alexander Scott. In that reading, he recognized what Cicero defined as a friend, a "second self." Cosby was the second self to Culp's Kelly Robinson.

For Culp and Cosby, the material was out of balance.

Culp: "There was a very quiet, dry, humorous, and gentle contempt for the references to race that were in the script. He would get to a line that contained such a reference and he would ad-lib it in another form, which indicated that he was hostile toward the line itself. This rang a bell with me, because I was hostile toward it too."[63]

The producers did not appreciate the ad libs.

Culp: "After the reading, I went to Friedkin and Fine's office, and said, 'Do you know what we just saw here?' 'Yeah,' Mort said, 'Bad acting.'

"They completely missed it. They were trying to have him read it as Black. And he wouldn't do it.

"I knew that Bill, in that first reading, which he did so badly, was a genius. I was in the presence of genius and I knew it. It disturbed me, when I went to talk to David and Mort about it, just a few minutes later, that they hadn't seen what I saw. They hadn't seen it at all. They couldn't recognize anything above their own level."[64]

Culp believed the tone of the script was wrong—there was an imbalance between the two principal players. The Friedkin/Fine script had Robinson at 75% and Scott at 25%. Culp instantly recognized that Alexander Scott was little more than a manservant to Kelly Robinson. And worse, he was written in a stereotypical manner.

Culp began to pressure Friedkin and Fine. He wanted Scott to be rewritten and given equal screen time with Kelly Robinson, which would allow Kelly and Scott the opportunity to create a true partnership.

This was an astonishing request coming from an actor looking to launch a series for himself. But Culp experienced a deeper understanding beyond Leonard's comment that "one of 'em is Black."

Culp: "Two guys who start out as equals, clearly become the closest of friends. They couldn't get any closer. Even if they were gay, they couldn't get any closer. And that had never happened before."[65]

Cosby: "At Bob's suggestion, we agreed to make the relationship between the White character and the Black man a beautiful relationship, so that people could see what it would be like if two cats like that could get along. If Bob hadn't been the great guy he is, I might have copped out."[66]

But he didn't cop out. And Culp got his way.

Bill Cosby would get a chance to play Alexander Scott.

2

The Road to Hong Kong

In the summer of 1964, one month before Kelly met Scott, before Cosby was signed to play opposite Culp, Leonard took his friend Earle Hagen on a scouting mission to Hong Kong.

"Cities have character," Leonard would later write. "Not all cities, but many. Paris has character. Take a shot on any Parisian street, and any arm chair traveler will place it immediately. The same is true for Venice, and for London, New York, Leningrad, Rio de Janeiro, Marrakesh, and Istanbul."[1]

And the same was true for Hong Kong. Better yet, Hong Kong was surrounded by the world of Communism; it was a hotbed of potential spy activity; and it was cheap. It would be the perfect place to test the waters for "Sheldon's Folly," a show NBC very much wanted, but did not believe could become a reality.

Yet Leonard had faith. He also knew he needed a title, and he needed it soon; something grand; something worthy to follow the screen credit "Sheldon Leonard Presents."

"He used to bring up the subject of shooting around the world," Hagen recalled. "It was at that time that the James Bond movies were getting popular. He said to me that we ought to take a trip somewhere. He asked where I was going to be on a certain date. I said, 'I don't know.' He said, 'I know where. You're going to be with me, and we're going to the Orient. I'm going to do a show called *I Spy*.'"[2]

I Spy was very nearly the first espionage series to hit American TV after James Bond went off with a bang on movie screens across the country. Very nearly.

The other project NBC was racing to develop, *Solo*, had hit a bump in the road. Even after an acceptable actor was found to fill the shoes of Napoleon Solo, the big name behind the series, Ian Fleming, was not allowed to participate. The movie producers who owned the film rights to James Bond were not happy about their author working both sides of the street. Fleming stuck with Bond, and Napoleon went solo.

But NBC needed a spy on the air for the fall of 1964, and *I Spy* had yet to be proven, and most certainly wouldn't be available until 1965.

So *Solo* was overhauled. The new title would be *The Man from U.N.C.L.E.* Norman Felton would helm it alone. Robert Vaughn would star.

While NBC was insistent that "Sheldon's Folly," in order to better exploit its far away scenery, be filmed in color, at great added expense, *U.N.C.L.E.* could be shot on the cheap in black and white. And there would be no need for travel. Its home would be at MGM, utilizing stages and back lots, in the tried and true way in which television had always been churned out.

There would be no risk, no delay, no folly. *U.N.C.L.E.*, although slammed by the critics at first sight, made it onto the air in time for the fall. Robert Culp even appeared in one of the first episodes, "The Shark Affair," playing a captain Nemo–type heavy. It was the least he could do for Felton after turning his nose up at the prospect of playing the lead.

Culp hoped that Leonard would not notice.

The ride begins, Hong Kong '64, as Culp and Cosby are pulled along in carts. (© 3 F Prod.)

Leonard didn't. When "The Shark Affair" was scheduled to air, in October 1964, Leonard would be on the opposite end of the earth, with Culp and Cosby, testing "the formula."

The formula for making the series, as Leonard saw it and sold it to NBC, was to shoot one-third of each episode overseas, and the remaining two-thirds back in Los Angeles. Using this ratio allowed for the combination of striking foreign visuals with slick domestic studio production. Each episode would also benefit by having big name guest stars—something that could only happen if portions of the show were shot locally.

T & L production executive Ron Jacobs recalls: "The biggest headache was doing something no one had done before. I once suggested to Sheldon that we do the entire episodes on location, instead of doing part on location and part back at the studio, several episodes at a time. It would have been cheaper *and* easier that way. But he said, 'No.' Sheldon wanted it to be different, and doing it that way was as different as you could get."[3]

By tying nine scripts to one exotic location, the second unit could film overseas three times a year, always bringing back one-third of each of nine episodes. Leonard's crazy system required nine scripts at a time, in fast order, to be approved by the network.

This was unknown and untried in the Hollywood system, much less the television arena. This was not only bluster, it was the greatest bamboozle of Leonard's career. Nine scripts approved as a group? With minimal network notes or comments? And the promise of the network to *not* require last minute changes?

Leonard loved the impossible. Round one was over. He had gotten the network to agree to relinquish power.

But if Leonard thought the network was his greatest challenge, he was about to get an education. At the end of the day, the lesson Leonard would learn was how to survive the impossible.

Round two, the formula needed to be tested.

Leonard's concept required casting for all nine episodes to be done prior to the onset of foreign filming, so that guest star "doubles" could be hired while on location to interact with Culp and Cosby.

Hair styles would have to match, and clothing would have to be selected for the doubles, then brought back to Los Angeles to create the illusion that the guest stars for each episode were on location, as well.

Pre and postproduction, then, had to be concerned about matching backgrounds, inserting shots, and making all of this seamless. If Kelly and Scott, while in Hong Kong, with the harbor serving as a backdrop, were to be filmed in a two-shot, then the reverse angle of the name guest star, filmed later in Los Angeles, would have to match perfectly. And that meant, in everything, by the weather, the lighting, the framing, and the sound.

The formula looked absurd on paper. The only thing left was to prove it could work. And that had to be done quickly.

Culp: "I remember wondering why we were in such a hurry. I couldn't figure out why, once we found Bill, everything moved so fast to get us to Hong Kong.

"It moved that fast because Sheldon was facing a closing window the following year in terms of selling it. Sheldon was, if nothing, a brilliantly smart tactician, and he could see that the window was rapidly closing on him. So he was spending money hand over fist to get us there to shoot this thing, to get us back, so he could cut it, in order to make this ridiculous gamble pay off. Sheldon was willing to put his money where his mouth was."[4]

An Affair Not to Remember

In October 1964, less than a month after *The Man from U.N.C.L.E.* made its television debut, Leonard, Friedkin, Fine, Culp and Cosby departed for the Orient.

Cosby: "There was nothing that I believed. That's how fairy-tale it was. That's how far away it was from anything I could imagine about this young man, born in a lower-economic split-family, and finding this new life before me. It was just way, way out of my thinking. Because I've never *been* here before. I mean—Sheldon Leonard... I had these people I didn't know anything about. Mort Fine and David Friedkin—I had no idea that they were responsible for

Typhoon Leonard, with Cosby and Culp, shooting the Hong Kong pilot (Sheldon Leonard Collection).

Gunsmoke. I am a guy who is literally stepping from a $5,000 home into a life of more than one fork."[5]

Leonard brought no heavy equipment, believing he could rent whatever he needed in Hong Kong. Once there, he visited Run-Run Shaw, the emperor of picture making for the teeming Oriental market, who had promised Leonard that he could rent a full line of equipment at what seemed to be a fair price. It turned out to be not so fair when everything they acquired from Run Run started to break down. Leonard and his team had been given "obsolete, ill-maintained junk," and they spent more time repairing it than using it. Whatever the cost, Leonard swore, he would never depend on rented equipment again.

The crew had planned for a seven day shooting schedule, but they hadn't taken nature into consideration. Why should they? October was known for being a time of pleasant weather in that region of the world. But, on the second day, as the company was shooting in the Tiger Balm Gardens—a fantastic setting filled with statues of gods and demons—a torrential rain started. Culp and Cosby huddled under an umbrella and rehearsed their lines as the camera shots were composed. Leonard appeared to be unconcerned, and even seemed to appreciate the unique and eerie quality the storm gave to the scene he was shooting.

Leonard was a leader. He had to remain strong. Showing weakness was not an option.

Yet, as the rain got worse, the crew and the cast barely made it back across the bay to their hotel.

A typhoon was soon raging in Hong Kong. For five days, no boats were allowed out onto the water. For five days, Leonard and his stars and his small crew were prisoners of their hotel rooms.

An essay written by Robert Culp for *Motion Picture Magazine*, for its February 1966 issue, had the actor recalling, "We were boarded up in the Peninsula Hotel, and we could look out the window through cracks in the boards and see people literally being blown away along the streets."

Culp: "Everything that could go wrong went wrong for Sheldon and my heart really went out to him. It was just a series of problems to overcome. Mr. Wang was our unit producer. But he wasn't good enough for what we needed. Stuff kept breaking down, the camera equipment, the sound equipment, the lighting equipment, everything!"[6]

Faulty equipment and a typhoon in Hong Kong weren't the only problems to be endured. Culp's intuition was sensing more dark and stormy clouds ahead.

Before filming had begun, Culp had reservations about the script for NBC's "test film." Culp saw "Affair in T'Sien Cha," the story of two American agents for Military Intelligence trying to find a missing train in the New Territory of Hong Kong Province, as simplistic, melodramatic, and extremely limited in the depth and breadth of the two leads. Culp didn't believe Friedkin and Fine had captured the voices, the rhythm or the sense of the characters; and he didn't trust Leonard as a director.

Culp: "I was worried about Sheldon. I knew damn well he couldn't pull this off as a director. He had only done half-hour shows, and a half-hour show on the stage, with three cameras, for Christ's sake, is not making a movie. And here we are, he was going to make a movie. But he wasn't up to it. Within a day I knew I was right."[7]

In the test film, Cosby, who had never acted before, came off stiff and uncertain. And Culp felt choked whenever he tried to bring the material to life.

Cosby: "The pilot that was shot, that thing was so horrible because of me. Because I didn't know anything about acting. If you have a bad script, and you take a bad actor, who doesn't know what he's doing, it can only make it worse."[8]

Culp: "Bill said, 'That thing was so horrible, because of me, because I didn't know anything about acting.' The point is, good writing makes good actors. It makes any actor better, not worse. It helps them. As good as Bill was going to be, and I could see it as clearly as I can see the sun is going to come up tomorrow, it isn't up yet, it's still night. And it doesn't help that I know it's coming up tomorrow, if what we need today is sunlight."[9]

Cosby's experience on the stage, playing to an anonymous audience hidden in the dark, did not help when it came time to face a camera and seasoned technicians and grips on a well-lit soundstage.

Cosby: "It was really weird, man. It took weeks before I felt able to do my thing without being self-conscious."[10]

There was only one moment in the entire episode where Culp and Cosby achieved a level of comfort that revealed the characters underneath. It was a scene shot on a railroad track overlooking Hong Kong bay. The two men, while searching for the missing train, walk and talk and kid one another. The hidden beauty of this scene is that Culp and Cosby composed it on the spot. The rest of the company would consider this an ad-lib. To Culp and Cosby, it was a rewrite. And Leonard, behind the camera, allowed it to happen.

Cosby: "Thank God Bob was the kind of person he is, that we could ad-lib. Bob was the person who gave the green light. Bob was the person I listened to, because we were on the set all the time. And I learned by listening to him when he talked to me, or whenever he talked to someone else. And he'd say 'Well this line doesn't make any sense, and there's another way to say this,' and then he'd mumble something; I mean, I was right there."[11]

Culp: "After the long scene on the railroad tracks, I asked the sound guy if I could listen to the rest of the dialogue from the show. I did, and then I knew how bad it was. It was fatally lame. But what could I do?"[12]

As filming progressed, the return to the states was delayed.

Cosby: "I got the word in the Peninsula Hotel, Camille was having our first child, and there I was in Hong Kong. Erikka was born."[13]

After two weeks in Hong Kong, suffering with bad equipment and dodging monsoons, the creative team and the stars returned to the comfortable climate and professionally controlled studio sets at Desilu for one more week of shooting.

Behind the camera, working under Leonard's guidance, was Fleet Southcott.

Having started as a camera operator in the mid–1930s for Hollywood B pictures, and remaining in that position for two decades, Southcott advanced up the ranks to director of photography when he ventured into television. First stop: *Gunsmoke*. Between 1955 and 1964, he supervised the filming of 351 black and white episodes of TV's top Western.

Now, as he made the move to *I Spy*, he would also make the transition to color photography. More challenging for him would be the task of lighting the studio back lot, as well as Los Angeles area locations, to exactly match the footage shot overseas.

The experiment continued.

By December, Culp was no longer confident that *I Spy* would ever go beyond its "test film" stage. He approached Leonard with these concerns. Leonard oozed his usual confidence. He reminded Culp that he had a "pay or play" deal with NBC, so not to worry about the fact that they hadn't been assigned a time slot yet.

Culp: "I asked him how many episodes he was going to make, because most people, normal guys, will say, 'three,' because the rest of the money is in their pocket for them in case it doesn't sell. I mean, what was he going to do with the film if it didn't get on the air, make guitar picks out of it?

"Leonard said, 'I don't care. I'm going to make all 18, or die in the attempt.' He was so adamant, I thought, 'I got it, I got it.' I didn't say it out loud. I said something like, 'Thanks, boss, I just needed to know.'"[14]

On Culp's way out, Leonard mentioned one more thing. He had instructed Friedkin and Fine to begin preparing the first batch of nine episodes. He told Culp this to further set his star's mind at ease. The writers of "Affair in T'Sien Cha" would soon be at work on more scripts, and were handpicking the writers who would supply the rest.

Leonard also believed in his editing team, who could splice with precision. Of significant importance, he believed in his music composer, Earle Hagen, who would score the test film.

Culp, on the other hand, believing the writing of the test film as "phoney" and Leonard's direction as "poor," had his doubts that the man who whistled the theme to *The Andy Griffith Show* could do enough to truly improve the project.

Robert Culp was determined to save *I Spy* from itself.

Although Bill Cosby didn't feel good about his performance in the *I Spy* test, he had a new baby girl to return home to, as well as a packed schedule for his comedy routines. His

The Cosby family—Camille, Bill and Erika—1965 (3 F Prod. Achieves).

second album, *I Started Out as a Child*, was released by Warner Bros. Records in time for the Christmas shopping season. It sold well, and the busy stand-up comic didn't have much time to worry about the status of *I Spy*. He left that to Culp.

The Test Film Gets Tested

Culp's intuition proved right. While the episode got the job done in introducing the characters and the format—that fusing of drama and natural comedy, which comes out of personality rather than situational one-liners—NBC shared Culp's concerns that they were not looking at a hit show.

Interoffice memos from the network at the time reveal the following sequence of events:

On October 13, 1964, NBC committed to Leonard for a full season for the fall of 1965, with a cut back to 18 episodes.

On November 6, 1964, Leonard was astute enough to send the network dailies from his

I Started Out As A Child, **1964 (under license from Warner Bros. Records).**

shooting in the Orient. A memo indicated that "NBC people highly enthusiastic with footage screened."

As a result, NBC made an air commitment for the show on November 20, 1964, to begin in September '65, with a time slot yet to be determined.

Leonard, perhaps knowing that his completed film would be viewed as a disappointment, delivered it to the network offices in New York just days before the start of the Christmas holidays.

It wasn't until January 23rd that the network had finished screening the "pilot," as it was called in their memos. As a result of those screenings, NBC gave the series a tentative timeslot, the worst they had to offer, Sunday nights from 10 to 11 P.M.

The next NBC memo, from February 4th, stated that a decision had been made to provide the series with a better timeslot, Wednesdays at 10 P.M. However, the report went on to say that the feelings regarding the "pilot" were "unanimously disparaging." The memo continued, "However, NBC [is] stuck with its commitment and, as a result, has definitely scheduled this."

The network had another problem.

The Man from U.N.C.L.E. was not doing well in its Tuesday 8:30 P.M. time slot. Routinely coming in third to *McHale's Navy* on ABC and *The Red Skelton Show* on CBS, the new spy series had failed to deliver an audience as big as Bond had in the theaters. Americans were not tuning in and now the NBC executives were looking at a pilot film with a pair of spies who excited them less than the *other* pair of spies already on the air. Someone had to be blamed.

A suggestion was made to replace Bill Cosby.

As 1964 came to a close, Culp had five months before he was due to fly back to the Orient and resume shooting *I Spy*.

Culp believed that if *I Spy* was going to make it, it needed a different direction.

Without authorization, and without notifying his employers, Culp took a very bold and unexpected step: Over the next four months, he wrote four scripts. One, "The Tiger," would be a rewrite of "Danny Doyle," the pilot script he had shown to Leonard six months earlier. "Court of the Lion" would be Culp's attempt to do James Bond. As he would describe it, "It had everything in it but the kitchen sink." The other two scripts, "So Long, Patrick Henry" and "The Loser," would prove essential in guiding the series toward the mood, the message, and the voice that would eventually become *I Spy*.

Culp, the writer, knew *I Spy* would not work if Kelly and Scott were overshadowed by the scenery and were reduced to being a device, a novelty for putting excitement and humor into an otherwise artificial story.

He also knew that the friendship and the shorthand language between friends would be the spine of this series; therefore, he began to have daily hour-long phone conversations with Cosby, as the comic traveled on his nightclub tour.

Culp was determined that the two men would connect, bond, and develop a common voice between them.

Cosby: "He said we had to be married. I didn't know what he meant. The sound of it made me nervous. It was later that I realized what he was saying was 'actor talk.' By then I knew he was right."[15]

Culp: "We had to pull the characters of these guys up and put them center and be as close as brothers could be. I couldn't tell anybody what I was doing, I had to prove it to myself before the fact. This is where I stuck my neck out further than anybody's ever done, certainly not before, and probably not since. I saw what those guys did with the pilot, and it was so goddamn awful that, if I didn't do something, we were sunk. I knew that Bill had no high bar to go to. No bar was set anywhere, for any of this stuff. But Bill's so sharp, so bright, so literate, that I knew, if I showed him the right thing, showed him the bar, he could clear it."[16]

Culp secluded himself in his home office for four months. A broken hand in a home accident didn't even stop him. Culp continued to type with one finger protruding from the cast.

Regarding the phone conversations, Culp said, "I was estranged from my wife. I didn't talk to my kids. Bill was the only voice of sanity, because there is no saner voice than Bill Cosby on the telephone. That was true then, it's true today. He was like a shrink to me.

"This was probably one of the first times something like this had happened to him, where somebody is coming to him for this kind of advice. I would bounce ideas off of him. We both knew that we were helping one another. We also knew that we were instructing one another. He was giving me information about him. We talked about his life, his family, his background, all the shit that needs to come out about one another if we're really going to create a bond. And we did it on the phone."[17]

Cosby: "Of course, I made Alexander Scott who I wanted him to be. And I wanted him to be this fellow who was highly educated, but people could reach in and touch him, no matter who you are. My philosophy was that his intelligence and his drive to be an educator—all that coming from where he was raised, that was in him. But he was not a person who took himself so seriously in terms of his credentials that you had to 'whoops' yourself around him."[18]

Two months into the process, Culp received a call. It wasn't Bill.

Culp: "Sheldon went right to it, man, he didn't mince words. He said, 'They want to fire Bill.' I never missed a beat. I said, 'Fine, no problem, fire him, and they'll have to fire me, too. We'll just wrap up the whole ball of wax right here.' Sheldon said, 'No, no, it's just that I wanted you to know. That's all.'

"What he wanted to do was to feel me out. Did I feel the same way he did? Because, frankly, he had been in contact with Bill a lot, too. And he had fallen for Bill, like a ton of bricks. It never wavered for the rest of his life. As much as he came to despise me, he loved Bill. He loved Bill like a son, truly.

"I never heard another word about it. Sheldon pulled something. I don't know what. He didn't have a fallback position. But he had me—and we were both in agreement."[19]

Earle Hagen was in Leonard's office when it happened.

Hagen: "I was with Skippy, Lenny's secretary, when the call came in from NBC. We only heard one side of the conversation. Sheldon said, 'Bill Cosby is the guy I want for this part.' There was some babbling. He said, 'I don't give a goddamn if we lose the South. I want Bill Cosby.' He waited, and then he said, 'In that case, we don't do the show.' And he hung up. He turned to the both of us and said, 'This is 1965, and they're giving me this stuff about 'those guys are going to be living in the same room and using the same wash basin?!' He never raised his voice in that call. He was very stern, and he gave them a little of the gangster touch. He wasn't trying to bluff them. He wasn't going to put a white bread graduate from Yale in that part. It took guts to do that in that day and time. He was a very strong person. Ten minutes later, the phone rang. It was NBC. Sheldon said, 'Okay.' He hung up and said, 'We're on.'"[20]

Leonard's timing had been good for his Mexican standoff with NBC. Something had happened in December of 1964 and the few months that followed.

Goldfinger had hit the theaters.

It was an immediate and massive hit, earning 51 million dollars at the box office in its initial release. This was more than the combined revenues from the previous Bond films *Dr. No* and *From Russia with Love*, both considered hits on their own merits.

Goldfinger triggered the spy craze.

The Ian Fleming Bond books were suddenly selling better than ever.

And even *The Man from U.N.C.L.E.*—benefiting from *Goldfinger's* largesse—finally began to do well in the ratings and catch on with younger viewers.

There was no way NBC was going to let *I Spy* go—even if it meant losing some Southern affiliates. Leonard gambled on that when he stood up to the network's demands concerning Cosby.

Leonard had won. And he had won big.

NBC would not only take the series and get it on the air, but they would loan Leonard the money he needed to realize his dream.

A mortgage agreement was created. *I Spy* was the collateral. Leonard owned it, and would have the freedom to determine how much he needed to spend. NBC would fund the loan with no interest due. In return, NBC would have the right to a minimum of five seasons of episodes. NBC would also have the right to broker the foreign sales of the series, and even oversee the domestic syndicated sales. Once the loan had been satisfied, the series would revert back in full to Leonard.

This had never been done before. No independent producer had ever owned a network series. No network had ever loaned money to a producer, or a studio, let alone with no interest due.

NBC did have one ace. Written into the security agreement, exhibit B, paragraph 13, it stated, "If Producer becomes unable to produce and deliver pictures in accordance with the package agreement, NBC will have the right, by giving Producer at least 72 hours notice, to take over and assume the complete production of the pictures, and Producer will turn over to NBC the supervision and control of production and delivery of the pictures thereof."

In other words, if Leonard screwed up, *I Spy* could be taken away from him.

While the drama over *I Spy's* future was playing out in Sheldon Leonard's office, Friedkin and Fine were struggling to find suitable material for the new series.

Between January and April 1965, a dozen writing assignments, approved and paid for by the team, had to be "cut off" at either story or first draft. A few more made it to a second draft script, and even went through a series of rewrites by Friedkin and Fine, only to be abandoned.

It is interesting to note that these assignments were not being handled by amateurs. Many of television's most prolific and successful writers had been brought in to help launch *I Spy*.

Few, however, were comprehending the blend of drama, action, and comedy required to make the new series viable. Perhaps one of the problems was that the only example of *I Spy* available to them for viewing was the problematic "Affair in T'Sien Cha."

John Meredyth Lucas, Steve Fisher, Roger Lewis, Charles Hoffman, and Adrian Spies, all working writers, all very much in demand, had all failed to turn in worthy material.

Robert Block and Harold Gast, both capable writers, had to be so severely rewritten that the credit they would receive was reduced from "written by" to "story by."

Edward J. Lakso and Emmy-winning writer David Karp, after succeeding in providing the series with one usable script each, both failed at their second attempts.

At this point, everyone was writing in the dark. The clear vision of the show had yet to be brought into focus.

In the meantime, Culp had returned to his writing.

The first script he completed, "So Long, Patrick Henry," was the story of a Black athlete who, frustrated by the racism he sees and feels in America, defects to China. The athlete, Elroy Browne, has sold out for money.

Unaware that he has become a pawn for Communist China, Browne is unhappy with the restrictions on his new life. Kelly and Scott are assigned to make contact and attempt to bring the lost sheep back into the fold.

Culp's story was topical and emotionally honest. It had elements of comedy, high adventure, drama, and politics, and it contained statements about racism and social unrest. It also predated the headline-grabbing event at the 1968 Mexico City Olympics, when Black athletes lowered their heads and raised angry fists of defiance during the rendition of the American national anthem.

The second script, "The Loser," achieved a different agenda for Culp. He had been told by the producers that Alexander Scott would "never get the girl." Annoyed, Culp wrote a script that, while not being a conventional love story, was a love story nonetheless, in which Scott's compassion for a nightclub singer goes so deep, it is as intense as romantic love.

Culp: "I finally, finally, finally finished 'The Loser,' and long before I turned it into them, the dreaded *they*, I mailed Bill a copy. I said 'This is my Valentine's present to you. You up front, I'm supporting, this is your story, baby. And, if we cast this right, I'm telling you, it's a 'mother.'"[21]

At the same time, Culp submitted "So Long, Patrick Henry" to Mort Fine.

Fine was "surprised."

In Culp's opinion, Fine seemed threatened that the star of the series would attempt to write a script on his own—and in secret. Fine did, however, agree that the script was good, and passed it on to Friedkin and Leonard.

Leonard was quick to call, telling the actor that he had no time for writing, but should instead be training and preparing for his role.

Culp: "He said, 'Are you working out? Are you playing tennis?' I'd say, 'Boss, I got to tell you, no. I got too many things on my mind.' He said, 'You got to pull that together, man, because tennis is growing. They'll be more and more people out there who will know you're not a pro, and it's not good for the show.'"[22]

Leonard was right. And, because Culp did not know how to play tennis, he hired Forrest Stuart.

Culp: "He came out to the house, and Forrest was a truck. He was really strong. I said, 'Don't teach me the game, teach me the moves, the look, that's all I have time for.' There was a tennis court on the property, and he and I worked out eight hours a day, day after day. And, man, when I was done, I could go through a wall."[23]

A second reprimand of a sort came from Mort Fine, who told Culp that the next time he got it into his head to write a script for *I Spy*, he had to work within the system.

Culp: "I said, 'What are the rules?' Mort said, 'I need an outline. Everybody does three pages.' So I gave him three pages the next day on 'The Loser.' He said, 'It's good, go ahead and write it.' I walked in the day after that and handed him the full script. He stared at it for the longest time, much longer than it took him to 'get it.' And, after all these colors had passed through his face, he said, 'You sonofabitch.' Just like that.

"I let a few more days go by so everyone could read it, and know what they had in their hands. I mean, 'The Loser' was so far over the heads of everyone who was writing for us at that time, including the writer/producers. They just didn't think in those terms, where you could mix all of those elements together and make 'em spell 'mother.'"

"A couple of days later, I handed the next two in. The subject of an outline was never brought up again. But there were no words of compliment, either. No 'well done,' no 'attaboy,' because anytime I did anything like this, it was a threat to their positions, and their egos. All of them—and I'm talking about three people: Friedkin, Fine and Sheldon. But they were in a position where they desperately needed the best material they could get their hands on. That's the operating concept here, without which, they would have found a way to kill it."[24]

Sheldon, Fouad, scouting locations, Hong Kong 1965 (Sheldon Leonard Collection).

Enter Fouad Said—The Schmoozer Gets Schmoozed

In early 1965, a young Egyptian immigrant—Fouad Said—eagerly read the Hollywood trade papers and had an idea.

He talked his way into a meeting with Leonard and began to schmooze, stating he could achieve *all* of Leonard's goals—inexpensively.

Leonard took convincing. He'd already been burnt by Run-Run Shaw and was not about to travel down that disastrous road a second time. But this kid had guts and imagination; and he kept coming back, day after day. Whatever the problem, the kid devised a solution. Good sound, good picture, good support—and all at a really good price.

Fouad was not without credentials. His spotty list of "accomplishments" stretched back to the mid–1950s, in Italy, when he, not even 20, bought his way into the business by helping to fund a cheapie called *Captain Fantasma*. Fouad's family had money, and that allowed him to be a producer and a film editor.

Two more Italian jobs followed, including the 1956 cult flick *I Vampiri*. Fouad got his first shot on camera with that.

Coming to America, Fouad was cinematographer and associate producer on another cult film, this time one of a slight controversial nature, *Virgin Sacrifice*. *Strange Lovers* and *The Right Hand of the Devil* followed in '63, and *3 Nuts in Search of a Bolt* in '64. Fouad shot camera on all.

With nowhere else to turn, Leonard hired the kid and gave him a title: "Location Unit Director of Photography."

What Leonard would learn, however, was that he'd just hired a genius.

Culp: "That was the goddamnest thing, he just walked in the door one day when I was in Sheldon's office. Sheldon said, 'Oh, by the way, this is the guy who's going to do picture and sound.' And I said, 'What? He's a *child*. What are you talking about?' He looked like a baby. God, he was handsome. But he's only about three feet tall!"[25]

Fouad's method would come to be known as "Guerrilla Filmmaking." Fouad's achievements are many and they are now routinely used in both television and motion picture production.

Production—as any Film or Television 101 class explains—is problem solving.

The streets in Hong Kong are crowded. In fact, they are jammed with people walking, talking, on bicycles, in market stalls, with live and dead animals, very curious kids, very curious adults, and very curious tourists. How do you solve the problem of the environment when every time the film van pulls up, a crowd gathers around it?

More to the point, how do you record your actors without drawing attention to them, when everyone can see the boom pole and/or the shotgun mike? Looping in the studio is one way—but looping is expensive and Fouad had promised a very good sound for a very good price. In other words, it had to be cheap.

Culp: "I think we did looping for the pilot, but I do remember Sheldon saying it would be a very rare instance when we would loop from then on. Both Bill and I despised the idea (of recording our words later). We worked so hard to get it to a place where it was starting to sing, and you can't loop that stuff. You lose it."[26]

At that time, there was nothing to solve this particular problem, so Fouad did it himself. He created a miniature wireless microphone to allow Culp and Cosby and any guest stars to be heard without drawing the crowd's attention. That microphone/radio system was the grandparent of the current wireless mike.

It was a start. But it still left the large problem of the bulky film camera, as well as the huge and very heavy arc lights.

Fouad stocked up on smaller, lighter, and cheaper equipment. In the minds of the established Hollywood community of technicians and craftsmen, the gear Fouad found for the trip was unproven junk. But in Fouad's mind, it was the future. Arriflex cameras and quartz and xenon lamps—light to carry, easy to conceal. And concealment would become a major concern, as Fouad was soon to find out.

Next stop, Hong Kong.

Back to Hong Kong

Robert Culp had to play several hours of tennis on the first day of shooting in Hong Kong. The location was a millionaire's mansion with a red clay tennis court that hadn't been used in years. It was Wimbledon perfect. The court had been rolled beautifully, and laid out with white lines all around. It looked like a perfect tarmac.

Culp: "The clay had disintegrated. It was sand. It was before eight o'clock in the morning, I stepped onto the court, and sank to the top of my shoes. Within ten minutes, I was covered with this red dust. It was a very hot, humid day, and, man, I'm telling you, after eight hours of that, breathing this red dust all day long, I went back to the hotel and I was bushed."[27]

That night, Culp woke up during a coughing fit.

Culp: "I coughed so hard, my throat closed up completely, and I thought, 'Jesus, I can't breathe. I gotta get to Bill.' He was in the next room, down the hall. I started for the door. That's as far as I got. Before I passed out, I thought, 'I'm gonna die.' When you can't breathe, and you're all alone, and you can't call for help, that's it.

"I don't know how long I was out. I woke up, I still couldn't breathe. I got into the bathtub and turned on the hot water, as hot as I could take it. I sat there for about 45 minutes. Something was in my chest, and I wanted steam. The spasm let up, and I thought, 'That was really weird.' I went back to bed and slept through the night. The next day, I had a fever."[28]

Culp saw a doctor, and was given the best antibiotics available at the time. He was being treated for a flu. Culp, however, was convinced he had inhaled a bacteria from the clay, causing the illness.

On the agenda for day two, a long chase sequence was to be shot for the episode "So Long, Patrick Henry." In the early hours at dawn, this physically grueling and complicated scene involved Kelly and Scott being chased by Chinese assassins through Hong Kong, across rooftops, up the side of a mountain, and into a slum village where they would finally make their stand.

Culp, still ill with fever, and short on breath, was relapsing fast.

Culp: "I said to Bill, 'I can't make it, I can't do this.' He said, 'Sure you can. I'll grab you from behind.' He reached under my coat and took hold of my belt. When I stumbled on top of the roof, he pulled me up."[29]

For the remainder of the chase, every time Culp began to fall, Cosby held him up—just as any friend and partner would.

While Leonard felt that Hong Kong had a great deal to offer to his cameras, crowd control had become a real problem.

In the mid–1960s, the British Colony was already inhabited by millions of people with very little to do. Its economy, though booming, could not absorb the countless refugees from China and southeast Asia.

A film company is an eye-catcher anywhere. In Hong Kong, this was free entertainment. So the idle crowds gathered.

They watched the crew going through incomprehensible but fascinating procedures: reflectors here, microphones there, and then, the most curious of all—Fouad Said's "sweat box."

Out of necessity, Fouad designed a box large enough to hide a camera and its operator, with holes cut into the sides for the lens. They'd put the box on the street, get the shot, and then move the box for the next set-up. It was clumsy, and time-consuming, but it seemed to solve the problem.

Sort of.

Yet it nagged at Fouad, that the gawking spectators were looking at everything, looking *into* everything, even looking into the sweat box.

Culp: "He was so sad that his idea for the box didn't work. It drew more people than the camera. And it was impossible in there, knowing the weather in Hong Kong. Anytime of the year, it's 95% humidity, and 95 degrees outside. Inside, it was just awful. It really *was* a sweat box."[30]

On one particularly hot day, onlookers stood for hours staring at the box, trying to understand why it was sitting in the middle of a sidewalk, and why it had a hole cut in its side. One after another, they peered into the hole, blocking the camera, and ruining the shot.

Finally, after hours of costly delays, the caged cameraman fainted from the heat.

Fouad began to think of modifications for his sweat box. In time, after numerous renovations, it would become known as the Cinemobile. But, for now, the prototype was merely referred to as "the white van."

Culp: "The Flying Tigers delivered the first one. It was a VW van, the smallest van you could buy. It looked like a James Bond cigarette lighter. It had all these teeny compartments, for filters, gobos, and a pocket in the back for the camera. It was the whole entire studio, including sound, in this little tiny van. He had redesigned it, retooled it, cut it, formed it, so that at the beginning, he had one 'Jenny' [generator]—the engine. He was using the VW engine to power it. It had one crucial flaw, the engine burned up because it couldn't handle it. It wasn't designed to take that kind of stress. Within a day or two, Fouad had to give up on trying to use it for anything else except driving it around. He got another Jenny and carried that separately. So we had two vehicles, and one where the back-ass end opened up like a Nazi machine gun to shoot the crowd. Then he'd close it up and be off to the next location, while Bill and I would be galloping down the street to change our clothes."[31]

Production is problem solving. Fouad had solved the biggest. But other problems kept coming.

In the hillside village where a scene from "So Long, Patrick Henry" takes place, a local actor was hired to play one of the doomed Chinese agents who would be shot by Kelly. A weak-looking Culp stood his ground, shot the agent, the agent fell down, then jumped up again. Take after take, the local actor kept hamming up the death scene.

At the same time, Cosby had to fall into the mud for each take, only to be cleaned up again to reshoot the scene with the Chinese agent who would not die.

Culp was tired and sick, Cosby and Leonard were annoyed. Finally, Leonard got an interpreter with the crew to explain to him why this Asian actor was unable to follow a simple direction and perform a death scene.

"He doesn't want to make it look too real," the translator said. "If the demons think he's helpless, they will steal his soul."[32]

Coughing, fever, mud, heatstroke—and now, demons.

Through the interpreter, and resisting the impulse to bay at the moon, Leonard firmly instructed the Asian actor to "act" as if he had been shot, and then stagger out of frame.

He did it. And that left three more weeks of location shooting in Hong Kong.

Michael Preece was responsible for script continuity. On any other show, that would mean he was the man on set keeping an eye on who, in a scene, is smoking or drinking, or who has a shirt that is tucked in, or untucked, or unbuttoned, and, if so, how far. Other shows would make mistakes. A cigarette being smoked by an actor would suddenly appear longer from a different angle. The level of the beverage in a glass being held by a performer would mysteriously rise or fall as camera angles would change.

But not on *I Spy*.

And, yet, on this series, the job of continuity was much more involved.

Preece had to keep detailed notes concerning the clothes worn by doubles, which would then be transported back to the states to be worn by the series' guest stars. Multiply this by everyone in the episode, and multiply that by nine episodes at a time, all being shot simultaneously and out of sequence.

Detailed notes also had to be kept concerning the backgrounds, even the color of a door that Kelly and Scott may have walked past, in case that door had to be reproduced at Desilu.

It was a big job. It was an important job. And Preece was very good at it.

There were only a handful of continuity mistakes on *I Spy*. This is amazing considering the scope of the production. And, of those dozen or so goofs, in the entire run of the series, two of them were in the pilot, the only episode filmed without Preece's guidance.

Preece: "It was complicated. It was a very bold venture. On rare occasions we would take a Polaroid picture for matching. The other unusual thing, unlike any other show I have ever been involved with, is we got nine scripts approved at a time. That is unheard of in television. But they did it. And we'd take those nine scripts with us. Of course, there had to be changes made on location for one reason or another, without network consent. And the network was agreeable to that."[33]

When on location, Sheldon Leonard made sure everyone stayed at the same hotel, cast and crew alike. Wherever he went, they went. Of course, some members of the crew were expected to share rooms.

Preece: "Sheldon put us all up at the Peninsula Hotel in Hong Kong, which was the best hotel there. I had a roommate, who was Harald Johnson, the costumer. He was a good costumer. Whatever was in style, whatever Culp and Cosby wanted, he was on top of. We all used to steal from him. It wasn't big stuff. Socks, things like that. There was this shirt that Culp had worn in one of the first episodes, a white shirt with blue sleeves, and I ended up with it. Harald was wonderful. But, he was also gay.

"One time I came back to the room and Harald had this young Chinese man in there on my bed. So the next season, I told Sheldon that I wanted my own room, that I didn't want to share with Harald. He said, 'When you didn't complain, we thought you liked that. Why didn't you say something in Hong Kong?' And I said, 'I didn't want to get the reputation of being a complainer.'

"I do remember, in Spain, we had to share a bed one night. It was a big bed, but I had to share it with Harald Johnson and Calvin Brown, a stuntman who was doing doubles for Cosby. Cal wasn't about to lie next to Harald, so I had to take the middle. I lied on my back with my arms folded over my chest, and my eyes wide open. I didn't sleep a wink all night."[34]

Calvin Brown: "Oh God, he told you about that? Harald would always be hitting on Michael. I said, 'This is one time when segregation is going to take over.' The White guys are going to sleep in the big room, and I'm in the small room by myself. And that's where that was."[35]

Culp: "Harald was weird. We used to call him Old Weird Harald.

"Harald had one great skill, which I spotted instantly, as soon as we went overseas. He had to match the wardrobe. He had the eye of an eagle when it came to clothes. We used to switch clothes just to screw him up, and he'd catch it.

"The man was a mule. He would have this pile of clothing on his back, walking down the streets of Hong Kong and Japan.

"We also didn't have dressing rooms. We dressed on the streets. We were in a hurry. We'd change our pants, and people would say, 'Those guys are in their underwear! On the sidewalk!'

"Bill didn't care and I didn't either. We were secretly proud of it, man. It's a macho thing. The hell with 'em."[36]

In addition to no dressing rooms, the company also did not have safety equipment.

For the episode, "Danny Was a Million Laughs," Fouad climbed out on a 16 by 2 inch plank at the top of the high-rise Peninsula Hotel. On the other end was a huge Asian grip, a sweating Buddha, who served as a counter-balance and anchored the plank so Fouad wouldn't kill himself.

Fouad, fearless and lightweight, crawled to the far end to shoot straight down at a black car that was rigged to explode. There were no ropes, there were no nets, there was nothing, except Fouad and the Buddha, and a teeter-totter of a plank.

Fouad's courage was proven. As would be his genius.

With the small amount of equipment Fouad had, he kept the filming moving along at a breakneck pace, and continued to pull rabbits out of his magician's hat. One of those rabbits concerned the contrast in skin tone between the two leads.

This is what separates an amateur from a pro. Anyone unfamiliar with the demands of film photography could not be aware of the pitfalls that exist. But skin tone, and the lighting created for it, is a difficult obstacle to be overcome by a director of photography. In this world, without prejudice, life was certainly easier in good old black and white.

Culp's skin was white. He had been working hard prior to his departure for Hong Kong, and, with the exception of the days when he practiced tennis, that work had kept him secluded indoors at the typewriter. Cosby's skin was black. Now try to place these two men, surrounded by intense light, standing side by side in a "two-shot," and watch how a camera iris will always adjust to the lighter colors, and how the visual specifics of anything or anyone darker will simply disappear.

Fouad made sure that did not happen.

In all the footage returned from this trip abroad, starting with the very first foot of exposed film, Cosby's face and features are beautifully photographed. Every nuance of expression is visible.

This was accomplished by silks, scrims and gobos, all used to perfection to filter and alter the degree of lighting.

Make-up would be another tool, albeit a short-lived one.

Culp was made-up to look darker, Cosby to appear lighter. But the make-up used, especially in these quantities, made Cosby itch and both men sweat. And both hated it.

When they returned to America, Culp was determined to find a better solution.

As filming continued, Friedkin returned briefly to his first love, acting, and cast himself to play a pivotal role in a script he'd written with partner Mort Fine: "A Cup of Kindness."

After production had begun, Friedkin confided to Culp that he was having second thoughts about his decision to appear in front of the camera.

Culp: "He was so nervous, he was shaking. Friedkin was concerned he might unintentionally sabotage that excellent script he and Mort Fine had written."[37]

Yet Friedkin's understated, beautiful performance helped make "A Cup of Kindness" one of the best episodes of the first season. Friedkin also saved Leonard a tidy sum: by playing an important role in the episode, Leonard could film more than the usual one-third of the script on location and made good use of Hong Kong's exotic background.

After three grueling weeks, the company returned to the controlled atmosphere at Desilu. They would have six more weeks of work with the main unit and the guest stars to complete the first batch of nine episodes.

Leonard, having no experience with one-hour directors, asked Culp to make some recommendations. Culp suggested two directors who could alternate duties for the first nine episodes — Mark Rydell and Leo Penn. Culp had also recommended his friend, Sam Peckinpah, who was currently experiencing a lull in his career.

Leonard said, "No."

The subject was dropped, for the time being.

Work continued under the guidance of Rydell and Penn with the continued problem of the photographic imbalance between Culp's and Cosby's skin tone.

Culp's solution was inexpensive and costly at the same time. He got a tan by both sunlight and sunlamp, and kept it going year round for the entire run of the series. The doctor's bills would come later for Culp's precancerous cells.

But, for now, he was beautiful, and the two-shot had been made possible.

Next, Leonard assigned a team of editors to work with the footage. And now it was time for Earle Hagen to wave his magic baton.

Hagen and Leonard had worked together many times before *I Spy*: the happy whistling heard in *The Andy Griffith Show*, the snappy tune for *The Dick Van Dyke Show*, the down-home country of *The Real McCoys*.

What Leonard wanted this time was something jazzy—like the dark and ominous *Peter Gunn* theme written by Henry Mancini. Hagen called it "semi-jazz."

Additionally, he wanted Hagen to score every episode individually. There would be no stock music in this series. Although musical themes would link the segments, each episode was to have music that would remain special and unique to it and it alone.

It was a massive undertaking for Hagen, who was already scoring music for a half-dozen other series.

Earle Hagen: "*I Spy* was the first real challenge for me. The changing panoramas of countries and plot lines were extremely daunting. It never occurred to Sheldon that I might not be able to deliver that kind of product. But then, it never occurred to me, either."[38]

Hagen and Leonard were so convinced that the music of *I Spy* would be a key component—as it was in the Bond movies—that Hagen was invited, all expenses paid, to join Leonard on his sojourns with the second unit. Hagen walked every land that hosted *I Spy*. He absorbed atmosphere, tasted the flavors, and heard the music in his head.

Back in the studio, he would compose what he heard and felt and, once a week, he would conduct his orchestra and create the signature sounds of the series to be. It was Leonard's determination that everything about *I Spy* would be outstanding.

When the footage was cut, and the music was scored, an inventive, eye-catching title sequence was devised. This innovative and original beginning was the first time a television show combined graphic art, live action and animation—all cut to a specific tempo. The rhythm track is right out of James Bond.

So is Kelly Robinson's silhouette.

He serves a tennis ball, pivots, hits a backhand, lobs, while the colorful names of major cities and global hot spots of the world appear behind him. With every upward swing of the racket, Hagen gives the pluck of a violin. The violin-tension mounts and plays off the notes of a saxophone.

The owner's name—above the title—appears: "Sheldon Leonard Presents." It is exactly as Leonard had envisioned. This would be the first time he had taken such a grand stand.

Next on screen is Robert Culp's name, in equal proportion and prominence, and then, Bill Cosby's name, a touch smaller, yet still out front and above the title.

Then, the graceful, catlike movement of Kelly Robinson's silhouette suddenly crouches. He turns, his racket is now a handgun and he fires. Abstract and elongated red triangles streak from the gun's barrel and form the words *"I Spy"* in perfect time with the main theme. There is a burst of violins over the black, white and red of the title. The music is urgent, exciting, melodic.

Kelly Robinson is introduced. He's cool, hip. There's a glint in his eyes and the barest beginnings of a jaded grin as he first lights a cigarette, and then the fuse to a bomb. He tosses the bomb to the camera and, after the flash explosion, the screen splits. The lower half of the screen showcases a fast montage of the episode to come. The top half stays with Robinson's extremely expressive eyes, watching and reacting to the adventure he is about to have—there's threat, danger, a fight, worry, and then, humor. The skin around his eyes crinkles as he smiles at the possibility of a little romance and a hint of a happy ending. It was unique, tense, hip, sexy, and smooth.

All of it, the essence of *I Spy* was caught in a spectacular visual worthy of a feature film. They'd done it.

3

The First Block of Episodes

In order of completion:

1. **"AFFAIR IN T'SIEN CHA"**; Written by: Morton Fine & David Friedkin; Directed by: Sheldon Leonard; Location: Hong Kong; First airing: 12/29/65

A train bound for Hong Kong disappears, and Kelly and Scott are assigned to solve the mystery. The investigation leads the agents to an ancient walled city and a pretty American schoolteacher. Along the way, several attempts are made on their lives by an assassin intent on stopping anyone from finding out about the train's secret cargo.

We are told here that Kelly has retained his amateur status as a tennis player, choosing to become a "tennis bum" after winning two Davis Cups, and that Scott, originally from Philadelphia, is a Rhodes Scholar, and is able to speak numerous languages.

Assessment

This was the infamous "test film." This is *I Spy*'s first breath of life, and it is a disappointment.

The idea of having Kelly and Scott search for a missing train is a curious hook.

There are a few comical moments, the first brush strokes of what is yet to be developed—the relationship between Kelly and Scott. The scene on the railroad tracks has the two men beginning their trademark banter. Scott reminds Kelly of all the sacrifices he has made for him, then says "Carry me."

In a scene with their contact, Edwin Wade (another terrific jaded, whiney portrayal by Roger C. Carmel), the gent pleads with Kelly to stop repeating everything he says. "Please! My wife does that. Why do you think I travel?"

The final fight scene, in the cramped confines of a sampan, is surprisingly vicious for a TV show filmed in 1964.

The location filming is impressive for its time, especially at the Tiger Balm Gardens. It is, as Leonard thought, eerie and strangely beautiful in the rain that became the typhoon.

However, the story is simplistic and lacks any real urgency.

The dialogue is often awkward and stilted.

Bill Cosby appears uncomfortable with the material and the direction.

The "danger" elements of the episode, where an enemy agent makes numerous attempts to stop Kelly and Scott from finding the train, are unbelievable.

Gavin, the enemy, a student at The Three Stooges Academy of Murder and Mayhem, blunders his way through the story.

In the teaser, his aim is off and he shoots Kelly's tennis opponent instead of Kelly. Next, he believes he can have another shot at Kelly while riding on a train. But, darn, another passenger, a tennis fan who wants Kelly's autograph, keeps getting in the way. Finally, worse still, he hatches a scheme to replace a kid's toy gun with a real one. Not only does the child not recognize the difference, he fires it repeatedly and never reacts to the kick of the weapon.

Gavin flunks. And, this time out, so do Friedkin and Fine.

The alleged "love story" (à la Bond) between Kelly and the schoolteacher is forced and unnecessary.

Wardrobe gets a smack on the wrist for the hideous cheongsam outfit on poor Vera Miles.

Vera Miles, "Affair in T'Sien Cha" (© 3 F Prod., courtesy Image Entertainment).

In the walled village, when Scott knocks on the mayor's door, the door is red. When the camera angles inside the mayor's humble home, at Desilu, the door is brown. This is a rare goof in a series so remarkably good at matching shots.

The Story Behind the Story

This episode was meant to launch the series—and very nearly sank it. When the brass at NBC saw the completed episode, the sound of jaws dropping echoed down, floor by floor, at 30 Rock.

Although "Affair" was the first episode filmed, it would be number 14 aired, completely buried in the 1965 Christmas season.

Culp: "Vera Miles was a big name, and an immense talent. I had asked for her. But the material was so poor, I was embarrassed for her, and for all of us. It was like we were all performing in a high school play."[1]

NBC Broadcast Standards, the in-house censors, had trouble with the graphic nature of the fight on the sampan between Kelly and the enemy agent. They had previewed the script and warned Leonard—before shooting it—not to make the scene too violent. When they saw it, they insisted that some of the "punch" be edited out.

CULP & COSBY ON SET REWRITE

In the first scene, as they are questioned by the police, Scott gives Kelly a rubdown; Scott's line, "He's the Green Hornet and I'm his faithful valet Kato" was not in the script. This was an ad-lib by Bill Cosby.

At the end of this scene, the line where Scott teases Kelly by interpreting a Chinese girl's statement, "She said something about skinny legs," as well as Kelly's response, "Ah, come on, they're not that skinny," were also ad-libs.

In the Tiger Balm Gardens, when Kelly shoves Scott against the wall to keep him from being hit by a falling statue, Scott quips, "Next time I'll take my chance with the statue." This too was not in the script.

The scene on the railroad tracks was entirely Culp and Cosby. All the lines from the script were replaced.

When they first approach the walled village, and encounter the gawking Chinese people, the set-up line for Kelly was in the script: "Tell them we were passing by and we heard their bell." Cosby, as directed by the script, was supposed to translate the line into Chinese, but, instead, repeats it in English. This prompts Culp to ad-lib, "In Chinese, you dummy."

When Kelly meets Rachel, the character played by Vera Miles, the line, "I don't mean to be rude, but you rock me," was finessed by Culp to, "I don't mean to be forward but, somehow on you, the pajamas look better."

After the fight on the boat, Vera Miles asks, "Is he dead?" Culp adds, "No, but I think I am."

She kisses him, then adds, "No, you're not." It was all made up on the spot.

Cast & Crew

Vera Miles was all over the dial in the 1950s and '60s, appearing on everything from *Wagon Train* to *The Outer Limits*. A former Hitchcock contract girl, she made many highly publicized appearances on *Alfred Hitchcock Presents*, as well as the director's films *The Wrong Man* and *Psycho*. She was 35 here.

Roger C. Carmel had been a familiar face on television since 1961. He'd made multiple appearances on *Naked City*, and would also appear in two more episodes of *I Spy*. He was 32 here. His real claim to fame was yet to come.

John Orchard, as Gavin, blended British upper class with cold-blooded sadism. He would become a familiar face through scores of TV appearances spanning the mid–1960s to the late '80s—and his most memorable role was the recurring character Ugly John on *M*A*S*H*.

Bud Molin was the first editor to be assigned the difficult task of cutting an episode of *I Spy*. This series would require a magician's hand in the splicing together of camera footage shot on opposite ends of the planet, and making all the sights and sounds appear as if they had happened on the same day, at the same place, with the same people.

The editors of this series, perhaps more than any other in the history of television, merit recognition.

Molin began in television, on the same lot where *I Spy* was shot. Desilu hired him to cut film for *I Love Lucy* and *The Loretta Young Show* in the mid–1950s. He would be the editor for Desi and Lucy's second feature film, *Forever, Darling*, and the Peabody Award–winning Desilu Playhouse segment *The Fountain of Youth*, directed by Orson Welles. When Leonard hooked up with Danny Thomas, and their factory of sitcoms made its home at Desilu, Molin began cutting episodes of *The Andy Griffith Show* and *The Dick Van Dyke Show*.

Leonard trusted Molin with his new baby.

Molin would return to cut sixteen more episodes, including the very next to be shot, "Carry Me Back to Old T'sing-Tao."

2. **"CARRY ME BACK TO OLD T'SING-TAO"**; Written by: David Karp; Directed by: Mark Rydell; Second unit directed by: Sheldon Leonard; Location: Hong Kong; First airing: 9/29/65

In America, Charley Huan made his fortune in noodles and illicit gambling. In Hong Kong, he makes a deal with Kelly and Scott: In return for a visa to Formosa, he will pay the IRS the one million dollars he owes in back taxes. To the agents' surprise, the income tax has been melted down and recast as a "black iron" stove ... or has it?

And then there is the viper in the bosom—or, in this case, three vipers—Charlie's sons-in-law, Harold, Mort, and Turkey. They have gold fever and will stop at nothing for a piece of that black iron stove, or, if need be, a piece of Kelly and Scott.

Assessment

"Carry Me Back" is a quickly paced, clever story that represents a major step in the "blendship" of Culp and Cosby.

The Story Behind the Story

Notice the scene where the pickup truck is chased by the convertible and crashes. It was shot next to Lake Hollywood, a reservoir in the Hollywood hills, less than fifteen minutes away from Desilu. This is also where the opening to *The Andy Griffith Show* was filmed.

Cosby: "There's a car-driving scene, and this car has to flip over one-and-a-half times. But Hollywood has not caught up with the times. There's no Black Stuntman's Union. That stuntman, who did the stunt for me, did it in 'black-face.' When I look at that, that was the most embarrassing thing to me. I said to them, 'If you tell me how much you paid that guy, I know some guys in my old neighborhood who will turn that car over right away!' So that was the beginning of Calvin Brown, moving in to become the stuntman. No more 'black-face.'"[2]

Director Mark Rydell: "Isn't that astonishing? It's not that long ago when we were in a primitive stage of emancipation for the Blacks in this country. It's just amazing to make people recognize how savage it was and how recent it was.

"What I remember mainly was the heroism of the producers in forcing the networks to accept a Black lead, which prior to *I Spy* had never been done. The courage of Sheldon Leonard and Mort Fine and David Friedkin prevailed, and they were pioneers of racial equality in television. They were really heroic and they stood fast under tremendous pressure. I admired them tremendously for their tenacity.

"And *I Spy* was a very daring show, besides the racial implications. It was the first show of its kind, to be adventurous in locations, even to this day. *I Spy* was a show that recognized the advantage of production value."[3]

Rydell did not go on location. Surprisingly, he wasn't even given the opportunity to preview the film from Hong Kong for this, or any of his episodes.

Rydell: "I wasn't shown the footage. I just shot my show. My shows were pretty much contained. As I recall, they were very independent and full and complete even without any additional footage from Hong Kong. Not that the location footage wasn't inserted, it was, but very minimally."[4]

Top: Philip Ahn, Pilar Seurat, "Carry Me Back to Old T'sing Tao" (© 3 F Prod., courtesy Image Ent.). *Bottom*: The Culp-Cosby Click, ad-libbing in 1965 (© 3 F Prod.).

"Carry Me Back" does not rely so much on the location footage, but on the cleverness of the material and the charm of the performances.

Culp: "We had fun on this, man. And, for the very first time, that divine bullshit, the jazz riffs between Bill and me, started to bubble to the surface."[5]

CULP & COSBY ON SET REWRITE

Moments not in the script, added by Culp and Cosby during the filming:

When Scott is bandaging Kelly, he asks his partner how he got a small scar on his shoulder. Kelly explains that it happened in the Middle East: "Three men on camels. We all knew one of us was a spy." The story meanders, apparently leading nowhere, when Scott insists on knowing who the spy was.

"*Me*," Kelly answers. "The other guy was a rug dealer and the third was looking for his camel."

In the hotel room, the first use of room 635 at the Peninsula Hotel, Kelly and Scott lie on their beds and plan a new strategy. Most of the dialogue is reworked, expanded, and Culp uses the phrase "wonderfulness" for the first time in the series.

Reviews

John Horne, a syndicated journalist, who reviewed this episode the morning after it aired, wrote: "In twisting an old yarn of Oriental guile, writer David Karp sped the hour with intrigue, surprise and humor. The light touch was the right touch. He also provided some neat tongue-in-cheek dialogue and plenty of exercise that made the stars act and sound like a couple of long-teamed working spies."

Cleveland Amory, of *TV Guide*, gave the series high marks in his October 1965 review. He called it "the best of the new shows we've reviewed." Amory was famous for using the royal "we" and "our." He went on to praise this segment as "one of our favorite early-season episodes." He predicted *I Spy* as a "can't miss."

Despite the positive reviews of this delightful installment, NBC never scheduled a repeat.

Cast

Philip Ahn (Papa Charlie) was a veteran at playing anything on television requiring an Oriental who could act (*Adventures in Paradise, The Islanders*, etc.). He was 59.

Bernard Fox (Harold), at age 37, would soon be Dr. Bombay on *Bewitched*, and Colonel Crittendon on *Hogan's Heroes*. Leonard knew him from his appearances on *The Andy Griffith Show* and The *Dick Van Dyke Show*.

Michael Conrad (Mort), at 39, would work regularly in television and movies for the next 20 years. He is remembered best as Sgt. Phil Esterhaus on *Hill Street Blues*, and added a new phrase to television oft-repeated tag lines: "And let's be careful out there..." He would return for another *I Spy*.

David Sheiner (Turkey), a gifted character actor, would return to *I Spy*. He was 32 here.

Pilar Seurat, at age 27, beguiling as Katherine, worked often in TV. Two years after this, she would be given a ghoulish death scene in an episode of *Star Trek* at the hands of an incarnation of Jack the Ripper.

David Karp, 43, made his only writing contribution to the series with "Carry Me Back" He had written for *The Untouchables*, and had won an Emmy for *The Defenders*.

Friedkin and Fine gave Karp a second assignment: "Double Eagle." He turned in the first draft on April 14, 1965, and a revision on April 30, 1965. The script was not produced.

Mark Rydell, 31 at the time, began his career in television as an actor on soaps. He turned to directing and worked on *Gunsmoke*, *Ben Casey* and *The Fugitive*, before arriving at *I Spy*.

His handling of the material in "Carry Me Back" is superb.

Sheldon Leonard would receive an Emmy nomination for his work directing the second unit for this episode, combined with two others: "So Long, Patrick Henry," and "A Cup of Kindness."

3. **"SO LONG, PATRICK HENRY"**; Written by: Robert Culp; Directed by: Leo Penn; Second unit directed by: Sheldon Leonard; Location: Hong Kong; First airing: 9/15/65. Repeated: 12/22/65.

One year ago, American Olympic star Elroy Browne defected to Red China. Now, heavily guarded, Browne and his fiancée, Princess Amara, arrive in Hong Kong where Browne's endorsement of the proposed Afro-Asian Olympics will result in a propaganda coup for the Reds. Kelly and Scott are sent to make contact, and ask a disenchanted Browne if he's ready to come home.

Ivan Dixon, Cicely Tyson, "So Long, Patrick Henry" (© 3 F Prod., courtesy Image Ent.)

Assessment

This above-average episode launched the series on NBC. It also bestowed a network imprimatur on Culp the writer.

The first 20 minutes of "Patrick Henry" fall into the "noir" category. Elroy Browne is not a likable character. He's temperamental, rude, and condescending. Kelly and Scott are not their usual easygoing selves and, in fact, Scott is not only moody, but angry.

This is notable, because this was the first impression *I Spy* would have on the American television audience, and, for that reason, "Patrick Henry" was a surprising choice for NBC to lead off with. The network did, after all, promote *I Spy* as a "comedy-adventure" show. Yet, here, the first quarter of the episode lacks excitement, warmth, and humor—the very elements of the *I Spy* brand and certainly the foundation of the Culp/Cosby pairing that the audience would find so endearing.

After the commercial break, however, the climate shifts slightly. Kelly and Scott join Elroy and his beautiful fiancée for drinks in a local club. Scott's anger is focused and aimed at Elroy: "The whole world's trying to keep bloody fools like you from selling themselves back into slavery. But you did it anyway."

The mood shifts again, this time to slight camp, as Kelly and Scott ham it up as harmless drunks for the benefit of the Chinese bodyguards waiting for Elroy outside the bar.

Next, in a 180-degree turn in mood, in a rainstorm, a chase begins and lasts for several minutes as the hunted agents try to elude their pursuers.

First-time *I Spy* viewers had their hands full in trying to pigeonhole this new series. By the time 11 P.M. rolled around, "Patrick Henry" had shifted gears from angry, to preachy, to exciting, to morbid, to humorous. As an example of the latter, young Rickey Der is delightful as Mickey, the bellboy obsessed with James Bond, signing his notes to Scott as "007" and quite proud of the fact that he's seen *Goldfinger* 27 times.

For the tag, Scott informs Kelly that, in gratitude for the boy's help, they will be taking Mickey to the movies.

"You'll like it," Scott says. "It's an English film. Lots of adventure and action and romance. This guy in the movie gets all the girls. And one of them's even painted gold."

The Story Behind the Story

Culp's original title, "I Am the Greatest," was scrapped. It referenced another Black athlete at that time: Muhammed Ali (who changed his name from Cassius Clay in 1964, and had recently adopted the signature catchphrase).

As to the geography of the script, and how he determined where to stage the story, Culp said: "When we went there the first time, I made a whole bunch of mental notes. There was poverty, a village on a hillside, and, with every rainstorm or typhoon, somebody would get washed away. The house supports were bamboo, for Christ's sake. What made it possible was being there. You can't get that from photographs. You can only get it by going."[6]

"Patrick Henry" was the first of seven scripts to be written by Culp.

Always an advocate for civil rights, Culp used the characters in this first script to voice the unhappiness of Black Americans toward their country. The script allowed three Black characters, Elroy Browne, Princess Amara, and Alexander Scott, to dominate the story.

And "Patrick Henry" is one of *I Spy's* bloodier episodes. Kelly and Scott eliminate a half-dozen enemy agents without so much as a blink. In an attempt to appease network executives' concern over losing their Southern affiliates, it is the White agent, Kelly, not the Black agent, Scott, who is the main perpetrator of the carnage in this episode. As written in the script, the cab and hotel shootouts, both emphasize that Scott's gun must be shot simultaneously with Kelly's. When only one shooter was needed, it was always Kelly. At one point, in the village, he says, "I'll do it, I've got the silencer."

CULP & COSBY ON SET REWRITE

Being that this was a Culp-written script, the voices for Kelly and Scott were right on the money, right from the start, right on the page. There is only one ad-lib of any consequence:

"Can't you ever bring a silencer," Kelly asks.
Scott's answer is, "It ruins the lining in my suit."
Kelly adds, "Mine, too."

Reviews

Weekly Variety, in its September 22, 1965, issue, gave *I Spy* a mixed review. Credit was given to NBC for having the "guts" to cast "a Negro in a feature role," but the critic expressed surprise that the show "would depict another ethnic group, the Chinese, with casting that was a throwback to Fu Manchu."

Daily Variety turned its assessment in for the September 16th issue, stating "The enchantment of distance from the Hollywood back lots with real Oriental atmosphere is a factor in [the series'] favor. Cosby proves he can be dramatic-oriented as well as to comedy." The review closed by predicting *I Spy* would "catch on."

Bill Ornstein, a critic for the *Hollywood Reporter*, wrote on September 16, 1965: "Sheldon Leonard has come up with an exciting, international intrigue series with interesting characters. The Hong Kong scenes give the overall effect authenticity without leaning on process shots. It should be a winner with viewers as well as those with a yen for a TV change-of-pace."

The *Los Angeles Times*, on September 16, 1965, wrote: "It's difficult not to go overboard on this one. The premiere story was written by Culp and his script was extraordinary. Ivan Dixon gave an outstanding guest star portrayal of a disenchanted Negro who attempts to negotiate a rich new life in Red China. Cosby's scene, where he puts down the defector, was brilliant, establishing him as a fine actor. Culp was equal to his script. A first-rate production, beautifully filmed in Hong Kong."

Jack O'Brian, a critic for the *New York Journal-American*, on September 16, 1965, wrote: "*I Spy* is slick, stylish, [and is] the best spy series we've ever encountered. The story was credible, the characters extraordinarily true, the backgrounds realistic, and the dialog, best of all, extended the sound and flavor of the management's respect for a viewer's intelligence. The performers were just right, wonderfully and precisely what your goosebumps ordered. Robert Culp wrote the script, which was crisp, tough, believable, and with touches of the sort of grim bantering that exists in the normal performance of any constantly dangerous duty. Bill Cosby, the comedian, is now the most unexpectedly proficient performer of the season. His style is light without being trivial. [The show is] a dandy."

Al Salerno, critic for the *New York World-Telegram and Sun*, on September 16, 1965, wrote: "*I Spy* breaks ground in all directions. A Negro, Bill Cosby, is co-starred. For a chap who never has done any TV acting, he scores well. Another Negro, Ivan Dixon, playing a guest role, is cast as the bad guy, who later straightens up and flies right in a first-rate performance. Action, excitement, and derring-do, often with tongue-in-cheek, as undercover agents make the world safe for NBC and producer Sheldon Leonard."

Ben Gross of the *New York Daily News,* on September 16, 1965, wrote: "Cosby is presented without any emphasis whatsoever on his race. His presence is merely taken for granted and thereby more is achieved for better racial relations than by a thousand propaganda exhortations. Sheldon Leonard's production is of top quality."

Ratings

According to *Daily Variety* (September 17, 1965), *I Spy*'s premiere episode dominated its time slot in two different ratings surveys.

The National Arbitron survey found *I Spy* to get a whopping 41% share, followed by *The Danny Kaye Show,* on CBS, with a 32% share, and *Amos Burke, Secret Agent,* on ABC, trailing at 21%.

A 26-city Trendex survey determined *I Spy* finished first with a 40.9% share, beating out *Danny Kaye* (30.3%) and *Amos Burke* (25.8%).

In the September 27th issue of the same trade paper, the first Nielsen report came in for the new season. For the week of September 12–19, the score from 30 cities had *I Spy* at number 20 out of 93 prime-time shows. Both *Danny Kaye* and *Amos Burke* failed to place within the survey's top 40 shows.

Cast & Crew

Ivan Dixon (Elroy) began on TV in 1957, soon appearing in three episodes of *The Outer Limits,* as well as turns on *The Twilight Zone* and *Perry Mason.*

After his stint on *Hogan's Heroes,* Dixon would spend less time acting and concentrate more on directing for television. One of his first jobs was on a comedy special for Bill Cosby in 1971.

Cicely Tyson (Princess Amara), fresh off her recurring role in *East Side, West Side,* would return in *I Spy*'s second season for a far more challenging character in "Trial by Treehouse."

Richard Loo is appropriately menacing. Culp and Cosby would never forget him, and, in particular, the way in which he pronounced some of his lines. Whenever either of the *I Spy* stars wanted to crack the other up, he would deepen his voice and send a menacing "Missa Brown" in the other's direction.

Loo was certainly one of the more familiar Asian character actors in American films in the 1930s and '50s, right alongside Philip Ahn. Loo's wife ran the very successful Bessie Loo Talent Agency in Los Angeles, concentrating on Asian talent. *I Spy* was a good customer.

Tiger Joe Marsh looks as if he stepped out of *Goldfinger,* providing an especially eerie moment when he stands in the pouring rain, a mountain of a man, unflinching, stone-faced, refusing to be moved. Tiger held the title as World Heavyweight Wrestling Champion in 1937. As a professional wrestler, he was required to become a member of the Screen Actors

Guild. He continued to wrestle into the late 1950s, when he finally gave his body a break and turned to other types of "acting."

Ricky Der (Mickey) had excellent instincts in front of the camera. He made his debut in an early 1960s Tarzan movie, then followed with a short run on a TV series called *Kentucky Jones*, starring Dennis Weaver.

As Kelly and Scott made room 635 of the Peninsula Hotel their home for their entire stay in Hong Kong, it is a shame that we did not see more of Mickey. But Mickey was the creation of Robert Culp, and it would have proved awkward for the producers of the new series to place that character into scripts written by other writers.

Leo Penn, the second director recommended by Culp, had been a victim of the 1950s blacklist—the unspoken, hidden list that held the whispered names, true or not, of anyone who had expressed any interest whatsoever in Communism.

In a directing career that spanned more than 30 years, Penn helmed over 400 television programs. Prior to working on *I Spy*, he directed episodes for *Bonanza, Ben Casey*, and *Voyage to the Bottom of the Sea*.

Bob Moore was the second film editor to be assigned the impossible—cutting together an *I Spy*. Like Bud Molin, Moore was a "cutter" on the Desilu lot, primarily employed by T & L Productions. His credits included *The Andy Griffith Show* and *Gomer Pyle*. He would alternate with Molin for the first entire block of episodes, and, before the end of the season, be entrusted with eight more hours of Leonard's experimental formula.

Earle Hagen's music is a delight. While the pictures brought back from the Far East begin the process, Hagen's score completes the magic of taking the viewer to Hong Kong in 1965.

Hagen: "Most Eastern cultures have their own scales. The Thai scale is very different from the Vietnamese, or Japanese scales. Once you are familiar with what makes a particular country tick, it's not so hard to write the style. I always chose to Westernize the music for the audience."[7]

Culp: "I didn't really understand the techniques involved, but what I do know about is what makes a picture work. I appreciate how much a drama is enhanced by its score. It's what I care about, and Earle Hagen made the picture work. Without him, I cannot imagine *I Spy* being able to achieve the rhythms that it did."[8]

4. **"DANNY WAS A MILLION LAUGHS"**; Written by: Arthur Dales; Directed by: Mark Rydell; Second unit directed by: Sheldon Leonard; Location: Hong Kong; First airing: 10/27/65

In Hong Kong, Kelly and Scott must protect mobster Danny Preston from himself. Until he is extradited to the U.S., Preston's fellow drug profiteers have reason for concern: Danny has quite a mouth. And now that mouth has made him a marked man.

Assessment

"Danny" is an unpleasant man in an uncomfortable episode.

The payoff here is in watching small, shallow people, like Danny and his henchmen, get the smug looks smacked from their faces.

"Danny" boasts many excellent moments, but those fragmented pieces never quite connect to produce a successful story.

NBC agreed, and did not choose to repeat the episode.

3—The First Block of Episodes

The Story Behind the Story

This episode contains the first mention of Scott's mother, and Scott's fondness for writing her letters.

Director Mark Rydell thought of Martin Landau when he read the script for "Danny."

Rydell: "I was really in control—unnaturally so—of any television show I ever did. I thought the director should do everything. And so I recommended him for that part."[9]

Landau: "When I played Danny, I took off on Sheldon. I knew Sheldon's personality from watching him in the movies. I designed Danny to be Sheldon. And about two days into the shooting, Sheldon came onto the set and said, 'Y'know, that's a very interesting character you're playing.' He got it, he actually knew that I had made that choice. I was sort of spoofing him. And it was too late for him to tell me not to do it. But I also think he was flattered."[10]

In Landau's opinion, *I Spy* had far reaching influence.

Landau: "We benefited on *Mission* by using cordless mikes and a bunch of stuff that they had developed. Arriflex cameras, and so on, that were not as common. It was all Fouad. It was radical, it was different, and we reaped some of the benefit of that. It was a direct result of the *I Spy* innovations."[11]

CULP & COSBY ON SET REWRITE

Culp and Cosby rewrote most of the dialogue in every scene, keeping the meaning, but substituting in words of their own to convey the message or the joke. For example:

After Danny flips Scott a coin, and says, "Here you go, boy, I'll put my shoes in the hall for you," Kelly whispers to Scott, "We could disconnect every bone in his body."

Both of these lines are in the script. Scott's reply to Kelly is not. He was supposed to say the bland, "Tell me about it." Cosby, however, gave the line a right cross: "No. Work before pleasure."

According to Culp, it was this script that provoked him and Cosby to join together in a united front against ever having to deal with dialogue like Danny's racist remark again.

Reviews

Hank Grant, in the October 29, 1965 issue of the *Hollywood Reporter*, wrote: "What more can we say about *I Spy* except that each show seems a more

Martin Landau, "Danny Was a Million Laughs" (© 3 F Prod., courtesy Image Ent.).

polished gem than the previous one and Bob Culp & Bill Cosby comprise the most perfect team in any type series. And Martin Landau never looked better as a villain than he did in Wednesday night's show."

Cast & Crew

Martin Landau (Danny) was 34 at the time of this performance. He had been gaining attention on television through high-profile guest appearances, including two on *The Outer Limits*. He had strong supporting roles in a number of films, such as Hitchcock's *North by Northwest* and the Burton/Taylor *Cleopatra*.

A few months before working on *I Spy*, Landau was approached by producer Gene Roddenberry to play an alien in a science-fiction television pilot. The character was named "Mr. Spock," and the series was *Star Trek*.

Landau passed on the role, due to Spock's emotionless character. In 1966, Landau accepted a weekly job in TV, which would bring with it plastic noses, fake ears, and a variety of wigs. He would play the incredible superimpersonator Rolland Hand on *Mission: Impossible*. His wife, Barbara Baines, was also an IMF agent. Landau's abilities would win him three Emmy nominations.

In 1989, Landau was nominated in the Supporting Actor category for his work in *Tucker*. He did not take home the Oscar, but did win a Golden Globe. The following year, he would again be Oscar nominated in the same category for Woody Allen's *Crimes and Misdemeanors*. And in 1995, the third time proving to be the charm, he would win the Supporting Actor Oscar for his role as Bela Lugosi in *Ed Wood*.

Rydell: "Martin Landau is one of the most generous, decent men around. He's up for sainthood."[12]

Jeanette Nolan (Aunt Helen) was 54. Her most famous role had been Lady MacBeth, opposite Orson Welles in his 1948 version of *Macbeth*. She would be nominated four times for the Emmy Award, and one of the nominations would be for *I Spy* (see "The Conquest of Maude").

Nick Colasanto (Genius) was 41 when he played this part. He is blessed with a fantastic death scene, a surreal moment as fellow bad guy Sam stares intently, knowing that Genius has been shot, and is already dead, but waiting, transfixed, for him to slowly topple from the chair. Colasanto would be on *I Spy* three times: He was a reporter in "Patrick Henry," and a cabbie in "My Mother the Spy." He would, of course, later tend bar as Coach, in *Cheers*. In 1985, he would leave that series due to illness, and die at 61 years of age of a heart ailment.

Arthur Dales (writer) would come back for one more *I Spy* assignment: season three's "Suitable for Framing." Like Leo Penn, Dales was a victim of the Hollywood blacklist, and therefore many of his credits have not been acknowledged. Among those that are include *Mannix* and *Ben Casey*.

5. **"A CUP OF KINDNESS"**; Written by: Morton Fine & David Friedkin; Directed by: Leo Penn; Second unit directed by: Sheldon Leonard; Location: Hong Kong; First airing: 9/22/65. Repeated: 5/4/66.

Agent Russ Conley, Kelly's mentor, arrives in Hong Kong. With him are sealed orders. The Pentagon's message: "This man double agent. Kill him."

Harder still for Kelly, Conley knew he was delivering his own death sentence, but came anyway. His reason: Only Kelly can help to prove him innocent of treason. And, for that, Kelly needs Scott.

David Friedkin, Emmy nominated in "A Cup of Kindness" (© 3 F Prod., courtesy Image Ent.).

Assessment

This excellent episode provided America its second look at *I Spy* on September 22, 1965.

Russ Conley is a tragic character, a man standing at the crossroads, carrying the weight of a death sentence on his shoulders, attempting to maintain a small ounce of dignity as he pleads for his life. The dark truth, he is setting Kelly up. As played by Friedkin, a man such as this shouldn't be able to smile or crack jokes. His situation is far too grave.

Culp is in perfect form throughout this episode. Notice, after he decodes the message telling him to kill the man who delivered it, how his stunned reaction quickly turns to one that is expertly guarded. It is Scott who breaks the silence, asking "What are you going to do?"

"I'm going to do my job," Kelly says sharply. "I'm going to kill him."

Watch how Kelly's eyes become downcast when he finds he is reluctant to kill his friend. And then how sinister he can become, when Russ is explaining his situation and pleading for help. Kelly leans back on the bed and says in a cold and dangerous tone, "So far you haven't saved your life."

Cosby's work in serious drama is such a stark contrast to his comedy: it is perfectly understated. He moves flawlessly from skeptical to compassionate. All he has to do is "glance" at Kelly and we know he has agreed to help. Scott has no reason to trust—or even want to help—Russ, other than that his help will protect Kelly.

And that brings us to the story's climax:

Kelly defeats Russ in hand-to-hand combat, and Russ falls to his death. Even though Russ betrayed and was trying to kill him, Kelly's face shows immediate and immense regret.

He cannot dwell on Russ because Scott's been shot in the leg. We have never heard the words "I'm sorry" expressed with deeper remorse and sincerity than when Kelly says them to Scott. "I'm sorry," stated over and over, carries the weight of guilt for putting Scott in jeopardy, for taking a bullet, and it's a two word confession by Kelly to Scott.

The Story Behind the Story

Friedkin and Fine, after an awkward start with "Affair in T'sien Cha," accomplished "wonderfulness" with "A Cup of Kindness." For their work here, both were nominated for an Emmy in 1966 in the category of Outstanding Writing in Drama.

LOCKED ROOM #1

The episode flows easily between drama and comedy, as it invents an *I Spy* signature—the "locked room."

In the first of many locked rooms, Leo Penn's direction is clever as the camera pans back and forth between two crates, following the whispered conversation of our agents, who remain out of sight.

The means to escape: a fertilizer bomb.

Cast

Irene Tsu was that girl under the bed with Kelly. She entered show business after winning the title of "Miss Chinatown" in a 1961 San Francisco beauty contest. Bit parts followed, including the 1961 film *Flower Drum Song*. Her first role of any consequence was for the 1963 comedy, *Under the Yum Yum Tree*. She is now a successful real estate agent in Beverly Hills.

Lee Kolima, looking very much like Tiger Joe Marsh from "Patrick Henry," played Kwan Tak, the hulk of an Asian with the shaved head who chases Kelly around the export office. Kolima was able to supplement his income for the better part of a decade playing menacing figures, like Kwan Tak. He played one named Bobo in two episodes of *Get Smart*, and a humorless mountain of a man named No-Fun in *The Wild Wild West*. In an episode of *The Monkees*, he was cast as Atilla the Hun. He would return to do another *I Spy*.

6. **"CHRYSANTHEMUM"**; Written by: Edward J. Lakso; Directed by: David Friedkin; Second unit directed by: Sheldon Leonard; Location: Hong Kong; First airing: 10/6/65. Repeated: 6/1/66.

Kelly and Scott are assigned to recover a map of defense installations stolen from a military courier near Hong Kong. But with the assignment comes bad company: They have been ordered to assist Maximillian d'Brouget, an eager but hopelessly confused counterspy.

Assessment

As one fan of the series wrote on an *I Spy* website, "We have the success of *The Pink Panther* and *A Shot in the Dark* to thank—or blame, depending on your point of view—for this atypical episode."

The character of Max d' Brouget is clearly modeled after Peter Seller's Inspector Clouseau.

"Chrysanthemum" is pure parody. Earle Hagen's wonderful score manages to sneak in Henry Mancini's signature notes from the theme to *The Pink Panther*. Max is Clouseau, and Kelly and Scott play a mixture of Dreyfus and Kato, the dutiful foils to Clouseau's dignified bumbling.

The episode does have some unavoidable laughs, most occurring in the last half. The situation becomes especially funny when Max leads Kelly and Scott to the water, where they "borrow" a series of boats and get drenched more than once.

Marcel Hillaire, "Chrysanthemum" (© 3 F Prod., courtesy Image Ent.).

The reason Kelly and Scott put up with Max, other than being assigned to, is the Frenchman proves himself at being hopelessly right. As Scott puts it, "He is strong with theory, but poor at execution."

The story also gives us a nice handling of the "character arc," this time taking place in Kelly. Kelly has a complete change of heart concerning Max. Once he discovers that Naval Intelligence counted on Max's failure and is displeased at his success, Kelly begins a slow boil. Max risked his life for these ungrateful people, and even that does not earn him their respect. Watch Culp's face. The nuance in his eyes, the steady stare, the slight change in the tone of his voice, the absolute contempt for his superiors.

The last half of the story and, especially, the final moments, make up for the awkward beginning, where writer and director seem to stumble over a pair of two left feet more often than the clumsy Max does.

The Story Behind the Story

The title of the episode refers to the code name Max is known by, as he is fond of wearing a chrysanthemum on his lapel. The title of the first draft script was "Butter Fingers," referencing Max's actual nickname with Naval Intelligence.

And Naval Intelligence is where this assignment comes from.

Many fans of *I Spy* are under the wrong assumption that Kelly and Scott work for the CIA. Even Bill Cosby thought this, at one time, describing the pair as a "CIA team" for an interview he gave to *Playboy* magazine. And John Tiger, the writer of seven *I Spy* paperback novels, also portrayed Kelly and Scott as being CIA operatives.

In fact, the agents work for Military Intelligence. This episode gives us our first true indication of this.

Commander Riddle, as we are told here, was the military officer who first teamed Kelly and Scott together.

Perhaps because one of the writer/producers was also serving as the director on this episode, there were no significant instances of ad-libbing by either Culp or Cosby. The script was shot as the script was written.

Many clever lines are lost, however, due to the heavy accent used by Marcel Hillaire.

Cast & Crew

Marcel Hillaire had been in TV since 1952. Thanks to the popularity of Inspector Clouseau, he had already played a French police detective three times, in a recurring role in *Adventures in Paradise* as Inspector Bouchard, then on *77 Sunset Strip* as Inspector Bordeaux, and in a 1964 film *Wild and Wonderful* as Inspector Duvivier. After his work in *I Spy*, he would be at it again, as Inspector Bevereaux in the 1966 film *Murders' Row*, then as Inspector Prideaux on *McCloud*, and then again on the same show as Inspector La Blanc. In 1978 he was Inspector Le Dious in a TV movie entitled *Evening in Byzantium*. Don't worry about him having been typecast, however. Hillaire also played a character named Phanzis in the final episode of *Lost in Space*.

Culp: "I was charmed by Marcel Hillaire, but he wasn't easy to work with. He was a blockhead—but that was the character, so it sort of worked out okay."[13]

Edward J. Lakso, the highly employed TV hack of the '60s and '70s, with credits on shows like *12 O'Clock High*, *Star Trek*, and *The Big Valley*, wrote the script. Mort Fine was particularly pleased with this piece, although he foresaw trouble in getting the written word onto the TV screen. In a February 15, 1965, memo, Fine wrote to Leonard, "This is a marvelously funny and inventive script. Of course, production problems are probable."

Lakso was offered another shot at writing for *I Spy*, but his second effort, "Where Is Diablo," planned to be shot in Mexico, was cut off after the first draft was turned in on August 19, 1965. He was not asked to write for the series again.

David Friedkin, experienced at directing light fare, took the helm for this episode, replacing Rydell.

Culp: "Mark Rydell broke it down to an 11-day shoot. Sheldon went through the roof. He took it from Rydell and gave it to Friedkin. Friedkin took 11 days. Eleven days is 11 days. Rydell was right.

"The episode was an interesting idea, but putting it on a Chinese junk drove it up to 11 days. It could have been done a different way. Put the camera on the pier; water is water and sky is sky.

"The story was kind of cute, but not very much fun shooting for us. It just about broke us in every way."[14]

7. **"DRAGON'S TEETH"**; Written by: Gilbert Ralston; Directed by: Leo Penn; Second unit directed by: Sheldon Leonard; Location: Hong Kong; First airing: 10/13/65. Repeated: 5/18/65.

In Hong Kong, Kelly meets an old flame. After she introduces her current fiancée, the man drops dead at Kelly's feet.

Prior to becoming a corpse, the man was suspected of dealing in weapons. He was also the agent's latest assignment. Now it appears he was the target of a secret society called the Blue Dragons.

Joanne Linville, Mike Faulkner, "Dragon's Teeth" (© 3 F Prod., courtesy Image Ent.).

Struggling with the feelings he still has for Alicia, his former love, Kelly joins Scott in searching for the reason for the "hit."

Assessment

"Dragon's Teeth" resembles the 1940s Charlie Chan movies. The piano-player/spy Johnny Sax hints at Hoagy Carmichael in *To Have and Have Not*. Police Captain Porter is trying for Sidney Greenstreet in *The Maltese Falcon*.

The teaser didn't do its job. Beginning from the fade in, we see the horrendous establishing shot of the party guests dancing to jazz piano, attempting to do the twist, and proving that only Chubby Checker could get away with that move. The shot is held for an awkward, stagnant, embarrassing eternity.

Kelly and Scott enter, decked out in timeless black tuxes, complete with ruffled shirts. They look sexy and debonair. We are given a glimmer of hope. But then all those terrible coincidences start popping up: The hip cat playing piano is a fellow spy. The pretty girl throwing the party is the first of many of Kelly's ex-lovers. The elegant gentleman the pretty girl is announcing her engagement to is a gun smuggler. The gun smuggler, of course, is Kelly and Scott's assignment. Immediately after saying hello, he drops dead.

Everyone Kelly and Scott talk to over the next 50 minutes turns out to be a member of the secret society; and, the mother of all coincidences, the leader of the secret society is the girl from Kelly's past.

Culp's performance for the first half of the party scene is over-the-top moody. Blame the director, the same man who staged the dance sequence. Leo Penn could have instructed one of the most skilled TV actors in 1965 to bring it down a notch.

Many of the sets and costumes in this episode are equally outrageous.

Inspector Porter wears a bright red vest.

Kelly and Scott visit two different rooms that have bright red carpeting.

Kelly wears a bright red tux in the tag scene.

Forgive us for seeing red, but the director should have had better—or, at least, some—input here.

"Dragon's Teeth" may occasionally embarrass, but seldom bores. It is so unintentionally camp, it's funny, proving that even mediocre *I Spy* can make for must-see TV.

The Story Behind the Story

Although Scott never put alcohol to his lips, this episode establishes that he makes it a point not to drink.

At the party, which opens the episode, Scott refuses a cocktail from a waiter. The script had him taking the drink. Cosby opted to change this.

Later, when Scott is ordered at gun point to drink a poisoned glass of champagne, he says, "But I don't drink."

Cosby: "My father drank, and it was my choice to play Scott that way."[15]

NBC Broadcast Standards took a pair of scissors to "Dragon's Teeth."

Culp: "Early in the show Bill and I arrive at a party, decked out in tuxedos. Joanne Linville greets us at the door, and, in the European manner, we buss each other on the cheek. The network had a shit hemorrhage because she kissed a Black man, and it was cut out. You have to pick your battles, and this wasn't one of them. So Sheldon backed off. He hated it, as much as everyone else did, including us."[16]

Culp and Cosby later learned that they were being quietly protected. Leonard knew his stars had to stay focused on their work, and sometimes the only way to do that was to isolate them from the world. They never saw the hate mail.

Culp: "Sheldon was the one who made the decision to keep all that shit away from us, and he was dead right. We wanted to know we had nothing but approval. If we had known [about the letters], it would have wrecked it all. It wouldn't have been fun anymore."[17]

CULP & COSBY ON SET REWRITE

Cosby adds the line, "The wonderfulness of your charm." He also uses the phrase "Go for yourself" for the first time in any episode. The producers and writers would soon pick up on the Cosbyisms, and work them into future scripts.

Cast & Crew

Joanne Linville was married to *I Spy* director Mark Rydell. Linville, a gifted actress, collected over 100 credits in TV and film between 1958 and 2001. From here,

3—The First Block of Episodes

she went on to play a Romulan commander and woo Mr. Spock in *Star Trek*. She was 37 at this time.

Walter Burke (Johnny Sax), usually cast as the little guy who gets pushed around, had a chance to play against type in the 1967 James Coburn spy-comedy, *The President's Analyst*, as ruthless and cold-blooded "FBR" (sic) Chief Harry Lux.

Ron Whelan, the Sidney Greenstreet–type who is a police inspector, worked in TV and film from the late 1930s until his appearance here. It was 1965 and, by the end of the year, he would be dead of leukemia.

Gilbert Ralston would return later to pen "Time of the Knife." His other TV credits include *The Naked City, Laredo*, and *Star Trek*.

8. **"THE LOSER"**; Written by: Robert Culp; Directed by: Mark Rydell; Second unit directed by: Sheldon Leonard; Location: Hong Kong; First airing: 10/20/65. Repeated: 5/11/66.

In Hong Kong, Scott is held prisoner by drug smugglers. The bounty for his life is three million dollars worth of heroin, confiscated by the American authorities. But the trade is impossible—the heroin has been destroyed.

As Kelly desperately searches for his friend, Scott awaits his death sentence, and meets Angel, an addict who sings for her supper—or, in this case, her fix. Whether "thin" or high, Angel can help no one, not even herself.

Bill Cosby, Eartha Kitt, their Emmy nominated performances from "The Loser" (© 3 F Prod., courtesy Ron Jacobs).

Assessment

The excellent "Loser" is a moody episode, steering clear of cliches, all very typical of the material Culp brought to *I Spy*.

Culp tackles two taboo subjects: drug addiction and a well disguised love story for Scott.

In a unique twist, Ramon, the antagonist, has a demon of his own to deal with, a silent and stern Asian man named The General.

And, as he had done with "Patrick Henry," Culp took another bold step in creating challenging roles for Black performers.

Good use of location photography, as Kelly and Scott are followed and chased through the city, highlight this episode.

The Story Behind the Story

Culp: "The Loser' deals with human irony. Scott thinks he's going to save the girl, but walks away with egg on his face. The title refers to everyone. She's a loser, and Scott tries to save her, and Kelly tries to save *him*.

"Kelly really *did* have a hair-brained notion of jumping out of the drum—like the nude jumps out of the cake. He had a gun. He thought it might work. And his legs went to sleep. I love that."[18]

A defining moment in establishing the character of Scott comes from Culp's script. Scott says, "I come from a long line of losers. Every time I see one, it hurts."

This is the only instance in the series where we get a hint as to why Scott does not drink.

Rydell's excellent direction of this episode was not lost on Culp.

Culp: "We never changed a goddamned word, except the 'Black Coffee' scene, which Rydell wrote. And I am forever indebted to him, because it was exactly what was needed."[19]

The "Black Coffee" scene has no dialogue. It features Angel, looking very thin, trying to sing. She breaks down on stage. Rydell felt the audience needed to see Angel being this vulnerable in order to sympathize with her. Culp agreed.

Culp: "She is in desperate need of a fix of heroin, and Ramon wouldn't give it to her—in other words, he's torturing her so she will be on their side. That abuse is what brings us to her."[20]

Rydell: "The screenplay is the single most important tool in the creation of a movie, but once that screenplay is finished, it has to be *turned* into a movie. The things that a director adds—to a scene or a character, enriches the process. The more you examine the material, the more ideas develop. And 'The Loser' certainly engaged us on a very deep level."[21]

With regard to casting the musicians needed for the episode, Rydell made some crucial choices:

Rydell: "I have a music background. I went to Juilliard, I'm a jazz pianist. I was thrilled with the idea of directing this show because of the jazz implications. I hired Jack Sheldon, the trumpet player, and his trio for Eartha. Jack, at that time, was a full-blown heroin addict, and he kind of credits this show with the beginning of the end of his drug addiction."[22]

Rydell's respect for Earth Kitt is boundless.

Rydell: "I think part of [the portrayal] had to do with my familiarity with that world—and I guided her towards the execution—but you have to give her all the credit. She's just a miracle, an amazingly remarkable woman. She has a lot of temperament, but that's what you want in a performer, someone who enjoys behavior, and she certainly has a wide range of emotions, including rage and anger and meanness."[23]

Cosby: "Mark Rydell was a director who tried to get things out of me, but I never wanted to play those things the way he saw them. Mark was telling me, 'You gotta have this *intensity*'—and Mark was from the Actors' Studio. But I wanted my guy to have a looseness about him, because life for Alexander Scott was really a part of something that was played cool."[24]

This would be Rydell's last turn at helming an *I Spy*.

Preece: "Mark Rydell was really involved in filmmaking. He said to me, 'Approach every show like it's the last one you're going to do.' But he fell behind with every episode of *I Spy* that he did. He was doing stuff that, today, would be commonplace. He was a very particular director."[25]

If *I Spy* put Bill Cosby on the map, "The Loser" provided the stepping stone on his journey to stardom.

Culp: "I am so proud of that. It made him a leading man.

"I knew they were never going to let Bill get the girl. This was too much for them to take. I was told by Friedkin and Fine, face-to-face, 'No, the audience isn't ready for that.'

"Okay, so what emotion resembles love? Compassion. I said, 'What if I put a woman in so much hot water, so much jeopardy, that you don't care how objectionable she is on the one hand, on the other hand she's a woman in trouble. His heart is going to melt. So, 'The Loser' was designed so that Bill doesn't get the girl, but he tries to save the girl. He puts everything on the line for the girl, and risks both of our lives for her. It *was* a love affair. It looked like a love affair, and, because of it, I knew we would have broken that barrier.

"All of a sudden, the barrier disappeared, and they were very grateful because it got all kinds of award nominations. From that point forward, Bill and I were equal as leading men."[26]

LOCKED ROOM #2

In this episode, Kelly and Scott are introduced to the second in a series of their famous locked rooms. Here, Culp's script solidifies the voice of the characters, that fluid, comfortable, intimate tone between two people who—in all the world—can depend only on one another.

The locked room scene begins as Kelly, having failed to rescue Scott, is tossed onto a bed next to his friend. Both are bound in straight jackets.

KELLY: "My legs went to sleep."
SCOTT: "Your legs went to sleep? YOUR LEGS WENT TO SLEEP?!"
KELLY: "You say that once more, I'm gonna punch you right in the mouth."
SCOTT: "Go ahead, take your best shot."
KELLY: "That did it. Untie my hands."
Scott attacks the knotted laces at the back of Kelly's neck with his teeth.
KELLY: "You'd better hurry, though. I think my punching arm is going to sleep."
SCOTT: "Why don't you just take a nap all over? I'll wake you up if anything happens."
KELLY: "Boy, this is the last time I'm ever going to get you out of trouble. The LAST TIME."
Scott pulls back, defeated, staring at the knots in the dim light. His next line is said without humor.
SCOTT: "Yeah, I'm afraid you may be right about that."
This cemented the buddy genre.

Reviews

In the October 16, 1965, issue of *TV Guide*, America's number one selling magazine, "The Loser" was given a prestigious half-page Close Up listing. This would be the first of over a dozen *I Spy* episodes to be acknowledged in this way.

Cast & Crew

Albert Paulson, a familiar face on TV in the 1960s and '70s, usually featured as crooks and losers, plays Ramon. He was 40.

Rydell: "I went to school with Albert Paulson. He was the most talented actor at the Playhouse. He was hampered by his inability to get rid of his accent, or he would have been perhaps one of the major actors of his generation. He was a giant."[27]

Eartha Kitt turns in a surprising and daring performance as Angel. Orson Welles, after catching Kitt performing in a Paris nightclub in the early 1950s, called her "The most exciting performer in the world!"

A jazz singer, appearing on TV variety shows for nearly a decade, Kitt was best known for her holiday chestnut, "Santa Baby." She had recently expanded her range to drama. Cosby, in particular, was struck by her.

Cosby: "I'm looking at Eartha Kitt, and Eartha Kitt is edgy. And I'm thinking, Orson Welles, 'Santa Baby,' and saying, 'this is fantastic.'"[28]

After *I Spy*, Kitt would replace Julie Newmar in something far less dramatic, as Catwoman on *Batman*.

With a hint of affection, Culp now says of Kitt, "She's still with us, and meaner than ever, just as mean as a snake."[29]

For her work here, Kitt would be nominated for an Emmy in the category of Outstanding Single Performance by an Actress in a Leading Role in a Drama.

Mako played Jimmy, who seals Kelly into a metal barrel. He was just getting started in a career that would span five decades. He would return to do two more episodes of *I Spy* before being cast the following year in *The Sand Pebbles*, where he would be nominated for an Oscar in the category of Best Supporting Actor.

Jack Sheldon, seen as the trumpet player, was a respected jazz musician who was also breaking out as an actor. He was one year away from having his own series, a short-lived comedy called *Run, Bubby, Run*. Jack Webb would cast him in seven episodes of *Dragnet* between 1968 and 1970. He would then spend over a decade on *The Merv Griffin Show*, as Merv's straight man, and leader of the band.

Bud Molin, responsible for the editing, was nominated by the American Cinema Editors (ACE) for an Eddie Award for his work here.

Bill Cosby was named Best Television Actor for 1965 by the ACE for his performance in this episode.

Mark Rydell, like Leo Penn, was under contract to shoot four episodes in the first block of nine. His contract was cut back to three when he turned in an 11-day shooting schedule for "Chrysanthemum."

Ron Jacobs: "Rydell was one of the most talented men I worked with. I had to tell him he was being cut. It was hard. I'll never forget it. But he was too particular of a director for what they needed—for the schedules and the budgets that they had."[30] Rydell would make the jump to feature films with *The Fox*. He would direct Steve McQueen in *The Reivers*, then John Wayne in *The Cowboys*. *Cinderella Liberty* followed with James Caan, then Bette Midler's *The Rose*, and Henry Fonda's last, *On Golden Pond*.

9. **"NO EXCHANGE OF DAMAGED MERCHANDISE"**; Written by: Garry Marshall & Jerry Belson; Directed by: Leo Penn; Second unit directed by: Sheldon Leonard; Location: Hong Kong to Japan; First airing: 11/10/65. Repeated: 5/25/66.

In Hong Kong, Kelly and Scott seek double agent Erik Thorsten, the only person the Communists will trade for Tommy Richards, a captured American pilot.

As the team searches for Thorsten, they receive unwanted help from the captured pilot's wife. Louise Richards is frustrated that the U.S. government has failed to secure the release of her husband after two years in a Chinese prison. She is now ready to take matters into her own inexperienced hands.

Assessment

"No Exchange" is entertaining, but below standard *I Spy*.

Once again, Kelly knows the "assignment" personally (following Russ in "A Cup of Kindness" and Alicia in "Dragon's Teeth"). The American pilot they are working to free is an old buddy of Kelly's, a plot device that seems contrived.

Later, the writers use a puppet show as a means for an informant to convey information to Kelly and Scott. This plot device, along with the Puppeteer's death, with the puppet acting out the melodramatic death scene, would be perfect for a more fantastic show, such as *The Wild Wild West*. It is grossly out of place in *I Spy*.

The Story Behind the Story

With this episode, we witness the first mention of Scott having attended Temple University. The secretary at the embassy recognizes him, and even knows that he played football, as a halfback, while in college. Bill Cosby also played football, as a halfback, while attending Temple University.

In the original tag scene, as written and filmed, Scott is on a date at the beach with the pretty embassy secretary we met earlier. A second pretty Black woman arrives, with Kelly, who is decked out in a new suit provided by the Hong Kong tailor he and Scott had visited during the course of their investigation. Both women are vying for Scott's attention. Kelly tells Scott of the second girl, a seamstress, saying, "She fell in love with your measurements."

If the scene had been kept, it would have marked Scott's first foray into a sexual situation. Perhaps the "She fell in love with your measurements" line was a bit much for the network censors.

An element in the telling of this story, which may seem unnecessary, is the framing device where Kelly is writing a letter to the Pentagon, trying to get reimbursed for a damaged wristwatch. While typing the letter, flashbacks take us in and out of their previous mission to locate Thorsten.

This was, in fact, an afterthought. The episode came in short, as a result of many lines from the script being cut or restructured in a simpler and shorter way, and the original tag scene being cut. And this resulted in the need to shoot additional material to make up for lost time. Eight pages were added by Friedkin and Fine, constituting the scenes in a Japanese hotel. These additions to the episode, as well as the voice over, were added on August 20, 1965, a full month after principal photography for the original episode had wrapped.

Culp and Cosby stuck to the new lines, but embellished slightly, filling in the necessary minutes.

Preece: "Sometimes we would have a show that was a little short, and they would be asked to improvise something to fill time. Part of my job was to time what they would do and make sure it added up to the minutes we needed."[31]

Culp & Cosby on Set Rewrite

A classic ad-lib: When Eric Thorsten, with a gun trained on Kelly and Scott, asks them which one wants to die first, they simultaneously point to each other.

When it is believed Scott may have killed Thorsten in self-defense, Kelly's line in the script is an accusatory "Do you know what you've done?"

Culp changed this to "We've really done it now."

This way, instead of agents behaving individually, the team remains as one.

Cast & Crew

Sue Randall (Louise Richards) was probably best known for playing Miss Landers, the first grade teacher Beaver Cleaver had a crush on in *Leave It to Beaver*. She was only 30 here, but would retire from acting two years later. In 1984, she died of cancer at the age of 49.

Kurt Kruger (Thorsten) appeared in the 1943 film *Sahara*. Having come to Hollywood from Germany, he was often cast as a Nazi, as he was in the 1957 film, *The Enemy Below*. In the 1960s, he turned to TV, again appearing often as a German soldier, spy, or other assorted heavies. In 1977, he abandoned show business for real estate.

Mako again plays Jimmy. He will return, as a much different character, for one of the Japanese block episodes.

Garry Marshall and **Jerry Belson's** writing talents would be better served in the 1970s sitcoms they wrote, produced, and directed, separately, including *The Odd Couple*, *Happy Days*, *Laverne & Shirley* (all featuring Marshall), and *The Mary Tyler Moore Show* (with Belson). Prior to this one and only assignment on *I Spy*, they had written together for *The Dick Van Dyke Show*.

Leo Penn, taking his fourth and final turn as a director for *I Spy*, would return to the series during the second season, as an actor. Look for him in "A Room with a Rack."

Preece: "At that time Leo had a little bit of a drinking problem, and would drink openly on the set. Also, Leo was extremely slow, and they were looking for people who could get it done fast."[32]

After *I Spy*, Penn would direct for *Star Trek*, *Columbo*, *Magnum P.I.*, and *Matlock*. Perhaps his most impressive credits lie in being the father of three sons, all very successful in the world of entertainment. Son Michael is a musician, recording hit albums in the '80s and '90s. Son Christopher has done well as an actor. And son Sean has received acclaim for both his acting and directing abilities, including an Academy Award as an actor in 2004 for *Mystic River*.

4

On to Japan

The world was quickly changing.
The Man from U.N.C.L.E. was beginning to catch on.

In the summer of 1965, CBS presented *Secret Agent*, the revamped version of *Danger Man*. Patrick McGoohan was back as John Drake, a dark, private, and somewhat humorless man. In glorious black and white, Drake traveled the world—never leaving England's Pinewood Studios—and had little interest in romancing women, or questioning the lethal means of his work.

All the components of Leonard's magic formula were still intact as cast and crew left for Japan and the filming of the second group of nine.

The last time Leonard had been in Japan was 1953, just eight years after the end of World War II. At that time, his impression of the Japanese people was that they were uniformly helpful, cooperative and eager to please.

In 1965, however, Leonard detected a shift in attitude.

Japan had prospered mightily and the *I Spy* boss now complained that the Japanese nationals he'd dealt with had reneged on agreements, raised previously agreed-upon prices, were utterly unfriendly and completely unhelpful.

In Nikki, an ancient village with legendary temples, the *I Spy* company had booked four days of shooting, and had reservations at the local hotel for 5 actors and a crew of 20.

And then all 25 reservations were suddenly gone. Their rooms had been given over to a convention of Japanese industrialists. No apologies. No assistance in booking elsewhere. Nothing.

The exceptional Leon Chooluck, Leonard's location manager, scrambled to find accommodations, and the company ended up being scattered in private homes. This proved extremely difficult in gathering everyone for the start of a day's work.

They lost two days, in that one afternoon.

During the shooting of a sequence in a fishing village on the Izu Peninsula for the episode "Court of the Lion," the local people resented the presence of the Americans. No one explained why they were offended. The locals just were—and made their displeasure known immediately. Usually demure women paraded half-naked in the background whenever they saw the camera, ruining far too many shots for Leonard to remain amused. He recounted that the women would actually heave their bare breasts at the camera just to infuriate him. More time lost, more money wasted.

Up next was an ordinary sequence in a club. Dancers had been hired, the set was dressed, then a gaffer hit a light switch only to discover the power had been turned off. Apparently, someone on the crew had inadvertently offended the building's janitor. The janitor exacted an interesting punishment: he cut the juice, and padlocked the power box.

Leonard steamed, and the problems escalated.

Next, Leon Chooluck was kidnapped.

Cosby and Culp, the Wonderfulness Boys, Japan '65 (© 3 F Prod.).

When Chooluck chose an exterior for a restaurant, the unchosen rival across the street was insulted and had arranged for the kidnapping. Calling the police, Leonard was told, would prove pointless. This section of the country was more or less run by the Japanese "mafia." To get Chooluck released, Leonard paid a ransom of many thousands of yen.

Leonard went on record to say that wherever the company traveled in Japan, they were threatened, strong-armed, harassed and demeaned. As a result, the second unit portions of several episodes represented a setback from the early success of the Hong Kong shoot.

Culp, already watching his boss with a critical eye, had a theory concerning the difficulties Leonard was encountering. It began with a historical observation.

Culp: "The British, wherever they went in their pursuit of empire, had very little use for the indigenous personnel. So the Chinese in Hong Kong were accustomed to rude White people—and, from their point of view, Sheldon could be really offensive in his gruff, no-nonsense approach to everything. Yet *he* was the one who was always talking about being polite in the Orient, because it is so important, and how we could lose face. And then he would butt heads with the Japanese, anyway."[1]

The trip was less traumatic for Culp and Cosby.

Culp: "The first thing I remember about Japan was that Bill took Camille and I took Nancy. This is something he and I discussed, because there had been no women with us on the first set in Hong Kong. It caused us to think about doing things that were not healthy. Both of us agreed that it would be really good to take our wives along."[2]

Leonard's daughter, Andrea Bershad, recalls, "Dad loved to travel with the whole crew, and invited the principals to take their wives with them, so there was a very nice social aspect. They could all be with their families and experience the opportunity to work hard and play afterwards."[3]

Families also need babysitters. Besides his multitasked position as script supervisor and continuity person, Michael Preece expanded his job description to include child care specialist.

Preece: "Cosby and Camille wanted to go out to dinner, but they had just had a baby. I offered to babysit. I had kids at home and I knew what to do, with changing diapers and all. So they went out to dinner and left the baby with me. Nothing happened, she slept the whole time. And they were back in 45 minutes. It endeared them to me, that they were worried about their child, and that they came back right away."[4]

As the trip to Japan unfolded, Leonard continued to protect his extended family from the difficulties that surrounded the shoot. He believed Culp and Cosby's only jobs were to concentrate on looking good, learn their lines and fine-tune their performances. To this end, Bill Cosby was quickly evolving as an actor.

Preece: "Culp basically taught Cosby all his acting tricks while we were doing that first year. By Tokyo, and, more so, by Mexico, Cosby caught on to all of it.

"At first, he was very concerned about remembering the lines, and a lot of his concentration went there. But, after a while, he learned that, through editing, he didn't have to deliver these long speeches. He could break them into pieces and, as script supervisor, I could cue him. Cosby caught on to a lot about filmmaking that he had been taught by Culp. 'If it's not good, ask for another take. If you don't feel right about something, say so.' Culp was very important in Cosby's learning."[5]

Leonard: "After eight shows, Bill was as advanced as many actors are after eight years."[6]

Culp: "I told Bill again and again, 'Don't try to act. You're not ready. It will come. Just follow your intelligence. Do what Scott's mind says is the objective; think the thought that the character is thinking. You can do that. It's easy, because it's second nature to you. You're the best storyteller in America today.' That's the only thing I ever told him. 'Trust the future. It will come.' And it did. He changed with every episode."[7]

Calvin Brown: "Bill trusted Culp—with everything. Bill would mess up a line, mess up a scene, and, on the next take, Bob would mess up, and then say that he needed to go and work on it a bit. Then he would take Bill back to the dressing room, and they'd redo their scene. He did this to help Bill out, and to show him what he should do. But no one else saw that."[8]

Culp was influencing Cosby in other ways, as well. The actor who had won himself a "bad boy" reputation on the set of *Trackdown* was already drawing the battle lines.

Culp: "We got to Tokyo and the four of us walked into the New Otani Hotel, where we had been booked by Sheldon and Leon. The ceilings in the hallways were built for little, teeny people. Bill and I were walking down the hall toward our rooms, and I looked at him, and he looked at me, and I said, 'Let's get out of here.' He said, 'What about Sheldon?' I said, 'Sheldon will just have to live with it. He can't run our lives completely, for God's sake.' I told Bill, if you're doing a movie, you're not forced to stay in a given hotel, unless it's the only one in town. So we took a quick cab ride to the Hilton, where the ceilings were tall enough.

"Sheldon hit the roof. Neither of us had ever seen him really cross before. We had caused him to lose face. We both said that we'd make up the difference of the cost between the hotels. It wasn't that. He had scheduled a shoot in the New Otani's gorgeous old gardens. And we screwed the whole thing up.

"We were both apologetic, but we held our ground, because Sheldon was Sheldon, and you had to do that or he would run all over you. So we stayed at the Hilton with our wives, and Sheldon and everybody else stayed at the New Otani."[9]

Leonard managed to soothe matters over with the management of the New Otani, and the *I Spy* company was allowed to shoot there, in the gardens, for the episode "Three Hours on a Sunday Night."

Culp would see Leonard's temper flare again, as a result of an incident that occurred during the filming of the Japanese block of nine.

Culp: "In 'The Tiger' I wrote close-ups of Bill's watch into the script, which was going to be a Rolex. Then I wrote a letter to Rolex saying I had done this, and it's going to be on, and gave them the date. I said it would be nice if you guys gave us each a watch. And I sent it to them. The watches came, and a couple of weeks later, Sheldon stormed into my dressing room and said, 'For Christ's sake, you asked them for watches because you wanted a Rolex?! You can't do that! It's against the law, you dummy!' He really tore me a new one. So I went sheepishly and collected Bill's watch, took mine, put them back in the box, and sent them back to the factory."[10]

Culp and Cosby had wanted a Rolex for themselves because they had admired the one Leonard wore. Leonard had excellent taste. Besides fine watches, he enjoyed wearing expensive clothing. One such item was a Vicuna coat Leonard picked up during the company's first tour of the Far East.

Leonard: "Vicuna is an expensive item. The Customs Department would want a big cut. How could I cheat them?

"On our return flight, we were scheduled to clear customs in Honolulu. I figured I could sneak my coat through customs by wearing it. They examine baggage, I thought, but they don't pay attention to clothes on your back.

"The plane made its stop in Honolulu, and we lined up for customs. I was wearing my lovely, warm vicuna topcoat. The outside temperature was ninety-two degrees, with ninety percent humidity.

"Sweat ran down my cheeks. Two paces behind me in the line, Bill bellowed, 'Hey, Shel. You look warm. Why don't you take your coat off?'

"The custom inspector's ears perked up.

"'Yeah, Shel. You're sweating. Take off your coat.'

"'I'll kill him!' I thought. 'With my bare hands! I'll strangle him, and get Greg Morris to play the part!'

"By now I was facing the customs inspector. I had no alternative under the circumstance.

"'I didn't list this coat,' I told him. 'Sorry. I just forgot to put it on my declaration.'

"'Yeah,' he responded. 'I was going to ask you about it, even before your friend started advertising. The first thing we look at is what people are wearing. They think they can get away with it, and they wind up in jail.'

"I paid the customs man. Cosby, the son of a bitch, had saved me from jail."[11]

Leonard loved everything about Cosby, including the teasing.

Preece: "I remember we had difficulty getting into a Japanese palace, and Sheldon really had to pull some strings. We were all sitting around, eating lunch, and they had served us these type of box lunches. Sheldon made a speech and said, 'Now don't leave a chopstick or a toothpick on the ground here, because these are sacred grounds.' And I remember, when we finished, as a joke, Cosby left his entire lunch box on the ground. That was Cosby. He was always joking and giving Sheldon a hard time. Nothing was sacred."[12]

Culp: "Bill never let up on him. If I had tried to kid Sheldon like that, he'd come after me with a meat cleaver. But Bill could do it. And Sheldon just plain loved it."[13]

While the father and son relationship between Leonard and Cosby quickly developed, the Culps' marriage was disintegrating.

The trip to Japan was a chance for the busy actor to have time with his wife. The four Culp children were left in safe care back in Los Angeles, and Robert and Nancy finally had time together. But part of that time was consumed by problems.

One problem occurred as a result of Culp trying to better acquaint himself with Laura Devon, a pretty blonde actress flown out to appear in the episode, "Tatia."

Culp: "You don't know these people, and you're supposed to have a love scene with them. You're supposed to feel something. I remember a scene in a restaurant at the New Otani. We were covering the scene at the table, and the director called lunch. Nancy was sitting over in the corner, getting ready to go to lunch with me. I sat and talked with Laura Devon for, I think, ten minutes. It was really the first opportunity we had to even talk at all. When she got up to go, I turned around and Nancy was not there anymore.

"We had a tremendous fight over it—pure simple jealous rage. And I remember being very shocked, because Nancy wanted to be an actress."[14]

According to Culp, another fight erupted during the trip due to a night where he indulged in what his wife felt was heavy drinking.

But, on another occasion, once the pretty blonde actress or alcohol weren't in the mix, Nancy displayed great support for her hard-working husband, especially when he made his debut as a director.

The episode was "Court of the Lion." Culp was wearing three hats. He wrote the script, he acted in the story, and now he would also direct.

Culp: "This was the summer of '65, and *I Spy* is not on the air yet. We're still in that period of limbo, like living in a vacuum until it happens. But, one of the things that it does is, if you have a lot of problems personally, it puts them on hold. And, if you have problems in a marriage, they go into the bell jar, because you have all this focus. Something is about to happen.

"When it came to going down to 'Court of the Lion,' everything had changed. Nancy set her mind. No guy was ever married to a more wonderful dame than my wife—when she was cool. And she knew what I was up against. She understood it, and how much was riding on it from my personal point of view. My first day as an honest-to-god director, which could change my life. And it did.

"At the hotel where we stayed, she took me to the bathhouse and she worked on my shoulders, which I've had problems with since high school. She worked everything, and put me to sleep. The following day, when I was in a jam and needed a woman to play a pearl diver, she jumped at it. She played it to the hilt. She just did it. That was a plus."[15]

While shooting the location portions of the episode, the series suffered its only fatality. A member of the crew, a local grip, was standing in the water just off the shore of the fishing village. He was attempting to place a hot lamp into a light stand. He dropped it.

Culp: "It went into the water and he was electrocuted. Strangely enough, no one else was affected. Only in a very close radius does that affect you in that way. As the short circuit electricity travels farther and farther away, it weakens. So, if you're standing six feet away, it might have shocked you, but you wouldn't have even fallen down. This guy, it killed him. That was the only time something like that happened."[16]

Culp would find out, much later, that the bad luck regarding the shooting of his "Court of the Lion" had just started.

By the end of one month's location photography, Leonard was not sorry to leave Japan, and would never entertain the thought of returning.

In September, the stars and crew were back with the main unit in friendly Southern California.

For one episode, "The Barter," Roger C. Carmel had been booked as the primary guest performer, marking his second of three appearances in the series.

Culp: "Carmel was one of two actors who provided Bill and myself with buzz words. The other was Richard Loo, who had been in 'Patrick Henry.' We used to always deepen our voices, and say in a sinister way 'Missa Brown' to one another. This was a signal when we were dealing with a performer who wasn't going to help us in a scene—an actor trapped so much in his own style, that he couldn't connect with the other actors. The burden would be on *us* to connect with *him*. The other buzz word was 'Roger C, Roger C,' meaning an actor who was in his own world, and everything he did was over the top. Whenever we came across someone like this, Bill and I would sneak a look to each other and say 'Roger C, Roger C.'"[17]

Enter Calvin Brown

I Spy achieved yet another first. Calvin Brown became the only Black stuntman to be given a permanent position on a network television series.

Brown: "I was the first Black stuntman in Hollywood, starting back in 1958. Dick Powell did a thing called *Zane Gray Theatre*, and he needed some African warriors, that were 6'3", slim, and under 25, and, at the time, I fitted the bill. As an extra, back then, I was only making $11 a day. But if you did a stunt, you went up to $100. So they needed someone to fall out of a tree. Well, I'm from Louisiana. We've been ridin' trees down—free—all of our lives. They asked all the 'Guild' members if they would do it, and no one would take it. So I said, 'I'll do it.' So the director said, 'We'll pay you a hundred...' and before he could even get the word 'dollars' out, I was up the tree. I had not seen a hundred dollar bill in a long time. So I did the fall. The director said, 'That was perfect, except for one thing, the camera jammed. Will you do it again for another hundred...?' And, before he could say 'dollars,' I was back up that tree."[18]

Now Brown was working as an extra on *Gomer Pyle*. For $25 a day, he played a nonspeaking part, as one of the marines in the barracks. One day, Leonard was visiting the set, and Calvin Brown caught his eye.

The two Alexander Scotts, Cos and Calvin Brown (courtesy Calvin Brown Private Collection).

Brown: "They couldn't find a Black guy who could double for Bill. So Sheldon came over and said, 'Calvin, have you heard of Bill Cosby?' 'No, I haven't.' 'I just signed him to do *I Spy*, and I want you to be his stuntman every week. You look like him, and you can do stunts.'

"So he told me to go talk to the AD and tell him that I was no longer an extra, but I was a stuntman for *I Spy*. And then he had me set up to do Judo school and Karate school, every evening after work."[19]

At night, Brown would practice. During the day, he would stick close to the set.

Brown: "When I got to meet Cosby, I found out he was a basketball nut. So, every day, we played basketball. And we got to know one another, and know one another's mannerisms. I saw his foresight, his insight, his intelligence, his mind, I could see that they picked the right person to do it. And when I saw him with Bob Culp, and Bob Culp fit in real perfect with that, they had a jewel of a team. Personality-wise, and friendship-wise, it was the two of them, and that's why it happened."[20]

Through basketball, Cosby and Brown quickly bonded. Communication was easy, and direct.

Brown: "Bill said, 'Calvin, I have never done anything in TV or in the movies. So you're gonna be my boss. With these stunts, whatever you decide that I should or shouldn't do, that's the way it's going to be. Don't get me hurt.'

"And I said, 'If I get you hurt, I have no job. So I'll protect you all the way I can.'"[21]

Brown was on the set, watching over Cosby, beginning with the shooting of the third episode. And Brown would also travel with the location crew, starting with the third trip abroad, to Mexico. He would never miss a trip after that, or the production of an episode, or a single fight.

Brown: "Every fight that you saw Alexander Scott in, I did some. The directors would get so mad at me, because, for instance, Bill would get up on a table and they'd say 'jump down.' And Bill and I had little signals, and I'd give him one, and he'd say, 'Well I can't do this one.' I'd say, 'Anytime you have Bob Culp's stunt double up there, I'll be there. Bill will not get hurt. I don't want him trying that stuff.' And, to this day, wherever we go, he says, 'This is Calvin, my stunt double and my boss. Don't even question what he says. If he says "no," don't ask me a thing about it, until he tells you what he will let me do, and how the scene can be shot.'"[22]

During this second block of nine episodes, Culp came face-to-face with his teenage fantasy: The temptress from "Terry and the Pirates," a cartoon strip he had read faithfully as a boy. Here was the Dragon Lady, both beautiful and mysterious. Culp had developed a crush on that character. For him, France Nuyen was the flesh and blood incarnation of her.

It was on the set of "Always Say Goodbye." Culp was already thinking about the casting of the next script he had written, "The Tiger," which was slated to follow. Pilar Seurat was being considered to play the pivotal part of "Sam" MacLean, a character romantically linked with Kelly. Seurat had appeared once before in the series, and Culp was on the fence concerning her suitability for the role. Then he saw Nuyen.

He immediately recognized her. Years earlier, while the young actress had been appearing in the New York stage production of *The World of Suzi Wong*, she had been featured on the cover of *Life* magazine. She was quoted in the article as saying "I am Chinese, I am a stone, I go where I am kicked."

Culp: "That line nailed me to the wall. I showed it to Peckinpah, who said, 'That is the most astounding revelation of the human psyche that I have ever seen in a woman—if true.'"[23]

That statement by Sam Peckinpah, that disclaimer, would turn out to be tragically important for Robert Culp. Peckinpah's implication was that Nuyen was not as she appeared.

The new Hepburn & Tracy, 1967 (Robert Culp Private Collection).

The statement, as quoted in *Life* magazine, portrayed Nuyen as a remarkably passive individual.

Culp: "Nothing could be further from the truth. But I didn't know that. Just because of that damn quote, I saved that magazine."[24]

And now here was the voice behind "that damn quote," France Nuyen, making a minor appearance in a minor episode of *I Spy*.

Leonard was on the set watching the work progress. Culp was there, as well, mystified by Nuyen. He approached Leonard with the idea that, without the Geisha outfit and headdress that Nuyen was wearing, her appearance could be transformed, allowing her to star in the much bigger role of Sam MacLean for "The Tiger."

Leonard agreed. She was hired.

Culp: "The mojo was already working when we did that episode. By the time we finished, France and I were seriously involved, and didn't know which way to turn. So, like most people who find themselves in that type of situation, we just stalled and stalled and stalled."[25]

The affair had only begun.

The Gentle Art of Self-Promotion

The grease on the wheels of any network enterprise is publicity. This is the animal that arouses the public interest, feeds the appetite it created, and promotes the program in the spotlight.

I Spy was a self-contained factory of possibilities.

Culp and Cosby, equals (© 3 F Prod.).

In July 1965, one month prior to the series' debut, *TV Guide* ran an article—actually a self-promotion letter from Leonard—about filming in Hong Kong. It was called "Having a Wonderful Time—Minus the Typhoons and Other Stalls in the Process."

Leonard wrote, "Even when the typhoon was over, the weather never really cleared up. In four weeks we got only one day of sunshine."

The schmoozer knew precisely what he was doing. Americans love underdogs—and if any show was an underdog, it was the great experiment of *I Spy*.

Editor Dick Gray wrote, in the July 10th issue of the *Atlantic Journal* newspaper, "Any NBC-TV station which does not broadcast *I Spy* will be doing a disservice to its viewers and to itself. The show is going to be a winner.

"If the writers and director let Mr. Cosby be as funny on the show as he is in real life, I don't see how it can lose.

"Mr. Cosby said, 'We are free to ad lib a lot. We will ad lib at the drop of a hat. Especially when we forget our lines.'

"Mr. Cosby happens to be the first Negro to star in a continuing network television series."

Industry trade papers had been tracking the development of *I Spy* prior to the *TV Guide* and the *Atlantic Journal* articles. *Variety* reported in its April 7th edition, "Cosby in 'Spy' Puts NBC Dixie Affils on Spot."

The article read: "When the clearances from southern affils are tabulated, television's test case on integration will be *I Spy*. The objections of the hard-core southern affils of *I Spy* casting is that it depicts a Negro and a White intermingling on an equal level. While some southern affils have grown more sophisticated, the taboo barriers are still strong. In years past, the failure of southern affils to clear for *East Side, West Side*, helped to shorten the life of this CBS-TV series. Objections of southern CBS-TV affils were that it was too sympathetic to the plight of Negroes. One of the reasons NBC-TV couldn't win sponsors to the weekly musical show of the late Nat King Cole was that southern affils failed to clear for

Cole. Southern clearance for Cosby and Culp in *I Spy* could tell which way the winds of change are blowing in Dixie."

The plight of the Negroes.

The costarring role of a Negro performer.

It appears archaic, strange, as if uttered by Civil War soldiers and onlookers from that other time and place when one didn't understand the meaning of equality.

But this was 1965, and the civil rights movement was strong and visible. The gentle insistence of the Reverend Martin Luther King Jr. would, eventually, begin to change the way in which America viewed its brothers and sisters.

Equality. Friendship. Love and respect for another, regardless of race or separate distinction. This message, part of the concept of a mere television series—a product of the TV industry, designed to, above all else, entertain—was about to do what no movement, no protest, and no war could do.

Hal Humphrey, in the *Los Angeles Times*, May 17th edition, stated: "The rest of the TV industry will watch with fascination to see how *I Spy* and its integrated co-stars are received by the viewing public. Culp says that Cosby already has vetoed any dialogue based on the racial issue—humorous or otherwise. Perhaps this is the best approach of all, to show an unawareness of the color differences between the two stars."

By August, TV supplements from various newspapers began running pictures from the series, and in the last days of summer, *Ebony* magazine would devote several pages of its September issue to Bill Cosby. The article was called "Comedian Bill Cosby Is First Negro Co-star in TV Network Series."

The article quoted Cosby as saying: "It's not what you'd call a stereotype role. Negroes like Martin Luther King and Dick Gregory, groups like the Deacons and the Muslims, all

Left: *Seattle Post Intelligencer*, September 26, 1965 (photo © 3 F Prod.). *Right*: Cover of *TV Week*, February 1966 (photo © 3 F Prod.).

4—On to Japan

are dedicated to the cause of Civil Rights, but they do their job in their way. My way is to show White people that Negroes are human beings with the same aspirations and abilities that Whites have."[26]

Five days before *I Spy*'s premiere on network television, the *New York Times* printed an article that stated that 180 NBC stations would carry "the first weekly network show to present a Negro as co-star." Absenting themselves from the count were the affiliates in Albany, Birmingham, and Savannah, Georgia, as well as stations in Daytona Beach, Florida, and Alexandria, Louisiana.

Stanley Karnow, in the September 25th issue of the *Saturday Evening Post*, delivered a three-page article that began, "For the first time, a Negro stars in a TV series—and he won't sing, dance or play the second banana."

These words, now, are so far removed from today's world, it is nearly impossible to believe them; but, for that time, at that stage of America's development, that was considered normal.

The article went on to state, "Budgeted at some $4.5 million and filmed on locations around the world, it is one of the most expensive TV series ever produced. But what sets *I Spy* apart is its costar, nightclub wit Bill Cosby. Among other things, he is a Negro. In *I Spy*, Cosby launches a racial revolution. For the first time a Negro will be featured on television as the star of a dramatic series—breaking a barrier that not even Nat King Cole, Sammy Davis or Lena Horne could overcome."

As *Variety* put it, "Bill Cosby is TV's Jackie Robinson. More significantly, Cosby's role is not fashioned to fit a Negro. Teamed with White actor Robert Culp, Cosby wrestles with villains and ogles pretty girls, just like any upstanding TV hero. At times, the show commits the heresy of subordinating the White man to the Negro. The abrupt change of roles could well provoke angry protests from TV audiences, particularly in the South."

Cosby was quoted by the *Saturday Evening Post*, saying, "What we're doing will offend all sorts of bigots, and not only in the South. There are folks in Philadelphia who'll write in to say, 'How come you have a colored guy kicking a Caucasian?' Some will even object to seeing a Negro in the same room with a White. But it will balance out. The pros will outnumber the cons.'"[27]

Again, and this cannot be understated, *I Spy* was an anomaly, something that appeared to be not normal. Yet those involved knew it was absolutely normal. The producers who thought it up, the two men who played it out, and the team of writers and directors who crafted the episodes, were all in uncharted territory in TV land.

Now it is normal, it is "okay" for a Black to bunk with a White man, sleeping side by side in adjoining twin beds, taking turns using the shower, and sharing—the great unmentionable in 1960s television—the toilet. In a time when, in many parts of the country, a water fountain couldn't be shared by two races, *I Spy* had its stars talking about who would be first in the shower.

Cosby: "If my material is without race, maybe I can promote equality better. After all, if something applies equally to Black and White, the underlying assumption is the sameness of both. I'll tell you this, I don't miss 'Amos 'n' Andy.' You can't trade on racialism till you cut out bigotry. That's got to come first."[28]

Leonard knew it. Culp and Cosby knew it. The rest of us would now decide.

On September 15, 1965, at 10 P.M. on Wednesday, *I Spy* premiered on NBC with the Culp-authored "So Long, Patrick Henry." It won its time slot with a staggering 41% share.

One week later, perhaps the best episode from the original block of nine gave American audiences "A Cup of Kindness."

I Spy would continue to beat all its competition, and then came the icing on the cake, the sought-after, hoped-for benedictions: the reviews.

Cleveland Amory, of *TV Guide*, predicted *I Spy* would be a hit. Other critics were nearly unanimous in agreeing that the show was sexy, smart, with an easy-flowing blend of humor and drama. Leonard's dream was realized by notices of the striking shot-on-location visuals, mature themes, and stand out performances.

Daily Variety wrote: "Any show that breaks down the studio walls in Hollywood and moves its cast and crew and gear to Hong Kong and other Oriental keys may catch on and hold fast. For frantic action and seething intrigue, few of the new season's dramatic shows will match it."

In a separate weekly *Variety* review, a different critic wrote, "This entry in the popular international spy cycle should deeply interest ethnologists. The network and producer Sheldon Leonard have, with more guts than ordinary observers could imagine, cast Negro comedian Bill Cosby in a feature role."

Ernie Kreiling, for *Citizen-News TV Week*, a supplement included in many Southern California newspapers, declared *I Spy* to be "the best television has offered." He went on to write that the new season's programs were especially light, with *no* characters that came across as real, most being of the "cartoonized variety." He cited, in particular, *The Munsters*, *The Addams Family*, *Gilligan's Island*, *The Beverly Hillbillies*, *Gomer Pyle*, *Lost in Space*, *Voyage to the Bottom of the Sea*, and *The Man from U.N.C.L.E.* He noted that *I Spy* was the exception to the rule, emerging as "the best of the season." He wrote, "*I Spy* met with almost universal acclaim from the reviewers and it's already outstripping its network competition in the early audience estimates."

For the *New York Times*, Joanne Stang wrote about Bill Cosby being the first "Negro" to star on a network series and how that must carry "an undeniable responsibility."

For the article, Cosby was quoted saying that he had "been trying to do the story lines without camping—to get a laugh as an actor, not as a comedian," and that it was not easy to do.

Stang noticed that the greatest asset on the series was Cosby's warm friendship with Robert Culp.

"Bob could make mincemeat of me in front of the camera," Cosby admitted, "but he's been very unselfish."

When asked how their friendship contributed to the show, Culp gave the answer he'd known from moment one: "It IS the show."

"The character I play is a highly educated man," Cosby said, "and I'm nowhere near that. And [Scott] is a Negro good guy working equally with a White man for a patriotic cause—a premise that may not be accepted by every Negro watching. In other words, though the part is never the usual put-down of the Negro people, I feel I have to be careful that it doesn't become an exaggeration of another kind."

For the October 23rd issue of *TV Guide*, Cosby admitted, "At first I was wooden. I spoke without expression. I had to learn that the face speaks, the muscles of your neck, your hands, your eyebrows, all act. As an insecure entertainer coming in to work as an actor, I need all the acceptance I can get. Bobby gives me that."

"I realized how strong we would be as a team," Culp said, "but at first, the other writers couldn't find the relationship. They all tried to put me in the front seat and Bill in the back seat and that isn't the idea."

In the *New York Journal American*, Culp said, "There are two stars on this show. I'm one, the other's Bill Cosby. Bill will do as much for the show as I will."[29]

In a brilliant move of timing, Bill Cosby's third comedy album, *Why Is There Air?* found its way onto record store shelves in early September 1965, midway into the preseason buildup to launch *I Spy*. It sold well, and Cosby's two previous albums were restocked and also

Why Is There Air? **1965 (under license from Warner Bros. Records).**

appeared on the charts. The series hadn't aired yet. Both Cosby and Warner Bros. Records had a great surprise in store for them.

On *Why Is There Air?* Cosby spoke with a new confidence and richer material. Bill Cosby began carving a place for himself, on multiple levels, in the world of entertainment.

I Spy was about to do the same.

5

The Second Block of Episodes

10. **"TIME OF THE KNIFE"**; Written by: Gilbert Ralson; Directed by: Paul Wendkos; 2nd unit directed by: David Friedkin; Location: Japan; First airing: 11/3/65. Repeated: 6/8/66.

In Kyoto, Japan, Michael Fane, a fellow agent and old friend of Kelly's, vanishes while carrying microfilm concerning remote-control missile systems.

Jean, Mike's girlfriend, believes he was killed in a fiery car crash. All that is left of him is in a carved Jade urn. Kelly and Scott must now find out what happened to the classified information Mike carried.

A man named Kurimachi may be of help, until he turns up dead, drowned in a bathhouse. When an attempt is made to frame Kelly for the murder, it becomes clear that the American agents are not the only ones in search of the military information.

Then, as the competitors come out of the woodwork, including a man named Corday and another named Kraft, it becomes apparent that Mike may not be dead.

Assessment

"Time/Knife" is well written and tautly directed. The first-rate use of location footage and Los Angeles sequences shot with Madlyn Rhue create the signature *I Spy* blend of flawless illusion. The slight-of-hand: Rhue was not on location in Japan.

In 1965, the women's equal rights movement was just beginning to form. Women, for the most part, didn't have careers, and their essential role was wife and mother—like every woman on television from Harriet Nelson to Donna Reed and June Cleaver.

Knowing this, we can better understand why Jean tells Kelly, "I belong to Mike."

And later, when she discovers that Mike is alive, he tells her to sit down. She tries to speak and he says, "Heel."

Look for many excellent nuances in the acting, courtesy of director Paul Wendkos in his *I Spy* debut:

Corday becomes a bigger, more confident man when he pulls out the much bigger concealed gun.

Kelly's reaction to finding Kurimachi floating dead in the bath is an eerie scene made better by an understated Culp, wrapped only in a towel, as he vaults out of the window and makes a hasty retreat to the hotel.

5—The Second Block of Episodes

Culp and Cosby fighting like brothers, July '66 (© 3 F Prod.).

The negotiations between Kraft, Corday, and Mike, are as cool and calm as an art auction until Kraft eliminates his competition.

And Jean, pressed against the wall, frozen in fear, averting her eyes while Kelly and Mike struggle for control of the gun that is pointed in her direction.

Everything works. The episode falls only slightly short of excellence.

Madlyn Rhue, John Van Dreelan, "Time of the Knife" (© 3 F Prod., courtesy Image Ent.).

The Story Behind the Story

This is the fourth time Kelly has had a personal relationship with someone who figures prominently in the story.

By this, the first script of the second block, Friedkin and Fine were already busy adding in the Cosbyisms: "go for yourself," "sorry about that," and "wonderfulness"—here stated as "The wonderfulness of your cleanliness."

Some of these lines were assigned to Kelly. Culp was clearly being encouraged to blend his character with Cosby's by his writer/producer bosses. The same men would later give him some knocks for doing so.

CULP & COSBY ON SET REWRITE

Not in the script:

After the police inspector gives Kelly a punishing lesson in martial arts, and Kelly falls back on the couch, mopping his head with a hand towel, there is a knock at the door. Looking toward Cosby, Culp adds the line, "I just got killed, you get it!" Continuing with the ad-lib, Culp tosses the towel at his partner.

After Kelly and Scott encounter Kraft, who enters through the door, and then Corday, who enters through the window and holds them at gunpoint, Culp contributes the line, "We've met Winken and Blinken, and I don't much care for them. I wonder who's playing Nod?" Cosby, glancing around anxiously, adds, "And I wonder what door he's coming through."

For the tag scene, after Jean throws Kelly onto the mat and tells him he's hopeless at judo, she leaves. The script has Kelly and Scott exchange a look, then calls for a "fade out." The rest of the lines we hear were added by Culp and Cosby, including Scott saying to Kelly, "The pitifulness of yourself. I think I ought to get you a pink belt with a noodle cluster."

Cast & Crew

Madlyn Rhue was 30. She had been performing in film and TV since 1958. Among many stand-out guest star roles, she played a prominent part in a *Star Trek* episode filmed one year after this. It would be the basis for the motion picture *Star Trek II: The Wrath of Khan*. She was still on the job as late as 1996, in the semirecurring role of Jean O'Neil on *Murder She Wrote*. She died in 2003 from pneumonia, complicated by multiple sclerosis.

Warren Stevens (Mike) had been working steadily in front of the camera since 1949 and would continue into the mid–1980s. He can be seen in scores of movies, including *Forbidden Planet*. On TV, Stevens can be seen on reruns of *Gunsmoke*, *The Twilight Zone*, and *The Outer Limits*. Shortly after the filming of this episode, at age 46, he would be seen competing with Captain Kirk for the affections of a space babe on *Star Trek*.

John Van Dreelan (the crafty Kraft) had a successful career that spanned 40 years, beginning in 1944. Fluent in several languages, including German, Van Dreelan escaped a concentration camp in Nazi-occupied Holland by disguising himself as a German officer, a role he would go on to play many times in TV and film. He was in great favor at Warner Brothers, and could have bought a house just from the money he made from appearing frequently on their trilogy of early '60s detective shows, *Hawaiian Eye*, *Surfside 6*, and *77 Sunset Strip*. He was 43 here.

Jay Novello (Corday) had one of those faces you couldn't forget, and his face was seen often in movies and TV, beginning in the late 1930s. He was 61.

Gilbert Ralston had written "Dragon's Teeth." This would be his final *I Spy* assignment before moving on to *Star Trek* and other shows of the period.

Paul Wendkos, coming onboard to direct the first of seven *I Spy* shows, practiced his craft with three Gidget movies, as well as dozens of TV credits.

11. **"TATIA"**; Written by: Robert Lewin; Directed by: David Friedkin; Location: Japan; First airing: 11/17/65. Repeated: 6/15/66.

In Tokyo, Kelly falls hook, line and sinker for Tatia Loring, a beautiful photographer, despite warnings from Scott that she could be a Communist spy.

A strange coincidence spells bad news for Kelly: Three American agents, all of whom were photographed by Tatia, are now dead.

Assessment

There is only one flaw in this nearly perfect episode: that a Russian spy, posing as a photographer, would have the opportunity to photograph four different American agents, all of whom she would target for murder. More so, it is incredible that Tatia would stamp her

Laura Devon, "Tatia" (© 3 F Prod., courtesy Image Ent.).

name on the back of the pictures, leaving a trail that even Inspector Clouseau could easily follow.

Kelly and Tatia appear to be kindred spirits: Both are attractive, ambitious, live life out of a suitcase, and ache to slow down, yearning for something real.

Kelly returns from his date with Tatia, blissfully in love, and is sobered by the news that John Irving, a fellow agent and friend, was murdered while Scott was taking a shower.

There is tension building. Usually Kelly and Scott think along the same lines. Not this time.

Scott challenges Kelly, saying, "Start thinking about Tatia. Straight up from the shoulder. Tatia. Girl agent. For them."

"We could be one big happy family if you would just shut up," Kelly shouts.

"You are really dumb, y'know," Scott responds. He picks up the telephone, informing the desk that he and Mr. Robinson will be playing some sound effects records, then he locks the door and stands firmly in front, blocking Kelly's exit.

The shoving match becomes a judo match. Scott pins Kelly down. "My shoulder," Kelly breathes.

Scott instantly lets up, with a look of concern, only to be met by a trick—a countermove as Kelly flips him.

The fight continues, ending with Kelly hurling Scott against a shogi screen—the strips of wood and paper ripping apart.

A battered Scott manages to say, "Go on, get out of here. Go get yourself killed."

But Kelly can't. Even after all the anger, he won't walk away from his friend.

The audience knows before Kelly does, Tatia is an agent. Kelly was a "kill mission."

Tatia, confused by her own feelings for Kelly, tries to stall her controller by telling him that Kelly has a code book that could be of value. The room where they will meet—her room—has been bugged. The ruthless men she works for are listening. And Kelly has come prepared to give them a show.

It's in his eyes. He's still in love with her, but he has to play it out, even though this is killing him. The point of no return comes: He tells Tatia that the embassy thanks her for her help. He gives her a passport, plane tickets and money.

"What are you doing to me," she asks. She sees the look in Kelly's eyes, then turns to the hidden microphone.

"I swear, I never had any contact with them. I never had anything to do with them," she repeats over and over.

Kelly has given Tatia the rope. Her colleagues will now hang her with it.

In the hallway, Scott is waiting.

"You want to hit me?" he asks.

"Just don't talk," Kelly says.

"C'mon, take a shot at me."

In a lightning move, Kelly swings. Scott steps away from the punch. He holds Kelly for a moment, and in the gesture reserved for family, straightens Kelly's suit, brushes imaginary dust from the shoulders, and makes sure his friend and brother is presentable.

Without a word, Kelly composes himself and walks out. Scott trails behind, giving him an arm's length of space.

The Story Behind the Story

"Tatia" introduces the series' long theme that the Russians know Kelly and Scott are American spies.

This episode also introduced an *I Spy* signature—the skin tight white jeans.

Culp: "I saw them. They were new. I had never seen them before. And I thought, 'Can I get away with this?' This will just be another problem for [wardrobe man] Harald Johnson."[1]

Preece: "The wardrobe was so important because the white jeans and T-shirts and boat shoes were not being worn by people on the street. I was affected. I must have had five pairs of those white jeans. You could only wear them one day because you'd sit down on something and they'd get dirty."[2]

Culp: "Poor Harald was up every night washing those things."[3]

At one point in "Tatia," the camera takes us into a bathroom. This is daring for 1965. We were still more than six years away from the first flush of a toilet on TV, heard but not seen, courtesy of Archie Bunker in the premiere episode of *All in the Family*. More daring, we see a man taking a shower, naked from the waist up. More daring still, the man is Black.

CULP & COSBY & FRIEDKIN ON SET REWRITE

The highlight of "Tatia" involves the hotel room fight. In a classic moment of conflict, one man has an agenda to leave the room, the other an agenda that both will stay.

Culp: "Bill said, 'There's only one way to do this. When these two men fight, they fight like brothers. You don't have any brothers, but I do. The intent is to kill. With brothers, every block in the world, every curve of your emotions, goes out the window. We should just go, and it should look like a fight to the death, which all of a sudden just stops.'

"We really went for it, and we got some bumps and abrasions from that. I had never seen that before. I think that it probably did come as a shock to many. It wasn't in the script. We did that."[4]

Earle Hagen: "Sheldon was very fond of 'Tatia,' because it was an episode where the relationship between the two of them happened. They had a fight—that was a great scene. Sheldon was very pleased."[5]

In the script, the entire fight sequence was written for laughs. As Kelly and Scott take swings at one another, they make jokes. At the end, Kelly cries "uncle," pulling himself out of the couch, springs and cushion trailing after him, as he pleads with Scott to give him another chance to prove Tatia's innocence.

The conflict of the fight, which Leonard loved so dearly, was the invention of his two stars.

At the end of the story, for the tag scene, the script places Kelly on the tennis court, playing badly. Scott, wanting to cheer his friend up, suggests that they go out and "get blasted." Kelly accepts, and the two men walk off, whistling. Culp and Cosby, with the support of their director, David Friedkin, saw a better way to play it.

Culp: "At the end of 'Tatia,' we improvised, 'Do you want to hit me?' Bill's recovery of that, and mine, and the thing where I walk down the hall ahead of him, that was all ours."[6]

There were other instances of on set rewriting, many of which brought forward some of the most memorable lines in the episode.

Before Kelly's date with Tatia, Scott receives a letter from his mother and shares it with Kelly. Scott then asks Kelly if he will be out late. In the script, Kelly replies by saying: "I'm going to try." Culp changes this to be: "You get one letter from your mom and you're starting to sound like her! Yes, I'm going to try for about 9 A.M.!"

During his dinner with Tatia, Culp adds the memorable lines, "Do I fit? Normally it would just be a game — played out to its inevitable conclusion. But, Tatia, I want to fit with you."

The next day, Kelly goes on a day-date with Tatia. The two actors stuck to the script, although Culp and/or director Friedkin added the following:

Kelly says, "Would you be able to give up your photography?" Tatia replies, "If I had to. For something lasting."

Kelly responds, "I never had anything lasting."

Tatia understands. "I haven't either."

Then, after a pause, after they look deeply into each other's eyes, Kelly finishes it with, "Tatia, I commit to you."

Robert Lewin was the lucky writer to be given credit for all of these indisputable improvements.

REVIEWS

Jack O'Brian, a syndicated entertainment columnist, wrote of this episode, "*I Spy* last night was beautifully off-beat romantic sexy-spy stuff. The more we see Bill Cosby, the more we're sure he's one of the finest young acting-finds of the season; decade maybe. That 'wonderfulness' razzles a neat sense of satiric dazzle. Culp & Cosby even imitate each other and it's grand fun."

TV Guide gave a critic's pick nod to "Tatia" with a half-page Close Up listing, the second episode of the new series to be so honored by the magazine.

CAST & CREW

Laura Devon traveled with the company to Tokyo, allowing much of this episode to be shot on location, creating the memorable images of Kelly and Tatia falling in love against a backdrop of scenic Japan.

Devon had a relatively short career in front of the camera. Beginning as a singer (and she sings a few lines of "God Bless the Child" in this episode), she turned to acting in 1962, then quit the business five years later, at age 27.

Richard Garland, who makes a memorable impression in merely two scenes, shared the fate of the character he played — an untimely and early death. He began his acting career in 1953, worked with Culp in a *Trackdown* episode, and won a recurring role on *Lassie* (as Clay), before dying at age 42 in 1969.

Robert Lewin, who had numerous TV credits, including episodic writing for *12 O'Clock High* and *Rawhide*, wrote "Weight of the World" for *I Spy* before penning this episode ("Weight" would be next up on the production roster). He would return again to write "Shana."

George W. Brooks makes an impressive *I Spy* debut here. Brooks was fairly new to film editing, but Leonard had a reason to take a chance on a "cutter" without a long list of credits. He needed someone who was hungry enough to travel for his work. Brooks was being groomed for the job of location film editor.

12. **"WEIGHT OF THE WORLD"**; Written by: Robert Lewin; Directed by: Paul Wendkos; 2nd unit directed by: David Friedkin; Location: Japan; First airing: 12/1/65. Repeated: 6/22/66.

Communist agents plan to test a plague virus at a scientific convention in Japan.

Kelly and Scott have been booked at the same hotel, in hopes of finding out what the Red Chinese are up to. For the mission, a reluctant Kelly has been given a young wife, an eager but amateur spy named Vicki. The agents also align themselves with Dr. Bingham, a scientist attending the convention. Despite the danger it may present for him, Bingham provides their only hope for isolating the plague.

Assessment

"Weight of the World" is one of the weaker entries of the first season. This is surprising, considering Robert Lewin, who wrote the excellent "Tatia," was also the writer of this material. In Lewin's defense, the script reads far better than the finished product plays.

But there may be another factor in why Lewin's material doesn't fare as well this time out: Culp and Cosby stuck to the script.

Paul Wendkos had given above standard direction to "Time of the Knife," but his work here feels uninspired. Not helping matters, the episode is almost entirely filmed at home, using very little footage of the country where it was supposed to take place. Except for a few establishing exterior shots, and one brief scene where Kelly and Scott are jumped by enemy agents and tumble into a swimming pool, all else takes place indoors.

The Story Behind the Story

I Spy continued to find new and interesting roles for Black performers, and no actor was more deserving than 66-year-old Rex Ingram, as Dr. Bingham.

Cosby: "Rex Ingram was probably my first role model come to life, because I had seen him in the movies, always so dignified and wonderful. And a leader. It's moments like that when I felt very, very special in life."[7]

What Went Wrong

Albert Salmi and Jeanne Arnold play the two western scientists who have sold out to Red China. The performances are less than ordinary and the casting of these two seems inappropriate.

In the script, the lead scientist on the Chinese team was Dr. Ch-en Hueng, an Asian. The woman accompanying him to the convention was a Chinese agent with a scientific background, and she, too, was Asian. For some reason, two Caucasians were given the roles. Also, as the scientific convention was to be devoted to the research of obesity, everyone present, including the Chinese henchmen, were described as overweight, giving the story an offbeat element of humor.

This plot point stayed in the story, but, again, some poor decisions were made when it came to the actual casting, being that the heavies were barely heavy at all.

Cast & Crew

Rex Ingram was born just before the turn of the century, and acted in silent and early sound movies, usually in parts that he felt were degrading to Black Americans. In 1939 he played the runaway slave Jim in *The Adventures of Huckleberry Finn*, receiving second billing to the man who was number one at the box office that year, Mickey Rooney. Following this triumph, Ingram was prominently featured in several films from the early '40s, including *Cabin in the Sky* and *Sahara*. By 1943, Ingram chose to turn down any work that he felt demeaned Blacks.

His career suffered a serious setback in 1948 when he was arrested in Kansas and charged with transporting an underage White girl (she was 15) across state lines. He spent a year and a half in prison and, after his release, struggled to regain acceptance in Hollywood.

After this performance, Ingram continued to work in television. He died in 1969 at age 70, from a heart attack.

Marlyn Mason plays Vicki, the young, perky, girly, baby agent trying to prove herself on this assignment. While Kelly's attitude may seem surprisingly chauvinistic, keep in mind the time and place of this story. Emma Peel was still six months away from making her debut on American television.

Mason did her first TV acting on *My Three Sons* in 1962 at age 22, and soon became a semiregular on *Dr. Kildare*. She would work with Culp again, this time playing his wife, in the mid–1970s Movie of the Week, *Outrage*.

Albert Salmi had been in TV and films since the mid–1950s. He accumulated over 100 credits on shows such as *The Twilight Zone* and *Combat!* He would continue to work as a character actor into the late 1980s. He committed suicide in 1990 at 62, having once said "I wish just one time my name would have appeared above the title."

Basil Wrangell joined the editing team with this episode. As a film cutter, Wrangell had edited the 1925 silent version of *Ben Hur*, as well as Tod Browning's 1932 sideshow attraction, *Freaks*. Throughout the 1940s Wrangell found work as the director of numerous B films. Returning to editing, he worked in television, cutting for *Maverick*, *Adventures in Paradise*, and *Combat!* Before finishing at *I Spy*, he would edit 17 episodes.

13. **"TIGERS OF HEAVEN"**; Written by: Morton Fine & David Friedkin; Directed by: Allen Reisner; 2nd unit directed by: David Friedkin; Location: Japan; First airing: 12/15/65.

In Japan, Kelly and Scott must infiltrate the Tigers of Heaven, a neo–Fascist group bent on discrediting the West.

This episode gives us a splendid example of Kelly's cover: the tennis bum sponging off the generosity of a wealthy host. That host fancies himself as a tennis player, and the opportunity to play against a trophy-winning semipro is irresistible.

Assessment

"Tigers" provides an interesting examination of the Imperial ideals and adherence to honor that sent Japan, with its two formidable allies, to wage war against the world.

It also examines the extremist point of view that has eerie echoes today, in a post 9/11 world; why a young, healthy, prosperous male is driven to kill not only himself, but others, in a rigid belief that the restoration of his country can be accomplished by holding the West— America—accountable for the ruination of his homeland.

In this story, the failure to complete a mission by two members of the Tigers of Heaven will result in the commission of "Bushido," on camera, and that, in itself, is extraordinary for this time period in television. The first suicidal cut is horizontal across the stomach; the knife is then dragged back to the center of the stomach and is pulled upward, completing the ritualized disembowelment.

One of the best examples in the series of the slight-of-hand directing that would place Los Angeles–bound actors into shot-on-location sequences is when Mr. Okura, the Westernized capitalist, is attacked by a Tigers of Heaven assassin, his own son, Toshio.

In the portion of the scene shot in Japan, Kelly and Scott follow Mr. Okura as he strolls through scenic gardens, then climbs a concrete stairway to pray at the base of a large Buddha. His would-be killer waits for him there. Both performers are doubles, and therefore must conceal their faces from the camera. But, here, they do so in a most clever way. It makes sense that the assassin would wish to hide his identity, so he keeps his face turned away. Mr. Okura is here to worship, so it does not seem unusual that he holds his clenched hands in front of his bowed head. By doing this, the camera is free to move as Kelly and Scott rush forward to save the older man from his attacker. Once all are present, the director and his editor switch to closer angles, allowing the footage shot in America to be cut in, now placing the guest star actors into the scene with Culp and Cosby.

So flawless. So brilliant. So *I Spy*.

The Story Behind the Story

For the second time in the series, it is mentioned that Scott attended Temple University, Bill Cosby's alma mater.

For the third time, Kelly and Scott receive their assignment from a military officer, a clue as to who their true employers were, something missed by many fans of the series.

The actors who play Mr. Okura and his son, Toshio, have very strong accents and it is hard to understand much of what they say. This is regretful, because the script for "Tigers of Heaven" has purpose. The third entry by Friedkin and Fine, both busy rewriting and polishing all the other scripts, is another solid entry.

CULP & COSBY ON SET REWRITE

Kelly and Scott are chased by an armed assailant on a motorcycle. In the script, there is this lead in: Kelly notices that there is no one on the street, and comments, "Tokyo is an amazing city because they roll up the streets at midnight." Then the motorcycle appears. The rest of the dialogue was from Culp and Cosby, including:

KELLY: "Is he crazy or what?" *Then, when the motorcyclist pulls out a gun, he adds, mimicking Oriental speak:* "No, he not crazy."

After both men are nearly killed, Cosby adds, "That's why there's nobody on the streets at night."

In the den of the Tigers of Heaven, Kelly challenges Toshio, in a stinging, edgy speech, to a samurai duel to the death. The sharp and deadly words belong entirely to Culp.

At the end, as Toshio prepares to commit hari-kari, the script gave Kelly the last word: "Your father would be proud of you, kid." It was a good line. A generous Culp turned it over to Cosby for Scott to say.

For the tag scene, a final ad-lib: When Scott is reading out loud from a Japanese newspaper, Kelly teases him, "I knew you couldn't read that stuff."

CAST & CREW

George Takei, one season away from cult TV fame on *Star Trek*, is cast as one of the obedient tigers. He was paid $250 for his day's work.

David Friedkin makes a cameo as a military officer on a date with a Japanese girl.

Allan Reisner directs his first of three *I Spy* episodes. Prior to this work, he had frequently directed for *Climax!* (1954), *Route 66* (1960), and *Ben Casey* (1961).

14. **"THREE HOURS ON A SUNDAY NIGHT"**; Written by: Morton Fine & David Friedkin; Directed by: Paul Wendkos; 2nd unit directed by: David Friedkin; Location: Japan; First airing: 12/8/65. Repeated: 7/6/66.

In Kyoto, Japan, Kelly and Scott attempt to locate a roll of valuable microfilm stolen from Army Intelligence. The trail leads to an underworld fence named Sorge, who will buy and sell almost anything, if the price is right. But Sorge is a tough customer to do business with.

Robert Culp, Sheldon Leonard, "Three Hours on a Sunday Night" (© 3 F Prod., courtesy Image Ent.).

Once contact is made, Kelly is given three hours to acquire $50,000, the price he must pay Sorge for the roll of microfilm—and for Scott's life.

Assessment

This episode makes maximum use of location footage, and contains all the elements that made *I Spy* popular: humor, action, sexual playfulness, big name TV guest stars, and the bond between Kelly and Scott.

There is also a very loud ticking clock as Kelly goes from person to person to try to get the ransom for Scott's life.

The Story Behind the Story

A case of TV déjà vu: The teaser for this episode is reminiscent of the opening minutes from "No Exchange for Damaged Merchandise." In both, an American military person is distracted by a pretty local girl, who takes a spill from her bike. Then, when he rushes to her aide, he gets slugged over the head by her accomplice.

In a nice example of series continuity, Kelly tells Sorge that he met Scott a few months back in Hong Kong, which we know was their last port of call.

The startling white jeans make their second appearance here, although briefly, along with the white boat shoes.

Regarding playing opposite Julie London, Culp had this to say:

"Bill came to my dressing room door, and said, 'Oh man, I hear who you're gonna play opposite now, and this is gonna be great. I'm gonna have to be on the set to watch all this stuff.'

"Julie London had been an amazing heartthrob, a young leading lady, coming off of a very successful career as a singer. But this was now, not then. Bill sat inches off camera and teased me. There's a thing when I have her on the floor, trying to steal her necklace, and out of the corner of my eye, I see Bill shaking his finger and saying 'Naughty, naughty.'"[8]

CULP & COSBY ON SET REWRITE

At the beginning of act one, Scott is preparing to take a bath and refuses the help of a Japanese maid when getting undressed. The script had Kelly saying, "That wasn't polite, Scotty." Culp replaced this line with, "Hey, man, if you can't learn to be a little more gracious, I can't take you to the good countries anymore."

The bit where Scott is writing a letter to his mom, and asks Kelly if he wants to add a P.S. to it, was not in the script. Nor was Kelly's line, "I'm going to have to write the Pentagon and tell them your mind has definitely turned bad."

In the script, when Kelly finally returns to free Scott, the action and dialogue played this way:

Sorge is keeping himself busy at his desk, looking over a stamp collection. Kelly enters. Scott is relieved to see his partner, but determined to play it cool. He had asked Kelly to bring him back some food, and now gives Kelly a hard time about not doing so, and asks,

"What kept you?" Kelly's answer, "Oh, little things. Try getting a fifty thousand dollar ransom in Tokyo on a Sunday night." Scott says, "A drag, huh?" Kelly adds, "Makes you know your friends. What you been doing?" Scott answers, "Nothing real constructive. I hate a day like this." Kelly agrees, "Know what you mean."

Culp and Cosby did it differently.

In the filmed version, the scene begins the same, and continues up to the point when Scott says, "What kept you?" But, this time, Kelly answers, "Do you have any idea how hard it is getting a fifty thousand dollar ransom in Tokyo on a Sunday night—even if you're only asking a dollar a person. And, one other thing, on top of everything else, I'm sick and tired of you sending me out to the deli. What have *you* been doing?" Scott motions toward Sorge and says, "I've been watching him licking his stolen stamps."

In the scripted tag scene, when Phyllis returns to find Kelly well, Kelly sulks. She says, "Talk to me." Kelly responds, "You didn't trust me, did you? You sent the police after your necklace. Here's your necklace. Be happy."

Culp changed it. Now, when Phyllis says, "Talk to me," Kelly answers, "I don't know whether I should or not. You let me walk out of there believing that you had faith in me. Then you turn right around and send the cops after me so you can be sure your wonderful necklace will be protected. Well here you are and here is your beautiful diamond necklace, and I hope the two of you will be very warm together."

Small changes. Slight improvements. A team working together to make *I Spy* as good as it could be.

Reviews

Once again, for the third time, *I Spy* had a half-page Close Up in America's number one selling magazine, *TV Guide*. These "spotlight listings" were used, both then and now, as a means to direct viewers to the most outstanding programs of the week.

Cast

Sheldon Leonard, by appearing as Sorge, allowed much of the episode to be filmed in Japan. The sequences with Julie London and James Shigata were shot in Los Angeles.

Julie London was a big catch for the new series. Beginning as a nightclub singer, she achieved some celebrity in a short marriage to TV's Joe Friday. The ex–Mrs. Jack Webb began a career of her own as an actress. She had a successful recording career in the 1950s, highlighted by "Cry Me a River," which sold over three million copies. She starred on the big screen in *A Question of Adultery*. With the changing music scene, her career was about to run out of steam for the 40 year old. Webb would come to the rescue in the '70s, casting her in the role of Dixie McCall on *Emergency*, opposite her current husband, Bobby Troup.

James Shigeta, as one of Kelly's wealthy but shallow friends, was born in Hawaii. He had been appearing in front of the camera since 1959 as anything but Hawaiian. Most frequently cast to play men of the Japanese persuasion, he became a heartthrob after his appearance in *Flower Drum Song* as the romantic lead.

15. **"ALWAYS SAY GOODBYE"**; Written by: Robert C. Dennis & Earl Barret; Directed by: Allen Reisner; 2nd unit directed by: David Friedkin; Location: Japan; First airing: 1/26/66. Repeated: 7/13/66.

Kelly must protect a womanizer from himself. James Winthrop, an American delegate, could disrupt an important U.S.–Japan financial conference as a result of his relentless girl chasing.

The plot thickens: A man named Oshima, who has nightclub connections and easy access to women of little virtue, is bent on placing Winthrop into the center of a scandal. Assisting him is Ito, a "paparazzi," Ganko, a bouncer, and Sada, one of those women of little virtue that Oshima knows.

It is also discovered that Winthrop has been misjudged. His true goal is not to chase tail, but to make contact with Eliska, a woman he knew from many years before, a woman who once claimed to have had his child, and who he had left behind in Japan without even a good-bye.

Assessment

Played for laughs, Kelly and Scott babysit Winthrop, believed to be a hopeless philanderer.

Most of the comedy revolves around Kelly having one bad experience after another: he's manhandled, arrested, drugged, has a "mickey" hangover, and must then rally himself to stand in for Winthrop.

The story behind all the silliness never quite catches fire. There are, however, several wonderful moments in this episode.

The drugged Kelly tackled by half-a-dozen scantily clad Japanese showgirls; Scott and Winthrop out-conning the cons in the bathhouse; Kelly not even denting the huge Ganko, while visiting the apartment of the pretty Sada.

And, of note: Sada is played by France Nuyen. Kelly shows only minor interest in her. The true-life situation would be far different for Robert Culp.

The Story Behind the Story

The title of the first draft script, dated April 7, 1965, was "Goldswinger." The James Bond movie with a similar title had come out four months earlier.

In March 23, 1966, *Daily Variety* reported: "Fine and Friedkin feel their show will 'go beyond the mild hysteria of spy series,' explaining 'Many times we stress the spy only tangentially. We have done stories such as the one about keeping a U.S. ambassador out of trouble with broads. Our guys are not supermen, nor comic-strip heroes. They are part of the contemporary scene, very human, and they make mistakes.'"

The teaser from the final draft script was filmed, but left unused. We are introduced to Ito. It is made clear that the opportunistic photographer and Kelly know one another, and Kelly is not very fond of him. When Ito tries to snap a picture of Kelly, he is told, "One of these days, Ito, I'm going to shove that thing right in your ear! Starting with the view finder!" Ito responds, "Just trying to help, champ. The chicks love to get their picture in the paper."

Much of the shot-on-location footage in this episode fails to convey the Japan that viewers around the world would expect to see. In fact, much of the Japan we are shown, from the exterior of the New Otani Hotel, to the exterior of Sada's house, where the police arrive in a military-style truck, look as though they could have been shot in Southern California, even though great expense was taken to make sure they were not.

Cast & Crew

Kent Smith (Winthrop), 58 here, had been appearing in front of the camera since the late 1940s. He had just appeared in *The Outer Limits*, and, after filming this episode, he would become a semiregular on *The Invaders*.

Dan Tobin (Winthrop's secretary) was David Friedkin's best friend. He was also a familiar face on TV and in the movies, going back to the early 1940s. Look for early but memorable appearances in *Woman of the Year* and *The Bachelor & the Bobby Soxer*. Shortly after this, he would appear in the brand new *Batman* as the guest villain "Mr. Jay." He was 55.

France Nuyen (Sada), 26 here, on her first of four *I Spy* appearances, had been on TV since the late 1950s, seen most frequently in programs with exotic backgrounds. She began her career in 1958's *South Pacific*, then went to work in a Broadway hit, *The World of Suzie Wong*, opposite a young William Shatner. She was two years away from being the third Mrs. Robert Culp.

Florence Marly (Eliska), 46, is the object of Winthrop's guilt. She had been starring in B movies since the 1940s, and finished her career with 1973's *Dr. Death: Seeker of Souls*.

Lee Kolima plays Ganko. If he looks familiar, he had previously appeared in "A Cup of Kindness."

Robert C. Dennis & **Earl Berret** would contribute three scripts to the series. They also wrote for *Batman*, *The Wild Wild West*, and *The Andy Griffith Show*. Their ability to combine espionage and humor would land them work on *Get Smart*.

Hugo Friedhofer, at his friend Earle Hagen's request, began his work with the series here, providing the new music. At age 64, he had been at it in Hollywood since the late 1920s, scoring *One-Eyed Jacks*, *Never So Few*, *The Young Lions*, and *Hondo*.

This was the first episode of *I Spy* not to be scored by Earle Hagen, who would write the music for 53 of the hour-long episodes. Friedhofer would be the second most frequent contributor to the show, scoring a total of 26.

16. **"THE TIGER"**; Written by: Robert Culp; Directed by: Paul Wendkos; Location: Washington, D.C. to Vietnam to Hong Kong; First airing: 1/5/66. Repeated: 7/20/66.

Kelly and Scott are sent into Vietnam. Dr. Owen MacLean, a missionary in the region, has gone into hiding. His daughter, American agent Sam-Than MacLean, has been kidnapped by Communist guerrillas, and is being used as the bait to lure her father out.

The mission is heightened by Kelly's past love affair with Sam. Complicating the rescue is Kelly himself. Both his mental and physical states are impaired following a rough assignment in the Orient.

Assessment

"The Tiger" is an atypical *I Spy* entry, and may not appeal to all fans. Its quality, however, is clearly apparent.

Like all of Culp's scripts, this has a darker feel than the average *I Spy* story.

At the Pentagon, Scott tells Col. Wise that he does not want to be assigned to work with Kelly again. He states that Kelly is unfit for duty, and suggests that his partner—known for pushing himself beyond the limit—might get them both killed.

This is the first introduction of "Gabe," their superior.

France Nuyen, Lew Ayres, "The Tiger" (© 3 F Prod., courtesy Image Ent.).

The Story Behind the Story

There is a reason why Kelly and Scott are separated throughout nearly the entire episode: The script was written by Culp before *I Spy* had been created and before Alexander Scott ever existed.

Culp: "Danny Doyle' was the title of my pilot, and it became 'The Tiger.' I lucked out on that one. I figured out a back story where Kelly is all screwed up in his head, and his bod, and Scott didn't want to go with him. Scott didn't want him to go *anywhere*, because Kelly needed to stay down and get some R & R. And the rest, in regards to 'Doyle,' was the same."[9]

The "Danny Doyle" script from 1964 is indeed, in many ways, identical to Culp's 1965 draft of "The Tiger." One small change, in "Danny," Gabe Wise was in the helicopter hovering over Southeast Asia; in "The Tiger" that part was reassigned to Scott.

Culp: "I was really concerned, because I was perfectly aware of the fact that I was splitting Cosby and me up for almost the whole length of the story, and it was not a wise idea. But I had this story that wouldn't allow him to be in it. I tried, but I said, 'This one is for me, all the way, and I want to pursue this because there is a very fine edge I want to walk.' With regard to shooting Sam, the audience would say, 'He would never do that ... would he?'"[10]

As a boy, Culp was fond of the comic strip *Terry and the Pirates*, which can be seen as having inspired much of the tone here. Dressed in a tight fitting jumpsuit throughout most

Robert "Terry & the Pirates" Culp, "The Tiger" (© 3 F Prod., Robert Culp Private Collection).

of the episode, Culp looks like he could have stepped out of the cartoon that was popular in the 1940s and '50s, and still in print in the '60s when this episode appeared.

According to Culp, the interior jungle set built on two adjoining stages at the Selznick Studio in Culver City marked a television triumph.

Culp: "Sheldon had spared absolutely no expense to create the largest jungle set that anyone in the world had ever seen. It was huge. And it had trees going all the way to the loft, which Kelly is stuck in when he parachutes into the area. It was really an amazing set, because it was indoors, and because it was a television show, for Christ's sake. He spent a lot of money, and he has my thanks for that."[11]

The exterior shots of the Vietnamese village, and the boat sequences, were accomplished on the Hal Roach studio back lot in Culver City, where Culp had previously shot *Trackdown*.

The infatuation Culp felt for Nuyen can plainly be seen in this episode. His every look, and the way his body language changes at the mere touch of this woman, is unusually intense, even for the method actor.

Sam MacLean, like Gabe Wise, would return to the series for the second season's "Magic Mirror."

Regarding the casting of Lew Ayers, Culp remembers:

"I wrote this character for a guy I knew, a neighbor who lived a block away—Lee J. Cobb. I took the script to him, but he didn't want to do it. He said, 'It's episodic. It's really lovely, but I don't think I should do that.' I tried to talk him into it, but I couldn't. [Casting Director] Mike Fenton brought in Lew Ayres. He was a wonderful choice. He wasn't the guy I had envisioned, but it worked. Ayres was a joy to work with. He was a real professional."[12]

REVIEWS

The day after "The Tiger" aired, Rick Du Brow, a reporter for UPI, in an article with the headline "Comedy Adds Appeal to the *I Spy* Twins," wrote: "Right under our noses, with hardly any warning, Robert Culp and Bill Cosby have been developing into a very high-class comedy team. They are funny fellows with a genuinely contemporary flair.

"I always remember best the shows' stand-up comedy routines between the two principals at the most unlikely times. Wednesday night, the routine came at the end, in a hospital, when Culp caught the entire droll mood of the series by saying to Cosby of their secret agent jobs: 'What would they do without us—those millions down there?' And Cosby added: 'Without us, they haven't got a chance.'"

William Donnelly, reviewer for the *Los Angeles Tidings*, on February 4, 1966, in an article entitled "*I Spy* Is an Oasis on TV Desert," wrote: "There was enough real human drama and exciting adventure on this episode for anyone's taste. Robert Culp proved he is capable of finding real depth in a characterization and again there was the sad, sardonic point of view. *I Spy* is a mature, well-acted, excellently-produced series. It is a promising oasis in television programming."

Daily Variety, on January 7, 1966, saw "The Tiger" as "an exciting action tale." The reviewer went on to write, "Bob Culp was skillful and convincing. Lew Ayres registers strongly as the idealistic doctor; France Nuyen is excellent as his half-caste daughter; Cosby has less to do this time out, but handles his role well. Culp's script was a good one. Direction was very good. While a good show, *I Spy* is at its best when Cosby and Culp are both involved in the spy stuff from start to finish."

CAST

Lew Ayres was a rising star as early as 1929, at the age of 21, when he played Greta Garbo's leading man in *The Kiss*. His breakthrough role came one year later in *All Quiet on the Western Front*. In the 1930s, his popularity grew when he played Dr. Kildare in the movies. His career was dealt a setback, however, at the start of World War II. When drafted, he became a conscientious objector and refused to fight. After movie theaters threatened to boycott his pictures, Ayres agreed to serve in the medical corps, where he practiced medicine under intense fire in the South Pacific.

After struggling to regain his career, Ayres was nominated for an Academy Award for 1948's *Johnny Belinda*. Sporadic work continued and Ayres was offered the chance to play Dr. Kildare on TV. He lost the part to a young Richard Chamberlain, however, when he refused to play for a cigarette sponsor. Once again, his uncompromising beliefs caused him professional setbacks.

This role on *I Spy* and other TV guest spots kept Ayres working into the 1970s, when he won a Golden Globe Award for his production of *Altars of the World*, an independent film intended to bring to the West the philosophies of the East.

William Boyett, the pilot of the rescue helicopter, is best remembered as Sgt. McDonald on *Adam-12*. He had also played a recurring part on *Sea Hunt*.

Robert Brubaker, as Col. Gabe Wise, rounds out the cast of familiar faces from TV. He had over three dozen credits by 1965, and had played a recurring role on *Gunsmoke* as Jim Beck.

17. **"THE BARTER"**; Written by: Harvey Bullock & P.S. Allen; Directed by: Allen Reisner; 2nd unit directed by: David Friedkin; Location: Japan; First airing: 1/12/66. Repeated: 7/27/66.

Kelly and Scott must aid Professor Shenko, a Communist political theorist, defect to the West.

Once the Americans have freed the elderly Russian from his bodyguards, the teenage daughter of Mr. Sommers, their contact, is kidnapped and used as barter for the return of the Russian. The agents' only hope for finding her is to put pressure on the messenger who brought them the bad news—a worm of a man named Merritt.

Assessment

An effective combo of drama and humor. The comedy stands out first, as Kelly and Scott shower Merritt with gifts and money to make it appear that he has sold out. The dramatic elements are also worthy of mention. When it is discovered that Mr. Sommers' teenage daughter has been abducted, note the sadistic intent in Scott's expression as he turns to face Merritt, and the way in which Kelly kicks Merritt to get his attention.

The Story Behind the Story

Look for one of the few examples of a body double who is not such a double after all. When Kelly and Scott escort Merritt to the harbor, the man standing in for actor Roger C. Carmel appears somewhat thinner, and has his jacket buttoned. Onboard the freighter, we see Carmel, dressed the same, but with a spare tire at his waist, a slump-shouldered stocky kind of a guy who could never button his one-size-too-small jacket.

Cast & Crew

John Abbott (Professor Shenko) was 60 here. Between the early 1950s and the late 1970s, he worked frequently in television. Like many who appeared on *I Spy*, he also worked on *Star*

Trek. The two series had much in common. Both were filmed on the busy Desilu lot, both would be immensely influential for their time, and both series would be often repeated over the years.

Roger C. Carmel, in his second of three *I Spys*, was less than a year away from gaining his greatest TV Land fame on *Star Trek*, as Harry Mudd.

Michael Forest (Igor) is also best known by fans of 1960s cult TV for a prominent guest appearance on *Star Trek*. In his case, it was for playing Apollo, the Greek god who falls for a mortal. The six-foot-three actor got his start working as a leading man for B-flick king Roger Corman.

George Takei plays a red herring. This was his second appearance on *I Spy*. He was weeks away from being cast as Mr. Sulu on, you guessed it, *Star Trek*.

Joan Blackman (Donna), the viper in the bosom, had a recurring role on *Peyton Place* for the 1965–66 season, as well as having played opposite Elvis Presley not once, but twice, in *Kid Galahad* and *Blue Hawaii*.

Harvey Bullock and **P.S. Allen**, known best for their comedy, wrote only one script for *I Spy*. Together, they also worked for *Hogan's Heroes*.

Allen Reisner would end his work with *I Spy* here. He would go on to amass nearly a hundred TV credits, for series such as *Mannix*, *Night Gallery*, and *Murder, She Wrote*.

18. **"COURT OF THE LION"**; Written and directed by: Robert Culp; Location: Japan; First airing: 2/2/66

In a small Japanese village, Kelly and Scott search for missing radioactive elements.

Once they arrive at the oyster farm, the agents encounter an Oxford-educated Zulu seeking revenge on White men by selling the industrial diamonds to the Red Chinese. The water beds of the farm serve as a hiding place for the radioactive material.

Assessment

Culp has much to be proud of with "Court of the Lion," not only from the point of view of a writer and actor, but also as a director. The camera angles are inventive and effective. There is a fluid feel to the shots and the editing. The performances are uniformly good. And, most impressive of all, the blended footage from Japan, the Desilu soundstage and a Southern California beach is flawless. The viewer would be hard pressed to tell that the entire episode was not filmed in Japan.

Godfrey Cambridge, "Court of the Lion" (© 3 F Prod., courtesy Image Ent.).

There is a hint of a love story here, for Scott, one of the creaky taboos still in place for this show and still disregarded by a Culp script. The girl on the beach delivering information to Kelly and Scott is killed. Scott runs down and holds her dead body. The inference is that he had been intimate with her. The dialogue line confirms it.

The only hole in the story is in the way in which Cethswayo hides the industrial diamonds—sprinkling a few grains at a time into hundreds, maybe thousands, of imitation oyster shells, then dumping them in the drink to be harvested later. Why not put the diamonds in a big chest, then bury it in the sand, like any other pirate would do?

The Story Behind the Story

Culp used elements from *The Seventh Samurai* in his story. He had wanted to write a James Bond–like script, "something big and fantastic," with an outrageous and colorful villain bent on world domination.

When Culp asked to direct this episode, he was surprised at how quickly Leonard agreed to his request. He was also impressed by Leonard's generosity, especially when it came to the quality and the expense of the yacht set that was built on stage.

From the beginning, the shoot was plagued with problems. At the Japanese fishing village, the crew had to contend with unhappy locals who did whatever they could to sabotage the shoot. And it was here that a local Japanese grip was electrocuted.

Two months later, in December, the day before shooting was to resume on a Southern California beach, where dialogue would be covered to match shots made in Japan, Los Angeles was hit by a phenomenon.

Culp: "We were supposed to start on a Monday. I had promised Hilly (Elkins), at the beginning of the year, that I would appear in his show on Sunday night, *Broadway Answers Selma*. I didn't tell anybody except Bill. I finished shooting Friday night. I ran to the plane and flew to New York. Today I would think about that much like Sheldon did. I would not look at that very kindly. But I was riding high on the hog, and I thought I could do everything.

"Sunday, late in the afternoon, I got a phone call from Sheldon, asking 'What are you doing in New York?' I said, 'I'm coming in tonight. Everything is okay. Planes fly every hour, Sheldon. Calm down. I knew you'd have a hemorrhage if you knew, so I didn't tell you. But I promised Hilly six months ago that I'd do this.' Sheldon just said, 'It's raining.' I said, 'So it's raining. We'll start on the stage.' He said, 'No, it's really raining.' And I said, 'I'll be there on time, because planes fly in the rain, Sheldon.'

"But planes don't fly in the rain. The heavens opened that weekend in Los Angeles. It rained more in two weeks than at any other time in the history of Southern California weather, all the way back to the 1880s. It never let up."[13]

Culp's flight was unable to land at LAX. After the plane was diverted to a neighboring city, Culp had to be driven back to Hollywood.

With less than 24 hours notice, sets had to be built on a stage to pass for a fishing village. Culp, who redesigned his production schedule daily, said he "learned a great deal about shooting in close-up."

But weather wasn't the only problem to be contended with.

Prior to casting this episode, stand-up comic Godfrey Cambridge approached Culp and asked for the opportunity to play Cethswayo, the deranged Zulu leader. Once filming began, Culp came to the conclusion that Cambridge was out of his element.

Culp: "He asked me how I saw it, and I said, 'I see a rumpled Albert Einstein, who is Black—grey hair, glasses, cane.' When he showed up on the set, in the double-breasted blue blazer, I thought, 'Fuck, what am I going to do? This is a disaster.' But he had me by the balls by then. And I had to figure how I was going to get a performance from him."[14]

Cambridge saw his chance to play a Black Goldfinger. The character of Cethswayo had to be modified substantially. But Culp still felt that Cambridge was trying too hard, and that his readings were coming off as "acting." For one scene, Culp required 27 takes before he was satisfied that he had gotten a good reading. By the final take, according to Culp, Cambridge was so exhausted that he no longer cared, and that became the take that was printed and seen in the show.

Surprisingly, after knowing of the struggle between actor and director, Cambridge comes off looking confident, and his elegance only seems to complement the character.

Cosby knew that the most demanding dialogue scenes would be given to him, freeing Culp to focus on directing. Cosby was unconcerned. When the time came, however, Culp felt that Cosby also required over two dozen takes to achieve the performance needed for one of the speeches. It was the only time Culp ever saw Bill Cosby become angry while on set.

Cosby: "I was just feeling that something magical would happen and I would get through it—because we would ad-lib. But when Bob wrote something, you said Bob's words. There was this scene, and it was an important scene, and a dramatic one, and Bob wanted it the way he wanted it, with the words, and I couldn't remember them. And this was the worst day of *I Spy*. I just went bad in all mental directions. And there was Bob, just as calm and as cool—I mean, looking at a guy who is supposed to be his buddy, and his friend, and his working cohort, and this guy can't make a commitment to learning the lines. And then, my low self-esteem caught up with a feeling of depression, and it just got to the point where I had about a half-inch of pride, which is necessary to accentuate failure, and make it worse. And we went into, maybe, triple overtime—because of me: The most selfish, self-absorbed moment that I think I've ever had with my friend. And the reason I am able to remember it is because Bob never said, 'Y'know, you're really a jerk, man. You know how important this was, and all you had to do was spend maybe 45 minutes.' I'm 67 years old now, and I still remember it."[15]

Preece: "Culp is a really good writer, and he had a vision of doing something that was not your typical episodic television. But the weather was just God-awful. It was extremely difficult, and it became a very, very strenuous time. I remember thinking, "Oh my God, please, can I take a week off."[16]

As the production fell behind and the budget escalated, the episode had to stop shooting two days short of completion. The *I Spy* team and its stars were set to travel to Mexico for location shooting of the third block of nine episodes, and the departure date could not be delayed.

A month later, Culp would return to finish "Court of the Lion," with both day and night shooting at Paradise Cove, a Southern California beach. But the problems were not over.

The actor Culp had earlier filmed scenes with, playing the village holy man, had vanished. After days of searching, the actor's agent located him in a hospital, deep in a coma, the victim of a stroke. Culp had no choice but to use a body double for the beach shots and to edit in a single close up of the actor taken a month earlier while on the soundstage.

To the director's credit, the effect is successful and even adds an unexpected element to the sequence where the holy man is praying for guidance before resorting to taking a life. The shot used of the actor, sitting on the floor, deep in prayer, was altered in post, changing it from a daytime shot to a nighttime shot, eliminating the background and replacing it with the darkness of the nighttime beach scene. An aura of light is created around the near frozen shot of the holy man, creating an impression that suggests he is, indeed, enlightened.

The final night of shooting went as badly as the rest.

Culp: "There was a sequence where Mako's character, Babyface, has everybody in the water, pulling the nets from the oyster beds. Scotty's out there, pulling like crazy. He's hip deep in water. It's January at Paradise Cove, the dead of winter, and it's at night. It's the last shot. Bill had the flu, and a fever of 102. He wouldn't tell me, and he wouldn't allow anyone else to tell me. He was going to die first before he would let me down."[17]

Censorship issues also had to be contended with. In the tag scene to the episode, Kelly was to be lying on the floor next to the pretty Japanese villager who had sought their help. It was a fun and flirtatious scene that the network censors felt was way too sexy. A mandate was passed down that the Japanese girl would have to be lying on a higher level than Kelly, and there would have to be a screen of some sort placed between them. Despite these demands, the playfulness and sexiness of the scene survived. It is also interesting to note that, as written, this scene was intended for the middle of the story. Once in editing, however, it seemed better suited to close the show as the "tag."

With all the agony involved in getting this installment of *I Spy* onto the screen, it is no wonder that Culp remembers Leonard saying, "Please don't try to direct anymore. I couldn't buy a better director at any price. But I need a live actor, not a dead director."[18]

For the February 6, 1966, issue of *TV Week*, Culp said, "As for directing, I wanted to see if I could take an idea from the start and see it all the way through. I found I can, and that's it. But no more. I'll stay with acting."

Cosby added, "There's not enough money to get me into directing. Why? I'd have to put up with people like me."

Cast & Crew

Godfrey Cambridge (Cethswayo), known primarily as a stand-up comedian, began his acting career off–Broadway, where in 1961, at age 27, he won an Obie Award for *The Blacks*, where he is transformed from a Black man to an elderly White woman. Contrary to the statement made in the *TV Guide* synopsis for this episode, Cambridge did not make his television dramatic acting debut here. That happened three years earlier, on *U.S. Steel Hour*. In the late 1960s, Cambridge would make several notable appearances in films, including *The President's Analyst*, as a Secret Service agent, *Cotton Comes to Harlem*, as a private detective, and *Watermelon Man*, as a White business man who wakes up and finds he's turned Black. He was working at the time of his death, at age 43, when he suffered a massive heart attack while on set playing Idi Amin in the 1976 TV movie *Victory at Entebbe*.

Miki Mayama, who plays the village girl who enchants Kelly, was a newcomer to acting. The following year she would make two brief appearances on *Star Trek* as Yeoman Tamura, as well as appearing in the short-lived series *Hey Landlord*.

Mako (Babyface) had made two appearances in *I Spy* as Jimmy. He is very effective as the expressionless and sadistic Babyface. Working steadily over the years, Mako would still be practicing his craft in the new millennia, playing Admiral Yamamoto in the big budget film version of *Pearl Harbor*.

Ed Parker, who has a small role as the hitman who commits murder in the teaser, then kicks Kelly's butt in a brief fight sequence at midstory, was not an actor. He was Robert Culp's karate guru. Culp chose him for this part, knowing Parker could convey the impression of hitting Kelly hard without really causing any damage. The effectiveness of the short sequence is enhanced by seeing Culp do his own stunts, at the trusted hands of his trainer.

David Friedkin also deserves credit for the success of this episode. Freeing Culp to return to his acting duties, Friedkin supervised the editing, pulling together all the fragmented pieces which were filmed over a extended period of immense difficulties.

Bud Molin was the actual editor, and would receive an Emmy nomination for his work here.

Ron Jacobs: "Crazy Bud Molin. You try cutting an *I Spy* show together, and see if they don't call you crazy. It was doing the impossible every day on every episode."[19]

6

South of the Border

In the fall of 1965, the espionage game was all over the dial.

The Man from U.N.C.L.E., still in search of its peak audience, began its second season on NBC, in its third time slot, Fridays at 10 P.M. *U.N.C.L.E.* made the jump from black and white to color, and, for the first time, found itself in A.C. Nielsen's Top Twenty.

The Wild Wild West premiered on CBS and was being marketed as "James Bond in the old west."

Get Smart, lampooning anything that was Bond, also made its TV debut.

Even the "law" behind *Burke's Law*, the millionaire Los Angeles chief of detectives, turned in his badge and became *Amos Burke—Secret Agent*.

The "Secret Agent" himself, John Drake, having proven his clout during a summer run, would return in January with new episodes.

And, with the success of that English import on CBS, rival network ABC was in discussions to bring on another popular British espionage series: *The Avengers*. John Steed and Emma Peel would make their U.S. debut in March of 1966.

American TV would soon, and quite suddenly, be crowded with spies.

On the big screen, James Bond was back. *Thunderball* was released in time for the Christmas season. It topped all the previous entries, earning $75 million at the box office. In 1965 dollars, this was a massive amount of loot.

To no surprise, Sheldon Leonard also had his sights on the big screen.

Neil Hickey, in the October 30th issue of *TV Guide*, reported that *I Spy* would soon end up in the movies. Sheldon Leonard was planning to shoot a feature-length version in the summer.

I Spy, at the time of Leonard's announcement, having only aired seven episodes on NBC, was already that hot. But it would take more than 35 years for the feature film Leonard envisioned to see the light of a movie house screen. The production schedule for *I Spy* didn't allow time for anything above or beyond the filming of the series.

In December, the *I Spy* company was en route to Mexico to begin location filming for the third block of episodes.

Las Brisas became a home away from home for the men and women behind *I Spy*. The visually distinctive resort—tucked into the side of the mountain overlooking Acapulco Bay, with its multiple "casitas" (little houses), private swimming pools and pink jeeps to negotiate the winding roads—was a priceless find. Resort managing director Frank Brandstetter proved to be a very accommodating gentleman to the visiting Americans and their camera equipment. The resort was open for filming and offered the show a series of unique and memorable visuals.

Director Richard Sarafian would now alternate with Paul Wendkos. Of the trip to Mexico, he recalls:

"Sheldon took me up to a vantage point overlooking Acapulco and said, 'Sarafian, some

6—*South of the Border*

BILL COSBY y ROBERT CULP
"Yo soy espía"

Two amigos in Mexico, Dec. 1966 (© 3 F Prod.).

people collect postcards, I collect vistas. Come with me.' He kept going higher and higher, from pool to pool on this hillside belonging to the Las Brisas Hotel. After each 20 or 30 feet, as we got higher up, he'd say, 'What do you think of this one?' I'd be a little out of breath, and I'd say, 'It's nice.' He'd say, 'Come on, I'll show you something nicer.' He'd lead me up to the next one and say, 'Now what do you think?' I'd say, even more out of breath, 'Well, it's a bigger shot. But, Sheldon, how big does it have to be?' And he'd say, 'The people who shoot postcards invariably come up with the best angles.' And I said, 'But, Sheldon, we're not shooting postcards.' He was crushed by that."[1]

As with any trip abroad, there are always problems to be solved.

Another country usually means another language and another culture. What Leonard began to understand, in this case, was the intent behind a very specific phrase: "No problem." Leonard was told this again and again. No problem. Actually, in the local dialect, it meant, "no hurry, no big deal."

In the teaser for "It's All Done with Mirrors," a freshly caught sailfish was necessary for the typical vacation photo every fisherman craves. Getting a sailfish was easy.

The fleet of sport-fishing boats loaded with tourists eager to string up their catches, was returning in the midafternoon. Leonard looked over the catch, and bought one very impressive fish, weighing in at 150 pounds. The late afternoon light, however, was turning yellow. Leonard asked his Mexican first assistant if the fish could be kept until the morning. And that phrase made its first ominous appearance.

"No problem," he was told. "It will be tied up in the water. It will be fine."

The following morning, the company returned and hauled the moored fish out of the water.

Any eleventh grader having read *The Old Man and the Sea* knew exactly what to expect: bones and gristle. Crabs, fish, and birds had left very little behind. As with Hemingway's Old Man, Leonard stared at the chewed and destroyed carcass. They would now have to wait for the tourist boats to return, to choose another fish, and thus lose a day.

"There should be plenty of fish to choose from," Leonard's first assistant said. And although it was unspoken, Leonard could hear that "no problem," just lingering in the air, as he continued to stare at the fish skeleton.

There is another problem that is unavoidable: the water. The dishes are washed in it; ice cubes for drinks are made from it. It is generally undrinkable to any visitor not from south of the border. Anglos call it "Montezuma's Revenge," but to locals, it's known as "La Turista."

Even in 1965, over-the-counter medicine was available, but La Turista runs its course, medicine or not.

In spite of the impressive variety of footage brought back from the Mexico trip—foot pursuits through Mexico City streets, jeep rides up and down the winding roads of the La Brisas resort, rendezvous at the top of Aztec pyramids, fight scenes on the slanted cobblestone streets of Taxco—many of those shots were filmed between frantic trips to the john.

And, beginning with this journey, the line at the john had grown.

George W. Brooks, the film editor who had spliced together "Tatia," and "Always Say Goodbye," was plucked from the air-conditioned comfort of Desilu studios and was now in Mexico as location film editor. It hadn't been thought about on the previous two journeys. No one could know there would be a need. But there was. And Brooks now had the job. He made sure that the footage being shot was of broadcast standard and would cut together.

Leon Chooluck, who had made his bones in Japan by surviving his kidnapping, was rewarded with a new title and the worst job on the planet: location production manager. Everything not provided by Desilu was his responsibility and burden. Every need, every complaint, every problem would fall directly into his lap.

The block of nine scripts that went along with the cast and crew to the locations had, first, been cleared by NBC, and then were submitted, in advance, to the local authorities. Mexican law required that the government censors approve all scripts.

Writer Dave Kaufman, in the February 22, 1966, issue of *Variety*, quoted Friedkin and Fine as saying, "They [the censors] pointed out where we were in error in terms of pride of their country or the historical truth, and we corrected [the scripts]. They have no problem about their nationals being heavies, so long as we don't make their police out to be fools."

The second unit, as always, had to be prepared for any last minute changes in the shooting schedules. A wire service report, dated December 16, 1965, stated that, while filming the episode "Crusade to Limbo,"—there was a "delay in the Company's production plans when permission to film scenes in the Museum of National History was refused. By altering the script, permission was obtained to shoot footage at the Pyramids."

What luck. Pyramids. Leonard was ecstatic.

Sarafian: "It was during the morning. It was incredible—the view of these ruins. I was there with Sheldon and his wife, Frankie, looking the place over for the best shots. He started to lead us up this pyramid with narrow eight-inch steps that seemed to go forever. Frankie is following in high heels. I'm lagging behind. He stops a third of the way up and calls back, 'Sarafian, can you hear me?' I'm huffing and puffing and way behind him, but I yell back, 'Yes, Shel, I can hear you.' He continues until he's half way up. Then he yells back, 'Sarafian, can you still hear me?' 'Yes, Shel, I can still hear you.' He continues and I'm trying to keep up. Then he reaches the top and yells down, 'Sarafian, can you hear me now?' And I yelled back, 'You know what, Sheldon? For the first time since I've known you, you look insignificant.'

"When we did the actual shooting, I had to climb that damn thing again."[2]

Preece: "I've nothing bad to say about Sarafian, except that he was too fat."[3]

Cosby: "I thought Sarafian weighed about 740 pounds."[4]

Preece: "He was overweight by a lot. And they were shooting on the pyramids with Howard Duff, and Culp and Cosby at the top. So, what did they do, they hired a director who wasn't in very good shape.

"Sarafian got half way up the pyramid and said, 'I can't make it, I'm too out of breath.' This was near Mexico City and it was a very high altitude. He said, 'Will you shoot it for me?' And he told me what he needed about the scene. I said, 'Sure.' So we started shooting. And we shot some more. And we shot some more. And finally Sarafian showed up."[5]

Sarafian: "It took a while, but I made it. Going down the pyramid was harder. The steps were short because of the size of the Aztecs' feet. And, besides being a big man, I had acrophobia. I had to have a couple of guys help me down."[6]

One of the "guys" who helped Sarafian, nearly made the trip ahead of schedule.

Culp: "The scene took place at the top of the Temple of the Moon. Originally, the pyramid was covered in marble, and to hold the marble in place there was a substructure of stones sticking out about a foot to anchor it. They're all over the temple walls to hold stuff that isn't there anymore. So the only thing that's left is all these jagged teeth, all the way to the bottom.

"We were standing at the top, and Fouad brought along the gaffer's son, a young man in his early 20s. We were all watching the set up, with our backs to the precipice. I realized the kid was shuffling his feet, and he stepped back a fraction of an inch too far, and he started to go. Just as he went, I grabbed him and pulled him back. If he'd fallen, he'd be completely gone, because those teeth would have torn him to shreds."[7]

As the month-long production continued, the *I Spy* company criss crossed Mexico, in search of the best visuals and highest vistas.

Sarafian: "It was more than extraordinary, because we would do nine at a time. Paul Wendkos would do four, and I would do four, and Friedkin might do one. We'd shoot a part of one, then Culp and Cosby would change their wardrobe, and then we'd shoot another. We didn't do it in a linear fashion. If I could take advantage of a certain location for one of my four episodes, I'd have Bob and Bill change clothes and put them against the backdrop.

"It was like a light cavalry outfit working with Fouad. It was a way of shooting that Hollywood had never seen before, working with short crews, working out of one truck, with a great gaffer named Homer Clement, who would prelight scenes, and doing four episodes at once. Fouad was so much of the package. Here was a guy who would crawl out on a window ledge and lean down over the street. He had so much balls. And it was his short crews, and his compact equipment, that made it all affordable, and, therefore, possible. We would never have brought an episode in for under $200,000 without Fouad."[8]

During the time of the Mexico shoots, Cosby told *TV Week* magazine, "The hardest part of the series is the lack of continuity in the scenes and our irregular shooting schedule."

For an actor, it was the hardest approach to shooting a series that had ever been attempted.

But hard work makes for hard play.

South of the Border, Behind Sheldon's Back

Sarafian: "In any movie, whether it is *I Spy* or anything else, if you're on the road, you become family. You take care of one another. You drink together. You play together. You go down to the beach, and you barbeque the fish. I can't tell you what a joy it was and what an adventure it was.

"In the evenings, we'd go out dancing. And Fouad was really very generous. He would find every stray in the hotel, and we'd take them with us wherever we'd go. We had the best time. It was one big party."[9]

Preece: "I was there when we all went to a whorehouse. They had trouble distinguishing between Howard Duff and myself. We looked a bit alike, except he was older."[10]

Culp: "All of a sudden I'm given a weekend off. I met a girl who was Swiss or Dutch. But she was very attractive, and very adventurous. There was also a girl there named "Suzy Creamcheese," famous for being on the American side of the jet set. My wife was coming down. France was already there. I was doing a lot of juggling. That was a real sailor's weekend."[11]

Preece: "In Mexico, on two different times, Culp used me as a 'beard.' He said, 'Can you pretend France is here to see you?' I said, 'What about me? I'm married, too.' And he said, 'Ah, nobody will believe that France is with *you—except my wife*.'"[12]

In a wire service story from December 16th, there was an item saying "Robert Culp became embroiled in a fight near the Maria Isabel Hotel with two Mexicans Tuesday evening. One of the assailants slugged Culp's wife Nancy, pulled a knife on Culp, and was detained overnight at the police station."

Leonard and the *I Spy* company denied the report. The Hollywood media was still watching him and his pet project very closely, as was NBC. The very last thing Leonard wanted was adverse publicity about anything concerning the show.

This desire to avoid negative attention, however, may have been the nexus for two fights—one more serious than the other—between Leonard and Culp, creating a wall between the two men that would last for the rest of Leonard's life.

Pistols at Dawn

Culp had not forgotten about Sam Peckinpah. He still hoped Peckinpah could direct segments, convinced that his friend's vision would be of immense help to the new series.

Leonard continued to refuse. And continued to not explain. In Mexico, strangely, came the Mexican standoff: Leonard didn't talk, and Culp didn't back down.

Worse, Culp—who had previously been proven right by NBC, when an episode he had written was used to launch the series—now injected a new irritant into Leonard's already sore spot. Culp wasn't just questioning the quality of many of the scripts, but he was getting Cosby to examine them, as well. The two actors had also been altering the scripts, making minor changes at first, but changes that would become more profound with each new teleplay to come down the chute of the TV assembly line system.

With the third block of nine, now shooting in Mexico, the producers began to notice a subtle conspiracy between the two leads.

Culp & Leonard, an uneasy alliance (© 3 F Prod.).

Cosby: "There were things that we did that were secrets between us. As an example: there are shows where we pay tribute to the *Treasure of Sierra Madre*, because both of us enjoyed the movie, and now we're ad-libbing, and I begin to give him a name like 'Dobbsey. Listen to it. It's Fred C. Dobbs, and it's *Sierra Madre*. It was just a lot of fun to be able to do that. And there Bob is, going right along with it—this guy's from Northern California, pole-vault champion, and this other guy's from North Philadelphia, also a track man—but the beauty of these two guys is to be able to laugh with each other, and to do things on the set that we loved and shared."[13]

The problem was, it was Sheldon Leonard's set. And Culp, unaware that the balance had shifted, cornered Leonard in an Acapulco parking lot to sell him on an idea for a new script to reunite Kelly Robinson and Sam-Than McLean.

As Culp pitched the story to Leonard, "Sam," fellow spy and Kelly's love interest from "The Tiger," would be brought back—meaning France Nuyen would be back, too.

Culp had worked it all out. Nuyen could fly to Acapulco now, film a handful of scenes for the opening of the story with the Second Unit, at a great savings to Leonard. The footage would enhance the episode, which could be written and completed later. This seemed like a solid idea to Culp.

It didn't to Leonard.

By this time, Culp and Nuyen were already heavily involved in a secret relationship that was becoming less secret all the time.

Culp: "Sheldon thought I was trying to con him, because I wanted to get a woman down there to satisfy my needs. That was not the point, and I said so. I got an opening teaser that I wanted to shoot with this woman on water skis—who then disappears. We're here, water is here, this is the place to do it."[14]

The problem was that the woman Culp had in mind, the woman who would disappear, wasn't disappearing fast enough for Leonard.

Culp: "We're out in public, in a parking lot—Sheldon wouldn't agree to do it. And I was deeply offended that he did not believe me that I would write what I said I was going to write—simply because it wasn't written yet. I said, 'Look, if it's a matter of money, I'll bring her down, for Christ's sake. I want her here, not just tonight, but I want her on the schedule.' When he said 'No,' I took it to be a repudiation of my word of honor."[15]

Leonard didn't just say "No." He shouted it. And he did so while the two men were out in the open, in public, where others from the cast and crew might hear.

Culp couldn't understand Leonard's refusal to see reason, or his anger over it.

Culp: "I thought, 'If that's all he thinks of me, then he's out of my life. He can't be my dad.' And Sheldon wanted to be everybody's dad. He wanted to be thought of as the ultimate dad figure. And he ain't up to the job with me. That's why we never got along. We were always water and oil. We never did mix."[16]

Andrea Bershad: "My dad had a warm attraction to Bill, which was mutual. But he didn't like Robert Culp as much. I'm not really sure why. Robert was kind of a womanizer at that time, and my dad's kind of a prude. But that was only part of it. It may have been chemistry—a clash of egos, his not accepting my dad's authority. Dad can be rather forceful, and he doesn't really like to be challenged."[17]

And so, the Mexican standoff: Leonard owned *I Spy*. Culp, on the other hand, felt he was more than just an actor on a TV series. In his mind, *I Spy* would never have happened if he hadn't sent Leonard that pilot script back in '64 or allowed Leonard to attach his name to the project to interest NBC. And it was his script, "So Long, Patrick Henry," which the network, by their own scheduling, chose as the one to set the tone and the rhythm for all the other scripts to come.

Leonard wouldn't question the professional integrity of Friedkin or Fine; why, then, did he doubt Culp?

Much later, Culp would refer to himself and Leonard as "two arrogant men."[18]

But at the time, in that parking lot, Leonard raised his voice. Culp fought back in a completely different way. He stopped speaking to Leonard.

Culp later said, if he and Leonard were on the same plane, within eyesight of each other, he (Culp) would turn away and scribble notes on his clipboard, something he always carried with him, pretending he was writing, rather than interact with his boss. In a car, he looked out the window and did not respond to one word spoken by Leonard, unless, for professional reasons, it required a response.

Culp made no eye contact when Leonard spoke to them as a group, never responded to any overture, and continued to freeze him out.

After the company returned to Desilu, during the final days of shooting their maiden season, the silence broke.

Culp: "Sheldon walked into my dressing room and said, 'Bob, this is ridiculous. We are grown men, we're involved in a very difficult project, we stand or fall together, and you refuse to communicate with me. It is really much too hard on everybody else, and too hard on the company, as a whole, and I think it should end.'

"He never apologized. At that point, I don't think he knew where it was coming from. He didn't know what he'd done. I never told him. Now, I simply said to him, 'You're right, it's over.' We shook hands, and that ended it."[19]

The hatchet would be buried, but not forgotten. The partnership between the two men would never again be the same.

Culp always saw his relationship with Leonard as being an "uneasy alliance, hardly brimming of trust."[20]

In the past, the two men at least made a pretense of being friendly. All that ended here.

Culp would complete his script and it was called "The Enchanted Cottage." Ironically, it dealt with two people, closely involved, unable to communicate, unable to understand each other, until one's betrayal of the other ends the story. He would submit it through the correct channels. It would be accepted and placed on the schedule to be produced, just as his other scripts had been: with no discussion and no request for a rewrite. The title would be changed to "Magic Mirror." It would not be filmed in Mexico, but in Spain. France Nuyen would reprise her role as Sam and share quarters with Culp. It would appear that Culp had won. But he would learn, in time, that this was merely a Pyrrhic victory.

Culp: "Years later, I realized that it really wasn't about Sheldon not trusting me as a professional. The fact is, he was the ultimate family man. My relationship with France offended him. Thinking back on it from this distance, I have no doubt that that was the real reason. He couldn't bring himself to contribute to what he perceived I was doing to my family, by having such a relationship. He knew Nancy many times over. And he could see that all the storm clouds on the horizon were very dark indeed. I was plowing right into them."[21]

7

The Third Block of Episodes

19. **"TURKISH DELIGHT"**; Written by: Eric Bercovici; Directed by: Paul Wendkos; Second unit directed: by Sheldon Leonard; Location: Mexico; First airing: 2/9/66. Repeated: 8/10/66.

Three internationally famous agronomists (specialists in the study of soil management), expected to attend a conference in Mexico City, disappear. Scott, masquerading as an American delegate, is also abducted and held prisoner by the alcoholic Karafatma, who intends to sell the captured scientists to a foreign government in need of their services.

As Kelly's search for Scott and the scientists is delayed by a series of dead ends, Dr. Rachel Alper, one of the kidnapped agronomists, unwittingly reveals Scott's identity to Karafatma, making escape for the captives appear impossible.

Assessment

I Spy's top trademarks—celebrity guest stars, foreign lands, espionage, drama, and humor—are well featured here.

Kelly's frantic search for his friend adds energy to the story, nicely interwoven with the cerebral interplay between Scott, Rachel Alper, and their host, Mr. Karafatma, and the sexual tension between Scott and Rachel.

Victor Buono is refreshing as the opportunistic Karafatma. His playful and constantly inebriated personality adds unexpected humor.

And could a more satisfying end have been designed than seeing the unconscious slavers sold into slavery?

The Story Behind the Story

Writer Eric Bercovici recalls his first meeting with the producers:

"I said, 'Why don't we reverse it? What about letting Cosby play the lead and letting Culp play second banana for a change?' And they said, 'Listen, we like the story, but we can't do it that way. Culp is our star, Cosby's not.' So I wrote it with Culp playing the lead. I turned the script in, and they called me in for a meeting, and they said, 'We need a rewrite. We think the script's okay, but we think Cosby should play the lead in this one.' And I said, 'Okay.' I went home and changed the names."[1]

"Turkish Delight" provides Scott with his first opportunity to be romantic on the show, and to kiss the girl.

Cosby: "I was always embarrassed to kiss on-screen. I thought that my wife would not like to see that. So I never could get into a love scene, 'cause, y'see, wives can see when you're 'play kissing,' and when you're really kissing."[2]

Earle Hagen's music continues to delight, with flavorful rhythms and memorable melodies.

Hagen: "It was tough duty operating out of Las Brisas, but

Top: Victor Buono, "Turkish Delight" (© 3 F Prod., courtesy Image Entertainment). *Bottom*: Cosby's first kiss with Diana Sands, 1966 (© 3 F Prod., courtesy Ron Jacobs).

somebody had to do it. I followed the Mariachi bands around with a bottle of tequila, which I would slowly empty."[3]

Culp & Cosby on Set Rewrite

An odd ad-lib takes place in the outdoor scene at the villa, where Rachel chides her three fellow prisoners for not being manly enough to attempt an escape.

The script has her say, "There isn't a man among you! You are decadent and soft. All of you!"

In the filmed sequence, in a scolding tone, she merely says, "Chickenhearts, all of you!" You may recall that "Chickenheart" was a stand-up comedy routine of Bill Cosby's.

Later, when Kelly is charging in like the cavalry, then finds that Scott has already freed himself, Culp contributes the line, "How come you always embarrass me when I'm rescuing you?"

Cast & Crew

Victor Buono began working in TV in the late 1950s. Look for a very young, rotund Buono in the 1961 film *Whatever Happened to Baby Jane?* His small screen assignments picked up with a recurring role on *77 Sunset Strip*, then he gained attention by playing larger-than-life evildoers, as he had on *Batman* in ten installments as King Tut, or in a pair of *The Wild Wild West* episodes as Count Manzeppi. He continued to work in TV and films until his death in 1982 of a heart attack at age 44.

Diana Sands, playing Dr. Rachel Alper, was a feather in the cap for the series' producers. She had been a star in theater since the mid–1950s, where she refused to be stereotyped and often played roles written for White actresses. In 1959 she won an Outer Circle Critics Award, playing a part that was written for a Black woman, in the stage production of *A Raisin in the Sun*. She would reprise the role of Beneatha Younger for the film version in 1961. She received two Emmy nominations during the early 1960s for *Beyond the Blues*, a music special, and for "Who Do You Kill?," an episode of *East Side/West Side*. The same year, 1963, she appeared in the film *An Affair of the Skin*. In 1964 she won an Obie Award and was nominated for a Tony for her continued work on the New York stage. In the late 1960s, she would create controversy by playing opposite Alan Alda in the stage production of *The Owl and the Pussycat*, with no explanation being given for the part of a White woman being performed by one who was Black. "Never mind the color," she would say, "Please just look at me." Her last movie, *Honeybaby, Honeybaby*, where she played the title role, was released posthumously in 1974. Sands died in September 1973 of cancer. She was only 39.

Cosby: "I was very proud to be on-screen with this fantastic actor. I mean, you're talking about going places and meeting people like Diana Sands. I was honored."[4]

Eric Bercovici was 32 when he penned this story for *I Spy*, and was fairly new to TV writing, having sold scripts to only a few series, including *Bob Hope's Chrysler Theater*.

Bercovici: "I saw one episode prior to writing for *I Spy*. The two characters were easily identifiable, or, in my case, interchangeable."[5]

20. **"BET ME A DOLLAR"**; Written by: David Friedkin & Morton Fine; Directed by: Richard Sarafian; Location: Mexico; First airing: 2/16/66. Repeated: 8/3/66.

Between assignments, and out of sheer boredom, Kelly bets that he can drop out of sight in Mexico and elude Scott for a period of one week. But the wager becomes a matter of life and death when Scott learns that Kelly is infected with fatal anthrax germs.

As Scott desperately tries to find his partner, Kelly baits him on in a high stakes game of hide and seek. On Kelly's team is Ramon, an industrious peasant boy, unaware of the deadly poison slowly killing his new friend.

Assessment

"Bet Me" offers a superior example of how the metaphor of a ticking clock can add excitement to a story, and push that story forward with urgency and purpose.

This is the first time we see Kelly and Scott on leave, without an assignment to occupy their minds or a life-and-death situation to dominate their time. Until Scott comes up with the idea of a game, Kelly is bored, restless, even depressed. Note how dark Culp's performance is, as Kelly sucks on limes and downs shooters of Tequila. Slumped over at the bar, he's coiled like a snake looking for something to bite—the quartered limes will have to do.

Just hours earlier, Kelly had been turning on the personality for a pretty woman. His tendency to please and impress any woman had even driven him to risk his life by breaking up a back alley knife fight. But now, after achieving his conquest and then losing interest in her, safe with his one true friend, he lets the inner darkness come out. Kelly, when dealing with his demons, can change dramatically from the joking, self-assured athlete, to a reckless and even self-destructive man.

Scott has seen it before, and knows how to shake his friend's blues away—with a mission—a challenge—and, on this day, a bet.

Once the bet is made, a unique and riveting storyline kicks in, allowing us to see the profound differences in the two men. And, by separating the team, as "Bet Me a Dollar" does, Kelly and Scott now work at cross purposes, demonstrating just how formidable the two are as a unit.

The location photography in "Bet Me" is especially impressive. A large portion of the show, far more than had been attempted in any previous episode, was shot on location, this time in Mexico City. After the restrictions imposed on the company in Japan, they were enjoying their newfound freedom, and appreciating working in an environment where they were not only welcomed, but embraced.

Richard Sarafian makes a strong debut on the series as a director. The camera angles and performances achieved while on location, which Sarafian, huffing and puffing, traveled to Mexico to oversee, are impressive.

"Bet Me" demonstrates an excellent work of writing by Friedkin and Fine, matching the level they achieved in "A Cup of Kindness" and "Tigers of Heaven."

The Story Behind the Story

Culp: "It was a very simple story, and it worked like a dream. I thought it was terrific. Marvelous.

"Sarafian, like any wise director in television, had come in early, hanging around for a bit, before he went to Mexico. He was there enough to see me struggle in vain with 'Court of the Lion.'"[6]

Sarafian: "In Mexico, at the floating gardens, at 800,000 goddamn feet, the air was so thin that I was having trouble breathing—and sleeping. I couldn't stay in Mexico City very long."[7]

Preece: "Sarafian used to walk around while they were acting and smoke cigarettes. He would never stand still. And he was fat. He had more problems than any human being at that time: a gorgeous wife who was costing him a lot, a Rolls Royce that was in the shop—and he was borrowing money to get it out of the shop. He was a charming guy, though. He was a very good guy, and I thought one of the best directors. He's wonderful."[8]

CAST & CREW

Pepito Hector Galindo, playing young Ramon, the shoe shine boy Kelly befriends, turns in a surprisingly touching performance, filled with both charm and humor, then sudden worry, anger, and regret. Since the young actor was available to work with the company both in Mexico and back in the United States, the episode benefits greatly.

Galindo worked briefly as an actor in American TV and films. His first appearance, under the name Jose Hector Galindo, was for *Daniel Boone* in 1964.

Richard Sarafian began directing in the mid–1950s.

Sarafian: "I started at Warner Brothers doing *Maverick*, *Bronco*, and the *Cheyenne* pilot. I directed for *Gunsmoke*, as well. I didn't know one end of a horse from another when I started. But they kept hiring me anyway."[9]

Sarafian graduated to the WB snoop shows *77 Sunset Strip* and *Hawaiian Eye*. There were no horses there, only actors with greasy kid stuff in their hair. He was 40 when he came to *I Spy*.

Hugo Friedhofer compositions excelled in this episode, his second *I Spy* assignment.

21. **"RETURN TO GLORY"**; Written by: David Friedkin and Mort Fine; Directed by: Richard Sarafian; Location: Mexico; First airing: 2/23/66. Repeated: 8/17/66.

In Mexico City, the State Department wants Kelly and Scott to learn what plans a former Latin American strongman, General Rafeal Ortiz, has for returning to his homeland, and to find out—"unofficially"—what assistance he will need from the U.S. to regain power. After two failed meetings, Kelly and Scott realize that the protective attitude of the general's wife, and a soldier of fortune named Matin Page, may force them to take more extreme measures in completing their mission.

Assessment

A successful blend of action, mystery, humor, and first-rate shot-on-location scenery. The plot reflects the often problematic U.S. policy of supporting dictators.

Dolores del Rio is elegant as Cerita, the ousted dictator's wife. She is willing to betray her husband in order to realize his dream of returning to power.

The location footage is the most impressive yet. Director Sarafian filmed half the episode in and around the town of Taxco, and at Del Rio's Mexican estate.

In a chilling re-enactment of the Abraham Zapruder film from 1963, the general's car, top down, drives into the plaza. Ortiz and his wife are in the back seat. She is wearing a pink dress. After shots ring out, the general falls into her lap. Kelly and Scott swarm over the car like the Secret Service did for President Kennedy. This visual is uncomfortably close to the actual footage from November 22nd, Dallas, Texas.

7—The Third Block of Episodes 123

The Story Behind the Story

The episode opens and ends with Kelly and Scott at the State Department office in Mexico City, telling their story to an accounting manager named Shelby. This footage, used as a framing device, was an afterthought. The episode had come in short. The new padded footage was shot at the same time as another Sarafian-helmed episode, "Crusade to Limbo," which also featured Shelby.

As for "Return to Glory," Sarafian recalls: "That was a difficult one, because Bob Culp didn't want to kiss Dolores del Rio. It was very embarrassing, because she felt that. Here is this wonderful icon from another time, who was quite an elegant lady. The only way you could tell her age was in her hands. Why Bob resisted a moment of kissing her is beyond me. I was always so saddened by that."[10]

Culp: "I used to always look at the production roster to see who they were going to pair me up with. And the ones that stand out as raising the hairs on the back of my neck were Julie London, Dorothy Lamour, and Dolores del Rio.

"Del Rio was a star when I was a kid. And she was 40 years old *then*. Now this is more than 20 years later, and I'm supposed to be making love to her. And, if Cosby had a ball teasing me over Julie London, you can imagine what he was going to do over this one. As it turned out, I really dodged a bullet on that one."

What about that missing kiss? It was to happen after Kelly enters the general's home, disguised as a Mexican laborer.

In the filmed episode, we see del Rio's character, Senora Ortiz, relaxing, listening to a boy play guitar. The moment has been staged for Kelly.

Senora Ortiz dismisses the boy, and takes Kelly into a hallway leading to the general's study. Once there, she tells Kelly to come to her room after he speaks to the general, so she may set his mind at ease regarding anything he may see or hear that will bother him. She adds, "It is important to me that you leave here with a feeling of friendship for us."

What we don't see—

The big comeback and the aborted kiss between Dolores del Rio and Robert Culp, Dec. 1966 (© 3 F Prod., courtesy Ron Jacobs).

what was written, but never filmed—comes next. Senora Ortiz slides her arms around Kelly's neck, then purrs, "Can you guess how important?" Before Kelly can answer, she kisses him on the lips.

After the kiss ends, the script has Kelly say, "What do we do now? Call in the boy guitar player?"

All deleted.

Culp's reluctance to play out the kiss, besides upsetting director Sarafian and hurting the feelings of del Rio, may have changed the mood in the *I Spy* writer/producers' office concerning the on set script changes and ad-libbing. Up to this point, Fine, Friedkin and Leonard seemed to approve, even encourage the contributions made by their two stars. But, by going against the script, a dramatic and eerie moment of the episode designed to occur right before the half-hour break was lost. Further, dialogue from this Friedkin and Fine script between Dolores del Rio and Mark Dana, from the very next scene, had to be altered to account for the changes. And a snub was perceived, directed at a famous movie star who was making a highly publicized return before the cameras.

No bullet was dodged here.

A fuse was lit instead.

Reviews

"Return to Glory," with the return of del Rio, was the fourth *I Spy* episode to be given a half-page Close Up listing in *TV Guide*.

Cast & Crew

Dolores del Rio, the first Latin movie star with international appeal, had been making Hollywood pictures since 1925 at age 20. She was a star in the 1930s, playing the romantic lead in *Flying Down to Rio*, the movie that introduced Fred Astair and Ginger Rogers. She played the protagonist in the 1942 Orson Welles thriller, *Journey into Fear*, and would sacrifice her second marriage by having a highly publicized affair with the boy genius director. At the end of that romance, she left Hollywood to live in Mexico. Over two decades later, at 60, after years of professional inactivity, the producers of *I Spy* convinced del Rio to return for this episode. This would be one of her last performances on film. She died in 1983 at age 78 from liver failure.

Victor Jory (Ortiz) was a boxing and wrestling champion in the Coast Guard before beginning his long career in front of the camera. He became a star early on, and even a romantic lead. But Jory seemed better suited for playing menacing characters, as he had in 1938's *The Adventures of Huckleberry Finn* as 'Injun Joe,' and as the overseer of Tara in 1939's *Gone with the Wind*. He was 63 when he did his work here.

Antoinette Bower had been on TV since 1959. This was the first of two appearances in *I Spy* as the flirtatious Shelby. She would be flirting with Captain Kirk two years later in a Halloween episode of *Star Trek*.

22. **"THE CONQUEST OF MAUDE"**; Written by: Robert C. Dennis and Earl Barret; Directed by: Paul Wendkos; Location: Mexico; First airing: 3/2/66

In Mexico, assigned to investigate security surrounding wealthy Maude Murdock, a visiting U.S. undersecretary, Kelly and Scott are being used as pawns by an American official. Sanders, who has sold out, says he wants Kelly and Scott to kidnap Murdock, as part of a "test." His real plan involves murder.

Jeanette Nolan in her Emmy nominated performance for "The Conquest of Maude" (© 3 F Prod., courtesy Image Ent.).

Assessment

Don't try to find anything of importance here. This is a successful blend of light and breezy *I Spy* fare.

The chemistry between Kelly and Scott has never been better, and their interaction with Maude Murdock, as well as Jaime, the cabbie they engage to help with their covert operation, is delightful.

Fun moments to watch for: how the embassy official goads Scott into staying on the case by remarking that he and Kelly have been referred to as "two clowns" who need to back off or get hurt; the surreal transition from Kelly telling Scott he has a great idea about how they can disguise themselves to gain entrance into the embassy party, to the shot of two midgets, dressed as we had last seen Kelly and Scott, miniature doubles of the two men, strolling out of the same hotel; and the first in a series of gags where Kelly and Scott argue about whose turn it is to make a sacrifice:

KELLY: "That barbed wire thrills me less and less. Let me have your jacket."
SCOTT: "No, man, what for?"
KELLY: "Well I can't use *mine*, I have to be beautiful for the girls."
SCOTT: "Whose jacket did we use to lay over the barbed wire in Hong Kong? You owe me one!"

The routine concerning their efforts to find a female dog to distract the male guard dog is also enjoyable. Of course, the plan doesn't work. The guard dog is also a female. "Who ever heard of a female guard dog," Kelly moans as the two dogs fight it out.

And, finally, when Jaime sees the middle-aged Maude, the alleged object of Kelly's affections, he comments, "She must be very rich, huh, Senior?"

The Story Behind the Story

Culp: "[Director] Wendkos again did a good job. He was a joy to work with. He was smart, bright, clever, witty—the kind of guy you like to run across at a cocktail party. And we were both fond of Miss Nolan. But the show was not worthy of her. It was a wonderful idea, but I thought it was just dumb as a post.[12]

CULP & COSBY ON SET REWRITE

When Kelly and Scott disagree over whose coat should be thrown over the barbed wire, and the script has Scott say: "Whose jacket did we use to lay over barbed wire in Hong Kong? You owe me one." Culp added, "Are you kidding? I had that rewoven for you. You can't even see the little holes in it."

As Kelly hangs from the tree and the guard dog bites at his coat tails, Culp added the line: "Here's another fine mess you've gotten me in to, Stanley!"

CAST & CREW

Jeanette Nolan, who played Aunt Helen in "Danny Was a Million Laughs," shines as the feisty, fun-loving Maude. In a career spanning nearly 50 years, she made over 300 TV appearances. She was nominated for four Emmy Awards, including one for playing this role. In later years, she was seen opposite her husband, John McIntire, in many TV shows and films, including the 1980s movie *Cloak & Dagger*.

Pedro Gonzales-Gonzales (Jaime) was born in 1926. He entered show business after getting attention from his appearance as a contestant on Groucho Marx's *You Bet Your Life*.

"If we got together as an act," Marx asked him, "what would it be called?"

Pedro answered, "It would be called Gonzales-Gonzales & Marx."

Marx's response: "Two men in the act and I get third billing!"

23. **"A DAY CALLED 4 JAGUAR"**; Written by: Michael Zagor; Directed by: Richard C. Sarafian; Location: Mexico; First airing: 3/9/66

After a jeep crash in the Mexican jungle, Kelly tries to solve a puzzle. A stranger—a giant of a man who saved Kelly's female passenger at the crash sight—is believed by the locals to be the reincarnation of the god Quetzalcoatl. In fact, he is Dimitri Balin, a renegade Russian cosmonaut, who is trying to evade a Soviet search party.

Dimitri, devoted to the study of archaeology, has been in hiding and living with descendants of the Aztecs.

Fellow cosmonaut turned amateur spy Nicolai Kirov has orders to bring his friend back home—or kill him, and anyone else who gets in the way.

Kelly and Scott now have orders to get in the way.

George Montgomery, Rory Calhoun, "A Day Called 4 Jaguar" (© 3 F Prod., courtesy Image Ent.).

Assessment

"Jaguar" suffers from a handful of implausible elements. First, the amazing coincidence that introduces our spies to a Russian in hiding and the other Russian who is out to get him. Second, Dimitri is described as a "giant," and possesses the strength to lift a jeep off of Kelly's date, Felicitas, who had been injured in the crash. When we meet him in the flesh, and that flesh belongs to actor Rory Calhoun, he is not nearly as big as the fantastic story told of him. And then, thankfully, the subject concerning his size is just dropped. Nicolai, the antagonist of the story, is a fool. He bungles his job more than once, failing to silence the hospitalized Felicitas, failing to kill Kelly and Scott, and then making the fatal error of assuming he can shoot Dimitri in front of his Indian worshipers without suffering grave consequences.

The Story Behind the Story

George Montgomery's availability to travel to Mexico allowed much of this episode to be shot south of the border, and the location production is very satisfying. This was the first segment to feature the famed Las Brisas resort.

Michael Zagor: "They called me in to do a story. They wanted to do one about a man running wild in the jungles, something to do with Aztec gods. I had done a bit of research on the Aztecs. They thought Cortez was a god, a White man with a black beard, and that's what this man was doing. The incarnation of the god Quetzalcoatl was supposed to come back on 'A Day Called 4 Jaguar.' Some days had names like that. But the story's all tinsel. The idea behind it was to lard it up with enough realism to make what is an improbable story somewhat more probable, or playable, anyway."[13]

In regard to the script and the episode made from it, Culp said, "It was really unfortunate. I don't get it."[14]

What Went Wrong?

Perhaps the all-time worst *I Spy*. Yet it was directed by Richard Sarafian, who had already proven himself to be one of the series' better directors, and written by Michael Zagor, who would go on to write some of the most successful scripts. So what went wrong?

One: Friedkin and Fine hatched the idea for this script and assigned it to Zagor. It was not his idea, therefore not necessarily a story he was passionate about writing.

Two: Wanting to impress his new bosses, Zagor may have tried too hard to make the script what he thought Friedkin and Fine wanted it to be—*Hearts of Darkness* set in the Mexican jungles, with Aztecs, and a White man, probably a Russian, living like Tarzan and being accepted by the Indians as a god. Zagor researched the history of the Aztecs and their gods, mixed in a healthy dose of cold war paranoia, then crammed as many of these unworkable elements into the teleplay as possible.

Three: The casting choices. Calhoun and Montgomery were competent actors, when allowed to play the type of roles they were comfortable with. This script needed more than that. The worst performance comes from Nicolai's Russian contact, who we see in two scenes. His bad-guy-Russian accent would better belong in an episode of *Rocky and Bullwinkle*.

Four: The cuts. Sadly, some of the more effective portions of the script were hacked away when the episode timed out long, including:

- From the teaser, as Kelly and Felicitas drive on the windy country road. It is established here, through dialogue spoken in the jeep, that Felicitas is of Aztec decent and is superstitious. Needed information, now gone.
- After the jeep crashes, Kelly finds three villagers and leads them to the sight of the accident to aid Felicitas. One of the three is a kindly man named Simon. When they discover that the jeep has already been moved off of Felicitas, and she mumbles something about "El barbado," two of the villagers exchange amused comments. Simon translates the phrase to Kelly, explaining, "It means 'Bearded One.' A stupid peasant joke, Senor. They say it must have been Quetzalcoatl." These two scenes, if left in, would have well explained why Kelly becomes so obsessed to find whoever or whatever it was that Felicitas saw.
- Later in the episode, Kelly and Scott try to buy the services of a group of Mexican villagers. They need guides to lead them into the jungle. The men are immediately hostile—all but one, the older villager named Simon. We even hear Kelly call him by name. But, because of the previous cuts, we never saw the scene where Kelly and he met and interacted.
- After the hostile villagers decide to take Kelly and Scott into the jungle, bound by ropes, the script tells us that Simon goes along, and, after nightfall, tries to free them. This was cut. And, moments later, according to the script, Simon, now on the run, meets Nicolai. The Russian has been following the villagers at a safe distance. Nicolai kills Simon, revealing himself to be even more cold-blooded than already depicted. Again, cut.
- Later, when Kelly and Scott tell Dimitri of Nicolai's sins, the scripts allows them to make their argument best with their fear that Nicolai has killed Simon. These lines, of course, had to be cut.

- When the Aztecs drag Nicolai off, to be punished for shooting Dimitri, the script called for Kelly and Scott to react to a scream, prompting them to look toward the flames. The look remains. The scream, out of the fear by NBC Broadcast Standards that it would be too disturbing, was omitted.
- As Dimitri is dying, he asks Scott not to block the sun from his sight. That remains. What comes next was cut. Dimitri says, "Quetzalcoatl was the sun, they say, bringing light to earth. Then his enemy struck him with his staff ... on the day called 4 Jaguar ... and all was ... darkness." The title of the episode was kept, but the line of dialogue that explained it was thrown away.

The script, while not Zagor's best work, is far superior to the completed episode. Despite an awkward start, Friedkin and Fine spotted Zagor's talent as a writer, and brought him back for multiple episodes.

Zagor: "It was not my finest hour. But I was way too long [with the script], and the cuts didn't help. How [Mort and David] spotted my talent, I will never know."[15]

As for that scream that was left out of the ending, Zagor jokes, "I do remember the scream, because it did happen—in my living room."[16]

Reviews

Jed Linde, a syndicated columnist for newspapers in Mexico, wrote: "Since this week's episode was made in Mexico, viewers here can see for themselves that *I Spy* rhymes consistently with *I Lie*. A Russian cosmonaut becoming the leader of a group of Quetzalcoatl worshipers in the non-jungles of supposedly Acapulco? Oh, come on!

"The plot is an invitation to sell one's TV and to start reading comic books."

Cast & Crew

George Montgomery (Nicolai) had been in movies since 1932, and would continue working until 1986, accumulating over 100 screen credits. Early in his career, he played opposite Betty Grable in *Coney Island* (1943). His personal life made the papers in 1963 when, after divorcing Dinah Shore, his housekeeper attempted to shoot him. The woman was suffering from obsessive infatuation, and had decided to kill Montgomery, then turn the gun on herself. Her efforts failed on both accounts.

Rory Calhoun (Dimitri) got into movies in 1941, moving to TV in '54. He worked most frequently in Westerns. His work rarely garnered critical acclaim, but he did land a short-lived TV series in 1958 called *The Texan*. He would also stand in for Ronald Reagan on occasion as host of *Death Valley Days*.

Michael Zagor turns in his first of seven *I Spy* scripts, six of which were to be produced. Like Culp, Zagor leaned toward creating darker episodes with complex stories and characters. Prior to getting this job, he wrote for *Ben Casey* and *Slattery's People*, and would now alternate jobs between *I Spy* and *The Fugitive*.

24. **"ONE THOUSAND FINE"**; Written by: Eric Bercovici; Directed by: Paul Wendkos; Second unit directed by: Sheldon Leonard; Location: Acapulco; First airing: 4/27/66

Kelly and Scott search the Mexican jungle for the wreckage of a plane that was carrying U.S. gold. With them is Jack Gannon, the plane's flight engineer, who is struggling with a memory block concerning the tragedy. Along for the trip, Gannon's fiancée—a woman from Kelly's past.

Dane Clark, Susan Oliver, "One Thousand Fine" (© 3 F Prod., courtesy Image Ent.).

Assessment

"One" is a 'should-have-been.' For one thing, it should have been better.

Kelly knows Jack Gannon and has deep feelings for his fiancée, Jean—the woman Kelly had to leave behind in order to become a spy. If you've lost track of how many times Kelly has bumped into friends and lovers from the past, see "A Cup of Kindness," "Dragon's Teeth," "No Exchange on Damaged Merchandise," "A Time of the Knife," and "The Tiger." In this case, the prior relationship is exactly why he is chosen for the assignment.

Kelly feels set up by his own people, and even by Scott. He wasn't told about Jean being part of the package. When Kelly wants to, he can be extremely charming, and then suddenly he can turn into the drag of the party, sulking, brooding, punishing, and all because a woman rubs him the wrong way.

Notice how upset Kelly becomes when he thinks that Scott has had a hand in setting him up.

The final scene at the airport tells us volumes of information concerning Kelly and Scott and how they mesh. Kelly decides to leave the service and marry Jean. Kelly hands Scott his letter of resignation before hurrying to catch his plane. Scott waits for Kelly to return. When Kelly does return, quiet and moody, as usual when a woman is involved, Scott sprinkles the torn letter into his partner's lap. The two men then silently drive off toward another assignment.

The Story Behind the Story

Eric Bercovici: "I wanted to write that one because I found out something about silver and gold. There is no '1000 Fine.' It doesn't exist. The highest grading of gold is point 999. I remember reading all about that at the time and thinking, 'This is interesting. Why not build a story about that minor piece of information?' What the hell, it intrigued me."[17]

"One Thousand Fine" offers us attractive coverage of the Las Brisas resort. The first 20 minutes is almost completely shot on location.

Culp: "We were at this outdoor café, and Stacy Harris got terribly drunk. He wasn't paying attention and he drank too much. It was like he couldn't even play the scene. It was really weird. Then there's the camera in front of him, and he had to deliver. I remember feeling sorry for him. I was a little pissed off, but it was really unfortunate."[18]

WHAT WENT WRONG

This episode is one of many cases where the script is better than the end product. Two brief pieces of dialogue from the final draft of the script, were edited out. Both concern the back story between Kelly and Jean. Had they been included, we would have had a better understanding as to why Kelly is so upset.

The first omission: While alone in the jeep, Jean turns to the sulking Kelly, with uncontrolled fury, and says, "How dare you?!" He doesn't respond. Not even an eyelid flickers. She continues, "It doesn't become you, Kelly—this injured air ... you were the one who walked away, swinging your tennis racket, off to see all the far away places with strange sounding names! Do you think you were the only one who was hurt?"

But Kelly isn't ready to talk. And he isn't about to stop punishing Jean.

The second omission: Jean asks Kelly why he hates her so. "Oh, come on, now," he says, "Isn't that a little melodramatic?"

"Is it?" she answers. "I look at you and I see a hard-eyed stranger. Where's the Kelly I used to know? The gay, out going Kelly who smiled while he broke my heart?"

"I wasn't the one who said 'Let's call the whole thing off,'" he retorts.

"No," Jean fires back, "You were the one who said 'Why do we have to rush into marriage? We can wait a couple of years. There are places to see and things to do!'"

"Your broken heart wasn't permanent," Kelly says, getting the last word in before they are interrupted.

The primary conflict between these two ex-lovers is that Kelly couldn't tell Jean why he had to go. He left her so that he could become a spy. But he planned to come back for her. She just didn't wait.

Now the set of lines which did make the cut, and occur three quarters of the way into the story, make sense. Jean adds two and two together and realizes the truth regarding Kelly's profession.

"One Thousand Fine" was originally scheduled to air on March 16, 1966. Two hours before the planned airing, the manned *Gemini VIII* space capsule orbiting Earth, encountered trouble. All three networks cut away from their scheduled programs, and this episode was bumped to the end of the season.

It is interesting to note that rival CBS was flooded with phone calls, protesting the preemption of *Lost in Space*, due to the network's sudden coverage of real astronauts who were nearly and permanently *lost* in space.

Cast & Crew

Susan Oliver (Jean), born in 1932, had over 60 TV credits, which included the pilot for *Star Trek*, where she played an alluring green-skinned alien. She also acted with Robert Culp in an episode of *Trackdown*. She was a regular on *Peyton Place* in 1966, gaining national attention when her character, Ann Howard, was killed off.

Oliver was also a pilot and walked away from the crash of a single engine plane she was flying, just months after filming this story about the survivor of a plane crash. In 1970 she won an aviation award for her flying achievements. She would also reach the 100 mark with her TV and film credits before her death in 1990 from cancer, at age 58.

Dane Clark (Gannon) worked in TV and films between 1940 and 1988. He started his career under his real name, Bernard Zenville, but became Dane Clark when Humphrey Bogart suggested the change. Among his many film roles, he was most proud of playing Abe Saperstein, the founder of the Harlem Globetrotters, in 1954's *Go, Man, Go*. Dane felt the movie, and the role he played, helped in a small way to oppose racial hatred. Clark was good friends with both Friedkin and Fine, who created and wrote his 1950s TV series, *Bold Venture*. This was the first of two roles for *I Spy*.

Stacy Harris (Hamilton) came from radio, where he acted as the voice of Batman. He got into television through his good friend Jack Webb, who cast Stacy in the very first episode of *Dragnet* in 1952. Webb would name his eldest daughter after the actor. Besides his work in Webb-produced shows, Harris was a regular on the *Wyatt Earp* series in 1960 and '61. He was still active in entertainment when he died of a heart attack in 1973 at age 55.

Eric Bercovici, who had previously written "Turkish Delight," would contribute to the story sessions for the second season without credit. From here, he would go on to write for *The Man from U.N.C.L.E.* and *Mission: Impossible*. In later years he would borrow some *I Spy* concepts and produce the short-lived Robert Conrad espionage series *Assignment: Vienna*, which was shot, in part, on location. He also wrote the miniseries *Shogun*. He and Jerry Ludwig, soon to become a fellow *I Spy* writer, would work again with Robert Culp in a Movie of the Week called *Strange Homecoming*.

25. **"CRUSADE TO LIMBO"**; Written by: Jack Tuley, Morton Fine & David Friedkin; Directed by: Richard C. Sarafian; Location: Mexico City; First airing: 3/23/66. Repeated: 8/24/66

In Mexico, Kelly bumps into Hollywood actor Sean Christie, a celebrity well known for his anti–American causes.

Christie's visit to Mexico is a secret, along with other Americans who are involved in his political obsession: the liberation of a Latin American country.

In order to infiltrate the organization, the agents must pretend to be left-wing radicals. Once on the inside, they discover that Christie and his naive colleagues are being manipulated by a ruthless man named Senor Munoz.

Assessment

The premise is stupid—that men of fame and wealth and celebrity would be willing to lead an invasion, carrying obsolete World War II weapons, storming a beach, under fire, and obeying orders from the sneaky Senor Munoz.

The lack of credibility begins with the opening scene:

Movie star Sean Christie is walking through a crowded park in Mexico City, in disguise—he wears sunglasses, you see—then he slugs Kelly, and he does this in order to *avoid drawing attention to himself.*

The rifles the "celebrity rebels" are given have no firing pins, and the grenades are filled with sand, and none of these morons notice.

Odder still, Munoz doesn't worry that an investigation concerning the slaughter of Americans on a Latin America beach would reveal that the weapons had been tampered with.

Like no episode that had come before, "Crusade to Limbo" requires viewers to check their brains at the door.

Regardless, "Crusade" is beautifully shot. What an utter waste it was that Culp, Cosby and Duff, not to mention Richard Sarafian, were willing to climb to the top of a pyramid for this substandard material.

The Story Behind the Story

Robert Culp had no worries about climbing the Temple of the Moon pyramid outside Mexico City.

Culp: "I was smitten by Tarzan when I was a kid. I love heights, always have."[19]

Director Richard Sarafian was another matter entirely: "I had to climb that damn thing twice."[20]

After the harrowing experience, Sarafian recalled:

"We took Howard Duff to a whorehouse, but he was married to Ida Lupino, and he didn't want to participate. So he sat in the bar with the Madam and had a lot of drinks."[21]

Michael Preece: "Howard Duff finally *did* go upstairs. But I don't remember if Sarafian did."[22]

Sarafian: "I was a good boy. I had a wife and five children. But, mainly, at the end of a day of shooting, and climbing pyramids, you're just too damn tired."[23]

CULP & COSBY ON SET REWRITE

Culp starts using the name "Jack," as in "It's a live grenade, Jack!" There are three instances of this in the episode, none of which are in the script. When asked by Christie who Scott is, Kelly was to say, "Alexander Scott." Instead, with great deadpan, Culp says, "This is Jack."

The absurdity of this story becomes very apparent in act four, when Christie takes Kelly and Scott to the armory to outfit them with uniforms and provide them with weapons. Culp and Cosby have a field day with the weapons that are rigged not to work. Every sarcastic look and line of dialog from this scene was an ad-lib, ending with Cosby saying, in a mocking tone, "About the only thing that works around here is a yell for help."

This is the seventh time that Kelly is friends with someone who figures prominently into the story. The only saving grace: When Kelly and Scott get roughed up and threatened by Christie's thugs, Scott remarks to Kelly, "I'm so sick of your friends." This was an ad-lib. And so was Culp's response, "I'm not feeling so good about it either."

Cosby: "How many times is Bob going to run into an old girlfriend? How many times is he going to run into an old friend—who was a spy, that he trusted—and I'm looking and saying 'Don't go there, don't do that,' and then he does, and I have to go get him. This stuff became tiresome."[24]

Reviews

Surprising, "Crusade to Limbo" earned *I Spy* a fifth turn at a *TV Guide* Close Up listing. It must have been the pyramids.

Cast & Crew

Howard Duff started in radio and played Sam Spade between 1946 and 1950. In the late 1940s he moved into motion pictures, with the lead in movies such as *The Naked City* and *Johnny Stool Pigeon*. He played opposite his wife, Ida Lupino, in *Private Hell 36*. The husband/wife B-movie stars achieved celebrity, and played themselves in an episode of *The Lucy-Desi Comedy Hour*. Shortly after *I Spy*, at age 52, Duff would get his own TV series, *Felony Squad*.

Frank Silvera, although light skinned and appearing to be Hispanic, was African American. He began in movies in 1948, and was featured prominently in Stanley Kubrick's 1955 film *Killer's Kiss*. Silvera was very heavily involved in civil rights causes from the 1950s through the 1960s, and ran an actor's workshop for minorities. Cosby had briefly turned to Silvera for acting lessons, until he realized he was getting lessons for free—from Robert Culp. But Cosby's admiration for Silvera remained.

Cosby: "The guys (Friedkin and Fine) were always writing. We'd come back from lunch, and they'd hand Frank five new pages. This was it. I felt like a little nine-year-old boy who

Frank Silvero (second from left) and Howard Duff (seated), on a crusade to limbo with Culp and Cosby, 1966 (© 3 F Prod., courtesy Ron Jacobs).

had come with his grandfather to watch him work. Frank looks at the pages, and the director said, 'action,' and Frank said those pages, and I *was* this nine year old, watching his grandfather. I was so proud then, it was Jackie Robinson stealing home and tipping his hat to me. And then, in the close-up, he did it again, just the same. Frank Silvera. He was wonderful."[25]

After "Crusade," Silvera would play banditos and other assorted heavies in shows like *The Wild Wild West* and *Hawaii Five–O*. He found regular work on *The High Chaparral*, until his death in 1970, at age 66, of accidental electrocution.

Jack Tuley had to be rewritten by Friedkin and Fine, who then took top billing, or blame, for the teleplay. Before coming to *I Spy* for this one job, Tuley worked for *Route 66* and *The Man from U.N.C.L.E.* After this, he would work for a producer who didn't mind far-fetched and illogical storylines: Irwin Allen, on *Lost in Space* and *Land of the Giants*.

26. **"MY MOTHER, THE SPY"**; Written by: Harold Gast; Directed by: Richard Benedict; Location: Mexico; First airing: 3/30/66

In Mexico, Kelly and Scott hunt for renegade American agent Angela March. Angela says she is tired of the killing necessary in the espionage game. She wants out. What she doesn't say is she is also nine months pregnant and about to deliver. The father of the child, double agent Ferenc Vlados, has also been searching for the mother-to-be, along with a ruthless enemy operative named Teba.

Assessment

It is an interesting concept to build a story around a female spy who decides to give up the business and go into hiding because she feels betrayed and, more so, is carrying the child of the man who betrayed her.

Sally Kellerman, as the woman in distress, displays remorse and emotional upset over her predicament. The moment when she reveals her pregnancy to Kelly and Scott is especially powerful, and comes as a true surprise.

Director Richard Benedict shows an impressive eye for unique and inspired camera angles, beginning with the scene where Angela shoots an enemy agent, using a gun concealed in her purse. The revealing shot of the agent being hit by the bullet is filmed through the bullet hole in the purse.

Sally Kellerman, "My Mother the Spy" (© 3 F Prod., courtesy Image Ent.).

The Story Behind the Story

There is a major continuity goof, and for a good reason. During the fight in the bar, a stuntman crashes through the street door, shattering and destroying it. Moments later, when Kelly and Scott return to the bar, the door is intact, as it had been before the fight ever took place. The reason: the fight, although it happens first in the story, was shot last. The stuntman was not supposed to crash through the flimsy, lightweight set door.

Calvin Brown, Cosby's stunt double, recalls:

"Cos' was the first Black to do a dramatic series—and I was the first Black stuntman to do a series. We were both under the microscope to see if we were going to work out. And a couple of the White stunt guys had gotten used to hitting me quite hard, quite often. So I went to Cos, and he said, 'They're just here visiting, doubling someone we hire week to week. But you're *here*. So do whatever you want to do.'

"I told Fleet Southcott [Director of photography], if I get out of character in this fight, just follow me all over the stage because Alexander Scott's gonna' be whuppin' butt. As soon as they said 'action,' the other stunt guy tee-ed off and he cocked me. The guy was wanting to fight. And so we did, all over the bar, behind the bar, and back up over the bar, and, eventually, I knocked the guy completely out. We had a standing ovation. They said the fight looked so real. And I said, 'Damn right it was real!' There was no missing it, because every time I swung, I hit him. And the word got around that Calvin is crazy, so don't hit him anymore.

"From then on, if I actually got hit, whoever did it would stop and say, 'Calvin! Calvin! I'm so sorry!'

"Hey, I know when it's an accident and when it's not. That's the thing. If I hit you back, then you know I know it's not an accident."[26]

CULP & COSBY ON SET REWRITE

Outside the hospital, Kelly and Scott wait for visiting hours. Scott goes on and on about how Kelly should compliment the baby, and cuddle it, and even "chuck it under the chin." The script continues by having Kelly look at his watch, interrupt Scott and say, "Time to visit." Culp changed this to: "I'll do anything if you just stop talking."

In a bar, where Kelly and Scott are being intimidated by a couple heavies, one of the men throws a glass of beer into Kelly's face. The script called for Scott to get splashed in the face, too. But Cosby, going against the script, blocked the beer being tossed at him with a bouquet of flowers.

Later, when Kelly and Scott return to the bar to confront the heavies, Cosby ad-libs, "Remember when you threw a drink in my friend's face?" He continues the improv by tossing a glass of beer into the heavy's face, but most of the beer splashes back on Cosby. Culp is quick to pick up on the opportunity, and ad-libs, "All right, the first man who laughs at my friend, gets it!" He then turns to Cosby, adding: "Stanley, can't you do anything right?"

Cosby fires back, "I tried to repay him."

Culp adds, "I appreciate the thought, but this is ridiculous."

CAST & CREW

Sally Kellerman (Angela) is best remembered for being the first actress to play Major "Hot Lips" Hoolihan. She did it in the 1970 film version of *M*A*S*H*. Prior to working on

I Spy, she stopped off at nearly 50 other TV shows between 1957 and 1966, including, just months earlier, the second *Star Trek* pilot, "Where No Man Has Gone Before."

Alejandro Rey (Ferenc) went on to be the playboy casino owner and benefactor to the convent where Sally Field flew high for three years in *The Flying Nun* (1967–70). He died in 1987 at age 57 of lung cancer.

Theo Marcuse, ever the hairless heavy, had nearly 100 credits in TV and film at the time of his death, just one year after shooting this episode. Prior to his performance here, he had been seen playing heavies on *Voyage to the Bottom of the Sea*, *The Man from U.N.C.L.E.*, and *The Untouchables*. He had become so popular in this type of role that, in the last year of his life, he played the commandant of Devil's Island not once, but twice, in two different series *(The Wild Wild West* and *The Time Tunnel)*. Both acting assignments were only weeks apart. On Halloween's Eve 1967, his final role was televised on "Catspaw," a witches and goblins tale on *Star Trek*. One week later Theodore Marcuse would perish in a car accident. He was 47.

Begonia Placios (the nurse) was married to Robert Culp's friend, director Sam Peckinpah. Culp was never able to get Peckinpah onto the show. He did, however, arrange for Begonia to get a day's work.

Richard Benedict only directed one episode of *I Spy*. He began his career in movies as an actor, having appeared in the cult science fiction film *It! The Terror from Beyond Space*. Then he changed directions and stepped behind the camera. He came to *I Spy* with TV credentials, such as *Hawaiian Eye*, *The Virginian*, and *Combat!*

Harold Gast wrote for *The Defenders*, *Ben Casey*, and *The Nurses*. This would be his only *I Spy* writing assignment, but he continued working in TV as a writer/producer for series such as *Judd for the Defense* and *Cannon*.

27. **"THERE WAS A LITTLE GIRL"**; Written by: Steven Kandel & Robert Bloch; Directed by: John Rich; Second unit directed by: Sheldon Leonard; Location: Mexico.; First airing: 4/6/66. Repeated: 8/31/66

Assigned to guard the teenage daughter of a U.S. cabinet member, Kelly and Scott discover that "babysitting" can be a very hazardous operation.

Kathy Sherman is spoiled, spirited, and even flirtatious. To make matters worse, she mistakenly buys a shipment of uncut heroin, baked into a piece of pottery, which sets off a series of attempts by the drug smugglers to recover their goods. The leader of the smugglers, Silvestro Porada, realizes that Kathy's death could become a commodity, allowing him to profit from creating an international incident.

Assessment

As with "Danny Was a Million Laughs," Kelly and Scott are assigned to babysit a difficult and demanding individual. While "Little Girl" may seem unimportant compared to many other *I Spy* episodes, it was clearly designed to amuse and titillate the younger viewers.

Monitoring the feedback left on *I Spy* websites, Sam, a female fan, writes, "I remember being so jealous of the actress playing the girl. The storyline worked on my pre-teen level, and the relationship between Kelly and Kathy. Culp as Kelly was great in any mood he chose—charming, exasperated, protective, pudding-hearted, but always appropriate. My favorite scene was when Senor Porada pulled his gun—the lightning reflex when [Kelly] jumped in front of his charge, was thrilling to me."

Tatia, another fan, writes, "Kelly handled Ms. Sherman's infatuation in a totally charming and rather adorable big-brother manner."

Silvestro Porada is one of the more ruthless bad guys Kelly and Scott have met. He is handsome and suave, but capable of murdering a child without so much as a blink of an eye. When Kathy cries, knowing she is about to be given an overdose of heroin in order to create a scandal, he merely says, "Splendid, the red and puffy eyes will look good."

As for the tag scene, in the pre-politically-correct arena, it was quite all right for a father to tell a nonrelated male to give his spoiled and flirtatious teenage daughter a spanking. Enjoy the moment. It is unlikely that you will ever see it in a TV show again.

The Story Behind the Story

The bulk of this episode was filmed north of the border. In a few instances, when the elusive Kathy breaks free of her babysitters, Culp and Cosby were allowed to run through an authentic Mexican village (Taxco, the hillside town seen in "Return to Glory"). Look for one example of clever intercutting between the use of a body double and the actual Kathy, as she allegedly strolls through Taxco with Kelly and Scott. All three then emerge onto "the compound," a village set on a back lot in Culver City.

Concerning a possible reason for this being director John Rich's only *I Spy* assignment, Michael Preece recalls:

"John Rich laughed at everything Culp and Cosby said. I remember them staring at me and raising their eyebrows, as if to say, 'Was that *that* funny?'

"They knew—we all knew—that you had to be careful with their humor. If Culp and Cosby did something and we laughed on the set, the rule of thumb was not to use it, that it wouldn't mean much to the audience, because it was an inside joke. And John Rich used to just roar with laugher—at everything. They didn't trust him."[27]

Culp & Cosby on Set Rewrite

After the incident where Porada pulls a gun on Kelly and Kathy in an attempt to retrieve the pottery, the heavy is thrown out. Kelly then returns to his room and informs Scott that they will have to take turns watching Kathy's door. In the script, Kelly asks, "Who takes the first shift?" Scott was to answer, "Well, Kathy has this little yen for you. You've just volunteered."

All starts as written, with Culp asking "Who takes the first shift?"

Cosby walks away toward the bedroom, groggy, grumpy and merely says, "Right."

Culp looks to see that Cosby has abandoned him in front of the camera, then calls out, "Stop snoring and answer."

Cosby doesn't.

After Kelly tries to stop the fleeing Miguel, and topples over a table, Scott asks him if he's all right. Culp's answer is not in the script. He holds his back and says, "Yeah, I'm all right. I've heard about how some people string along for years on one kidney."

Moments later, after the broken pottery, a mask which has been nicknamed "Herman," is discovered to contain heroin, Culp ad-libs to Kathy: "I'm sorry, sweetheart, but Herman was a junkie."

As Kelly and Scott search for Porada's mountain hideout, they look toward the difficult climb ahead of them. Culp ad-libs to Cosby, "And *you* were the one who said I should wear my boots." Cosby responds, "Well *you* were the one who said you wanted to look like a cowboy."

Cast & Crew

Mary Jane Saunders was 22 when she played the teenage Kathy. She began as a child actress, and went on to have a recurring role as a teen on *Tales of Wells Fargo* (1961–1962).

Harry Raybould, the cruel Senior Porado, was 33. He had appeared in *Gunsmoke* and was soon to play a green-skinned alien in *Lost in Space*. Raybould bore a striking resemblance to Mike Faulkner, the actor who had previously appeared in the *I Spy* episode "Dragon's Teeth." Look closely at the two men. Some believe Faulkner and Raybould were one and the same.

Jose de Vega played the young Miguel. At the time of this filming, at 31, he was older than he looked. Attractive, youthful, and ethnic, he had played a Puerto Rican in *West Side Story*, a Hawaiian in *Blue Hawaii*, and an Indian in *The Wild Wild West*. He would go on to play a Mexican in *High Chaparral*. He died in 1990, at age 56, of AIDS.

Robert Bloch only wrote one script for *I Spy*. He had penned *Psycho*, the novel, based on the movie, as well as writing scripts for *Alfred Hitchcock Presents* and *Thriller*. After this, he would move on to *Star Trek*.

Unhappy with Bloch's approach to the telling of the story, the producers entrusted the script to Steven Kandel.

Steven Kandel would write (or cowrite) five *I Spys*. Busy working on other scripts for the series, Friedkin and Fine handed this problem over to Kandel, who they no doubt felt would be the right writer for the task due to his past credits, which included one of the Gidget movies.

John Rich's comedy credits went all the way back to *Our Miss Brooks*, and more recently, *Gomer Pyle*, and a dozen outings with *The Dick Van Dyke Show*. In later years he would direct for Norman Lear's *All in the Family*, *Sanford & Son*, *The Jeffersons*, and *Good Times*.

28. **"IT'S ALL DONE WITH MIRRORS"**; Written by: Steven Kandel; Directed by: Robert Butler; Second unit directed by: Sheldon Leonard; Location: Acapulco; First airing: 4/13/66. Repeated: 9/7/66

In Acapulco, Kelly is lured into a trap by a beauty named Vanessa, then delivered to Zoltan Karolyi, the Russian mastermind of brainwashing.

The not-so-good doctor's goal is to condition Kelly to both cause an international incident and to kill his partner and friend—Scott.

Assessment

Simply excellent.

In 1965, the same year this episode was written, Michael Caine starred in *The Ipcress File*, dealing with a crook turned secret agent, involved in grueling mental torture. In *The Manchurian Candidate*, brainwashing was used to create an assassin. Perhaps because of the popularity of those movies, and with the spy show craze in full swing, numerous hours of TV drama were devoted to the art of washing one's brains.

Fay Spain, Carroll O'Connor, "It's All Done with Mirrors" (© 3 F Prod., courtesy Image Ent.).

In this episode, a clever use of sound and sights, manipulated by inventive editing (some images last on the screen for less than one tenth of a second) create an effective and believable atmosphere for the brainwashing sessions.

The story is fleshed out through excellent performances by Culp, sweating, writhing, and even withdrawing into a fetal position during this grueling ordeal, and Carroll O'Connor, as Dr. Karolyi, perfectly underplaying his part to create stark contrast between the distress of the subject and the calm pleasure of the sadist in charge.

Watch how Kelly struggles to resist the intrusion into his mind, then battles against the programmed instructions he's been given to kill Scott, who he has been programmed to believe has turned traitor.

Equally impressive are the reactions from Scott, as Kelly's erratic and dangerous behavior becomes more pronounced. In particular, note the quality of Cosby's acting in the restaurant scene, when Kelly's drinking gets out of hand and Scott becomes the victim of a rash of insults.

Another dramatic moment occurs when Scott meets with his superiors, a cold blooded trio of senior agents (looking very much like some of the suits we would meet decades later in *The X-Files*).

"Washington advises we cut our losses," one says.

"You're going to have to spell that out," Scott responds. We discover here that Scott and Kelly have been working together for three years. Scott believes that the bond between them will override any brainwashing that was done in less than two days. He asks for time to bring Kelly back. When asked how he can trust Kelly, Scott answers, "Trust him? I need him. He's the only guy who wears a shirt the same size as mine."

Culp and Cosby also wore the same size shirt, and, as a result, would often trade clothes.

Sitting in his bungalow at Las Brisas, on the telephone, we learn something more about the complex and disciplined Alexander Scott, as his face brightens when he hears his mother's voice, as "little-boy" happiness replaces the worries of a grown man. When Kelly enters, holding a gun, the smile slowly fades. Scott tries to keep up a front for his mother's sake, and tells her that Kelly sends his love. But the true drama of the moment is watching this very real character saying good-bye to his mother, believing that he may be doing so for the last time.

The climax of the episode, beautifully shot by Leonard on a vista overlooking Acapulco, is one of the most dramatic moments of the series. Kelly orders Scott to jump off the cliff. "That would be suicide," Scott says. "If you want me dead, you're going to have to do it yourself."

The Story Behind the Story

Writer Steven Kandel: "Carroll O'Connor was marvelous in that. Culp and Cosby ad-libbed, and they improved it, which is all right with me."[28]

CULP & COSBY ON SET REWRITE

While the script for "It's All Done with Mirrors" is well above average, some of the best moments came from the stars.

Kelly's line, when meeting Karolyi, about being willing to "shave points off his game," and that it looks like he has been cast in a mad scientist movie, were not in the script.

The dramatic moment when Kelly pours champagne on Scott's hand and up his sleeve, along with the dialogue that accompanies the action, including Scott's line, "Don't put that stuff in my glass," were contributed by Culp and Cosby.

Much of what was said during the very heavy final moments, when Kelly aims a gun at Scott, but Scott is defiant enough to jump down Kelly's throat over the line, "You're all alike."

And then, there's that last moment: Kelly surrenders the gun to Scott, steps up onto the wall, intending to jump to his death. Scott grabs him and pulls him to safety. Both actions, also not in the script.

Notice the tender gesture by Cosby when he pulls Culp's shirt down, to help him compose himself, to allow him to feel safe in the arms of family.

CAST & CREW

Carroll O'Connor (Dr. Karolyi) is, of course, best remembered as TV's Archie Bunker (1971–1983). Prior to his appearance on *I Spy*, he was a high school teacher who moonlighted at acting. His work in television and film began in 1953, but he continued his teaching duties until 1958, at which time he was gaining regular employment as an actor in series such as *The Naked City*, *The Outer Limits*, and *The Fugitive*. After playing Zoltan Karolyi, O'Connor tore up the scenery as a homicidal mortician in an episode of *The Wild Wild West*, as well as colorful roles in features such as *Kelly's Heroes* and *Waterhole #3*. A man of great decency, he was devoted to his wife Nancy for 50 years, until his death in 2001 from a heart attack at the age of 77.

Richard Bull (Blaine) may look familiar to anyone who ever watched *Voyage to the Bottom of the Sea*. He was the ship's doctor.

James Frawley (Greenburg) had a brief stint in acting, appearing in front of the camera from 1964 to 1966. In '66, he switched to directing, beginning with two years on *The Monkees*, where he would direct 32 episodes, and appear in three. In later years, he would direct for *Columbo, Law & Order, Ally McBeal*, and serve as coexecutive producer on *Judging Amy*.

Roy Jenson (Tate) was a stunt man turned actor, with hundreds of screen credits, usually playing tough guys who can take a beating. He was 31 here. He would return to *I Spy*.

Lawrence Montaigne (Smollett), one of the enemy agents, might look more familiar if you put a pair of pointed ears on him. One year after this, he would make his first of two appearances on *Star Trek*, first as a pointed-eared Romulan, then as a pointed-eared Vulcan.

Robert Butler had begun directing in 1959 with an episode of *Bonanza*. He followed that with multiple assignments on *The Twilight Zone, Ben Casey*, and *The Dick Van Dyke Show*, where he proved he could guide comedy as well as drama. One year before getting this assignment, he directed the pilot for *Star Trek*. His most recent credit is for directing chores on the TV series *The Division* in 2001. At age 74, and considering television's tendency to seek out younger talent, getting that job was no small accomplishment

Bud Molin, George W. Brooks, and **Basil Wrangel**, three of *I Spy's* top four editors, broke with tradition and shared the chores, working together to make the magic cut here. The fourth man on the editing team, Bob Moore, was working on another episode.

8

Wrapping Season One

With the final day of production for "It's All Done with Mirrors" completed on March 7, 1966, *I Spy* wrapped filming of its first season.

Culp and Cosby would have less than three weeks off before reporting back to work on March 28th to film location sequences for a pair of second season entries in Las Vegas, Nevada.

The Ratings

NBC was extremely pleased.

I Spy won its time slot, week after week.

Newsweek, on January 31, 1966, announced that in the overall Nielsens, in ranking 93 prime time programs, *I Spy* was in the top 20, no small achievement for a series airing at 10 P.M.

Daily Variety, on November 23, 1965, called *I Spy* "one of the better series of the season," and reported that it was the second highest rated 10 P.M. program, slightly trailing *The Fugitive*.

TV Guide, on November 20, 1965, reported that Home Testing Institute's TVQ, the only ratings survey to break the audiences into demographics, had found that, with viewers 18 to 34, *I Spy* was the number one rated series on television. *The Man from U.N.C.L.E.* had come in at number two.

On February 6, 1966, *I Spy* was on the cover of *TV Week*, a television supplement found in many newspapers across the country. Reporting the results of an independent survey, *TV Week* readers ranked *I Spy* as the "third most liked program," a slim one-tenth of a point behind the tied leaders, *Get Smart* and *Hogan's Heroes*.

The Race Issue

Regarding the networks' worry over the race issue, the test results were also in.

Ebony magazine (September 1965) quoted Sheldon Leonard: "Everybody told us we were going to have trouble with the sponsors. But we have more sponsors than we need."

Newsweek (January, 31, 1966) quoted Bill Cosby: "Without Leonard, there would have been no Negro Scott. No other producer had the guts. Sure, they'd call a Negro when they needed a slave, but this is the first time they called one up to play a spy instead of a problem."

From the same article, *Newsweek* wrote: "Cosby has accomplished in one year what scores of Negro actors and comedians have tried to do all their lives: he has completely refurbished the television image of the Negro. He is not the stereotyped, white-toothed Negro boy with a sense of good rhythm. He is a human being, and a funnier, hipper human being than anyone around him."

Newsweek reported Culp as saying: "We're two guys who don't know the difference between a colored and White. That's doing more than 100 marches. We're showing what it could be like if there had been no hate."

TV Guide (January 15, 1966) quoted Cosby: "We don't have any race jokes in the scripts. Even in real life, race jokes would be embarrassing to Bobby and embarrassing to me."

From the same issue, Paul Wendkos said: "They always take the off-beat way. But underneath their hip, existentialist veneer is a sense of irony just this side of bitterness—the irony of the artist in show business, the irony of racial inequality."

And Sam Peckinpah said: "Bob is incensed by prejudice. He doesn't recognize it; he doesn't understand it."

And Mort Fine said: "There is a wide audience acceptance of the camaraderie between Culp and Cosby. People want to do the right thing, White to Negro."

The *New York Times* (October 17, 1965) quoted Cosby: "When we go off on these overseas location trips, I have a feeling that perhaps never occurs to a White performer. As an *I Spy* star, I'm part of the NBC team and, as such, I'm not deferred to, but respected and protected. This is difficult to express, but that's an odd feeling for the average Negro. The money doesn't really matter, it's the dignity I'm working for."

TV Digest (February 1966) quoted Cosby: "It's all kind of wild. I played a personal appearance in Lubbock, Texas, and drew 7400 people. Let's face it, a lot of them came to see that *I Spy* guy. Before TV, as just plain comedian Bill Cosby, I'd be lucky to pull half that number."

Look magazine (May 30, 1967) quoted Sammy Davis Jr. saying: "Bill Cosby carries as much weight on his shoulders as any Negro known, and he wears it as well and as lightly as any man could."

The *St. Louis Globe Democrat* (February 12, 1966) wrote: "*I Spy* has already been renewed for another season. If TV follows its usual course, there will be several more series with integrated co-stars."

The newspaper quoted Cosby as saying: "If [the programmers] have any sense, they'll set up a situation comedy series about a Negro family. Let it be about a family—mother, father, sister, brother. That way TV can take viewers into a Negro home and let all the people see how it looks, what they eat, how they talk, hear some of the problems, and so on."

Newsweek (January 31, 1966) quoted Cosby: "I am now waiting for a producer to call and say, 'Let's make a movie where Cosby lives next door to Jack Lemmon. Let's show that their kids play together. And the next step is to do interviews without having to talk about problems."

Variety (October 1966) reported that the success of *I Spy*'s first season had "sparked new station allegiances." For its second season, the series would be telecast by 204 NBC affiliates, "about as high a station lineup any network can secure."

Indeed, many of the Southern affiliates who had boycotted the series during its first year were now picking it up. Now 204 stations gave *I Spy* the potential of reaching 98% of the U.S. market.

Look magazine (May 30, 1967) wrote: "Judging from the remarkable spread of acceptance for his work in what has been heretofore exclusively a White man's part, some 25 million Americans, Southerners included, don't notice anymore. Yet, until Cosby made the breakthrough, a top Negro performer seemingly had as much chance of erasing TV's most noticeable race taboo as Crazy Horse would have had if he'd been appointed a US Cavalry General for tactical excellence at the Little Bighorn."

New York Journal American (February 27, 1966) wrote that the critical and ratings success of *I Spy* would make it easier for other "Negroes" to follow.

The newspaper quoted Cosby as saying: "Maybe the barriers have been let down a bit

The first *TV Guide*, 1966 (courtesy *TV Guide*).

Herald Examiner examines *I Spy*, 1966 (courtesy Hearst Corporation).

for [other Blacks] to get the chance. They'll be free to succeed or to fail on their own. That was all I asked."

Reactions

Robert Culp had felt the rewards and the demands of being a star once before—during the run of *Trackdown*. So he was prepared for the sudden change in an actor's life when they are part of a weekly television series that is a success. But Bill Cosby had never experienced anything like this before. Nor had his family. Nor had his friends.

Cosby: "Everybody's stunned. As a matter of fact, there's a story. I come home, and I *always* go home to Philadelphia. And Mr. Tripplett is there. Now Mr. Tripplett, I grew up with his children. I come from the street in the neighborhood, growing up, and every day this man sees me, watches me play baseball, knows his son and I play for the same neighborhood basketball team. And Mr. Tripplett sees me now. And I say, 'Mr. Tripplett, how are you?' And he said, 'I'm fine, Mr. Cosby.' I said 'Mister Tripplett—this is Cosby.' And he just looked at me. And we both realized.

"I don't know how I could have become 'Mister' Cosby. But to him, me being on that TV, and all of a sudden, I come home, and I'm 'Mister' Cosby."[1]

FROM THE MAIL BAG

"Dear Sheldon, I have never been so excited over a television series. Your cast, your script, your direction, and your production are all 'A' NO.1. When the inevitable question arises, as it does every year; 'why is television filled with junk?' all of Hollywood can now point with pride to *I Spy* in answer. As a television viewer, I sincerely thank you."—M.R., Los Angeles, CA.

"Dear Sirs, May I compliment you on your fine production, *I Spy*. Your combination of excellent acting, wit, and well-written, ever-changing plots make for some very enjoyable evenings. I have no criticism of your program, however, I have a suggestion. I know that you do much of your filming on location and I think that maybe you have overlooked an ideal spot right here in the United States—Mackinac Island, Michigan. My roommate and I have been there nine times and I have just about covered every inch of the island on foot. If you ever need two girl guides, you have our address." J.C., Kalamazoo, MI. "ps: The Grand Hotel has a fine tennis court."

"Dear Bright Spot In A Bleak Season, I do not watch much television anymore, due to the lack of good shows on this season. I find homework more interesting than most programs. Your show is one of the exceptions. I do not know if it is your very interesting plots, your terribly fine actors, or the fast-moving action that makes your show so interesting. My guess is that it is a combination of all three." J.L., Long Beach, CA.

"Mr. Leonard, I enjoy your production, *I Spy*. At risk of being jingoistic, I detect a thread of common-sense running through the dialog ... And after all of these years of expecting nothing but the opposite type of propaganda from your baliwick, (sic). Thanks again for a fine show." D.N., Sacandaga, NY.

"Hey! I cry every Wed. because I have classes and can't stay home and laugh, cry, and rejoice over *I Spy*. This show is without a doubt the top TV show of all time—and much of the credit belongs to Bill Cosby and Bob Culp. I have been a fan of Mr. Culp's for more years than I like to think of, and he is really something else. Add the adorable and talented Mr. Cosby, and location-photography, and you have the greatest hour of TV ever. I catch the show when college is not in session, and summer will find me glued to the set—so keep it up." H.N., Radnor, PA.

"It must have been a great challenge for you to use Bill Cosby on *I Spy*, and I am sure you must have sweated as to the resulting comments therefrom. It is evident that your courage has paid off. May God's blessing continue to shine upon you." L.F., Hollywood, CA.

In reply:

"Dear Miss F: And may God's blessings shine upon you, too, for being so thoughtful. Sincerely, Morton Fine, Producer, *I Spy*."

The Awards

On May 22, 1966, the 18th Annual Emmy Awards were presented on NBC.

Sarafian: "Bill told me, 'I called up Dad and I said, 'Pop, you and I are going to need to get dressed up. I want you to go to Brooks Brothers and buy two coats, two suits, two ties, two belts, two pairs of socks, two pairs of shoes, two pairs of gloves, and two hats, and come out here, because I'm going to be the master of ceremonies on the Emmys.' He said there was a long pause, then his father said, 'Can I have a vest?' He couldn't understand all the success. He said, 'My son is becoming another Bob Hope.'"[2]

As cohost, Cosby shared the stage with Danny Kaye.

Culp: "I'm sure there must have been some drama going on for Bill, being up on stage, cohosting the Emmys with Danny Kaye, after being relatively unknown a year earlier. But Bill is so adroit, so adept, and was even then, in his 20s, that he could handle any situation. Bill is fast, fast, fast on his feet. It is instinctive for him. Even when he was 12, Bill could MC a show better than Danny Kaye."[3]

The nominations for *I Spy's* first season were plentiful.

Eartha Kitt was up for Outstanding Single Performance by an Actress in a Drama for the episode "The Loser." Jeanette Nolan was also nominated in the same category for her appearance in "The Conquest of Maude Murdock."

Earle Hagen was nominated for Best Music in a Series.

Mort Fine and David Friedkin were nominated for Outstanding Writing Achievement in Drama for "A Cup of Kindness."

In a unprecedented move, the industry bent the rules in order to nominate Leonard for directing portions of "Carry Me Back to Old Tsing-Tao," "So Long, Patrick Henry" and "A Cup of Kindness."

This had never been done before. Leonard was not the principal director on these episodes. He directed only one third of each, so the Academy, incredibly, combined the three episodes to give Leonard the equivalent of a 60-minute show, therefore justifying the nomination. But the true intention was to pay tribute to Leonard's advancement in second unit film making.

I Spy, itself, was up for Best Dramatic Series.

And then, there was Culp and Cosby, competing against one another, for Best Male Dramatic Lead in a Series.

Culp: "Nancy wants me to win. But she is also terrifically fond of Bill. So she is torn. I'm torn. But it's easier for me than it is for her."[4]

One giant step for Black Americans, the first Emmy, 1966. Bill gets a kiss from his wife Camille. (3 F Prod. Archives).

It is now part of history. Bill Cosby won that night. It was a first. His first, and the first for any Black actor in American television.

Culp: "My wife was quite miffed that life hadn't turned itself around and given me the 'attaboy' instead of him. And I was a little surprised by that. When it happened, Nancy went so far down the tubes, she was so livid, that I had to spend the rest of the evening saying,

'Calm down, you have to calm down, you've got to take this in stride.' I was so furious with her—not over losing, not with my best pal in the world getting the reward instead of me—no, I was furious with her because it was like she was in somebody's house instead of out in public."[5]

Cosby's gratitude was evident at the podium—with Leonard, first, then NBC, then, and mostly, with Culp.

Culp: "I felt just as pleased as if I had won. Bill's accomplishment was Herculean. It was so huge. The guy started with nothing, and he won the entire game. I was just simply delighted. There is nothing else to say."[6]

There *was* more to say. In the surrounding months, *I Spy* received further honors:

The American Cinema Editors nominated Bud Molin for an EDDIE Award his work on both "Court of the Lion" and "The Loser."

Bill Cosby would win the EDDIE for Best Actor on Television, for his performance in the Robert Culp scripted "The Loser."

Earlier in the year, there had been two other significant nominations: The Screen Producers Guild nominated *I Spy* for Best Produced Series of 1965. And, at the Golden Globe Awards, *I Spy* was nominated for Best Series OF 1965.

The recognition of their colleagues was astounding.

9

Basking in the Sun

In April of 1966, as the cast and crew of *I Spy* were shooting the first of the second season episodes, Warner Brothers released Bill Cosby's fourth album, *Wonderfulness*. It was an immediate hit, shooting into the top ten of the Billboard LP charts.

It was not alone.

Cosby's first three albums, all having recently achieved gold record status, were clustered in the top 40. Unlike the other albums, *Wonderfulness* was Cosby's first record to be recorded after he became an international star.

The new album reflected his understanding of where that popularity had come from. Even the title was influenced by the television series. The expression "wonderfulness" was part of the Culp/Cosby banter on *I Spy*.

More influences from the series showed up on the record. The final cut, "Niagara Falls," was all about "My boss, Sheldon Leonard." After telling the audience at Harrah's, Lake Tahoe, how Leonard had hired him to be a network TV star, Cosby did his best Sheldon Leonard impression as he retold a story that his boss had told to him. The album also featured the classic "Chicken Heart" routine.

Pop Art Spies

The peak year for TV and movie espionage was 1966. Nearly every spy show to hit the air—as were the motion pictures to use the spy game as their theme—was a success.

During the summer, on the big screen, American audiences would flock to see James Coburn in *Our Man Flint*, the first of two Derek Flint adventures.

Dean Martin began with the first of four assignments as supersleuth Matt Helm in the Irwin Allen production of *The Silencers*.

On television, along with the continuing success of *I Spy*, *The Man from U.N.C.L.E.*, *Secret Agent*, *The Wild Wild West*, and *Get Smart*, there was a new addition to the world of cloak and dagger: *The Avengers*.

The series began its alphabet network run in March of '66. Like everything to do with spies, it was instant pop culture.

The I Spy *Family*

All those who worked on *I Spy* have one thing in common: they describe the show as being a family affair.

Covert & casual: the second season look, fall '66 (© 3 F Prod.).

The families of Friedkin and Fine remember the profound effect *I Spy* had on its producers, and vice versa.

David Friedkin's son, Gregory: "It had to start somewhere at the top. I know when my dad directed he gave equal attention to the grip or the star. He had a great passion and respect for humanity, so whether you were in crafts services or a producer, it didn't matter to my father. He was going to talk to you in the same way. The whole thing that happened in the '60s, on all levels, was so unique. On this show, there was an element of optimism. Good vibrations. A sense of real affection. And almost a love/friendship vibe between Culp and

Wonderfulness ad, 1966 (© Warner Brothers Records).

Cosby, and that was so perfect for the times. The timbre of the '60s was infused into that show."[1]

David Friedkin's son, Anthony: "My father was part of the actors' movement in the '30s, a theater troupe that went all over the country. Dad befriended a Black actor in the troupe. And, when they were in the South, apparently you could not walk down the street with a Black person. They were harassed, arrested, and thrown in jail. So Dad experienced the horrible racism in this country, and he brought that awareness to *I Spy*.

"Dad used to say, 'Write the way you talk.' It should come from your heart. Be genuine. I found treatments that he wrote, and they bring tears to my eyes. He talks about light coming through a window, the delicacy and the color of the light, and the tone and the mood it would create. This man was a visual artist. He loved Salvador Dali, Matisse, Picasso. Also, he loved Culp's scripts. He respected Culp as a writer."[2]

But David Friedkin was only one-half of the team, and, like his partner, had to report to the man at the top: Sheldon Leonard.

Mort Fine's wife, Bernice: "Culp's a little aggressive and liked to write, and I think they tried to hold him back."[3]

Culp agrees that, while the scripts he wrote were produced, and with few modifications, he never felt that the producers would encourage him to continue.

Friedkin and Fine, however, *were* encouraged to write. Their contract with NBC required that they write one out of every five scripts to be bought for the series during its first two seasons, plus oversee all the changes being made to the other scripts that they would buy. For Mort Fine, this was an easy contractual stipulation to comply with.

Bernice: "Mort loved to go to the office. He liked to get in early, because at 9 A.M., the telephone starts ringing. He would always go in about 6, so he'd have some hours for himself. Whatever anyone wrote, the two of them would go through it, and plug in what was needed. They never let one go by. I think he liked being a producer, too. He liked the control of it."[4]

Friedkin, however, did not enjoy the responsibilities of being one of the three men with the "control."

Anthony: "My Dad never felt comfortable as a producer. He never really liked wearing that uniform."[5]

Gregory: "No question about it, Dad was a reluctant producer. He was poetic and artistic. Then he was an actor on Broadway. Business and paperwork and numbers meant nothing to him. He was really a writer-director-actor kind of a guy."[6]

Bernice: "Unlike David, Mort never wanted to be a director. For him, it was all about the writing."[7]

Mort Fine was the type of writer who enjoyed the challenge of trying to change good words into great words. Being a producer allowed him the power, and the final say, in doing so, provided he could get his actors to speak the words he wrote.

David Friedkin was the type of writer who liked bringing the words to life, on the set, working with the actors and the technicians of the production company. But directing could often be a double-edged sword.

Gregory: "Sheldon's little phrase was, 'ah, that's artsy-fartsy.' To my Dad, it wasn't. It was crucial. And I think that's one reason the show has the quality that it does. Which was great for Sheldon and the network."[8]

And, when the quality was noticed, it was also great for Friedkin and Fine.

Anthony: "I remember what an event it was in the house to watch the show. We'd have friends over nearly every week when *I Spy* was on."[9]

Bernice: "Mort loved that show. And the people. I don't remember any severe arguments that he came home and cried about."[10]

Fine was born and raised in Baltimore, Maryland, a stone's throw away from Sheldon Leonard's Brooklyn, New York. Friedkin was Kansas City born. His time in New York was as a struggling and sensitive actor. The things that didn't aggravate Fine, sometimes did aggravate Friedkin.

Anthony: "There were some really challenging moments for my father because his personality was very different than Sheldon's. Dad was a very gentle, articulate man, not a passive-aggressive game-player. Dad would come home and relive the day passionately with us. He'd tell us if he had a conflict with Sheldon over a certain shot: He'd want to put the camera on a hill and do a slow zoom-out, but Sheldon would say, 'Ah, we don't have to do that.' I think a lot of the creative tension on the set was Sheldon and my father. But, somehow, they were able to take that tension, and make the show great."[11]

Gregory: "Sheldon was like a coach, the owner of the team. Mort and my Dad, not only wrote the team plays, but allowed Culp and Cosby to pick up the ball and score a touchdown."[12]

The Family Grows

Calvin Brown was also a part of the family.

Brown: "*I Spy* was a big, big family type thing. Sheldon Leonard was Daddy, and he watched over all of us.

"I was unofficial stunt coordinator, as far as Bill was concerned. Paul Stader, who doubled for Culp, was the 'official' stunt coordinator. But Stader did some stuff that was uncharacteristic of Sheldon Leonard and Bill Cosby. I happened to see a production report, and I was getting paid $50 a day less than every other stunt guy that was coming in on the show. I'd say, 'I'm fighting this particular stunt guy, why is he making $50 more than me? I'm Alexander Scott. I think it should be the other way around.' So I told Cos'. And he said, 'Show that to Sheldon.' So I showed it to Sheldon, and I said, 'Is it because I'm Black? I think it's very unfair.' And Sheldon said, 'I think it's very unfair, too.' He called the production coordinator and said, 'I want Calvin's salary upgraded—from day one.' So I got all my money back for the whole year. And that's when we changed stunt coordinators. Sheldon was a sweetheart. You couldn't beat him with a stick. I know that when he died, Bill said, 'I just lost a second father.'"[13]

Hurricane Sheldon & the Writers' Room

In early 1966, two things of note happened.

Triple F Productions changed its name. It had to. It was learned that there was another Triple F Productions in existence, one that had nothing to do with *I Spy*, but, no doubt, would have liked to. So Friedkin and Fine and Leonard rechristened themselves as Three F Productions.

Problem solved.

Also in early '66, the three "F's" put together an event unique in the history of television.

Writer Steven Kandel was there: "One thing Sheldon instituted, which I thought was brilliant, was a brainstorming session for story development. The writers who proved to 'get' the show, were invited to come back for a weekend session, 48 hours, locked in a room, two secretaries, two stenographers to take down notes, lots of refreshments, and an absolutely free-swinging story session. Throw up an idea, somebody will grab it, bounce it, change it, twist it, take it back, play with it, then throw it up in the air again."[14]

The plan was to map out the 1966–67 journeys of Kelly and Scott.

In today's world of television writing, the way shows are planned is to have a half-dozen or more writers map out a season under the guidance of a "show-runner." Weekly series are staff driven, with little room for freelance material. In 1966, there was no set staff and the scripts were primarily written on a freelance basis.

Rick Mittleman, a comedy writer who would make the leap into *I Spy* during the second year, remembers: "You had a producer, like Mort Fine, and you had a director, like David Friedkin, who got a coproducing credit, and that was it. There were no writing staffs then. That came later with Norman Lear."[15]

Kandel agrees: "It was unique. I had never seen it before. Sheldon did not do it on his other shows. But it was successful on *I Spy* for an odd reason."[16]

That reason was the nine-script block that *I Spy* needed to film overseas: locations had to be arranged; talent needed to be booked far in advance; travel arrangements had to be made; along with body doubles and matching clothing for Leonard's crazy formula to work again.

Leonard took all of this into account. The road trips were meticulously planned, yet fluid enough to turn and change directions, if necessary. While it did have a schedule and known direction, this particular hurricane did not have a calm eye of the storm. Hurricane Sheldon had a tornado at its center—the marathon script idea session. This is one more innovation credited to *I Spy*.

But change—by its nature—is usually not easily welcomed.

Barry Oringer was one of the writers in the room: "When I went to work on *I Spy*, I thought I'd have a meeting with the producer, bring in a few ideas and we'd start to toss them around. So I showed up, expecting to just meet with Fine and Friedkin, and maybe Leonard. But there were a whole bunch of writers in the room. Michael Zagor was there, Steve Kandel was there, some others were there, and to my shock and horror, instead of having an intimate meeting about my proposed project, the way they were working was like a comedy team, and the half-dozen writers and the producers would kick around one idea after another. Immediately I was flung into the ongoing process with everybody throwing around these ideas and jokes and laughing, and I'm absolutely paralyzed."[17]

Kandel remembers that Oringer tried to contribute, but that he was not prepared for the frankness of the others in the room: "Barry was a very sweet guy, but he just felt attacked and overwhelmed. And, of course, he *was* attacked. Things were said like 'What are you doing?!' and 'That's fucking stupid!'"[18]

Oringer admits: "I was still very, very shy. And I couldn't speak. Literally, I sat there and didn't say a word, and sweat proceeded to pour down my head and I thought, 'I'm not going to be able to get through this meeting. I can't contribute anything, I'm not going to survive.'"[19]

Jerry Ludwig began writing for *I Spy* late in its second year and, therefore, was spared the tornado. But the talk on the Desilu lot was all about that first, bizarre brainstorming session.

Ludwig: "They had been there all morning long, getting some stuff done, and Oringer finally got weary of the whole thing. When they broke for lunch, he took anything that he needed out of his brief case, like his wallet and keys, and then left his attaché case next to his chair. When everybody came back from lunch, Oringer didn't come back."[20]

Oringer remembers the moment as being surrealistic, like walking in his sleep: "At a certain point, it was so uncomfortable, I got up, walked out of the room, walked down the corridor, out of the building, out of the studio, and that was it. I told my agent, Marty Shapiro, 'I can't work on this show. Cancel the deal and forget it.'"[21]

Ludwig said: "The meeting went on, and then at a certain point in the afternoon, Sheldon asked, 'Where's Oringer?'

"And somebody said, 'I think he went to the bathroom.'

"And somebody else said, 'Well, that was like half an hour ago.'

"Then someone says, 'Well, his attache case is still here.'

"And so they just went on. He was represented by his attache case."[22]

Eric Bercovici, who had written two of the first season episodes, added: "That became a legend at *I Spy*. We all admired Barry, because he got up and walked out."[23]

Bercovici had been in countless standard story meetings: "Those are always difficult. Every writer in Hollywood can understand—you go in with your story that you've built with these little walls and they immediately say, 'Why do you need the corners? Why do you need the keystones?' or 'The punch line is really funny, but the setup line isn't funny at all, so why do we need that?' And then you realize that you're dealing with people who don't have the vaguest idea of what they should know."[24]

But this was not a standard meeting. This was a marathon.

Steven Kandel adds: "At the end of the 48 hours, we had 30 perfectly good stories that had been really worked over. But two of the writers, Barry being one of them, couldn't take the psychic battering and fled."[25]

Despite this, Oringer was offered—from the marathon session—two stories to write. In time, he would write more.

Kandel sums it all up: "We had 30 stories, and then they were divided. Everybody had participated, but when you got the story, you also got the story credit. Everybody got an equal amount of scripts to write. They could do the production planning from that. It made the production of a series on location possible. It made for much better stories. Of course, the only way it was possible was because there was no network intervention. Nobody had to get clearance on the stories. It was wonderful."[26]

Hurricane Sheldon's plan, to fulfill the order from NBC for 28 new episodes, was to shoot eight in the United States, followed by ten in Italy, and ten more between Spain and Morocco.

"The Warlord," written by Robert Culp, one of the eight slated to be filmed in America, utilizing studio soundstages and back lots, all dressed to pass for a remote area in Burma, was cut from the schedule because it was too expensive.

The episodes to be shot at home were now reduced to seven.

Season Two: Hitting the Road

For the first block of episodes for season two, Leonard made the decision to take advantage of local scenery and shoot in Los Angeles, Palm Springs, and Las Vegas, all at a time of year when the weather would be sunny and mild.

Ronald Jacobs who, by today's standards, would have been classified as a producer, instead performed throughout the first season with the usual 1960s credit of associate producer. For the new season, he received an increase in prestige and would carry the title "Production Executive." He reported only to Leonard.

There was another change in credit.

Leonard wanted Fouad Said to continue as part of the road package. The American Cinematographers Union said "no."

Culp: "It was pure and simple racial discrimination from the Cinematographers Local.

Ron Jacobs and Leonard, watching the rushes, 1966 (© 3 F Prod., courtesy Ron Jacobs).

They were not going to let someone with the 'N' word be a cinematographer. God, it might as well have been called 'the Redneck Society' back then."[27]

Cosby: "I think that Fouad's attitude about it was, he just kept looking the other way. I don't think Fouad allowed himself to take in that what 'they' were doing was to *him*. It was like they were doing it to someone they 'thought' was a Negro."[28]

Ron Jacobs: "We called him 'Crazy Fouad.' We would always test his equipment on the back lot of Desilu before sending him overseas with it. And sometimes the crew would try to sabotage the tests. Lights would be turned away, while the camera was rolling, and so on. They felt threatened by what he was doing. But I don't think it was racial. It was just the old school guys trying to slow down the winds of change."[29]

Sarafian: "In that first season, there were those who didn't respect Fouad or what he was doing. Some of the crew members would rebel and damage Fouad's equipment—like stepping on microphones and crushing them into the ground. The old-timers were that threatened."[30]

Leonard wasn't. To the contrary, he needed Fouad. *I Spy* was not possible without him and the energy he brought to the show.

Sarafian: "Fouad drove that crew. He was the dynamo behind the machine. And he'd work so hard that at the end of each season, he'd have to go to Switzerland and have his blood changed."[31]

Culp: "I have watched that man shoot first camera all day long, stop at lunch to repair the camera, keep going until nightfall, and, before having anything to eat, work all night long on sound. At the end of the first year, he checked himself into a sanitarium in Switzerland. He was a wreck. It would have killed an ordinary man."[32]

But Fouad was not an ordinary man. After checking out of the sanitarium, a revitalized Fouad created one more innovation. Genius struck again.

Preece: "During the first season, he just used a white van with equipment jammed into it. For Palm Springs and Las Vegas, he began using the Cinemobile."[33]

Sarafian: "Cinemobile was like a Swiss watch."[34]

In a March 1968 *TV Guide* cover story on *I Spy* (one of three in as many years) Fouad discussed his accomplishments.

Fouad: "My truck houses two generators, six Arriflex cameras, wireless mikes, quartz and xenon lamps, dolly and track, and the top deck of the van lifts 23 feet above the roof in 18 seconds for a camera platform. The truck fits into the belly of a cargo jet and can be flown anyplace in the world in 24 hours. Hollywood uses 70 men. I need only 11."[35]

Fouad told the story of a famous movie director who, as an apprentice, had scratched his initials on the stand of an arc light—and then found the same stand and light still in use 30 years later.

Fouad: "Those klunky arcs weigh 400 pounds and give off no more light than two of my quartz units. Each [quartz] unit weighs 14 pounds. You can hold it in your hand."[36]

New technology. New innovations. Another problem solved. Another problem to face.

The Cinematographers Union could—and did—stop Leonard from hiring Fouad to work as a director of photography in the United States.

Leonard, therefore, hired Fouad in a different capacity.

Fleet Southcott, *I Spy's* stateside director of photography, would lead the camera team while on the road in California and Nevada. Fouad would be the "Location Consultant."

Leonard, the innovator, had deftly sidestepped the union rules. As loyal to Fouad as "Foo" was to him, he created a position no one could object to.

Fouad Said, small cameraman, smaller camera (courtesy *TV Guide*).

10

The Fourth Block of Episodes

29. **"LORI"**; Written by: David Friedkin & Morton Fine; Directed by: Paul Wendkos; Location: Paris, Washington D.C., Las Vegas; First airing: 9/21/66. Repeated: 4/19/67.

Assigned to protect John Keegan, surviving member of an elite six-man demolition squad, five of whom have been murdered, Kelly and Scott learn that the prime suspect is Jim Rogers, a former classmate of Scott's. Also part of the picture puzzle, Roger's sister, Lori, a popular nightclub singer whom Scott admires.

Keegan is now in Las Vegas, where Lori is performing. Kelly and Scott's fear: Jim is not only nearby and behind the mayhem, but Lori is somehow involved.

Assessment

This time it's one of Scott's old friends who may be causing trouble. Friedkin and Fine displayed a fondness for this type of plot device. While in many ways their instincts can be admired, some of their techniques had a tendency to be overplayed.

This is an effort to duplicate the success of "The Loser." The final tip of the hat is John Keegan's last line, "Who's the loser now, Scotty." But there's more.

I Spy's producers fashioned a story involving a pretty night club singer, who Scott has feelings for, who is not only talented but high-strung. (Angel from "The Loser" was a drug addict; Lori is a recovering alcoholic.) And, like in the superior Culp-penned episode, there are plenty of blues being sung here, smoke being blown, and booze being poured. It's all very moody and adult, but, this time, it's all surface.

The problems begin in the teaser: A fellow agent is knifed in the back, and, before he can pass along information to Kelly and Scott, he drops dead at their feet. This is *Get Smart*, not *I Spy*.

In act one Kelly and Scott are at the Pentagon, being brought up to speed. It goes on forever, and you need to be taking notes to follow along. The short version is six agents went through a special training program to detect underground nuclear testing. Four are dead, one is missing, and number six is their assignment—keep him alive.

Look for a rare *I Spy* continuity problem when Scott, sitting in the background on the couch, holds a newspaper, then suddenly the paper is lying in his lap, then back in his hands, then in his lap again.

In Vegas, the problems continue.

The character of Jim Rogers gets lost in this story. This is the first man we've met from Scott's past. He should have stayed there.

Nancy Wilson is no Eartha Kitt. She overacts rather than reacts.

Keegan's choice to dump Scott's body at Hoover Dam, a tourist attraction, defies belief.

Bill Cosby and Nancy Wilson, "Lori" (© 3 F Prod., courtesy Image Entertainment).

Keegan's choice to let Scott live until they get to Hoover Dam further defies belief. In summary, there are good shots of Hoover Dam.

The Story Behind the Story

This was the second telecast for year two.

"Lori" was meant to kick off the second season. The agents travel to Vegas. They make reference about having recently been in Mexico. The series made an effort to have good continuity, but the network had doubts that this story could launch a new season, and therefore changed the running order.

Look for Calvin Brown, Bill Cosby's stunt double, in a rare cameo appearance.

Brown: "David and Mort were just angels. But they would never give me a part. I'd say, 'I can do this.' And they'd say, 'No.' The one time they let it happen, they had me sitting in a bar, and Bill was in the foreground, talking, and they got letters saying, 'How could he be in two places at once.' And so that was the end of that."[1]

REVIEWS

Daily Variety reviewed the episode on September 23. The critic wrote: "Nancy Wilson took her first plunge into drama.... As with most beginners, she attacked the part rather than played it. Director Paul Wendkos should have braked her over-zealous embrace of the role. It wasn't a strong vehicle that Morton Fine and David Friedkin rolled out. The scene was Las Vegas and the real action didn't kick up until late in. What about the trade saying that you grab 'em early or lose 'em?"

RATINGS

When aired, on September 21, 1966, *I Spy*, as it had done during its first season, easily won its time slot.

A.C. Nielsen gave "Lori" a 40 plus share. Over 40% of all the television sets in America, that were on that Wednesday night between 10 and 11 P.M., were tuned to *I Spy*.

The audience was divided up as follows:

I Spy, NBC: 40.9%
ABC Stage 67, James Mason in "Dare I Weep": 27.1%
The Danny Kaye Show, CBS: 25.2%
All remaining stations: 8.9%

The top five programs to pull in the largest audience share for the week were:

Sunday Night Movie, Bridge on the River Kwai, *ABC: 67.0%*
Saturday Movie, Rock Hudson in The Last Sunset, *NBC: 44.6%*
Voyage to the Bottom of the Sea, *Sunday, ABC: 42.4%*
Tuesday Movie, Debbie Reynolds in My Six Loves, *NBC: 41.3%*
I Spy*, Wednesday, NBC: 40.9%*

FROM THE MAIL BAG

"Dear Sir, I am a young man studying for the Catholic Priesthood in the Dominican Order. A good number of us in the house experience the acting of Kelly and Scotty regularly every week—by free choice and not by mere mechanical habit. I find your show very interesting and highly entertaining, to say the least. It is very human. I am writing this letter because I am bewildered. How would Lori's witnessing the killing on the balcony jeopardize her singing career? Please, if you can spare the time, I would greatly appreciate an answer to my problem. Forgive me if I am just too slow to see the reason for myself." Brother J.D., River Forest, Illinois.

In reply:

"Dear Brother J: You had reason to be confused. So was my family. After the show, I sat them around me—told them something like this: 'In the editing of the picture, because we had shot so much film, and because we had to cut it down to air time, some of the exposition got lost.' They were unimpressed.

"Lori was indeed witness to the initial murder. Compounded to her being drunk, since initially she said she knew nothing of the murder. Later—well, then it was too late, and she was on her way to a smashing career. John Keegan took advantage of her vulnerability. He used her as a courier all over the world; her brother as a go-between. Knowing, because he was part of the cadre, of the cadre's disposition around the world, Keegan had them killed one by one by other enemy agents. Keegan's hold on Lori's brother was the fact that Keegan had a hold on Lori; the brother was willing to implicate himself to protect Lori.

"My family smiled kindly, drank their milk, went to bed. They didn't believe me, because hardly any of this was clear in the film. Sincerely yours, Morton Fine, Producer—*I Spy*."

Cast & Crew

Nancy Wilson (Lori) was a jazz singer who had a top ten pop hit in 1964 called "How Glad I Am." She appeared frequently on television, singing on various variety shows, and would be given her own syndicated variety series for one year, the same year as her appearance here. She tried her hand at light comedy on *Burke's Law* in 1963, but made her dramatic acting debut with "Lori." In the '70s, she would appear with Bill Cosby on one of his variety specials, and on an episode of *The Cosby Show* in 1984.

Greg Morris is best known for playing Barney Collier on *Mission: Impossible*, which had just begun production and would run from 1966 through 1973. He came to Sheldon Leonard's attention through three appearances on *The Dick Van Dyke Show*. He would later have a recurring role in *Vegas*, playing a police detective. He died of cancer in 1996 at the age of 63.

Malachi Throne (Keegan) had nearly 50 TV and film credits at this time, and would amass well over 100 in a career that began in 1959 and is still going. He played False Face, a guest villain on *Batman*. A few weeks after this job, he would be off to film a two-part *Star Trek*. Between 1968 and '69, he would costar for two of the three seasons of *It Takes a Thief*, as Noah Bain, the CIA man who kept a close eye on Alexander Munday (played by Robert Wagner), a thief turned spy.

Ben H. Roy became the fifth film editor to work for *I Spy*. Leonard knew him from *The Andy Griffith Show*. He would immediately be given a second episode to cut, "Trial by Treehouse." But there were some editing mistakes with this first assignment (the before mentioned scene at the Pentagon), and Roy's stay at *I Spy* would be a brief one.

30. **"SPARROWHAWK"**; Written by: Marion Hargrove; Story by: Walter Black; Directed by: Paul Wendkos; Location: Las Vegas; First airing: 10/26/66. Repeated: 5/17/67.

In Las Vegas, Kelly and Scott become reluctant bodyguards to a teenage Middle Eastern king on holiday. Bashik, the royal pain, has been marked for death.

The surprise double-cross is a double threat: Bobby Seville, a hip Vegas nightclub singer whom Bashik befriended and idolizes, and the very unpleasant Colonel Halouf, who heads up the young king's security force.

Assessment

This is the third time Kelly and Scott have had to babysit a difficult individual—and, sadly, the third time is *not* the charm.

The story is unforgivably awkward.

A coincidental chance meeting connects the two American spies with the boy king and his ruthless protector, Colonel Halouf. Then, because Kelly tries to give Bashik instruction on how to swing a golf club, he and Scott get guns stuck into their ribs. Next, they are taken against their will to the house serving as a summer retreat for the king's entourage, where the snaky colonel, by merely making a few phone calls, is able to break Kelly and Scott's cover wide-open. That easy. That stupid.

We move on. Bashik now insists that Kelly and Scott work for him. It will be fun.

The idiocy continues on Lake Mead as Bashik, goaded on by Bobby Seville, shakes off his bodyguards and takes to the lake for some water sport. The bad guys—proud graduates of the Three Stooges Academy for Murder and Mayhem—in a speedboat, pursue the waterskiing boy king, trying to arrange an accidental death. The speedboat is not that speedy. Kelly and Scott have time to arrive by car, park the car, rent a boat, and cast off, intercept the boy king, shoot their guns and chase away the bad guys.

The desert trek is even worse.

After driving "twenty miles off the main road," the cars are disabled. Kelly, Scott and Bashik head back on foot. After a commercial break, they look as if they have been wandering for a week.

The helicopter hovering above—in the middle of nowhere—continues to illustrate how the Stooge Academy graduates carry out a mission. It's called "Helicopter 101."

"Why not leave them there to die?" asks the traitorous Bobby Seville.

"Never leave anything to fate," the evil Colonel Halouf replies. And, after landing to see if the three bodies in the desert are alive or dead, the man who doesn't believe in leaving anything to fate chooses not to put his gun to the heads of Kelly, Scott and Bashik, then kill and bury them. Instead, this Stooge graduate prefers to save the three men from dying slowly in the sun, and drag them to his tiny helicopter, only to fly them someplace else where he can lay them out to die in the sun.

Of course, his plan doesn't work.

In the end, the bad guys are knocked out by a windstorm of sand being kicked up by the blades of the small whirlybird.

Among all this lunacy, there is one moment to watch for, a glimpse of Middle Eastern philosophy regarding treachery. Colonel Halouf says it.

"I and my brother against my cousin. I and my cousin against the world."

The Story Behind the Story

The network was less than thrilled with this episode, which they pushed back from being the first of two filmed for the new season to the seventh aired. Sadly, the NBC programming department lost all reason when they decided to repeat it in May 1967, leaving far superior second season episodes with only one airing.

An interesting tribute by Sheldon Leonard to his former partner is seen in the episode. The Sands Casino marquee advertises its star attraction: Danny Thomas.

RATINGS

Another impressive night at the Nielsen's for *I Spy*. The time slot was won with a whopping 47.9% share. Nearly half of the TV sets turned on in America were tuned in to Kelly and Scott.

The race played out like this:

I Spy, *NBC: 47.9%*
Tony Bennett Special, *ABC: 22.4%*
The Danny Kaye Show, *CBS: 20.8%*
Remaining channels; 11.3%

When ranked by the highest audience share, and out of over 90 prime-time series on all three networks, *I Spy* came in third for the week. The big weekly winners stacked up as follows:

Jackie Gleason Show/The Honeymooners, *Saturday, CBS: 49.7%*
The Dean Martin Show, *Thursday, NBC: 49.2%*
I Spy, *Wednesday, NBC: 47.9%*
Tuesday Night Movie, Kirk Douglas in For Love or Money, *NBC: 47.8%*
Lucy in London, *Monday, CBS: 45.1%*

Cast & Crew

Clive Clerk (Bashik) was a newcomer to TV, with only a handful of credits. He had just started a one-year stint on the soap *Days of Our Life*.

Walter Koenig (Bobby Seville) is best remembered as wearing a Beatles wig for the second season of *Star Trek* (1967). He would grow his own hair out to continue playing Ensign Chekhov for the remainder of the series. He would work elsewhere, including a recurring role on the 1990s sci-fi series *Babylon 5*. He was age 30 here.

Michael Constantine was 39 when he played the backstabbing Colonel Halouf. He had already achieved nearly 50 TV and film credits. Bigger roles would follow, including another *I Spy*.

Walter Black began the script for "Sparrowhawk," but had to hand it over to Marion Hargrove. Black had many TV credits, including drama (*Rawhide, Bonanza*), comedy (*My Three Sons, Gilligan's Island*) and animation (*Johnny Quest*). He would survive his sacking to go on to work for series such as *The Streets of San Francisco* and *S.W.A.T.*

Marion Hargrove, a well-known writer at the time, had seen a few episodes of *I Spy*, liked the show, and asked his agent to arrange for a meeting with the producers. When he came in, rather than wanting Hargrove to pitch new story ideas, Friedkin and Fine asked him to "doctor" Black's teleplay.

Hargrove was a newspaperman turned war correspondent turned novelist turned screen writer. His difficulties adjusting to military life in World War II became the basis for his best seller *See Here, Private Hargrove!*, which was later turned into a motion picture. He wrote the screenplay for the 1960s James Garner film *Cash McCall*, and won the Writers Guild Award for his 1962 screenplay of *The Music Man*.

31. **"LISA"**; Written by: Jackson Gillis; Directed by: Richard Sarafian; Location: San Pedro, California; First airing: 12/7/66. Repeated: 6/14/67

Kelly and Scott get a job scrubbing the decks of a fishing boat in San Pedro, California. Their mission: plug a security leak. Someone is using Aram Kanjarian's fishing fleet to get America's top secrets to Russian trawlers.

It has also been learned that Stevens, Aram's business partner, has made travel arrangements for Aram's mail-order bride to come to America from Greece. The American spy network has discovered that she will be carrying a microdot, hidden in her luggage. The big question: Is she working for the enemy, or merely being used by them?

Assessment

There are numerous red herrings to be caught in this excellent fisherman's tale, and more than one will turn out to be a shark.

The microdot, incidentally, is the classic Hitchcock "MacGuffin." What information it contains, and why it is so important, is never explained.

The plotting for this story is both complex and subtle. It is only though repeat viewing that some of the plot points can be fully appreciated:

- It might seem odd that Kelly and Scott are already working on the fishing boat when Lisa arrives. The U.S. spy network only got a heads up about Lisa as she was leaving Athens. So how did they move so quickly? The answer: Lisa had to make a stop in New York, where she picked up Bessie, an undercover American agent posing as an immigrations assistant. Bessie stalled Lisa's departure for L.A., allowing Kelly and Scott time to get into position.
- Aram's partner, Stevens, while given little screen time, is an important red herring. Later in the story, Aram and Sam, his true Communist colleague, kill Stevens in order to make him a scapegoat. Once we learn about this, knowing how loyal Stevens had been to Aram, and how long they had worked together in the fishing business, a light is put on the darkness of Aram's true character.
- Scott, the good agent that he is, offers to stay behind at the airport, alone, to collect Lisa's belongings. The scene in the taxi is brief, but tells us that Scott has searched through Lisa's packages and luggage.
- Look for the other subtleties used to convey Frank's importance to the story. Frank is, after all, Cyrano de Bergerac. He has romanced Lisa for Aram through his letters. When he sees her at the airport, and realizes how young and innocent she is, his happiness turns to jealousy and shame.
- When Kelly is tossed into the boat's cabin to join Scott, both bound by ropes, he asks Scott a question the viewer may also be contemplating: Why are they being put on ice, instead of just being killed? We never hear an answer, but notice the sly looks between them as Aram comes to their rescue. The heavies didn't kill them because Aram wants to get out of the spy game and be with Lisa. In order to do this, he has to give the Americans a Russian spy. Kelly and Scott were allowed to live, and to escape, so that they would shoot at a shadow of a man in the warehouse, then find the body of Stevens.

This story is all about decoys. Lisa and the microdot were a decoy. Stevens is also used as a decoy. If it doesn't make sense that Russian spies, wanting not to be discovered, would kill Bessie, understand that these two Russian spies, Aram and Sam, already know their operation has been blown. All they are concerned with now is finding a patsy to pin the rap on—Stevens—and all they do, including killing Bessie, including killing Stevens, is designed to send the Americans in the wrong direction.

Look for the second appearance here of Kelly's white jean jacket—and in combination with a sleeveless white T-shirt, white jeans, and white boat shoes, he may be dirty, but he is very much a fashion statement and leader for 1966.

The Story Behind the Story

The scheduling department at NBC pushed this segment way back, from the third filmed to the 13th to be aired. Perhaps the subtleties of the plot were lost on them.

CULP & COSBY ON SET REWRITE

Kelly's line to Bessie, "You've lost a little weight, haven't you?," which so perfectly conveys the affection between the two agents, was not in the script. She nudged him back in response, also not in the script. This exchange helps us to appreciate Kelly's loss when Bessie is murdered.

When Sam holds a gun on Kelly outside the party, the arrival of more guests prevents Sam from pulling the trigger. The script has Kelly say, "Now shoot me," knowing full well that Sam won't. Culp does one better, changing the line to sting, like a slap to Sam's face: "Go ahead and shoot me, sweetheart."

In the cabin of the boat, as Kelly and Scott, both bound from behind, talk, the following lines were not in the script:

SCOTT: "Now will you please put your teeth on these ropes and start gnawing away."

KELLY: "Wait a minute! The last four times *I've* been gnawing on *your* ropes. *You* gnaw on *mine*!"

SCOTT: "Don't give me that. The last time we got caught in that den by those heavies, who was the guy who chewed away his molars?"

KELLY: "Oh. That's right."

SCOTT: "That's right. Now I want teeth of iron. Of iron!"

LOCKED ROOM #3

Friedkin and Fine began the famous "locked room" gag with their script "A Cup of Kindness." Culp, simultaneously, was hatching one of his own for "The Loser."

Culp started the "friendly bickering" between Scott and Kelly, regarding whose turn it was to help the other, during his locked room scene in "The Loser." It was brought back and emphasized even further in the script for "The Conquest of Maude," when Kelly and Scott try to decide who's turn it is to put a coat over the barbed wire.

Both routines return here, with this on set rewrite, and are given the definition that will allow them to continue on a frequent basis throughout the remainder of the series.

CAST & CREW

Jack Kruschen (Aram) would amass over 200 TV and film credits in a 50-year career that spanned from the 1940s to the 1990s. He was nominated for an Academy Award for his work in the 1960 film *The Apartment*, as the kindly doctor who lives next door to Jack Lemmon and treats Shirley MacLaine after her suicide attempt. He appeared in over a dozen early episodes of *Dragnet*, before coming to do this, his first of two *I Spy* appearances. He looked old for his years, only being in his mid–40s here.

James Best (Sam), born in 1926, grew up in Kentucky. He was a prolific actor on TV and in films during the 1950s and into the 1980s. Before *I Spy*, he appeared on *Wagon Train*, *The Twilight Zone*, and *Have Gun—Will Travel*, as well as doing three guest star spots on Culp's *Trackdown*. But he was best known as Sheriff Roscoe Coltrane on *The Dukes of Hazzard*, a part he played ten years after *I Spy*.

Rita Shaw (Bessie) was 54. She had already been a regular on six TV series, but is best remembered for her seventh, *The Ghost and Mrs. Muir*, from 1968 to 1970, as housekeeper Martha. She can also be seen playing housekeepers in many other homes, including the one used for the 1960s movie *Mary Poppins*.

Jackson Gillis, for the most part, wrote good scripts for less than good TV series between the early 1950s and the early 1990s. Some of the best *Lost in Space* stories were by Gillis, who also bettered such shows as *The Man from U.N.C.L.E.* and *The Wild Wild West*. He began his work on TV with *The Adventures of Superman* in the early 1950s, and then moved on to *Zorro*. Later, after writing a second segment for *I Spy*, he would become a staff writer for *Columbo*.

32. **"TRIAL BY TREEHOUSE"**; Written by: Michael Zagor; Directed by: Richard Sarafian; Location: California; First airing: 10/19/66. Repeated: 5/24/67.

Kelly and Scott pose as factory workers to find a madman who is involved with terrorists.

The madman: A social misfit named Bernie. His sponsor: A refined Black mercenary named Edward Prince Edward. The terrorist clients: An assorted group of thieves, as well as interested parties from a foreign nation, who see an advantage in having a major American city plunged into darkness.

Assessment

While the setting lacks glamour, this excellent drama makes up for it with sensational character development.

We see Scott in a way we've never seen before, living as a blue-collar worker with a wife and son. He punches a clock in a factory, he punches his coworkers, and very nearly punches his make-believe wife. He is bitter, chauvinistic, and argumentative. He is anger personified, even stating, "Hate is a beautiful basis for a friendship."

There is a love story here, despite Scott's moodiness. He doesn't like this assignment. It angers him to have to play house, and he takes it out on Vickie.

Bill Cosby, Cicely Tyson, "Trial by Treehouse" (© 3 F Prod., courtesy Image Ent.).

Yet Vicki tolerates the behavior. She sees that Scott acts fatherly toward her son. She also sees that the emotionally distant boy, who escapes into cartoons on TV, begins to respond to the pretend father.

As for the single mother, she planned to marry a government agent, who was murdered while trying to infiltrate Edward Prince Edward's terrorist organization. Vicki, used to driving a desk for the department, asks for—and gets—the assignment as a field operative. She intends to avenge her fiancée's death.

Bernie is not only a misfit, he's a sadist. Notice the creepy shadow of a bird fluttering in terror as Bernie opens the cage. He is a young man only a mother could love.

Mom Nettie is kindly and maternal. She behaves like a friendly aunt to Vicki's young son. But she can turn lethal, if need be. She explains it well to Vicki when she says, "You understand what it is to love something violent." She has already said she would be willing to kill in order to protect Bernie; and then she reminds Vicki to put a blanket over her own son. "Children shouldn't sleep without a blanket," the one mother tells the other, at gunpoint.

Edward Prince Edward has made himself a cultured and refined man, but the fears and resentments from his childhood still haunt him. He grew up in Jamaica, poor, envying and hating the rich men who held all the power. Electricity, a rare commodity when he was growing up, symbolizes power to him more than anything else.

And, with this unique characters in place, the episode boasts many effective moments.

The morgue scene. Notice Scott's face when he is looking at Kelly's body, and the weight of responsibility he feels for the death of his friend.

The laundromat. Scott tells Vicki about losing someone he cared for, someone who was like a brother to him.

Outside the laundromat. Scott runs into a live Kelly, disguised as the leader of a motorcycle gang. Cosby's underplayed reaction, facing the friend he believed to be dead, is both a surprising and bold choice for the small screen where subtle nuances are often missed.

The only flaw that can be found with "Trial by Treehouse" is the performance of young Douglas Leonard as Vickie's son. Uncomfortable in front of the camera, he lacked the presence needed to match this otherwise excellent story of espionage, hatred, sacrifice, and love.

The Story Behind the Story

The title refers to a conversation between Scott and Vicki, where she confronts him over his chauvinistic attitudes when it comes to the espionage game.

"It's like when I was a kid, and the boys didn't want the girls to be in the treehouse," she says.

"That's because girls always want to play house," he tells her, "And that doesn't work for boys, especially when they want to play war."

Michael Zagor: "'Trial by Treehouse' was a script I wrote because I wanted to do a love story for Bill. Nobody else seemed to be doing it. It was kind of a taboo. Cosby liked the script and said to me, 'Hey, man, I like what you did, and I'm even going to do some of your lines.'"[2]

After the success of "The Loser," Cosby had been asking the producers for a conventional love story. *Newsweek*, for it's January 31, 1966, issue, quoted Cosby as saying, "If Alexander Scott doesn't go out with a girl once in a while, people are going to wonder about me. As far as White girls go, I want Scotty sterile. I believe in my women first."

Sheldon Leonard responded, "We want him to have girls. But there has to be sweetness and dignity to it."

Director Richard Sarafian recalls: "'Trial by Treehouse' was about something. It was character driven. Some times you pull the lever and you hit some good ones. Michael Zagor wrote me a wonderful note afterwards that he was so pleased with the results."[3]

As to the excellent casting, Sarafian says, "What I remember of Raymond St. Jaques is his dignity and his voice. It was such perfect casting for the part he played. Among the Black actors doing television at that time, he stood out. With people like St. Jacques, you don't direct them, he just comes in and holds his own.

"Michael J. Pollard is such a wonderful child. That performance he gave in *Bonnie & Clyde* was so much him. But that's the character. You wouldn't get the standard performance, the standard reading, because he was such a unique personality. And totally misunderstood in Hollywood, because he was so anticonventional. He lived a real gypsy life. And he was so destructive. I'd asked him afterwards, 'Michael, would you like to go out and have a drink?' And he'd say, 'I can't do that, I keep falling on my head.' Poor Michael."[4]

And, at the head of the cast, was Bill Cosby.

Michael Zagor: "Bill was magnificent. I couldn't have asked for anything more."[5]

CULP & COSBY ON SET REWRITE

After Scott visits the morgue and sees Kelly dead, he runs into his friend and partner again, this time alive. For this, Culp and Cosby added two delightful lines of dialogue:

KELLY: "The next time you go staring and staring at a dead man, try to remember that he might be holding his breath and turning blue."

SCOTT: "Had I known you were alive, I would have left the thing open for three hours, so help me."

Later, when fighting the heavies in Edward Prince Edward's darkened home, Cosby asks Kelly, who now is in disguise wearing glasses, "Where did you get those glasses?" Kelly, still fighting off attacker, answers, "Oh, I thought no one would hit me. But it didn't work out that way."

And, finally, for the tag scene, after Scott says his good-byes to Vicki, then joins Kelly in the car, he tells Kelly that he and Vicki plan to meet up again in six months and see what happens. Kelly's response, courtesy of Culp, is, "I wish you a lot of luck. From my experience, after you get to know them better, after six months, they get different."

RATINGS

"Trial by Treehouse" destroyed its time slot competition. A.C. Nielsen divided up the TV sets as follows:

I Spy, *NBC: 42.2%*
The Danny Kaye Show, *CBS: 29.2%*
ABC Stage 67; *15.4%*
All remaining stations; *14.5%*

In regard to audience share, *I Spy* again made up part of the top five prime-time shows for the week:

Saturday Movie, The Proud and the Profane, *NBC: 45.1%*
The Jackie Gleason Show, *Saturday, CBS: 44.5%*
Bob Hope Special, *NBC: 43.2%*
Friday Movie, Marlon Brando in One-Eyed Jacks, *CBS: 43.1%*
I Spy, *Wednesday, NBC: 42.2%*

Fewer people watch television at 10 P.M. than 8 P.M., especially on a work night, or a school night, and especially back in 1960s America. Yet, when all the noses were counted, for the entire week, Nielsen still placed *I Spy* high in a line-up of over 90 prime-time shows. It made number 12.

REVIEWS

From the *Lutheran Monthly*, November 1966: "Too long a time from now, many of us are suddenly going to realize that we could have stepped up the pace in race relations by making *I Spy* 'required viewing' during the late '60s! The deep-running current in *I Spy* that seems to sweep submerged icebergs of racial prejudice in front of it, lies in the subtle welding of Cosby and Culp into one unit of humanity. Bill is as gifted as Bob. Bob's lines match Bill's for sparkle, intensity and wit. With each passing episode of *I Spy*, I am less and less conscious of varied skin pigmentation in the actors cavorting across the tube in my house. Summarizing: Adopt the statements, listen to the speeches, read the resolutions, but experience *I Spy*!"

FROM THE MAIL BAG

"Dear *I Spy* and Company: I love *I Spy*! It's the greatest show on air! I have watched *I Spy* every Wednesday since I first saw it! But ... the new season of shows are not as exciting as they were before. Kelly and Scott don't seem to be getting into any danger at all! Especially the one 'Trial by Treehouse.' There was only one fight against the enemy. I certainly think *I Spy* is the best of all shows and it is the only program I watch until eleven on a school night! Robert Culp and Bill Cosby are excellent actors and should start having more action and get into more danger! Please reply!!!!" D.F., Corning, New York.

In Reply:

"Dear Miss F: *I Spy* is indeed fortunate to have a fan such as you. I was deeply touched by your letter, and hope this season brings you many hours of enjoyment watching our show. Sincerely, Morton Fine, Producer—*I Spy*."

"Dear Sirs: Please rerun the *I Spy* episode called 'Trial by Treehouse.' Thank you." P.P., Houston, Texas.

"Dear Executives: We recently took a poll at our college in New England—a poll of the 2500 students—and your TV show *I Spy* was voted NUMBER 1. Please keep up the good work. Avid Fans, Taunten, Massachusetts."

In reply:

"Dear B.D. Thanks much. And bless each and every heart, of each and every avid fan, avidly. Sincerely, Morton Fine, Producer, *I Spy*."

CAST & CREW

Michael J. Pollard (Bernie) was 27 when he played this role, as well as a part he took just a few weeks later on the original *Star Trek*, where the 27 year old played a boy who was 14. His first big break in television came when he replaced Bob Denver on *The Many Loves of Dobie Gillis*. Denver, who was stealing the show with his character Maynard

G. Krebs, was drafted into the army, and Pollard was brought in to play his weird cousin Jerome.

Pollard gained attention and found steady work on TV shows such as *Lost in Space*, and films like *The Russians Are Coming, The Russians Are Coming*. Michael J. is still active, playing an existentialist fireman in Steve Martin's *Roxanne*, and, more recently, appearing as Stucky in 2003's *House of 1000 Corpses*.

Cicely Tyson had previously appeared in the first season episode "So Long, Patrick Henry." She began her career as a model for *Ebony* magazine, then turned to acting. After *I Spy*, she won further acclaim, along with an Academy Award nomination, for her work in the film *Sounder*. Two years later she won an Emmy for her work in the TV movie *The Autobiography of Miss Jane Pitman*. She was married to jazz musician Miles Davis in the home of Bill Cosby, with Cosby serving as best man and giving the bride away.

Cosby: "Cicely, for me, is an activist, and a role model, and a performer, and it is always an honor to work with her. I don't care what she does, even if she's just handing out coupons, she's wonderful."[6]

Raymond St. Jacques (Edward Prince Edward) had received national attention one year earlier when he was given a recurring acting job in the final half-season of *Rawhide*. In a supporting role, he was cast against type by playing a Black who spoke with an English accent and was, of all things, a cowboy. He enjoyed regular employment in TV and films spanning the early 1960s to the late 1980s, including a recurring role on the prime-time soap, *Falcon Crest*.

Marge Redmond (Nettie) had much experience on TV, including appearances on *The Virginian*, *The Munsters*, and *Dr. Kildare*. Later she would play Sister Jacqueline on *The Flying Nun*.

33. **"WILL THE REAL GOOD GUYS PLEASE STAND UP"**; Written by: Rick Mittleman; Directed by: Richard C. Sarafian; Location: Palm Springs; First airing: 11/2/66. Repeated: 5/31/66.

In Palm Springs, two enemy agents assume the identities of Kelly and Scott in a deadly plot to kidnap a Unites States rocket scientist and his daughter.

Meanwhile, the real Kelly and Scott are being kept on ice in the desert community.

Assessment

This is a clever premise, maximizing the Culp-Cosby teamwork and using—twice—the signature feature of *I Spy*: a locked room.

It is interesting to see Lee Philips and Hari Rhodes as a pair of Soviet spies learning to mimic Kelly and Scott. By watching the impersonators, both competent and attractive actors, it is soon quite clear that Robert Culp and Bill Cosby pulled together a chemistry, an indefinable warmth, that was not only unique, but could not be duplicated.

The time frame of the enemy agents' training seems remarkably short. Yet the Russian agents learn to mimic everything about Kelly and Scott in a few days, then make their way into the United States. A clue to how this is done: The tennis court they practice on looks very much like the tennis court Kelly practiced on, with surrounding land that resembles southern California or Mexico. We may assume the Russians, and their training camp, are already in the area.

If you glance away from your TV for more than a few seconds, you may miss this crucial point: The plan, of course, is not just to kidnap a scientist, but to frame and discredit Kelly and Scott.

10—The Fourth Block of Episodes

The Story Behind the Story

The producer/writers were trying to create continuity. Kelly and Scott mention the assignment they recently completed in Las Vegas, as well as talking about the trip they will take to Palm Springs, creating a clear geography for the series. It was a good plan, if NBC had only cooperated.

Watch for David Friedkin, making a cameo appearance in the tag scene, as a waiter.

LOCKED ROOM #4 & #5

Number 4 is a garage with a reinforced door. The plan for escape, start a fire. The hope, stay alive until rescued by the Fire Department.

Number 5 is a storage room in a toy factory, devoid of furniture or boxes. There is, however, a ventilation conduit. Kelly's swimmer's physique is the perfect fit.

CULP & COSBY ON SET REWRITE

In the first locked room, after Kelly and Scott throw themselves repeatedly against the garage door, a bruised looking Culp and Cosby added the following:

KELLY: "If we keep giving this thing a couple of cracks each hour, how long do you think it's going to take us to get out?"

SCOTT: "What month is this?"

In another ad-lib, Kelly says, "Do you remember in the old days, the heavies always tried to make us jump off a cliff? Nowadays, all they can think of is to lock us in a garage."

Scott's idea to build a chair from a crate and an innertube was an ad-lib, along with the following lines, as Scott begins rummaging through the empty cardboard boxes and their stuffing:

KELLY: "No, don't tell me, let me guess, now you're going to make a sofa."

SCOTT: "No, a primitive yet effective device for escape."

KELLY: "Escape?! All right, it's about time. Beautiful. This is my man. He knows how to escape."

The plan involves building a cardboard chimney to a high window, then starting a fire. When Kelly and Scott find themselves trapped in a second locked room, the opening lines are not to be found in the script:

SCOTT: "Kelly, wake up."

KELLY: "Where are we?"

SCOTT: "In another locked room."

KELLY: "Oh ... We're not going to have to do that smoke stuff again, are we?"

RATINGS

According to A.C. Nielsen, Wednesday night at 10 P.M. divided up as follows:

I Spy, *NBC: 48.7%*
The Danny Kaye Show, *CBS: 28.6%*
ABC Stage 67, Oscar Wilde's "Canterville Ghost": *10.1%*
All remaining TV stations in America: 14.7%

I Spy also had the highest audience share of any prime-time program aired during the week. The top five were:

I Spy, Wednesday, NBC: 48.7%
NBC Tuesday Night Movie, Forty Pounds of Trouble; 48.6%
NBC Saturday Movie, Audrey Hepburn in Roman Holiday; 42.7%
Bonanza, Sunday, NBC: 41.8%
The Ice Follies, Wednesday, NBC: 41.1%

From the Mail Bag

"Dear Sirs: I had to write and let you know how surprised I am that your show was not taken off the air at the end of last season. It is one of the very finest shows on TV. I felt sure that some misguided persons would take it away, as they have taken so many fine series. Your show is the only truly entertaining ADULT show on the air, combining just the right amount of comedy, drama and action. I wish you many more years of success for a very selfish purpose, namely, my own enjoyment. Thank you for providing one hour every week when I can forget all my troubles and live in a world of intrigue and humor." Mrs. G.H.C., LaGrange, Illinois.

"Dear Mr. Leonard: *I Spy* is THE GREATEST show ever. Have only missed three shows since it started. Don't know which I love most, Cos or Culp. Many thanks for so much pleasure, having *Spy* on makes everything worthwhile." C.L., Sacramento, California.

"Gentlemen: I, a sophomore in high school, wish to congratulate you on your program. It combines adventure, comedy, suspense, and action in a way that makes it one of the few enjoyable programs on the air. I hope that *I Spy* is allowed to stay on and that the people responsible for its production receive the reward they so justly deserve." R.R., Greenville, South Carolina.

Cast & Crew

Lee Phillips (Kelly #2) acted in TV and films between 1948 and 1966. In the late 1950s, he began shifting the focus of his career in TV to directing, primarily for Sheldon Leonard on *The Andy Griffith Show*, *The Dick Van Dyke* Show, and *Gomer Pyle*. His appearance here, at the age of 39, would be one of his last as an actor. He would continue working prolifically, as a director, into the 1980s.

Hari Rhodes (Scott #2) began appearing on TV in the mid–1950s. He found guest work in a dozen series, including *Ben Casey*, *The Outer Limits*, and *The Fugitive*. In January of 1966, he became a supporting regular in the TV series *Daktari,* which ran until 1969. It was during this time that Rhodes, the third Black actor to be cast in a prime-time drama, came to *I Spy* to mimic Cosby, the one who started it all. He would later appear in the miniseries *Roots*, as well as costar in his own, although short-lived, series, *The Protectors*.

Henry Wilcoxon (scientist Lazlos Gagny) played Mark Anthony in Cecille B. DeMille's 1934 *Cleopatra*. He continued to work frequently with DeMille, but only sporadically as an actor after the director's death. He was age 60 here.

Sarafian: "He was a man of enormous dignity and stature. Because of that episode, I had the honor of directing Henry Wilcoxon, and that was the beginning of a lasting friendship."[7]

Leon Askin (Boris) is best known as General Burkhalter from *Hogan's Heroes* (1965–71). He was born in 1907 and remained active as an actor until his death in 2005. He performed to critical and popular acclaim on Broadway, as well as amassing hundreds of credits in both American productions and films shot in Europe. He was also a director.

Rick Mittleton was a first time *I Spy* writer. Prior to this, he had written for Leonard on *The Dick Van Dyke Show*. A three-time Emmy winner, he would go on to work for *MacGyver*, *Simon & Simon*, and *Remington Steele*.

10 — The Fourth Block of Episodes

34. **"SO COLDLY SWEET"**; Written by: Steven Kandel; Directed by: Paul Wendkos; Location: Palm Springs; First airing: 9/14/66. Repeated: 4/26/67.

In Palm Springs, Kelly and Scott don't like their assignment. Conflict #1: Is Marisa Terizcu, a defecting Russian agent, misleading the Americans? Conflict #2: If so, Kelly and Scott have been ordered to kill her. Conflict #3: Marisa is getting to Kelly.

Local scenery—Diana Hyland showing Robert Culp some skin, 1966 (© 3 F Prod., courtesy Ron Jacobs).

Assessment

Despite some minor flaws, this episode is as striking as the first image of Diana Hyland, poolside.

Scott has seen it all before. Kelly's in love.

Watch for subtle nuances in Cosby's performance concerning his annoyance over Kelly's love spell. The first and second occur in the woods, right before shots are fired. And, later, when talking to fellow agent Bennet, Scott refers to Kelly as "lover boy."

It is a nice touch that the Russian agent who claims to be tired of all the killing, and who seems ready to fall in love, is just that—but in love with General Sorin, not Kelly. There is an electric pause when Kelly has a gun pointed at the back of Marisa's head. In an instant, Culp's facial expression visibly hardens to stone. He is ready and willing to kill her, should she make the wrong choice.

The flaws in this story involve the arrogance and clumsiness of the Russian agents. These are the foreign exchange students of The Stooge Academy. Case in point: The sight of them walking en masse outside the hotel, carrying rifles, seems particularly stupid, considering they are covert operatives on foreign soil.

Also, for a sadistic and proudly efficient rifleman like Dinat to miss his easy mark in a hotel parking lot seems unreasonable.

And then the chase. We see a Russian on a motorcycle, firing a gun at the car he follows. No surprise, he gets blown away.

And then the shoot-out. The general fatally underestimates his opponents. The Stooge Academy owes him a refund.

The Story Behind the Story

NBC chose this scenic episode, with ample doses of action, danger, sex, betrayal, and skimpy swimwear, to open the sophomore season. But, before that could happen, some changes had to be made.

THE CENSORS

NBC's Broadcast Standards Department sent the following memo, detailing concerns over the "So Coldly Sweet" script, and we quote:
- "Costuming should be handled with restraint and good taste, in particular, *Marisa's swimsuit.*
- "Although plot consideration necessitate the knifing of Bennet by Dinat, staging indicated here is much too sensational to be acceptable. Please delete Bennet's: 'Mouth opens, gasping for air, he arches—half-turns and we can see a knife hilt protruding from under his ribs.' This type of action must be deleted. The removal of the knife by Dinat must be handled with an off-camera technique and his 'wiping (the blood off) on Bennet's shoulder' should be deleted. In short, this scene must be substantially tempered in order to be acceptable and acceptability must be reserved until the rough-cut has been screened.
- "The blow which renders the policeman unconscious should be handled with caution.
- "When Dinat tries unsuccessfully to shoot Scott, Kelly and Marisa, and is himself hit in the return fire, it should be sufficient that he be downed with the first shot. Dinat 'moaning,

starts to get up, holds out a hand,' and Surin 'looks at him, levels the rifle, fires, killing him,' is unnecessary and should be deleted. Further, please delete Dinat's 'screams' and his 'clawing at his face when he is hit.' Again, this scene will be acceptable only if handled without the sensationalism indicated in the script.
- "The demise of the heavy riding the motorcycle is overly sensational as described and unacceptable. It should be sufficient for Marisa to fire at him and, perhaps because of a blown tire, the motorcycle may crash, thus immobilizing him and relieving the need for him to 'scream, throw up his hands,' etc.
- "When the limousine crashes, delete action wherein 'Surin is hurled, flaming, like a burning doll.'
- "Please substitute 'No, you *fool*,' in place of Marisa's line, 'No, you *idiot*!'"

Reviews

In a September 16th review of the season opener, a critic for the *Hollywood Reporter* wrote that the second season opener had "a plot that was long on dialogue and short on action, but nevertheless paced briskly enough to sustain viewer interest. The excellent photography affording viewers some fine scenery, not the least of which was guest star Diana Hyland, no less alluring in full dress than in an eye-popping bikini."

Rival trade paper, *Daily Variety*, in its review from the same day, wrote "Sheldon Leonard struck hard to open the new season with a new twist—a shapely babe in a bikini coming out of a pool. That grabbed the males and it was up to Bob Culp and Bill Cosby to hold the others for the rest of the hour."

From the Mail Bag

"Gentlemen: Your show this year is disgusting! We strongly take exception to the bikinis on your show. You're ruining a good show." Mr./Mrs. S., San Diego, California.

"My Dear Sir: May I say the program *I Spy* is an insult to the public. At the beginning it showed a girl's naked navel and about a 3" bikini. How disgusting can you get? That is not fit to be in anyone's home. I never saw anything in such poor taste." Mrs. H.B, address unknown.

"Dear Sirs: It seems to us that a network with your responsibility to the public would have more common sense and good taste. We are referring to the almost bikini-less bikini featured on your show of Sept. 14. While that almost bottomless bikini might be at home on the Riviera where everyone is dressed the same, it is indeed shocking to have it walk into your living room. At times, we imagined she had nothing on at all. While this swimming pool sequence lasted only a few minutes, it spoiled the whole show, as far as we are concerned. Please keep TV in good taste. Are your censors getting lax? I'll be asking my friends how shows in the future are, and if the show is 'straightened up,' we might even start watching it again." Mr./Mrs. B.G., Warren, Michigan.

"Dear *I Spy*: The overdone love-making and 'smooching,' the indecent dress (bikinis are OK if you can turn the pages of a magazine, but not sit in front of a TV screen exposed to nudity and weak sentiment), has lessened our enthusiasm for *I Spy*." Mrs. F., and Family, San Francisco, California.

"Dear Sirs: Was it necessary to expose Diana Hyland in a bikini to make the opening more attractive? I couldn't believe it! I take the Legion of Decency pledge in my church each year. If you continue to find it necessary to have indecent exposure on the show, I shall have to boycott it." Mrs. M.S., city unknown.

"Dear Sirs: Why must Kelly wear a low-necked shirt? And why TWO bikinis? Women don't like them. And we buy more vitamins than men." Mrs. L.W.C., Shreveport, Louisiana.

"Dear *I Spy*: Your opinion of your own show must be very low if you have to have 'bikini' shots on your first new season show. We are opposed to BIKINI and KISSING close-ups as you had. Just thought we'd let you know. Dissappointed (sic) Teens, Pat 19 yrs, Gary 17 yrs, Sandy 16 yrs."

In reply:

"Dear Pat, Gary and Sandy, My apologies if *I Spy* offended in any way. We are always interested in your comments; rest assured that we are thereby guided. Cordially, Morton Fine, Producer, *I Spy*. PS — You signed your card 'dissappointed.' Disappointed has only one 's.' Just thought I'd let you know."

"Dear Sir, I'd just like to say I think *I Spy* is great. I thought "So Coldly Sweet" was very good. Keep up the good work." K.J., Mt. Holyoke, Mass.

THE RATINGS

Old broadcasting proverb: More letters means more viewers. With all those people writing in about this episode, *I Spy's* second season starter, the ratings couldn't have been better. The whole Nielsen pie, known as 10 P.M. Wednesday night, sliced up as follows:

I Spy, *NBC: 49.2%*
The Danny Kaye Show, *CBS: 25.7%*
ABC Stage 67, *Alan Arkin, John Gielgud, Alan King and Lee Grant in* "Love Song of Barney Kempinski": *17.4%*
All other channels: *7.7%*

The five shows to grab the largest audience shares for the week were:

I Spy, *Wednesday, NBC: 49.2%*
Bonanza, *Sunday, NBC: 48.1%*
Jackie Gleason/The Honeymooners, *Saturday, CBS: 43.8%*
Saturday Movie, *John Wayne in* Donovan's Reef, *NBC: 42.7%*
Gomer Pyle, U.S.M.C., *CBS: 41.4%*

CAST & CREW

Diana Hyland (Marisa) was 30 at the time of this filming. She had been a regular on the TV soap, *Young Dr. Malone* (1961–62). Later, after her appearance here, she played Susan Winter on the prime-time soap *Peyton Place*. In 1976 she began a May–December romance with 17-year-old John Travolta, after they met in the TV movie *The Boy in the Plastic Bubble*. The following year she was cast opposite Dick Van Patton as Joan Bradford in *Eight Is Enough*. She had only completed four episodes when it was learned that she had breast cancer. After her death in 1977 at age 41, it was explained on *Eight Is Enough* that Joan had also died of cancer, leaving Van Patton to raise his kids alone. Hyland won a posthumous Emmy for her work in *The Boy in the Plastic Bubble*, which a distraught Travolta accepted on her behalf.

Charles Korvin (Sorin) was a Hungarian born actor who was signed to a contract at Universal in the 1940s and played a romantic lead opposite Merle Oberon in three pictures.

In 1951 he was blacklisted for refusing to testify before the U.S. House of Representatives Committee on Un-American Activities. Ironically, he was given an opportunity to return to acting by playing a Russian agent in the 1952 film *Tarzan's Savage Fury*. Making the transition to TV, he kept active thanks to *Studio One*, which hired him seven times, and *Zorro*, which also put him to work on seven occasions as 'The Eagle.'

Michael Conrad (Dinat) appears for the second time on *I Spy*. At the time of his death in 1983, of cancer, he had achieved over 100 credits, not counting 50 plus episodes of *Hill Street Blues* as Sgt. Phil Esterhaus.

Bob Moore would leave the series after cutting this episode. It was his ninth. His association with Leonard would continue, on *Mayberry R.F.D.*

35. **"LITTLE BOY LOST"**; Written by: Chester Krumholz; Directed by: Paul Wendkos; Location: Los Angeles; First airing: 12/14/66.

From Malibu to Santa Monica, California, Kelly and Scott try to stay one step ahead of enemy agents while searching for a missile expert's runaway son.

Thirteen-year-old Alan Loden has endured his busy father's indifference for too long. Jealous of the attention Dad shows to his work, Alan steals a top-secret prototype from the research center. And now the race is on.

Assessment

Some interesting and heartfelt moments occur in this fabulous episode, as Kelly and Scott question the father about his boy. Dr. Loden admits to not knowing who his son's friends are, what his hobbies are, or anything else about Alan other than the boy's age and the color of his hair. The subtle reactions from both Kelly and Scott raise the level of this material above TV clichés regarding children who are given everything money can buy—except love.

The ante is raised when we are introduced to the trio of Soviet spies. One agent, in particular, utilizing the art of the garrote, stays in top form by decapitating pineapples. The inspired casting of Ron Howard as Alan allowed the viewers to immediately connect and worry for the boy.

At the amusement park, Culp and Cosby are at their best, amusing one another and young Alan with their charm and wit.

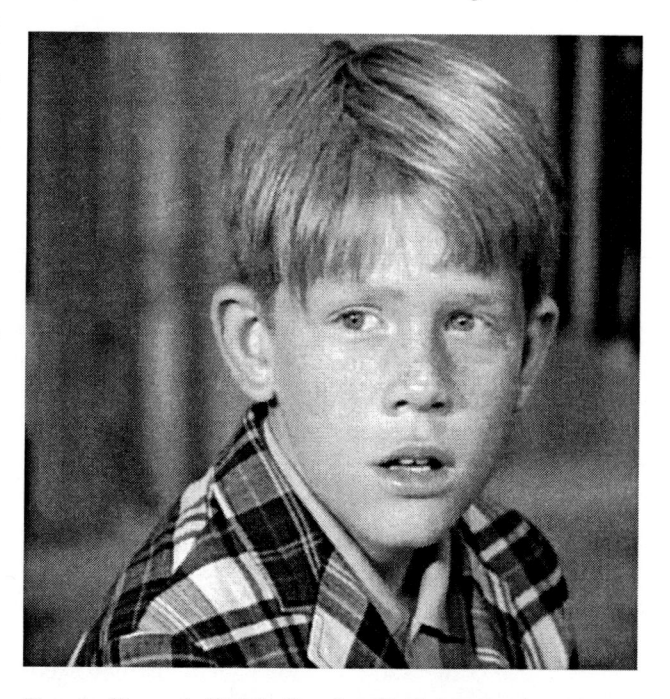

Ronnie Howard, "Little Boy Lost" (© 3 F Prod., courtesy Image Ent.).

The Story Behind the Story

The location photography at Santa Monica's Pacific Ocean Park is top notch. The park is filled with people, running and laughing and riding the attractions. The casualness of it all takes us back into a different world, with the sights and sounds of a theme park that no longer exists.

Preece: "We stole a lot of stuff. I remember us hiding cameras everywhere. The park was open."[7]

THE CENSORS

NBC Broadcast Standards Department had only one serious issue: "Please handle costuming of Carol in her 'modest bikini' with caution."

And they hadn't even seen the letters yet regarding "So Coldly Sweet."

THE RATINGS

I Spy continued to dominate. Nearly 46% of all the TV sets running between 10 and 11 P.M. on Wednesday night were dialed in to see Opie Taylor meet Kelly and Scott. According to A.C. Nielsen, 100% divided up as follows:

I Spy, *NBC: 45.9%*
The Danny Kaye Show, *CBS: 29.2%*
ABC Stage 67, Arthur Kennedy in "The Brave Rifles": *19.1%*
All others: *8.5%*

Only three shows pulled in a higher percentage of the audience during the entire week. The top five attractions:

Tuesday Night Movie, The Doomsday Flight, *NBC: 62.6%*
Bonanza, *Sunday, NBC: 47.6%*
How The Grinch Stole Christmas, *Sunday, CBS: 47.5%*
I Spy, *Wednesday, NBC: 45.9%*
Saturday Night Movie, *White Christmas, NBC: 45.5%.*

The big winner of the week, *The Doomsday Flight*, a first-run Movie of the Week, was written by Rod Serling and starred Jack Lord. The story, pure fiction, gave television its first handling of a skyjacking. Serling later stated he regretted writing the script. The reason: real life skyjackings began happening shortly after the movie aired.

This was a powerful indication of how television could influence society. *I Spy*, with its positive portrayal of the friendship of two men, had already proven this, but in a positive manner.

CAST & CREW

Ron Howard is famous for three things—playing Opie Taylor on *The Andy Griffith Show* (1960–1968), playing Richie Cunningham on *Happy Days* (1974–1980), and being the Academy Award winning director of *A Beautiful Mind*.

Richard Anderson (Dr. Loden) had just finished playing Lt. Drumm in the final season of *Perry Mason* (1965–66). He was a few months shy from playing Richard Kimble's brother-in-law in the highest rated hour of television in the history of TV at that time—the final episode of *The Fugitive*. In the 1970s, he was Steve Austin's boss on *The Six Million Dollar Man*.

Sarah Marshall was 33 when she played Carol Baines. One year later she would play Dr. Janet Wallace, a love interest of Kirk's on *Star Trek*.

Oscar Beregi (the Soviet spy leader) has been seen in numerous *Twilight Zone* episodes, along with being a regular during one year of *The Untouchables* (1961–62). More often than not, he played villains and Nazis. His final appearance was as a cruel jailor in 1974's *Young Frankenstein*.

Chester Krumholz, on his only *I Spy* assignment, delivered a story rich with emotion, action, humor, danger, and betrayal. He had previously written numerous episodes for *Ben Casey*. After writing "Little Boy Lost," he would go on to *Mannix* to write one called "Little Girl Lost."

Paul Wendkos, on his 11th and final *I Spy* directing assignment, would go on to do smaller films, such as *Brotherhood of the Bell* and *Guns of the Magnificent Seven*, as well as directing for Quinn Martin on both *The FBI* and *The Invaders*.

Preece: "Paul Wendkos was a suggestion of mine. I thought he would be ideal for the show. And they liked him. They would give him better scripts because they felt he was better than the other directors they had. But then he got a little too artistic for what they thought *I Spy* was. He was too time consuming."[9]

Cosby: "We laughed, and joked, and many times at the expense of the visiting director. Poor Paul Wendkos. I never liked him because he'd come on the set and give you the feeling that he really should be at MIT [Massachusetts Institute of Technology] or something. He was just 'slumming' down here. Is he still alive?"[10]

11

Growth, Genre, Gratitude, and Gondolas

June 1966. *I Spy*, like *The Man from U.N.C.L.E.*, *Get Smart*, *The Avengers*, and *The Wild Wild West*, was enjoying its highest numbers yet.

Patrick McGoohan, however, was ready to move on and pull the plug on *Secret Agent*. CBS wanted more, but McGoohan already felt trapped by a role he had been playing on and off on British TV since 1962. Under pressure to continue as undercover man John Drake, McGoohan would soon return in something a bit off-kilter, but representative of how he was feeling—*The Prisoner*.

For all the TV shows involved in spying, as well as those spies on the big screen, James Bond, Derek Flint, and Matt Helm, business had never been better.

The Sore Spot, the Ad-libs

I Spy had made it through its awkward adolescence. The growing pains were over. Or were they?

In an article written by Bill Cosby for an August 20, 1966, edition of *TV Week*, the comedian-turned-actor said, "In the beginning I was careful to keep my Bill Cosby comedian personality strictly separate from the personality of Scott. After awhile, though, I began to realize that Scotty was a man with characteristics and I had to develop them. I also felt that separating my comedy self from my dramatic self was not right. In the end I just relaxed and let things come naturally. As a result Scotty has become a very real person to a lot of very real people. It's hard to keep pushing yourself into different areas, but you have to if you want to be around in a few years. In this business, if you stand still, you disappear!"

New directions meant that Cosby, following Culp's lead, was ready to take a bigger stake in the handling of his *I Spy* character.

For the episodes filmed in Mexico, Culp and Cosby felt the quality of the scripts could be improved.

Culp: "Just about this time, the third block, we would be given the scripts about a week before we'd shoot them. They didn't want us to have them sooner than that. We would read them, come in, take one look at each other, and, without words, lock arms, walk to David and Mort's office and say 'this is not acceptable work.'

"By that time Bill knew as much as I did about what would work and what wouldn't. We were never in disagreement about this. If we could see anything there that was going to be funny or cute or clever or dramatic, then we'd keep quiet.

"To get us to do this, it's got to be pretty bad. We know how hard it is to do this stuff.

Cosby and Culp arriving in Venice, Italy, via gondola, in 1966 (© 3 F Prod.).

Bill took his cues from me on that, and I have the highest respect for people who write. Nothing comes higher in my mind on the list of things that I respect in this life. And, just because I don't like a couple of scenes, I'm not going to casually march upstairs and say, 'Gee, I hate your work.' But some of this stuff was unplayable. Some of it was just embarrassing. I mean, really bad. And all the guest artists in the world are not going to fix that. They can't make the drama work. And, as far as the comedy was concerned, almost always this stuff was in an area of *not* funny.

"Mort and David would say, 'This one didn't turn out quite as well as we thought it would.' That was their standard response—that and 'We'll try to do better,' and 'We've got some coming up now that we think are good.'"[1]

Ever since the disastrous "Affair in T'Sien Cha," Culp had little faith in Friedkin and Fine.

And while the team bettered themselves in his eyes with the Emmy-nominated "A Cup of Kindness" and the excellent "Bet Me a Dollar," he still found their work, or the work they sent out, as being less than satisfactory. He saw "Always Say Goodbye" as "silly and pointless," "A Day Called 4 Jaguar" as "really unfortunate," and "The Conquest of Maude" as "just dumb as a post."

The producers did not appreciate the criticism. Writer Ernest Frankel, who would work for Friedkin and Fine during *I Spy's* third season, and who would be elevated by Leonard and assigned to produce the fourth year, knew of the frustrations the creative team were feeling regarding the input from their stars.

Frankel: "Mort and David were consummate professionals. Somehow they managed to write *The Pawnbroker*, a critically-acclaimed film, without instruction from Culp and Cosby."[2]

The sad truth was, Friedkin and Fine had greater admiration for Culp's writing, in regard to *I Spy*, than he had for theirs.

Culp: "A good writer can write a *Mission: Impossible*, and make it not just be about a bunch of sticks of wood prancing around and jumping up and down, but real honest-to-God human beings with human emotions.

"You have to take those ridiculous characters of Kelly and Scott, who never lived, who never existed, and give them, within the story structure, enough underpinning around them to allow them to appear real. In other words, to break through to a suspension of disbelief. Because there isn't anything that is more unbelievable, really, than James Bond. It's silly. James Bond is fucking silly. Yet, there's a way to make it work.

"Mort and David didn't know what that way was, because they had never done that. And I had. I had been writing stuff like that for as long as I could remember. Mostly it didn't get on. But I had been writing it. And what I know about turning fantasy into reality I learned from Edgar Rice Burroughs. It was an early concept that I recognized in myself, from the time when I was 14, my mission in life is to take fantasy and turn it into reality. I remember saying that out loud to myself."[3]

Fantasy into reality. To take the action and humor of James Bond and make it real. That was Culp's vision for *I Spy*. And that was his goal from the moment he wrote the first words to "So Long, Patrick Henry" and "The Loser."

But Culp's vision for this new series that he was committing his life to was a singular one. He had partners. His partners would say that he had bosses. And his bosses had a vision and a plan of their own.

Friedkin and Fine had an executive producer to satisfy, as well as the network, and sponsors, and critics, and the A.C. Nielsen company. And they had themselves to satisfy, as well, and that meant telling the type of stories they enjoyed watching at the end of a hard day. Tried and true stories. Stories by the numbers. Boy meets girl—girl is a spy—girl betrays boy—boy betrays girl one better, and wins in the end. It worked, and it worked well. It was called "Tatia."

By substituting the "girl" out for another guy—an old friend or colleague of the boy, it could work again. They had proven that. It was called "A Cup of Kindness." And then it was called "A Time of the Knife." And then "The Conquest of Maude." And then "Lori." And then "So Coldly Sweet." Each time a slight variation on the formula. But each time remaining true to that formula—a formula that brought in good ratings and pleased the higher ups that needed to be pleased. That was how television worked—back then—for Friedkin—for Fine—for Leonard. But not for Culp.

Culp: "I learned a great deal from Sam Peckinpah. From him, I began to understand the kind of irony I should be dealing with as a writer. He said: 'If you have a wonderful story and you can't find the irony, then pass. Go on to the next story. Because you'll never make it. You can't beat it, unless the irony's built in.'"[4]

This is where Culp felt he differed with Friedkin and Fine. While he admired much of the work they had done, he didn't believe the stories they wished to tell were right for *I Spy*.

Culp: "The requirement, intellectually, for writing *The Pawn Broker*, or that Western series that they had for a year or so, *that I liked*, was very different than what was needed for *I Spy*. *The Pawn Broker* was for two Jews in New York City. *I Spy* wasn't.

"As for that Western they did: If you have a flare for a half-hour black and white Western, which is what this was, you can be very limited with your understanding of human drama and still get away with it. There was a hell of a difference with what they wrote, and did, on their television series, and what Peckinpah wrote and did, just a short while later, for *The Westerner*. Those stories were about real people, not about cardboard figures."[5]

But *The Westerner* had failed to find an audience. Peckinpah had failed to please his network. He had failed to work within the system, and to tell the type of stories American TV audiences, by the tens of millions, wanted to watch.

These were things Leonard had always succeeded in doing. And, with *I Spy*, and with Friedkin and Fine, Leonard was succeeding at doing them again.

So the two opposing agendas continued. And the visits from the two actor/stars to the producer's office continued, as well.

Culp: "It didn't happen every week, and it didn't happen every third week, but every month or so it *would* happen. We just reached the boiling point as to the crap they wanted us to put up with. We'd ask them, 'Can't you get some better writers? What the hell is wrong?'

"This was a constant irritant. And it was a constant irritant to them, too. Writer/producers have to have a sense of power, and it isn't good for their stars to be coming up and complaining constantly. But we had to complain. And we complained bitterly. And it's too bad. But it kept our petulance in check, and it kept it in house, and that's very important. You don't take this stuff outside. You don't let the world know about it."[6]

Culp had learned that from Dick Powell. Keep the family squabbles behind closed doors. He was being professional.

Leonard saw him as being something different. *I Spy* may have been a young and hip series, but the man at the top of the chain of command was, in this aspect, old school all the way.

Writer/producers write and produce. Actors act. Period. And that was Leonard's final word on the subject.

Culp: "All the negativity that came was largely from Sheldon. He was the only one with the authority to dish it out. Freidkin and Fine were 'hired help' just like us. So when Bill and I said something to them, we always framed it as an entreaty, to fix this, to make it better. We did not yell. But we'd speak authoritatively about the scripts — 'They've got to be better. This is garbage. Christ, this is the same thing we did last week.'"[7]

Culp hoped Friedkin and Fine would listen. He had no such expectations concerning Leonard.

Culp: "Sheldon *could* tell good writing from bad, but not how it got that way. He thought that the difference between good and lousy writing was a fluke — an accident."[8]

Ernest Frankel: "Sheldon graduated from Syracuse University with a degree in English literature. He was chief reader for the Schuberts before Mr. Culp got out of knickers. Actor, writer, creator, director, producer, Sheldon had six top ten shows on the air at one time. Yet, Culp has the temerity to question Sheldon's credentials as a creative person! Culp believes he knew more about writing, about drama, about comedy than Sheldon did!"[9]

As the second season began, Culp was working on two more scripts. But with a mere two and a half weeks off between the filming of season one and two, time was short for a perfectionist like Culp to be turning out material enough to do what he felt would be needed to raise the creative bar for the series.

Instead, he would have to settle for the five scripts each year that Friedkin and Fine's contract with NBC required them to write, as well as the ones their handpicked group of writers contributed. He would settle for them, and then he and Cosby would change them.

Leonard: "Culp and Cosby had been injecting a lot of ad libs into their work. Most of it was good, very good, in fact. No less could be expected of Bob Culp, who had a talent with words, and Bill Cosby, who was a world-class champion at this kind of stuff. However, ad libs can be dangerous."[10]

Culp: "Sheldon hated improvising on principle."[11]

Frankel: "It was not improvisation he did not like, it was the banality and repetitious nature of his stars' banter, the predictability of their reaction to jeopardy, the repetitive exchanges, the elimination of plot points that left the viewer scratching his head with confusion; the inability of his stars to understand that both drama and comedy have to be set up with transitional scenes, containing some clear exposition, so that the primary scene following will have impact."[12]

Leonard agreed with Ernie Frankel, who he would eventually see as the solution to the "ad-lib problem."

Leonard: "It's easy to be amused by a witty ad lib and to overlook the damage it's going to do to the structure of the tale you're telling."[13]

But Culp and Cosby had a problem of their own—and that was the caliber of these "tales" that were being told. So they did what they felt they had to do.

Culp: "We had no compunction about anything except getting what the scene was about. That finally became the mantra, and the raison' d'etre for us doing the show. We'd go in, we'd read the scene out loud, then we'd go over into a corner and say, 'Okay, now what is this really about?' 'Well, it's about this, this and this.' 'Alright, then we don't need all of this other shit.'

"We would get pretty harsh with a lot of the dialogue, and the writers just couldn't abide that. One guy, Barry Oringer, became so angry, and so disenchanted with us for messing around with his dialogue, that he almost quit."[14]

It had gotten that bad. Culp knew it. Cosby did, too. But the creative differences continued.

Culp: "We had every right to do it because our necks were on the line. And we could make them look better than they really were—Barry Oringer included."[15]

Oringer: "I was not crazy about the ad-libbing. When the two of them were together, and there wasn't another character in the scene, they would pretty much run amok with the ad-libs. It was different in the scenes featuring other characters. Those actors did the lines I had written for them. Naturally I thought those scenes were a lot better. But, you know, every writer is like that. When you're a young writer, you get all ego involved."[16]

Culp: "Both of us had a really sharp eye for a good line of dialogue, and we would keep it every time. As to the stuff we didn't keep, most of it was very pedestrian, some of it was banal, and banal went out first, and then pedestrian.

"The thing that Bill and I could do together, that nobody else could do, simply wasn't there. So we put it there."[17]

Michael Preece, in his capacity as the series script continuity person, was caught right in the middle. He was the only member of the crew to be present for both the location filming and the studio production on every episode ever produced, with the exception of the very first.

Preece: "I would have to give my working scripts to the editors, because I'd write into the scripts everything Culp and Cosby said, and changed. That would be the only record, the only guide for the editors to follow."[18]

Preece was also privy to the reasons for the changes.

Preece: "Cosby said that a 52-year-old Jewish man couldn't write dialogue for a 27-year-old Black man. That was his biggest objection to Friedkin and Fine, especially Mort—that they would try to write hip dialogue. He just felt it didn't work."[19]

Jerry Ludwig, a writer who would begin with the series during its second season, and continued providing material thereafter, saw Cosby, not Culp, as the instigator of many of the script changes that were being made.

Ludwig: "Cosby was the guy who was pissing on the scripts. He is gifted, I agree. But the odds on someone standing there, on the hoof, and coming up with something in the moment that is better than something that a writer sat in a room for a month working on, something that was reviewed by other writers, is unlikely. And sometimes they would lose the point of what we were writing about. There was a mutuality. They would encourage each other to be bad guys—what I designate as being bad guys."[20]

One *I Spy* writer Culp especially appreciated was Michael Zagor. But even Zagor took issue with the arbitrary last minute rewriting of his material.

Zagor: "Bob and Bill were famous for just improvising. I thought some of what they did was an improvement. And then you kind of resent it in a way, because you'd worked hard on these lines."[21]

In time, most of the writers and directors and crew members came to believe that Culp and Cosby were, in fact, improving the material. Even Zagor, who labored over his scripts as much as Culp labored over his own, could see some merit to what they were doing.

Zagor: "A lot of that 'riffing' back and forth between them really gave the show its flavor."[22]

And Ludwig: "Okay, the guys mumble our lines, or some of our stuff would get lost. But, overall, they were obviously a great pair, and they brought roundness to their characters. They were real people, and most of all, there was a genuine affection. It wasn't two actors who were acting like they were friends. It was two guys that loved each other—and it showed."[23]

And Oringer: "My view of what Culp and Cosby did has certainly mellowed over the years. In regard to the show, I thought they did very well with it."[24]

Some of the directors learned to use Culp and Cosby's skills at improvising as a tool for getting through the difficult and fragmented shooting process.

Preece: "Sometimes a show was a little short, and they would be asked to make something up, to improvise something to fill time. That would be part of my job, to time what they would do, and make sure it added up to the minutes we needed. So we'd put them at a table in a restaurant, and tell them to give us three minutes, or whatever we needed. And we'd just photograph them doing an ad-lib."[25]

Sarafian: "I never felt it was wrong. It was the style of the show. It was up to the director to let it happen or not. The two of them loved to ad-lib, and they felt they had to, due to what they felt about the scripting. It got out of hand sometimes, and it was just a question of editing it down to keep the scene intact to what its intentions were. But, when you had the two of them, it was worth taking the chances, working free like that with the improvisations. Let's face it, they came up with some wonderful stuff."[26]

Steven Kandel: "They improved it, which was alright with me. Mostly, they ad-libbed when they didn't like the dialogue or when they felt the dialogue didn't accurately reflect their relationship. They were very secure about that, because that relationship was real.

"Overall, they were pretty good with my dialogue. I once had a talk with Culp about ad-libbing, and I said, 'Look, I don't give a shit if you ad-lib, as long as you improve it. If you don't, I'm going to come in and haunt your dreams.'"[27]

In the end, most surrendered to Culp and Cosby and the magic they created. Most, but not all.

Leonard: "What had started as harmless interjections became increasingly intrusive ad libs, often inconsistent with the story line. Eventually it reached a point where they were totally unacceptable."[28]

As *I Spy* moved toward the network premiere of its second season, the battle lines were clearly drawn.

The Solidification of the Buddy Genre

I Spy invented what Hollywood now calls the "buddy genre." Two guys, on the road, sharing an adventure, sharing laughs, sharing babes, and risking their lives. It would show up at the end of the 1960s as a Western in *Butch Cassidy and the Sundance Kid*. Later, it would return, and the buddies would usually be portrayed as cops. They were called *Starsky and Hutch*, or they reported for work on *Miami Vice*, or did their time in *48 Hours*, or dodged bullets in *Lethal Weapon*. Often, as in the last three examples, they were portrayed as Black and White, just as *I Spy* had done back when it all started.

There had been books, movies, and TV shows about two buddies on the road before *I Spy*. But the intent was different. The mood and the feel were not the same. The chemistry hadn't been discovered. The genre had yet to be born.

Zagor: "It is very much an American tradition, with stories like 'Tom Sawyer and Huck Finn,' two guys out on the road having an adventure. But the difference in this was that Cosby was not a foil for Bob. They were very much equals. There was a lot of respect and friendship between them. That kind of camaraderie was new, especially because it was a White man and a Black man."[29]

Ludwig: "We anticipated Butch and Sundance by several years. We were really ahead of the game. Kelly and Scott—They were just best friends."[30]

Writer Eric Bercovici: "No question, *I Spy* was ahead of its time. *I Spy* was an original show. And originality is pretty scarce in television—especially today. It created the buddy genre."[31]

Oringer: "Culp and Cosby *were* that show. And I greatly admire what they did. It was a terrific show. It was a fun show. And it was really unique."[32]

Writer Rick Mittleman: "The key to that show was the banter. Even when Kelly and Scott were on the verge of dying, the back-and-forth quips was what drove that show. This was the first time the buddy genre was used, and, more importantly, the first time that a Black actor got costar billing. Culp and Cosby were terrific in their roles."[33]

Kandel: "They would need to feel at ease with their 'two-scene,' as much as possible. And their ability to feel at ease made the series a hit."[34]

Preece: "The main reason the show was a success was the way in which they expressed themselves. They created a language of their own. And Culp was the one who got a lot of that out of Cosby. He'd say, 'Just be yourself; don't try so hard to go against who you are, and be doing what they're telling you to do in the script.'"[35]

Culp: "The fascinating part about Bill's dialogue, when we began to improvise, was that he brought a new sound, a new sense of delivery to the American language. If I didn't join him in that, it was going to wreck him, and make an asshole out of me. The point was for us to work together.[36]

Cosby: "When you have a relationship, two people begin to sound alike if you really love each other. And what we had, the two of us, *was* a relationship. I'd never met anybody like him. The man—who he is, what he is, what he stands for, there's integrity there. I believe in his holding himself *accountable* as an actor and doing the most beautiful and correct thing. He laid in, and stayed in. And that's why, it always upsets me when people say, 'well now, he's copying you.' No. No. I took from him. And I did."[37]

Culp: "Our relationship had such power that it overrode everything. We were individually very powerful personalities. Put them together with an enormous affection and enormous respect—not for ourselves, but for each other—and you have an incredible force."[38]

Culp and Cosby, and *I Spy*, were an incredible force.

White and Black now stood together on an equal basis. The walls of the studio system had been breached. A prime-time network TV series was now, for the first time, independently owned and operated. And it traveled. New technology had been designed and imported. And a new genre had been launched.

No one knew to call it a genre yet. It had snuck up on everyone—including those who had invented it.

Equal Footing

In September of 1966, Bill Cosby slammed two home runs. He won an Emmy, and he was on the cover of *Ebony* along with his wife, Camille, and their new baby daughter.

Included in the article were numerous pictures of the happy Cosby family, and candids of *I Spy's* second season. Of particular note was the snapshot of "Uncle Bob" with the youngest member of the Cosby clan.

After receiving the Emmy for his work in *I Spy*, the series itself paid tribute to Bill Cosby by increasing the size of his name in the opening title sequence. Leonard's name was first, then Culp's name was in equal size to Leonard, and at this point Cosby's credit would now be of equal size and grandeur to the other two men.

Seven episodes had already been delivered to NBC and, for those, the credit sequence would remain the same as it had during the first year. Beginning with the eighth episode delivered, the new titles would be in place. NBC didn't air the segments in the same order as they were produced or delivered. Cosby's name would grow and shrink, and then grow again, between September and December of 1966.

Regardless, a gesture had been made. Sheldon Leonard appreciated Bill Cosby. NBC appreciated him, as well. But there was someone else whose appreciation allowed Cosby's name to grow in stature.

Robert Culp.

Culp's contract guaranteed him that his name would come first and be 50% larger than that of his costar. The contract had never been changed.

Further, Culp was not informed that a change in the opening title sequence had been made.

He made no complaint.

He made no threats to quit.

He made no demands for more money.

Robert Culp was a completely satisfied friend.

As *I Spy* prepared to begin its second season run on NBC, a report was made in the August 6, 1966, issue of *TV Guide* that "The *I Spy* company will film shows in North Africa and Spain for the upcoming season, and hopes to go to Greece, Scandinavia, the Middle East and Russia for 1967–68 segments."

The North African segments would be delayed, again, until the start of the third year.

What is more significant about the *TV Guide* announcement is that plans were already underway for a third year of *I Spy*—and the first episode of the second season had yet to air.

On to Italy

In early June 1966 the *I Spy* company departed for Italy. The final California-based episode, "Little Boy Lost," had finished filming on June 1st. "Bridge of Spies," the first segment to be shot in Venice, would begin production on June 6th. The five days in between were spent on good-byes, packing, and travel.

At this time, Culp's personal life shattered like a splintered pane of glass. His ten-year marriage to wife Nancy was in the debris, as well as his full-time role as father to four children.

More pain followed. Due to *I Spy's* overseas schedule, Culp's love affair with France Nuyen was subjected to a six-week separation.

But there was something deeper. Robert Culp the writer had been wounded, as well.

His script, "The War Lord," an immensely personal labor-of-love that had taken one year to see life, and had been planned to be part of the first block of the new season—had been pulled from the schedule. The reason: too expensive.

Everything in the business of television is reduced to "the bottom line." And, with "The War Lord," there were too many scenes, too many sets, and too many costumes.

Sarafian: "I think they would have gotten more from Bob Culp, but they couldn't afford Bob Culp. His scripts were too dense with too much detail. You couldn't shoot a Bob Culp script in the allotted amount of time."[39]

But Friedkin and Fine, and even Leonard, could not deny Culp his due. The scripts were good. The stories felt important. And the rewards were apparent.

Sarafian: "Culp had a lot to contribute. So going over budget once in a while was okay. And they would allow for it."[40]

They would allow for it when they could. "The War Lord" felt like one of those times. But it was looking as though its time hadn't come.

With Culp's spirits dampened, travel arrangements were made. Next stop: Venice.

Alf Kjellin had traveled with the company to direct "Bridge of Spies" in Italy, in its entirety. Second unit portions of "A Gift to Alexander" were filmed next before the company moved on to Rome.

Once there, Robert Butler flew in to direct "Sophia," giving Kjellin a week off to prepare "Vendetta." Second unit footage was then shot for additional episodes to take place in the Italian capital, including "Father Abraham," "Tonia," and "Rome Take Away Three." Kjellin would handle these duties, and would even double as an actor, playing a pivotal role in "Rome" as a doomed American embassy official.

During this time, Butler prepared the next phase of production—for Florence.

Also during this time, Culp was busy writing—not a script, but a letter to his wife Nancy.

Leonard was opposed to Nuyen traveling with the company. Culp was still married. So was Nuyen. Period.

In the romantic setting of Rome, Culp made the decision to do something about it.

The tabloids picked up on it first. *Screenland* magazine led the pack. In an article entitled "The Oriental Girl Robert Culp Left His Wife For," the magazine "reported" that Culp had moved out of the Woodland Hills home he shared with Nancy and their four children and taken an apartment in Beverly Hills at the beginning of the year. They were legally separated, but neither had yet filed for divorce. France Nuyen, however, had. Her marriage with a Los Angeles–based psychiatrist had faltered. Nancy Culp was hoping for a reconciliation.

The text from the gossip magazine read: "One of his *I Spy* locations had taken the actor to Italy, and the two had made tentative plans for Nancy to join him there. Certainly this meant that Bob had changed his mind about a divorce. Nancy's hands trembled that day when she put down a letter with an Italian postmark. She had already made reservations to fly to Rome. However, the penned words bitterly had shattered her hopes. He didn't want her to come. What he wanted was his freedom."[41]

The article ended with the end of the marriage. Nancy Culp filed divorce papers that very month of July.

As the month progressed, halfway around the world, actress Joey Heatherton joined the company, and the second unit moved on to Florence where Butler would film portions of the two-part episode, "To Florence with Love." While en route to do so, the second unit took advantage of the train, and filmed the journey as part of the episode. Sequences were also shot in the Florence rail terminal.

Some final second unit shots were taken in and around a small hillside village for the episode "One of Our Bombs Is Missing." The company flew home to finish this block of episodes at Desilu.

Filming at the studio would continue for the remainder of July, all of August and September, and into the first days of October. The company would film five days a week, 12 hours a day, taking weekends off.

Culp was reunited with Nuyen. Both marriages were over.

12

The Fifth Block of Episodes

36. **"BRIDGE OF SPIES"**; Written by: Steven Kandel; Directed by: Alf Kjellin; Location: Venice; First airing: 11/9/66. Repeated: 6/7/67.

In Venice, Giana Paluzzi, an enemy agent who works undercover as a tour guide, tricks an infatuated Kelly in her lustful desire to find and kill American agents.

Unable to determine the source of the costly security leak, Kelly and Scott turn their suspicions on each other.

Assessment

The excellent "Bridge of Spies," in its title, makes reference to one of the rendezvous points within the story. In the 17th century, the Bridge of Sighs was so named by the prisoners passing from freedom on one side to prison cells on the other. British poet Lord Byron made it famous: "I stood in Venice on the Bridge of Sighs, a palace and prison on each hand."

From there, the episode continues to live up to the series' prime directive—incorporate spectacular locations as an integral part of the story. Venice does not disappoint. In the 1960s, her beauty was still shining, a very romantic city where, in this instance, romance is a distant second to murder.

Giana Paluzzi is a true femme fatale. She beckons a fellow spy to come closer, fatally stabs him with her stiletto, and slinks away. We see her kill again, this time disguised as a nun. She strikes quickly, quietly, with skill and a great deal of pleasure.

Giana is an enemy that harkens back to film noir: Her body is the lure, her weapon is the stiletto, and, true to the genre, she loves killing more than romance.

Kelly, on the other hand, just wants to have sex with her. For television in the mid–1960s, this is bold and Bond-like.

Of special notice: Kelly's rendezvous with Giana, off camera, in a hotel room. While the two are otherwise engaged, Giana's weasel-like colleague sneaks in and repairs the bugging device planted in Kelly's dad's pocket watch. Never before on *I Spy*, or on any other American-produced television show, had it been made so clear that the viewer was watching a voyeur, who was listening to the activity of sex.

Again, it is demonstrated that the Soviets know very well who Kelly and Scott are. This time, they attempt to eliminate our heroes.

There is an interesting twist in character here, revealing another layer to the relationship between Kelly and Scott. Usually, Kelly is the moody one. In this episode, Scott sulks when Kelly has no interest in sightseeing.

Back in their hotel room, after the death of two agents, the atmosphere turns dark. "One of us has got to be leaking information," Scott says in an accusatory way, adding, "And it isn't me."

Kelly becomes angry, but the suspicion is short-lived. After a moment, while both men sulk and refuse to look at each other, they decide at the same time—without a word being spoken—that there must be another answer. As if they could read each other's minds, they begin searching the room for a bug, offering us an underplayed yet highly-effective insight into this intimate partnership.

In the earlier episode "Time of the Knife," Kelly and Scott discover

Top: The body count in Venice, 1966—Culp and a dead Barbara Steele (© 3 F Prod.). *Bottom*: Barbara Steele, "Bridge of Spies" (© 3 F Prod., courtesy Image Entertainment).

a dead agent, quickly pat down the body to remove any indication of the person being an American operative, then quickly walk away. This continued as the standard M.O. for *I Spy*, and remained largely, if not completely, unseen in other TV series.

In "Bridge," Kelly and Scott witness two different agents, at two different times, killed in broad daylight.

The second kill ties in with the symbolism and the play on words of the title. The man, holding flowers, is metaphorically in the middle of the Bridge of Sighs. And, for a moment, like Byron's poem, he stands between two places—not a palace or a prison, but this world and the next.

He's shot. Kelly and Scott hurry to their fallen colleague, find out what they can, pat him down and, then, simply leave. Kelly sums it up best: "He's dead. No cops. Split."

In the final moments of the episode, two more bodies are left in the streets of Venice: Giana and Metkovic.

Kelly merely glances at the lovely Giana, now a dead enemy. Metkovic, her colleague, shot in the back as he tried to escape, does not even rate a blink.

A split second after the double kill, Kelly conceals his gun under his coat, and with Scott by his side, they turn and walk away. There is a casual urgency to their stride, but nothing out of the ordinary.

The way in which Kelly and Scott move, the awareness of their environment, the body posture and their look, typifies what John LeCarre wrote in *Tinker, Tailor, Soldier, Spy*. "It's the way we look at things, isn't it? We don't stare. We don't seem to be looking. We just know how to see."

Culp, an unidentified actor, and Cosby face sudden violence, sudden realism, Venice, 1966 (© 3 F Prod.).

In the late 1960s, gunplay on most other television series appeared staged and utterly unrealistic. With *I Spy*, however, the violence—while neither glamorized nor glossed over—was utterly matter-of-fact. It was part of that world. In direct contrast to the camp violence of *The Man from U.N.C.L.E.*, the team of Kelly and Scott helped the viewer feel the tension, experience a world of always seeing but never looking, living life on the move, with your guard always up.

In the final moment of this episode, a daring political statement was made. The American spies are as cold-blooded as the Russians. The fellow agent Kelly and Scott had been trying to make contact with, who has fled Russia, is as beautiful and alluring and deadly as Giana. She too carries a stiletto, with a gleam in her eye and a desire to use it.

The Story Behind the Story

This episode establishes that Kelly's father is deceased.

Recalling the impetus for writing his script, Steven Kandel agrees that Scott is "acting like a cross lover."

Kandel: "I was exploring the relationship between them because that was the most important and interesting thing in the series. There was a lot of negative mail saying that 'they're supposed to be John Wayne, what the hell is going on?' But there were a lot of other letters that said, 'It's real. I really thought they were people.'

"What I wrote was what I wanted to write, that the relationship was central. It was not just that they were a functioning team, but that they were, in the human sense, highly dependent on one another. And the fact that they were racially identified, made the relationship stronger, because it was the two of them against the world. That was not part of the series, but it was certainly part of the national psyche. This was the first time to have this kind of pair bonding, a Black man and a White man. It was extremely important because they were a beleaguered outpost in the march toward civilization. So, of course, it was terribly important. The sense of deep bonding between them was essential to the series, and essential to the characters' self-identification. I always felt that."[1]

Assessing director Alf Kjellin, Michael Preece recalls: "Alf was a very warm man and organized director. Very precise. Outside of maybe Sarafian, Alf was the best director we had."[2]

And then there were the women.

Preece: "I remember Venice very well. It started with a scene on the beach for "A Gift to Alexander." The script called for this pretty young girl for Kelly and Scott to flirt with. But the woman the Italian Extras Guild had sent out wasn't very attractive. So we needed to get someone else, and we saw this very pretty young girl lying out on the beach, and I was asked to approach her and see if she would be willing to be photographed. I introduced myself and asked her if she wanted to be in an American TV show called *I Spy*. And she knew the show, because she was American. So we put her in the scene. During that same week, we were shooting "Bridge of Spies" with Barbara Steele, another very attractive, tan, dark-haired woman. While this is all going on, I had this opportunity to spend some time with the first girl, and I remember taking her up on a platform overlooking the water, and there was Barbara Steele, sunbathing with no top on. So Barbara Steele is half-naked, and this girl laid down next to her, and I took a picture of them. I wish I still had that photograph."[3]

The Censors

NBC Broadcast Standards had a few issues with the script for "Bridge of Spies":

- "Per discussion with Mort Fine, demise of Janos should be handled with caution to avoid sensationalistic effects, such as Janos' "arching backward, his mouth open, face horrified." Also in the same scene, the weapon should be something less sensational than an icepick.
- "Caution on costume worn by Giana—avoid the *overly brief bikini*.
- "Caution on Kelly's attempt to 'fervently embrace' Giana.

Culp & Cosby on Set Rewrite

The first two scenes in the hotel room between Kelly and Scott retain the idea behind the scripted dialogue, but all the lines are the creation of Culp and Cosby, including those from a rigid looking Kelly, sitting on the bed, suffering from a hangover: "Don't be talking to me while I'm doing my sitting up exercises." Scott says, "But you're not doing anything." Kelly answers, "I'm sitting up, aren't I?"

When Kelly leaves the hotel room, he manages to get a smile out of the otherwise sulking Scott. Culp says, "Alright, alright, Ollie, there's hope for you yet."

After their contact is killed, Kelly quickly removes any identification from the body. The script did not direct Kelly to do this, nor did it have the line that Culp says to Cosby, "He's dead. No cops. Split."

The climatic argument between Kelly and Scott in the hotel room was an ad-lib. The script had the two men come to blows, much as they had done in "Tatia." It worked well in that episode, but the Culp and Cosby's idea works better here, as both men become angry with one another, then immediately stop talking, and stop looking at one another. Kelly lies back on his bed and smokes, Scott throws a pillow on the floor. And then, just as suddenly as they got angry, both men come to the same realization at the same moment, without even a look between them: The room must be bugged. Instantly, and silently, the two men cool down and resume working as a team, as they search the room.

And, finally, after Giana and her colleague are killed in the streets, the script merely called for the shot to fade out. It was Culp and Cosby, or director Kjellin, who chose to add the bit of action where the two men quickly conceal their weapons, rise up and walk away from the dead bodies, casually, but hastily, continuing with the cold-blooded theme that is prevalent throughout this excellent episode.

From the Mail Bag

"Dear Sir: I viewed 'Bridge of Spies' last night, and was not too happy about it. Some of us become a bit discouraged that it takes our agents so long to 'catch on,' as in this episode. It would seem incredible that a trained and tried 'agent' would take so long to discover 'the leak.' I remember Kelly falling for a beautiful agent, and thereby causing the death of one or more of our own agents, was done last year. So, supposedly, he and/or the writer would learn." P.A.A., San Francisco, California.

"Dear Sirs: I watch *I Spy* weekly and it is my personal belief that this series is the greatest thing that ever happened to television. 'Bridge of Spies' was great. But what I'd really like to comment on in this episode is the music. It was 'out of sight,' especially the part when Kelly and Scott were to meet their contact on the bridge, who was to have a bouquet of flowers.

I think if this music was recorded, it would really sell, and sell big. Keep the good work up. I also think that Robert Culp and Bill Cosby are a couple of handsome guys." M.A., Los Angeles, California.

"Dear Sir: Just a note to tell you how much I enjoyed last night's show of *I Spy*. My thanks to Viceroy, Jolly Green Giant, and Ramada (Inns) for their sponsorship of this consistently fine program. Also, may I extend a word of appreciation to the writers of the *I Spy* scripts. They seem to have found the kind of material which Bill Cosby and Robert Culp do best with." G.W.C., location unknown.

"Dear Sirs: I would like to personally thank you for having such consistently good scripts and actors on your show. In my opinion, *I Spy* is the best show on the air. It may also interest you to know that *I Spy*, Bill Cosby, and Robert Culp were ALL voted on the top ten list at my school, and only one person spelled Bill Cosby wrong." N.L.B., location unknown.

Cast & Crew

Barbara Steele (Giana) was a star in Italy, and had become known in America through her Italian made horror movies. Her break-out role was for *Black Sunday*, considered by many as the quintessential Italian film concerning witchcraft. American International Films, which packaged many of Steele's movies for distribution in the U.S., brought her to America in 1961 to star in Roger Corman's *The Pit and the Pendulum*. After returning to Europe, and filming an episode of Patrick McGoohan's *Danger Man*, she appeared in Fellini's *8½*, as well as more than a few movies dealing with the occult. Playing Giana in "Bridge of Spies," at age 29, would mark a rare appearance on American television, and only due to the show being shot in her native land. Frustrated over being typecast, Steele made less frequent appearances and began applying her skills to endeavors behind the camera. She won an Emmy in 1989 for producing the miniseries *War & Remembrance*.

Carlo Croccolo (Metkovic) was a busy character actor in Italian cinema and TV. *I Spy* represented his only time at working for an American film company. He was 39.

Alf Kjellin began his career in cinema in Europe as an actor, building a resume of over 50 credits, including an attention worthy performance in 1965's *Ship of Fools*. On one of his trips to America for an acting job, he was given the opportunity to direct for *Alfred Hitchcock Presents*. *Bonanza*, and *The Man from U.N.C.L.E.* soon followed.

Kjellin was a perfect candidate to helm episodes for *I Spy* because of his familiarity with filmmaking in Europe.

Earle Hagen again does a masterful job of scoring the episode, reworking some of the musical themes from the first season's Mexico episodes, but giving them new arrangements to allow the music to feel very much at home in Italy.

37. **"A GIFT FROM ALEXANDER"**; Written by: Barry Oringer; Directed by: Alf Kjellin; Location: Venice; First airing: 10/12/66

In Venice, a character named Luchesi wants Kelly to steal a book containing a hidden manuscript that will make a deceased Soviet writer famous.

Luchesi and his two associates, Plotkin and Kraus, want the document back for reasons other than what they say, and Kelly is being asked to seduce the woman guarding the book, a surprisingly attractive and sensitive Soviet military officer named Alina.

Assessment

An uneven episode that, while trying to amuse, often fails. On many levels, the campy "A Gift from Alexander" can be compared to "Chrysanthemum."

The first half is awkward, filled with heavy exposition in the dialogue.

We are reminded here that the Russians have broken Kelly and Scott's cover. The tennis player and his trainer may fool agents working for other world powers, but their only real use—when it comes to the Soviets—is to act as decoys.

Some moments of comedy do prevail. When the three Russian misfits are trying to appeal to Kelly to seduce Major Linkolva, Plotkin shares information he has uncovered while researching the tennis bum. Reading from a card, he says, "In 1964, you won third place in the *Playgirl* poll to determine the man most likely to tempt respectful women into scandal and disgrace!"

These three bumbling con artists have no idea they are addressing an American intelligence agent. They just want a playboy with questionable morals to seduce a shy Russian military bookkeeper.

The tongue-in-cheek antics of the three Russian criminals—Plotkin, Kraus, and Luchesi—clash with the more inspired moments between Kelly and Alina. It is not until Kelly becomes infatuated with the lovely Major Alina Linkolva that the story gains any real sense of purpose.

The scenes shot in Venice are scenic and, sadly, too short. The love story could and should have been played bigger, exploiting a city famous for providing a backdrop for young love, and better featuring Anna Karina. There is definite chemistry between Culp and Karina. It is a shame so much screen time was given to the clumsy villains, and not more for the relationship between an American agent and a Russian soldier.

THE STORY BEHIND THE STORY

An interesting continuity problem occurs when Kelly enlists the aid of some Italian ruffians to break up a chess parlor. The thugs, as seen in the portion of the show filmed off a canal in Venice, barely resemble the men who, a moment later, walk into the chess parlor. Worse, their clothes don't even match.

Writer Barry Oringer recalls his first *I Spy* assignment: "They took one of the stories that was developed at that marathon writers meeting. They gave me the basic sketch of an idea, and I went from there. It was based on a minute or two conversation on the phone, and then I sat down and I figured out the rest of it. I thought it was pretty good. It was not my absolute favorite script, but it was fun."[4]

And then there were the women.

Preece: "Anna Karina was the love of my life. She came out to L.A. to finish that episode, and we spent some time together. A truly beautiful woman."[5]

Culp: "Very beautiful. And very nice. She was a big thing over there. And a great pleasure to work with."[6]

THE CENSORS

NBC Broadcast Standards had many problems with the script for this episode:

- "Caution on the *bikini bathing suits*—please avoid the overly brief type.
- "Kelly's reference to the thugs being 'living nuts,' should be changed to 'weirdos, kooks,'

etc., to avoid referring to mental ill health in a flippant way.
- "Do not show the toilet facilities in the bathroom interior.
- "The scene between Kelly and Alina should be tempered to avoid Kelly's attempted seduction and Alina's apparent willingness.
- "Caution on their position on the sofa, and do not have Alina 'change into something more comfortable.'
- "Scott's line, 'He was railroaded into the laughing academy,' is unacceptable as a flippant reference to mental ill health. Please delete 'laughing academy.'
- "Please delete the following underlined from Scott's speech, 'a bunch of lunatic con men.'
- "Please substitute something such as 'fool' for Benkovsky's use of 'idiot.'

As always, NBC was protecting us idiots.

Anna Karina and Robert Culp, pure chemistry, a gift from *I Spy*, 1966 (© 3 F Prod.).

THE RATINGS

For Wednesday at 10 P.M., A.C. Nielsen did the arithmetic as follows:

I Spy, *NBC; 42.5%*
The Danny Kaye Show, *CBS; 29.7%*
ABC Stage 67, Donald O'Conner in "Olympus 7–100": *14.4%*
All others: *14.9%*

The top five programs of the week, in regard to the largest audience share, were:

Friday Movie, Dick Van Dyke in Bye Bye Birdie, *CBS; 51.4%*
Jackie Gleason/The Honeymooners, *Saturday, CBS; 45.6%*
Friends & Nabors, *Wednesday, CBS; 45.0%*
Voyage to the Bottom of the Sea, *Sunday, ABC; 42.7%*
I Spy, *Wednesday, NBC; 42.5%*

Jim Nabors, still riding high on *Gomer Pyle, U.S.M.C.*, had the cover of *TV Guide* the week *Friends & Nabors*, his first highly promoted variety special, aired.

CAST & CREW

Anna Karina is beguiling as Alina. Born in Denmark in 1940, she gained notoriety as a top model in Paris at age 18, before entering films the following year. Nearly a 100 foreign film and TV credits span 1959 to 2003. She was already a star in European cinema, although unknown in the United States. For this role, at age 26, she worked on location in Venice, as well as traveling to Los Angeles two months later to complete the assignment.

All other actors appeared in either the Venice portion of the episode or the U.S. portion, but not both.

Of the three bad guys, two were *I Spy* veterans.

Michael Constantine (Plotkin) had been in "Sparrowhawk."

Jay Novello (Kraus) appeared in "Time of the Knife."

Laurie Main (Luchesi) was the newcomer to the series. He had guest starred in TV shows such as *Daniel Boone* and *Hogan's Heroes*. Between 1953 and 2002 he achieved over a 100 TV and film appearances.

Alan Oppenheimer (Colonel Benkovsky) has a massive list of over 200 credits in TV and film and is still active.

Oppenheimer: "That was my first guest star role. I'd been out here like two weeks. My agent sent me in to meet Mike Fenton, and I'm talking to him, and he says, 'Well, let's go meet Alf Kjellin, he's the director.' And we go in and Mike, God bless him, says, 'I don't know if Al is right for this role.' So he covered his ass right away. And Kjellin says, 'Well why don't we just let him do what he does'—which put Mike in his place. And I read the part, and did this Russian character, and Kjellin says, 'I think you'll do just fine.' That was it. You didn't have to pass muster with anyone else.

"So I go into the show, and I had a very *very* long monologue to do. But, in those days, I could learn anything over night. When I finished, the crew broke into applause, and I thought, 'Oh my God, isn't that wonderful.' It wasn't until much later, I thought to myself, they only broke into applause because they didn't have to stand there for another hour while this actor fumbles through retake after retake. It had nothing to do with my performance, they were just glad to get that scene out of the way.

"Well, it aired, and the next morning, NBC called Sheldon Leonard's office and said, 'Bring that character back.' So, they wrote the next episode that I was in—'Blackout'—which featured the character."[7]

Hugo Friedhofer composed the lovely score.

From the Mail Bag

"Gentlemen: I would very much appreciate if you would let me know the name of the Russian melody played repeatedly during the performance of 'A Gift from Alexander.' M.H., Woodside, California.

In reply:

"Dear Sir: Thank you for your inquiry as to the name of the Russian melody played in 'A Gift from Alexander.' This is an original song written for *I Spy* by Hugo Friedhofer. I am afraid it is unpublished and not available at this time. Thank you so much for your interest. Sincerely, Judith Seal, Secretary to Producers, *I Spy*."

38. **"SOPHIA"**; Written by: Morton Fine & David Friedkin; Directed by: Robert Butler; Location: Rome; First airing: 9/28/66. Repeated: 5/10/67

En route to Rome, Kelly and Scott take a break from spying to play daddy.

Years earlier, Scott sent in his ten bucks a month to become the foster father of an Italian orphan—a girl named Sophia. The foster daughter, whom Scott has never met, has become a lovely and engaged young woman. Big problem: Her fiancé is Gino, a wise-guy thief. Scott is also leery of the help being offered by another wise guy—Kelly.

Assessment

"Sophia" has nothing to do with Kelly and Scott's line of work, and even less to do with pleasing the average fan of the series. Regardless, there are a few moments of cleverness.

Scott is challenging Gino on how he makes a living. More so, on how he expects to be able to support Sophia. Gino answers the question *with* a question: He challenges Scott right back about how *he* makes a living. Scott points to Kelly and says that he works as the trainer to a traveling athlete. "Oh," Gino says, "a tennis bum."

Whenever Kelly is trying to "help," it is enjoyable watching Scott become increasingly protective of Sophia. Scott knows what his partner is capable of, and he is determined not to let the "tennis bum" lay one finger on his foster daughter.

The Story Behind the Story

NBC liked this segment so much, they moved it forward several notches in the order in which it was produced and aired.

Shot entirely on location in and about Rome, Fouad Said was given the director of photography credit.

CULP & COSBY ON SET REWRITE

In an episode brimming with ad-libs, one in particular bears mentioning.

Kelly and Scott are incarcerated for a second time. The script had Kelly pacing. But Culp chose to lie on a top bunk bed and stare at the ceiling. Cosby lies underneath, and kicks the bottom of Culp's bunk. Cosby says, "How can you just lie there?" Culp responds, "Well, they wouldn't give me no award for pacing—so I'm going for a new category. It's called, Best Performance By A Leading Half-Wit While Lying On His Back In A Jail Cell, Looking At The Ceiling, Being Pitiful!"

Culp had missed winning the Emmy for his work on *I Spy*, losing to Cosby, just days prior to departing for Italy.

THE RATINGS

I Spy's highest rated episode to date. The Wednesday night Nielsen pie was sliced as follows:

I Spy, *NBC: 54.4%*
The Danny Kaye Show, *CBS: 23.5%*
ABC Stage 67: *17.1%*
All others: *10.6%*

More than half the TVs turned on at 10 P.M. that night were tuned to *I Spy*. Only two programs received a higher audience share for the entire week, and those were both movies. No other regular weekly show had a bigger percentage of the viewing public than *I Spy* did.

The five shows:

Friday Movie, The Geisha Boy, *with Jerry Lewis, CBS: 54.8%*
Saturday Movie, Alfred Hitchcock's Rear Window, *NBC: 50.6%*

I Spy, Wednesday, NBC: 50.4%
Sunday Movie, Doris Day in Move Over, Darling, ABC: 49.8%
Jackie Gleason/The Honeymooners, Saturday, CBS: 44.2%

REVIEWS

For this installment, *TV Guide* praised *I Spy* in yet another Close Up listing (the sixth for the series).

But not everyone who tuned in was singing along with "Sophia," Earle Hagen's original song for this episode.

FROM THE MAIL BAG

"Dear Mr. Leonard: I enjoy the show *I Spy* very much. But THE MUSIC IS TOO LOUD! Sometimes it is louder than the spoken words and I can't hear what the actors say. Music is supposed to be 'background,' not to take over the show." E.E., Norfolk, VA.

"Dear Sirs: I have just finished watching *I Spy* for the 62nd time. In other words, every time it has been on, including the repeats. You've got the greatest theme song I've heard yet. Don't ever change it. Don't even try to do it over again. Don't even change the beginning where the tennis figure comes out. Don't ever turn sour like *The Man from U.N.C.L.E.* and write some ridiculous plots. If a writer approaches you with an idiotic episode, TEAR IT UP! I must admit, when you were in the Far East, it was the best 'period' of *I Spy*. Mexico and the United States were pretty good, too. *Italy is rather YUK*! Thanks for some 62 weeks of wonderful suspense and entertainment." H.S., address unknown.

"Gentlemen: The specific purpose of this letter is to express my increasing disappointment in this season's offering from *I Spy*. While creating good entertainment week after week is bound to tax even the best of abilities, the shows this season have been consistently poor from the scripts up. Admittedly, each of the scripts has a relatively good basis, but they appear to have been enlarged upon and finished by 'hack' writers. The acting ability of Robert Culp is unquestioned—but why has he become a perpetually love-stricken playboy with lines more suited to and expected from Bill Cosby? What happened to the moody, matter-of-fact, exciting, young man of last season? The talents of Mr. Cosby are equally unquestioned. However, an Emmy does not necessarily an actor make. Suddenly, he's the straight man, the worrier, and the deliverer from evil. His gift for comedy is equal to and balances out Culp's dramatic delivery. Why switch the roles? Two hard-working men, deadly serious about the business of spying, hip enough to break the drama with identification with the scene of today, have become a couple of slip-shod hippies engaged in skipping around the world with perpetual and 'hopeless' love affairs and glib dialog. What happened to my show?" J.R., Los Angeles, California.

In reply:

"Dear Miss R: A letter such as yours cannot go unanswered. It hurt. I rely on a cliché to help me out: It's impossible to please everyone—and I don't expect this facile answer to please you. Yet it is the truth, from here. The show's success this year exceeds that of last. That's my yardstick, but I must be honest, my argument is specious. I know what you mean. And you are right, moderately. But I believe my show is entitled to experiment, to find out what the weaknesses are, the strengths. I believe, too, we have aired shows this year at least as good as the best of last year. On the other hand, we have put on shows this year the likes of which we will never do again. Your letter is meaningful. I thank you for it. It's kind of a yardstick, too. Please do let me know when we have pleased you. Sincerely, Morton Fine, Producer—*I Spy*."

Cast

Rafaelia Carra, playing Sophia, at 23, through numerous appearances on TV variety shows, was already a star in Europe. She would continue working there in a career that spanned the late 1950s through the early 1980s.

Caterina Boratto (Contessa D'Orsini), prior to World War II, had caught the eye of Louis B. Mayer, who offered her a contract with MGM. Caterina, however, decided to return to her native Italy when war broke out. Once home, she resumed a long career in television and film, which had begun in 1937. She was 51 at the time of this appearance.

Gordon Mitchell (Angelo) was an American body builder and actor of minor accomplishments who moved to Italy in the early 1960s to find frequent work in the popular Steve Reeves' Hercules movies. After the period piece muscle-man epics ceased to be a fad, he successfully made the switch to playing heavies in spaghetti Westerns.

Enzo Cerusico (Gino), through no fault of his own, became a player in the decision that would eventually end *I Spy*. Stay tuned.

39. **"VENDETTA"**; Written by: Marion Hargrove; Directed by: Alf Kjellin; Location: Rome; First airing: 10/5/66. Repeated: 5/3/67.

In Rome, Kelly is kidnapped and brought to trial at a countryside estate. His accusers: a family out for revenge. They believe that Kelly murdered their son, who served under him during the Korean conflict. Kelly's only defense: Scott.

Assessment

The on-location photography, the authentic Italian performances, and the personal revelations within this story help to make "Vendetta" a tense and engrossing drama.

"Vendetta" is an atypical *I Spy* segment, and some of the story elements are hard to follow due to the heavy accents of the principal players. Even thought the script is crystal clear concerning the motives behind Romolo shooting his twin brother in the back 16 years ago, you may need to listen carefully—the reasons for murder were cowardice and dishonor. Romolo, a coward under fire, killed his brother because he was afraid. He blamed Kelly so he would not lose face and dishonor his family.

Here, as in "Bet Me a Dollar," we are shown the complexities of Kelly Robinson and why, when he is not occupied by work, he can be his own worst enemy.

In the new millennium, Robert Culp said, "Kelly would be dead of alcoholism. Either that or he might be a kept man. But they'd have to lock him up to keep the booze away from him."[8]

Kelly does seem to have two Achilles heels: wine and women—usually without a song.

In this episode, as in "Bet Me," Kelly is bored and looking for trouble. He decides to sit by the pool and drink his lunch. Once there, he catches the eye of a pretty, young Italian girl. She invites him to join her for a day of sightseeing, but it is all a setup. He will be abducted, imprisoned, and subjected to a trial by a family needing to justify their desire to kill him.

For the tag scene, Kelly is again drinking and still can't resist the come-on of a pretty girl. Scott refuses to watch. He knows Kelly will pay dearly. This time the payment is a sock in the jaw from a jealous boyfriend. Scott catches Kelly as he falls, just as he had earlier, just as he no doubt will do again.

Many TV shows during the 1960s took their turns at doing episodes built around a "kangaroo court." It seemed to be a popular theme and the variations could often be fascinating. Marion Hargrove gives it a good turn here, creating a parallel in his story with that of Romulus and Remus, the architects of betrayal, as well as introducing information regarding Kelly's military past.

We find out that Kelly served as a young lieutenant in Korea (both Kelly and Culp would have been 22 during the final year of the Korean conflict).

The Story Behind the Story

For the third time in this new block of episodes, all was shot on location.

This would be the second Italian-themed episode to be aired by NBC, pushed forward in the rotation by six positions.

It was a thrill for Robert Culp to meet and work with Victor Francen. Culp had admired Francen's work in many movies he had seen as a boy.

Culp: "He had a strong presence. He was a powerful actor. In many ways I learned a lot about acting from watching him, and other performers like him from that time. When we met to shoot 'Vendetta,' I told him that I enjoyed his work. He could tell I was a fan. I didn't hide it very well. And he was most gracious about it. He felt honored to be appearing in our show. He knew all about it. So we were both somewhat humbled.

"I thought 'Vendetta' was very well done. I liked that only Italian was spoken in the teaser. That was very daring. A good job, all around."[9]

CULP & COSBY ON SET REWRITE

Ad-libs are kept to a minimum for this episode. However, when Scott attempts to rescue Kelly from the loft where he is being kept prisoner, both are discovered, and cut off with no route for escape. That is in the script. This isn't:

KELLY: "Gentlemen, I don't think you've met my failure."
SCOTT: "How do you do? I've come to rescue him."
KELLY: "And I've embarrassed him again. And I'm sorry."

RATINGS

I Spy won its time slot, as usual, but its lead was cut down by a special segment of *ABC Stage 67*, which brought that series its best numbers yet. The program, entitled, "The Kennedy Wit," was produced and narrated by Jack Parr, and featured films, stills and recordings from JFK campaign speeches, news conferences, informal moments, and interviews.

The Wednesday 10 to 11 P.M. time slot was tracked by A.C. Nielsen as follows:

I Spy, *NBC: 38.5%*
ABC Stage 67, "The Kennedy Wit": 30.8%
The Danny Kaye Show, *CBS: 22.2%*
All others: 9.4%

12—The Fifth Block of Episodes

Even with *ABC Stage 67* having a good night, *I Spy* still had one of the biggest audience shares of the week. It came in seventh, bettered by three network movies, *The Jackie Gleason Show* featuring *The Honeymooners*, and just slightly by *Bonanza*, and *The Man from U.N.C.L.E.*

CAST

Victor Francen (Don Federico) was nearly 80 at the time of this filming. He had 100 credits in Italian cinema, and scores more in American-made movies from the 1930s through the '50s, including *Confidential Agent,* from 1945, and *Hell and High Water*, from 1951. This episode was his last known work on film, although he would live until 1977.

Massimo Serato (the elegant and fair Emilio Paolo) was 50. Three years later he would appear in an episode of *It Takes a Thief*, entitled

Victor Francen and a fan, "Vendetta" (© 3 F Prod.).

"Three Virgins of Rome." His other 150 credits in film and TV were all Italian productions.

40. **"TO FLORENCE WITH LOVE"** part 1; Written by: Norman Borisoff; Directed by: Robert Butler; Location: Rome to Florence; First airing: 11/23/66

In Florence, Kelly and Scott must guard a priceless da Vinci painting being returned to Italy as a goodwill gesture. The owner and courier is an American girl unaware that thieves surround her every move.

At the end of World War II, or so the story goes, Katie Cartwright's mother visited Florence and had a romance with a married man. Unable to divorce his wife due to Italian law, the wealthy gentleman gave a gift to his lover to remember him by—Leonardo da Vinci's original painting of the Madonna. Flash forward to 1966. Katie wishes to bring the da Vinci home to Florence and personally present the painting to an Italian museum. The American government considers this to be a priceless public relations coup, and assigns Kelly and Scott to watch over Katie and her Madonna.

Kelly is more protective of Katie than the painting. She meets Aldo, the son of the man who originally gave the Madonna away as a gift. Aldo is the stunning image of his father, as Katie is of her mother. The romance that was forbidden between the elder lovers may now blossom between their offspring.

During all of this, the painting is stolen, then recovered. After it is presented to the museum, Aldo tells Katie that the painting on display is a fake. This means the authentic work of art will need to be found, recovered, and exchanged for the bogus Madonna, now under tight museum security. What follows, in part two, anyway, is a heist caper.

Assessment

The pacing is a bit slow. This story began as an idea for an hour-long TV episode, then was tricked up with an eye toward developing it into an *I Spy* feature film, then downgraded and retooled as two one-hour episodes.

Let's back up. In late 1965, Sheldon Leonard announced his plans to produce an *I Spy* movie for the big screen, to be shot during the summer of 1966. "To Florence with Love" was briefly considered as the basis for that project. But, with all the traveling, *I Spy* took longer to shoot than the average TV series, and the break between the production of season one and season two was a mere two-and-a-half weeks. The feature film was shelved and the script being prepared for it was placed into production as a two-part story.

In part one, the location sequences are impressive, as we travel from Rome to Florence. Notice the scenes shot on the train. An Arriflex camera and quartz lights made this possible. Fouad Said made it possible. What a difference an outcast director of photography, a little camera, and a real train can make.

The Story Behind the Story

By making this a doubleheader, the cost of bringing out a bigger star like Joey Heatherton was justified, and the story was able to retain the plot complications given to it when it was being structured as a feature.

In regard to spending time in romantic Florence with the beautiful Joey Heatherton:

Preece: "I must have been better looking than I thought. I was just the script guy. And you wouldn't think the script guy should do so well. But Joey made me do things I shouldn't have done. She was a wild little girl."[10]

Culp: "That actress was so spaced, wherever she was, she wasn't in Italy. She was sure pretty, though. Somebody took a still of us by Michael Angelo's doors depicting the levels of hell. She wasn't there, Jack."[11]

RATINGS

"To Florence with Love" got off to a great start when part one aired a few days before Thanksgiving, 1966. The Nielsen findings for Wednesday at 10 to 11 P.M. were:

I Spy, *NBC: 42.4%*
The Danny Kaye Show, *CBS: 26.1%*
ABC Stage 67, Olivia de Havilland in *"Noon Wine": 24.9%*
All remaining channels: *9.6%*

Disconnected, Culp & Heatherton in Florence (© 3 F Prod.).

For only the second time in the season, *I Spy* just barely missed making the top five shows of the week to pull in the highest audience share. The top five were:

Saturday Movie, Fame Is the Name of the Game, *NBC: 53.1%*
Sunday Movie, Can-Can, *with Frank Sinatra, ABC: 44.2%*
The Jackie Gleason Show, *Saturday, CBS: 44.5%*
Friday Movie, Barabbas, *with Anthony Quinn, CBS: 42.8%*
Bonanza, *Sunday, NBC: 42.7%*
I Spy *(at number six), Wednesday, NBC: 42.4%*

Cast & Crew

Joey Heatherton had a youthful mystique about her, a Lolita-like "sex-kitten" image, which eventually took her to the Las Vegas stage, clad in miniskirts and go-go boots.

Joey's father was a song-and-dance man and, at an early age, she followed in his dancing footsteps, becoming one of the children in the New York stage production of *The Sound of Music*. She appeared in a small handful of lightweight films, such as 1964's *Where Love Has Gone*.

Arthur Batanides (Rocco) was well known to Sheldon Leonard from his four appearances on *The Dick Van Dyke Show* and *The Andy Griffith Show*. In 1966, he had already played nearly every TV show of the decade. He would be back to play more heavies on *I Spy*.

Mario Badolati (Bonfiglio) had appeared in *Love with the Proper Stranger* with Steve McQueen and Natalie Wood, as well as a 1966 episode of *Mission: Impossible*.

Norman Borisoff was well qualified when it came to the subject of Italian art, having written the early 1960s documentary *The Titan: Story of Michelangelo*. Leonard knew him through his association with *The Andy Griffith Show*.

Bud Molin, who had been honored with a pair of EDDIE Award nominations for his work on *I Spy*, left the series after assembling part one of "Florence." His talents took him into feature films, as the editor on *They Call Me Mr. Tibbs*, then often working for Carl Reiner, cutting, among others, *Where's Poppa*, *The Jerk*, and *Dead Men Don't Wear Plaid*.

41. **"TO FLORENCE WITH LOVE"** part 2.; Written by: Norman Borisoff; Directed by: Robert Butler; Location: Florence; First airing: 11/30/66

In part two, Kelly and Scott are conned. They believe they are breaking into a museum to replace the gallery's forgery with the real da Vinci painting. The truth: There is no honor among thieves.

Assessment

It is a hard concept to buy that Kelly and Scott would think the only way to return the authentic Madonna to the museum would be to break in, and to do so with the aid of a group of art thieves. They say they must do this in order to allow the museum curator to save face. Yet, after all their hard work, they end up going to the curator anyway and embarrassing him over his poor security.

Reality must be suspended further for us to buy into the idea of a pair of pros like Kelly and Scott partnering up with a hopeless amateur like Katie.

When asked about this unbelievable plot device, Culp smiled, shrugged and said, "I didn't write it."[12]

The Story Behind the Story

Watch for Robert Culp doing his own stunts during the pole-vaulting sequence.

Culp: "I was a pole-vaulter in school. It changed my life and made me who I am. So, for this, I went out and I got a pole-vault and I started practicing sprints. I was working out

Heatherton and partners in crime, Culp and Cosby, Florence, 1966 (© 3 F Prod.).

on the field and I pulled something in my groin. I was 35 years old and I shouldn't have been doing this. My body was telling me that. So I babied it, and I told myself 'I can do this, even with the pulled groin muscle.' So I ran up, I did it, and I just barely got over."[13]

RATINGS

For the airing of part two of "Florence," the numbers were significantly down from those of part one. During the Wednesday night time slot, Nielsen ranked the shows as:

ABC Stage 67, "The Life & Legend of Marilyn Monroe": *39.7%*
I Spy, *NBC: 29.1%*
The Danny Kaye Show, *CBS: 23.1%*
All remaining channels: 11.0%

Although critically acclaimed, *ABC Stage 67*, which featured a series of one-hour dramatic anthologies, had failed against its competition. A few weeks earlier, as an experiment, ABC tried a documentary called "The Kennedy Wit," under the banner of *Stage 67*. The ratings improved. Now the network tried it again with a biographical profile on the legendary Monroe, narrated by John Huston. This time ABC struck gold and toppled *I Spy* from the top of the hill.

Norma Jean was a worthy opponent. But she was helped along by a two-part *I Spy* story that only hardcore fans of the series would be interested in seeing wrapped up.

FROM THE MAIL BAG

"Dear Gentlemen, Concerning the show of *I Spy* on November 23rd, my wife and I are definitely opposed to your two-part drama policy set by this program. We feel this is an attempt to force us to watch the following episode, which seems very degrading to the program. *I Spy* is a program capable of holding peoples' interest without such tactics." J.D.B., Fullerton, CA.

"Dear Mr. Leonard: Years ago, in the early days, I watched *Gunsmoke* every week. It was a good program—then. You know what happened? I stopped watching it because I couldn't stand a half-hour of material dragged out to one hour. You want to know what else? One hour's material dragged out for two hours will make me drop *I Spy* from my watching, too." D.H., San Diego, CA.

CAST & CREW

Joey Heatherton continued to enjoy popularity through sexy Serta mattress commercials and frequent appearances on Dean Martin's variety hour. In 1971, her good fortunes began to change. First, her football star husband, Lance Rentzel, was arrested for exposing himself to a young girl. Divorce followed. Next, Joey found herself out of fashion with the changing times.

Arthur Batanides (Rocco) would still be acting in the 1980s, playing Max Kirkland in the *Police Academy* movies.

Mario Badolati (Bonfiglio) would pass away several months after the completion of this two-part episode.

Norman Borisoff, the writer of this two-part episode, would be placed on a second *I Spy* assignment immediately following this job. That script, "39 Ways to Go," would remain unproduced. Borisoff would go on to write for *The Saint* and *Starsky & Hutch*.

Bob Lewis, after Molin's departure, stepped in to finish the cutting on "Florence." Leonard knew him from *The Andy Griffith Show* and *Gomer Pyle*. What is wrong with this episode has nothing to do with the editing, yet this would be the only work Lewis would do for the series.

42. **"FATHER ABRAHAM"**; Written by: Steven Kandel; Directed by: Tony Leader; Location: Rome; First airing: 12/21/66

Kelly and Scott, entrusted with the life of a fellow agent who is being used as bait in a plot to foil enemy spies, are foiled themselves by the colleague's well meaning but overbearing father, army general Shaw.

Shaw is unaware that his son, Gary, a brilliant research chemist, is on assignment to give bogus information under torture.

Assessment

With the exception of a few shots actually taken in Rome, this episode is dull. The writing, direction, and even the acting, on the part of the guest performers, are heavy-handed and, therefore, ineffective.

Steven Kandel, responsible for some of *I Spy's* best studies on the relationship between Kelly and Scott, reworked many of the elements from his superior story, "So Coldly Sweet." The situation here is reversed. Instead of a Russian feeding false information to the agents of the West, we now have an American feeding bogus scientific lingo to Soviet spies.

In an effort to add a personal stake in the story for Kelly and Scott, a former buddy and spy hands them their assignment; kidnap, torture and break a young rocket fuel specialist. Gary Shaw, their assignment, is a friend.

The father/son issue is way over-the-top. General Shaw is too quick to believe that his son is capable of nothing good. And Dad is a bull-headed, hard-nosed, military man who warrants little, if any, sympathy or understanding. It is asking too much from the viewer to care once the end of the story finally arrives and we get to see the general gain respect for his boy.

"Father Abraham" is an example of a story that tries to get personal, and tries to be important, but fails on both accounts.

The title references the biblical character of Abraham, who is told by an angel to sacrifice his son.

The Story Behind the Story

Either NBC or Three F Productions was taking great liberties in the information they were feeding *TV Guide*, which proclaimed this episode as being "filmed on location." Less than a quarter of this episode was actually shot in Italy. Some well-staged sequences create the illusion that Kelly and Scott are escorting Gary on a day of sightseeing and barhopping in Rome. Truth is, actor Tony Bill, who plays Gary, never left the magical world of Desilu.

For the first time in the series, Kelly and Scott encounter a pair of rogue Soviet agents who are unaware of the Americans' true identity. This was not a mistake on the part of the series. It was an indication that Vacaro and his associates were working outside of the Soviet inner circle.

CULP & COSBY ON SET REWRITE

The script, and the filmed episode, have Kelly and Scott strolling through Rome with a drunk Gary. At one point, not in the script, Gary pauses and leans over a wall, as if he is going to vomit. Culp says to Cosby, "It's your turn to hold the forehead. I held the forehead in Japan last year."

Later, after Kelly and Scott are knocked unconscious in their hotel room, the script has both wake up seconds apart, responding to a ringing phone. In the filmed episode, Culp and Cosby had a better idea. Kelly wakes to the phone, answers it, then goes into the bathroom and returns with a damp washcloth. He drops it onto Scott's face. A grumpy Scott removes the cloth from over his eyes and says:

SCOTT: "Now ... have I ever done that to you?"

KELLY: "You know, there have been times I've enjoyed your work, Thelma. This wasn't one of them. Come on, Thel. Up you go."

SCOTT: "You just wait until I wake up first one time."

The improvisation continues. As Culp helps Cosby into the bathroom, he notices a stain on his pants, and says:

KELLY: "Look what happened to my pants! How am I going to get that off? That's all your fault. Every time you go bad, I've got to send my stuff to the cleaners."

Later, after Kelly and Scott locate the villa where Gary is being tortured, the agents must climb over a high stone wall—*four different times*. Culp had the idea to use a trampoline to give himself a boost at jumping up. Watch closely, as they leave the villa. Scott struggles to get over the wall. Kelly runs toward it, leaves camera's view for a split second, then springs up to the wall, easily pulling himself over. Michael Preece remembers Cosby wishing he had thought of bringing a trampoline of his own. Then comes the ad-lib:

KELLY: "And you did not trust the magnificence and brilliance of my plan."
SCOTT: "No, because I'm tired of leaping across this wall on my shins."

The Censors

NBC Broadcast Standards wrote:

- "The scenes in which Vacaro tries to force information from Gary must avoid the detailed presentation of brutality. Your utmost restraint and caution will be necessary to insure acceptability of these scenes. In particular, Gary's painful reactions should not be sensationalized with screams, writhing, etc.
- "Please reduce the number of deaths to one or two rather than three."

The Ratings

Nielsen rating results for Wednesday night, December 21, 1966, 10 to 11 P.M.:

I Spy, NBC: *39.0%*
The Danny Kaye Show, CBS: *33.5%*
ABC Stage 67, Geraldine Page in "A Christmas Memory": *19.9%*
All others: *8.7%*

I Spy was down a bit, due to unusually strong competition from *The Danny Kaye Show*, with its Christmas special, featuring Peggy Lee and Wayne Newton, and *ABC Stage 67*, with the premiere airing of Truman Capote's "A Christmas Memory." Nonetheless, *I Spy* won the time period, and rounded out the top ten shows of the week, concerning highest audience share.

From the Mail Bag

"Dear Sirs, I have always enjoyed your show—it tops my list of favorites. The combo of Cosby and Culp is superb! And the performance of Tony Bill was *quite* up to standards. Is it possible to have Mr. Tony Bill return to *I Spy* on additional guest shots?" Mrs. A.S.G., La Plata, Maryland.

"Dear Sirs: I have decided Robert Culp needs a haircut. When a man's hair curls around and over his ears, it's about time for clippers. He looks very untidy in his personal grooming because of this. Thank you." Miss C.B.E., Walla Walla, Washington.

"Dear Whosit: Thanx for your consistently enjoyable program, which most of my friends and even my husband take time to watch. We like the acting, humor, marvelous naturalness of the stars' relationship. Please don't stop." Mrs. N.O., Chatswork, CA.

"Dear Sir: The following is to be considered as a letter of protest! I am a faithful fan of the program *I Spy*, but I have had it up to here! In plain and simple language, it amounts to this: CUT ROBERT CULP'S HAIR!! He looks plain sloppy. You can't convince me that a tennis player would have hair as long as that. Incidentally, I'm no old fogey, I'm 23 years old and enjoy the life of a single girl. From my own point of view, Culp's sex-appeal goes down the tubes every time I see that unkept, messy mop of Vitalis hair. Ug and Arg! For curiosity, I'd like a reply. That way, I'll know if this letter gets farther than the janitor's box!!" Miss K.M., Fresno, CA.

In reply:

"Dear Miss M, your letter got further than the janitor's box, its contents noted and I have just talked with Mr. Culp AGAIN about his hair. Thank you so much for letting us hear from you. Sincerely, Morton Fine, Producer, *I Spy*."

Cast & Crew

Tony Bill was 26 when he took this role. He had been appearing in TV and films for several years, including six appearances on *Dr. Kildare*, as well as dressing up in drag for Blake Edwards in the Steve McQueen, Jackie Gleason comedy, *Soldier in the Rain*. In the early '70s he changed his career emphasis to producing. His third film was 1973's *The Sting*, the highest grossing film up to that time, which also brought him an Academy Award. He continued to act, as well, appearing in Warren Beatty's 1975 comedy, *Shampoo*, playing a director. In 1980 Bill became a director for real with *My Bodyguard*. He is still active as a producer, director, and occasional actor.

Austin Willis (General Shaw) came from Canada, where he was already a TV personality, hosting that country's version of *Your Hit Parade*. He would have recurring roles in three short-lived American-made series. In the last of the three, he played a navy admiral. He looked older here than his 49 years.

David Sheiner (Vaccaro), age 38, was last seen as Turk in "Carry Me Back to Old Tsing-Tao."

Tony Leader would only direct one episode of *I Spy*. Michael Preece has a theory as to why.

Preece: "Tony Leader was too meticulous. He wasn't freewheeling like Culp and Cosby. He would say, 'Any resemblance between this script and what you're doing is purely coincidental.' He was one of the more strict directors, not understanding ad-libs."[14]

Leader started as a director and producer on radio. On TV, usually under the name of Anton M. Leader, he directed segments of *Gilligan's Island*, *Mr. Lucky*, and *Lost in Space*. In 1965 he won the Western Heritage Award for "Horse Fighter," an episode of *The Virginian*. He would continue directing for *Star Trek*, *Hawaii Five-O* and *It Takes a Thief*, before retiring in 1971.

43. **"ROME TAKE AWAY THREE"**; Teleplay by: Bill Billinger, Morton Fine & David Friedkin; Story by: Bill Billinger; Directed by: Alf Kjellin; Location: Rome; First airing: 12/28/66. Repeated: 6/21/67.

Investigating a serious security leak in Rome, Kelly and Scott encounter a blackmail plot involving a U.S. embassy employee being threatened with scandal.

Behind the blackmail is hoodlum Coly Collisi, a deported American filled with hatred for his former homeland.

Kelly and Scott attempt to gain Collisi's trust, offering their services as bodyguards. Their true goal is to get proof that the gangster is responsible for the death of a State Department official, or to eliminate him.

Assessment

"Rome Take Away Three" was filmed only in part on location. But the scenes shot in Los Angeles have better production value than most: a hilltop skeet shooting scene in Griffith Park, and a beach sequence at Malibu's Paradise Cove.

"Rome Take Away Three" is hard-hitting, cold-blooded, spy-versus-spy fare. In this story, Dean Sherman has sold out, and now he wants to die. He hires a mercenary to kill him, hoping that this type of death by an unknown assailant will spare his wife and children the disgrace of having to discover that he betrayed them and their government.

But Kelly and Scott save Dean, then ply him with alcohol. He admits he fell for a woman, an agent, and then allowed himself to turn over government secrets because he was being blackmailed. Before Kelly and Scott can persuade him to divulge the name of his blackmailer, the self-loathing Sherman jumps to his death.

A string of three bodies explains the title, and leads our agents to Coli Collisi, the American-hating, ruthless trader of information.

Kelly and Scott manage to gain employment with the thug. Their real goal is to find out if Collisi is the one who broke Dean Sherman, and, if so, to eliminate him.

When they beat and torture Collisi, this is a stark example of how ruthless Kelly and Scott can be. They toss him into the trunk of a car, take him to the scene of a murder, and frame him for the killing. It would be unsatisfying for them to merely kill Collisi. Instead, they drag him around the room, wiping his fingerprints on the furniture, then drop him on the couch next to the woman he had strangled. They want to see him get convicted for murder and sent to the Italian gallows.

In 1966, on any other American TV series, this degree of brutality was not only unseen, but unthinkable. *I Spy* was opening a nasty door to the depiction of espionage, crime, rage, and violence.

The violence was in the script, Culp and Cosby intensified the acts, making them more brutal, more real, more disturbing.

RATINGS

"Rome Take Away Three" had one of the best ratings of *I Spy's* entire second season. Nielsen found that more than half the TV sets running at the time in America were tuned to this episode. The results were:

I Spy, *NBC: 51.1%*
The Danny Kaye Show, *CBS: 32.8%*
News Special, *Year-End Review, ABC: 9.0%*
All others: *10.5%*

I Spy, more so than any other prime-time program, on any network, drew the highest audience share of the entire week. The top five were:

I Spy, *Wednesday, NBC: 51.1%*
Tuesday Movie, *Sandra Dee in* Tammy Tell Me True, *NBC: 45.9%*
The Jackie Gleason Show, *Saturday, CBS: 49.5%*
Green Acres, *Wednesday, CBS: 44.4%*
Hollywood Palace, *New Year's Eve, Saturday, ABC: 44.3%*

FROM THE MAIL BAG

"Dear Sirs, I saw your December 28 *I Spy* show with Nehemiah Persoff, and me and my family thought it was just great, as usual. I think Bill Cosby is the best actor and comedian on TV. Keep up the good work!" J.G., location unknown.

"Gentlemen: I was very disappointed in *I Spy* of December 28. The show depicted a situation in which the agents were absolutely positive of the identification of a particular

12—The Fifth Block of Episodes 215

criminal, but were unable to come up with definite proof of his guilt. They therefore manufactured evidence by planting him into position, unconscious, at the scene of the murder he had ordered committed, so he would be 'caught red-handed.' I think that this is an example of unethical procedure. It was also a violation of the right of an individual to a fair trial. What I am objecting to is the way the 'solution' was presented as a justifiable one. I enjoy watching your show because it is usually characterized by a refreshing sense of proportion, and I trust I will enjoy it in the future for this quality, despite its absence in one episode." T.P., Redwood City, California.

"Dear Sirs: My friends and I saw your December 7 ('Lisa') and December 28 shows and agreed these were to be seen again. Could you please show them in the summer. Thank you very much." L.M., location unknown.

"Dear Sirs: This show is tremendous. It's so packed with action, and Bill Cosby and Robert Culp have such a spontaneous reaction to each other, and they are marvelous actors. I have never seen two people act so well together." J.B., Minneapolis, Minnesota.

"Dear Sirs: I'm writing to tell you how much I enjoy *I Spy*. It's a great television series. Not too dramatic, and not too funny. Well, anyhow, you should know what I mean. The time *I Spy* is on is perfect, because it doesn't

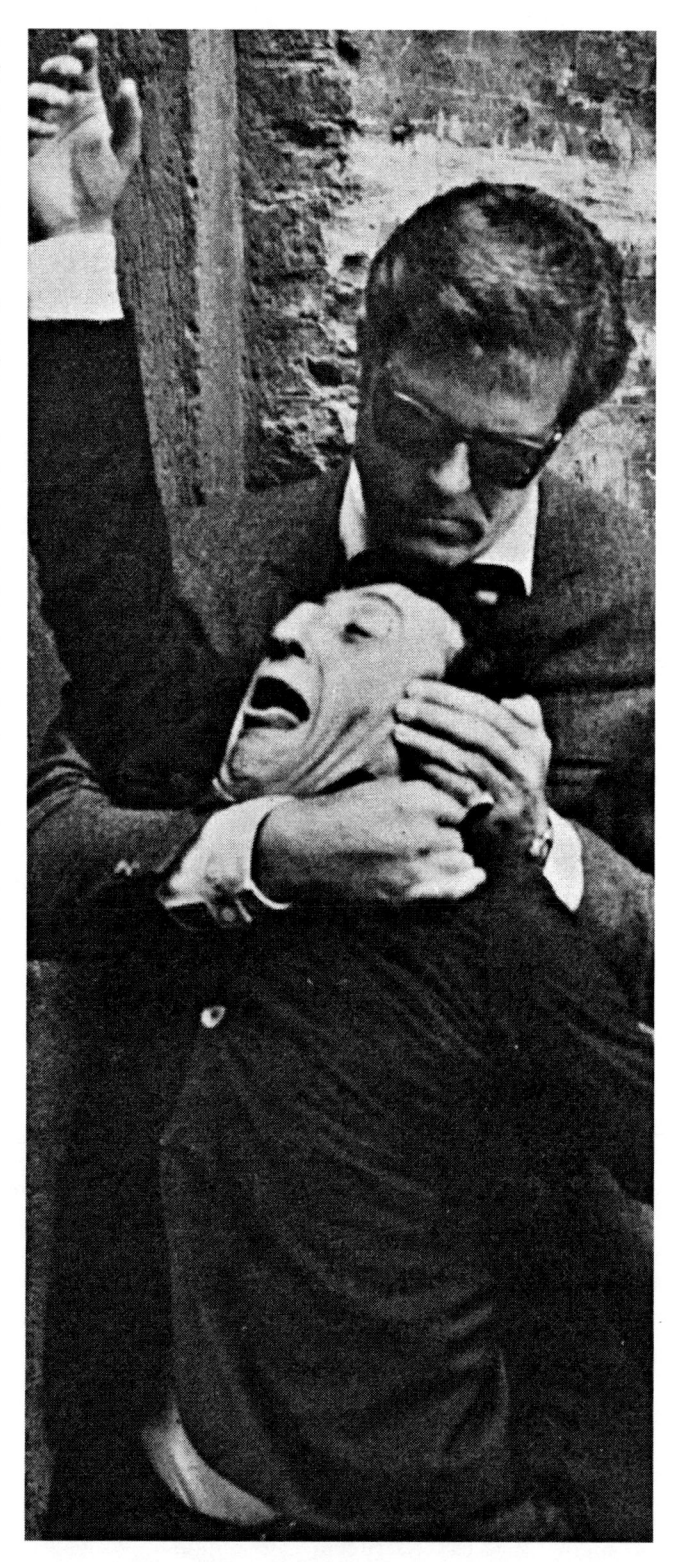

Culp looking at his unidentified victim, into the face of death, the future of TV violence (© 3 F Prod.).

interfere with my homework or anything like that. I'm 14. Robert Culp and Bill Cosby are perfect for the roles they both play. Thanks for listening." F.M., Mineola, New York.

Cast & Crew

Nehemiah Persoff (Coli Collisi) would chalk up over 200 credits in TV and film, spanning the late 1940s into the late 1990s. He was featured prominently in 1950s films *The Harder They Fall*, *The Wrong Man*, and *Al Capone*. On TV, he appeared in nearly every drama in production from the 1950s through the 1990s. He was 47 here, and would return for a second *I Spy* during the series' third season.

Ulla Stromstedt (Tilde), one year prior to this, was a regular on *Flipper*. Beautiful and certainly not without talent, she would never achieve stardom.

Elisha Cook (Erick Magnuson) would serve as one of the three to be taken away from Rome. He started acting on the stage at 14. He had many death scenes in over 200 TV and film roles, including one in *The Maltese Falcon*. He was 63.

Alf Kjellin (Dean Sherman) was the very same Alf Kjellin who directed this episode. A competent actor, Kjellin's willingness to play the doomed embassy man allowed impressive sequences to be shot in Rome with his character being tailed by Kelly and Scott.

Bill Ballinger only worked for *I Spy* once. He wrote the first draft of "Rome Take Away Three." Friedkin and Fine decided the teleplay needed serious reworking and Billinger ended up sharing the writing credit with the two producers.

44. **"TONIA"**; Written by: Michael Zagor; Directed by: Alf Kjellin; Location: Rome; First airing: 1/4/67. Repeated: 6/28/67.

In Rome, a Communist Party leader with a grudge to settle against Kelly, attempts to break up Kelly and Scott. His primary weapon, playing on Scott's fondness for Tonia, a lovely revolutionary. His killer punch, frame Kelly for Tonia's murder.

Assessment

"Tonia" is beautifully written. Alf Kjellin's direction is consistently good in both Rome and at Desilu. Leslie Uggams, new to acting, makes an impressive appearance.

Michael Zagor had an agenda to write a love story for Bill Cosby. "Trial by Treehouse," produced earlier in the season, was just that, albeit a reluctant love story. Now, with this script, Alexander Scott would be a willing participant from nearly his first glimpse of the girl named Tonia. For that reason, this episode leaves its mark on history.

Scott believes his introduction to Tonia is a chance meeting. Actually, it has been orchestrated by a Communist leader named Zugman. Tonia is a pawn. Zugman is seeking revenge against Kelly and has devised a plan to break up the team of Robinson and Scott.

It is rare that *I Spy* makes reference to the race of the two leads. This is one of the few instances. Tonia, the daughter of an American USO performer who chose to stay in Italy after the end of World War II, speaks not only the English she learned from her mother, but the bigotry. She has inherited a low opinion of White America. She accuses Scott of being someone who "carries the tennis racket of the White man." By the time she sees the true Alexander Scott, both are falling in love.

Cos and the Communist, with Leslie Uggams, Rome, 1966 (© 3 F Prod.).

It's Kelly turn to disapprove. He should know more than anyone, spies do not have the luxary of falling in love.

When Tonia is killed by Zugman, Kelly is framed for the murder. Zugman feels close to victory, but he underestimates the friendship and the trust between Kelly and Scott.

The stand-out scenes between the stars include the dramatic moment in the bar where Kelly voices his disapproval over Scott's feelings for Tonia, and the confrontation scene in the billards room, where Kelly is accused of the girl's death and Scott must decide if he believes his partner is innocent or guilty.

Watch for a rare moment in *I Spy* of Scott losing his cool.

The stellar performance, however, is that of David Opatashu as Zugman, who disguises the Communist leader's ruthlessness behind a facade of calm.

RATINGS

Wednesday night, 10 to 11 P.M., according to Nielsen:

I Spy, *NBC: 37.6%*
ABC Stage 67, *Cliff Robertson, "Trap of Solid Gold": 25.9%*
The Danny Kaye Show, *CBS: 25.2%*
The rest: *14.1%*

When compared to all the other prime-time shows during the week, *I Spy* had the seventh largest share of any program on any of the networks.

From the Mail Bag

"Gentlemen: I know he is supposed to be a 'tennis bum,' YOU know he is supposed to be a 'tennis bum,' but we never SEE him as a 'tennis bum.' It might re-identify his cover a little, if Kelly and Scotty had an episode involving training for, or actual participation in, a tennis match. Also, I have particularly enjoyed the episodes set in Italy. None of your episodes have I not enjoyed—but I get the impression Mr. Cosby feels slightly self-conscious in the role of a lover, as he has been cast recently. But he really should not—if he is as much a man as he appears on TV. It seemed unnatural when Kelly got all the girls and Scotty did not. Anyhow, I've said my piece." Miss M.A.V., location unknown.

"Dear Sirs—'Tonia' was the best *I Spy* of this season! It ranks second only to last year's 'It's All Done With Mirrors.' This show was *unbelievably fantastic!* Everything about it was perfect. Michael Zagor should get an Emmy for his script. Please tell him that I think he's a fabulous writer! Leslie Uggams was *great* as Tonia! It goes without saying that ROBERT CULP (m'-man!) is *the greatest actor on television*. He can handle any part with *brilliance!* On this show he proved it again! My friends, all *I Spy*-nuts, and I all agree that he and Cos' (as we call Bill C.) were *too much* on 'Tonia.' I admit that I really cried when Scotty 'thought' that Kelly killed Tonia! I couldn't believe that Scotty would doubt Kelly! When we finally found out that he *didn't* believe it, *WOW!* I felt so sorry for poor Kelly! That was a *fantastic* situation to get them into! Beautifulness!

"If Bobby Culp doesn't get an Emmy *this year*, you should sue the Academy. Practically all the kids in my school will resort to hysteria, especially yours truly here! Show this to Bob Culp:

"Dear Bob (M'man)—YOU ARE THE *GREATEST*! I *LUV* YOU! Please send me an autographed pic of you! I'm 17, and have blue eyes and brown hair. (Big deal, you snort. Oh well). *You are my favorite* of *favorites*! The wonderfulness of yerself! Thanks for making *I Spy* what it is—the hippest, most intelligent and meaningful show on TV today!" E.K., Brooklyn, New York. "P.S.: *Please* get the Emmy! If you, down at *I Spy*, ever need any publicity or anything in Brooklyn, remember me. P.S.: Say 'hi' to Cos'! I *luv* him, too!"

"Dear Mr. Leonard, Sitting here this evening watching *I Spy* with Leslie Uggams playing a dramatic role, I feel compelled to write this short note. Robert Culp is becoming more unbelievable because he seems too much the comic these days. He hardly ever finishes a sentence anymore. The pausing, and hedging, and slurring of words, which was once so natural in little bits, is now sickening. This letter will probably mean nothing to you, and your million-dollar staff, but it rids me of a frustration created by all of you. Since I don't watch the show every week, I'm sure you won't concern yourself over lil' ole' me. So no hard feelings and away I go! Sincerely, One-Less-Aggravation from One-Less Aggravator," location unknown.

To: RCA/NBC, Mr. R. Sarnoff, Pres.
"Dear Sir: I'm a White man, not that it's important, *but*—I'm writing this in praise of Bill Cosby. I suppose you have other letters in his praise—but, if not, please read this one. Bill is a great guy—his acting and feeling on *I Spy*—Jan. 4, 1967—was great. I wish I could express myself better, but what I'm trying to say—Bill Cosby is a credit to all Americans. I know he's an actor, but such a kind, relaxed, wonderful guy—a great American. God bless him. I hope this helps all Negroes and Whites. This is a very modest letter—not proving a thing—but I would like you to show it to Bill. PLEASE!" D.A.C., St. Petersburg, Florida.

In reply:

"Dear Mr. C: Mr. Sarnoff has referred your letter of January 6 to NBC since it concerns broadcasting and I thank you for your generous comments on Bill Cosby and *I Spy*. I am sure Mr. Cosby and all connected with the program will be pleased to know your feelings, and thus, I have forwarded your comments to Triple-F Productions in Hollywood. Thank you again, for taking the time to write. Your enthusiasm and interest are most appreciated. Sincerely, Thomas Baum, NBC."

Cast & Crew

Leslie Uggams traveled to Rome for location production with Cosby and Culp. The balance of the show was filmed at Desilu.

Uggams began her show business career at the age of six when she was cast in a guest spot as Ethel Waters niece in *Beulah*.

Appearances at the Apollo Theater in Harlem followed, and Uggams was frequently featured as an opening act. Television came next. She began appearing on programs from the early '60s, singing on various variety shows. *I Spy* marked her dramatic acting debut at the age of 23. In the fall of 1969, she would be given her own variety series on CBS. She was heralded as the first Black female performer to star in such a capacity in prime time. The series lasted only three months. In 2001 she was nominated for a Tony as Best Lead Actress in a Play for *King Hedley II*.

Cosby: "Her performance was wonderful. Beautiful. She was a pleasure."[15]

David Opastashu made nearly 150 TV and film appearances between 1948 and 1989. He started in radio in New York City, during World War II, reading the news in Yiddish. By the 1950s and '60s he was appearing in TV all over the dial. The same year as his appearance here, at age 48, he played the ruler of a planet engaged in a 500-year-old war on *Star Trek*. In 1990, for his final TV performance, he won an Emmy for guest staring on the series *Gabriel's Fire*.

Ronald Freinberg made his television acting debut in this episode. He worked often on TV during the 1970s, showing up in *Hawaii Five-O* and *Mission: Impossible*, among others, usually playing individuals who were mentally challenged.

G.D. Spradlin, playing Kelly and Scott's regional director, was a lawyer turned oil man turned politician turned actor. He began on TV in the mid–1960s. He was 46 here, and would work well into the 1990s. Jack Webb enjoyed featuring him in the color episodes of *Dragnet*, and you can spot him playing the general who sends Martin Sheen up the river in *Apocalypse Now*. He would work with Culp again on the pilot for *Greatest American Hero*.

Bob Fritch, the third "Bob" to cut for *I Spy*, would edit two episodes for the series, starting here, and ending with "Child Out of Time." His work on both would be flawless. He had been a cutter for Leonard before on *The Andy Griffith Show*. He was also the man who edited the 1943 film, *My Friend Flicka*.

45. "ONE OF OUR BOMBS IS MISSING"; Written by: Barry Oringer; Directed by: Earl Bellamy; Location: Italy; First airing: 11/16/66

Kelly and Scott are sent to retrieve an atom bomb from an American plane that crashed in the Italian countryside. But both plane and bomb have vanished without a trace.

Angelo, a resident of the village near where the plane went down, divulges to the agents that the entire aircraft—piece by piece—has been distributed to the poor townspeople. And

Angelo is claiming to have the bomb. He offers to make a deal: The U.S. gets the nuclear weapon—if Kelly marries Angelo's daughter.

To prove that he truly has the weapon, Angelo brings Kelly and Scott a piece of it—and, in doing so, has inadvertently removed the safety, starting the self-destruct countdown.

And this is called a ticking clock.

Assessment

In the entertainment industry, this type of premise is known as a "high concept" story, meaning it is so unique anyone could describe it in one or two sentences.

The episode is rich in clichés. Scott pulls one of several wires free from the bomb, hoping to deactivate it and not vaporize every one within a 50-mile radius. We've seen this gimmick before. It was used, incidentally, in *Goldfinger*. Culp and Cosby's acting, especially here, is far above the cliché and overall goofiness of the rest of the episode. Kelly and Scott both expect to die. They don't share the village priest's faith. Father Bellini has prayed for them, and assures Scott that whichever wire he pulls will be the right one—and it is. Scott collapses on the bomb, unable to speak, unable to move. Kelly trembles and stutters, appears faint, and can't believe Scott picked the right wire. Father Bellini corrects him. The right choice was made by someone higher up.

The Story Behind the Story

Writer Barry Oringer recalls: "It was not my original idea. It came out of that marathon session. But I had a lot of fun writing it."[16]

When reminded that Earl Bellamy was nominated for an Emmy for his direction on this episode, Oringer laughed and said, "I was burnt up that *I* wasn't nominated."[17]

Despite receiving an Emmy nomination, this episode was passed over by NBC for a repeat showing.

"Bombs" had a severe problem, and his name was Earl Bellamy.

Bellamy was a director in a hurry. He stayed on schedule, within budget, and pleased his employers, as well as cast and crew, because everyone got to go home on time—or even early. The show paid the price.

Case in point: In the horrendous teaser, as Kelly and Scott entertain a pair of lovely ladies in their hotel room, both men pair off with their dates to slow dance. The camera stays on Scott and the lovely woman in his arms. Watch the shadows on the wall of Culp and his date, doing something reminiscent of the jitterbug. Clowning around as they were, off set, their shadows were being picked up by the camera. Yet Bellamy, in a hurry to move on, provided the editors with no other takes, and no other coverage.

There is a bad cut in the opening of act one. Ambassador Perkins is seen with his arms down at his sides. Then, suddenly, as the shot changes to a closer angle, his arms are crossed. Either the editor missed it or didn't care—both unlikely, considering the episode was cut by an old pro named Basil Wrangell. More likely, Mr. Wrangell had little to work with. There were no other shots. There were no "reverse angles," or "singles," or alternate "masters." What they had was a well-liked director we will refer to as "One-Take Bellamy."

And Bellamy would return for the third season.

12 — The Fifth Block of Episodes

CULP & COSBY ON SET REWRITE

Not in the script:

Scott refers to Kelly twice as "Hoby." The name was that of the character Culp played on *Trackdown*.

Cosby also works in a reference regarding his own past. When speaking to the two babes in the teaser, Scott says, "Do you guys like football? I was one of the great halfbacks of our time."

Culp, like Cosby, makes a personal statement. When Scott is trying to convince Kelly he should marry Maria, Culp, now going through his second divorce, adds the line, "You know what it is when you go into a bad marriage? You know what that's like? I can tell you, man. When you walk out of the courtroom, ..." The sentence trails, Culp never gets a chance to finish.

LOCKED ROOM #6

The gag is clever: Kelly and Scott are literally gagged, preventing the usual joking around and ad-libs. The script called for them to be gagged. Message from Barry Oringer?

RATINGS

"One of Our Bombs" proved to be anything but—at least, in regard to the ratings. For Wednesday night at 10 P.M., Nielsen claimed the audience was divided as follows:

I Spy, *NBC: 46.9%*
The Danny Kaye Show, *CBS: 27.7%*
ABC Stage 67, *Anthony Perkins in "Evening Primrose": 9.2%*
All others: 18.2%

I Spy was also the leader when it came to the highest audience share captured by any prime-time program during the week. The top five were:

I Spy, *Wednesday, NBC: 46.9%*
Sunday Movie, *The Courtship of Eddie's Father, ABC: 46.8%*
The Jackie Gleason Show, *Saturday, CBS: 46.0%*
Saturday Night Movie, *Come September, NBC: 45.6%*
Bob Hope Special, *Wednesday, NBC: 42.8%*

FROM THE MAIL BAG

"Dear Sirs: Congratulations on your fine program, November 16. Not only was it exciting all the way through, but the ending, where Scott could have pulled any of the five cords to de-activate the bomb, had a deep religious significance." B.H., Artesia, New Mexico.

"Dear Sirs: Congratulations on showing the possible proper race relations on November 16. The friendly relations between a colored *beautiful* woman and White man (Culp) and between a colored man (Cosby) and a White girl. The further shift to a romantic scene between White and White, and Negro and Negro, proved what most intelligent Civil Rights workers have been saying all along: 'Just because your sister goes to school with a Negro, doesn't mean he'd want to marry her (or vice-versa).' I believe a show such as this will help pave the way for more peaceful race relations." J.L., location unknown.

"Dear Sirs: I had great respect for *everyone* connected with *I Spy* until the episode about the lost atom bomb was presented on November 16. The climax of the episode: the bomb must be found and de-activated in time or the entire area will be destroyed, thousands of people will be killed, and there will be tremendous radio-active fallout. But instead of mentioning the above, all Kelly can manage to say is 'If the bomb is not found before it is set to go off, many people will be embarrassed.' I am ashamed for the entire production staff of *I Spy*, the writer of the script, and I am surprised that Robert Culp would say the line. I honestly feel an apology is due to the viewers. Certainly the lives of thousands of people are more important than the prestige of a few American officials." Miss. H.H., Hewlitt, New York.

"Dear Sir: Your program with the atom bomb story was gripping and excellent ... and especially making a priest into something not so inane, as they usually do—and to have him ask for help from 'His Manager,' at the moment of greatest suspense and crisis ... terrific! I also might add, I like the friendship existing between the colored man and White man in this series ... not phoney ... just two good pals who respect each other as individuals ... with disregard for color ... another true Christian concept ... done with great skill. Keep it up and you will win more awards ... for there is a dearth of stupid TV this year—so programs such as yours stand out even more." Mrs. C.J.N., Marion, Mass.

"Dear Sirs: Here sits an undyingly loyal Culp-Cosby fan. I undauntedly proclaim to friends, who have witlessly become Channel 4–10 P.M. deserters, that *I Spy* has the most well-written, most human, easiest-to-enjoy dialog (or banter, which is more accurate), on TV today. Now sirs, in deference to your great talents, one comment: The 'Don Camillo' parish priest, Communist Mayor bit is fine for light satire and is cute comedy, but oh, sirs, for *I Spy*? Really!" Mrs. D.E.V., Bergenfield, New Jersey.

"To Whom It May Concern: The credibility of some of the recent productions, particularly 'One of Our Bombs Is Missing," is so low that the program is beginning to resemble a fairy-tale. The increasing lack of credibility destroys the drama and infringes mightily on the fine performances rendered by Messrs. Culp and Cosby. May I suggest that more attention be paid to the scripts so as to avoid the widening of the credibility gap." R.C.G., Boston, Mass.

"Dear Sirs: The final straw came tonight when I saw the first few minutes of *I Spy*. I am very disappointed with the way it is has turned out this season. The plots are too silly, Kelly and Scott are too free with important government material to be real, and they are joking around too much." P.L., Pasadena, California.

"Dear Mr. Leonard: Please accept the following as constructive criticism—I have watched your program *I Spy* quite regularly since its beginning, but it is getting more difficult for me to watch, for Mr. Culp has been copying Bill Cosby's 'slurry' type of speech. I believe he has been doing it unconsciously because of his apparent admiration for Mr. Cosby, but it doesn't become Mr. Culp as it does Mr. Cosby. Also, it takes away from Mr. Culp's individual talent, which is great." C.E.K., St. Louis, Missouri.

"Dear *I Spy*: I'm very fond of this program. The scenery is beautiful. Please work on your sound. A lot of the time, I can't tell a word being spoken." M.D., Radnor, Pennsylvania.

"Gentlemen: We think *I Spy* is better than ever." J.H., Los Angeles, California.

Cast & Crew

David Mauro (Angelo) also played the butler who fancied himself a tango dancer in "Rome Take Away Three."

Dewey Martin (Father Bellini) was the most successful of the actors to be seen here.

12—The Fifth Block of Episodes

In 1952 he was cast as one of the leads in the film *The Big Sky*. For two years during that decade, he was married to Peggy Lee. But, after a promising start, he was relegated to playing smaller guest star roles in TV series of the period. He was 33 here.

Earl Bellamy was a latecomer to the series, beginning his work as an *I Spy* director here. But, before the end of the third season, he had directed 14 episodes, more than any other individual.

Beginning with *Seminole Uprising*, a low budget Western feature, Bellamy directed many TV Westerns, including *The Lone Ranger*, *Wagon Train*, and *The Adventures of Rin Tin Tin*. In the area of comedy, he knew Sheldon Leonard through his work for *The Andy Griffith Show*, but also directed for *Gilligan's Island*, *Leave It to Beaver*, and *The Munsters*. For this episode, surprisingly, he received an Emmy nomination in the category of Outstanding Directorial Achievement in Comedy.

13

Exposure

In January 1966 CBS added *Daktari* to its prime-time schedule as a midseason replacement. In the cast was Black actor Hari Rhodes, who would make a guest appearance in *I Spy's* second season. *Mission: Impossible*, new on CBS, featured a Black actor—Greg Morris—who would also appear that year on *I Spy*. NBC launched *Star Trek*, and had a Black among it's interracial cast. Nichelle Nichols, as Lt. Uhura, was the second Black woman to be featured on a network prime-time drama. With *Hogan's Heroes* and *I Spy* going into their second years, this brought the number of Blacks on prime time to five.

I Spy was still the only series to present a Black actor in a lead role. *Star Trek, Daktari, Hogan's Heroes,* and *Mission: Impossible*, were clearly dominated by a White cast. The color of television was expanding and, while these other shows should not be ignored for the contributions they made, *I Spy* remained the only example of the coming change in television.

Jack T. Sullivan, from the October 23, 1966, issue of the *Boston Sunday Herald TV Magazine*, wrote an article entitled "Casting of Negro Actors Shows TV Has Grown Up." Sullivan commented: "Maturity and television seldom get together. Yet in one instance a great maturity has been shown—the employment of more Negro actors in regular weekly series. Television's silly *Amos 'n' Andy* approach to life now is very much a part of the past. The pioneer move was in casting Bill Cosby in *I Spy*. At first many officials in the industry were apprehensive. They wondered how the program would go, or not go, on stations in the South. Now, as we move ahead into the show's second season, they know. The ratings, north and south alike, show that it just about owns the Wednesday night 10-to-11 time spot. Television at last has grown up in a very important segment of its existence and responsibility."

Supporting Sullivan's observation concerning *I Spy's* impressive ratings was a report from *TV Guide*: "According to TvQ (Home Testing Institute), *I Spy* was the most popular series on TV with the most desirable age group. For the 18–34 age group, the choice group for advertisers, the top six shows were the five network movies and *I Spy*."

As a result of all this news, a November 19, 1966, issue of *TV Guide* reported that Bill Cosby was being rewarded. "Job security, show-biz style—Bill Cosby has a 10-year recording contract with Warner Bros., and NBC is considering signing him to a 20-year pact. Cosby will do a special for NBC next fall."

If nothing else, success on TV inspires imitation. Richard K. Doan, in the December 3, 1966, issue of *TV Guide* reported that David Suskind was producing an hour-long pilot, to be shot on location in New York, called *N.Y.P.D.* Doan wrote, "The hour long play will borrow an *I Spy* idea. The central figures will be one White, one Negro."

More Press, of a Sort

TV Picture Life, February '66: "We Spy on the Spies: Bob Culp, Absence Makes the Heart Ache."

"Culp: 'When I was first offered *I Spy*, Nancy was against my taking it. I had quite a job convincing her that I should sign on for the show—and I did convince her only after I promised I'd have a stipulation that read I could only be away from home a maximum of one month out of every three. The producers wanted me to be away even more than that."

Inside Movie Magazine, July '66: "How the Spies Make Love."

"Cosby: 'This may be disappointing to my eager public, but I actually make love the same as any other guy. I'd give you a few more details, but my wife might read this. Maybe you'd better ask my buddy, Bob Culp.'"

"Culp: 'I'm married. So I won't get that personal, either. If you think Bill's wife is tough, you ought to see mine. One thing I must make perfectly clear: I've never used a gun or any other type of weapon on a woman.'"

TV Radio Mirror, September '66: "The Letter That Broke Six Hearts."

"Mrs. Robert Culp: 'We have been sort of split up since January. But I got a letter from him in Italy where he's filming segments for his TV series. He told me I might as well face the facts. I'm going to retain an attorney.'"

Photoscreen, December '66: "Bob Culp: A Woman's Love Is Not Enough."

The four Culp children: "Where's daddy?" ... it began.

Photoplay, January '67: "The Love They Couldn't Hide Anymore."

"Would you believe Bob Culp and France Nuyen are altar bound? Until recently, the so-called insiders in Hollywood considered this as unlikely as Richard Burton divorcing Liz Taylor for Mother Goose."

Motion Picture Magazine, March '67: "I'm Not a Wronged Wife: Mrs. Bob Culp's Own Story of the Divorce."

"Nancy Culp: 'You cannot be good friends after ten years of marriage. Anyone who says you can be friends after a divorce never had a marriage that amounted to anything.'"

TV Picture Mirror, May '67: "Bob Culp, France Nuyen, Reaching for That Dream."

"Every decade or so, Hollywood is ripped open by a great love affair, a heart-rending divorce that scandalizes even the most jaded residents of the town, and a new love team takes its place in the headlines. Now a new team has joined the ranks of the helpless passionate lovers."

Photoplay, December '67: "I Hate a Woman Who Clings."

"Bob's divorce in 1966 and his new romance with France has given him a great sense of freedom and exhilaration. Relaxing, playing, sharing things together, has even affected his acting, he declared.

"Culp: 'Now I see on the screen the man I've been looking for twenty years. It's a kick.'"

Robert Culp's press agent, Jay Bernstein, had been doing his job.

Culp: "I believe that gossip is primal, self-protective, greedy, and it is a force."[1]

On to Spain

Robert Culp once stated that while on location shooting for *I Spy*, the happiest he had ever been was at the end of 1966, during the six weeks in Spain. He found the country to be

Ollie & Stan, Spain '66 (© 3 F Prod.).

scenic, majestic, and hospitable. He was also pleased with the quality of the scripts that were to be shot at that time. France Nuyen, who was traveling with him, would costar in "The Magic Mirror," one of the episodes being filmed, which Culp himself had written.

There were, initially, nine segments to feature Spain as a backdrop. Just days before the company departed, that number was increased to ten.

Culp: "'The War Lord' was really important to me for a lot of reasons. I knew it was a virtual impossibility when I wrote it, but I said 'I've got to do this anyway.' We couldn't do it in L.A. because we didn't have any money, and it was twice too much money."[2]

Besides laboring over the script, Culp had spent several hours a day, on numerous days spread over a year, testing make-up with John Chambers, an expert on facial prosthetics. Chambers had donated his time, telling Culp that, if he were able to get the script onto the schedule, he could compensate Chambers for his work with a job on the production. Then, in April of 1966, as production on the second season began, all the hard work and sacrifice seemed for naught.

Culp: "Sheldon knew that I had spent, by then, eight months in the backyard of Johnny Chambers, who later got the first Academy Award for make-up. He knew how much 'The War Lord' meant to me, and he had to throw it off the schedule."[3]

And that was that. Period.

Culp: "Leon Chooluck was the one who got 'The War Lord' on. It never would have been made without Leon. On his way to the airport, Leon stopped in my dressing room, and he said, 'Have you got a copy of that "War Lord" script.' 'Yes! Absolutely yes! How many do you want?' Leon said, 'Keep your fingers crossed.' And the next thing I heard, less than a week, it was on the schedule for Spain. I just went crazy."[4]

For the first time since the series had begun, Culp was truly happy. This would be one extended location shoot he was actually looking forward to.

As the month in Spain progressed, Culp and Nuyen were inseparable, and Bill Cosby shared his hotel room with four women: his wife, Camille, his mother, Anna, and two young daughters. Erikka had been born while Cosby had been filming in Hong Kong. Erinne came on July 23, 1966, just days after he returned from the shoot in Italy. And now the whole family had traveled with him to Spain.

In an interview with JoAnne Stang in *Good Housekeeping*, he told what it was like on location overseas with two offspring to contend with.

Cosby: "You can imagine what happens to the closets when we move into a hotel. I end up giving my clothes to the wardrobe man. There are diapers and rubber pants, booties, and little woolen hats. It takes me two days to get a shower."[5]

There were times, during the extended visit, when the magic in the air became almost surreal.

Preece: "One night we went to a restaurant, Culp, Cosby and myself. And Boris Karloff was at our table. At the same table was Peter Lawford, who was also out for an episode. Orson Welles was at another table, because he was out there doing a movie at the time [*Chimes At Midnight*], and at another table was Richard Harris, who was there doing *Camelot*. I remember thinking, 'My God, I've never been in a restaurant where there were so many famous people at one time.' Not in Hollywood, not anywhere, but there it was in Spain, in Seville.

"And Karloff was telling humorous stories about all the time he had to sit in make-up being made to look like a monster—because Culp was about to go through some of that for his script, 'The War Lord.'"[6]

It was a time of magic. *I Spy* had never before looked or felt so good.

14

The Sixth Block of Episodes

46. **"CHILD OUT OF TIME"**; Written by: Morton Fine & David Friedkin; Directed by: Alf Kjellin; Location: Madrid; First airing: 1/11/67. Repeated: 7/12/67.

Because of her amazing retentive powers, the ten-year-old daughter of a former Nazi collaborator becomes a pawn in her greedy mother's plot to sell World War II secrets to the highest bidder.

Having realized that names of men guilty of wartime atrocities would someday bring a high price, Gerta had her daughter Leno commit the valuable list to memory. Kelly and Scott are now entrusted with the girl's safety, as it becomes apparent that she is being pursued by agents from both sides.

Assessment

"Child Out of Time" offers up a first-rate mystery with a list of Nazi war criminals at its center.

This episode was shot entirely at Desilu, prior to the company departing for Spain. Regardless, this is *I Spy* at its best.

The writing, directing and acting are superb.

The camera work is also above standard when compared to previous Desilu interior-bound episodes. Notice the maverick filmmaking technique involving a handheld camera used to open the teaser. And, in defiance of network censors, the baseboard wood carvings of two women, breasts exposed, are featured in the foreground of a dialogue scene between Kelly and Scott.

It is a disturbing sight when the camera pushes in on the face of the ten-year-old girl, deep in concentration as she recites something from memory, oblivious to the assassin who just fired a shot that nearly killed her mother. Then again, the camera singles her out as she later finds her mother lying on the floor, dead. Perhaps the most shocking moment comes when Kelly places a gun to the back of Leno's head and threatens to blow her brains out if the Israeli agents don't lower their weapons. She doesn't even blink.

The depiction of Leno is both eerie and moving. Even her mother refers to Leno as having one serious flaw: "She feels nothing. How could she with me as a mother?" Yet Scott, played so perfectly by Cosby, the man who would one day be charming children in Jell-O commercials, will break through and touch something human in this distant and robotic little girl. Kelly and Scott's adversary is Peter Karl, who is both frightening in and out of the nylon stocking he uses as a disguise.

The Israeli agents, Lew and Tedor, are interesting and unexpected characters. They will do whatever they must to get the list—kill Kelly and/or Scott, or torture the information out of the young girl. Leno is the key to a larger issue, and, for the Israelis, does not beg the moral question, "is it worth a life to avenge a life?"

The banter between Kelly and Scott is top notch. The frustration they feel is offset by a series of unexpected yet needed moments of humor, when armed men pop in and out of their hotel room.

Kelly's disgust of Rienzi, the Nazi on the run, is also well played. When Rienzi admits that he and his colleagues faked their deaths to escape prosecution, Kelly says to Scott, "Do you remember what I said I'd do if I ever ran into one of these guys?" Kelly settles for a quick backhanded slap across the Nazi's face, knocking him down. Clearly disapproving, Scott asks, "Do you feel better?" "No," Kelly answers, wishing he could go further.

Kelly reveals another dark layer of his character in the scene where the older Gerta caresses his face and tells him how fond she is of having young lovers. Though she is crusty and with a hard edge, Kelly appears to be under the influence of a narcotic as this woman, who appears to be 20 years his senior, strokes his cheek and purrs about her fondness for younger men.

We are given more family background on Kelly, as well, as he confides in Scott that he visited the ruins of concentration camps shortly after the war. Kelly was in his early teens. His father was a military lawyer, assigned to inspect the records at these camps. The father, determined that his son would learn a lesson in life, had young Kelly look at the records and the photographs so that he would know what human beings are capable of.

The Story Behind the Story

Culp: "That was us doing 'The 39 Steps.' Nina Foch was terrific. I really liked working with her."[1]

As in a previous episode, Cosby, in an ad-lib, makes reference to Robert Culp's last ongoing TV character, Hoby Gilman. On two separate occasions, Scotty calls Kelly, "Hoby."

RATINGS

I Spy had new competition on Wednesday night. *ABC Stage 67* made way for the new *ABC Wednesday Night Movie*.

In the days before HBO and Showtime, before VCRs and DVD players, the movies being shown in prime time by the three networks were always big ratings grabbers.

NBC was the first to discover the possibilities of running not-too-old theatrical films on TV. It seemed like a no-brainer just a few years later, but it was pure innovation when *The NBC Saturday Night Movie* found its way onto the schedule in September 1961, giving the network its first viable competitor to the CBS king of Saturday nights, *Gunsmoke*.

Gunsmoke had been the number-one rated show on television for the previous four seasons. But, once up against a series of big-screen, big-budget, big-name movies, Marshall Dillon and gang dropped to number three in the year-end Nielsens, then down again, the following year, to number ten, then down again, the year after that, to number 20. For the next 17 years, Saturday night would be movie night on NBC.

ABC was next. *The ABC Sunday Night Movie* premiered in September of 1964 and gave the alphabet network a well-aimed shot at NBC's powerhouse Western, *Bonanza*. The Sunday movie would stick around for 23 consecutive seasons.

The following year, the same year *I Spy* premiered, NBC rolled out a second weekly night at the movies: Tuesday. The network had been having trouble with the ABC hit, *The Fugitive,* which had placed at number five in the Nielsens for the previous year. Now, going head-to-head against a series of movies, *The Fugitive* dropped completely out of sight, and out of Nielsen's Top 25.

CBS got into the game in September 1966, and made up for lost time, by premiering two weekly series of movies in the same week: *The CBS Thursday Night Movie* and *The CBS Friday Night Movie.*

And now, at the halfway point of that season, ABC brought out a Wednesday night movie to do battle with *I Spy.*

Regardless, *I Spy* won its time slot. Surprisingly, Danny Kaye, hosting Liberace and Vikki Carr that night, proved to be the greater opponent.

According to Nielsen, the television sets tuned in on Wednesday night between 10 and 11 P.M. were divided up as follows:

I Spy, *NBC: 36.8%*
The Danny Kaye Show, *CBS: 28.6%*
Wednesday movie, Ulyses, *with Kirk Douglas, ABC: 24.9%*
All others: 12.3%

THE CENSORS

From NBC Broadcast Standards and Practices:

"The Broadcast Standards objection to Scott and Kelly sharing information on the locations of surviving Nazi death-camp officials with Israeli agents was based on the belief that our government would not place itself into the position of assisting another government that has used extralegal methods of bringing war criminals to justice. As discussed, I agreed that if you provide us with verification that our government would indeed permit the sharing of information under like circumstances, our objection would be withdrawn." Don R. Bay, Broadcast Standards.

FROM THE MAIL BAG

"Dear Sirs: I am writing to protest the latest episode of your program, where two agents, presumably American, hand over information to agents of a foreign power. Such a program condones an action which is basically immoral; the agents are working to supply information to the agency that hires them, not to a foreign power. Even more basic, they are Americans, not Israeli agents. The more subtle issue of the propaganda value of the program, I will not question. Let me state, however, that this particular episode of *I Spy,* I found extremely offensive." Mrs. A.J.A., North Hollywood, California.

"Gentlemen: 'Child Out Of Time' was one of your best ones. Miss Foch, in particular, was absolutely brilliant—but it was a great mistake to make that child work with a German accent: the resulting distraction nearly wrecked the show." J.S.R., New York City.

"Dear Mr. Leonard: Thanks for maintaining *I Spy* to its achieved level of entertainment. Thanks to Cosby and Culp—the 'vitamin C's'. I hadn't intended to write, but after tonight's episode wherein the script calls out 'Hoby,' that was motivation for me, being one of the original 'Texas Ranger' fans. So, Mr. Leonard, keep up the good work—I appreciate it!" M.R., Campbell, California.

"Dear Mr. Friedkin: Put a shirt on Robert Culp. What is the bit with he and/or Cosby going shirtless? Is it to please the sex-frustrated females, the perverts or homosexuals???? Both he and Bill are splendid actors and *I Spy* will go on forever, but it is disgusting to see either of them parading around dressed to please the sex-crazed watchers. It may please pink shirt Johnny Carson, but real males find it disgusting." F.M.W., Lima, New York.

Cast

Nina Foch, the greedy and doomed Gerta, was a leading lady in the 1940s. Look for her opposite William Holden in the 1948 film *The Dark Past*, and with Bela Lugosi in *Return of the Vampire* from 1944. In the 1950s, she made the move to television and had amassed over 100 credits by the time she came to this role. She appears older here than her 43 years. Shortly after this, Gene Berry would strangle her, making her the very first victim of a murder to be solved by Peter Falk's Lt. Columbo in 1968's *Prescription: Murder*.

Eileen Baral, ten-year-old Leno, had been acting for only a few years, with appearances on *Wagon Train*, *Bonanza*, and *Perry Mason*. She would find regular work on *The Nanny and the Professor*, from 1970 through '71.

Charles Macauley, 39 at this time, played the Nazi assassin Peter Karl. Watch for two very different looking Macauleys in a pair of episodes from the original *Star Trek*. A talented actor, Macauley appeared as Laundru in "The Return of the Archons," and as Jaris in "Wolf in the Fold," filmed in 1966 and '67. Continuing to work through the 1990s, he would appear in three *Columbo* episodes, as well as seven *Perry Mason* TV movies.

Paul Lambert, 44, played Lew, the lead Israeli agent. He made his film debut in *Spartacus*. He had been acting for nearly a decade on the stage and New York–based TV, which included a record 14 appearances on the prestigious *Playhouse 90*.

Richard Morrison played Rienzi. He first appeared in the 1963 film *Swingin' Affair*, and can also be spotted in reruns of *Daniel Boone*, *Mission: Impossible*, and *Hawaii Five-O*.

Peggy Webber (Sister Agatha) had crossed paths twice with Robert Culp on *Trackdown*. In the pilot, "Badge of Honor," she played Hoby's sister Norah. Culp had the character return in the episode he wrote for the series, "Back to Crawford."

A favorite of Jack Webb, she was cast in over 100 *Dragnet* episodes between its run on radio and television.

47. **"MAGIC MIRROR"**; Written by: Robert Culp; Directed by: Tom Gries; Second unit directed by: David Friedkin; Location: Spain; First airing: 3/15/67. Repeated: 8/9/67.

In Madrid, Kelly and Scott are ordered to check reports that deposed ruler General Juan Vera intends a political coup to regain power in his country.

Two factors complicate the mission: Russian ballistic missiles and Sam-Than MacLean, a fellow agent and Kelly's soulmate, who may have switched sides.

We first met "Sam" MacLean in "The Tiger," where it was established that she and Kelly still had feelings for one another. Both were determined, however, to remain professional and resist involvement. The situation has now changed.

Assessment

The images in this stand-out episode are truly stirring. The seething hatred in Kelly's face as he talks to Sam on the phone, tells her that he's coming back, and warns her that, if she blows his cover, he'll kill her, are seared into the viewer's memory.

Another chilling visual occurs with Kelly and Sam's uncomfortable reunion at the general's party. They dance and talk of the betrayal they feel, yet smile at one another for the benefit of the other guests.

Juan Vera himself is a character rich with complexities and driven by a lust for power. He has made a deal with the Russians and, as a result, has regained power in his country. Vera's plan is well thought out and a win-win for him. By letting Kelly and Scott complete their assignment and gain pictures of him with the Communists, he wins again. The Americans will not let the Russians deliver the missiles by creating a blockade, just as they had done around Cuba four years earlier. Vera will have gained all, and paid nothing. Vera also wins Sam. Kelly is the only loser here. The sight of him—silent, crushed, riding with Scott in the back of the limousine—is poignant. He puts on his sunglasses and turns off the world. Scott is uncharacteristically slumped, unable to look in Kelly's direction.

The Story Behind the Story

The script for "Magic Mirror" was originally titled "The Enchanted Cottage," and began in December 1965, while Culp was in Mexico shooting episodes for the first season.

Culp wanted to provide Nuyen with the most challenging role of her career, and he was confident his sixth script for *I Spy* would be his best yet.

Days prior to shooting, and during a brief stopover in England, Culp and Nuyen came down with a severe case of food poisoning. Both were extremely sick with fever and stomach pain when they filmed the exterior sequences for the teaser of this episode.

Watch the dialogue scene, in particular, between Culp and Nuyen in the car outside the Madrid airport, or the sight of them being playful and running together at the Royal Gardens. No one would ever know that these consummate professionals were ill.

Another location used in the making of this episode was the Royal Palace of Spain. This was the very building where Queen Isabella gave permission to Columbus to sail the sea of blue in 1492. At the time of this filming, it belonged to Generalissimo Francisco Franco.

Robert Culp acknowledges that the story for "Magic Mirror" would have been better suited for a feature film, rather than a 51-minute TV episode. The characters are complex and the motivations behind their actions are often vague.

Both Culp and director Gries felt Nuyen was baffled by her character.

Ricardo Montalban, "Magic Mirror" (© 3 F Prod., courtesy Image Ent.).

Culp: "I remember

the final scene in the story—outside the mansion. The general has arranged for a limo to take Kelly and Scott away—wherever they want to go. Sam is there. The general is momentarily distracted, talking to someone else, and it gives Kelly one last chance to try to reason with Sam. She is in emotional shock. She has dealt with so much over the last 24 hours that she—for some reason Kelly can never understand—decides to go off with the bad guy. But this scene was all about that thing France said—in *Life* magazine—'I'm Chinese, I'm a stone, I go where I am kicked.' It was about what I thought she meant when she said that. And France was having trouble connecting to it. We found a place to be alone and we ran lines. She kept pulling away from the way the scene was written. She wasn't getting it. So I was hammering at her, trying to help her see what it was about, and how she should play it. Unbeknownst to me, after that, she went to Tom Gries, the director of the episode, and said, 'Keep that sonofabitch away from me.'

"Tom told me this many years later after France and I had been married and divorced. If I had known earlier—if I could have seen the writing on the wall—it would have changed everything."[2]

Michael Preece shines a bit more light on the character conflicts that were taking place behind the camera: "At first, Culp and France were like 16-year-old lovers. But, after that, I got the feeling that she had grown away from him a little bit—even *before* they got married. And I was surprised they got married. They were completely different, as people. Her acting was just something she liked to do, I think, because she was pretty, and she was a decent actress. But for him, acting was far more important. An obsession."[3]

The motivations of the characters in "Magic Mirror" were very clear in Culp's mind. Their actions made sense.

Culp: "Sam is all the things that she said she was in the teaser—tired, beyond tired—and she has lost whatever it was that she had of her own self. It is something that can happen with spies. Burned the fuck out. 'I don't care. No one will let me not care. This may be permanent, or it may be temporary—I have no idea—but, at the moment, I don't care who wins, I don't care who loses, I don't care about the sides, I don't care about anything.' This is the place she has reached when she finds out that her aunt, this woman who is sacred to her, is being violated by this man."[4]

As to why Sam thinks allowing Vera to romance her will free her aunt, Culp puts it plainly:

"The general says it was only a matter of time before he would send her aunt away. This is what Sam is doing—making it happen sooner. And that was her objective. She didn't figure on a suicide attempt. She must have figured that the alcohol would enter into it, and there would be a big scene, and then the general would send her aunt away. And that would be the end of it. Then she would slip out somehow."[5]

And then there is that ending. Why does Sam go off with the general, the man she blames for her aunt's death?

Culp: "By the end of the episode, all is burnt out of her character. She is disinterested. She is just following the line of least resistance. Maybe she will get out of it, maybe she won't. I guess she didn't, because we never saw her again."[6]

Oddly, the subtleties of the script may have benefited "Magic Mirror." Culp has said that he has received more mail on this episode than any other that he wrote, and most of that mail was from women who had their own theories as to what the motivations of the characters were and what the message of the story was.

With this episode, the opening title sequence of the series was changed. Instead of Kelly's eyes viewing a montage of the adventure to come, the producers replaced this with a recap of great moments from the show's past.

LOCKED ROOM # 7

Despite the dark tone of this episode and the melancholy ending, "Magic Mirror" contains a favorite comedy moment involving the signature locked room. Cosby had given Culp a cartoon he had found with two half-starved, bearded men, shackled to a wall in a dungeon. In the caption under the drawing, the first man says to the other, "Now here's the plan..." Cosby suggested to Culp that he work the gag into his next script. It was done so here.

CAST & CREW

France Nuyen had appeared twice before in *I Spy*. She would appear once more, in a different role, in the third season.

Ricardo Montalban was 46 when he played the somewhat older General Juan Vera. The charismatic and powerful actor was one of the few on television who could play a man who was both articulate and intimidating, capable of obtaining such power, and using it, yet convey compassion and sex appeal.

Montalban began in films in 1942 and had amassed over 100 different character performances in movies and TV by this time, with another 100 plus to go.

During the year of this episode, he would portray another general, this one named Khan, on another series shooting at this time at Desilu. Fifteen years later, he would reprise that role in the big-screen treatment of *Star Trek II: The Wrath of Khan*.

His most famous role, however, would be that of the elegant white-suited Mr. Roarke of *Fantasy Island*.

Virginia Grey (Aunt Grace) was a contract player at MGM in the 1940s. The studio placed her in numerous starring roles in "B" pictures and supporting roles in "A" pictures. In the 1950s, '60s and '70s, she continued to act regularly in films and on TV.

Ken Tobey (Gabe) would return for more *I Spys* during the third season, playing the same character, but undergoing a name change to Russ. Culp, who added so much to the series as a writer, gives us the one element the series lacked, a superior for Kelly and Scott to report to, and rebel against; a man who could hold his own with the two clever and glib agents. Ken Tobey was that man.

In 1966, Tobey was halfway into a successful TV and film career that would see him collect more than 200 credits. Among those, he had his own short-lived TV series, "The Whirlybirds" (1956–59), a contemporary Western using helicopters instead of horses.

Roy Jansen, playing Russian agent Rochensky had appeared in "It's All Done with Mirrors," as a fellow agent.

Tom Gries, prior to coming to *I Spy*, directed segments for *Combat!*, *Route 66*, and Jack Lord's rodeo cowboy series, *Stoney Burke*. He won an Emmy in 1964 for *East Side/West Side*. "Magic Mirror" may be among the best directed episodes of *I Spy*, yet Gries, after completing his double assignment of this and "The Trouble with Temple," would never return to the series. Culp was allowed to select him for this project and the director claimed that scheduling was the reason he didn't return. Culp believed it had more to do with a personality clash between Gries and the producers. Gries went on to direct the feature film *Will Penny* with Charlton Heston, as well as the 1976 made for TV movie, *Helter Skelter*. He died the following year, from a heart attack, while playing tennis. He was only 55.

Preece: "Tom Gries was another one of the more efficient and good directors they ever had."[7]

Earle Hagen's score is haunting and played sparingly, yet is immensely effective, especially in the final moments in the limo and in the steam room.

14 — The Sixth Block of Episodes

48. **"THE TROUBLE WITH TEMPLE"**; Written by: Morton Fine & David Friedkin; Directed by: Tom Gries; Location: Madrid; First airing: 1/25/67. Repeated: 7/19/67.

In Madrid, American schlock filmmaker Nick Fielding is dealing in the wrong kind of film—that of secret NATO maneuvers. Scott discovers this and is captured. Kelly, unaware of his partner's situation, is busy being charmed by Temple Jones, Fielding's discontented mistress—a Marilyn Monroe–type aspiring actress. Although Fielding bullies and demeans her, Temple has earned the right to talk back to him. But when she shows an interest in Kelly, Fielding's homicidal jealousy kicks in.

Assessment

The trouble with "Temple" is that it is slow in getting started and the guest performances lack the quality of subtlety.

Carol Wayne, as the not-so-smart but not-so-stupid Temple either amuses and touches you, or annoys you, depending on your taste for stereotypic platinum bombshells. Temple is a paradox: both childishly simple, yet emotionally complex, or, at least, *wanting* to be emotionally complex. On the plus side, Wayne's Temple displays a frightened, yet determined young woman who is both tender and sad.

Jack Cassidy, as Fielding, is smug and egotistical. The only surprising wrinkle is his

Carol Wayne, Jack Cassidy, "The Trouble with Temple" (© 3 F Prod., courtesy Image Ent.).

willingness to make a fool of himself over his woman. The fight scene between Fielding and Kelly is sudden, violent, and works extremely well.

Location scenery is both effective and quite stunning, notably when Temple and Kelly stand by a stone wall with an ancient Spanish city looming in the background.

"The Trouble with Temple" does what *I Spy* episodes are supposed to do—combine espionage, danger, humor, sexuality, and scenery.

The Story Behind the Story

As with "Magic Mirror," it was felt this episode had too little physical action to justify cutting a montage of clips for the opening title sequence. Instead, clips were shown from previous episodes.

Recalling the casting of "Temple":

Culp: "Jack Cassidy was a very interesting actor to work with. For a little guy, he was over the top."[8]

Preece: "Jack Cassidy thought he was funnier than he was. I remember thinking, 'This jerk is married to that pretty girl—Shirley Jones. How could such a nice lady be married to this guy?' He was completely smug and full of himself. He had a sarcastic mouth. I remember standing there and thinking, 'God, will this guy ever stop.'"[9]

Culp: "Friedkin and Fine had this thing for Carol Wayne, because she was young and attractive, and she was clearly going to have some sort of career. She was very nice, very sweet. She couldn't possibly be as dumb as she played, because she really played dumb to the last notch. But they were very hot on her."[10]

Preece: "Everybody had a crush on Carol Wayne. I remember standing out on a parking lot, and she was in a bus changing clothes. You could see her naked. Everybody was watching, so I assume she didn't mind. She had an incredible figure."[11]

CULP & COSBY ON SET REWRITE

Not found in the script, when Kelly rescues Scott:

SCOTT: "Don't talk to me. Your timing is so bad on rescuing people. You are without a doubt the lowest at timing."

KELLY: "I'll give you timing. All last year I rescued you—right on the dot—and every time you'd embarrass me?!"

SCOTT: "You're either too early or too late—and, this time, you're too late. My whole life was passing before me."

Also, at the end of the tag scene, after Scott finds out that his Aunt Ruth married Harry instead of George, doing away with the need for Scott to send the silk shirts he had Kelly pick out as a wedding gift:

SCOTT: "Now I've got to take these and..."

KELLY: "You don't have to take these. They're gonna stay here. These are the ones you gave me."

SCOTT: "You can't have those."

KELLY: "Don't be silly, man, you asked me to pick 'em out."

SCOTT: "Yeah, but that doesn't mean that you get to have them."

KELLY: "You had an Uncle George for a moment there—and then you lost him—and now I have two wonderful silk shirts."

Reviews

"Temple" marked the seventh time *I Spy* was given a half-page Close Up listing by *TV Guide*, America's number-one source of TV news and reviews in the 1960s.

Ratings

During the week "The Trouble with Temple" aired, the pie for the time period *I Spy* shared, according to Nielsen, was divided up as follows:

I Spy, *NBC: 35.5%*
Wednesday movie, *Elvis Presley in* Flaming Star, *ABC: 30.7%*
The Danny Kaye Show, *CBS: 25.4%*
All others: *10.5%*

Cast

Carol Wayne was 24 when she played Temple Jones. She, and her look-alike sister, Nina, were brand new on the scene in 1966. Carol appeared in a handful of movies and TV shows, including *Bewitched* and *The Man from U.N.C.L.E.* While her statuesque figure and little girl voice would gain her work, it would also limit her career. She would be best known for performing in over 100 "Tea Time Movie" skits with Johnny Carson on *The Tonight Show*. Carson would play TV matinee movie host and commercial spokesman Art Fern, and Wayne was his curvaceous and tempting Matinee Lady. Carol Wayne died in 1985, at the age of 43, of an accidental drowning. Foul play was suspected, but the case was never solved.

Jack Cassidy, 39 here, began his career in front of the camera in 1957. At this time, he had a recurring role on a new TV series, *He & She*. Cassidy was indeed married to actress Shirley Jones, and their two sons, David and Shaun, would both be future TV and pop music idols. Father Jack would go on to do three guest appearances on *Columbo* in the 1970s, tying Culp as the most frequent villain to play on the series. In 1977, after a night of heavy drinking, Cassidy fell asleep on a couch with a lit cigarette in his hand. The ensuing fire took his life. He was 50.

Kurt Kasznar, playing Dr. Ibanez, a crooked man of medicine who administers the truth serum to Scott, had a long and impressive list of credits from the stage, radio, film, and TV. He would be best known for playing Alexander Fitzhuh, the Dr. Smith–type lovable villain on producer Irwin Allen's *Land of the Giants*.

49. **"MAINLY ON THE PLAINS"**; Written by: Morton Fine & David Friedkin; Directed by: David Friedkin; Location: Spain (Madrid from Seville); First airing: 2/22/67. Repeated: 8/16/67.

On the plains of Spain, Kelly and Scott are assigned to befriend a weary antimissile systems expert, Don Ernesto Silvando. A friendship with the aging genius is desired by both sides of the iron curtain.

But Don Ernesto has his own loyalty test. The challenge for Kelly and Scott will be to learn that only a Sancho Panza could believe and follow a Don Quixote.

Assessment

An off-beat but enjoyable story, we see another side to Kelly and Scott. This time they use their winning personalities to make friends for America.

This episode has many endearing qualities, beginning with Boris Karloff. His portrayal of Don Ernesto is warm, complex, and most certainly memorable. And this brilliant scientist is not as crazy as he often appears. The strain to decide which side of the iron curtain will benefit from his knowledge may have proven too great for him, but madness, it has been said, while not always having a means, often has a purpose. In the end, by adhering to the rules of chivalry and a challenge of combat, he may allow fate to make the decision for him.

"Mainly on the Plains" offers a series of spectacular locations. The imagery is as memorable as the story, most notably the somewhat crippled Karloff leading a charge against giant windmills, backed up by a reluctant Kelly and Scott.

There is much humor to this story, as well, but perhaps the funniest is the aftermath of a farmer's efforts to chase off trespassers, his gun loaded with buckshot, and the bull's-eye target being Kelly's backside.

Sprawled over the car, Kelly winces in pain as a gleeful Scott plucks out the pellets with a tweezer, saying, "She loves me, she loves me not."

Some moments do not work, particularly those with too-easy escapes and inept villains. And, while most of the events in the episode are humorous, or curious, they do become predictable. Every time Kelly and Scott get Don Ernesto back into his car, he pulls off the road and gets into more trouble.

Regardless, Friedkin and Fine's script is tender and heartfelt, and "Mainly on the Plains" is a stand-out entry for the series.

The Story Behind the Story

An entire days filming for "Mainly on the Plains" was nearly lost. After the footage was returned to Desilu for editing, it was discovered that the radio microphones used for two key dialogue scenes had been picking up interference, therefore leaving the recorded sound filled with flaws. Earle Hagen was given the chore of finding a way to salvage the footage.

Hagen: "The dialogue in the Spanish Garden was so bad, I finally said to Dave Friedkin, 'I'll put a music cue in there, and you can bring it up to fill in the gaps in the dialogue.' We couldn't go silent because, when they started to speak, you'd get the noise back in. The cue was enough for them to lean on to cover up most of the noise."[12]

Technical problems aside, "Mainly on the Plains" remains a very special episode for many who were associated with the series.

Culp: "The Boris Karloff episode is very dear to both Bill and me because it's a great story—not very well done, but one we related to—and we worked with him. It was awesome. It was really exciting.

"He was the ultimate trooper. We had a scene, just him and me, around an enormous fountain where they had laid track for the camera. We were supposed to walk around it, doing a page or two of dialogue, as the camera tracked along with us. But he was having trouble getting around it without losing breath. And we had to do it a couple times. I sensed he was having trouble, so I sat down—and only then would *he* sit down. Then we did another take, and this time we sat down twice, but he always waited for me to sit first.

"I was very touched by his ability to concentrate, because he could scarcely walk. He had injured both of his legs severely as a young man playing soccer. And he had steel braces that covered his legs under the trousers. I guess part of the thing he had was emphysema, or something like emphysema, so he was short of breath to start with. Plus he had a back injury from when he was playing Frankenstein. But he never said a word, never whined for a second.

"I remember when we actually encountered the windmills, which was sort of the heart of the story, and he charged toward them. Here's this guy who could scarcely get around the fountain in the scene earlier, and he's galloping down to the windmills, waving his cane. I was really concerned. I thought he was going to fall down and kill himself. But he did it, because the scene required it. He was a hell of a guy. He really was a marvelous, glowing, gentleman. He was a pleasure to be with."[13]

Cosby: "We were in Spain, out on the plains. They'd wrapped because the sun was gone. But it's gone in terms of the light for the camera. You can still see. And Bob is sitting in the back seat of the car, and Boris is sitting up front. And they put his topcoat over him, just over his shoulders. And we are *way* in the countryside, and the car is rolling, and I'm sitting right behind Boris, and he's rolling, ever so slightly, with the car. There's the head of Boris Karloff. And there I am. And it's getting dark. And I turned to Bob and I said, 'If he turns around and says, "Arrrrgh," I'm going to punch Frankenstein in the face.'

"I don't know if Bob told you the quote that he said to us. He said, 'I've watched you boys, and when you stop doing the jokes, I'll say my lines.'"[14]

The ultimate trooper, Boris, 1966 (© 3 F Prod., courtesy Ron Jacobs).

Preece: "It meant so much to Culp and Cosby to be working with Karloff. For that episode, they stayed to do all their off-camera readings. And they weren't doing that by that time, not in the other episodes. They had too many other things to do, and were quite busy. I would often do it for them. I'd stay behind the camera, whichever side the director instructed me to, and stand on a ladder, and place my script before me. And I had a white glove and a black glove, and I'd use hand signals to let the other performers know whether I was speaking for Culp or Cosby, because they were off doing whatever they did. But with Boris Karloff, they would stay. They were into him so much."[15]

Preece remembers one more thing concerning the shoot with Karloff: "Boris knew *I Spy* was very popular, and he was so thrilled that he was actually remembered and that we wanted him for this part. He loved doing this episode."[16]

THE CENSORS

The NBC Broadcast Standards Department had several cautions about the script for this episode. One read: "Removal of buckshot must be handled in an off camera fashion, and area should be played as lower back. Kelly's line, 'Tell them I said I regret I have but one ... ow ... to give for my country,' should be revised to add the word, 'life,' so that it does not play as a derriere gag."

Needless to say, Culp and Cosby did not adhere to the censor's concerns.

Reviews

"Mainly on the Plains" was the eighth episode of *I Spy* to claim a *TV Guide* Close Up listing—the second episode in a row, following "The Trouble with Temple."

Cast & Crew

Boris Karloff was a late bloomer in Hollywood. He was 44, with 80 films to his credit, by 1931 when *Frankenstein* was released. He would reprise the role of the monster for *Bride of Frankenstein* and *Son of Frankenstein*, but declined to return for any of the other sequels or parodies.

Educated in England, Karloff was of East Indian heritage. A man of slight frame and of medium height, via make-up, padding, and lifts, he was made to appear as a towering monster. The illusion was highly effective—but at a price.

The weight of the costume, along with the added weight of the actress Karloff had to carry up a castle stairway, injured his back so severely that he suffered from chronic pain for the remainder of his life. He would have three back surgeries and find walking, or even standing, to be quite difficult in his declining years. Many of his final performances, even predating his work in *I Spy*, were done from the confines of a wheelchair.

Besides playing Frankenstein's monster, Karloff scared moviegoers in *The Mummy* and *The Mask of Fu Manchu*. On Broadway, he spent the first half of the 1940s in *Arsenic & Old Lace*, playing Jonathan Brewster, the sociopathic murderer who had undergone so many plastic surgeries that, upon seeing him for the first time in many years, his brother, Mortimer, exclaims, "Good grief, you look like Boris Karloff!" Karloff was prevented from being featured in the 1944 film version that starred Cary Grant because of a contractual commitment to stay with the stage production.

In later years, Karloff would host a spine tingling TV series called *Thriller*, as well as provide the voice of the green-skinned Scrooge in *How the Grinch Stole Christmas*.

As for being the subject of the 1962 novelty record, "The Monster Mash," which became a two-time top ten hit, Karloff sent word to Bobby "Boris" Pickett, stating, "Tell him I enjoy his record." Karloff eventually sang the song himself on a TV special.

His movie swan song was for director Peter Bogdanovich in the 1968 film *Targets*. Karloff died one year later of emphysema, less than three years after filming this episode of *I Spy*. He was 83.

Art Seid made a promising debut on the series as the editor of this episode. He began cutting film in the late 1930s with The Three Stooges shorts. Along with his ongoing Stooge duties, he handled the splicing of many B flicks through the 1940s, before moving to television in the 1950s. He served as supervising editor on *You Are There!*, *Broken Arrow*, and *The Third Man*, before advancing in the ranks and becoming a producer on *Perry Mason*. Seid returned to the editing chair for *I Spy*, but had his eye on something bigger within the organization. Stay tuned.

50. **"THE WAR LORD"**; Written by: Robert Culp; Directed by: Alf Kjellin; Location: England to Burma; First airing: 2/1/67. Repeated: 7/5/67.

Assigned to rescue Katherine Faulkner, an impulsive young English girl being held hostage in the back country of Southeast Asia, Kelly and Scott parachute into Burma with $500,000 in ransom money. Once there, they learn that the woman they've come to rescue has no intention of leaving.

Katherine, one more of those women from Kelly's past, has fallen for the man thought to have kidnapped her, Chinese warlord Chuang-Tzu. Because of this, Katherine has fleeced her wealthy father and his government to sponsor Chuang-Tzu's guerrilla warfare.

Assessment

Typical of the writer's scripts for the series, "The War Lord" is dark, grand in scope, and rich with multidimensional characters.

Part of the complexity of Culp's writing is his willingness to use his characters with equal conviction making both conservative and liberal statements. Katherine is a peacenik. Her beliefs are well represented by the writer, notably in a scene where she begs Chuang-Tzu to spare the life of a Communist soldier.

As a gift to her, he does, thus proving the old proverb, "The way to hell is paved with good intentions." Tzu's kindness is rewarded by treachery when the pardoned soldier leads an attack on the palace resulting in Tzu's downfall and death.

Kelly has met Katherine before. He certainly knows her flare for drama and her willingness to deceive her rich and powerful father, as long as the cause fits her fancy.

Kelly sees the change in her—the deeper, committed Katherine; the mature and calm Zen-like Katherine; all due to Chuang-Tzu, who has taught her more about life than anyone else she had ever met.

The great unsaid in this story is another step into the field of equality. A White daughter of an English peer is in love with a Chinese warlord. Her previous life of entitlement was empty and shallow. In another twist on the "enchanted cottage" theme, the writer has placed them in a secluded, ancient palace, hidden and overgrown by jungle.

They are safe here. There are no judgments here. There are no society mirrors to shatter their illusion here. But, as in all elusive dreams, their Eden cannot last.

The Story Behind the Story

Of the seven scripts Robert Culp would write for *I Spy*, this would be the most renowned and bring him an Emmy nomination for Outstanding Writing Achievement in Drama. Yet "The War Lord" almost didn't happen.

Culp was hesitant to turn the script in, concerned that Leonard would not cast him in the part of Chuang-Tzu, allowing him to play opposite himself in the same episode.

While waiting, Culp began to plot a way to convince Leonard, Friedkin and Fine that he could perform both parts. He had heard that makeup artist John Chambers was considered one of the best creators of prosthetic facial pieces. The two men met and agreed to work on creating a look that would alter Culp's appearance just enough to allow the actor to play both Kelly Robinson and Chuang-Tzu.

For several months, Culp visited Chambers at his Studio City home. There, every Saturday, in the garage, facial molds were cast in this trial-and-error process.

Toward the end of the filming of the first season, Leonard stopped by Culp's dressing room. He had just seen the first cut of "Court of the Lion," the episode that marked Culp's directorial debut. Leonard told Culp that the episode was "very good," but he wanted Culp to promise to never ask to direct another episode. The line he used: "I need a live actor, not a dead director."

If Leonard wanted a "live" actor, Culp was going to give him two.

A few day later, the script for "The War Lord" was submitted to Mort Fine. Along with the script came a request from the writer to be allowed to play the part of Chuang-Tzu.

"The War Lord" was assigned a production number, but production was delayed over budget concerns.

In late 1966, when Culp and Cosby boarded a plane to fly to Spain, "Warlord" was back on the schedule due to Leon Chooluck's genius. Further, the schedule for the production was set at a staggering 11 days. The normal amount of time allotted for shooting an episode of *I Spy* was seven.

The 11-day shoot had been given a green light; John Chambers was brought in and paid for his magical transformation of Culp; and Leonard never asked to see the 8mm test of Culp in makeup.

Although Leonard and Culp did not always agree, Culp is quick to say he always suspected Leonard was behind the resurrection of his pet project, and that the *I Spy* boss enjoyed making "grand anonymous gestures."

Foaud Said was director of photography on this episode, as it was shot entirely in Spain. The camera work is certainly above standard for a TV series of this time.

The reduced costs of shooting in Spain allowed the grand palace sets to be created, as well as those of the Asian village and the board room in Hong Kong.

Culp: "When we got there and I saw what these people had built—it would have cost Sheldon three episodes, for Christ's sake, to build these sets. The stuff inside the temple, the passageways, it was all spectacular."[17]

The costumes and the background players during the opening scenes shot in the Asian village add a sense of realism to "The War Lord." The handheld camera work allows this sequence to look and feel like a documentary. By allowing us to see the children being bathed, and a dog tied to the side of a shack, eating scraps, from the first frame, the viewer knows this episode was not shot on a back lot at Desilu.

While working on "The War Lord," Chambers received a message that a producer named Arthur Jacobs was trying to reach him from London. Chambers had never heard of Jacobs and, having been burned so often by wannabe producers looking to make cheap monster movies, was unsure whether he should return the call. Culp, on the other hand, knew very well who Arthur Jacobs was, and advised Chambers to respond quickly and request airline tickets to London. When "War Lord" wrapped, Chambers flew to England to meet with Jacobs, and was hired to create simian faces for *Planet of the Apes*.

Many years later, Culp was asked to present a Life Achievement Award to John Chambers. He hadn't seen the makeup artist in years, and was surprised to see Chambers arrive at the ceremony in a wheelchair.

The fumes Chambers inhaled for his entire professional career, the very same fumes Culp remembered smelling in Chambers' garage workshop back in 1965 and '66, had ruined the makeup artist's lungs, damaged his liver, and attacked his nervous system.

Culp threw away the speech he had written, then stepped to the podium and talked without a script, from the heart, about the generosity, the talent, and the sacrifice of a true artist named John Chambers.

A final note: The part of Katherine Faulkner was originally written for Julie Christie. But, in early 1966, Christie won an Academy Award for her appearance in *Darling*, and became unavailable for television work.

Culp: "Jean Marsh is a terrific actress, but she did not possess the same quality as Julie Christie. That was my character—'I don't give a shit' drop-dead-gorgeous rich girl. When Jean Marsh showed up, she's a very normal looking person. Makeup did a great job, and Foo

Fouad's Rembrandt moment, Jean Marsh with Culp, the war lord, in Spain, 1966 (© 3 F Prod., courtesy Robert Culp).

said, 'Don't worry about it, I'm going to light her like Rembrandt.' And he did. The one close-up that really mattered, it worked."[18]

Reviews

Yet another Close Up listing in *TV Guide*. This was the ninth in less than two years, already a record for an entertainment series. It was also the third episode in a row to be so honored.

At the time of its initial airing, "The War Lord" was reviewed by both the *Hollywood Reporter* and *Daily Variety*.

From the *Hollywood Reporter*, February 2, 1966: "Filmed in Spain, this *I Spy* segment has its usual quota of nail-biting scenes. The big honors go to Culp who not only wears his Chinese make-up well, but also performs with restraint a role that could have been overacted."

From *Daily Variety*, February 3, 1966: "Bob Culp dominates this intriguing episode, [giving] a particularly powerful portrayal of the relic of the past living in the world of today—the remnant of a feudal system. Culp handles the dueling very well, and in realistic makeup essays the part of the War Lord with conviction. His story is replete with unusual characterizations as well as action."

RATINGS

According to A.C. Nielsen, *for Wednesday, 10 to 11 P.M.:*
I Spy, *NBC: 37.2%*
The Danny Kaye Show, *CBS: 27.5%*
Wednesday movie, Jerry Lewis in It's Only Money, *ABC: 20.5%*
All others: *16.3%*

Cast

Jean Marsh was born and raised in England. She was relatively unknown in Hollywood, having done one *Twilight Zone* in America while performing on stage, but otherwise mostly seen in British-made series such as *Danger Man*, *The Saint*, and *Doctor Who*. She was 32 at the time of this filming. She would go on to create and star in the acclaimed PBS series *Upstairs, Downstairs* in the early 1970s. Culp was impressed with the unexpected quality and nuance Marsh brought to Katherine, illustrating the profound change in ideals and personality of her character.

Cecil Parker (Sir Guy Faulkner) was a distinguished English actor. Culp felt he was excellent at bringing the "upper class arrogance and furious determination" needed to the scene in order to kick-start the story. Parker, who had extensive stage experience, compiled over 100 credits in film and TV during a career that spanned the early 1930s through the late 1960s.

51. **"A ROOM WITH A RACK"**; Written by: Michael Zagor; Directed by: David Friedkin; Location: Spain; First airing: 2/8/67. Repeated: 7/26/67.

In the room and on the rack is Kelly. He is being tortured to give up a secret formula. Kelly resists, but is broken by the ordeal. Scott's challenge, keep the enemy at bay until Kelly can rebuild himself.

As Frenchman Maximilian de Brouget had been in "Chrysanthemum," we will discover that Kelly is being used by his own agency. The formula he carries in his head is fake. The Military Intelligence director in Madrid, the uncaring Anderson, arranges for Kelly to be released from the hospital even though his doctor advises against it. Anderson wants the enemy, who tried to crack Kelly in the first place, to take another stab at it.

Scott takes Kelly to the ranch of the wealthy Don Jose for a little R & R. They meet up with an old friend, the free-spirited Lindy, who will prove to be of great help to them before this adventure is over. While there, they also spot Kelly's tormentors, who wait their chance to strike again.

Assessment

Culp is in top form in this excellent episode. Watch for the absolute terror he conveys when, while at the party, he spots the "Bald Man" who had orchestrated his torture. He collides with a waiter, sending a tray of hors d'oeuvres flying, then withdraws into a corner, staring at his tormentor, unblinking, truly terrified. Next comes his indecisiveness on how to proceed—his panic in the bullring and the self-loathing that follows. Finally, when returned

Sancho Gracia, Jose Pepe Nieto, Salome Jens, "A Room with A Rack" (© 3 F Prod., courtesy Image Ent.).

to the torture chamber and left alone for the night, he sobs uncontrollably. The brave acting choices are excellently conveyed in what is certainly one of Culp's best performances.

For once, a woman from Kelly's past does not create a problem for him. Lindy is a bright and refreshing character, fleshed out by the talented Salome Jens. She turns out to be a true friend and worthy of Scott's trust when he reveals to her the true nature of his and Kelly's work.

As we have seen in the past, Kelly can turn vicious. Notice, after he guns down three of his tormentors, including their leader, the Bald Man, how he takes his desire for revenge a step further. As he walks by the Bald Man, Kelly kicks him in the face. It is done quickly, without premeditation or justification. Scott doesn't even give it a second look. They make a joke and exit the room.

"A Room with a Rack" returned *I Spy* to the type of episode chock-full of exciting visual images. For this reason, the opening title sequence, as it always had until recently, included images highlighting only the story to come.

The Story Behind the Story

Zagor: "I remember Kelly losing his nerve. It worked. Bob is a wonderful actor. He starred in 'The Sound of One Hand Clapping,' my very first *Ben Casey*. And, for this, he was simply brilliant."[19]

Salome Jens: "I loved the show, loved the character, loved the writing. What was most wonderful about the experience was those guys [Culp and Cosby]. Bill kept me laughing all the time. His on-going commentary as we drove to the set everyday was just hysterical. We just had the time of our lives.

"As a director, David was such a prince. He connected with actors, and he trusted you. That was a happy show. Those people had integrity, they hired good actors, and took steps to make it a quality show. And the fact that they traveled to these wonderful, exciting places. It was the first time I had gone to Spain, so I think maybe it was one of the nicest experiences I ever had filming."[20]

Culp: "I had worked with Sal Jens before, and she was really one of the dames. Boy, she was terrific.

"The scene I remember loving most—Bill walks into the dungeon, and I'm on the rack, and he asks, 'How have you been?' And I say, 'Shorter.' I loved that line."[21]

With this episode, we meet Anderson, their regional supervisor. There is no affection between Kelly or Scott and Anderson. He is a heartless man who will do anything to get the job done. An interesting choice was made in having Anderson call Scott by his first name, Alex. Scott, or "Scotty", seems to prefer that his pals not use his Christian name. Anderson is clearly not a pal.

Anderson, under a new "code name," will return for a pair of episodes in the third season, with a surprising twist.

Mostly shot in Spain by Fouad Said, under the supervision of Friedkin, only three scenes with Anderson (his office, a gym, and the various hospital sets), plus the hospital sequences with Dr. Minores, were filmed in Los Angeles.

If you listen closely to the audio track to the movie playing at the local cinema, you can recognize it as an episode of *The Untouchables*, dubbed in Spanish. That series, along with *The Man from U.N.C.L.E.*, would often combine two-part segments and release them overseas as feature films.

Bill Cosby wears a short-sleeved sweatshirt in the gym scene, which has "Temple University" spelled out on it. He also shows off his abilities at gymnastics.

Salome Jens was flown from New York to L.A. to shoot one scene to finish the episode. The scene, the last in the script, has Kelly and Scott meet up with Lindy at a hotel bar where she was told, by Scott, to wait for them. She is drunk and must be carried out by Kelly. The set up for this scene remains in the finished episode, when we last see Lindy. Scott tells her to go to Madrid and pass information on to Anderson, then to wait for him and Kelly:

LINDY: "Where do I meet you?"
SCOTT: "Casa de Botin. Order a big pitcher of sangrias."
LINDY: "What if you're late?"
SCOTT: "Drink slow."

However, the punch line to this, and a chance for Lindy to return and see that both Kelly and Scott made it back all right, was left out due to time constraints.

Culp & Cosby on Set Rewrite

The scene where Kelly and Scott are using sticks to scrape bullshit off the bottoms of their shoes was pure improvisation.

After Scott rescues Kelly from the stretching rack, Kelly sits up on the wooden frame and rubs his sore wrists, and complains, "I was doing *ok* in there. I might have made it. Now

14—The Sixth Block of Episodes

I'll never know." Cosby adds the comeback: "You want to get back in it? I'll run you down a couple times. Make a basketball player out of you."

REVIEWS

TV Guide presented *I Spy* with its tenth Close Up listing. This would be the fourth such acknowledgment in as many weeks.

CAST

Salome Jens (Lindy) had played opposite Culp in "Corpus Earthling," a segment of *The Outer Limits*. She played opposite another prominent leading man of the 1960s, Rock Hudson, in the John Frankenheimer film *Seconds*. During the mid–1970s she would have a recurring role on Norman Lear's *Mary Hartman, Mary Hartman*. And in the 1990s she appeared on 15 episodes of *Star Trek: Deep Space Nine* as a female shape shifter.

Keith Andes (Anderson) had been quite successful in film and TV, often playing the handsome lover, as he did opposite Marilyn Monroe in 1952's *Clash of Night*. On TV, he was featured in three series of his own, all short-lived. One year after this, as well as appearing in more *I Spy* episodes, he would play an alien jungle native on *Star Trek*.

Leo Penn plays Dr. Minores. Penn was better known as a director, having called the shots in four of the very first *I Spy* episodes.

52. **"GET THEE TO A NUNNERY"**; Written by: Marion Hargrove; Story by: Barbara and Milton Merlin; Directed by: Alf Kjellin; Location: Spain; First airing: 3/1/67. Repeated: 8/2/67.

In Spain, Kelly and Scott shadow British agent George Ponsonby Rickaby Hackaby. The sneaky Brit is sniffing out a secret worth 14 million dollars. The key to the puzzle is the silent gardener working at a nunnery.

One must pay close attention and follow the bouncing ball.

The gardener at the nunnery was the art curator for a Nazi general during World War II and therefore came to possess millions of dollars worth of stolen paintings. He has been hiding in the convent, claiming to have taken a vow of silence, staying close to the masterpieces. He has covered them with amateurish art of his own. It is his obsession to protect his secrets. He has even assumed a name that was given to a saint who was tortured and killed for refusing to divulge information.

George Hackaby believes the gardener can lead him to the stolen

Peter Lawford, "Get Thee to a Nunnery" (© 3 F Prod., courtesy Image Ent.).

art. A greedy doctor, who treats the gardener after he is beaten by a German thug and his henchmen also believes the silent man can bring him great wealth. And that henchman, well, he actually works for the not-so-good doctor, who somehow knows about the gardener's secret even before Hackaby does.

Assessment

The manner in which the story is told is overly complicated. More time is spent on dialogue designed to create the competitive relationship between Kelly, Scott and Hackaby, than to help us keep track of who is who and what is what.

Oddly, after devoting so much of the story to developing a relationship between Hackaby, Kelly and Scott, the English agent vanishes for nearly the last third of the story.

It is amusing to see the American agents dress up as nuns in order to gain access to the convent, as well as get into a fistfight with the corrupt doctor and his henchmen, slugging it out while still wearing the religious habits.

Otherwise, "Get Thee," despite *TV Guide*'s raves from so many years ago, never quite connects.

The Story Behind the Story

In the original script by Barbara and Milton Merlin, the location was Casablanca. It had been the plan to move the *I Spy* company to Morocco after filming in Spain for the final episodes of season two. When this changed, Marion Hargrove was brought in to do a quick rewrite.

Additionally, in the Merlins' script, the British agent is not sealed up behind a brick and mortar wall at the halfway mark of the story. Instead, he is killed.

In the original script, it makes perfect sense to spend half of the episode exploring the relationship between the British spy and the American spies. Only then can the audience feel the impact of his death, and cheer on Kelly and Scott as they attempt to complete the assignment. However, once Lawford was cast, and in hopes that he might make additional appearances in the series, a decision was made that Hackaby should not die. Hargrove, in doing his rewrite, should have changed the structure of the script, and kept Hackaby in the main story, rather then sealing him up behind a wall. It all feels rather pointless to spend so much time with a character, only to lose him for nearly half the story.

In the Merlins' tag scene, Kelly and Scott decide to give their dead friend credit for finding the paintings, out of final respect. In Hargrove's version, they give Hackaby the credit just to annoy him. While Hargrove wrote a punchier script, his handling of the story was far inferior to that of the Merlins.

REVIEWS

Eleven Close Up listings in just two years. And this would be the fifth in a row. No entertainment program—and perhaps, even, no news program—has been more acknowledged for its excellence by the critics of *TV Guide* than *I Spy*.

Cast & Crew

Peter Lawford (George Hackaby) was 44 here. He is best remembered as being a member of the famed Rat Pack with Frank Sinatra, Dean Martin, Joey Bishop, and Sammy Davis Jr. He was also famous for being married to President John F. Kennedy's sister. In an effort to keep the president clear from scandal, he visited Marilyn Monroe, along with Robert Kennedy, on the night that she died. Years later, Lawford married Mary Rowan, daughter of comedian Dan Rowan, of *Laugh-In*.

Besides his high-profile appearances with Rat Packers and Kennedys and Rowens, Lawford had two series of his own prior to working here: *Dear Phoebe* (1954–55) and *The Thin Man* (1957–59). A few months before filming this episode of *I Spy*, he would appear with fellow Rat Packer Sammy Davis Jr. in a segment of *The Wild Wild West*.

Always one to enjoy a cocktail, Lawford would die in 1984 at the age of 61 from liver and kidney disease.

Culp: "I never knew Peter at all, except through conversations with Sammy [Davis]. I remember talking with him about Sammy one morning when we were shooting at the studio. It was a thoughtful conversation, which I really didn't expect from Peter Lawford. He was a nice guy. I liked him"[22]

Preece: "Peter Lawford was never sober, the poor guy. He was an unfit man."[23]

Vincent Gardenia, the corrupt doctor, had appeared in multiple episodes of *Ben Casey* and *The Naked City*. He would receive an Academy Award nomination for 1973's *Bang the Drum Slowly*. At that time he was also cast for one season on the top rated show on TV, *All in the Family*, and he appeared in Culp's 1972 film, *Hickey & Boggs*. In 1987 he received a second Academy Award nomination for *Moonstruck*. In 1989 he won an Emmy for the TV movie *Age-Old Friends*. He died in 1992 of a heart attack. He was 70.

Barbara and Milton Merlin, a husband and wife writing team, had provided scripts for *Bonanza* and *The Virginian*. They wrote the first draft script here, which was then turned over to another writer. The Merlins were downgraded to a "story by" credit and would not return.

53. **"CASANOVA FROM CANARSIE"**; Written by: Rick Mittleman; Directed by: Hal Cooper; Location: Spain; First airing: 3/29/67. Repeated: 9/6/67.

In Spain, Kelly and Scott keep a watchful eye on vacationing Herbie Rimstead, a former Pentagon file clerk who was recently replaced by a computer. The nerdy Herbie has total recall. Kelly and Scott are worried he'll spill it all to a lusty, busty Russian.

Assessment

For anyone tired at the end of the day and not looking to be challenged by their TV set, this is a pleasant and harmless episode.

Wally Cox, playing the file clerk named Herbie, was instantly recognizable to TV audiences of the 1960s, having had his own popular series, *Mr. Peepers*. We need little explanation as to who his character is to understand him—he is Wally Cox, innocent, meek, nerdy. Other than some back story, such as how he worked at the Pentagon, had access to highly classified information, then was replaced by a computer, we are ready to proceed. We will find out that Herbie, his confidence low, and having plenty of free time on his hands, has traveled to romantic Spain looking to discover what kind of a man he truly is. A pair of

Wally Cox, Letricia Roman, "Casanova from Canarsie" (© 3 F Prod., courtesy Image Ent.).

Spanish spies, in cahoots with the Russians, are interested in finding out what kind of a man Herbie is, too. Kelly and Scott's only instructions are to keep the wolves away.

Once we know the set up, it's just a matter of sitting back and enjoying the ride.

The Story Behind the Story

According to this episode, Scott became an agent on May 15, 1964. Kelly was sworn in on August 12, 1964. We can gather that in October '64, by the shooting schedule of the pilot, they were working together in Hong Kong.

I Spy was featured on the cover of *TV Guide* the week "Casanova" first aired. The article concerned the difficulty of shooting in foreign lands under a variety of circumstances. It is ironic that, during a week when *TV Guide* was drawing attention to the travels of *I Spy*, the episode being aired was shot entirely on soundstages in Hollywood.

For the article, Dick Hobson wrote, "Sheldon Leonard, the NBC series' Executive Producer, insists that *I Spy* stay out of Hollywood studios as much as possible and use the real world for its setting."

An exception to this, clearly, would be "Casanova from Canarsie."

Rick Mittleman: "After the show had been on for a couple of years, and the expensive traveling was becoming prohibitive, this was designed to be a 'bottle show,' to be shot on stage. Mort Fine was looking for a story for Wally Cox, and I came up with something that seemed to work. Wally had a great character—or, I should say, a great persona."[24]

Michael Preece: "Wally Cox was a sweet man, and one of the great guys. But he was unlike his persona about being shy. He had a drinking problem, too, and died very young.

"They wanted a comedy, so they hired Hal Cooper, who was a comedy director."[25]

LOCKED ROOM #8

We get to see Kelly and Scott trapped in another of their famous locked rooms. This is the one with the giant crate of oranges and a window so high up that Kelly and Scott decide to build a mountain of citrus for climbing.

CULP & COSBY ON SET REWRITE

Upon arriving at the restaurant, Kelly and Scott spot Herbie and Consuela sharing drinks at a table. Kelly says, "What do you think? Plan X?" Scott replies, "Plan X it is." Culp and Cosby changed this to:

KELLY: "What do you say? Plan X?"
SCOTT: "Plan X?"
KELLY: "Yeah, X."
SCOTT: "Don't tell me Plan X. Don't give me no letter, man. Tell me what you want to do."
KELLY: "How come every time I give you one of the hippie things, you embarrass me? Plan X. That's when we both, or one of us, messes up."
SCOTT: "That's Plan Y, man."

After knocking Herbie out for the second time, and sitting by his side in their hotel room, and listening to the unconscious Herbie call out, "Momma," Cosby gets silly, turning to Culp and saying:

SCOTT: "You don't have a bottle?"
KELLY: "Don't start with that. Don't start with that."
SCOTT: "He's calling for his momma. Why don't you get him a bottle of milk?"

When in the locked room, they build a mountain of oranges, in hopes of climbing up to the high window. When Scott tries to run up the mountain, the oranges slide out from under his feet and he lands face down in the scattered pile. The ad-lib: Kelly joins him, picks up an orange, then says: "Usually when I want orange juice, we slice them first, then we put them in a machine. Listen, if we had a bunch of eggs, we could put them inside [the orange] with a straw, and open a stand or something."

Culp was making reference to the two main ingredients of an Orange Julius, a drink sold at stands all over the Los Angeles area in the 1960s.

In the tag scene, after Herbie pays Kelly back, by smashing a vase over Kelly's head, and knocking him out, Cosby pinches Culp's cheek, ad-libbing:

SCOTT: "How do? Now say after me: Mamma. Mamma."
KELLY: "Mother."
SCOTT: "No. Mamma. Mamma."
KELLY: "Mamma."
SCOTT: "Yeah."

CAST & CREW

Wally Cox, besides typecast as *Mr. Peepers*, was also the voice of *Underdog*. He had played the recurring role of Harold Harrison on *77 Sunset Strip* in 1963, and had even recently appeared on *Lost in Space*, as a nerdish alien creature named Tiabo. A literate and thoughtful man, Cox had written a pair of children's books. From 1966 to 1973 he reigned as the top left hand square on the popular NBC daytime game show, *Hollywood Squares*, until his untimely death at age 49 of a heart attack.

Cox was best friends with Marlon Brando. When Cox died, Brando kept his ashes. When Brando died, his instructions were that both their ashes be scattered in the same place.

Joan Marshall was Ellie, the embassy girl who likes to wear miniskirts. She costarred in a syndicated series entitled "Bold Venture" for one year (1959–60). It was written and produced by Friedkin and Fine. After that, she became a favorite of the Warner Brothers TV factory, turning up on *Maverick, Bronco, Surfside 6, 77 Sunset Strip,* and *Hawaiian Eye.* One month prior to being seen here, she played a space-age prosecutor trying to nail the hide of Captain Kirk to the wall in *Star Trek*. She was 35 and only one year away from retiring from acting.

Marshall would marry film director Hal Ashby, who would use stories of her early days in Hollywood as the basis for the 1975 Warren Beatty film *Shampoo*. Marshall made a cameo appearance in the movie, as one of the customers in the trendy Los Angeles beauty salon.

Will Kuluva, playing Smerlov, Conseuela's superior, had over 50 TV and film credits in 1967. He began acting before the camera in 1949 and was 60 at the time of this performance. The notches on his thespian bedpost included numerous appearances on *The Untouchables*.

Sandy Kenyon, playing Barnes, Kelly and Scott's local contact, was another familiar face on TV. In a career spanning more than 40 years, Kenyon accumulated some 150 TV and film credits. At this time, he was a regular performer on the short-lived *Love on a Rooftop*. He had also appeared on Leonard's own *The Dick Van Dyke Show*.

Rick Mittleman wrote the equally-light "Will the Real Good Guys Please Stand Up." In the '70s, he would write for *The Mary Tyler Moore Show, The Odd Couple,* and *M*A*S*H*. In the '80s, he would be a staff writer for *MacGyver*.

Hal Cooper, directing his only assignment with *I Spy,* had also worked under Leonard on *The Dick Van Dyke Show*. He would go on to work for Leonard again on *My World and Welcome To It*, as well as directing episodes for *All in the Family*.

Basil Wrangell, after cutting 17 episodes of *I Spy*, more than any other editor, would leave the series here. At 62, the talented Wrangell would take an early retirement.

54. **"BLACKOUT"**; Written by: Barry Oringer; Directed by: Alf Kjellin; Location: Spain; First airing: 3/8/67

In Spain, Kelly has been assigned to wine and dine and pick the mind of a Russian ballerina, suspected of being an agent. Now she is dead in Kelly's bed and he is suffering a "blackout" of all activities from the previous evening. He has 24 hours to come up with an answer, and only Scott can help.

Assessment

The opening of "Blackout" is striking. With Alf Kjellin calling the shots, the feel is very much that of a European art film. Clever editing and effective music help to weave the present day story in with the flashbacks of the picture puzzle that brought Kelly to this compromising situation.

As Scott and Kelly retrace the latter's steps, excellent location photography showcasing the city of Seville added greatly to the production. And, finally, the episode benefits from Alan Oppenheimer reprising his role as Benkovsky, this time in a much more serious vein. He is a worthy adversary for Kelly and Scott, an enemy who has earned their respect.

Alan Oppenheimer, Lawrence Dane, "Blackout" (© 3 F Prod., courtesy Image Ent.).

The Story Behind the Story

The direction and editing in this episode is stylistic — very cinema verité. This was the look Friedkin was proud of, and Leonard would refer to as "artsy-fartsy."

CULP & COSBY & OPPENHEIMER ON SET REWRITE

For the tag scene, the script remains somber. The slight humor that was seen at the end of the episode, between the Americans and Russian agent, was added later, once it was decided to have Benkovsky a recurring character. The improvisation plays like this:

IVAN: "Hey, fellas, where do you go now?"
SCOTT: "I'm going to shave, and then going to go over and see this new Sidney Poitier picture."
IVAN: "Sidney who?"
SCOTT: "Sidney Poitier. He's an actor. He's playing in a spy picture, and I'd just like to see what I would look like if I was in the movies."
IVAN: "Can I come along?"
SCOTT: "Well, sure, Ivan."
IVAN: "We go dutch?"
KELLY: "Nah, if you're gonna hang with us, I think we'd better go Russian."
IVAN: "What's that?"
KELLY: "You pay."

For the record, Poitier had not played a spy before the cameras. No Black actor had, other than Bill Cosby.

Oppenheimer: "Culp and Cosby had a lot of fun—because the closing, at the end of the show, was seldom written and often ad-libbed. You know, they go back for that last 30-seconds of the show that is kind of like fun between the two guys. They didn't know where they were going to go with that, they just found stuff on each other. And it was fun to watch.

"When I did that first show, when it came time for my close-up, Culp and Cosby went to the dressing room. They didn't want to be bothered. And so I did my close-up reading with the stage manager. I had no problem with that. But, when they brought me back the second time, Culp and Cosby never left the set—they worked with me. They said, 'This guy might be decent, we'd better stay here and see how it goes.' The second time they respected me and they were there for those off-camera lines.

"It was a good set to work on. The crew was wonderful. They were all terrific. And I had great respect for Oringer's writing."[26]

Cast & Crew

Zohra Lampert drew attention for her work in a pair of well received films, *Pay or Die* (1960) and *Splendor in the Grass* (1961). She was nominated for a Tony for the Broadway production of *Look, We've Come Through* (1960). She also was working regularly on TV. Born in New York, the daughter of Russian immigrants, she was a perfect fit for the role of Zili. After the start of the '70s, however, she was relegated to smaller supporting roles. You can catch one of her rare lead performances in the 1971 film *Let's Scare Jessica to Death*. She was 29 here.

Alan Oppenheimer, now with over 300 TV and film credits, and still counting, would go on to act opposite Sheldon Leonard in a TV series called *Big Eddie*.

Oppenheimer: "In 1992 or '93, I'm up for an Emmy as guest star on *Murphy Brown*. And Sheldon Leonard is up for an Emmy for a guest star. So I went up to Sheldon and I said, 'You know, Sheldon, you gave me my first guest star role out here.' And he said, 'Well, let me tell you something, you were going to be spun off into your own series from that part.' I said, 'What?!' He said, 'Yes. But, because it was the cold war, NBC, at the last minute, got cold feet about making a show about a Russian.' Here it was, 27 years later, and I found out that my first job almost got me my first series. That really floored me when Sheldon told me that. But NBC got cold feet about it. That guy on *Man from U.N.C.L.E.* wasn't a real Russian. I was a real Russian. He was whatever—Twentieth Century Fox Russian."[27]

Alf Kjellin would go on to direct a pair of *Columbo* TV movies in the 1970s, as well as work on other series of that era. This was his final *I Spy* assignment.

Preece: "I think the only reason he wasn't brought back for the third season is that they were looking for somebody who could get it done in less time, for less money."[28]

55. **"NIGHT TRAIN TO MADRID"**; Written by: Steven Kandel; Directed by: David Friedkin; Location: traveling to Madrid; First airing: 3/22/67. Repeated: 8/30/67.

USO comedian Frank Bodie is his own worst enemy. He's an international scandal waiting to happen. Kelly and Scott's job is to keep him on the right track as they solve a murder on a train.

Bodie tells the three showgirls in his troupe that he's going to cut the act down to one. When one turns up dead, Kelly and Scott have no way of knowing if she was killed by one of the other girls or by a Russian spy, also on board. With our various conflicts well in place, and red herrings in every travel compartment, the train begins its journey.

Assessment

"Night Train to Madrid" succeeds through its simplicity. Well-defined characters, perfectly cast, with opposing agendas, attempt to outwit one another, as our good guys try to solve the murder mystery. Agatha Christie would be proud.

Alfred Hitchcock proved in 1938, with "The Lady Vanishes," that a suspense story could be filmed in the confinement of a moving train and still hold the audience's interest.

Don Rickles, "Night Train to Madrid" (© 3 F Prod., courtesy Image Ent.).

The best example of mixing comedy and suspense on a train was the 1976 film *Silver Streak*, which also borrowed the *I Spy* angle of teaming a White guy (Gene Wilder) with a Black guy (Richard Pryor) for thrills and laughs. For good measure, the producers even threw in a former TV spy, Patrick McGoohan, as the heavy, plus a beautiful damsel in distress, murder, trickery, and mystery. If the recipe tastes familiar, this episode of *I Spy* had already been served nine years earlier.

Don Rickles was the perfect choice to play the caustic USO comedian. With Rickles as the loud-mouthed public relations nightmare, the audience doesn't need to see an example of Frank Bodie's stage act. Anyone who had seen Rickles perform on stage (and that included anyone with a TV set) would immediately visualize what a Frank Bodie show would be, an uneasy mix of insults and crude remarks, with a trio of beautiful dames, serving up the perfect menu for a camp of rowdy service men. As with the casting of Wally Cox in "Casanova from Canarsie," the viewer immediately accepts and relates to who the character is supposed to be, allowing the writer and director to jump-start the story.

The Story Behind the Story

Working title of this script was "Frank Sinatra Goes USO."
No, Sinatra was not being considered for the guest lead. But Sinatra's volatile temper was well known.
When Leona discovers Joanne's body and tries to scream, actress Barbara McNair recalled that she was unable to cry out. Friedkin, directing, told her he would have a scream dubbed in. Instead, Hugo Freidhofer, who was scoring this episode, put in a blast of a trumpet.
Art Seid edited. Look for an editing mistake, in the fight scene between Scott and Kutna at the end of the story. Kelly is standing at the end of the corridor, on lookout. In one brief

moment, in a wider shot, we see that Robert Culp is wearing white sneakers instead of the brown loafers he was wearing throughout the story.

Look for a young Gregory Friedkin as a Spanish police officer, outside the train, and then in the corridor of the train, during act 3. He is the one with no lines.

The *TV Guide* synopsis stated this episode was filmed on location, but didn't specify what that location was. The answer: Desilu Studios, Hollywood.

Barbara McNair: "That show had been done in so many exotic places that, when they asked me to do it, I thought, 'Oh boy, I get to go to some foreign locations.' But then we spent the whole time in a railroad car.

"I was a big, big fan. And I was a big fan of both of those guys. I thought they were just terrific actors. And I had known Bill from having worked at Harrah's. I had never met Culp before, but both of them were just a joy to be with. They were just wonderful.

"We had a lot of fun on the set. Every time we sat around and waited for them to set up, it would become a contest to see who could outdo the other—Culp, Cosby, or Rickles."[29]

Kandel: "It was an interesting problem shooting it. Don Rickles was supposed to be obnoxious. And he certainly was. He had to be toned down. At some point, people were saying, 'Let's kill the sonofabitch.' But it was fun, and, with Rickles, you know who you're dealing with. It worked beautifully."[30]

Preece: "Leonard and Don Knotts and Andy Griffith came onto the set. And Rickles just let those guys have it, all for fun. God, it was one great one-liner after another. He was on everybody, Culp, Cosby, even me."[31]

Andy Griffith and Don Knotts weren't the only visitors to the set that day. Bill Cosby's mother was also present.

Cosby: "Andy was standing there talking to me, and she walked up, and didn't know it was Andy. I said, 'Mom, this is Andy Griffith.' And she said, 'Oh my God.' And she slapped him in the face. I swear to God, she short-circuited. I said, 'Andy, I'm sorry.' And he said, 'I appreciate it.'"[32]

Cosby's mother was having a harder time accepting the changes in her son's life than he was. In regard to Cosby appearing on the cover of *Ebony* magazine, and her picture being included in the article, Cosby commented: "Once again, I'm from the housing projects. I think my mother's with me on this. She doesn't believe *any* of this. When my mother died, she left each one of us $48,000 apiece, in case we needed some money to fall back on."[33]

Culp: "That was fascinating about his mom—slapping Andy Griffith in the face. And the comparison to her 'shorting out.' My kids scarcely came to the set. But one time they did, in a limo, to watch a couple scenes and have lunch. My son Jason, who was only about five, was in the backseat. Bill came out of his dressing room the same time I did, and I was walking over to the limo to say good-bye to them. And he came up beside me, and leaned in close to Jason, and started to say something, and Jason spit at him! The window blocked it—so it didn't hit Bill. But he spit at him. And I was so shocked. And it took a shrink to explain it to me, that there is a short circuit where you do something inappropriate because the excitement is so overwhelming—that it is like a short circuit to your system, that you go completely out of character. Boy, oh boy, oh boy."[34]

Regarding the week when Don Rickles spent filming with the *I Spy* company, and when Andy Griffith was getting his face slapped by Anna Cosby, Culp remembers:

"Sheldon wanted to come down on the stage the morning that Don went to work and sit down with everybody and have a nice heart-to-heart. That was Sheldon's idea. But doing that to Rickles would have simply compounded the felony to the degree that the guy would have been wrecked for the whole week. We were all thinking, 'Sheldon, just get off the thing and let him go to work.' Bill, realizing that something had to be done to break through, went to the prop man and rigged this gag, just after Sheldon had done this whole heart-to-heart thing. Rickles opened the box up and it was a World War I German helmet, with the spike on the top. And he broke up, and everything was okay after that. But that was Bill's idea, not Sheldon's. The look on Rickles' face—going from thinking 'I'm never going to get out of this alive' to laughter—was really great for everybody. And he was terrific."[35]

McNair further recalls her week of shooting with the *I Spy* family: "I thought David was very efficient as a director. Sometimes you work with directors who have to do things again and again. But when he came in, he knew what he wanted and he knew how to shoot it, and we didn't spend a lot of extra time going over and over things.

"At the time, there was a lot of resistance to put Blacks on TV, and here you had an interracial couple—not married couple—but interracial buddies. It was a first. I knew at the time that it was such a daring thing to do. I really could begin to see things opening up for Black people. So it was wonderful to be in that era where you could be one of the ones to help open the door."[36]

The Censors

The NBC Broadcast Standards Department had a few concerns about the script. From their notes:

- "Bodie's line, 'Smelly broads,' is in poor taste and should be deleted.
- "Bodie's speech, "All three of you can stick this in your cleavage," is in poor taste and should be deleted."

Culp & Cosby on Set Rewrite

When talking to Frank Bodie, and Bodie is convinced he is a great asset to the United States, and someone is therefore trying to harm him, the script has him say, "If I were gotten out of the way, it would be a master stroke." Kelly responds, "For who?" Cosby, in an ad-lib, corrects him by saying, "For whom."

When Kelly returns to the compartment he is sharing with Scott, after handcuffing the wrist of the dead Joanne to the arm of the seat in Kutna's compartment, the script has Scotty ask, "All nailed down tight?" Kelly's response was to be, "Oh, yes. I used my Junior G-Man handcuffs, too." Culp changed this line to, "Nailed down and clamped down with chains. If that guy is going to get out of this one, he'll have to have hacksaws for teeth."

Cast

Don Rickles was 40 at this time. Leonard had direct experience with him through the comedian's two appearances on *The Dick Van Dyke Show*, as well as one stopover each on *Gomer Pyle* and *Andy Griffith*. Other sitcoms to feature the nightclub entertainer: *The Addams Family*, *The Munsters*, and *Gilligan's Island*. Immediately following his work here, Rickles would make a stand-out series of guest appearances on *Get Smart*, playing Maxwell Smart's old army buddy, Sid. In 1968, ABC gave Rickles his own variety program, *The Don Rickles Show*, where he would turn his venom lose on a studio audience. The attacks lasted only four months. Another *Don Rickles Show*, this time a sitcom on CBS, lasted yet another four months in 1972. Sheldon Leonard was the producer of that bomb. *C.P.O. Sharkey*, on NBC for two years (1976–78), had the king of insults playing a chief petty officer in the Navy.

Michael Strong was 42 when he portrayed the Russian agent Kutna. He was a guest star in episodic TV during the '60s and '70s. He started on the soaps, the daytime serial *The Edge of Night*, from 1957 through '59, followed by a stint on the nighttime *Peyton Place*. A few months before playing Kutna, he appeared in an episode of *Star Trek*. After *I Spy*, he would continue snagging guest spots in many more series, including multiple appearances in *Hawaii Five-O*. He died in 1980, at age 56, of cancer.

Barbara McNair played Leona, the only one of the three showgirls to survive. Prior to *I Spy*, she was often seen performing on various variety shows. In 1969, and for two seasons, she would host her own variety series, the syndicated *Barbara McNair Show*. In 1970 and again in '71, she would play the love interest of Sidney Poitier in the two sequels to *In the Heat of the Night*.

Marianna Hill, the sneaky Joanne, the showgirl who snubs Kelly, then kills Nora, achieved nearly 100 TV and film credits between 1960 and 1990. Prior to *I Spy*, she was so well liked at certain shows that she made multiple appearances: four on *77 Sunset Strip*, three on *Run for Your Life*, and two on *Batman*. She also had to fight off the affections of Captain Kirk in *Star Trek*.

Diahn Williams, playing Nora, was performing before the camera from 1963 to '76. Her first role of any consequence was in a short-lived 1963 TV series on NBC called *Harry's Girls*. Williams played one of three dancers working for a nightclub comic. This time the comic was played by Larry Blyden. After this *I Spy*, she would come back to do another.

Larry D. Mann is seen in the teaser as the unhappy Arbuckle. He was a familiar face on TV in the 1960s, appearing often on *Bewitched*, *Gunsmoke*, *The Man from U.N.C.L.E.*, and *Hogan's Heroes*, along with nearly every other show in production. He was 44 at the time of this appearance.

56. **"COPS AND ROBBERS"**; Written by: Jerry Ludwig; Directed by: Christian Nyby; Location: Philadelphia; First airing: 4/12/67

Scott's home in Philly is the setting. A trusted old friend has gone bad. In exchange for a roll of microfilm, he'll return Scott's mother and sister—alive. The obstacle preventing Scott from making the trade: Kelly.

Assessment

This is first-rate episodic TV, and first-rate *I Spy*. The reasons:

- It's a personal drama for Scott. His profession has endangered his family.
- It's a personal story for Kelly. His best friend slugs him, steals from him, and appears to have betrayed him. Then he finds out the truth. His best friend was trying to protect him by keeping him uninvolved.
- But the best of all is that we get to meet "Mom."

The Story Behind the Story

Jerry Ludwig: "I had done one script for *The FBI*, which hadn't even been on yet. Mike Zagor, who I had known for years, made the introduction for me to get into *I Spy*. That's where every writer wanted to be. That was the hippest game in town.

14—The Sixth Block of Episodes

"I prepared three or four story ideas, I ran them past Eric Bercovici, who had also written for the show, and was a friend of mine, then I went in, and tried them out on Mort Fine and David Friedkin. They were marvelous guys, both. And they led me to Sheldon's office and I made my pitch. And almost invariably, you get turned down. You're by definition *not* on the inside and you don't know where they are, or where they're going, but there was enough in what I said to where they thought 'maybe the guy's got something.' So they said, 'We've been talking about doing something with Scotty's mother. Scott [has] been seen talking to her on the phone, and gets her letters and stuff like that. We always refer to her but we've never seen her on camera. And we were thinking of doing something like that. Maybe sort of a *Desperate Hours* kind of show."[37]

Jim Brown, "Cops and Robbers" (© 3 F Prod., courtesy Image Ent.).

Desperate Hours was a 1950s movie concerning gangsters who invade a house and hold the family inside captive. At the story's center is the interplay between the hostages and the gangsters.

Ludwig: "That's what they said, *Desperate Hours*, Cosby's movie. So I went away, and it was one of those golden things where everything fell together. I came back in and I told the story, from beginning to end, and when I stopped talking, there was a pause, and then Sheldon, in that Brooklyn voice, which I can still hear in my ears at this moment, said, 'Very unusual young man.' That was blow time! That was it.

"He talked to Zagor and he said, 'Can the guy write it?' And Zagor said, 'yeah.' And Sheldon said, 'Well, if he can't, will you back him up,' meaning, 'Will you make good on it?' And Zagor said that he would. Zagor didn't even know what he was agreeing to.

"I wrote the show, I had it all, it worked out great. The only change Sheldon made was an interesting thing. There's the point where Scotty wants to free his mother and his sister, so he's taken the microfilm capsule that was hidden in the sock in the drawer and now he's over in a bar making the phone call, you know, the usual kind of ransom trade thing like: 'If you let them out, I'll come in, to trade it.' And Kelly has deduced where Scott has gone and is behind him now and puts a beer bottle into his back. But I wrote it as a gun. And Sheldon says 'No, he'd never do that to his friend. But a beer bottle would work.'

"Sheldon never took away something and left a hole. When we were sitting in story meetings and you hit a wall or an obstacle, Sheldon would say, and we all did the voice, 'We are resisting the story.' I just loved the man. He was fabulous.

"The big finish of 'Cops and Robbers' was a chase through the old neighborhood, and there's this big billboard that was called for in the script. You see, when they were kids, they used to play around it. And Scotty could climb the back of the billboard, and go up one side and come down the other. And that's how he ends up getting Jim Brown in the end, with the shoot out.

"As I turned in my draft on 'Cops and Robbers,' they called the Morris office and made a multiple assignment deal. So I'm talking to them about the second one. I'm coming out of the meeting, and I'm going across the lot to get to my car, and all of a sudden I notice the billboard there in the middle of the studio lot, and I thought, 'Jesus, what a stupid place to put a billboard up, in the middle of the studio. Who's going to see that? Oh god, it's me! I got them to build this thing, and now I'm taking it seriously!' That was the moment when I really felt like a writer."[38]

Culp & Cosby on Set Rewrite

When Kelly gets off the elevator, where he had been riding in silence with a beautiful woman, the script has him give one more try to get her to smile. When she does, Kelly was to have said, "Thank-you, my dear. Now fly from me." He then walks away, satisfied, as the elevator doors close. Culp, instead, said, as he tried to keep the doors from closing, "There. See how easy it is to make a man's day. We don't have much time. Room number, or key ... anything!"

At the end of the script, after Scott failed to get his mother to accept the truth about his profession, he says to Kelly, "I couldn't make her understand." Kelly says, "Maybe she just doesn't want to." And they walk away, past several children who are playing stickball in the street.

Cosby says his line, but Culp changes his, saying, "Don't be silly. She understood. She just didn't want to let you know she knew about it—so you wouldn't worry. You've got a very fine lady there, m'man." And then, the on set changes continue, as Culp and Cosby jump into the game of stickball with the children.

Ratings

I Spy was in top form for its season finale. The Nielsen findings, for Wednesday at 10 P.M.:

I Spy, *NBC: 46.6%*
The Danny Kaye Show, *CBS: 27.1%*
Wednesday movie, Ferry to Hong Kong, *ABC: 19.8%*
All others: *6.5%*

I Spy also topped the list of shows with the highest audience share for the entire week. The top five were:

I Spy, *Wednesday, NBC: 46.6%*
The Jackie Gleason Show, *Saturday, CBS: 44.4%*
Friday movie, All in a Night's Work, *CBS: 43.0%*
The Andy Griffith Show, *Monday, CBS: 42.6%*
The Dean Martin Show, *Thursday, NBC: 42.3%*

Cast & Crew

Jim Brown, Pro Football Hall of Fame honoree, was a fullback with the Cleveland Browns from 1957 to 1965. He tried his hand at acting in a supporting role in *Rio Conchos* in 1964, while still playing with the Browns. At the age of 30, Brown left football behind for a career in show business. His first job was for *I Spy*. Next came *The Dirty Dozen*, followed by four films in 1968, including *Ice Station Zebra*, *The Split*, and *Riot*. The following year he would give one of his best performances in *100 Rifles*, followed by another memorable appearance, as the lead in the 1970 film *Tick Tick Tick*. As the '70s progressed, the caliber of the films Brown made were diminished by Black exploitation fare such as *Black Gunn*, *Slaughter*, and *Slaughter's Big Rip-off*.

Cosby: "It was just great being beside Jim Brown, and looking at him, and respecting him."[39]

Beah Richards, playing Scott's mother, was 66. She had been nominated for a Tony in 1965 for Best Actress for *The Amen Corner*. Less than a year after appearing here, she would be nominated for an Oscar for her turn as Sidney Poitier's peacemaking mother in *Guess Who's Coming to Dinner*. Not bad, in the same year, playing the mom of the two most successful Black actors in the world.

Richards would work with Culp again, for a mid–1970s Movie of the Week, *Outrage*.

Two decades after her work here, still active as an actress, Richards would win an Emmy for her guest appearance in the situation comedy *Frank's Place*. In 1999, despite being severely ill with emphysema, Richards would be nominated for a second Emmy, this time for her appearance in *The Practice*. In 2000, just days before her death, she would win again.

Culp: "She was a wonderful actress. She was marvelous. I remember her very fondly. And I was delighted that we had a woman of her caliber on the show."[40]

Cosby: "I did that. I picked Beah Richards for that role. You look at what I do. I don't hire any weak people for me to stand and talk to."[41]

Rupert Crosse was 39 when he appeared as the sadistic Chester. On TV since 1959, he had made more than one appearance each in *Ben Casey* and *Dr. Kildare*, as well as taking a turn in a handful of other shows. His break-out performance came shortly after this, in the 1969 Steve McQueen vehicle, *The Reivers*. In 1971, he costarred opposite Don Adams for one season, as half of a pair of bungling detectives, in *The Partners*. Rupert's health diminished at the same time his career was foundering. He died in 1973 at age 45 of cancer.

Hazel Medina, playing Scott's younger sister Jo, was a newcomer to acting. She was reunited with Bill Cosby on a 1988 episode of *The Cosby Show*.

Christian Nyby was a newcomer to the series, but not to the world of film. In the 1940s, Nyby was a top film editor, having cut together such black and white classics as the Cary Grant World War II film *Destination Tokyo*, a pair of Humphrey Bogart movies, *To Have and Have Not* and *The Big Sleep*, and the Howard Hawks Western *Red River*. Making the move to TV in the 1950s as a director, he helmed episodes of *Lassie* and *The Roy Rogers Show*. Multiple assignments on *Bonanza* and *Gunsmoke* followed, leading him here.

15

Wrapping Season Two

The Press

I Spy, for the second time, had the cover of *TV Guide* on March 25, 1967. The article concerned the hazards of shooting while on location, and featured a photograph of Culp and Cosby on motorcycles from "Mainly on the Plains."

The May 30th issue of *Look* magazine featured a pictorial article on Cosby entitled "Cool Talk from a Hot Property." In the piece, which featured pictures of the "hot property" with his wife and children, emphasis was again made on Cosby making "the breakthrough," opening the door for Blacks to be cast in starring roles on network television.

The August 19, 1967, issue of *TV Guide* featured a three-page picture article entitled "Cosby Comes Back to 11th and Green," and covered the actor's recent visit to his old Philadelphia neighborhood to film a special for NBC. The special, the first perk guaranteed under his new contract with the network, was set to air the following season as a lead-in to an *I Spy* episode.

By signing a contract with Cosby that was separate from his deal with Sheldon Leonard, NBC had made an unusual move.

According to Ruth Englehardt, the business affairs attorney for the William Morris Agency who handled the majority of the contracts for the show, Leonard had mixed feelings about NBC's action.

NBC had a hit series that was just ending its second year on the network. Leonard expected *I Spy* to run for another five. NBC agreed. But now the network appeared to be wooing one half of the Kelly-Scott team away.

The network, of course, had no wish to see the series end. They just wanted to ensure that, when it did, Cosby would remain the exclusive hot property of the National Broadcasting Company.

The side deal guaranteed Cosby three hour-long variety specials for the coming season, to be aired in prime time, a number that was later increased to four. It also called for him to develop and star in a half-hour comedy series of his own once *I Spy* had ended.

Leonard was happy for his friend. But, at the same time, he was livid with NBC.

A Tribute Book

I Spy may have been the very first series to have a tribute book written about it. In 1968, while still in production, *Star Trek* would go one better with Stephen Whitfield's *The Making of Star Trek*, an exhaustive look into the production of the now classic science fiction series. But a full year earlier, in the late summer of 1967, Ed Goodgold got there first. His

The second *TV Guide* cover, 1967 (courtesy *TV Guide*).

TV's Swinging Spies, 1967 (© 3 F Prod.).

lightweight book, *I Spy: Robert Culp & Bill Cosby TV's Swift and Swinging Spies* (Grosset & Dunlap, 1967), sold for a buck and featured hundreds of pictures from the series, biographical sketches of both stars, backgrounds on their characters, and glimpses into the making of the series. The tribute book would be released in time to coincide with the start of the third season.

Bill Cosby's Revenge

Cosby's fifth album was released while NBC repeated what the network felt were the best of the second season episodes. *Revenge* (Warner Bros., May 1967) shows the comic achieving new heights as a stand-up performer. For the first time, the album is a cohesive work, with the separate comedy bits connecting into one another, feeding one another, benefiting from one another. "I told you that story so I could tell you this next one," Cosby says at one point.

Almost the entire album deals with the humor and charm that comes from childhood. Two classic Cosby characters are created here, Old Weird Harold and Fat Albert.

Revenge was Cosby's greatest hit as a recording artist. The record shot to number two

Revenge, 1967 (under license from Warner Bros. Records).

in the Billboard album chart shortly after its release in May 1967, blocked from the number one position by *Sounds Like* from Herb Alpert and the Tijuana Brass. *Revenge* quickly achieved Gold Record status, as had Cosby's previous four albums.

Bill Cosby Is a Very Funny Fellow, Right?, his debut record, was still on Billboard, 69 weeks and counting; *Wonderfulness* was also present, in its 56th week; *I Started Out As a Child* was in its 89th week; and *Why Is There Air?* held on, at an impressive 95 weeks on the charts.

The Ratings

For its second season, *I Spy* ended the year with a Nielsen placing of 29 (out of 93 prime-time series).

For its entire second year, according to A.C. Nielsen, *I Spy* averaged a 40 to 50 percent share for its time slot, often the greatest share of any show for the week. And yet the same A.C. Nielsen now ranked *I Spy* at 29.

Here's how it works:

Fewer people watch TV at 10 to 11 P.M. than earlier in the evening. Nearly all of the top 30 shows on all three networks began their broadcasts at 9 P.M. or earlier. There were two exceptions: *I Spy* and *The Dean Martin Show*, which made it into the top 30, nose to nose.

In the previous season, *I Spy* had knocked off two competitors, *Long Hot Summer* and *Burke's Law* (retooled as *Amos Burke—Secret Agent*). Now, in its second year, it sent the four-year-old *Danny Kaye Show* on CBS to cancellation, as well as the critically acclaimed anthology series, *ABC Stage '67,* and had been keeping the new *ABC Wednesday Night Movie* from gaining a foothold.

Bottom line, *Dean Martin* and *I Spy* were working out well for NBC just where they were—both achieving the impossible, week after week, at a time when most good Americans were off to bed.

And so said Nielsen's findings. But Nielsen wasn't the only ratings service busy counting noses.

According to a March 18, 1967, *TV Guide* report on the ratings, while comparing the findings of both Nielsen and Home Testing Market's TvQ for the month of December 1966, *I Spy* ranked fifth with TvQ, of all shows to be carried on network TV, regardless of the age group.

This was startling news. A 10 to 11 P.M. show showing up as the fifth most watched weekly broadcast on television.

But the TvQ report had more data to be considered.

Nielsen was not yet tracking the demographics—the age group and gender of the audience. Home Testing Market was.

In that same report, TvQ found *The Monkees* and *I Spy* to be the most watched shows among teenagers.

I Spy was rock solid.

The Awards

In early 1967, as the episodes filmed in Spain were receiving their first airing, *I Spy* won the Golden Globe Award for Best Series on TV of 1966. Bill Cosby and Robert Culp were both nominated for Best Actor on TV, losing to Dean Martin.

History is made again: Bill Cosby wins his second Emmy, 1967 (3 F Prod. Archives).

In June, as the second season episodes were being repeated, the series had another good night at the Emmy Awards, being honored with six nominations: Best Drama Series; Outstanding Writing Achievement in Drama, for Robert Culp's "The War Lord"; Outstanding Directing Achievement in Comedy, for Earl Bellamy's "One of Our Bombs Is Missing"; Best Music in a Series, for Earle Hagen for the second year; and Best Actor in a Series Drama, for both Culp and Cosby.

Again, for the second year, Culp and Cosby competed against one another and for the second year, history was made. Cosby won.

At the time, Cosby had this to say: "Bob and I are a team. And that's why I don't feel anyone should split us up and give an award to just one guy.

"Bob told me what acting really meant. He wouldn't let a director make me do something I couldn't handle yet. He protected me that first year. And he still does. Bob knows as well as I do that the strength of the series happens to be the relationship between the two men."[1]

Later, Culp would add: "After the second time, he came over to me while we were having lunch and started to apologize. And I said, 'Don't. Don't you ever do that. This is for the show. This is for what we have done together. It couldn't be as important if it went any other way. It's got to be like this.'"[2]

And then, the greatest honor any TV show could receive, *I Spy* was given the going over for the June 1967 issue of *Mad Magazine*.

If it all had suddenly stopped here, *I Spy* would already have left its mark.

16

Tie-Ins

I Spy *in Print*

The bastard child—or, in this case, children—of any television series are the tie-in products. *I Spy* had its share.

In this case, some of the bastard children deserve an inkling of respect.

I Spy NOVELETTE
by John Tiger
Popular Library, 1965

Kelly and Scott are dispatched to Paris to investigate the death of a fellow agent who was poisoned by nerve gas. They quickly learn their cover has been blown, their hotel room bugged, and they're being followed by agents of a powerful underground organization known as Force One.

At a slim 142 pages, Tiger's novelette manages to capture the mood and voice of some of the earliest episodes of *I Spy*, but on a much larger canvas.

Tiger makes one mistake. He states that Kelly and Scott are CIA, not Military Intelligence.

I Spy #2: "MASTERSTROKE"
by John Tiger
Popular Library, 1966

Kelly and Scott are tailing the man who they know is responsible for creating China's first hydrogen bomb.

Not quite the achievement of the previous book, "Masterstroke" is nonetheless an easy read with a complex and well thought out storyline.

Tiger had clearly seen more episodes of the series by this time. He was now comfortable with the voices and mannerisms of the series' characters. It is easy to visualize Culp and Cosby delivering many of the lines of dialogue from this paperback thriller.

I Spy #3: "SUPERKILL"
by John Tiger
Popular Library, 1967

Force One, the radical Nazi terrorist organization determined to reverse the outcome of World War II, last seen in Tiger's first *I Spy* novelette, is back. Their goal is to blow half the planet apart and bring those who are left to their knees. Their plan involves placing small nuclear bombs in the abdomens of numerous unsuspecting military personal and fanatical suicide bombers, as a means to get the bombs onto various military bases.

I Spy #4: "Wipeout"
by John Tiger
Popular Library, 1967

Tiger's fourth entry is the best yet, staying faithful to the premise and style of the series.

The antagonist is Arthur Traft, a botanist, a nobody, an angry insignificant man who is in the right place at the right time with the wrong idea. "Attila" is a man-made plague—a combination of chemicals which, if unleashed into the environment, would wipe out all plant life on Earth. Traft sees this as an opportunity to blackmail the United States government into paying him $10,000,000 in exchange for the stolen sample of the virus.

New, this book sold for 60 cents. Quite a bargain for saving the entire planet.

I Spy #5: "Countertrap"
by John Tiger
Popular Library, 1967

Tiger's fifth novel is a winner. Gone was the massive intelligence operation that would involve hundreds of agents, and military units from all corners of the globe. "Countertrap," while providing an interesting and fantastic premise, managed to remain smaller, more in line with the styling of the television series on which it was based. This assignment is all about Kelly and Scott, as they travel from Canada to Germany, then infiltrate the Soviet Union.

Within the Soviet Union, an attractive American newswoman is preparing to interview the prime minister. A high-ranking Soviet official, with influence over the KGB, is planning on assassinating the Russian leader. A gun is hidden in the TV camera, and can be fired by remote control. As the soviet prime minister is being interviewed, live on TV, with the camera pushed in tight for a close-up, he will be shot. An entire nation will witness the murder. When the smoke has cleared, it will be revealed that the camera belongs to an American TV network.

I Spy #6: "Doomdate"
by John Tiger
Popular Library, 1967

The best of the seven Tiger *I Spy* novels. The plot has to do with two die-hard Nazis who have a brilliant plan to trigger World War III. If you're going to read one, read this.

I Spy #7: "Death-Twist"
by John Tiger
Popular Library, mid–1968.

Tiger falls back on his tendency to write too big for the premise and the characters of the popular television series (as he did in books two and three).

I Spy was always about Kelly and Scott. Tiger, too often attempted to make it about the giant spy network, with its tentacles intertwined into all the various branches of the military and big government. His plots often involved the potential destruction of the world.

World domination was a James Bond theme. Not an *I Spy* theme.

John Tiger was the pseudonym used by Walter Wager, who sold his first novel, *Death Hits the Jackpot* in 1954. The story was about two CIA agents who use the agency's money for gambling.

A prolific writer, Wager has written numerous books, mostly thrillers, as well as articles on the arts and travel, topics that made him an ideal choice for writing an *I Spy* book.

Three of his novels have been made into movies. The movie titles are: *Die Hard 2*, *Telefon*, and *Twilight's Last Gleaming*.

Under the name of John Tiger, he also wrote two novelettes for *Mission: Impossible*.

Lighter Reading

I Spy: A WHITMAN AUTHORIZED TV ADVENTURE.
by Brandon Keith
illustrations by Al Anderson, Ernie Koller, and John Miller 1966

Kelly and Scott, stationed in Japan, are assigned to get close to the widow of a scientist who was defecting from the Soviet Union. Their job is to learn if the dead man carried anything of value out from behind the Iron Curtain. Progress on the case is painfully slow and is only achieved after Scott slips into Russia, disguised as a VIP traveling from Africa.

Lighter Reading Still

I Spy #1
Gold Key Comics, 1966

The story, dealing with an American scientist who is suspected of wishing to defect to Red China, takes place in Hong Kong. The writers and artists were working off the first block of nine episodes for their inspiration.

As with most Gold Key TV tie-ins, *I Spy* is given the full treatment here in promotional photographs from the series, including front and back covers, and inner sleeves designed to serve as pin-ups.

I Spy #2
Gold Key Comics, 1967

Much on par with the first. However, this issue contains two separate stories.

"The Missing Man," set in Japan, and "The Tell-Tale Camera," focuses on the security leaks within a U.S. naval base in the Philippines.

The Whitman hardcover, 1966 (© 3 F Prod.).

I Spy #3: "A Deadly Friend"
Gold Key Comics, 1967

Kelly and Scott are in Venice. Their new local contact meets with them to pass along their new assignment. They are to kill an American scientist with the Atomic Energy Commission, who has turned traitor. He is also an old friend of Kelly's.

Both agents struggle with the assignment. To Scott's surprise, Kelly decides to carry

Gold Key comic 3, 1967 (© 3 F Prod.).

out the order to terminate a security leak, although saying that this will be the last assignment he ever takes.

"A Deadly Friend" feels like an *I Spy* story. A real deal at 12 cents!

I Spy #4: "Duet for Danger"
Gold Key Comics, January 1968

This and the previous comic are the most satisfying of the six to be published by Gold Key. The story involves Scott's determination to rescue an old friend, who is being held behind the Iron Curtain on bogus charges of espionage.

I Spy #5: "The Maximum Guerrilla"
Gold Key Comics, May 1968

Kelly and Scott travel from Venezuela to Brazil. They attempt to apprehend a renegade Green Beret training officer, who is leading a small but efficient army of rebels against the U.S. sponsored governments in that region.

I Spy #6: "Live Bait"
Gold Key Comics, August 1968

Kelly and Scott travel on a train bound for Munich, Germany. Lights go out as the train enters a tunnel, then stops. Kelly and Scott are separated—Kelly is gone.

Whether Scott finds his partner or not is irrelevant. This would be the last *I Spy* comic.

Winning the Spy Game

I Spy Board Game
Ideal Toys, December 1965

Ideal Toys' *I Spy* board game was designed for children. As the show was broadcast at 10 p.m. on Wednesday, a school night, this was an unusual marketing tool. Who would think there would be paying customers for such an item? Sheldon Leonard and Ideal Toys did. And they were right. The numbers were good enough to prompt Ideal to also release a card game and a gun and holster set.

I Spy Card Game
Ideal Toys, December 1966

True junk-in-a-box, the *I Spy* card game was out in time for Christmas. It was the biggest bastard child of all.

I Spy Gun & Holster Set

Ideal Toys, December 1966

Finally the toy company came up with something any self-respecting boy between the ages of six and ten might be interested in playing with. The packaging was ideal.

Top: ***I Spy*** **board game, 1965 (© 3 F Prod.).** *Bottom*: ***I Spy*** **card game, 1966 (© 3 F Prod.).**

I Spy *Long Play Records*

A few weeks after unveiling Bill Cosby's *Wonderfulness*, Warner Bros. Records released *I SPY: Music from the Television Series*, composed and conducted by Earle Hagen. Sheldon Leonard provided the liner notes, admitting, "I still have chills up and down my spine when they play the *I Spy* theme for me whenever I appear on different variety shows."

Joe Price, music critic for *Daily Variety*, reviewed Hagen's album in the April 5, 1966,

I Spy soundtrack LP 1, 1966 (under license from Warner Bros. Records).

edition: "Composer-conductor Hagen has melded jazz, suspense, blues, chase and Oriental music (the real stuff) into one sensational, swinging package. Disk can't miss."

A second *I Spy* soundtrack LP by Hagen was released to coincide with the start of the third season. This time Capitol Records was the releasing label. Capitol also issued a 45 rmp "single" of the title theme.

Hagen's music fit the show like a glove. When separated out, as presented here, it still plays like a dream. These were not bastard children. They were legitimate. And one grew up to gain great prestige: *I SPY: Original Television Soundtrack*, from Film Score Monthly-Silver Age Classics. The limited edition CD release came out in 2003.

A Spectacular Parody

A true *I Spy* fan has one more collectable to bring delight.

In the June 1967 issue of *MAD Magazine*, *I Spy* received the greatest honor a TV show could hope for. The royal treatment—a spectacular parody.

Look for six pages of wonderfulness.

The characters are named Killy and Scoot. The parody opens with a picture perfect characterization of Robert Culp playing tennis. He swats at the ball. He's up, he's down, he's up again, this time with a gun in his hand. Then he shoots, and we see the title, "Why Spy?"

Killy takes a break. He smokes and juggles a bomb with a lit fuse. He says, "I sure hope you enjoyed that opening ... because it's the only action you're going to see in this program! And now, here's tonight's bomb."

After the expected explosion, Killy and Scoot meet with their regional director. He tells them that they are the only agents who can handle the job.

"What's that," Kelly asks.

The answer: "To make an hour show out of ten minutes of plot."

Artist Mort Drucker and writer Stan Hart proved to be oh-so-familiar with their target. One might even suspect they were fans.

The June 1967 issue of *MAD Magazine*, as well as all seven *I Spy* paperbacks, six comic books, the Whitman hardback reader, and numerous NBC promotional photos can easily be had for $15 each in this age of eBay. All come up for bidding regularly at the Internet auction house.

The NBC promotional poster from 1967 and the soundtrack albums can usually be won for a bid of $25 each. The games are a bit more expensive. Figure $50 each. The rarest and the most expensive of all the bastard children is the handcuffs and gun set. This juvenile brat will cost $300 to bring home.

17

Morocco to Greece

In the summer of 1967, James Bond returned to movie theaters around the world with *You Only Live Twice*. With an initial take of $36 million, the receipts dipped slightly from the previous installment. Nonetheless, the Bond franchise was still healthy.

Competing for a slice of Bond's pie was James Coburn's international superspy Derek Flint, returning with *In Like Flint*, the successful sequel to the previous summer's hit. *Casino Royale*, starring David Niven as another James Bond, competed with the main franchise. Dean Martin returned for a third time as Matt Helm in *The Ambushers*. And, later in the year, Coburn was seen in another espionage action-comedy, *The President's Analyst*. Although having peaked the previous year, the world of 1960s TV and film spies remained a popular craze.

The Faces of a Changing World

Changes were on the horizons of television for the fall of 1967. Two more actors, Robert Hooks and Don Mitchell, would be stepping through the door that Bill Cosby, along with a handful of visionary White men, had pushed open two years earlier. Both were Black males and both would be playing recurring roles on prime-time network dramas.

On ABC, in *N.Y.P.D.*, Hooks would portray a New York City police detective. Over at NBC, on *Ironside*, Mitchell would be a law student and part-time assistant for a wheelchair-bound Raymond Burr, acting as a special consultant to the San Francisco P.D.

Returning for another season were Ivan Dixon on *Hogan's Heroes*, Hari Rhodes on *Daktari*, Greg Morris on *Mission: Impossible*, and Nichelle Nichols on *Star Trek*. All were supporting roles, as Mitchell's part would be in *Ironside*. Only Hooks, like Cosby, would be cast in a costarring capacity. Like Cosby, the character Hooks played carried a gun and used deadly force against bad men, regardless of race.

Although Hooks was only the second Black actor to share equal billing with White performers on a network television series, there would be little fanfare. The idea of a Black man playing a lead was no longer controversial. Since September 1965, a mere 24 months earlier, the world had changed.

A Sensible Schedule and a Perfect Plan

Thanks to an early renewal from NBC, the *I Spy* company got a jump on the third season. Three scripts, to be shot in the Middle East, had been written before the end of season

Cosby and Culp in an NBC publicity photo, Morocco, fall '67 (© 3 F Prod.).

two. They would now be used to lead off the 1967–68 season. Also ready was a transitional script that would move the espionage team from Morocco to Greece.

By the early months of 1967, Friedkin and Fine were quick to hand out assignments for several more scripts, all to be filmed in Greece.

At a time when most of the other series were just beginning to shoot their new season, *I Spy* would have nearly a dozen episodes in the can. Production would begin in April, allowing cast and crew to avoid the harsh heat of the North African summers. May would be ideal for Greece. In June, they would be home when the mercury in L.A. rarely climbs higher than 70 degrees.

For August and September, when the climate in Los Angeles is at its hottest, the company hoped to film within the Soviet Union, and then on to Northern Red China. More Los Angeles based shooting would be planned for October through December, months that are normally dry and mild, completing the episodes started overseas and wrapping the season well in time for the year-end holidays, avoiding Los Angeles' rainy season.

It was a sensible schedule and a perfect plan.

Someone once asked a Holy Man, "What is the one thing man does that God finds funny?" The answer was simple—"God finds it funny that man makes plans."

First stop on the Third Season ride was Morocco. Mort Fine's son, David, recalls: "Mort was proud of the Marrakech stuff, because he'd always talk about *The Man Who Knew Too Much*, the second Hitchcock version, and that they'd shot on location, and nobody had done that before."[1]

The images were startling and would prove to be exceptional to the average American

Producer and star, Fine with Cosby, Athens, 1967 (© 3 F Prod.).

viewer. Never before had a TV series used as many locals—and all clamoring to sell their wares. Culp and Cosby were filmed at the local Camel Market where the extras juggled, danced and bartered for the camera.

Leonard: "If you opened your mouth, you might lose the gold fillings in your teeth. The thieves would take anything that wasn't nailed down. They even stole reflectors, which are five-foot-by-five-foot squares, painted in a glistening silver to reflect sunlight to the areas the cameraman wants to brighten."[2]

Leonard recalled the story of how guest star Maurice Evans had to wear specially-made orthopedic shoes due to foot trouble. Each time he was needed for filming, Evans would take the orthopedic shoes off so that he could wear the shoes that matched his costume. The first time he did this, the orthopedic shoes were stolen. The second time, the replacement pair, which he had provided for, were stolen. And the third time, his final pair, his emergency pair, were also stolen—this time by the local urchin Leonard had paid to guard the shoes.

Before filming was complete, Evans, a distinguished actor and a sophisticated Englishman, was reduced to wearing a pair of sneakers with his dinner clothes.

Evans' problems were not over. He would later claim to have been abandoned by the company. They would depart Morocco. He would miss his flight. Days would drag by, with an exasperated Evans writing letter after indignant letter to Leonard and Leon Chooluck, blaming them for his predicament and demanding that they provide him a way out.

But, for now, all were together — almost.

Bernice Fine: "We lost Sheldon in Marrakech. And we were told to all stay together. So, we went into a market, and Sheldon was *gone*. Frankie nearly had a conniption. My God, we heard they'd cut people's tongues out. So Mort said to Frankie, 'It's okay. Don't get upset. Tomorrow is the slave market. We'll buy him back.' Frankie almost hit him.

"Sheldon finally showed up, and he was scared to death. He was always looking at something. And that's what he was doing — and we just walked on."[3]

Leonard couldn't be blamed for having been distracted. The sights and sounds and flavors of Morocco were all around them.

Calvin Brown: "The food was good — but I don't eat spicy foods. That's Cosby. That was Cosby and Culp. They were the ones who would get sick eating all that kind of stuff. And Sheldon would go along with them. Bill would start it, because, as long as Camille wasn't around, Bill would eat anything. He'd eat raw minnows out of a basket in Spain — and they'd all get sick. And goat heads out of a vendor's cart in Marakesh, Morocco, that had turned black! And all the flies were buzzing around it when you opened the top up! Like I said, he would eat anything."[4]

Less amusing were the encounters with the Moroccan police, which Leonard described as being "brutal toward their own people."

Leonard had made a spur-of-the-moment decision. He had seen a ten-year-old boy wash his feet in a public fountain and thought this would make an interesting and unusual foreground shot.

The wide-eyed boy was filmed and was then invited to share lunch with the crew. One of the policemen, on duty with the unit, ordered all spectators back behind restraining ropes. Invited by the Americans, the boy didn't think that the policeman's order was meant for him.

It was.

Using his baton, the policemen beat the child to his knees. When Leonard protested, the cop was confused. He couldn't understand why an American was so concerned about an unimportant ten-year-old peasant boy.

Different cultures made for good television. In some cases, they also made for hard memories.

After two-and-a-half weeks in North Africa, Leonard chartered a plane for the journey to Greece.

The Seventh Sojourn

Hong Kong, Japan, Mexico, Las Vegas to Palm Springs, Italy, Spain, and now, North Africa to Greece.

The seventh block of episodes promised to be the most rewarding. But the seventh would also prove to be the most costly, the most risky, and the most likely to never see completion.

En route to Greece, the Americans were informed that they would not be allowed to land in Athens. The airport had been closed, as had the borders. The military had overthrown the government. No one could enter or leave the country. This was devastating news to Leonard, who knew that this was more than a mere delay, it could mean bankruptcy.

The prep for the productions in Greece had scripts and locations for the islands of Mykonos, Delos, Hydra, Crete, Santorini, and Rhodes. Leonard had chartered an 18-ton interisland vessel, the *Lina B*, to do double duty as both transportation and hotel/restaurant. Fifty-six people would live onboard. The charter had been paid in advance and had provisions for a 32-day itinerary. And now, due to a military coup, all those plans were in jeopardy.

Once again, Leonard took a gamble.

Although all planes had been refused permission to land, Leonard wagered he could guilt the new government into giving that permission if the only alternative was a fiery plane crash, and the ensuing bad publicity regarding American celebrities dying on location.

He was wrong.

With fuel running dangerously low, emergency calls were made and the plane was finally allowed to land in Lisbon, Portugal.

No sooner had Leonard's feet touched ground than phone negotiations began with the new Greek government. The progress was minor, and the production company was hemorrhaging money.

Leonard schmoozed his way up the line. From new government officials, he went on to a one-star Greek general. This was the snake-oil salesman's finest hour.

Surrounded by uninterested people, Leonard made an impassioned plea: The episodes would be excellent public relations for Greece. All those pictures, all those ruins, all those American TV sets tuned in to the beauty of Greece.

Leonard was told, "Call back tomorrow."

And so he did.

Leonard upped the ante.

I Spy was a hit—25 million Americans watched it every week, which, in Leonard-speak, translated to 25 million potential tourists.

Twenty-five million potential tourists—and he was told, "Call back tomorrow."

And so he did.

Leon Chooluck calculated every "call back tomorrow" cost them $30,000. In today's dollars, that equates to $100,000 per day.

Looming over Three F Productions was the NBC contract for 26 episodes for the new season. Thus far, they had shot only three and a quarter. If Leonard failed to deliver, if the "no play/no pay" option kicked in, and his reputation would be ruined. Furthermore, NBC, by being the lender of the money used for producing the series, had the contractual right to take *I Spy* away from him. Leonard was desperate.

After another day, and another "call back tomorrow," and another $30,000 lost, Leonard traded in his one-star general for a two-star general.

The answer hadn't changed. "Call back tomorrow."

Leonard: "Understandably, this sent a chill down my spine. I told [the General] I didn't think I could wait because the American media were hungry for my story. He promised he would have definite news for me the next day which could save me the expense of all those phone calls. Okay, put another thirty thousand dollars on my bill."[5]

It was time for "The Mole."

Leonard let loose Leon Chooluck, with all the money that could be stuffed into his clothes and carry-on baggage. He was told to go and buy friends.

It was a dangerous assignment. Chooluck could be robbed, arrested, or killed, but somebody had to talk sense into the new Greek government.

On April 27, 1967, *Daily Variety* reported: "Bill Cosby and Bob Culp, stars of *I Spy*, appeared to be lost in the wilds of the Mediterranean early this week. The pair was to have left Friday from filming episodes in Africa to do more in Greece. They were unheard from during the Greek revolution, and people around NBC were getting nervous. Yesterday, however, they called—to say they're missing a location manager who presumably *did* make it to Athens."

Chooluck had an ace up his sleeve. He was Greek-American. He knew people in the old country, like his cousin, the army colonel.

The colonel got Chooluck in. Introductions were made. Palms were greased.

Leonard had a new friend, a three-star general, now on the payroll of Three F Productions. The company was given permission to fly to the island of Rhodes. They were the only commercial plane allowed in.

Once there and settled into a hotel, they were told to wait.

And wait they did, for another two days, another $60,000 lost, hoping their new friend would deliver the *Lina B*.

After 47 hours, Leonard and several colleagues rushed to the hotel's window and saw the *Lina B* on the horizon. The general had delivered.

Calvin Brown: "Those islands were just fantastic. That was as good as it got. Next to that, Marrakech. They were really foreign to me, coming from being a little country boy from Louisiana. I had never dreamt that I would be in those places. And I was treated like Cosby on the show. We were a team, and it was unbeatable. Everything was good, a lot of fun, no hang ups, no problems whatsoever.

"But when we went into Greece, that uprising was happening. And they'd take all of our guns at night and then give them back to us at the beginning of the next day. And if one would come up short, we'd all be leaving the country or going to jail. We never lost a gun. They were prop guns, but you get a bullet for it, and it's gonna work. So having all these armed men around, that was a scary situation."[6]

The *I Spy* company spent four weeks on the various islands of Greece, with additional filming in Athens.

For the trip, Leonard brought along only two directors to alternate the episodes. Earl Bellamy and Christian Nyby both had been tried out during the previous year, and were believed to be the best candidates.

Richard Sarafian had originally been offered a chance to travel with the unit, but had declined the invitation.

Sarafian: "I got one I didn't like and said, 'Sheldon, I can't do this. I'd rather do *Batman*.'

"And he said, 'Sarafian, you're being very unprofessional. It would be more professional of you to politely rewrite it.'

"So I said 'okay' and I read it again and said, 'It still stinks.'

"And he said, 'You're still being very unprofessional.'

"So I went and did *Batman*. But I missed the gang. I missed Bill and Bob and Sheldon, and I missed out on traveling with them. That episode was to be filmed in Greece, and I missed out on that trip."[7]

Despite the days of wracked nerves, military coups, recalcitrant officials, and money lost, somehow, in the end, the schmoozer came out ahead.

Fouad Said had shot the magnificent islands with a master painter's eye. The Aegean had never before been photographed so beautifully, and the ruins reminded the American viewers of just how old this land really was.

The gambler, the mole, and the general had provided *I Spy* with the most spectacular scenery to date. This was Leonard's great addiction—exotic locations, beautiful vistas, and problems to solve.

18

The Seventh Block of Eleven Episodes

57. "OEDIPUS AT COLONUS"; Written by: Marion Hargrove; Directed by: Christian Nyby; Location: Marrakech, Morocco; First airing: 11/27/67

In Morocco, Kelly and Scott are given the unpleasant assignment to assassinate an elderly Muslim revolutionary in order to head off a holy war.

After a slow start, the agents meet with Russ Conway, the stern Military Intelligence director who had begun as "Gabe" in earlier episodes. Their assignment: kill Jahbad, the Muslim leader, who was supposed to be languishing in a British jail, but has been spotted in Morocco, and may be planning an Islamic jihad.

Attempting to carry out their instructions, Kelly and Scott enter Jahbad's home where they are captured, and, to the agents' surprise, allowed to live. Jahbad wants the Americans as witnesses to the dramatic final act he has planned for himself.

Assessment

"Oedipus at Colonus" offers an intriguing and surprising story, as well as striking location photography. With the exceptions of the two scenes featuring Conway, the entire episode was filmed on location in Morocco.

The script effectively combines elements of classic literature with diverting moments of contemporary comedy and sudden, graphic violence.

Indeed, this is the most violent *I Spy* shot to date, with the majority of the carnage saved for the end when more than a dozen Arab leaders are knifed and machine-gunned to death in an enclosed courtyard. The slaughter goes on for nearly a minute. When it ends, Kelly and Scott step into the courtyard, surrounded by the bodies of the slain.

Maurice Evans brings great dignity to this ironic story. Delia Boccardo, as his granddaughter, is beguiling. Ken Tobey marks a welcomed return as the stone-faced "Russ." And, as the *TV Guide* synopsis from 1967 points out, we are allowed an unusual opportunity to see the young Arab who made *I Spy* possible. Fouad Said plays Mousa, their local contact.

The Story Behind the Story

The original title of this episode was "The Sword of God," one of the many names Jahbad is known by. "Oedipus at Colonus" is the title of the book that Jahbad is reading, which provides a clue to the end he seeks.

Adonis (Culp) in Greece, 1967 (© 3 F Prod., courtesy Robert Culp).

The "Oedipus" myth deals with a son who unknowingly kills his father and marries his mother. In a later book, Oedipus, having fallen on hard times, travels to the city of Colonus to die. Scott knows of this book and is able to translate it. Neither he nor Kelly realizes the significance of the material until it is too late.

A second clue to Jahbad's plans is when he allows his bodyguard to select the type of automatic rifle he wishes to use. Kelly and Scott observe this from the shadows. The cleverness of the writing leads Kelly and Scott, and us, to believe that the guns will be used in a holy war. We later learn that Jahbad is selecting the instrument of his own death.

NBC, indicating their displeasure with "Oedipus," pushed the episode back 11 positions in the rotation, and declined to give it a repeat showing.

Locked Room #9

A tiny room in the mansion, with two cots with wire support, and only one way out: for Kelly and Scott to be executed.

Culp & Cosby on Set Rewrite

The teaser, surprisingly, was scripted. Part of the following wasn't:

Ken Tobey, "Oedipus at Colonus" (© 3 F Prod., courtesy Image Ent.).

In the basement storage room, as the agents search to discover how Perizadah left the room, Kelly inspects a large shipping trunk with a false bottom. He asks Scott a question—crossword puzzle style: name a small tropical grain, used for food and manufacturing of oil, in six letters. The script has Scott immediately say, "Sesame." Cosby changes this. Culp immediately plays along. Now the ad-lib:

Scott thinks hard, then says, "Wheat." Kelly calls down to the trick bottom of the trunk, "Open wheat!" He then looks up and scolds, "That's five letters!"

Now back to the script. Scott says "Sesame," allowing Kelly to call out, "Open sesame," and fall through the trick bottom.

Having failed to escape from their locked room, Kelly and Scott are asked to turn around and offer up their hands to be tied behind their backs. They believe they are going to be taken out and executed. And this is an invitation for some ad-libbing:

KELLY: "Hey, you know what?"
SCOTT: "What?"
KELLY: "This is one way to get out of a locked room."

From the Interoffice Mailbag
(The Maurice Evans Controversy)

April 23, 1967:

"Dear Sheldon: It is really becoming a bore. Alan and I are still unable to get out of Casablanca, and you must consider me on your pay-roll until we are returned to New York. Yesterday's five hour wait at the airport was followed by a four hour wait today. The best I have been able to do is to secure reservations for tomorrow morning as far as Madrid. If there are connections there, we will continue on to New York, otherwise it would seem useless to go via either Paris or London. Sincerely, Maurice Evans, Room 126, Hotel El Mansour, Casablanca."

April 25, 1967:

Mr. Evans sent a list of his expenses for reimbursement, including 13 days per diem totaling $597.57, plus reimbursement for round-trip airfare New York to Casablanca, $1,422.20, plus $150 for replacement of stolen shoes and orthopedic arch supports.

May 5, 1967:

To: Sheldon Leonard, Western Union Telegram:

"Received Maurice Evans letter with hotel, taxi, per diem, lost shoes, bills. Should we issue payment? Fenton."

May 9, 1967:

Western Union Telegram:

"Advise Fenton regarding Maurice Evans—stop—absolutely not—stop."

May 16, 1967:

To: Sheldon Leonard, From: Leon Chooluck:

"When Mr. Evans had completed his role in Marrakech, he asked that we arrange a very complicated itinerary for himself and Mr. Foster—Casablanca—Sevilla—Lisbon—Madrid—and then, Mexico! The plane to Sevilla was late due to engine complications—and when the same flight left the following morning, they refused to take that flight due to their own fears! (One of our own personnel, Paco Ariza, was booked on the same flight, so we know all the facts.) Our responsibility to Mr. Evans ended, since we easily could have returned him direct to Lisbon and New York on the regular flights. His per diem was paid to include one additional day to cover travel time. In regards to his shoes and arch supports—suggest you advise him that we will turn it over to the Insurance Company, but I know the answer will be 'personal property of actors is not insurable.' Your actions should be guided by the above facts. Leon."

May 23, 1967:

To: Jean Boskin, From: Mike Fenton:

"Please be advised that Maurice Evans is to be reimbursed for two air-tourist transportations—New York—Casablanca—New York—in the amount of $942.80. Would you please see that a check in that amount is issued to Mr. Evans." Mike Fenton.

CAST & CREW

Maurice Evans gained attention in the 1930s as a true thespian, heading Shakespearean stage productions on both sides of the Atlantic. In 1953 he played Sullivan for the film *The Story of Gilbert & Sullivan*, before returning to the Bard. In the late 1950s and early '60s he brought numerous Shakespearian plays to American TV, playing the leads for *Hamlet* and *Richard II*. He won an Emmy in 1960 for his title performance in *MacBeth*. But Evans never turned his nose up at a chance for a colorful acting assignment. He would play a criminal known as "The Puzzler" in a pair of 1966 *Batman* episodes. He also appeared in *Rosemary's Baby* and was an ape in the 1968 film *Planet of the Apes*. Perhaps his best-known performance was as Samantha's warlock dad in *Bewitched*, 1964–72.

Ken Tobey returns. We first saw him in the Culp-scripted "Magic Mirror." He was known as Gabe then, but a change in name was required by the "creators" of the series in order to bring the character back.

Marion Hargrove turned in his fourth *I Spy* assignment. He would write a fifth, "She Sleeps, My Lady Sleeps," using San Francisco as a setting, but it was not produced.

Christian Nyby, alternating with Earl Bellamy, would split all the directing chores for this block of 11 episodes.

Preece: "They took to Earl Bellamy and Christian Nyby immediately. Bellamy was a no-problem get-it-done kind of a guy. Nyby wasn't, but he got it done anyway. If those guys had done the first year, I'm guessing the show wouldn't have gone on. They were the type of directors that some might call 'hacks.' They weren't the Mark Rydells or the Dick Sarafians or the Paul Wendkoses, who really took it more seriously. We were always done by five o'clock with Nyby and Bellamy. Those episodes are all right, but they were just run-of-the-mill directors."[1]

58. **"THE HONORABLE ASSASSINS"**; Written by: Les & Tina Pine; Directed by: Christian Nyby; Location: en route to Marrakech; First airing: 10/16/67

Dorothy Lamour is still on *The Road to Morocco*. Her first companions were Hope and Crosby. Now she travels to Marrakech with Kelly and Scott. The Americans are supposed to protect her aged father from assassins. But that is only the tip of this iceberg in the desert.

It is a case of accidental involvement that finds the agents being sidetracked into someone else's shenanigans, involving the usual treachery and gunplay. Roop, the man we are lead to believe is the evil one, is actually not. The old man, the one Kelly and Scott and Halima, as played by Lamour, are trying to protect, is the bad guy. He has sold out both his daughter and his honor.

Assessment

It's a "*Road* picture," and like all of the Crosby-Hope-Lamour outings, it is filled with humor, in-jokes, scenery, a quest, and a chase. Also, it is lightweight material, meant only to amuse and entertain. It succeeds.

The Story Behind the Story

The "blendship" of Kelly and Scott has never seemed better. Yet NBC was unimpressed by the three episodes filmed in Morocco. All were pushed back in the rotation, and two of the three were not given a repeat showing.

While some portions of this episode were filmed in Morocco in late April 1967, the majority, including all of the portions featuring the two primary guest stars, were shot back in Los Angeles, onstage, and at a reservoir in the San Fernando Valley known as Hanson Dam.

Look for a rare continuity problem with the white truck being driven by Roop. In the portions of the episode filmed in Morocco, including when the truck drives into the city of Marrakech, the vehicle used had a shorter-than-standard engine chassis. For the scenes filmed at Hanson Dam, a white truck with a longer front hood was used.

According to Sheldon Leonard, that is Camille Cosby in the teaser, dressed as an Arab woman. She is holding the camel's harness, looking out for her husband, who is seated on the hump. This shot was taken in Morocco. All other camel scenes were filmed at Hanson Dam.

Locked Room #10

This time, containing drums of olive oil, perfect for treating candles, provided Scott can find a suitable wick. A reluctant Kelly literally gives the shirt right off his back.

Culp & Cosby on Set Rewrite

All of the dialogue regarding the snakes in the room was improvised by Culp and Cosby, including:

Scott's line, after seeing the snakes, then looking back up to the sleeping Kelly: "What did you drink last night?"

Kelly asking Scott, "Hey, remember that record that guy made about being in a crib and snakes under the crib?"

And Scott's reply, "That's not too funny now."

That record, of course, was a Bill Cosby comedy album.

Moments later, Roop looks in the room and, reacting to the dead snakes, asks, "Could they have been meant for Hadji Quazzani?" That was in the script. Kelly's reply was not: "Well they certainly got to the wrong address!"

From the locked room:

SCOTT: "Quite an interesting place."

KELLY: "Ah ha, well, it's our famous locked room, but other than that..."

This ad-lib constitutes the coining of the phrase, "famous locked room." More ad-libs from the locked room:

SCOTT: "You got a hole in your shirt."

KELLY: "Where?"

SCOTT: "There."

And, after Scott sticks his finger through what may or not be a tiny hole, making it into a big hole, he rips the shirt from Kelly's body.

KELLY: "Oh, that one."

SCOTT: "Yes."

KELLY: "Listen ... you tore my shirt off."

SCOTT: "I fixed the hole."

Later, after Kelly and Scott escape the locked room and are riding the camel, they encounter German tourists.

The attractive girl in the convertible says, "What do you do on a camel?"

Kelly was supposed to say, "Just riding to Marrakech." Instead, Culp ad-libs, "Well, everybody does different things on a camel. I mostly watch the ground go up and down a lot."

From the Interoffice Mailbag

"Dear Mr. Fenton: Since living in Maryland for the past few years, the Western Union operators seldom receive telegrams in 'show-biz' (as they call it) talk—so, when your wire was read to my secretary in my absence, re: your reimbursing me for first-class, round trip transportation, the operator was laughing so hard, she could hardly read the message! I suppose the wording does sound a little strange to some of the small-town people! In any event, I do thank you, and will count it as part of the contract.

"You wrote that I should be able to do an Arab accent. I am sure there will be no problem at all. However, I would greatly appreciate it if the Director of the segment (I think it was printed in *Daily Variety* that it would be Mr. Nyby,) would call me some time this week, as I would like to ask a few questions—such as, if I might learn the dialogue I have—or will it be changed—etc. etc. Sincerely, Dorothy."

"Dear Miss Lamour: There will be a technical advisor available commencing Monday, who will be able to assist you with the phonetic pronunciation of any Arabic words that you may find you are not familiar with. I shall be in touch with you on Monday, and hope that your journey here was a pleasant one. Best regards, Mike Fenton, Casting Director."

Cast & Crew

Dorothy Lamour proves to be a very good sport. The part of Halima is not a flattering one. When she first lowers her veil and reveals her face to Kelly and Scott, the men exchange put-off looks. Halima even hints at wanting to seduce Kelly into helping her, but admits that she knows she is far too old and unappealing. She was 53.

Lamour came to fame in a sarong, in the 1936 Paramount film, *The Jungle Princess*. More sarongs quickly followed, including a 1937 sarong in *Hurricane* and a 1940 sarong in *Typhoon*. It was also in 1940 when she first teamed up with Bing Crosby and Bob Hope for *The Road to Singapore*. Seven films later, Dorothy would be reduced to a mere guest star appearance for the final *The Road to Hong Kong*, released in 1962. A handful of rare appearances would follow over the next 20 years. The end of her road came in 1996 at age 82.

Nehemiah Persoff makes his second appearance here, not at all looking or acting like the ruthless character he played so effectively in the previous season's episode, "Rome, Take Away Three." A versatile actor, he was a favorite among TV producers, appearing in over a hundred TV shows between the 1950s and '70s.

Les & Tina Pine only sold a few scripts together. Tina, under the name of Tina Rome, had attempted an acting career. She had modest success. Les had been writing scripts for *Peter Gunn*, *The Naked City*, *Mr. Lucky*, and *Ben Casey*, before taking on his wife as a collaborator and writing this one teleplay for *I Spy*. A script for *The Big Valley* followed.

Jack Kruschen, "The Medarra Block" (© 3 F Prod., courtesy Image Ent.).

59. **"THE MEDARRA BLOCK"**; Written by: Barry Oringer; Directed by: Earl Bellamy; Location: Marrakech; First airing:10/2/67. Repeated: 4/29/68.

The Medarra Block is a wooden puzzle. One agent has already died in an attempt to solve the mystery. Now Kelly and Scott turn to a Jewish scholar for help. But by making Isaac Mendoza their friend, they have put his life in danger.

Assessment

"The Medarra Block" should amuse anyone who enjoys a mystery, or solving puzzles.

Several minutes of actual footage from Morocco is nicely integrated with studio interiors and back lot shots.

And we have Ken Tobey back as Conway. It is only one brief scene, but the gifted actor carries so much attitude with him that he is a joy from start to finish.

These attributes notwithstanding, "The Medarra Block" is of mild interest, only.

The Story Behind the Story

Writer Barry Oringer: "I come from an orthodox Jewish family, so my family really appreciated the episode. I really admired Cosby in this. At the beginning of the show, Cosby and Culp are being pursued by some bad guys, and find refuge in this synagogue. Kruchen, who plays the caretaker of the synagogue, shelters them. As part of the prayer service, Kruschen says 'Happy are they who dwell in thy house,' and Cosby says 'Amen.' But he says it with a very, very little-known and very authentic old-world pronunciation of the word. My grandfather, who was an old-world orthodox Rabbi, said that's the way he *should* have pronounced it. Cosby went to the trouble of doing some of his own research, clearly, and finding out how that word would be pronounced in that setting. I thought that was terrific."[2]

Two nice bits of series continuity: First, while Scott is practicing balancing a plate on his head so that he can keep a promise made to his mother about bringing home culture from each place he visits, Kelly asks, "What did you bring home from Las Vegas after we visited there?" Las Vegas was the location of two second season episodes.

The other, less obvious: As Kelly and Scott are driving through Morocco, Scott is trying to figure out the schedule of religious holidays in that country. He states that it is now mid–April. Mid-April *was* when the company shot the location sequences in that region.

LOCKED ROOM #11 / CULP & COSBY ON SET REWRITE

In the basement of a church, the script includes the lines about how much Kelly and Scott hate locked rooms and preferred it when the bad guys used to try to force them to jump off cliffs. Also in the script, Scott tells Kelly it is his turn to come up with an escape plan, and the line, "Last time we escaped from a locked room, I got the guard so mad at you he threw the keys at you. That counts as MY turn!"

What is not in the script is Kelly's first idea for an escape plan, including that he and Isaac will hide, and that Scott should lie in the middle of the room, and then, when the bad guys return, jump up and scream, then run around and get them to chase him, then knock them all out, making it safe for Kelly and Isaac to come out of hiding. Cosby listens, unhappily ponders the idea, then adds the line about it being a rotten plan.

Later, Cosby adds, "I did not like your plan, sir," prompting Culp to say, "Oh, no, I was still groggy. But now my brain cells are leaping right up. How would you like to be in show business? I'm talking about a disappearing act." Cosby puts his hand on Culp's forehead, checking for a temperature.

Ratings

Carol Burnett, who had been gaining attention on television for several years, was now being launched by CBS with her own weekly variety series.

Burnett had earned her chance. She was coming off a handful of popular prime-time specials. But, still, Burnett was unproven, and would be doing battle with ABC's big Western, *The Big Valley*.

With its big star, Barbara Stanwyck, and its cast of attractive supporting players, Richard Long, Peter Breck, Lee Majors and Linda Evans, *The Big Valley* had been pulling in big numbers. During the previous year, in its second season, the colorful Western had often won its 10 to 11 P.M. time period. On the average, it pulled in a 30% share.

CBS had reason to be apprehensive. And then things for the network, and for *The Carol Burnett Show,* got worse. NBC announced it was moving the powerhouse *I Spy* to Monday nights. Burnett would not only have to go head to head with Stanwyck, but with Culp and Cosby, as well.

TV insiders were predicting that Burnett would crash and burn.

But in those first few weeks of the 1967–68 season, something surprising happened. A vast majority of the television sets turned on between 10 and 11 P.M. on Monday were tuned to CBS. Americans love backing an underdog, and viewers wanted to see how Burnett would fare. The new Queen of Comedy fared extremely well.

According to A.C. Nielsen, *I Spy,* previously number one, would have to settle for second place. And *The Big Valley*, always a solid number two, if not in first place, would have to settle for third.

The audience share divided up as follows:

The Carol Burnett Show, *CBS: 43.5%*
I Spy, *NBC: 26.9%*
The Big Valley, *ABC: 22.2%*
All others: 7.4%

Point of reference: In today's TV market, a 26.9% share is better than the number one rated show on TV pulls. There were far fewer channels to choose from back then. *I Spy's* audience was still huge.

Cast & Crew

Jack Kruschen (Isaac) is likable, playing a character very much unlike his temperamental and deadly serious Aram in the previous season's "Lisa."

Oringer: "Jack Kruschen was one of my favorite actors on television. He's terrific here."[3]

Arthur Batanides (the enemy leader) had previously appeared in the two-part "To Florence with Love," as well as the episode shot prior to this, "Oedipus at Colonus." He would return for "Philotimo."

Norman Fell is here, and, if you look hard, you may spot him under all the makeup, as Karim, the man who is shot to death in a Marrakech cafe. Fell had already costarred in two short-lived TV series. And this was the year he appeared in *The Graduate* as a not-so-friendly landlord. He is best known for work yet to come. He would play Mr. Roper, another not-so-friendly landlord, on the late 1970s sitcom *Three's Company*.

Richard H. Calhoon started his work as an editor with the series here. He cut his teeth at cutting in the 1930s and '40s on scores of B films, before moving into television in the 1950s, editing episodes of *Broken Arrow*, *Perry Mason*, and *The Fugitive*. He would quickly became a favorite at *I Spy*, and would cut eight out of 26 third season episodes.

60. **"THE BEAUTIFUL CHILDREN"**; Written by: Berkely Mather; Directed by: Earl Bellamy; Location: Casablanca to Greece; First airing: 9/18/67. Repeated: 4/22/68.

When the identity of an agent working behind the iron curtain is about to be uncovered, Kelly and Scott are assigned to bring him across the Greek border to safety. The agent, however, is reluctant to be rescued.

Andreas, a Greek patriot, has dedicated his life to the dangerous undercover work of aiding in the escape attempts of "The Beautiful Children," young Greeks who were kidnapped and are being forced to serve Communist interests. But now Andreas is believed to be a traitor.

Assessment

Kelly and Scott must get out of Casablanca in order to travel to Greece for the assignment. The teaser ends on a clever note, Kelly's incredulous reaction to a humorless fellow agent's warning that they take care, for, in Casablanca, the "spies are everywhere." If the line sounds familiar, it comes from a rather famous 1940s movie named after that city.

Act 1 continues to amuse, as we witness Kelly and Scott's efforts to get out of town, and to do so unobserved.

The first moments in Greece are delightful, as the agents connect with their local contact, Zarkas. He promises to take them to a hotel where every room has running water. The abandoned inn is in serious disrepair. Entering a dank bedroom, Scott asks where the running water is. Zarkas replies, "Wait until it rains."

Twenty minutes in, and the good parts are over.

What follows is a road trip as Zarkas takes Kelly and Scott to their destination, the Greece-Bulgarian border.

A few minutes of screen time are spent on setting up a rather pointless joke, telling us that the truck they drive has no mirrors, but they shouldn't worry about being followed because "the one above" watches over them. We find out that The One Above is an elderly, giggling, toothless man, who hides under the tarp above the cab and uses a rifle to shoot out the tires of cars that follow too closely. It doesn't seem to matter to director Earl Bellamy that, from where The One Above is positioned, there is no way that he could see a car following, much less shoot at it.

The main plot concerns Andreas and his mission: to retrieve hundreds of Greek children who had been stolen by the Communists. Why were the children stolen and brought to Bulgaria? We watched the episode and we have to tell you, we're not sure.

The plot thickens when Andreas fails to cross back into Greece with the children he rescues. Each time he tries, the Communist guards patrolling the border appear and he barely escapes, always returning to the direction he came from.

Now the big surprise: Andreas' father has been preventing him from returning to Greece. The father is convinced that his son is a traitor.

Why does he believe this?

Twenty percent of the audience NBC had the first time this episode ran did not stick around to find out. They switched channels at the halfway mark to watch Carol Burnett instead.

The Story Behind the Story

Leonard appeared to be very unhappy with Mather's work. In the "coverage notes" he gave to Mort Fine, Leonard wrote: "There is a very disturbing lack of action in this script. Everything has been expository or lightweight. Their trip to the country side is enlivened only by the incident of The One Above. It's very dull and very uneventful. I do not understand why Kelly and Scott came to the border. What the devil was their purpose? We must believe that it is their intention to get Andreas out, and yet they seem to have no function here except they're spectators. The more I read this script, the more it's apparent that it's badly in need of additional incident. There are unnecessary words, unnecessary scenes. I don't understand the end of the 4th act. I don't understand the reason why [the father] thought his son was a traitor. He says twelve of the beautiful children have named him. Named him what? The beautiful children trusted him to get them over the side. What the devil did they name him as?"

Despite these notes, Leonard did not request that the script be cut off at first draft. The material was revised, slightly, then placed into production. Mather would return to fulfill his two script contract and write "The Seventh Captain."

NBC was fond of this mediocre episode. While the network chose to push the previous three segments back in the rotation, this episode was pulled forward, making it second in the line up for the new season. It was also given a repeat airing.

Perhaps the Programming Department felt the viewers who tuned out for the last half of the episode would come back to see what they had missed.

THE RATINGS

Carol Burnett's lead had diminished slightly, even with the advantage she was given with viewers abandoning this below-standard episode. The end results were:

The Carol Burnett Show, *CBS: 34.4%*
I Spy, *NBC: 31.1%*
The Big Valley, *ABC: 22.3%*
All others: 11.2%

CAST & CREW

Harold J. Stone, making his first of three appearances as Zarkas, accumulated over 200 credits in films and on TV between 1946 and 1986. He had appeared with Robert Culp in three episodes of *Trackdown*. Leonard would bring him back for a recurring role in the short-lived but critically acclaimed 1970 sitcom *My World and Welcome to It*.

Paris Alexander (Andreas) worked exclusively in Greece for his career in front of the camera. He made one American movie, shot in Greece, 1962's *It Happened in Athens*.

Anna Brazzou played Phyllida, the token babe. She had appeared in a low budget 1967 film called *Bikini Paradise*.

Berkely Mather was an English writer. He had worked for *The Avengers* and *Dr. Who*. Because he was not a member of the Writers Guild of America, Friedkin and Fine were able to save Leonard some money. Instead of the usual $5,000, Mather received $3,500.

Van Cleave, his first time composing for *I Spy*, provided the new music. His credits included writing scores for numerous episodes for *The Twilight Zone*, and the motion picture, *White Christmas*.

61. **"LET'S KILL KARLOVASSI"**; Written by: Michael Zagor; Directed by: Christian Nyby; Location: Greek islands; First airing: 9/11/67. Repeated: 12/18/67.

Arriving at a resortlike community in the Greek islands, Kelly and Scott anticipate an easy assignment until their contact turns out to be the beautiful and cunning Maria Galonis. She orders them to assassinate Denis Karlovassi, an extremely likable man, who she claims is an enemy agent.

Maria is a driven woman. Four years earlier, her husband and only child were killed by an East German border guard. She has since surrendered to a lust for vengeance. Her decision to have Karlovassi killed, while seemingly practical, has a darker intent.

Assessment

NBC chose well by picking this episode to open the third season. The material is both engaging and surprising, two elements found in many of Zagor's scripts. There are no clichés used here, no clear-cut good guys or bad guys, and the characters all delight and surprise. The locations, of course, are spectacular.

The Story Behind the Story

Kelly and Scott have been ordered to kill before. In "Cup of Kindness" Kelly was given instructions to terminate a fellow agent suspected of being a traitor. In "Oedipus from

Ruth Roman, Walter Slezak, "Let's Kill Karlovassi" (© 3 F Prod., courtesy Image Ent.).

Colonus" their kill assignment was a Middle Eastern holy man. Kelly comments to Scott that they have been fortunate and have never had to make a hit. In a way, that is true. Their assignment in "Kindness" does die, but Kelly kills in self-defense. In "Oedipus," the holy man dies by his own hand.

Regarding his script, Michael Zagor offers this:

"Mort and David liked the script for that one quite a bit. A lot of my first drafts got shot, and it made me very happy, but it also made me nervous because I felt that things could be better. Mort and David would rewrite some of my stuff, and I always trusted them. But, in the opening of this script, I had Scott and Kelly being picked up off the boat by somebody in a very old car. Sheldon's one comment on the script was 'There are no cars on Mykonos!' I was so embarrassed.

"So I went to Sheldon and told him that I had never been anywhere. I said, 'Sheldon, I've been writing the show out of *Europe on Five Dollars a Day*. Why don't you send me to the Greek islands so I can get some really good stories?' He said, 'I would think that a young man interested in his career would wish to pay his own way.' Sheldon was a lovely man, but writers' travels were not in the budget."[4]

From the Interoffice Mailbag

To: Dick Heffernan, Ashley Famous Artist, From: Walter Slezak:

"Dear Dick—This morning—just after my wife mentioned at breakfast that she would like to visit the Grecian Isles someday—your letter with the script arrived. I read it—It's a good script, I think—and will play well. So I sent you a wire: Accept Deal. There is only one small item I wish you could take care of for me—it concerns my wife. As you may or may not know—we are extremely happily married and I *never* travel alone—so the only courtesy I would like extended: in the hotel where we shall live—a double bed instead of a single. And, when we live on the boat—a *double* cabin—and the freedom of the dining room for her. *She is a very light eater!* The rest, with 25 dollars per diem and five dollars on the boat, is okay—as I treat the whole thing more or less as a paid vacation. Now about the costumes or clothes situation—I don't know where they will be made or purchased—but since I made the film for Paramount last summer, I have lost about 38 pounds—and will have lost another fifteen by the end of April—(hopefully)—so let me know, if they want my measurements or if they will clothe me in Athens—which of course would be more sensible. With Best Personal Regards—I am yours, Walter."

Reviews

On September 13, 1967, two days after the airing of "Let's Kill Karlovassi," both *Daily Variety* and the *Hollywood Reporter* reviewed the episode.

The critic for *Daily Variety* found the season debut to be slow in starting, and overly complicated. "The scenic beauty of the Greek Islands both enthralls and fascinates," he wrote, but then added, "For the first half hour it's walk and talk, walk and talk."

The critic had trouble keeping track of who was working for whom, and who was to be trusted, or not trusted, and wrote, "It's all Greek to me."

John Mahooney, critic for the *Hollywood Reporter*, took a different stand and predicted that *I Spy* would likely "parlay its new time to a greater ratings lead and continued popularity."

He continued: "One of the greatest charms of *I Spy* are the interludes of conversational scat which confirm the relationship between partners and make the series so convincing.

Fouad Said's color photography, aided by a compact and lightweight location unit, sustains a crisp and fluid coverage which abets the immediacy of the show. Earle Hagen's musical scores are a continuing marvel, adapting the idioms of the various locales while maintaining dramatic aptness and interest."

RATINGS

According to A.C. Nielsen, *I Spy* failed to dominate its new time slot. For the first time (this episode was aired before "The Medarra Block" and "Beautiful Children"), the series came in number two. The premiere of *The Carol Burnett Show,* on CBS, won the hour.

The Carol Burnett Show, *CBS: 40.8%*
I Spy, *NBC: 28.6%*
The Big Valley, *ABC: 20.2%*
All others: 10.4%

Again, by today's standards, the audience share *I Spy* garnered in its new time slot would be considered a resounding triumph. And, as further reports by Nielsen would confirm, *I Spy* was outpulling all its competition, including *Burnett*, with viewers in the demographically desirable age range of 12 to 40.

CAST

Ruth Roman (Maria Galonis) achieved over 120 film and television credits between 1948 and 1989. Her striking looks, whiskey voice, and confident manner made her a bankable guest star. She found regular work on the short-lived series *The Long Hot Summer*, which went head-to-head against *I Spy* in 1966 and was quickly cancelled. She was 45 here.

Walter Slezak (Karlovassi) played the Nazi sailor who had everyone jumping during Alfred Hitchcock's mid–1940s classic, *Lifeboat*. He had been appearing in films since 1922. He won a Tony in 1955 for his performance in the Broadway production of *Fanny*. He published his autobiography in 1962, and was age 65 when he appeared in *I Spy*. His daughter, Erika, has been featured since 1971 on *One Life to Live*. In 1980, Slezak's last acting job was on *The Love Boat*. According to IMDB, he committed suicide three years later.

62. **"LAYA"**; Written by: Morton Fine & David Friedkin; Directed by: Christian Nyby; Location: Athens; First airing: 9/25/67. Repeated: 3/18/67.

In Greece, a stunning but low-priority foreign embassy clerk becomes the key figure in a deadly game of espionage.

Ordered to glean information from Laya, Scott finds himself in love and unable to complete the assignment. In Scott's eyes, the biggest threat may come from Kelly, who is determined to finish the job for him.

Troy Duncan, the regional director from "A Room with a Rack," and now apparently operating under a different code name, places Scott on the assignment. But Laya proves to be too pleasing, and Scott struggles with a decision involving his future with the department.

Unbeknownst to Scott, he is being set up. An enemy agent named Hamilton is pulling Laya's strings. She objects to his means, which involve killing one of his own men for having failed at a job, but she doesn't refuse Hamilton—at least, not right away.

Assessment

"Laya" is beautifully written and exquisitely filmed.

But, if the premise sounds like a reverse take on the first season episode "Tatia," it is.

Regardless of the intended tie-in, and the Greek scenery notwithstanding, we can't help but feel we've been here before—more than once.

Remember the formula: Boy meets girl—girl is a spy—girl betrays boy—boy must now betray girl—or some variation thereof.

More specifically, in "Tonia," a second season episode with a similar title, Scott was given an assignment to get to know a beautiful Black girl, and then we discovered that *her* assignment, in turn, was Scott.

In that episode and this, both women reported to ruthless White men who were bent on destroying the American agent. In both stories, those men were responsible for the tragic outcome in store for the women. And, in both episodes, like Scott had opposed Kelly in "Tatia," Kelly was forced into being the voice of reason, opposing Scott and the love he believed he felt.

"Laya" is a good episode. It would have been a great episode if "Tatia" and "Tonia" hadn't come first.

Michael Rennie, Janet MacLachlan, "Laya" (© 3 F Prod., courtesy Image Ent.).

The Story Behind the Story

Earle Hagen recalls: "In 'Laya,' there is a scene done with an Arriflex camera, when the assassin goes into Culp and Cosby's room and does everything with a knife. It's very stylized. I think they got the idea for the fight from James Bond—in the railroad car in *From Russia with Love*. That had no music, it was just sound effects. I wanted to go the other way.

"I said to David, 'I found a track in Greece, a clarinet. I knew I would use it someday. It's really theatrical, and I don't want any sound effects—except the door lock when Culp walks in.' He asked if I wanted him to build it (the soundtrack). I said, 'If you build it, you're going to want to use it. And what I have in mind won't work effectively if it's not dead silence.' He said, 'Okay.' I ran into Sheldon, and he said, 'I hear you don't want any sound effects. What are you going to do?' I said, 'I'm not sure yet.' Sheldon, too, said, 'Okay.'

"I sat at a moviola and cut it to fit the picture. As far as the feathers flying, I didn't try to choreograph it, just imitate it. I cut the clarinet piece from five minutes to two-and-a-half, for that whole sequence. Then I wrote an orchestra accompaniment to it. It was effective and made out of nothing. When we recorded it, without the clarinet track, the guys thought I was crazy. Then, when I played it back with the clarinet, the woodmen looked at me and said, 'Did you do that? Who did that?' I said, 'Some guy with a wooden clarinet on the isle of Rhodes.'

"You could do stuff like that then, without going into long explanations, which I couldn't make clear anyway. It was a matter of trust. I had enormous creative freedom. That's why everyone who worked on that show just worked their tails off.

"That sequence is probably why I won the Emmy."[5]

CULP & COSBY ON SET REWRITE

After Kelly is attacked in the hotel room, and the pillow is ripped apart by the attacker's knife, feathers fly. The On set rewrite begins when Scott returns to find Kelly alone in a room filled with feathers.

SCOTT: "Did you have a nightmare or something?"

KELLY: "Yeah, a monster came in here—and I thought I was going to throw this stuff all over the floor and make him fall down. It didn't work."

SCOTT: "You're supposed to do that with Jell-O, not feathers."

KELLY: "Is that what went wrong?"

The reference is to a comedy routine on one of Bill Cosby's 1960s albums, where he tells how, as a kid, he would spread Jell-O on the floor to cause any monsters to slip and fall.

Later, in the script, Scott asks Laya to show him how people dance in her country. His line reads, "I want you to dance for me. I want to take the thigh bone of an elephant and beat it against a huge drum and I want to dance."

Cosby changed this to: "I don't know anything about it except for what I've seen in the movies. I'll teach you the way we dance in North Philly. The Boogaloo. We put on a Stevie Wonder record and we stand up and we don't touch. It's a way of expressing oneself—You are freer."

But the big change, the greatest addition to Friedkin and Fine's good script, the defining lines that make the entire episode fall together, come when Culp and Cosby pay tribute to "Tatia," the episode this story borrows from. Culp begins:

KELLY: "Boy, you know all the jazz musicians there are in the world, and all the languages there are, and how to make a bomb in a locked room. You're the most brilliant dummy to ever come down the street. That's you. In this business, my friend, you can have whatever you can pick up and carry off. But you can't have the love of a good woman. That is definitely out. You are talking to the expert. You know I know. You were there."

SCOTT: "Of course you know you killed that girl, too. That's what they do to traitors—they kill them."

KELLY (*unable to accept it*): "No ... that's not necessarily true—*ever*."

The phone rings. It is Laya on the line. Scott agrees to meet her. Culp also adds the line that ends the scene, the perfect thing for Kelly to say, the only thing he can say, considering the mistakes he himself has made in the past.

KELLY: "Just be careful. Will you *please* be careful."

But Scott has already left the room.

Cast

Keith Andes reprises a role he began with "A Room with a Rack." He had a different name there—Anderson. Friedkin and Fine liked the character, and the actor who played him, but the budget didn't provide for paying Michael Zagor, the writer of that previous episode, more money for creating a character. So they renamed Anderson to Troy Duncan. Troy would return for "Now You See Her, Now You Don't."

Michael Rennie had starred in the TV series *The Third Man*, as well as playing Klatu in *The Day the Earth Stood Still*. In an acting career that spanned from 1936 to 1970, he accumulated over 130 credits. He was 58 here. A heavy smoker, Rennie died four years later from emphysema.

Janet MacLachan, who played the title character, was 34. She had been acting on TV for two years, including an appearance on the prestigious *Alfred Hitchcock Presents*, as well as the original *Star Trek*.

Shelby Flint, singing Earle Hagen's original song, "The Voice in the Wind," for this episode, was a pop singer who had a top 40 hit in 1962 with "Angel on My Shoulder."

63. **"NOW YOU SEE HER, NOW YOU DON'T"**; Written by: Jerry Ludwig; Directed by: Earl Bellamy; Location: Athens to Menkov to Delos; First airing: 10/23/67. Repeated: 5/13/68.

Kelly and Scott comb the Greek island of Mykonos for Kate Stanford, a space agency mathematician who mysteriously disappeared while on a European vacation. Their local contact, Troy Duncan, has put them on the assignment. But every time Stanford is found, and the Americans attempt to free her, the kidnappers are one step ahead. Someone on the inside is tipping them off.

Assessment

"Now You See Her, Now You Don't" is an entertaining story, with a big surprise of an ending. Generous doses of action, a charming guest performance by Barbara Mullen as Kate Stanford, along with plenty of scenic photography of Athens, Mykonos and Delos, make this an above-average entry.

There are some awkward moments of action, courtesy of director Earl Bellamy, including the speedboat rescue of Stanford from the yacht where she is imprisoned. The shoot-out on Delos, however, more than makes up for the clumsiness of the previous action sequence.

And then there is the splendid betrayal, when Kelly and Scott discover that Troy Duncan, a.k.a. Anderson, has gone bad.

The Story Behind the Story

Writer Jerry Ludwig recalls the origin of his script:

"They wanted to go to Greece, and they just said 'Greece and *The Lady Vanishes*.' So I suggested she be a scientist. And they said, 'Good.' I went away and figured it out and came back. That's the shorthand way to sell a story in TV. That's the way *I Spy* operated. The episode Friedkin acted in was *The Third Man*. The Karloff episode was *Man of La Mancha*. Most of the shows that we did were those kind of derivations. That's television.

"They told us pretty much where they would be shooting. I'd never been to Greece, and yet I feel I have because I did so much research to write that episode. My original title was 'Nobody Dies on Delos.' For whatever reason, be it superstition or what have you, anyone who was sick, or looked like they were in danger of dying, was taken off the island. So death was not part of the experience of this place."[6]

Fortunately, NBC aired the two episodes from the third season featuring Keith Andes in proper order, ending with his death. For the syndicated rerun package, however, because the episodes were run in a sequence following the misleading production numbering, this order was reversed.

LOCKED ROOM #12

In a church by the sea, Kelly and Scott are tied back-to-back, with hands and ankles bound. Kelly tells Scott he has a lighter in his pocket. Then the fun begins.

CAST & CREW

Barbara Mullen effectively looked older than her 53 years at the time of this production. This would be her final appearance in front of the camera, in a career that kept her moderately busy from 1941 until 1967.

Tom Pace played Jimmy Mitchell, and this would be one of the few times a character he played would have an actual name. Usually, he was assigned parts described as "Radioman," "Driver," and "German Soldier." Prior to *I Spy*, because of his ability to speak German, he was cast in nine episodes of *Combat!* He remained close to the *I Spy* company during its stay in Greece, and would return to do two more episodes. Look for him, briefly, in "Philotimo" and "The Lotus Eater."

Keith Andes makes his last of three appearances on the series. He would continue acting for another 13 years, playing roles that, sadly, became increasingly minor.

Art Seid became supervising editor with this episode.

64. **"PHILOTIMO"**; Written by: Ernest Frankel; Directed by: Earl Bellamy; Location: Bulgaria to Greece; First airing: 10/9/67. Repeated: 5/6/68.

Kelly and Scott touch off an international incident when they aid a famed child prodigy in defecting from his native Bulgaria. After bringing young violinist Stefan Petkov into friendly Greece and presumed safety, the two U.S. agents and the entire State Department are accused of kidnapping the boy.

In a surprising turn of events, Stefan is using Kelly and Scott in order to make a propaganda statement and damage the Americans' credibility.

Assessment

"Philotimo" succeeds on many levels.

Young Stefan cons not only Kelly and Scott, but Greek police officer Zarkas, as well. Frankel's skill at plotting, character and pacing totally misleads all involved, including the audience.

Escape and return is the plot. Politics and national pride—or "Philotimo"—is the theme.

Stefan enters Greece empty-handed. His plan is to return to Bulgaria with top secret materials. The final touch is the boy denouncing the West, and loudly charging the agents of holding him against his will. He says Kelly and Scott, and all Americans, deal only in lies.

Another very dramatic moment occurs when Constantinos, the efficiently deadly opponent, turns his gun on Kelly and pulls the trigger. Robert Culp gives us a multifaceted reaction, beginning with a freeze. The trigger is pulled. Kelly remains frozen, expecting to be thrown back by the impact of the bullet. But there is *no bullet*. Kelly doesn't wait to think about it. As Constantinos' finger tightens on the trigger, Kelly springs like a cat, spinning as he flies through the air, landing in the farthest corner of the room available, up on a bed, pinned against the wall.

Constantinos turns toward Scott and now tries to shoot him. Did the gun jam?

Cosby's reaction is just as perfect as Culp's. Scott remains completely still as he waits to die. The gun again fires, but Scott feels no impact of lead.

Scott doesn't give his would-be killer a second chance. Moving with exceptional speed, he gets the gun away from Constantinos. He takes aim and pulls the trigger twice, meaning to kill the man. But the gun remains useless.

Scott examines the gun that did not kill, and deduces that the weapon had been loaded with blanks.

The agents now know that they have been tricked. And, we, the audience, now know it, as well.

The Story Behind the Story

The title, "Philotimo," as explained by Zarkas, is a Greek word meaning "love of self-respect." Kelly and Scott both respect themselves and the flag they salute. Those feelings influence their decision to help Stefan flee from Communism, which, in turn, is the very mechanism that allows Stefan and the Communists to easily trick them.

Zarkas admits that he, too, is a man driven by the righteousness of what he believes in. And, like Kelly and Scott, he, too, has been tricked.

And then there is Stefan. The young boy has some philotimo of his own.

CULP & COSBY ON SET REWRITE

If watching Kelly try to start the motorcycle, which takes a while, seems like an add-lib, it is ... in part. The script indicated that he would have difficulty getting the engine to kick, allowing him time to make a small speech about it being "nearly dawn and I'm leaving four thousand bucks worth of Uncle Sam's automobile I'm signed out with."

But, once the engine sparks, everything else is as real as it appears. Watch the expression on child actor John Megna, frozen, not sure what to do, totally unaware of the Culp/Cosby banter, as Cosby kids Culp, with, "Here we go; Ease it in there, Randolph; There it is; I can feel it moving; We're moving now."

And all of this before the bike lurches forward a single inch.

Another amusing ad-lib also comes at the expense of young John Megna. Stefan is locked in the cabin on the boat. The camera stays with him, as we hear Kelly on the other side of the sturdy looked door. Megna knows that Kelly and Scott are to break in and rescue his character. What follows is not in the script:

18—The Seventh Block of Episodes

KELLY'S VOICE: "Alright, stand back, Stefano. I'm going to take it out."
We hear Culp slam against the door with a hurtful "Yah!" And then another slam, and another pained "Yah!"
KELLY'S VOICE: "Hold on, Stefanelli. I'll get you out in a second. Wait. One more time. I'll get it this time."
Then another loud thump, and another pained "Yah!" And then the muffled, broken, "Oohh."

And, finally, the grading at the top of the door shatters out, as Cosby smashes it open with a fire extinguisher. Megna jumps. Is it acting? Or were Culp and Cosby messing with the overly serious young actor? Part of the fun will be in never knowing.

Right after the gun filled with blanks is shot at Kelly and Scott, and Constantinos is taken out, Culp ad-libs to Cosby, "Did you notice there are no bullet holes in the wall behind where I was standing? Did you not wonder why? Did you not notice the big red 'S' on my chest?"

This unexpected ad-lib appears to have caused Cosby to drop his next line. The script has Scott examining the gun, and then he is supposed to say: "This is the gun we took from the guy on the motorcycle."

This line would have reminded the viewers where the gun filled with blanks came from, and that would have explained why this gun, which Constantinos took from Scott, failed to kill Kelly or Scott. In fact, an entire puzzle unravels with that line. But it was never spoken.

Cosby dropped the line, perhaps because Culp veered off the script.

Michael Preece, busy scribbling the very funny ad-lib about "the big red 'S' on my chest" into his copy of the script, didn't catch the error.

Earl Bellany, a director notorious for rushing through the day, didn't bother to ask for a retake.

Ernest Frankel, a very precise writer, and former military officer, who believes in "no horseplay" when there is a job to be done, can still be heard steaming.

And then there is that final speech from Kelly to Stefan. Perhaps this is an amends to Frankel from Culp for the damage done earlier.

The script gave the idea for the line, with Kelly saying, "But Stefan, despite yourself, you'll take back a few memories ... and I hope that, even in your dull, grey world, you can't shake them!"

Culp changed it to: "You'll take back something else, Stefan. You'll take back memories. The mind's a funny thing. It plays tricks on you. It remembers what happened, whether you like it or not. And you *will* remember Scotty and me ... I hope."

Cast & Crew

Ken Tobey, who three times before had played "Gabe" a.k.a. "Russ" (Kelly and Scott's bossy regional director), was intended for the part of this Russ. But this Russ dies before the end of the story. Tobey had been working out too well to be sacrificed, so, instead, this Russ was given the surname of "Hamilton" and a different actor was cast to perform the death scene.

Barney Phillips, who plays new/dead "Russ," accumulated a long list of guest star appearances on TV during the 1950s, '60s and '70s. One of his first prominent jobs was as the second of Joe Friday's four partners in *Dragnet*.

Harold J. Stone makes his second of three appearances as Greek police detective and renowned anti–Communist Zarkas.

John Megna, as Stefan, was the real-life brother of actress Connie Stevens. He began in show business with a part in the 1961 Broadway production of *All the Way Home*. This led to his being cast as Dill, the toothy, gawky young summer visitor in the 1962 Oscar-winning film *To Kill a Mockingbird*. TV appearances followed, including a 1966 episode of *Star Trek*. One year later, at 15, Megna had grown out of the youthful cuteness that had established his appeal. In later years, he would focus primarily on stage directing. Magna died in 1995, at age 43, of AIDS.

Eleanor Summers (Maria) and **Arthur Batanides** (Constantinos) had appeared together in the two-part episode "To Florence with Love." By being cast to play opposite one another again, we can't help but feel we've seen these two characters before. This would be the last of five guest spots for Batanides in *I Spy*, more than any other actor—other than Ken Tobey—would achieve. Besides the "Florence" two-parter, Batanides was also featured prominently in two episodes from Morocco, "Oedipus at Colonus" and "The Medarra Block." He played bad guys in all.

Ernest Frankel, the writer of "Philotimo," was recommended to Sheldon Leonard by Art Seid, the supervising editor for the series. Seid had previously worked as one of the producers of the long-running *Perry Mason* and, at that time, had hired Frankel as a writer. Seid knew that Frankel was exceptionally fast at producing scripts.

In early 1967, Leonard mentioned to Seid that he was one script short for the batch to be shot in Greece, but needed it written quickly. Seid suggested that Frankel be called in.

Frankel had never seen the series, but his agent at William Morris briefed him as to what it was about before arranging a meeting with Leonard. On his way into the meeting, Frankel met old friend Marion Hargrove, who was also writing for *I Spy*. Hargrove gave Frankel additional information on the show.

Frankel pitched the story for "Philotimo" and Leonard bought it, but asked that the script be written in five days and, if he could do it, he would be rewarded with more work.

Frankel took the dare, and delivered on time.

Leonard was good to his word. The writer was given four more *I Spy* assignments.

65. **"THE SEVENTH CAPTAIN"**; Written by: Berkely Mather; Directed by: Earl Bellamy; Location: Greek islands; First airing: 11/13/67. Repeated: 5/27/68.

In the Greek islands, Kelly and Scott want to know what happened to six enemy agents who disappeared. Also present, their old friend Zarkos. But this time, Zarkos, the renowned Communist hater, seems less willing to help.

Assessment

Berkely Mather and Earl Bellamy redeem themselves by collaborating on this excellent entry.

"The Seventh Captain" provides some of the best photography from the Greek islands. Underwater sequences filmed in Florida enhance the visuals, reminiscent of *Thunderball*.

In this ticking clock episode, Bill Cosby makes some interesting acting choices: his reaction to having his character, the always sober Scott, being drugged; and his panic at waking up inside a hollowed out statue which is being filled with cement.

The urgency conveyed by Culp as Kelly attempts to save Scott is splendid. Having freed him from the vertical grave, Kelly leads a dazed Scott to a waiting boat. When Kelly releases Scott's hand, in an unscripted moment, Cosby stumbles off the sea walk and into waste-deep water. The looks exchanged by Cosby and Culp are priceless.

"The Seventh Captain" features Zarkas for a third time, revealing him a much darker character than we had believed. The story provides a unique hook for the Zarkas trilogy: This secret society of patriotic Greeks and obsessive traditionalists exacts an interesting revenge. When one of their own is killed, tradition demands the death of seven enemies for the one.

The visual impact of the female dancers swaying in rhythm atop the ruins is eerie and memorable.

Harold J. Stone, "The 7th Captain" (© 3 F Prod., courtesy Image Ent.).

However, the final struggle ends with Zarkas flung over Kelly and down the cliff to his death. This is one of film's most tired clichés.

The Story Behind the Story

Sheldon Leonard was not as critical of the second script turned in by Berkely Mather, although Leonard noted the plotting to be "awkward and confusing." He also wrote, "This script badly needs a good heavy quite early in or else we've got another one of those god damn intellectual puzzles."

To its credit, NBC ran all three of the Zarkas episodes in proper sequence. The network chose to repeat all three episodes, as well, also showing them in the intended order.

For the syndicated rerun package, the episodes were shown in the order of their misleading production numbers, resulting in Zarkas being introduced, then killed, then resurrected.

CREW

Ivan Tors provided the underwater sequences. Tors, producer of *Sea Hunt* and *Flipper*, had overseen the underwater shots for *Thunderball*.

Paul Stedes, the second unit director was a stuntman and diver who had coordinated underwater stunts for Tors. He would do likewise for *Voyage to the Bottom of the Sea* and *The Poseidon Adventure*.

Robert Drasnin provided the new music. He had also scored episodes of *The Man from U.N.C.L.E.*

66. **"THE LOTUS EATER"**; Written by: Elick Moll & Joseph Than; Directed by: Christian Nyby; Location: Greek islands; First airing: 12/11/67. Repeated: 6/3/68.

The mysterious disappearance of Kelly somewhere in the Greek islands sends Scott on a weeklong search for his partner, who, when found, announces he has quit the service.

Located living in a secluded beach cottage, Kelly is strangely hostile toward Scott, especially when questioned about Irena, a beautiful Greek singer with whom he's been keeping company.

Adding to Scott's worries, their old nemesis, Sorge, has been seen in the region.

Assessment

"The Lotus Eater" is successful, despite separating Kelly and Scott, the magic formula of the series.

Cosby and Culp are individually brilliant in this story. The nuances of their performances are always consistently good throughout the series. But here, they raise the bar higher still.

A breathtaking scene opens the teaser. Scott climbs the cobblestone walkway up the side of a mountain that overlooks the Aegean Sea. When Scott finally locates his partner, a tanned and relaxed Kelly informs him that he has "come in out of the cold." He is no longer in the espionage game.

The Story Behind the Story

The title comes from Homer's "The Odyssey," and refers to an island off Greece where Ulysses and his men paused to rest. After eating something called "Lotus," a food with an unusual effect that causes men to become complacent and completely lacking in ambition, they stayed for seven years.

Culp: "I remember 'The Lotus Eater' well. I was both excited and scared to death by that scene I had to play where Kelly crawls on the floor and confesses his fears. I had never done any kind of drugs. I didn't even try pot until *Bob & Carol & Ted & Alice*—and that made me feel like I was going deaf for a couple hours! But I had to try something in this scene, and there was no time to refine it. It just had to be done. It was frightening. I hoped they were telling the truth and not just trying to spare my feelings, but everyone seemed to feel it worked. I hope so."[7]

CULP & COSBY ON SET REWRITE

In the script, after coming down from his high, Kelly asks Scott if what he remembers as happening really took place. Scott lets Kelly know that it did. And now the ad-lib:

KELLY: "Isn't that awful. I must have been doing everything: 'Oh wow,' and the beads, and everything. I'm ashamed."

SCOTT: "I hope so."

KELLY (*holding up a handgun Scott left out*): "On the other hand, for shame on yourself, because you left this around, and I could have ... (*seeing that Scott holds the bullets*) ... Oh, is that right? Did you really do that?"

SCOTT: "Old John Wayne movie."
KELLY: "Certainly. I was doing, 'Oh wow,' and the beads, and you were doing an old movie."
SCOTT: "Well, I had an excuse."
KELLY: "What was that?"
SCOTT: "You were high. And you had an excuse."
KELLY: "What was that?"
SCOTT: "You were high."
KELLY: "Certainly."

Cast & Crew

Sheldon Leonard reprises his role as Sorge, last seen in season one in "Three Hours on a Sunday Night." Returning the character was possible as he was created by Friedkin and Fine, who were doing the rewrite on this script. They decided that the "heavy" could easily be played by Leonard, saving the company money and adding continuity to the series.

Vivian Ventura (Irena) was 20. Born and raised in England, she made her film debut with a small role in one of that country's popular 1960s "Carry On" films. A role on the British-made *The Saint* followed. Next, it was off to America to appear in *The Wild Wild West*, *The Man from U.N.C.L.E.*, *Get Smart*, as well as half a dozen small features, before landing a job that took her back to Europe for *I Spy*.

Elick Moll and **Joseph Than** wrote the script, their first of two contributions to the series.

Back in the days when a writer in his sixties could find work in the freelance market, Elick Moll, arriving at the door of *I Spy*, was 66. He had written nearly a dozen small features in the 1940s and '50s, along with a handful of assignments on TV. Joseph Than, 64 at this time, had been successful in Europe as a writer of films and television. The two teamed up for this assignment, taking advantage of Than's knowledge of the Greek territory.

67. **"RED SASH OF COURAGE"**; Written by: Oliver Crawford; Directed by: Christian Nyby; Location: Greece; First airing: 10/30/67. Repeated: 5/20/68.

While investigating mysterious crashes of allied flights over Greece, Kelly and Scott's visit to a small village brings unexpected trouble from the enraged father of a beautiful peasant girl.

Pappas, the town's mayor and father of Stephanie, wants Kelly drawn and quartered for spending a night alone with his virginal daughter.

Assessment

Played strictly for laughs, "Red Sash" succeeds, if nothing else, in being amusing. Culp and Cosby, with good support by guest stars "Roger C, Roger C" and Louise Sorel, make the good time they are having quite contagious.

The plot is not terribly important. The enemy agents and their jamming device is Alfred Hitchcock's "MacGuffin," a plot device that helps set things in motion, but has very little to do with the story itself.

In fact, this story has very little to do with *anything*. It merely offers an amusing diversion for television watchers. A year or two after you watch this episode, you can watch it again — and most of it will seem new to you. You will have retained that little of it.

"Red Sash" is somewhat pleasant, very much frivolous, and completely forgettable.

Louise Sorel, Roger C. Carmel, "The Red Sash of Courage" (© 3 F Prod., courtesy Image Ent.).

The Story Behind the Story

THE MYSTERY LOCATIONS

With the exception of two establishing shots, "Red Sash" was filmed entirely in and about Los Angeles.

The lake near the villa, as well as the abandoned farm, were filmed in Upper Franklyn Canyon.

The villa itself was actually the Claretville School, off Mulholland Drive and Las Virgenes Road.

The chase takes place on Stokes Road, near the school.

The village courtyard was shot at the 40-acre "Culver City Compound," a movie location long since bulldozed.

All other sets were built on stages 1A and 1B at the Desilu (now Paramount) Gower studio.

CAST & CREW

Louise Sorel, playing the mayor's daughter, Stephanie, began her work in TV in 1963. Sorel had nearly two dozen credits before coming to *I Spy*. One year later, she would visit another cult TV show of that era, *Star Trek*, winning a stand-out role in the haunting "Requiem for Methuselah."

Roger C. Carmel, since his last visit on *I Spy*, found a role that would possibly make him more recognizable than any other he would ever play—as Harcourt Fenton Mudd on three episodes of *Star Trek*. Following this appearance, he would costar in the Desi Arnaz–produced series, *The Mothers-in-Laws*. He left after one year in a salary dispute with Arnaz.

By the early 1980s, Carmel's career was sliding downhill fast and much of his employment was limited to voice-over work and Mexican fast-food TV commercials. In 1986 he died unexpectedly of heart disease.

Oliver Crawford, writing his only script for *I Spy*, was one more writer associated with this series who was a survivor of the 1950s Hollywood blacklist. Only 10% of those on the Joseph McCarthy anti–Communism hit list ever recovered to continue their careers.

At the time, Culp would have enjoyed knowing that Crawford had written for the *Terry and the Pirates* TV series, which had a short run in the early 1950s. In the 1960s, he was gainfully employed as a writer on *Ben Casey*, as many more who came to *I Spy* would be. At this time, he was also given a three script assignment for *Star Trek*, making him the third person from this episode to have been connected with the science fiction series.

19

A Change in Plans

Leonard & Leon Chooluck in Russia

June 1967. Lucille Ball sold Desilu to Paramount Pictures. Paramount, in turn, had agreed to be absorbed by Gulf-Western Corporation. The little mom-and-pop television factory, home to so many sitcoms and hour-long dramas, would no longer exist. By the time the *I Spy* company returned from Greece, the ten-foot high brick wall separating Desilu from Paramount was gone. Triple F was now renting space from a component of a major corporation.

On April 20, 1967, a letter sent from a Three F Productions office worker to Leon Chooluck, who was still on location, gave indication as to the changes in store:

"Dear Leon: Thought I'd drop you a few lines and let you know what's going on in this miserable Desilu-Gower Studio, which is now being run like a factory, what with all the efficiency experts hired. We have to answer for everything from now on, such as buying office supplies, goodies to eat, etc. Everything must come through the accounting office, and I suppose the next thing will be that we won't be able to flush the toilets or use too much toilet paper ... unless we check with Accounting. Everyone is quite upset about the new regime ... and everyone thinks it *STINKS*!!!!!

"I have been fighting for weeks (and I mean fighting all these big wigs) about not having an office for you. I told them that in six weeks you will be back and *no office*. Mention this to Sheldon and see what he might have to say.

"Hope you are feeling ok ... and please take care of yourself."

The TV series that had helped to change an industry was now having to deal with an industry that was determined to continue changing. Otherwise, it was business as usual as the *I Spy* cast and crew finished the seventh block of episodes — meaning, it was madness.

Meanwhile, Leonard, the travel addict, had fixed his eyes on the two most difficult places to film: Red China and the Soviet Union. He had been corresponding with high-ranking officials of both governments for some time. The Chinese, in particular, seemed very interested.

Leonard asked if he could shoot at the Great Wall.

He was told "yes.'

And the Forbidden City?

Again, the answer was "yes." Anything Leonard wanted, he could have — with one small condition: The government insisted that any film shot in China be processed there as well.

Leonard investigated processing facilities and what he found was not encouraging. Their final product was substandard, and would not meet American network specs.

The Schmoozer tried a compromise. He would shoot the best China had to offer. He would show the world this beautiful and inviting country. Twenty-five million people alone would be watching in America. The film would be processed in America, but Chinese officials would view the footage before it was cut. Leonard gave them his word.

Sheldon Leonard & Leon Chooluck, scouting Russia, 1967 (Sheldon Leonard Collection).

The Chinese declined.

Leonard, reluctantly, said good-bye to the Great Wall.

But Leonard was a gambler. If one slot machine wasn't paying off, move on to the next. His back-up was the Soviet Union.

The Russians had fine laboratories. Any film shot and processed in the Soviet Union would meet NBC standards. And, like the Chinese before them, the Russians would surely see the advantages in having a hit American television series film episodes within their borders. To be exact, 25 million advantages.

When Leonard first approached the Russians, he thought he would have to do his salesman's dance to help them understand who he was and what his TV series was all about. He didn't. The Russians knew all about *I Spy*.

The Soviet Information Service was already watching Leonard's series. And it didn't like it.

Leonard did a gold-medal 180-degree turn. He proposed that the stories would emphasize the benefits of cooperation — and not the differences — between the super powers. "After all," he told them, "we share a common goal: survival. And our survival, the survival of the whole human race, depends on peace."

Well, using the word "peace" wasn't exactly the best way to sell a concept to Soviet officials.

Leonard pitched a curve ball.

The U.S. and the Soviets have a common enemy. The stories would focus on that. The American and Russian intelligence agents would link arms. They would fight side by side, as they had done against the Nazis. Period.

This time the Russian officials liked what they heard. They agreed to allow the Americans into their country—with a few minor conditions: The Russians wanted their own writers to collaborate with Friedkin and Fine to develop plots. Leonard would have the final word. The Russians, however, would control what words he was allowed the final word on.

Leonard balked. He needed this deal and the publicity attached to it. He knew the locations were more important than the scripts. And, besides, Culp and Cosby would rewrite everything the Russians wrote anyway.

So Leonard agreed. And the Russians agreed—with one more small condition: Russian labor would be used in all categories except principal casting, directors, producers, head cameraman and head electrician.

Now Leonard was concerned. Meeting and negotiating with the Soviet officials in Moscow, he noticed that the local laborers seemed unmotivated. As there was little chance for personal advancement in the Russian system, laborers were reluctant to give any extra effort.

Leonard had been successful in the highly competitive world of television long enough to know an absolute truth of the industry: A show does not get made if the producer does not have a team of devoted, ambitious and slightly crazy people supporting him. In America, it was more about ego than cash. In Russia, personal ego was a low priority.

Hoping to be proven wrong, Leonard submitted a typical *I Spy* script to the Soviet Film Production Office. Two days later he received the result: it would take 19 days to shoot the script in Russia using Soviet technology and Soviet labor. This same script had recently been produced in Greece in eight days.

This was not good news.

Regardless, having full cooperation of the government, Leonard, his wife, Frankie, and Leon Chooluck began to scout locations. They were provided with a pleasant, helpful, multilingual, middle-aged guide named Sonya. They stayed in Moscow's best hotel, The Rusya, overlooking Red Square and Lenin's Tomb.

And, in the 1967 world of the cold war, they had been given one more present, something they knew nothing about, something hidden in their hotel suite.

One night, alone, the Leonards discussed their desire to see the town of Bershad in the Ukraine. Leonard's family was from Bershad and he wanted to visit his roots.

The next morning, Sonya volunteered that it would be impossible to travel to Bershad, but they could arrange the trip for another time. Somehow she knew about the Leonards' private conversation from the night before.

The Leonards now knew their hotel room was bugged.

And the Russians weren't the only ones treating the producer of a television espionage show as if he were the head of a real-life spy organization.

Leonard contributed the article "In Russia, *I Spy* Was Out in the Cold" to the *New York Times* (May 1968). In part, he wrote, "When I called my activities to the attention of a prominent personage in our own country's policy making area, he called back from Washington to tell me that unnamed figures, on the highest level, would not take kindly to my project, because 'it might imply that this Administration is soft on Communism.' He said, 'If I were you, I wouldn't plan any picture-making in Russia before you make sure the passports for your group haven't been cancelled."

Disappointed and saddened, Leonard decided not to film in the Soviet Union. He focused on the immediate problem: how to fill the void in *I Spy's* schedule.

Anticipating immediate problems, Friedkin and Fine had prepared several scripts that could go into production in California. "This Guy Smith," a bit of a dog, was an unused script from the second season. It had been written to be shot at a mountain resort with a lake. The second, "A Few Miles from Nowhere," written in March of 1967 for a desert community, could easily be restaged for a mountain retreat and was quickly revised to be shot in conjunction with "Smith."

Robert Culp had just turned in his seventh script, written to be filmed on a farm, which he described as "Anywhere USA."

Leonard dug out a script he'd bought from a fan of the show. "Oliver's Twist," by M.J. Waggoner, was set within a U.S. base where Military Intelligence trained their recruits.

San Francisco was perfect. It had numerous facilities and most of them had a spectacular view of the bay. One base in particular, the Presidio, looked as if Military Intelligence might very well conduct such classes there.

Friedkin and Fine gave the script to Steven Kandel for a quick rewrite. He turned "Oliver's Twist" into "Tag, You're It."

Kandel: "We had a meeting with some favorite and fast writers. Sheldon had a kind of long lunch that went into the afternoon in his office, and he said, 'I want to do a little polishing, because we've got some location problems.' Some of the scripts had to be changed to adjust to new locations, because they *did* have location problems. There was a lot of juggling around. 'Tag, You're It' was a rewrite. I did it quick. I did a lot of quick rewriting. If you have a production problem, I will adjust the script. You don't always get credit for that, but you do get paid."[1]

Elick Mull and Joseph Than, who had written "The Lotus Eater," were given the green light to write a script called "An American Princess." When Friedkin and Fine, two Jews, informed Mull and Than, two Germans, what "American Princess" meant in America, they immediately changed the title to "An American Empress." It was to be shot in San Francisco.

Michael Zagor, who had proved to be such an asset to *I Spy*, would write a script called "Anywhere I Hang Myself Is Home." It, too, would be set in the San Francisco area.

Marion Hargrove would contribute "She Sleeps, My Lady Sleeps," an odd story involving the return of the character played by Peter Lawford, George Rickaby-Hackaby, this time involved in the occult. An old Victorian house overlooking the bay was the primary setting of the trick-or-treat tale.

No television show had ever been shot in San Francisco. The Steve McQueen movie *Bullitt*, one of the first to take cameras onto the streets of San Francisco, was still one year away. The city, to most Americans, would be as exotic and beautiful a location as any of the others visited by *I Spy*.

So Kelly and Scott went to San Francisco in late July of 1967. That summer would also be known as "the summer of love." The Bay Area was ground zero for the hippie event. *I Spy* would be there.

Hargrove's "She Sleeps, My Lady Sleeps," turned in on June 11, 1967, and revised on June 23, failed to make the cut. The script for "An American Empress" was turned in on July 10th, 14 days before it would begin filming. "Anyplace I Hang Myself" came in on the 11th. "Tag" came in on the 14th. Revisions would be needed on all three, plus they would have to be cast. The trip to San Francisco was scheduled for the last week of July and the first few days of August, with additional sequences to be shot back at Paramount throughout August. It was a mad dash.

At the same time, another race was taking place. "A Few Miles West of Nowhere," and "This Guy Smith" were picking up shots at the studio. The Lake Arrowhead location shooting was scheduled for late August.

In early September, "Home to Judgment" would be shot on a farm on the border of Los Angeles and Ventura counties.

"Apollo," the last episode to be filmed of this emergency block, would be shot in Los

Angeles at the downtown train yards and at the Rocketdyne Jet Propulsion facility in the Santa Suzanna Pass. That final script, written by Ernest Frankel, who had already proven himself as a quick thinker and an even quicker typist, was turned in by August, just a few weeks before it was set to go before the cameras.

It would be close, but the Company would continue shooting without any break in the schedule. Russia and China had been replaced, *I Spy* style.

20

The Eighth Block of Episodes

68. **"THIS GUY SMITH"**; Written by: Jackson Gillis; Directed by: Ralph Senensky; Location: Lake Arrowhead; First airing: 2/5/68. Repeated: 7/8/68.

Kelly and Scott search a mountain resort for an enemy known only as Smith.
While on the assignment, Kelly has been enjoying the company of Sally Holmes, a local real estate agent. When she is killed, the local police think the agents are responsible.

Assessment

"This Guy Smith" is an enjoyable mess.

At the beginning, it seems unlikely that the explosion of a boat could put Kelly into the hospital with cracked ribs. His and Scott's boat was nowhere near the craft that blew up.

Don't blame Earl Bellamy for this one. Director Ralph Senensky began and ended his association with *I Spy* here.

While Kelly sees what he can learn by snooping around with the pretty realtor, Scott is searching for an elusive man named Dr. Franks. He thinks he has a lead. For this reason, Delaney, the owner of the lodge and one of the bad guys, arrives at the absurd decision to kill Scott on the property, in broad daylight, with a pitchfork. At best, this is a sloppy method of murder. While hotel guests regularly arrive and depart from the lodge, Delaney walks Scott out onto the tennis court to kill him. The pitchfork just happens to be there. Delaney's excellent plan, one that can be found in that handbook from the Three Stooges Academy of Murder and Mayhem, of course, fails.

Back to Dr. Franks. Scott is searching for him because the informant, that guy who was blown up in the boat in the teaser, mentioned both Franks and a guy named Smith. Perhaps the mysterious doctor lives just outside of town. Bingo! Franks does, and he is not very good at laying low. He has nailed a sign to a tree just to the side of the main road. On it is his name, and an arrow pointing up the dirt drive.

Sally turns out to be "this guy Smith." Having decided to get out of Dodge, even though no one seems to be close to discovering her secret—including Kelly—she arranges her own death.

For some reason, after going to all the effort to drop out of sight (which included picking up a girl who was hitchhiking and killing her so that she could leave a body behind), Sally remains close—then resurfaces. She forgot to do something—kill Kelly.

Naturally, instead of just shooting him, she first has to explain her evil plan. This allows Scott time to turn up, and he gets the jump on her.

"This Guy Smith" has lovely location photography, and the delightful interaction between Kelly, Scott and Russ Conway—whose appearance here was an afterthought, but a much

The defiant ones, summer 1967 (© 3 F Prod.).

appreciated framing device. Why the script was put aside during season two and replaced with "Cops and Robbers" is abundantly clear.

The Story Behind the Story

Kelly and Scott are packing for a trip to San Francisco when Russ intrudes and arbitrarily decides to help them unpack. This episode was clearly meant to be aired before San

Francisco was used as a backdrop. But, as they often did, the programming wizards of NBC chose to air "This Guy Smith" after all three of the San Francisco episodes had been broadcast.

The continuity Friedkin and Fine tried so hard to achieve was also lost once the series went into syndicated reruns, by improper sequencing of the episodes. This time, however, F & F had no one to blame but themselves. Their own misleading production numbering was the culprit.

Gillis's script was thin and the episode came up short on running time when the first edit was completed. So, on September 25th and 26th, additional scenes were written featuring Kelly and Scott in their hotel room, recalling their previous assignment to Regional Director Russ Conway.

Diana Muldaur, "This Guy Smith" (© 3 F Prod., courtesy Image Ent.).

"Smith" was shot at Lake Arrowhead. Cast and crew stayed at The Village Inn. The inn is also featured in this production.

Cast & Crew

Richard Denning (Delaney), beginning in 1937, had a long and satisfying career in front of the camera. He racked up over 100 credits in the movies. On TV, in 1952, he starred in the series *Mr. and Mrs. North*. In 1959, he played an airborne medic in another: *The Flying Doctor*. He was 53 when he appeared here. By 1968, Denning wished to retire and move to Hawaii. At that moment, he was made an offer he couldn't refuse. The producers of a new series wanted to cast him as the governor of the 50th state. He agreed, but only if he didn't have to appear in every episode. The producers kept their promise and Denning appeared half-a-dozen times each season—for twelve years—on *Hawaii Five-O*. His retirement was postponed until 1980.

Diana Muldaur (Sally) is a former president of the Academy of Television Arts and Sciences. She also has well over 100 credits in TV and film. She had a recurring role for half a season on *Dr. Kildare* in the early 1960s before becoming a highly sought after guest star. She was 29 when she worked here. In the same year, she traded kisses with Captain Kirk in a *Star Trek* episode. He must have liked it, because she was brought back the following year to do it again.

Ken Tobey is back as Russ. This was his fourth *I Spy*. The best was yet to come.

Michael Preece (in charge of script continuity) appears as the highway patrolman who talks to the bus driver regarding the crash, and death, of Dr. Franks.

Jackson Gillis had written the previous year's "Lisa." This would be his final *I Spy* assignment. He would go on to write several episodes for *Columbo*.

Ralph Senesky had cut his teeth as a director working for producer Quinn Martin on *Twelve O'Clock High* and *The Fugitive*. He only directed one episode of *I Spy*. He fared better with *Star Trek*, where he did seven, including the two that featured Diana Muldaur.

69. "ANYPLACE I HANG MYSELF IS HOME"; Written by: Michael Zagor; Directed by: Christian Nyby; Location: San Francisco; First airing: 1/15/68. Repeated: 6/24/68

Suddenly afflicted with an eerie compulsion to take his own life, Scott undergoes medical treatment that has him reliving his days of training with Kelly.

Prior to Scott's suicide attempt, the team returned to San Francisco for what Kelly jokingly refers to as a "class reunion." Russ Conway is here. And so is Dr. Akita. Both had been involved in the training of Kelly and Scott several years earlier. Through flashbacks, we see how the two partners first met, and learn that both had been given a posthypnotic suggestion by Akita to kill themselves rather than remember an event from that time.

Assessment

Michael Zagor scores again with another script rich with the complexities of a personal and urgent story. As with most of Zagor's work, even the lesser characters have believable ambitions and curious frailties.

Zagor borrowed from the best. Orson Wells' *Citizen Kane* is the story told through multiple flashbacks and allows each ego-driven character to tell their own version of the events.

Via flashbacks, we witness the first meeting between Kelly and Scott and see that their friendship was not love at first sight, or even like at first sight. Both are strong-willed men, and when strong-willed men meet, they often butt heads.

And, speaking of butting heads, we get our first look here at the core relationship between Russ and his two subordinates, Kelly and Scott. Despite Russ's gruffness, he not only respects the agents, he likes them.

The best moment, as it should be in any good story, is last. It is Kelly's turn to fight the hypnotic demons programmed into his mind all those years ago.

Oblivious, he stands on a ledge at the top of Coit Tower, ready to jump. Scott climbs out onto the ledge. But the scene takes a surprising turn. Scott doesn't rattle off the expected clichés about why Kelly shouldn't jump. Instead, bothered by the height, Scott asks for help. Kelly aborts his plan to jump, and offers Scott a hand.

In a beautifully underplayed moment, the only thing that matters to a suicidal Kelly is that his friend needs him.

I Spy, again, clearly defined friendship in a way that no television show or movie had done before. The looks, gestures and actions between these two friends were not only visible, but believable.

The Story Behind the Story

In the flashback scene where Russ addresses the trainees, he tells them "We're a little more military than the CIA—and a lot less publicized."

In "This Guy Smith," Kelly and Scott talk about how long it has been since either was in San Francisco. In this episode, we discover that San Francisco is actually where they first met.

Again, although Friedkin and Fine had very clear ideas as to the order in which *I Spy* episodes should be broadcast, their wishes were seldom fulfilled. The NBC programmers chose to air "An American Empress" first, a story that has Kelly and Scott preparing to *leave* San Francisco. Next, the network ran "Home to Judgment," which features Kelly and Scott on the run in Idaho. Then this episode aired, with the two back in the Bay Area, and behaving as if they hadn't been there for quite some time.

Ken Tobey's character is incorrectly listed in the closing credits as "Jeff." Reason: Jeff was the name of the character in the Michael Zagor script. When Tobey was cast, he, Culp, Cosby, and director Nyby knew to rename the character "Russ." But nobody bothered to tell the production house doing the titles for the episode.

Henry Silva, "Anyplace I Hang Myself Is Home" (© 3 F Prod., courtesy Image Ent.).

Richard H. Cahoon, under the supervision of Art Seid, does an outstanding job of editing, borrowing ideas from "It's All Done with Mirrors," an episode cut long before he or Seid joined the team. Many of the flashbacks, particularly of the objects from the not-so-good doctor's office, are seen on screen for less than a second, accented by Earle Hagen's perfectly eerie score.

The final scene from act 4, where Kelly climbs to the top of Coit Tower for his attempt at suicide was a last minute substitution. The script had called for the Golden Gate Bridge. Cost factors concerning the amount of personnel needed to pull off such a filming caused the change.

Michael Zagor: "It was very hard to tell a story like this in 1960s TV—with all the flashbacks. I felt fortunate to be able to do it. Mort and David, and particularly Sheldon, went to bat for me."[1]

Cast & Crew

Henry Silva (Dr. Akita) was in *The Manchurian Candidate*, the movie that inspired this episode.

Frank Sinatra was the star of the spy thriller that involved hypnotic conditioning for assassination. He appreciated Silva's talents, and brought him back for the Rat Pack pictures *Ocean's Eleven* and *Sergeants 3*.

Silva had been a graduate of the Actor's Studio. In the 150 TV and film credits Silva amassed between the 1950s and 1990s, he most often played heavies. He was 39 at the time of this production.

Denny Miller (Wally) was a UCLA basketball star when he was spotted by a Hollywood talent scout and cast to play the King of the Apes in the 1959 cheapie, *Tarzan, the Ape*

Man. TV work followed and within two years he had the regular role of Duke Shannon on *Wagon Train*. He left that series in 1964 to be promoted to the second lead, opposite Juliet Prowse, in *Mona McCluskey*. It was no laughing matter that the comedy only lasted one season. He was in his early 30s here.

Mary Murphy (Cass) was a Paramount contract player in the early 1950s that, due to her pleasing looks and spunky style, was expected to go far. She acted in *The Wild One* with Marlon Brando, as well as appearing opposite her future husband, Dale Robertson, in 1954's *Sitting Bull*. But the movie career didn't pan out, so she made the move to TV in the late '50s, and was cast as a regular in the 1961 series *The Investigators*. She was 36 here.

Carl Brandt assisted **Earle Hagen** with the score.

70. **"TAG, YOU'RE IT"**; Written by: Steven Kandel; Story by: M.J. Waggoner; Directed by: Earl Bellamy; Location: San Francisco; First airing: 1/22/68. Repeated: 9/2/68.

In San Francisco, Kelly and Scott reluctantly agree to help train new agents for the department—then learn they have become moving targets for an assassin's bullet.

Oliver, a renegade trainee, is actually an enemy agent who has infiltrated the Military Intelligence recruitment program. The espionage training exercise allows an opportunity to not only eliminate American agents, but frame two others—Kelly and Scott.

Assessment

"Tag, You're It" is superb. The episode has a surprising amount of humor, considering the seriousness of the storyline. The comedy is balanced with dramatic and tense moments, and all play out to a satisfying end.

We get a second look at the inside of the training program for Military Intelligence. Kelly and Scott are the seasoned veterans sharing their knowledge with the young hopefuls. Something goes wrong, and suddenly Kelly and Scott are running for their lives in San Francisco.

The ruthlessness of their work is best summed up by training instructor Brandon, who is quick to believe Kelly and Scott could kill one of the recruits for sport. He tells them, "In your wanderings, you two have done in a number of people. It's easy, it's routine. The habit of killing can become very strong, very effortless."

Scott, explaining to Oliver that there will be no trial for either he or Kelly, says, "The department is shy. We avoid publicity. Nobody is ever fired. They're either eliminated—or incarcerated."

"All quite legal," Kelly adds. "A team psychologist commits us to a small private hospital for the seriously disturbed. The beds are soft, the food's good, and nobody goes home again."

The Story Behind the Story

Of the three episodes shot in the Bay Area during late July and early August 1967, "Tag, You're It" would best showcase the city. It would give the audience a glimpse into the summer of love, by taking cameras into the famed Haight-Ashbury district and allow Culp and Cosby to interact with the hippie community.

The script for this episode began under a different title, courtesy of a different writer. "Oliver's Twist" was sent in to Three F Productions by an aspiring writer named M.J. Waggoner, living in Texas. Something about the writing, or the story, caught Leonard's eye, and he promised to buy the script if Ms. Waggoner could correct the formatting problems and address any other notes Leonard might have. She did, and Leonard, as always, remained true to his word.

Friedkin and Fine, however, found it rough going in trying to get the script they wanted from a novice screenwriter.

Script Writing 101

Other than the setting being Washington, D.C., instead of San Francisco, the teaser and act 1 of "Oliver's Twist" are nearly identical to that of "Tag, You're It." But, in Waggoner's script, at the end of act 1, when Oliver shoots at Kelly and Scott near the fountain, Scott is hit in the shoulder. From there, the story goes in an entirely different direction. At the beginning of act 2, Kelly and Scott are hiding out in a seedy hotel. Kelly, then, goes in search of their pursuer, alone.

This scene and everything that follows could not be used when the decision was made by the producers that Scott not be wounded. And there was good reason for this: In "Twist," Scott is very nearly taken out of the story before the halfway point; he and Kelly are separated; and, with no other red herrings in play, Oliver is discovered as being the obvious bad guy and the story comes to a hasty conclusion. The structuring of Waggoner's script was better suited for a 30-minute program, rather than one that was 60 minutes in length.

In a letter to David Friedkin, dated April 1, 1967, Waggoner conceded to being unable to completely comply with the script notes given to her by the producers. She wrote, "I have cleared up the two points Mr. Fine mentioned: (a) Seriousness of Scott's wound, and (b) Why doesn't Oliver kill Kelly immediately. As for 'stretching it,' everything I have come up with is either superfluous, pointless, maudlin, or asinine, even though the sample scripts you sent to me were of great help."

Friedkin and Fine brought in Steven Kandel.

Kandel: "It's always startled me how many writers don't have a clue about the actual physical aspect of production. It's odd, but that's a fact. They will write things with a blind disregard for either budget or time or physical possibility."[2]

Kandel's teleplay, written in haste, as all the San Francisco episodes were, turned out to be a bit on the short side. To pad the show, the coffee shop scene with the bickering waitress and cook was added. That sequence was written by Friedkin and Fine on September 9, 1967, more than a month after the episode had finished production. The extra scene was shot at the studio on September 26th.

Much of the comedy with Cobalt-Blue was improvised. The character *is* in Kandel's script, but used to far less effect.

"Tag" has a severely-flawed opening teaser.

In the script, Kelly and Scott creep through the woods and are jumped by unknown assailants in nondescript uniforms. Our attention, however, is drawn to a lone man in a suit, casually reading a newspaper and sitting in front of a one-story military installation–type building. We continue to intercut between the man and the action. It is even stated that Kelly and Scott look toward this mysterious man, as if he is the reason for their battle with the assailants.

Next, Scott tosses a hand grenade toward the man. It makes a whirring sound. The man looks up. Scott looks up. Kelly looks up. Their assailants look up. We see the grenade explode over the target in a cloud of white powder. It was all a training exercise.

But the filmed teaser fails to convey the most important aspect of the material: We never see the mysterious man, the target, until the very end of the teaser, when he looks up at the whirring sound. We have no idea who he is.

What Went Wrong

For the last half of the third season, *I Spy* had a new supervising editor. And, at this point, a sloppiness found its way into the cutting of the series.

Art Seid was that new editor in charge. And Leonard trusted Seid implicitly.

Michael Preece: "Art Seid was a jerk. One time there was this script that I had timed to make sure it was long enough to fill out the hour, and he raised a stink with Sheldon that I had timed it wrong.

"Sheldon came to me and said 'This is four minutes short, your stopwatch must be broken—*or something*.' So I went to Seid and said, 'How come you told him this was short, when you didn't even use this four-minute scene we shot?' And he said, 'That scene wasn't very good, so I decided to cut it out.' And I said, 'Well, that scene was part of my timing!'

"So he was taking it onto himself to make these editing decisions, and cut out scenes. Whether they're good scenes or bad scenes, they're still needed to make the episode come in at the right length. But he misled Sheldon, and, as a result, Sheldon was upset with me at the time.

"So that's why I never liked Art."[3]

Ernest Frankel, who worked closely with Seid, also had an opinion concerning the supervising editor's approach to his work.

Frankel: "In Art's mind, he never worked for anybody. He worked for himself. He would do whatever he wanted to do."[4]

From the Mail Bag:

"Dear Sirs, Who was the girl in the fountain on *I Spy* on Monday night? Terrific!" Bob H., Spokane, Washington.

In reply:

"Dear Mr. H: In answer to your letter, the girl in the fountain is LEIGH FRENCH. Miss French can be seen each week on *The Smothers Brothers Comedy Hour*. Thank you for your interest in our show. Sincerely, Nancy Fitzgerald."

Cast & Crew

Leigh French didn't have to travel far to play the talkative wannabe actress Cobalt-Blue, who takes a dip in the fountain. She was a member of the San Francisco–based improvisation group, The Committee. And, as you might expect, most of her work here was improvised. Her work on *The Smothers Brothers Comedy Hour* included a recurring segment, "Have a Little Tea with Goldie."

John Smith (Oliver) was born Robert Van Ordon, but changed his name to John Smith when he learned that he could be the only one in the business with such a name. The good-looking and athletic blonde found that TV roles, especially in Westerns, were easy to come by. He was seen on *Gunsmoke* and *Colt 45* before being cast in a regular supporting role as Sheriff Lane Temple in *Cimarron City* (1958). After one year, he was given his own series, sharing the dual lead with Robert Fulton in *Laramie*. The one-hour Western lasted four seasons.

Paul Mantee (Pirelli) got his big break when he was cast in the lead for a film that went out of its way to find an "unfamiliar face." The role was for 1964's *Robinson Crusoe on Mars*, which would become a cult classic. More than 100 TV and film appearances followed, including his work here, at age 36. In 1976, he would play one of the lead investigators in the television adaptation of Vincent Bugliosi's book *Helter Skelter*. From 1986 to '88, he was a regular on *Cagney & Lacey*, playing Detective Corosso.

Peter Duryea (Halsey) was the son of well-known Hollywood character actor, Dan Duryea. Peter's time in front of the camera was relatively brief, from 1964 to 1971. He was the first actor to play the part of the helmsman on the Starship *Enterprise*, on *Star Trek*. Jack Webb was fond of Duryea and often cast him in the 1960s version of *Dragnet*, then *Adam-12*. He was 28.

Norman Burton played Barton, the head of the training program. He achieved over 100 credits in film and TV, and might be best known for playing CIA agent Felix Leiter in the James Bond film *Diamonds Are Forever*. In 1977, he was Wonder Woman's boss for one year, appearing in that series with Linda Carter. He was 44 at the time of this appearance.

Richard Webb, playing Ross, the senior agent who is killed by Oliver, was best known as TV's *Captain Midnight* from the 1950s. He would appear in more than 100 TV programs and films, including a 1967 episode of *Star Trek*. He was 52 here. He committed suicide in 1993 after a long, debilitating respiratory illness.

Roy Jenson (Abrams), 32 here, was a stuntman turned actor. From 1951 to 1999, he garnered an impressive 200 credits in front of the camera. This was his third *I Spy*. He played Tate, a similar character in "It's All Done with Mirrors," as well as a Russian agent in "Magic Mirror." And he was the third of four men in this episode to have walked across the Desilu/Paramount lot in 1967 to be in *Star Trek*. He played a savage alien there.

Roger Bowen (Rudin, the agent who meets Oliver on a cable car) was a writer who moonlighted as an actor. He would write seven novels in his career, as well as material for the stage and for TV. In front of the camera, he is best remembered as Col. Henry Blake in the 1970 film version of *M*A*S*H*.

Steven Kandel wrote eight *I Spy* episodes, seven of which were produced. He also did uncredited rewrite work for the series. He was the fifth person associated with this episode to work on *Star Trek*. He invented Harry Mudd.

71. **"AN AMERICAN EMPRESS"**; Written by: Elick Moll & Joseph Than; Directed by: Earl Bellamy; Location: San Francisco; First airing: 12/25/67. Repeated: 8/12/68.

In San Francisco, Kelly and Scott meet a lovely and mysterious Chinese woman. When Confucius say "Girl is more than pretty face," look out for the famous locked room. This pretty face is an empress in exile, whose followers are involved in a Chinese government power struggle.

Assessment

A question arises. One wonders why the writers would resort to a plot device introducing danger and excitement into Kelly and Scott's lives that has *nothing* to do with their work as spies—a job that already provides a full agenda of both.

The must for any writer in television should be to know how their script benefits a series.

What new information does it give us about the characters? What point does it make? Or, at least, does it excite or amuse as well as the best from the past?

"An American Empress" merely entertains. It is pleasant and good to fall asleep to.

Those still awake will find the pictures of San Francisco to be pleasing. And it is a also pleasure to see France Nuyen—who so often was given roles that didn't require her to express happiness—actually smile.

"Empress" doesn't try to be anything more than a diverting and pleasant 60 minutes of television, counting the commercials.

The Story Behind the Story

Earl Bellamy handled the direction. Note in the teaser: Kelly rescues Mei Lin, pulling her out of the path of a double-decker tour bus. As Kelly and Scott and Mei Lin talk, we see the people on the top floor of the bus, looking toward actor and camera, and using cameras of their own to snap pictures of the big event. All looked well to "One-Take Bellamy." He yelled "print" and the company moved on.

NBC clearly liked "Empress." They chose to air this episode before any of the others to feature the Bay Area, or even "This Guy Smith," the episode that was meant as a lead-in to the trip to San Francisco. And *TV Guide* liked it, too.

Not bad for a last minute substitution.

LOCKED ROOM #13 / CULP & COSBY ON SET REWRITE

The script gives us an airtight room containing a shrine for the dead Tu Po. His body and his coffin are here, as is his faithful Siamese cat. There is a small gong, and, as Kelly and Scott will discover, a trapdoor leading out of the room. Oh yes, and there are candles, using up the precious oxygen.

What the script does not give us follows:

As Kelly tries to kill the flames on the candles, all mounted high up on the wall and barely within his reach, hot wax rains down.

KELLY: "Man, I have seen fiendish Oriental devices before, but spitting candles?! That's something else entirely. Oh, man, look at that. That's my best psychedelic tie. Waxed! And now the shirt, too."

Culp stays busy after this, picking dried wax off his clothes and his hands. He doesn't see what Cosby is doing, which is inspecting the gong. The script called for Cosby to hit the gong, not comment on it. And this nearly throws Culp off:

SCOTT: "We need to ring for room service."

KELLY: "We need to what?" (*looking to see what Cosby is doing*) "Oh, cut that out. Wax all over everything. Here we are inside of our famous locked room—with insidious spitting candles."

Watch Robert Culp, once again handling his own stunts—as he falls through the trapdoor that gets him out of the locked room. It may seem easy enough. But notice how small the opening is. And notice, when we see the trapdoor open for the cat, and for Scott, that it drops from one side, and not necessarily that quickly. Standing on this thing could easily cause the intended victim to pitch forward, as he drops, slamming his face into the portion of the floor that does not fall away. Culp could have broken his chin, or his nose. But, the former pole-vaulting contender makes it all look effortless.

Reviews

"Empress" earned *I Spy* its 12th Close Up listing in *TV Guide*, the first of the third season. Far better episodes had been passed by, but, for whatever reason, this one caught the editorial eye of the number-one selling magazine in America.

Cast & Crew

France Nuyen (Mei Lin) would stay married to Robert Culp for two years. She immediately followed this work with an appearance on *Star Trek*, where she plays an empress of another kind—spoiled and very alien. She was 27. She would make three appearances on *Hawaii Five-O*, as well as stopping off at *Kung-Fu*. Beginning in the mid-1980s, as she alternated her time between acting and furthering her education to become a clinical psychologist, she gravitated toward playing doctors, and did so on three different TV series, as Dr. Kiem on *St. Elswhere* (1986–88), Dr. Chen on *Santa Barbara* (1989), and Dr. Carrol on *Knots Landing* (1990). She also appeared in *The Joy Luck Club*. In 1989 Nuyen received a Woman of the Year Award in Los Angeles for her work with abused children and women behind bars.

Benson Fong (Cheng) got his start in the Charlie Chan movie series. He played Tommie Chan, Number Three Son, in *Charlie Chan in the Secret Service* and *Charlie Chan and the Chinese Cat*, both from 1944. The character proved so popular that Fong was given a spin-off series of his own, making four movies without his dad. Twenty years later, well on his way to achieving 100 credits in TV and film, he made his appearance here, at age 51. Fong was also a restaurateur, owning California's popular Ah Fong's Restaurant chain.

Philip Ahn (Tu Po) had over 200 film and TV credits in his career. He would go on to play Master Kahn on *Kung-Fu* (1972–75). He had previously appeared in *I Spy* during season one.

Elick Moll and **Joseph Than** were 66 and 64, respectively. After *I Spy*, they would briefly write for *Hawaii Five-O* before retiring from television.

72. **"A FEW MILES WEST OF NOWHERE"**; Written by: Jerry Ludwig; Directed by: Arthur Marks; Location: Small California mountain town; First airing: 1/29/68. Repeated: 7/1/68.

Kelly and Scott's investigation of a murder takes them to a California town which is to be the site of a nuclear power plant. But the locals, under the influence of Pierson, a paranoid land owner, have isolated themselves into "survivalist mode." They are armed and determined to keep the government out.

Kelly befriends Cathy, who works for Pierson. She would like to help, but Pierson has her under his thumb. He also has the loyalty of Cathy's brother, Tiny.

Assessment

Jerry Ludwig, a self-confessed advocate for giving television what television wants, purposely filled his *I Spy* scripts with tried and true TV and motion picture formulas.

Ludwig: "This was actually my second script, written before 'Now You See Her, Now You Don't.' At the time we were working out the story, it was being called 'Rotten Town.' If my first script borrowed from *Desperate Hours*, and 'Now You See Her' was inspired by *The Lady Vanishes*, then this was *A Bad Day at Black Rock*."[5]

Ludwig drew from many sources. See if you can spot the clichés:

Andrew Duggan and Debbi Storm, "A Few Miles West of Nowhere," (© 1967 3 F Prod., courtesy Image Ent.).

- The Damsel in Distress, who is a Pretty Single Mom, but can't get a date.
- She has an Adorable Child, who can't get a dad.
- She has a Slow-Witted Big Brother, who really is big.
- And he's nicknamed Tiny.
- There's Big Daddy, whose wife actually calls him "Daddy," who is intent on running the town with an iron fist.
- And then the Cowboy Hero (Kelly) comes to town.
- And his Trusted Companion (Scott) rides along.
- Big Daddy sends in the Not-So-Good Good Old Boys, i.e., the mob mentality, the bigotry, the chains, the baseball bats.
- All encounter the Child in Danger, who can only be saved if the bad Not-So-Good Good Old Boys and the Cowboy Hero, along with his Trusted Companion, can put aside their differences and work together.
- The required big ending, as Tiny, the Slow-Witted Big Brother, is shot repeatedly in the abdomen, but keeps advancing, and, before dying, crushes the life out of Big Daddy.
- The Good Guys win.
- Then the Cowboy Hero tells the Pretty Single Mom that he might be back this way again. With his Trusted Companion at his side, he rides off into the sunset.
- The Pretty Single Mom chokes back the tears and waves good-bye.

It is to some surprise that an episode that is built almost entirely on cliches can turn out somewhat good, but that's exactly what "A Few Miles West of Nowhere" does.

One reason is there are some original and daring ideas for 1967:

- Big Daddy and his followers are a radical cult of survivalists, who are at war with the government.
- Big Daddy does all of this because he is sexually dysfunctional.
- The Cowboy Hero and his Trusted Companion literally run a gauntlet as they are being stoned.
- Robert Culp's masterful handling of the fight in the gas station, as he takes off his expensive watch, signaling to the audience that he's about to beat the gas station attendant to a pulp, and then that spin, those kicks, that deadly elegance.

"A Few Miles West of Nowhere" can be an entertaining episode, provided one doesn't demand complete originality.

The Story Behind the Story

Jerry Ludwig: "They shot it up in Arrowhead. The sexual dysfunction of the major villain was interesting, because you couldn't do hardly anything—the censorship thing in Hollywood was still there. But I think we managed to convey that this guy was such a sonofabitch because he was just plain warped."[6]

But the episode came in short. Culp and Cosby's improv skills would be needed, so the two leads met with actor Leonard Stone on a Paramount soundstage made up to look like the corridor of a motel and a motel room. On October 4, 1967, they shot a couple of scenes, mostly ad-libbed, including the thumb dunking scene.

Culp & Cosby on Set Rewrite

Back in the hotel room, after the vandalism of their car, Kelly looks at his broken tennis racket. The ad-lib is from Culp: "There it is, folks, my best psychedelic racket to date. This tears it. I'm going to put in a requisition and get all steel rackets—and they'll pay it, too, because *this* was in the line of duty!"

For "Apollo," the very next episode to show Kelly with a tennis racket, he would have a brand-new metal one.

Later, in the same room, after Scott has injured his thumb, Culp contributes: "If I've told you once, I've told you a thousand times: If you're going to whip a man about the face and lips, you must pick the soft spots, never the hard part on the *top of the head*."

The improvisation continues: Kelly fills a drinking glass with hot water. It's dunking time. But, first, the thumb needs to be popped back into place. Kelly takes hold of the thumb. Scott plays a coward. He insists Kelly let go. Kelly tricks him into thinking that he will. And then POP.

And, in the shack containing the secret weapons, most of which look like World War II rejects, or older (there is even a tommy gun), Culp picks up a mortar shell and uses it as a mock microphone, saying, "Good evening, ladies and gentlemen, welcome to the world famous Hostile Room of the Hotel Paranoia, where the very wonderful Bonnie & Clyde dropped off a lot of their old equipment."

Cast & Crew

Andrew Duggon (Pierson) was 44. He had been appearing in front of the camera since 1948, including countless guest turns on television. He had recurring roles on four series, most notably, *Bourbon Street Beat*, from 1959, and *Lancer*, a Western on CBS from 1968 through '70, where Duggon costarred with James Stacy, and played a Ben Cartwright type. The fatherly Duggon often appeared as U.S. presidents, including two turns as Dwight D. Eisenhower, in *Back Stairs at the White House*, a 1979 miniseries, and again in 1987, in *J. Edgar Hoover*. He played a make-believe president for *In Like Flint*, the James Coburn spy spoof in 1967.

Diahn Williams (Cathy) had already appeared in *I Spy* for "Night Train to Madrid." She would continue acting in television and became a regular on the daytime soap *Summerset*, from 1972 to 1974.

Richard Kiel (Tiny) once said he was often mistaken for Ted Cassidy (Lurch from the *The Addams Family*) and Fred Gwynne (Herman from *The Munsters*). The 7'2" actor began his career in 1960. He played the alien who comes to Earth looking for a food source in "To Serve Man," one of the best-known episodes of *The Twilight Zone*. He was Voltair, the associate to the tiny terror, Dr. Miguelito Loveless, in four episodes of *The Wild Wild West*. But his greatest claim to fame is for playing Jaws, the steel-toothed assassin from a pair of James Bond films, *The Spy Who Loved Me* (1977) and *Moonraker* (1979).

Ken Swofford (Clay, the redheaded redneck) has had a 40-year career in television and films. He was well liked at *Gunsmoke* and would appear in nearly a dozen episodes. He was a regular on *The Virginian* for one season, immediately following his work here, before having two years of celebrity on *Fame* in the 1980s. He was 35.

Leonard Stone (Charlie, the motel operator) racked up over 150 appearances on TV and in films, plus regular work on three different prime-time series. True couch potatoes may remember him from a role he played during the same year as his work here, as Farrum, a space circus operator, in two episodes of *Lost in Space*. He was 44.

Arthur Marks is best known for his Black exploitation films from the 1970s and '80s. They include *Detroit 9000* and *Monkey Hustle*. This would be his only work directing for *I Spy*.

73. **"HOME TO JUDGMENT"**; Written by: Robert Culp; Directed by: Richard C. Sarafian; Location: Idaho; First airing: 1/18/68. Repeated: 6/17/68.

Kelly and Scott bungle an assignment and become the hunted rather than the hunters in a deadly cat-and-mouse game across a midwest prairie.

Physically exhausted and outnumbered, they seek refuge at the lonely farmhouse of Kelly's Aunt Alta and Uncle Harry, and decide to make a stand against their heavily armed pursuers.

Assessment

From the photography to the scoring, acting, writing, and excellent direction, "Home to Judgment" was *I Spy*'s finest hour.

Culp and Cosby agree.

The subtext of the story is about a man's aching desire to return to the less-complicated times of his life, a desire that is thwarted by his own ambitions, dreams, and history. He is desperate now to escape the life he has worked so hard to create.

Everyone associated with the making of this episode—the producers, crew, cast, editors and musicians—knew this one was special. And their best efforts are evident throughout.

Will Geer, Robert Culp, "Home to Judgment" (© 3 F Prod., courtesy Image Ent.).

The Story Behind the Story

Michael Zagor: "Bob Culp is an amazing writer. I learned so much by reading what he wrote—the way he would convey his visual ideas. Reading a Bob Culp script is like reading a textbook on how to write quality television."[7]

Michael Preece: "Richard Sarafian was brought back for 'Home to Judgment.' That was a big episode, and they wanted a really good job. Sheldon felt it was beyond both Chris Nyby and Earl Bellamy."[8]

Richard Sarafian: "Culp was a terrific writer. His scripts were very good. One of the things I liked about that script was it was surreal. I would call it a diamond in a gold band, as compared to some of the other stuff we were doing. You get lucky once in a while. I'm sure I was Culp's second choice for that. His first choice was always Sam Peckinpah.

"Una Merkel was a wonderful little pixie of a character. She was so darling.

"Will Geer hadn't worked a lot for many years, because he was blacklisted. I'll take the credit for getting him a stand-out job at a time when he was struggling to get over all that negative business. Mort Fine agreed to the casting. He was very sensitive to what went on in the mid–1950s."[9]

Mark Rydell: "I remember the moral courage (concerning the casting choices) on *I Spy*. I wanted to hire Will Geer for the grandfather in *The Reivers*. CBS had a great deal to do with the production of that picture, and they told me I couldn't hire him. And I remembered what Sheldon and the others did. So I said to CBS, 'Okay, I want you to know that I'm going to call a press conference and say that the blacklist still exists. And I'm going to do it tomorrow. I'm planning to expose you.' And the next day, they hired him. It was a 20-year blacklist for him, and he went on to a very distinguished career. And that's due, in many parts, to the heroism of the *I Spy* producers."[10]

At the midpoint of the third season, the world of *I Spy* had become a blur for Robert Culp. By his own admission, excluding weekends and holidays, it had felt to Culp that he and Cosby had a mere 12 days off in three long years. The production records for the series indicate that it *was* an exhausting schedule.

Robert Culp, the globe-trotting actor, was as tired and confused as Kelly Robinson, the globe-trotting spy.

Culp had been struggling with the idea for his seventh *I Spy* script. In early 1967, the story, or what Culp had of it, had to do with an old prospector, someone reminiscent of his grandfather, who was searching for an abandoned mine. It was to be something along the lines of *The Treasure of Sierra Madre*. But the story elements wouldn't come together.

Hoping to break his writer's block, Culp took a drive out to Malibu to visit Sam Peckinpah. Along the way, on the heavily traveled canyon road, he spotted an old farmhouse and barn surrounded by fields of crops. It was a setting that could have passed for the late 1930s, when he last saw his Uncle Harry and Aunt Alta on their farm in Idaho. And yet here it was, in 1967, on the outskirts of Los Angeles.

Culp pulled off the highway and scouted the property. There was a dog lying in the shade near the farmhouse, but he saw no people. The sight of the property released a flood of memories, and, almost as quickly, Culp had the story he wanted to tell.

Culp based two of the characters in the script on his grandfather and grandmother. But he chose, instead, to name them after his aunt and uncle. The farm was fashioned after the property where his Uncle Harry and Aunt Alta lived in those long distant days of the 1930s.

In this labor of love, Culp assisted in the decorating of the house. The guns used in the episode were his. The .33 rifle had belonged to his grandfather. The .22 had been his, as a boy, a gift from his grandfather. And the pictures on the table in the living room of the old house were that of his grandmother and grandfather.

Culp had ideas concerning the casting, as well. He had wanted Walter Brennan to play his Uncle Harry. But Brennan was busy on a series of his own, *The Guns of Will Sonnet*. So casting director Mike Fenton, on the recommendation of Richard Sarafian, brought in Will Geer.

For Aunt Alta, Culp had wanted Ula Bondie. But she was ill.

Una Merkel was booked instead. Culp was concerned that Merkel was best known for playing second banana in a series of early talkie comedies. He was convinced she would not be right for the part.

Culp later acknowledged he was wrong. After a day of filming, he knew that Geer and Merkel were perfect in the parts. Both professionals brought elements to the roles that Culp hadn't envisioned. At one point, he admitted, Merkel's performance even brought him to tears.

To direct "Home to Judgment," Culp had indeed wanted Sam Peckinpah. Again he made the request. Again Leonard refused. Culp's next choice was Richard Sarafian.

Culp was immediately struck by the excellence of Sarafian's work. The director connected with the script more than any other he had handled for the series. In Culp's words, with "Home to Judgment," Sarafian proved he had "the eye of a painter."

Leonard himself vetoed the idea of beginning the episode with Kelly and Scott jumping from a freight train, as Culp had written. The concept was just too expensive. Leonard suggested an old car, with the hood up, overheated. That is what we see in the first seconds of the episode.

From that point on, it is Culp's writing, barely altered and preserved through the detail of Sarafian's fine direction.

The episode was allowed nine days of production—two days more than the norm. With all the differences they may have had, Sheldon Leonard never shortchanged Robert Culp on the productions of his scripts. They were given the grand treatment—as grand as mid–1960s TV would allow.

Cast & Crew

Will Geer (Uncle Harry) is best known as Grandpa Walton in the long-running 1970s series *The Waltons*. In addition to over 100 episodes of *The Waltons*, he amassed another 100 plus appearances in films and various other television series during a career that began in 1932. In the 1950s, Geer was indeed blacklisted for refusing to testify before the House Un-American Activities Committee. His career stalled. Geer's immense talent outlasted the list and his acting career survived the unjust action. He would remain busy as an actor right up until the time of his death, in 1978, while *The Waltons* was still in production. He was 65 here, 76 then.

Una Merkel (Aunt Alta), as Culp remembered, came to fame playing secondary roles in 1930s comedies. She had actually been appearing before the camera since 1923. She won a Tony Award in '56 for the stage play *The Ponder Heart*. In '62, she was nominated for an Academy Award in the category of Best Supporting Actress for *Summer and Smoke*. By 1967, she had achieved over 100 film and TV credits. Her excellent work here would be her last. She retired immediately after filming "Home to Judgment." She was 64.

Robert Donner, the killer disguised as a mailman, was 36 at the time of this production. He had been in one previous *I Spy*, playing the role of Dr. Bustard in "Dragon's Teeth." He would go on to work with Will Geer in *The Waltons*, where he played the recurring role of Yancy Tucker. He also had a recurring role on *Mork & Mindy* as Exidor.

Richard Sarafian, writer/director/actor, would contribute his eighth and final directing assignment for *I Spy*. After his work here, he made the transition into feature films and received acclaim for his early 1970s cult favorites, *Vanishing Point*, from 1971, and *The Man Who Loved Cat Dancing*, from 1973. Look for him as an actor in *Bugsy*, playing "Fat Man in the Sauna."

Robert Culp would stay true to his words to Bill Cosby, when, after turning in the script for "Judgment," he said, "I'm finished." This would be his final script for the series. The Emmy-nominated writer would remain unproduced until the early 1980s, when he would contribute two scripts for his next series, *The Greatest American Hero*.

Earle Hagen, in Culp's opinion, did his best work for the series with the musical score he wrote for "Home to Judgment." Culp was not surprised that Hagen would finally win an Emmy for *I Spy*. He was, however, bothered that the award was not for "Judgment," but for "Laya," an episode Culp found to be "unmemorable."

Richard H. Calhoon, under the supervision of **Art Seid**, handled the editing duties on this episode, which is perfect in all ways.

74. **"APOLLO"**; Written by: Ernest Frankel; Directed by: Earl Bellamy; Location: Los Angeles; First airing: 11/20/67. Repeated: 6/10/68.

Kelly and Scott must break up in order to break open a planned sabotage of an American aerospace project.

It seems Kelly knows his best years as a tennis player are behind him, but it appears he needs someone, anyone, to blame it on other than himself. Scott is the target of Kelly's criticism, and the trainer acts as if he's had enough. He blames Kelly's bad performance on the tennis court as a result of the athlete's excessive boozing and womanizing, and he tells him so, within earshot of the press. So Kelly decks him.

Now Scott is out of a job. It is quickly established that he is in dire need of money. He even has an ex-wife he has been keeping a secret. But a chance meeting brings her out of the woodwork, and now she claims Scott owes her thousands of dollars in back alimony.

The ex-wife's name is Margo. She is a nightclub singer. Kelly has a girl with him, too, named Bronwyn, who, with Kelly's help, will manage to get a job at the same aerospace facility where Scott has recently found work. She, of course, is an enemy spy. Kelly and Scott, of course, know all about it.

Now the opposition moves in. Scott is offered $10,000 to steal industrial secrets. But the enemy, lead by a lesbian named Bobbie, have something more horrific in mind.

Bobbie's plan not only includes stealing classified information concerning the Apollo program, but blowing up a jet propulsion facility near Los Angeles.

Assessment

Writer Ernest Frankel instills some personal urgency, and a very loud ticking clock, into this otherwise convoluted tale of espionage.

The episode has three things going for it: the then-current topic of the space race and man's soon to be realized trip to the moon (Apollo 11 would make it in July 1969); some daring choices between the actors and director, including the decision to have Pippa Scott play Bobbie as a lesbian; and rare aerial shots of the Rockadyne jet propulsion facility in the Santa Susanna Mountains, as well as the filming that was permitted at the facility itself.

There is also an amusing bit at the end, when Kelly teases Scott about the latter thinking he might want to settle down and have a regular job: "You could be happy here—What did you call this place? Downey?"

The Story Behind the Story

Sheldon Leonard may have lost the chance to film in China and Russia, but he was the only producer to ever gain access to both the Rockadyne facility in the Santa Susanna Mountains and the aerospace facilities in Downey.

Robert Culp does many of his own stunts, both running along the top of freight cars, and doing gymnastics on a skeletal structure of criss-crossing pipes on a towering platform at Rockadyne. A stuntman was used for the more dangerous shots, but Culp can clearly be seen doing much of the physical work himself.

And then there's that song that Margo is singing in the nightclub. If it sounds familiar, it's not because it was a hit. But it did help win its composer an Emmy. That's "Voice in the Wind," the song written by Earle Hagen for the episode "Laya."

RATINGS

A.C. Nielsen's findings for the split in the audience share for Monday night from 10 to 11 P.M. were:

The Carroll Burnett Show, *CBS: 35.0%*
I Spy, *NBC: 26.3%*
The Big Valley, *ABC: 22.9%*
All others: 15.8%

Cast & Crew

Pippa Scott (Bobbie) made her film debut in John Ford's *The Searchers*. She was a regular for one season (1962–63) on *The Virginian*. She was 32 when she played the unfeminine Bobbie.

Nancy Kovacs (Bronwyn) got her start on *The Jackie Gleason Show*, as one of his pretty, bouncy Gleason Girls. During the same year as this, she appeared in *Star Trek*, playing a bewitching alien medicine woman in designer animal skins. In 1969, at age 33, sans the animal skins, she was nominated for an Emmy for a guest shot in *Mannix*.

Ron Rich (Roger) got off to a great start. In 1966 he played Luther "Boom Boom" Jackson, the football player who thinks he cripples Jack Lemmon in *The Fortune Cookie*, then spends the rest of the movie looking after him. Despite the promising beginning, other movie offers did not follow. Rich made his TV debut here. The *Wild Wild West* and a pair of *Mission: Impossible* segments came next.

George W. Brooks ended his 13-episode run on *I Spy* with a less than perfect segment that, nonetheless, featured top-notch editing. Having seen the birth of the buddy genre firsthand, Brooks would make the jump to directing with a couple of TV buddies who owed much to *I Spy*: *Starsky & Hutch*. He would follow that with more directing assignments for some buddies of a different sort, on *Charlie's Angels* and *Hart to Hart*.

21

The Grind Continues

Back to Mexico

While the eighth block of episodes were being filmed at various sights in California, the mad dash continued to fill the holes in the schedule, created by the loss of Russia and China as potential locations.

More scripts were needed—and quickly.

Nine teleplays would be prepared. Eight would be filmed. One, "Suitable for Framing," was a reject from the second season, and would go through a series of hasty rewrites.

Another, "The Name of the Game," had actually been written in May for possible inclusion in the eighth block. But, when the decision was made that *I Spy* would return to Mexico for the ninth, it was felt that "Game" would be better suited for that locale.

A third script, "The Defector," submitted to the series by a novice writer, would get an overhaul by Friedkin and Fine. It would become "The Spy Business."

These three, and the rest of the scripts, as well, would be written or rewritten between June and October 1967.

September 21st marked the final day of production for "Apollo," the last episode of the eighth block. Earl Bellamy was the director. It was also the first day of filming for "Carmelita Is One of Us," a show that would be included in block number nine.

At midday, Bellamy wrapped photography on his episode, then Christian Nyby stepped in to begin the local portion of the shooting on "Carmelita." That work would require three-and-a-half days. The balance of the episode was put aside and completed later while the crew was on location in Mexico. A half-day of work on "The Spy Business" followed on September 27th, also with Nyby calling the shots. Everything else to do with that segment would be shot south of the border.

At midpoint on the 27th, Earl Bellamy returned, taking over from Nyby, and starting "Turnabout for Traitors." He would spend two working days on that project, finishing up halfway through the day on September 29th before shifting gears and shooting sequences for another script, "Suitable for Framing," continuing through the 6th. As with the other three episodes not yet finished, the bulk of the work on this latest segment would have to wait.

The following day, October 7th, Culp and Cosby and company departed for Mexico, where they would remain for a month and a half. Once there, Bellamy and Nyby would trade off, each taking turns at having the second unit and the actors at their disposal, finishing the four episodes they had begun in Los Angeles and breaking ground on four more, all to be completed once the company returned to the studio in late November.

It would have been helpful to the actors if the four episodes already partially filmed could have been completed before filming was to begin on the next four—but that wasn't how *I Spy* worked.

Throughout this process, Culp and Cosby, as they had done for three years, would

21—The Grind Continues

The grind continues. Culp, Said, Leonard and Cosby in Acapuleo, Mexico, 1967 (courtesy *TV Guide*).

continuously shift gears, shooting portions of different scripts, out of sequence, all designed to take advantage of scenery and the availability of guest performers. The burden was on the two stars to keep focused, jumping from one story to the next, then back again.

It is not surprising that for Robert Culp much of the third season blurred together. What is surprising, however, is that both his and Cosby's performances remained consistently good, if not excellent.

Shooting a weekly television series is a grueling process, even when the *I Spy* formula for filming was not in play. It is hard on all involved, but perhaps the greatest weight lies on the shoulders of the lead players. That is the case today, but it was even more so in the 1960s.

At that time, budgets were much smaller than by modern television standards. And, in contrast to the practice on most of today's series, the storylines would often be built around only one or two actors. Think about David Jansen of *The Fugitive*, or Ben Gazarra of *Run for Your Life*, or Mike Conners of *Mannix*. The burden must have seemed insurmountable for these men. They carried their shows and, therefore, were featured in very nearly every scene shot. There were no half-day schedules for them. No four-day workweeks. It was five to six days a week, often 12 hours a day, week after week, month after month. Additionally, at that time, there were more episodes being produced for each television season, so this work schedule would go on for eight or even nine months without a break.

The workload was worse for Culp and Cosby. They shared the lead, but rarely was either excused from appearing in a scene to be shot for any given episode.

By the very design of *I Spy*, Kelly and Scott were inseparable. In most of the episodes the two men would travel side by side, dodging bullets, swapping jokes, trying to break free of their famous locked rooms, and always demonstrating that unique thing called "blendship."

The schedule was relentless. Add to that four or more months a year of travel, living out of a suitcase, away from the comforts of home and the support of loved ones. Increasing this burden, Culp and Cosby were also rewriting. When they weren't rehearsing a scene, or shooting a scene, they were dissecting it, rethinking it, restaging it.

As the two stars struggled to make it to the finish line, and wrap the final episodes of season three, Freidkin and Fine burned the midnight oil, as well.

Like their stars, *I Spy's* two writer/producers were feeling the strain. David Friedkin, the least likely of the two to blow off steam, except at night over cocktails, held his worries and tension within. All of this had a price.

Anthony Friedkin: "Dad got very ill. Colon cancer. There was a surgery, but he was seriously ill for a long time. It hit him hard."[1]

This is why there would be no episodes directed by Friedkin during season three. But he was still writing. And, with his partner, the producers designed the journey to Mexico.

If nothing else, they had a method to their madness. Or, at least, a timeline.

Friedkin and Fine had a very clear idea for the sequence regarding Kelly and Scott's travels, which was not indicated by the manner in which the episodes were shot, or even numbered.

Kelly and Scott begin in Guadalajara, on stakeout at the airport, for the start of "The Spy Business." The "business" involving that story takes them out of the city, by a four-hour car drive, to Lake Patzcuaro, and a natural body within the lake known as Janitzio Island.

They are then in Guanajauto for "Happy Birthday, Everybody." In that episode, they drive a red convertible sports car, which they keep for "Carmelita Is One of Us."

They are still in Guanajauto for the beginning of "Carmelita," then quickly leave town, sans the convertible (which had to be ditched after a colleague's dead body was stuffed into the front seat.) They are en route for Guadalajara.

For "Suitable for Framing," they are still assigned to Guadalajara, but with a new convertible, which they will also ditch after a body is stuffed in its trunk. During the story, they journey to Mexico City.

At the beginning of "Turnabout for Traitors," Scott is returning to Mexico after a short vacation to see his mother in Philadelphia. He arrives in Acapulco, where he is to hook up with Kelly at the Las Brisas resort.

Following the conclusion of "Turnabout," they will remain at Las Brisas for the next three episodes, ending with "Shana."

A logical sequence is indicated by the scripts, but not by the shooting schedule. In reality, Culp and Cosby were bounced around, from town to town, from script to script, from director to director, in a disjointed frenzy of production.

It was madness.

Culp: "By the final episodes of the third season, for the first time, Bill and I were wearing on each other. We needed time off, time apart."[2]

Steven Kandel: "They got testy with one another toward the end. Who could blame them?"[3]

Preece: "I felt the tension, so I assumed others on the crew felt it too. That was the beginning of their not eating lunch together, and no longer rehearsing together before they got on to the set. Culp seemed to become more moody and more reclusive. Both of them got that way."[4]

Cosby: "I never said that I was tired of Bob. I was just tired. It became a grunt. Look, you come to work at seven, and then, as the season goes on, you're not finished until seven. You're putting in 12 hours. A television series, after awhile, gets to a point where ... hey, man, the best way to say it is: The director that we both loved more than anybody was Bellamy! Earl Bellamy. That's the man. When we saw Bellamy's name, we knew we were going to be home before the sun went down. Maybe he didn't win any awards, but he won it for us. Man, it's the 'Get to Go Home' award.

"It was wearing. Twelve hour days ... and rewriting the scripts. You know, after awhile, in my close-up, I would say 'Look, let the other actor go home. I can do it without the actor.

Let somebody else read the line, because I know who my character is.' You know, that kind of thing. I never got tired of Bob, I don't know what he's talking about."[5]

The company would return home to Paramount studios to continue the maddening agenda.

On November 20th, director Bellamy was back for shooting on a soundstage. Only one day of production was required to complete "The Name of the Game," an episode that had, otherwise, been shot entirely in Mexico at some point in the last month and a half.

The next day, the two stars had to switch gears again. Christian Nyby was back, taking charge so that work could resume on "Pinwheel," one of his segments that he had begun in Mexico. Bellamy would rest.

Next up, "Happy Birthday, Everybody," with Bellamy again at the controls. Nyby would rest. Culp and Cosby wouldn't. For three days, they connected back with the script about a maniac bomber out to kill a retired State Department worker and his family. That work ended on December 1st.

After a weekend break, Nyby returned, again switching off with Bellamy, to finish "Shana," an episode he had begun down south, with only two additional days of local shooting required. Culp and Cosby had to get back into the mind frame they had started earlier in November, and think only about Shana, the beautiful Black woman who was being tortured by enemy agents aboard a yacht anchored off Acapulco. In the most dramatic scenes of that episode, Kelly and Scott struggle with their decision to allow Shana to suffer.

On December 5th, the final day of shooting, Kelly and Scott are bound and gagged in what would be the last of their famous locked rooms for the season. Once out of their prison, Culp and Cosby would be free of the exhausting schedule and the maddening lack of continuity that the formula for the shooting created.

The third season, which had begun early, had ended.

But not quite.

As the footage from Mexico was combined with the shots at Paramount, there were a few rough spots that still had to be smoothed out. Looping sessions were scheduled; second unit work was done in Mexico with a pair of Kelly and Scott doubles; and even an unexpected extra day of filming was needed at Paramount.

"Happy Birthday, Everybody" had come in short. No surprise. The script was overly simplistic and light on pages. So, on December 28th, a very ill David Friedkin helmed the shooting of a pair of scenes designed to pad an already overly-padded segment. Culp was away on his honeymoon with France Nuyen and unavailable. Instead, Friedkin made do with Cosby and Ken Tobey, trading lines in a phone conversation. He also shot a bit of fluff with a child actor, who appears to be having trouble sleeping, then rises to practice taking swings at a piñata.

It was unexciting stuff. But it gave them the needed minutes.

And that was a wrap.

22

The Ninth Block of Episodes

75. **"THE SPY BUSINESS"**; Written by: Morton Fine & David Friedkin; Story by: John Shannon; Directed by: Christian Nyby; Location: Guadalajara to Lake Patzcuaro to Janitzio Island; First airing: 4/1/68

A Communist defector arrives in Mexico. One of his bodyguards is a double agent. Kelly and Scott must find out who it is—a trusted American agent or a longtime friend of Kelly's. Time is short for unmasking the traitor. Enemy assassins are close behind.

Assessment

This is a powerful story with elements of irony and tragedy.

Kelly resists believing that his old friend and colleague, Mike Woods, could be a double agent. He goes into this assignment determined to prove Mike's innocence and hang everything on the other questionable American agent, Russian-born Chanetsov. With Chanetsov, Kelly has an excellent scapegoat, and this episode has a gold star red herring.

Scott is determined not to let Kelly take the easy way out, revealing a story rich in conflict.

One might think Michael Zagor or Robert Culp wrote this script. The characters are that complex and fully developed. The story is that dark. But credit must go to Friedkin and Fine, working from a script submitted by a novice writer.

The Story Behind the Story

"Spy Business" benefits greatly from scenic photography taken around Lake Patzcuaro and its largest island, Janitzio. As Kelly tells us, the region lies approximately four hours by car from Guadalajara. Visitors will be pleased to find that the area has changed little since the *I Spy* company filmed there in late 1967.

THE CENSORS

NBC Broadcast Standards and Practices wrote: "Don't let enemy agent become human torch, as suggested in script."

That scene involves the siege of the house on Janitzio Island. One of the attackers has a Molotov cocktail in his hand. Scott shoots him, just in time to keep the attacker from hurling the flaming bomb at the house.

Culp and Cosby go back to Mexico, '67 (© 3 F Prod.).

In the script, this bit of action takes place at night, and is described as follows: "Henchman drops the bomb, which shatters, splashing flame. He screams. His sleeve catches fire. He runs back to his other henchmen, lights up the area. Other heavies are now revealed. Gun fight."

To appease Broadcast Standards, the scene was changed to take place in the daylight. The henchman falls over an embankment, out of our view, then there is an explosion. Effective for 1968 TV, but not as effective or horrific as it could have been. NBC got their wish and their watered-down version.

CULP & COSBY ON SET REWRITE

At the start of act 1, Kelly and Scott approach the airport worker they saw pick up a crumpled note from the runway. He is now in the airport terminal, in a phone booth, changing out of his workman's overalls. The script has Scott say, "Now why would a man change his clothes in a phone booth?" Kelly was to answer, "I have no ready answer for that. We should ask."

Need we say, the writer/producers of *I Spy* should never have fed a straight line like this to Culp and Cosby. Culp, instead, says, "I wouldn't know unless he has a big red 'S' on his chest." Cosby taps on the glass of the phone booth and announces, "Excuse me, Mr. Reeves, can we get an autograph."

George Reeves, of course, played TV's Superman.

REVIEWS

Thirteen was a lucky number for *I Spy*. With "The Spy Business," the series earned a 13th Close Up listing from *TV Guide*. Thirteen in just three years—an entertainment industry record unbroken to this day.

CAST & CREW

Dane Clark (Mike Woods) had appeared in the first season episode "One Thousand Fine." With over 200 credits from a career that spanned from 1940 through 1988, Clark is given better material here, and a character who displays a broader range of emotions. He was 55 at the time of this filming.

Cosby: "Dane Clark! I'm growing up watching him in the neighborhood movie theaters, and now here he is, and he's calling me 'Billy.' I'm having a good time. Dane Clark. Amen!"[1]

Paul Richards (Chanetsov) had a successful career playing a variety of character roles on both television and in the movies. He began in 1951. By 1974, at age 40, he already had 150 credits. He would die that year of cancer.

George Voskavek, playing the Russian defector, Hasel, began his career in entertainment in Czechoslovakia as the founder of a theater group. He was also a writer. When the Nazis invaded in the late 1930s, Voskavek immigrated to the United States where he found work acting in the movies. He was 62 at the time of this production, appearing somewhat younger than his years.

76. **"HAPPY BIRTHDAY, EVERYBODY"**; Written by: Morton Fine & David Friedkin; Directed by: Earl Bellamy; Location: Guanajauto; First airing: 2/26/68. Repeated: 7/15/68.

Kelly and Scott must protect a retired agent and his family living in Mexico from a madman. Frank Hunter, a specialist in killing with high explosives, is out for revenge.

Assessment

Simplicity often served *I Spy* well, but here is a case where there was just too little happening in the story to sustain interest.

Kelly and Scott are sight seeing when they spot Frank Hunter, a man they believed to be in prison. Further inquiry will tell them that Hunter escaped and has sworn revenge against Tom Mathews, a retired State Department agent now living with his wife and young son in Mexico. Mathews had put Hunter in jail.

Hunter is an expert with explosives and, unbeknownst to Kelly and Scott, has a suitcase filled with nitroglycerin.

It doesn't take great skills at deduction to put two and two together and come up with four. Hunter is in town to seek revenge against Mathews. His weapon of choice will be an explosive. And, of course, it's up to Kelly and Scott to save Mathews and his lovely family from a horrible death.

That is as far as Friedkin and Fine went in developing their story or any of the story's characters—except for one minor hook: Hunter has put the nitroglycerin in a piñata. Mathews son, Paul, will celebrate his birthday the following day and, in Mexican tradition, will be blindfolded, given a stick, and asked to break open the piñata.

Now we have a ticking clock. And a child in jeopardy.

But the banality of the writing is so severe it is embarrassing.

The cast appears lost, not knowing what to give in order to fill in the blankness of their characters or the empty corners of this story. And the director was offering little help here. Bellamy was back on the job.

Of course, Culp and Cosby hold their own. At this point, they could make up dialogue on the spot, anywhere, anytime, anyhow. And that's exactly what they did. But a new directive from the top—from Leonard and his supervising editor, Art Seid—mandated that the ad-libs, if at all possible, be left on the cutting room floor. This script, in desperate need of those Culp/Cosby witticisms, is left to stand on its own.

Jim Backus, Jeanne Bal, young Tony Fraser, and even Gene Hackman are also left standing on their own, empty-handed, with little to show to the camera beyond the expected cliches.

The Story Behind the Story

"One-Take" Bellamy strikes again. Notice the scene where Kelly and Scott walk and talk, as Scott conveys the information he was given over the phone by Russ. Local spectators, amused by the antics of the production company, and perhaps star struck by the chance to be caught on camera with two American celebrities, closely follow Culp and Cosby, grinning and chattering amongst themselves. Culp, as one point, while still delivering his lines to Cosby, glances behind himself to see what the fuss is all about.

He and Cosby are what the fuss is all about.

Earl Bellamy's reaction was to yell "cut and print!"

Perhaps Bellamy thought we would think the teenage girls following Culp and Cosby were doing so because they found Kelly and Scott to be really cute.

In Bellamy's defense, it is a nicely composed shot. It is charming moment, and it doesn't detract at all from the storyline, what little of it there is.

In Bellamy's further defense, "Happy Birthday" is beautifully shot, especially in regard to the gunfight scene with Hunter in and about the church and the cluster of mini pyramids.

The editing, however, handled by Richard Calhoon and Art Seid, demonstrates many questionable choices. Case in point, why do Calhoon and Seid cut to a shot of the sleeping Paul Mathews right smack in the middle of a dialogue scene between Kelly and Scott, which takes place miles away, then, after showing that nothing of interest is happening with Mathews, cut back to Kelly and Scott. If this was meant to build tension, it fails as badly as the script.

Another editing screw up—unless "One-Take" Bellamy failed to provide the editing team with proper coverage: The script tells us that Hunter sneaks into Paul's room and prepares to suffocate the boy under a pillow. He is interrupted when Tom enters. Hunter retreats into the shadows, then hears Tom and Paul talk about the birthday celebration for the next day, including the ritual of the breaking of the piñata. And this is where Hunter gets the idea to plant the explosives.

The problem is, we never see Hunter place a pillow over the head of the sleeping Paul. We do see the boy sleeping. We see Hunter enter the room. We see Hunter pause by the bed. Then, hearing that Tom is approaching, we see that Hunter hides. We see Tom enter, and we see that he sees that Paul is sleeping with a pillow now covering his head. But we never saw how the pillow got onto Paul's head.

But there is more.

David Friedkin directed a final day of pick-up shots with Bill Cosby, Ken Tobey, and Tony Fraser on December 28, 1967. This was the last day of production on the third season.

It is curious that for the pick-up shots, Ken Tobey appears only in voice. We see Scott, talking to Russ Conway on the phone. From the other end of the conversation, we see only Russ's hand, along with the photographs he lays out on his desk of Frank Hunter and Tom Mathews.

Financial records from the series tell us that Tobey was paid his normal rate for this appearance, so an issue of money certainly did not keep his face off-camera. And production records document that Tobey was indeed present for the pick-up shots made on December 28th. That *is* his voice, as well as his freckled hand laying the pictures on the desk top.

The choice to keep Tobey's face off-camera was made by the editors—Seid and Calhoon.

Cast

Jim Backus (Tom Mathews) began appearing in films in 1948. At that time, he had already been performing on the radio, and onstage. He first supplied the voice for Mr. Magoo in 1950, continued to do so in films, and then later on television, well into the 1980s.

Another character Backus would spend decades portraying was Thurston Howell III, from *Gilligan's Island* (1964–67), and its spin-off TV movies and animated series.

Besides Magoo, Backus was the voice for the cartoon bird riding on the back of a jetliner for Western Airlines' TV ads ("The only way to fly!"). He had his own short-lived television series, *The Jim Backus Show*, in 1960. He was 54 at this time.

Gene Hackman (Frank Hunter) had been appearing on television since 1959, mostly in minor supporting roles. His break-out performance was in the 1967 hit, *Bonnie and Clyde*. By the time this episode was repeated, Hackman had been nominated for an Oscar. A second nomination came his way in 1970 for *I Never Sang for My Father*. Two years later Hackman would win the Academy Award for *The French Connection*. He would win a second Oscar for his part in Clint Eastwood's *Unforgiven*. Hackman was 37 at the time of his appearance here.

Cosby: "These great guest stars kept coming—I mean, like Gene Hackman. To get a Gene Hackman, and the word is the guy's going to be a star—and you get to work with him. That's a nice time."[2]

Jeanne Bal (Shirl Mathews) is most famous, among TV boomers, for playing the Salt Vampire in the very first episode of the original *Star Trek* to be aired by NBC in September 1966. She had begun her TV career just six years earlier in the part of Pat Becker, a semiregular supporting role on a sitcom entitled *Love & Marriage*, then moved on to *Bachelor Father* in 1961, and *Mr. Novak* for the 1963–64 season. She wrapped up her brief TV acting career in 1970.

77. **"CARMELITA IS ONE OF US"**; Written by: Robert C. Dennis & Earl Barrett; Directed by: Christian Nyby; Location: Guanajauto to Guadalajara (plus catacombs under Guadalajara); First airing: 4/8/68

Kelly and Scott turn into a pair of doting babysitters when a ten-month-old child is used as a courier of top-secret data. As the agents flee with the baby across the Mexican countryside, a ruthless enemy, posing as the child's mother, is in hot pursuit.

Assessment

This episode is in trouble from frame one.

"Carmelita" has one of the worst opening teasers of the entire series. The photography and the editing are sloppy, and even amateurish. And the writing is unforgivably confusing.

This sloppiness continues into the first part of act 1. One must wonder if the director, a seasoned pro like Nyby, was even present for the location photography.

At one point, the wireless microphones cut out, causing the audio levels to dip while Kelly is speaking. And yet this footage was used for the final cut.

Rudy, driving a motorcycle with a sidecar, is being chased through town by a large black sedan, late 1950s in design. It is the same visually distinctive car we saw Frank Hunter driving in "Happy Birthday, Everybody." Cheap. Sloppy. Foolish.

Later, Kelly and Scott park their car near Rudy's house. In an unscripted moment, a Mexican peasant boy jumps into the front seat, offering to watch the fancy car, for a fee. This was not in the script, nor was it planned as an ad-lib. Culp and Cosby, focusing on what they are supposed to be doing, which is proceeding to Rudy's house, don't even acknowledge the boy. Moments later, we will find a dead body in this car, with the boy nowhere to be seen. Yet the master shot was used, either because it was the only one made, or the backup take had other problems. Again, cheap. Sloppy. Foolish.

Things finally improve.

"Carmelita," although poorly executed in the beginning, provides an excellent premise for *I Spy*.

Kelly and Scott are on the run, being chased across the Mexican countryside. In their custody, Carmelita, a baby girl who is being sought by the enemy agents for reasons unknown.

Along the way, the guys must milk a cow to get food for the baby. They must tear up their T-shirts to make diapers. They give one another tips on the handling of such a small infant, even quoting Dr. Spock (a renowned baby expert at the time, not the pointed-eared alien from *Star Trek*). And, when they seek shelter from a storm at a nunnery, they are imprisoned in a locked room—by a nun, no less, who believes them to be kidnappers.

"Carmelita" is an excellent vehicle for Culp and Cosby. The writers were two seasoned pros, Robert C. Dennis and Earl Barrett. The director, Christian Nyby, had already delivered some of the best episodes of the third season. What could possibly go wrong?

Plenty.

The Story Behind the Story

In the script, Scott is the one driving the motorcycle. Kelly is sitting in the sidecar, holding the baby.

For the filmed sequence, because Culp was better at driving a motorcycle, the roles were reversed, as was all the dialogue.

A major continuity mistake is made in this episode, in act 1, as if act 1 needed more problems.

Notice that when the babysitter leaves Rudy's house with the infant, she takes the baby carriage that is parked at the bottom of the stairs. She then goes to meet with Kelly and Scott. Kelly and Scott then hightail it back to Rudy's house, where the baby carriage has magically reappeared at the bottom of the stairs.

LOCKED ROOM #14 / CULP & COSBY ON SET REWRITE

In the script, the nun asks Kelly how many teeth the baby has. Kelly should know, as he claims to be the baby's father. Scott holds up two fingers on each hand, and acts as if he's scratching his chin. Kelly says "Two." Wrong answer. The baby has four teeth, two on top, two on bottom.

What isn't in the script is the best moment, when, after the nun walks away, Scott blames Kelly for blowing it by not reading his signal correctly. Again, Scott holds up his fingers, two on each hand, close to his face, as if he's rubbing his chin. Culp responds, "It's your fault. Your fingers were mumbling."

WHAT WENT WRONG

The opening of the story, from the script, suffers from a bad rewrite. In pages dated August 28, 1967, added in to the August 14th draft, the confusing tone of the teaser is set. There is no dodging the bullet, this is truly bad writing: clumsy and ineffective.

On top of this, something went badly wrong on location, beginning with the clumsily-written teaser. Either the cast, or the director decided to simply ignore the awkward dialogue and try to make up something better, or the wireless microphones were cutting in and out, as we would hear them do later in the episode, therefore requiring footage be thrown out in editing, or, perhaps still, the technical crew were rebelling.

First, this is what we are supposed to be following in the teaser:

- Rudy is established as being an American agent, working with Kelly and Scott.
- Rudy's assignment is to get close to Alma Rosa, an enemy agent, and steal classified information from her.
- Kelly and Scott are there, in the marketplace, to keep an eye on the operation. And then things go wrong.
- Alma Rosa discovers that Rudy has been playing her and has stolen from her.
- Rudy's wife, Lupe, the mother of his baby daughter, shows up, suspecting Rudy of

having an affair. She sees Alma Rose lashing out of Rudy, adds two and two, and does some lashing out of her own.
- Rudy does what any man would do. He runs.
- Kelly and Scott try to calm Lupe down, and assure her that Rudy was only cheating on her for the good of his country ... or, more correctly, their country.

It is a funny scenario, butchered by a hacked-up writing job, or, at least, a hacked-up rewriting job. But, if nothing else, we now understand what's going on.

For the filmed teaser, all of this is a muddled mess.

From here, we move on to the catacombs. It is not in the script.

In his autobiography, Leonard recalls how fascinated he was by the catacombs, and how fortunate the company was to be able to film there. Leonard even claimed that his company spent several days in the burial tunnels where "great sequences were captured on film."[3]

Calvin Brown was there, with Culp and Cosby, as they shot underground. He recalls that, in the sequence, Kelly and Scott were searching for something. But mostly he recalls the catacombs:

"You went down into the hole on a ladder, and you came back out on the ladder. If you toured down through there, you could see the soldiers who had been killed, still in their uniforms. And a lady who had died in childbirth, and she had a little fetus tied to her wrist. And they looked just like real people. The moisture and the type of earth down there kept them as if they were out having a sunbath. Bill told Camille not to go down, but she was so nosey that she went anyway, and she was sick for the next day."[4]

Culp and Cosby appear very uneasy about being involved in this portion of the filming. Culp even verbalizes his disapproval, speaking as Kelly, scolding Scott for dragging him into such an unpleasant place just for the purpose of "sightseeing," and making him see things that he found to be so disturbing that he will no doubt have nightmares for days, or weeks, or years to come.

None of these lines were scripted. The entire sequence that survives from the underground shoot was an ad-lib.

Michael Preece: "They wouldn't let us take lights down into the catacombs. We shot quite a bit, but much of it wasn't usable because of the lighting."[5]

And so only a single minute of Leonard's "great sequences" show up on screen. We see nothing of interest, nothing that conveys the eeriness and history of the tombs, and, if one wasn't told that Kelly and Scott are walking past actual mummies, one might assume those human figures are merely a row of ash-colored statues. Sadly, by the time we are told what they are, through more crackling audio, the mummies are no longer onscreen.

As for the intermittently poor audio, Preece recalls: "One of the big problems on *I Spy* was with the wireless mics. I remember Bob Trask was the audio mixer, and he had huge problems with that."[6]

Earle Hagen recalls the work spent in post to clean up the bad sound:

"Sometimes they'd ADR the dialogue [use filters and equalizers to try to clean up the sound], they'd loop it [have cast members come into the studio later to rerecord their voices], and get some dialogue back in. But that was the nature of the show. It was the first to use radio mics.

"We used to pick up radar sweeps and rock'n'roll stations. It wasn't discriminating. The problems in postproduction were enormous, especially with sound. So what you got was the best that they could do. I tried to cover up whatever I could."[7]

There may have been one last problem plaguing the location portion of this shoot.

In his autobiography, Leonard recalled how, when shooting in Guadalajara in 1967, the

Seven-Day War broke out in the Middle East. On the morning of the day after Israel "trashed" the Egyptian military, Fouad Said, who is Egyptian, approached Friedkin, Fine, and Leonard, his "three Jewish bosses," and said, "Today all shots will be out of focus."

He then walked away.

Leonard recalled that this had happened while the three producers stood in a huge central market, planning camera setups.

The tragically compromised opening teaser of this episode takes place in a huge central market. And it was in Guadalajara.

Perhaps a bit of the mystery has now been solved.

This problematic episode was buried opposite the Academy Awards broadcast on ABC.

Cast & Crew

Marie Gomez, the evil Alma Rose, worked mostly in TV Westerns, such as she had on *The Wild Wild West* and *Hondo*. She was also cast in a recurring role for several episodes of *The High Chaparral*.

Nate Esformes, playing Arista, Alma Rose's accomplice, had a long list of TV credits. At this time, he had already visited *The Monkees*, *Felony Squad* and *The Flying Nun*.

Paul Bertoya (Rudy) had recently been featured in the 1967 cult classic *Hot Rods to Hell*.

There were no big names in this guest cast, but all were able and willing to travel to Mexico for a chance to be in *I Spy*.

Richard H. Calhoon was the editor, working under **Art Seid**. **Chrystian Nyby** was the director. And **Fouad Said** was the location director of photography, and in charge of field technical support. The buck must stop on their desks with this problematic episode.

With all the sloppiness out of the way, by act 2, things glide along as they should with these four pros.

78. **"SUITABLE FOR FRAMING"**; Written by: Arthur Dales; Directed by: Earl Bellamy; Location: Guadalajara to Mexico City; First airing: 3/25/68

Kelly and Scott are assigned to a bogus U.S. senator, unaware that he's part of a far-fetched assassination plot.

To get things rolling, a physically ravaged street bum is selected by Andrew, a traitorous assistant to the real senator, to undergo plastic surgery and impersonate the politician. The timing is important, for the senator is in Mexico City preparing to shake hands with the president of the United States, who is on a goodwill visit to that country.

Assessment

First, the good news.

"Suitable for Framing" is fast moving, scenic, and has generous doses of intrigue, action, and humor.

Now, the bad news. What were they thinking....

The type of story they were trying to get was something along the lines of Hitchcock's *The 39 Steps*, *Saboteur*, and *Foreign Correspondent*.

What they got were villains fresh out of the Three Stooges Academy of Murder and Mayhem, Division of Political Assassination.

The idiocy of their plan:

- Alcoholic, broken-down street bum can pass himself off as a U.S. senator.
- Back alley doctor who performs abortions is now capable of delicate facial reconstruction.
- Back alley doctor is so good that, upon removing the bandages from his patient for the first time, there is no swelling, bruising, or stitches.
- The real U.S. Senator, while traveling abroad on official business, has no security, no staff, no entourage whatsoever, except for a personal manservant, who's selling him out.
- Bad Guys, following instructions from Stooge Field Handbook, stuff dead manservant into trunk of Kelly and Scott's car, even though Kelly and Scott do not yet suspect anything is amiss.
- Kelly and Scott now suspect something is amiss.
- Bad Guy Andrew, played by wimpy actor who portrayed the neurotic Mr. Peterson on *The Bob Newhart Show*, knows Kelly and Scott are en route to meet their contact *even* before *they* know.
- Bad Guy Andrew impersonates Kelly and Scott's contact, a Mexican dentist. He somehow even knows the secret handshake (a dental bridge that Scott is carrying that will fit into a mold of a human mouth, which is locked in a glass cabinet).
- Kelly and Scott evade the police, take off on foot, and flag down a car on a remote highway, which is driven by Andrew's evil colleagues, and has the body of the real senator stuffed in the trunk.
- Kelly and Scott, top U.S. agents on assignment in Mexico, have no clue that the president of the United States is visiting that country. A Mexican bartender turns on a TV and they see coverage of the presidential motorcade. Now, finally, they know.
- When Kelly tries to call the embassy in Mexico City to warn them of an impending assassination attempt, no one will accept the call.
- Kelly can't think of anyone else to call, not Washington, not the Pentagon, not the local police, *not even a script doctor*.
- Bad Guy Andrew, back again, still working out of his Stooges Handbook, has rigged a handgun in a briefcase to fire through a tiny hole. He then hands it off to the alcoholic street bum/bogus senator, to carry with him in an official greeting line, so he may pull the trigger mechanism and shoot the president at close range.
- And Andrew trusts the alcoholic to do this!
- And, finally, the alcoholic, who has no political agenda, nor has even discussed money, or how he expects to get away, is *willing* to do this.

What were they thinking....

The Story Behind the Story

The first draft of this problematic script was dated October 11, 1966, with a rewrite turned in on November 2, 1966, while the second season was still in production.

A rewrite by Friedkin and Fine was done on March 21, 1967, during the hiatus between seasons two and three, indicating that they were attempting to salvage the substandard material — just in case Russia were to fall through.

Russia did.

Another rewrite was attempted on August 16, 1967. Five weeks later, sadly, the script was in production.

A final attempt to polish the material was made on November 27, 1967, after the fact, after the shoot in Mexico, with only days left for shooting any portion of any episode for this season. This was a last minute attempt to make something out of nothing. It didn't work.

What were they thinking....

In many ways, this entertaining but hopelessly dumb story can be compared to the equally entertaining and hopelessly dumb "Crusade to Limbo."

And, like in "Crusade," where Culp, Cosby, Duff, Sarafian and crew climbed a scenic pyramid to shoot inane dialogue, Fouad Said does something inventive and risky in this episode, and all in an effort to shoot some more equally inane dialogue.

Check out the scene where Kelly and Scott get a lift from the bad guy in the red car. The camera seems to be attached to the hood, allowing us a nicely framed three-shot of the men inside the vehicle as they drive along a country road at a good clip. That was Fouad, strapped to the front bumper—one year before Jack Webb and his technical people figured out how to build a rig on the front of a car for filming of *Adam-12* (which would premiere in September 1968).

THE CENSORS

In the script, it is suggested that stock footage of a presidential motorcade be used, and that we see a glimpse of the current president of the United States, Lyndon B. Johnson.

Of course, NBC Standards and Practices had concerns. The network censors wrote, "We recommend that another high-ranking official, such as the Vice President, be the object of the assassination plot."

Interesting that NBC didn't mind Hubert Humphrey being a target.

Like a fine Ed Wood movie, this episode is so bad, it is funny.

CULP & COSBY ON SET REWRITE

Look for two examples of Culp and Cosby thumbing their noses at the material.

In one sequence, shot in Mexico, Kelly and Scott are being chased through a giant indoor market place by police. Culp and Cosby pause, as instructed. Culp, wearing a wireless microphone, delivers his scripted line, asking his partner, "What kind of rap do you get in Mexico for a corpse in your car?" Cosby is supposed to say, "Life, unless you go through the Auto Club," but instead says "Life, and a good beating." At this point, Cosby drops out of character, unable to suppress a smile and have a chuckle. Then the two men walk off. No other take of this scene was made, indicating that Earl 'One-Take' Bellamy was on the job.

Later, after riding in the back of a donkey drawn cart, wearing Mexican sombreros and ponchos, Culp is being silly with his hat, the chin strap hooked under his nose. By doing this, the hat is nearly pulled down over Culp's eyes. When he pushes the brim of the hat up, the strap tugs against his nostrils.

Cosby hasn't looked Culp's way and therefore hasn't noticed. Once they climb out of the cart, Culp ad-libs, "The problem with these hats is either you can't see, or you can't breathe." Cosby looks to see how Culp is wearing the hat and reacts by laughing, then pointing to the hat strap and saying, "That's supposed to go in the back." Again, it is more Culp and Cosby then Kelly and Scott. 'One-Take' does it again.

The week NBC aired this episode, *I SPY* was featured on the cover on *TV Guide* for the third time in as many years. This ensured a bigger audience. So, after careful thought, the network chose to televise this.

What were they thinking....

Cast & Crew

John Fiedler (Andrew), as mentioned, was on *The Bob Newhart Show* in the 1970s. He was also one of Felix and Oscar's poker buddies on *The Odd Couple* series from the same time. He got his start on radio, then moved into television with a recurring role as Cadet Higgins on *Tom Corbett, Space Cadet*. During the same year as his appearance here, at age 42, he played the incarnation of Jack the Ripper on *Star Trek*. He would go on to provide the voice of Piglet in over a dozen Winnie the Pooh movies and two animated TV series.

Dan Tobin, playing both the real and the phoney senator, had previously appeared in *I Spy* for the first season episode "Always Say Goodbye."

James Best, the back alley doctor, whose miraculous talents as a plastic surgeon would have qualified him an office in Beverly Hills, had he been real, appeared in the second season episode, "Lisa," as a homicidal enemy agent. He dies there, as well.

Arthur Dales had written the first season episode, "Danny Was a Million Laughs."

79. **"TURNABOUT FOR TRAITORS"**; Written by: Ernest Frankel; Directed by: Earl Bellamy; Location: Acapulco; First Airing: 2/19/68. Repeated: 7/22/68.

In Mexico, Kelly is being framed. The culprit is Clive Hampton, a British agent who has damning evidence proving that Kelly is a traitor. Hampton is a double agent, and figures that once Kelly is sentenced to do the time, he will have no choice but to do the crime.

Assessment

This story offers an engrossing hour that holds the viewer's interest, but never tips its hat as to what the outcome will be, or who is truly behind the frame job.

The supporting cast is effective. The sights are dazzling. The storyline, and the challenge it presents to Kelly and Scott, is unique and effective.

"Turnabout" breaks a great taboo of *I Spy*, it separates Kelly and Scott for much of the episode. And, just as "Bet Me a Dollar" did during season one, and "Trial by Treehouse" during season two, and "The Lotus Eater" at the start of season three, all which separated the team, this script and episode succeeds in creating a taut and satisfying chapter in the series.

Kelly's reaction, when a knife is thrown into his back, is superb. You'll need to sit down for this one, just as Culp did.

And, the icing on the cake is Jose Chavez as Goza, Kelly's light-fingered ally. He is delightful.

The Story Behind the Story

Good use is made of the Las Brisas resort, which was also featured in episodes from season one. This time out, we see much more of Acapulco than any episode from that first year, including a sequence shot at Fort San Diego.

Earl Bellamy and Art Seid are behaving themselves here. The direction is flawless, the editing top notch.

Bellamy, when not in his hometown, when not in hurry to get himself and his cast and crew off work at a decent hour, was capable of very impressive work—as seen here, and with another episode that was very nearly entirely shot on location—"The Seventh Captain."

Seid, when given good footage to work with, from a good script, could cut together film as smoothly as the next editor. But, when irked by what he felt was shoddy workmanship, be it bad writing, bad directing, or misbehaving stars, Seid would be inclined to make little effort to clean up someone else's mess.

There are no messes here. Everything works, and Bellamy and Seid do their jobs.

Cast

Peter Donat (Hamilton) is a cousin of Academy Award winner Richard Donat (*Goodbye Mr. Chips*). His career spanned from 1953 to the present, with over 100 credits. In the 1990s he played William Muldar in seven episodes of *The X-Files*. He was 39 here.

Jose Chavez (Goza) was never without work south of the border. He has over 300 film and TV credits of Mexican origin. Shortly after his work here, he would start popping up in American productions, as well, usually when the films would take advantage of Mexican scenery, beginning with *Butch Cassidy and the Sundance Kid*, *The Wild Bunch*, and *Two Mules for Sister Sara*. He can also be seen in *Romancing the Stone*. He was 51.

Regina Torme (Elena), like Chavez, was pulled from the Mexican talent pool. Her career was just getting started. She has since been featured in 13 Mexican television series.

Ross Elliot, playing Nate, the senior American agent who doubts Kelly's innocence, and dies because of it, appeared in over 250 different TV shows and movies. He also had a recurring role on two series: as Virgil Earp on *Wyatt Earp*, and the town Sheriff on *The Virginian*. He got his start with Orson Welles as a member of the Mercury Theater. He was part of Welles' famous *War of the Worlds* radio broadcast in 1938.

80. **"THE NAME OF THE GAME"**; Written by: Jerry Ludwig; Directed by: Earl Bellamy; Location: Acapulco and surrounding area; First airing: 3/11/68

In the jungle north of Acapulco, Kelly and Scott become "the naked prey" in a deadly game of hide-and-seek. The hunter: an American general, forced into retirement, who now has paranoid delusions that he's been betrayed.

Assessment

Robert Culp once said, when discussing his own script, "Home to Judgment," that *I Spy* worked best when kept simple. With such a strong relationship as the one between Kelly and Scott, the essence of the series was best realized when the script allowed time for the stars to interact.

Once again, as in "Carmelita Is One of Us," and "Suitable for Framing," Kelly and Scott are on the run. Yet unlike "Carmelita," with its clumsy opening and the poor production quality that weighed it down, or "Suitable," which chokes on its own complexities and both contrived and inane plot twists, "Name of the Game" makes sense, remaining a perfectly primal story of competition and madness.

The Story Behind the Story

The inspiration for Ludwig's script was the 1932 film *The Most Dangerous Game*, involving a megalomaniac who hunts human beings on his remote island.

That movie, based on a story by Richard Connell, was often ripped off, and officially remade twice, first in 1946 as *Game of Death*, and then again in 1956 as *Run for the Sun*.

Ludwig recalls his passion for wanting to write this story: "There was a general named Walker, who, at the time, was our man in Germany. He was saying, 'If the Communists mess with us, I'm gonna mess with them.' This army general took it upon himself to decide whether or not to start World War III—until the government removed him. He was the model for the Lloyd Nolan character.

Lloyd Nolan, "The Name of the Game" (© 3 F Prod., courtesy Image Ent.).

"Nolan played so many lovable Irish cops over the years, that that's what he brought to the part. You start out willing to trust this man, and then you discover you'd better not.

"The dinner table scene worked very well. When someone like Manion starts talking in terms of good and evil, and starts thinking in that way, you're in trouble. Anyone who disagrees with him *can't* be a good American. They become traitors.

"As a writer for *I Spy*, even though you're doing the pitter-patter between Culp and Cosby, you could also deal with subject matter that was very meaningful—some heavy stuff."[8]

Cosby: "I really enjoyed the one with Lloyd Nolan, with him hunting us. And my not realizing—Bill Cosby not knowing that this was a story that had been done at least 1,500 times. It's wonderful. I love writers like that. You steal from the best. Don't come in with bad stuff that you've made up."[9]

CULP & COSBY ON SET REWRITE

In the past, we've heard Ken Tobey's character referred to as Gabe, then as Russ, then as Russ Conway. Here, Kelly calls him "Russell-Gabriel."

The character, once known as Gabe, had begun in a Culp written script, but was renamed by Friedkin and Fine when they resurrected him, and the same actor, to continue with the series.

Culp reclaims the character here, saying lines that were not in the script, and saying them in a place where his words would be difficult to edit out. So Kelly calls Tobey's character Russell-Gabriel, not once, but twice. He even goes out of his way to introduce the character to Scott, mocking the situation. "Say hello to Russell-Gabriel," Culp says, jokingly.

Upon viewing the rushes, Leonard was no doubt steaming.

CAST

Lloyd Nolan began his long career in front of the camera in 1935. By 1985, he had appeared in nearly 200 films and TV shows. He was 65 here. Shortly after this, Nolan would costar with Diahann Carroll in *Julia* (1968–71), a series made possible by *I Spy*.

Nolan's final performance, shot just months before his death in 1986, would be in Woody Allen's *Hannah and Her Sisters*.

Barbara Angely (Tracy) spent her career in front of the camera in Mexico. *I Spy* was the only American production she appeared in. Here, she was a stunning 24.

Ken Tobey makes his seventh appearance as "Russell-Gabriel" Conway. He would return for "Pinwheel."

Earl Bellamy directed a total of 14 episodes of *I Spy*. This would be his last. Bellamy, a true TV hack, would go on to direct for *Hart to Hart*, *Starsky and Hutch*, and *Fantasy Island*.

81. **"PINWHEEL"**; Written by: Barry Oringer; Directed by: Christian Nyby; Location: Acapulco; First airing: 4/15/68. Repeated: 8/19/68.

Kelly needs a wife. The setting: romantic Acapulco. The wife: an inexperienced and overly enthusiastic cutie named Melanie. The mission: playboy millionaire Andrew Wellington, suspected of being an enemy agent with top-secret Soviet documents in his possession.

Assessment

This one is slick and entertaining. From a technical point of view, "Pinwheel" is as flawless as any other stand-out episode of the series. The bulk of the episode was filmed at Paramount under the careful supervision of Fleet Southcott. And "Pinwheel," a light romantic comedy, seems to work best as a stage-bound production.

The writing is crisp and clean. The performances are natural and enjoyable. The chemistry between Melanie and Kelly sparkles. Culp and Cosby shine. The location footage, although limited, is bright and lively. Earle Hagen's music is melodic and rhythmic, helping to make this light-natured, scenic heist caper feel all the more like a 1960s vehicle for Cary Grant, in the tradition of *Charade* or *To Catch a Thief*. And, always a bonus, Ken Tobey is back as Russ Conway, clicking so effortlessly with Culp and Cosby. The entire endeavor is smooth and delicious, even if the relationship between Melanie and the reluctant Kelly and Scott recalls the less successful first season entry, "Weight of the World."

The Story Behind the Story

THE CENSORS

NBC Broadcast and Standards Department had a few concerns about this episode, and how the "making love" sequence would be handled. They requested that, "Staging should not produce an overly suggestive sequence, and the line 'on a circular bed' is unnecessarily pointed and should be deleted."

The lines Broadcast and Standards were most concerned over:
KELLY: "What's she doing in his bedroom?"
SCOTT: "Spying."
KELLY: "That's spying? On a circular bed?"
SCOTT: "That's how girls spy."

Regarding a later part of the script, Broadcast and Standards wrote, "Again, Kelly's reference to the 'circular bed' is unnecessarily pointed and overly suggestive. An acceptable substitution would be 'Well, watch yourself with him.'"

The scene which was causing all the fuss, had read:
KELLY: "And what will you be doing, Melanie?"
MELANIE: "Whatever my country demands, buster."
KELLY: "Yeah, well, stay away from the circular bed."

Culp & Cosby on Set Rewrite

Not in the script:
Kelly is practicing his Western fast draw with a gun and holster he has strapped on. Scott remarks, "Hoby, Hoby."

This is not the first time in the series Cosby had done this. The reference is to Hoby Gilman, from *Trackdown*.

Cast & Crew

Arlene Golonka (Melanie) was 28. Her acting career spanned the years 1959 through 2001. She would finish with over 100 credits. At the time of this episode, she was a well-respected TV guest star, playing prominent roles in, among other series, *Get Smart*. Sheldon Leonard enjoyed Golonka's performance here so much that he would cast her in a recurring role as Millie, for the retooled *Andy Griffith Show*, now to be called *Mayberry R.F.D.*

Marino Mase (Andrew Wellington) was also 28. He had been a prominent Italian actor since 1961, still working often in that country, with nearly 100 credits. He had appeared in *I Spy* once before, in a smaller role, as Mikos, for the episode "Laya."

Victor Sen Yung (Han) was the second actor to appear in *I Spy* who had played a son to Charlie Chan—this time, Number Two Son, Jimmy Chan.

Yung first stepped into the role for the 1938 B film, *Charlie Chan in Hawaii*. He would play the second banana role six more times by 1940 before getting a series of spin-off movies of his own, with Jimmy Chan now in the lead.

In 1957, Yung began keeping house on *Bachelor Father*. The following year, he did double TV duty when he was also cast as Hop Sing, the housekeeper in *Bonanza*. This was his second time working for *I Spy* (he had a small role in "Weight of the World").

Ken Tobey made his eighth and final appearance as Russ-Gabe Conway. With 100 appearances already under his belt, he would go on to collect another 100 before retiring in 1994. Tobey passed away in 2004, at age 85, from natural causes.

Saul Caplan edits his only episode of *I Spy* and does a flawless job.

82. **"SHANA"**; Written by: Robert Lewin; Directed by: Christian Nyby; Location: Acapulco; First airing: 3/4/68. Repeated: 7/29/68.

In Acapulco, Kelly and Scott try to prevent a disillusioned American Black beauty from selling out to the Communists.

Shana Davis has stolen a flask of experimental rocket fuel. Her hope, to hand it over to the Russians in exchange for her brother, an American agent imprisoned behind the iron curtain.

Assessment

As with "Tatia," writer Robert Lewin created a very personal story for the two leads. It is rich with conflict, and demonstrates a seamier side of the spy business.

Shana is a beautiful Black woman. Scott is taken by her.

Shana's race factors into this story in that Scott uses their "kinship" as a means to gain her trust, telling her that she and he are "folk," meaning that she should believe what he tells her because he speaks to her as Black to Black.

But Shana doesn't buy in to it. She believes America has turned its back on her brother, and she is now willing to turn her back on America—and Scott.

Avoiding the expected, when Shana is captured by enemy agents and is tortured to reveal where she has hidden the rocket fuel, it is Kelly—not Scott—who is the more anxious of the two.

Kelly wants to rescue Shana.

Scott decides they must do nothing. He is sure the enemy will succeed where he failed and force the information out of her. The plan, then, is to intercept the message and beat the enemy to the hiding place.

I Spy's third season would end on a strong note.

The Story Behind the Story:

Look for a continuity goof. When we see Kelly and Scott bound and gagged in the famous locked room, their white jeans are filthy. Immediately after they escape, and are driving in a jeep, their whites are clean and pressed.

Also, from the locked room:

When Kelly gets oil on his watch, it stops running. He says that Rosy will kill him. Scott says that Rosy bought Kelly a cheap watch, and even implies that it may have been stolen.

So who is Rosy?

Watch "Happy Birthday, Everybody" again, if you dare. Rosy is the bargain shopper whom Kelly is seeing, and about whom Scott clearly has less than flattering opinions.

LOCKED ROOM #15

A grease pit of a garage. The way out includes a can of oil, a car jack, and a beam.

CAST & CREW

Gloria Foster (Shana) began working in films in 1964, one year after winning an Obie Award for her performance in the play *In White America*. *I Spy* represented her first work in television. She was 34. Foster would appear opposite Cosby three more times in *To All My Friends on the Shore* (1971), *Man & Boy* (1972), and in *Top Secret* (1978).

Foster played her most famous role at the end of her career as The Oracle in *The Matrix*. In 2001, she died from diabetes while filming the sequel, *The Matrix: Reloaded*.

Cosby: "I picked her—many times. Strong business. I knew her from *Medea*, New York City. If you're lookin' for the best actress in New York—Gloria Foster!"[10]

Albert Dekker (Indris) was a star of Broadway, as well as films, who occasionally appeared on television. Two of his most memorable performances were for *The Killers* in 1946 and his final film, *The Wild Bunch*, released in 1969, just months after his death. Dekker was 62 here. He would die one year later of asphyxia, the result of an accidental hanging.

Mary Wickes, played Mildred, one of the two unflappable ladies who drive their car into the middle of a shoot-out. Beginning in 1938, she had a long and successful career portraying women just like this. In addition to 100 other TV and film appearances, she acted in ten television series. Among the series were *The Danny Thomas Show*, in the 1956–57 season, where Sheldon Leonard first met her. Right after her appearance here, at age 57, she would be in the cast of *Julia*.

Florence Halop, Clara, the other tart lady, also worked regularly from 1951 through 1986. Leonard knew her from a guest spot from 1965 on *The Dick Van Dyke Show*. Later, in the mid-1980s, she played the gravely-voiced, heavy-smoking bailiff on *Night Court*, until dying of lung cancer. She was 44 here.

Robert Lewin wrote the haunting and romantic "Tatia," in addition to "Weight of the World." He would go on to contribute scripts to *Cannon*, *The Paper Chase*, and *Star Trek: The Next Generation*.

Christian Nyby finished his run with *I Spy* here, having helmed 11 segments. Among Nyby's *I Spy* triumphs, "Let's Kill Karlovassi," "Oedipus at Colonus," "The Lotus Eater," "Anyplace I Hang Myself Is Home," "Pinwheel," and "The Spy Business." He would go on to work for *Kojak* and *Moonlighting*.

Cosby: "Chris Nyby was a wonderful director."[11]

23

Wrapping Season Three

The Press

It had taken eight and a half months, but *I Spy's* third season was now in the can, and the series continued to be the darling of the press.

On March 25th, *I Spy* made the cover of *TV Guide* for the third time in as many years. But there was other less industry-related press, as well.

TV AND SCREEN WORLD, March '68: "Sex and the Swinging Spy."

"For Cosby, an agent needs a girl. So romance has been written into Bill's future. *I Spy* episodes will now feature love interests for Bill."

MOTION PICTURE MAGAZINE, March '68: "First After-the-Wedding Interview with Bob Culp."

"It was in romantic Mexico that Bob went to film several episodes of *I Spy*. And, naturally, France accompanied him. 'I had been pushing her to get married for six months,' Bob said, 'And I doubled my efforts when we got to Mexico.'"

TV AND SCREEN WORLD, March '68: "Robert Culp: Caught in the Venus Fly Trap."

"They rushed to the altar the moment the ink on Bob's divorce paper was dry."

TV RADIO MIRROR, March '68: "Bob Culp's Inter-Racial Marriage to France Nuyen."

"The setting was the living room of *I Spy* producer Sheldon Leonard's home.

"Culp: 'Sheldon had offered some time ago to have the wedding at his home — if we decided not to elope. I told Leonard on the set Monday that he'd better be home Saturday because we were getting married.'

"There were two dozen guests. Bill Cosby was the tranquilizer. He kept everyone amused. First thing Bill did following the ceremony was offer Bob a big cigar. Cosby lit up, saying, with a smile, 'I'm glad my son finally got married.'"

MOVIE LIFE, April '68: "Bob Culp/France Nuyen: Even Society Couldn't Stop Their Wedding."

"The dangers of a mixed marriage: France was Eurasian and Bob a Caucasian."

TV AND SCREEN WORLD, April '68: "Robert Culp, France Nuyen, Love Is a Many-Splendored Thing."

"What really hurt was the reaction of some bigots to their romance. They resented France because she is Eurasian. In some ways, they aren't the ideal mates. France is fatalistic; Bob is filled with anxiety, a perfectionist, and worries about everything. France is cheery, outgoing; Bob tends to brood and withdraw into himself. She loves parties; he doesn't. She's a mystical Oriental; he's a typical Western man of action. Granted that love can overcome many, many obstacles, but only time will tell if their love is strong enough to endure the rat-race that is Hollywood's quicksand of pressures and tensions."

Culp and Cosby wrapping the third season, end of '67 (© 3 F Prod.).

SILVER SCREEN, May '68: "Lovers Who Mixed Race and Religion."
"France Nuyen-Culp says, 'I don't consider myself Eurasian or Chinese or French. I consider myself a human being.'"

Guest Appearance and a Special

On January, 29, 1968, Culp appeared on the second episode of *Rowan and Martin's Laugh-In*, aired on the same network, on the same night as *I Spy*. He would return for a second appearance several weeks later, this time bringing along France Nuyen.

On March 18, 1968, NBC aired the first of four prime-time specials with Bill Cosby. It was televised on a Monday night, right before the series that made him famous.

On March 30, Culp made a cameo appearance on *Get Smart* for an episode entitled "Die, Spy," a spoof on *I Spy*. In the 30-minute comedy, Max plays a ping-pong champion who travels the globe with his hip Black trainer.

Cosby Can Sing

Bill Cosby had a pair of new albums, and a single out.
Cosby's sixth comedy album, *To Russell, My Brother, Whom I Slept With,* was another instant best seller. It made the Top 10 of Billboard's album charts, and, like his other five LPs, achieved Gold Record status.

358　　　　　　　　　　　　　I Spy

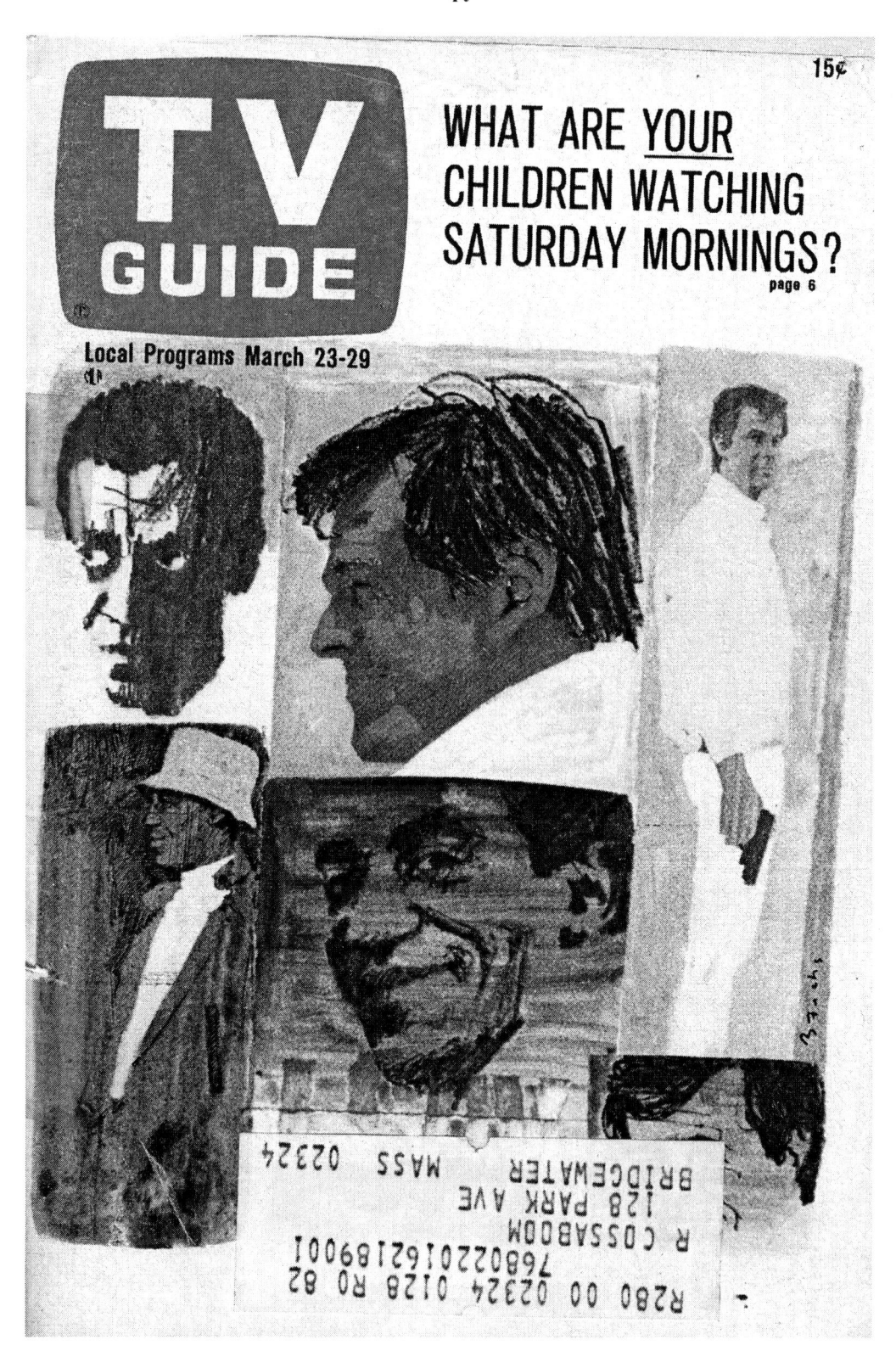

The third *TV Guide* cover, 1968 (courtesy *TV Guide* and by permission of Bernice Fuchs).

Several weeks later, a new album called *Silver Throat* was hurried out to coincide with Cosby's first variety special on NBC.

Upon its release, and even today, the initial reaction is profound surprise. *Silver Throat* is blues, mostly rhythm and blues, that is. And, with the exception of one novelty track, the record is played straight.

Then comes the other surprise. Cosby can sing. Even Bill Persky and Sam Denoff, coproducers for *The Dick Van Dyke Show*, who provided the liner notes for the back of the album cover, were stunned. They believed they knew Cosby well. But he had never told them he could sing. The comedian-turned-actor had never worked music into his performances, not on record, not on stage, not on TV. Yet here he was, singing his heart out, and singing the blues all the way to the bank.

Silver Throat was a hit, enjoying a 26-week stay in the Billboard album charts, and peaking at number 18.

The album can also be credited as the project that got Cosby into the "Top Pop Singles" charts. The track pulled from the album to be promoted as a single was "Little Ole Man," utilizing the tune to "Uptight, Everything's Alright," by Stevie Wonder, with new words by Cosby. The single had an 11-week run in Billboard's Hot 100 Pop Singles charts, in September and October of 1967, and peaked at number four, sitting pretty right under two songs that would trade off at topping the charts, "The Letter" by the Box Tops, and "To Sir with Love" by Lulu, and a third song that would make it as high as number two, "Never My Love," by the Association.[1]

It was an offbeat and unexpected project by Cosby. And it worked.

And, by the way, the picture on the front of the album came from that certain spy show that made Bill Cosby a household name. It was a promotional still from the first season episode "The Conquest of Maude Murdock," and featured Cosby, staring at the camera as if posing for a Wanted Dead or Alive poster, wearing a large Mexican hat and a handlebar moustache.

The Ratings:

Depending on which chart was read and believed for the 1967–68 television season, *I Spy*, in its new Monday night time slot, was either an indisputable hit, or a slight disappointment (although far from being a failure).

According to A.C. Nielsen, the show was down in the ranking of over 90 prime-time series, now coming in at number 42. *The Carol Burnett Show*, on CBS, was consistently the winner of the Monday night 10 P.M. slot.

TvQ, the only competitor of A.C. Nielsen, however, still placed *I Spy* in the Top Ten survey.

And, in 1968, as *I Spy's* third season was wrapping up, Nielsen, like TVQ, began preparing alternate charts, ranking TV programs according to viewer demographics. The results were eye-opening.

In the July 27, 1968, issue of *TV Guide*, for a report entitled "Who Watches What," the Nielsen demographics for the months of March and April of that year were examined. *I Spy* was number eight among teenage viewers, ages 12 to 17. Other shows in that top 10 list were *Star Trek*, *The Monkees*, and *The Smothers Brothers Comedy Hour*.

In a second top 10 list, ranking the favorite shows among adult viewers, ages 18 through 34, *I Spy* again came in at number eight. More importantly, on this chart, only two other series placed higher: *Mission: Impossible* at number five, and *The Dean Martin* Show at number seven. The other programs that scored better than *I Spy* were regularly scheduled weekly movies.

I Spy was gold, and NBC knew it.

Third time is the charm; Earle Hagen gets his Emmy, 1968 (courtesy Earle Hagen).

For the history books. Cosby (with Don Adams and Lucille Ball) wins his third Emmy in a row, 1968 (Emmy Awards, 3 F Prod. Archives).

The Awards

On May 19, 1968, the Emmy Awards were handed out for the 1967–68 season.

For the third consecutive year, *I Spy* was nominated for Outstanding Dramatic Series on Television. It would lose for the second time to *Mission: Impossible*.

For the third consecutive year, Earle Hagen was nominated for the music he composed for the series. This time he won, for the score he wrote for "Laya."

For the third consecutive year, Culp and Cosby would compete in the category of Outstanding Performance by an Actor in a Lead Role in a Drama Series. And, for the third time, Cosby would beat out his partner.

Cosby: "The three Emmys became sort of ridiculous, because I'm winning and nothing for Bob, and nothing for Bob, and nothing for Bob. Hollywood, to this day, still has not given him his due."[2]

Rounding out the evening, *I Spy* received one nomination for a technical award for Robert Guhl, the audio engineer on the episode "Home to Judgement."

Surprisingly, Culp's excellent script for "Judgment" was overlooked.

Friedkin and Fine's work was overlooked, as well.

24

The Fourth Season

Changing of the Guard

In January and February 1968, plans were already underway for the fourth season. But there would be some changes.

David Friedkin and Mort Fine had decided not to return to the series, and to take a break from television.

Michael Preece: "I knew Mort Fine was not well. And David seemed run down a bit, too. I wouldn't say they were burned out, because they went on to do other things. And they weren't that old. But they were tired."[1]

Ernest Frankel: "Friedkin and Fine *were* burned out. They left because they'd had it. And they'd had it with Culp and Cosby. It wasn't that Bob and Bill misbehaved on set—they didn't. They were too professional for that. It was the ad-libbing. And Sheldon didn't help David and Mort there. He couldn't stand confrontations, he couldn't go down on the set and say, 'Look guys, you didn't get here by ad-libbing, so let's just do the show. He couldn't."[2]

Friedkin and Fine felt they were between the proverbial rock and a hard place.

David Friedkin's son, Gregory: "I had a feeling, then, that everyone was fed up with Sheldon. For my father, anyway, that was the bigger issue."[3]

During *I Spy*'s third season, Friedkin had already been letting go. He had no choice.

Ron Jacobs: "I remember David Friedkin had some health problems—bleeding ulcers."[4] And he also had colon cancer.

But the men near the top chose to keep their personal lives, and health issues, to themselves. They had been part of the Hollywood system long enough to know that a producer does not continue producing when he allows the ambitious men around him to see any sign of weakness.

Leonard never showed weakness.

And Friedkin and Fine did their best to play by Leonard's rules.

Only one person on the entire *I Spy* team saw the producers as being anything other than men who were comfortable at running the show.

Culp: "David and Mort were laid back. They were easygoing. They had opinions and they were not stupid, neither one of them. They were both bright as hell. But they were soft."[5]

Frankel: "David and Mort had more to wrestle with than the other producers on the lot. Those other producers didn't have the problems that we did on *I Spy*. Guys like Bruce Geller and Ivan Goff had actors who *did the scripts*. David and Mort didn't."[6]

It's called "creative differences." And Culp and Cosby had been winning.

Leonard: "Eventually it reached the point where they were totally unacceptable. An episode was shot in Guadalajara in which Gene Hackman, as a recently released criminal, has set a diabolical trap to destroy Jim Backus, the agent who sent him to prison. Culp and

Cosby chase the Hackman character into the surrounding hills and wound him fatally in a gun battle. The dying criminal tells them that they are too late. He has already loaded the piñata hanging in Backus's living room with nitroglycerine, and when the sun rises, Backus's children will be blindfolded and given clubs that they will swing wildly, trying to break the piñata. When a club strikes it, it will burst, but instead of showering down gifts and candy, it will shower down death."[7]

Leonard's description of the terrible "Happy Birthday, Everybody," one of the last episodes from season three, conveys his fondness for the Friedkin and Fine script.

Creative differences. The splinter under Leonard's nail had to do with what Culp and Cosby allegedly did following the scene he so colorfully described.

In the script, Hackman's character, with his last dying breath, tells Kelly and Scott they will not have time to stop the family from being killed. The family is a father, mother, and one child (not "children," as Leonard remembered). Kelly and Scott race back to Guanajauto (not Guadalajara, as Leonard remembered). But their car runs out of gas, beginning a series of comical events (which Leonard failed to remember). Each scripted event delays the agent's efforts to make like the cavalry charging over the hill. And, with this, the ticking clock is supposed to tick a bit louder.

Then, according to Leonard, the ad-libbing started. And, as a result, the ticking clock risked being silenced.

Leonard: "Culp turns to Cosby and, in his best Oliver Hardy manner, snarls, 'This is another fine mess you've gotten us into, Stanley.'

"Backus and his kids are about to be blown to bits—and they're making jokes!"[8]

Cosby: "I don't know what the arguments were. I was a child when all these domestic fights were going on. And those locked rooms and the banter, the two of us being Laurel and Hardy. We did do a tribute to Laurel and Hardy in *our I Spy*, calling each other 'Ollie' or 'Stanley.' Bob loved 'Well this is another fine mess...' We took from those guys."[9]

Cosby didn't see what the fuss was. But, perhaps without realizing it, he had referred to the series as "our *I Spy*."

As far as Leonard was concerned, it was *his I Spy*.

Leonard: "I wasn't on the location when the bit in question was shot, but I saw it two days later in the projection room. I sent a second unit back to Mexico to re-shoot it with doubles, a correction that cost the show twenty thousand dollars."[10]

That's $20,000 in 1968 currency. Leonard's wallet was getting thinner by the minute.

Close examination of the episode, however, shows no clear need for "body doubles" to be doing anything. There is an abundance of footage of Kelly and Scott—the real Kelly and Scott—in their little red convertible, racing down Mexican country roads—running out of gas—finding gas—then racing some more.

In comparing the episode with the script, Culp and Cosby say very nearly every line that is written.

Any ad-libbing they may have done, including the "This is another fine mess" line, did not make it into the episode. Art Seid, under the direction of Leonard, was making sure of that.

And much of the comedy written into the climactic moments of the script also failed to make the cut.

But the mood of the script, at this point, clearly was light in tone. Culp's ad-lib, as Leonard remembers hearing it, was not out of context with the scripted material.

So what was the real problem?

Leonard was feeling the pressure, too. *I Spy* was a demanding series. He had designed it that way. This was his formula, his structure, and, therefore, his burden. And he bore it well. Leonard, after all, loved solving problems.

But there was one problem—one member of the *I Spy* family—Leonard could not control. Robert Culp was the one individual who had openly challenged Leonard's authority and vision.

The events had dramatically accumulated: Culp had doubted Leonard's direction for "Affair in T'Sein Cha"; he had doubted Friedkin and Fine's take on the characters; he stepped out of his assigned role as an actor, and went head-to-head with the writer/producers, by writing his own scripts; he had refused to stay at the New Otani Hotel, and had encouraged Cosby to leave as well, thus jeopardizing the deal Leonard had made to shoot there, and, worse, causing his boss to lose face; he had put Leonard into a difficult position over his affair with France Nuyen, and he had embarrassed Dolores del Rio.

To Leonard's ears, Culp had let his character and Cosby's character become interchangeable.

And then there were the ad-libs.

Now Robert Culp was in a no-win position. When a relationship has deteriorated this much, any reason will do for a divorce.

But unlike his two producers, Leonard could not walk away. He had a contract with NBC telling him he had to stay. Friedkin and Fine did not.

On December 26, 1967, in a correspondence to a writer wanting to make a submission to *I Spy*, Mort Fine wrote that he would be "taking a hiatus from television for an undetermined length of time." And that went for his partner, too.[11]

Friedkin and Fine had been offered a contract by Universal that would allow them to write and produce a series of television movies. Having stayed on *I Spy* for three seasons, they had already satisfied their obligations to the show. The show, however, would always have an obligation to them.

By the terms of their financial agreement, as cocreators of the series, Friedkin and Fine were guaranteed 20% of the profits from the show, whether they remained or not. The only stipulation: After three seasons, they had to find acceptable replacements for themselves. And that they would do.

Ernest Frankel would comprise half of the new producing team. As a writer, Frankel had won favor with Friedkin and Fine and, especially with Leonard, by proving he could deliver scripts fast, and write in the manner that was felt best for the series.

He had never produced before.

Frankel: "Sheldon told me, 'I can teach you everything there is about producing in one afternoon. Surround yourself with people who know their jobs. Make the location become part of the story. If there's a fiesta in town, shoot it.'

"He also said, 'And make your TV leads behave.'"[12]

The other half of the "show running" team would be Art Seid.

Seid was, primarily, a film cutter. But he had one producer's credit from *Ben Casey*. And he had spent more than a year with *I Spy*, working his way into Leonard's favor as the series supervising editor, and the man who would snip away the ad-libs.

Immediately following the start of the new year, Friedkin and Fine handed over the producing chores to Frankel and Seid.

Earle Hagen: "I know Ernie and Art had already planned out what was going to be done for the first 13 weeks. Ernie's a different kind of guy. He wouldn't stand for anybody screwing around with the scripts. He doesn't get into fights with stars. He has his own way."[13]

Years later, while Frankel was producing a series called *Moving On*, there is a story of how he pinned series costar Frank Converse against a wall. Frankel wanted Converse to quit messing with the scripts. He told the actor that there was only one person in charge. Converse was given a choice: Leave the scripts alone, or Frankel would leave the series and let Converse explain things to the network.

The message was delivered. The two men had a drink together and got on with the show. Converse did the scripts as they were written.

Frankel, a former Marine colonel, was not one to mince words.

Frankel: "I worked very hard on the show when preparing to do it. Preparation for an *I Spy* episode is like going to college. You have no idea of the breakthrough element that was the show: You're going to go around the world, carrying all that gear—and you're going to do it with a bunch of television actors."[14]

Perhaps as a result of his military background, Frankel was key on organization.

Frankel watched all 82 episodes of *I Spy*. He wanted to know everything about the show, everything that worked, and everything that didn't.

Frankel: "Robert Culp was perfect for that role. And having the good relationship with Cosby made their on-camera chemistry together exceptional. But there was more: Because of Mort being the kind of person he was, and David, and Sheldon, and Bob, and Bill, it gave the show a unique personality."[15]

Frankel had put his finger on it. By observing the others, he saw something the five partners in *I Spy* had missed. *I Spy* worked, and it did so because of an uneasy mixture of drastically opposing agendas. Robert Culp wanted the series, its stories, and its characters to be real—sometimes dark, sometimes edgy, but always filled with irony. Leonard wanted *I Spy* to entertain, and stay clear of making statements. Fine wanted to tell stories that were by the numbers, tried and true, and geared to please the greatest amount of viewers. Friedkin wanted the show to reflect a touch of artistry. And Cosby wanted to promote positive race relations by portraying a Black man that Blacks and Whites, alike, could relate to and be at one with.

Different agendas, even opposing agendas, created a series that, far more often than not, worked, and worked beautifully.

Frankel was determined to see that *I Spy* continued to work. In order to not upset the balance that was Leonard, Friedkin, Fine, Cosby and Culp, he would have to be the voice of Friedkin and Fine. He, and he alone, would have to bring to the table what his writer/producer predecessors had always brought. He would also have to be the glue that would keep the other top members of the team from pulling further away from one another.

So Frankel designed his plan.

Part of that plan determined how he and his producing partner would divide up the responsibilities. It worked like this:

Frankel: "Art would come in at six and leave at four. I'd come in at nine and stay until we wrapped. He was all post production, and I took care of production. Art and I had an agreement and an understanding between us. I didn't argue with him about post, and he didn't argue with me about the scripts.

"I gave out the script assignments, but I included Art and Sheldon so they would know what I was doing. Art sat in on the script meetings because he had a good story mind, as all good editors do."[16]

The first order of business was to determine locations for the tenth and eleventh blocks of episodes.

England would be one, Thailand combined with Australia would be another. The latter is a country that offers a variety of unique and stunning locales. Among the many places where filming would be attempted was the Great Barrier Reef.

Scandinavia was being considered for the latter part of the season, among other visually distinctive locales.

The second chore involved the writing of the scripts.

Ernest Frankel inherited several teleplays, leftovers from the Friedkin/Fine watch. These stories could be rewritten to fit the locations being planned. The easiest to modify would be his own script, "The Choice." As written in June 1967, the story takes place on a freighter, as Kelly and Scott deal with terrorist hijackers who have taken over the ship.

"The Choice" was an exciting tale, and would make a unique and enjoyable episode of *I Spy*.

Frankel had also written a new script, entitled "The Day They Gave the Bride Away." It was designed to play equally well in either England or Australia.

Leftover from season three, Marion Hargroves' "She Sleeps, My Lady Sleeps," was retooled for England.

A pair of scripts by Rick Mittleman were also ready. "I Lost It in Tangiers" uses a backdrop of Morocco, designed to take advantage of leftover footage shot while the company visited that country. Soundstage work could complete the episode.

The second Mittleman script, "Pluck Went the Strings of My Heart," like Frankel's latest, could be shot in either England or Australia.

Michael Zagor, writer of six previous episodes, had also completed a new script, "A Place for the Devil."

Jerry Ludwig, writer of four produced *I Spy* episodes, had turned in a script "Better Never Than Late."

Ludwig: "I said to Sheldon, 'Let's do *The Hound of the Baskervilles*, and send the guys out onto the English moors.' The two of them would stand there looking at a footprint, and up would come the line, 'Those are the prints of a great beast.' And he thought that was good. It was a kick."[17]

Barry Oringer, who wrote four *I Spy* episodes, contributed a new script entitled "Night Is Coming." Again, with English-speaking secondary characters, it could be shot in either England or Australia.

Friedkin and Fine had approved all of these scripts, and had also been involved with the rewriting. They were watching over their child.

Starting with the new year, Frankel and Seid moved into their offices on the Paramount lot. In addition to the scripts left by Friedkin and Fine, the new guard gave out several assignments to writers of their own choosing.

On January 23, 1968, the Writers Guild was notified that work had been assigned to Norman Hudis, Jerry Ludwig, and the team of Robert C. Dennis and Earl Barrett.

Dennis and Barrett were *I Spy* veterans with three scripts for the series under their belts.

Ludwig, in addition to "Better Never Than Late," contributed a second script entitled "Call Monica," which was set for England. In the story, Scott is wounded and confined to a hospital. Kelly dominates the story, continuing the assignment on his own. He has a romantic encounter, and then, as in the spectacular "Tatia," struggles with a betrayal. The excellent script was the best Ludwig had done to date.

Hudis was the newcomer. A former journalist, Hudis had been writing films in England, primarily comedies, including six from the *Carry On* series. He had also written for *Danger Man* and *The Saint*. His script for *I Spy*, set in England, was entitled "The Mission Is the Mission."

One month later, on February 26, 1968, Frankel and Seid informed the Writers Guild that they had given additional assignments out to Orville Hampton, Leigh Chapman, Joe Bonaduce, Ellis Kadison, and Steven Kandel.

Now there would be more new blood in the show. With the exception of Kandel, who had written seven episodes for the series, these would all be fresh faces in the writers' room.

Hampton had primarily written for the movies, with nearly 50 film scripts to his credit. He had recently moved to TV, and to espionage, providing a script to *Mission: Impossible*.

Bonaduce had written for the Westerns *Bonanza* and *Loredo*, as well as Leonard's *The Andy Griffith Show* and *The Dick Van Dyke Show*.

Kadison had written for *The Invaders* and the classic anthology series *Climax!*

Chapman had written for *Burke's Law*, *The Wild Wild West*, and *It Takes a Thief*.

Kandel's new script was set for England, and was based on a group of British aristocrats who, in the late 1930s and early '40s, were pro–Nazi, and had been involved in espionage. For his story, a comedy, Kandel recalls, "Kelly and Scott spend a weekend in the country with a group of aristocratic twits who are unwittingly aiding the efforts of a Soviet block agent."[18]

But there was another story Kandel wanted to tell, a subject that he felt *I Spy* was ready to take on.

Kandel: "The story was about a U.S. diplomat who's going to be 'out-ed.' It dealt with gay politics. That was a long time ago, and it was a little too hot. And it was too bad, because it was a good story and it related to reality.

"It was a well-known fact that it was common to use boys as well as girls to lure American diplomats, and American agents, and I felt it played off in a way with the relationship between Culp and Cosby, making the distinction between a masculine relationship and a gay lover relationship. Anyway, I liked the story. I liked it a lot.

"Kelly and Scott were brought in because the diplomat in question was alleged to have taken some documents, relating to a friend of theirs, who then had been killed. When they got in to it, they discovered that the diplomat *hadn't* taken the documents. But he *had* been compromised, and they discovered an attempt to 'out' him. They questioned themselves at the end. Did they have the right to destroy this man's career, or, on the other hand, did they have the responsibility to protect U.S. security. It was an interesting moral dilemma."[19]

But Leonard wasn't buying.

Kandel: "I had a huge fight with Sheldon on that story. He said, 'I just don't want to do it.' And I argued with him, marching around the lot, and finally he said, 'Fuck it! It's my ball and my bat!'

"And I said, 'Then it's your right to strike out.' And we left it at that."[20]

Leonard preferred that Kandel work on an idea that he had about an exploding golf ball. It was an idea he had pitched to nearly every writer on the series, including Ernest Frankel.

Frankel: "Sheldon had a great sense of what makes drama. But he also had a blind spot. He would fall in love with a story point and never let go of it. Sheldon said, 'I got a thing that would be great. Let's put them on a golf course instead of a tennis court. And there would be an exploding golf ball.'

"His thought was that the golfer would hit the ball, and then it would explode on target down the fairway. And then I said, 'It wouldn't happen that way. The golf ball would explode as soon as the club hit it.'

"Sheldon didn't agree. He still wanted me to write it. He said, 'What do you think?' And I said, 'Not much.'

"It broke his heart. He could never find a writer for his exploding golf ball."[21]

Even without the exploding golf ball, Frankel and Seid had 16 scripts on hand, enough for two blocks of eight.

Frankel was also not opposed to slotting in a new script by Robert Culp.

Frankel: "He has a sweetness and consideration for others. He's a very good actor, very talented in many ways. He writes very well, too. I did not ask him to write a script for the new episodes, but he was welcome to do it. I had no objection to that."[22]

During January and February, Culp rested. According to his secretary, Joy Keller, he was thinking about writing again, and perhaps even trying his hand at directing another episode for the series.

Cosby used his time off to get caught up on the other areas of his multidimensional career. He had recording sessions to complete, club dates to honor, and the second of four NBC specials to shoot.

And that left April. Midmonth, the company was due to depart for England to film the on-location portions of eight episodes. After returning home for additional production, they would depart for Bangkok, Thailand, and then Australia.

The End of I Spy

For the better part of three and a half decades, Robert Culp was under the impression that NBC cancelled *I Spy*.

Bill Cosby was, too.

It is what they had been told, over and over again, by both the media and Three F Productions—And that meant Sheldon Leonard.

Others involved with *I Spy* were sure the series ended for other reasons.

Each believed what they had been told, and each had been told what they were most likely to believe.

To understand why *I Spy* ended, we must first understand why a short-lived series called *My Friend Tony* began.

In late 1966, *I Spy* was riding high in its second year, and Leonard was a major player in television.

Culp: "Leonard was the single most powerful purveyor of television at that time in the world. Sheldon was totally gung ho. In today's parlance, guys who move swiftly move at a snail's pace compared to Sheldon. Things happened because he ordered them, like a general. And, by God, they happened."[23]

NBC wanted to keep "the general" happy, no matter what, and that meant agreeing to give him a second weekly hour on the network. They invited him to submit some ideas, and they would select one. Leonard already had something in mind.

A few months earlier, Leonard had met Enzo Cerusico in Italy during the shooting of the *I Spy* episode "Sophia." Something about Cerusico struck Leonard, and the veteran producer immediately became professionally infatuated with the young actor. So much so that Leonard boasted to Cerusico that he would find a project for him in America.

In 1967, Cerusico was flown to Los Angeles to star opposite veteran actor James Whitmore in a pilot. The premise involved a crime-solving team. As Leonard pitched it, in typical Leonard style, "Whitmore was the brains. Cerusico the legs." Period.

Leonard: "There was nothing startlingly new about the idea, but then there's nothing new about flour, eggs, and butter."[24]

Leonard wasn't done. After a puff on his cigar, he would say, "However, [flour, butter and eggs] can be combined, and recombined, into an enormous variety of eatables."[25]

Leonard's confection was *My Pal Tony*, as it was being called then.

NBC wasn't drooling.

Regardless, they selected *Tony* as the best of the projects Leonard had offered. It was no *I Spy*. But if it kept *I Spy* going, then it might be worth doing.

Based on the proposal, and the attachment of James Whitmore, and the promise of a hot new discovery that the kids would really go for, the series was tentatively scheduled to play for the 1967–68 season.

The general was ready to move forward. NBC was less sure.

24—The Fourth Season

TV Guide announced in its February 25, 1967, issue that *My Friend Tony*, as it was now being called, would be postponed until the 1968–69 season. Clearly, the network was stalling.

Although NBC had delayed the dreaded date, they attempted to appease Leonard and promised that *My Friend Tony* would absolutely be provided a time slot for that following year.

Problem solved—for now. NBC could announce its schedule for the fall of 1967. *I Spy* would be part of it. *My Friend Tony* would not.

One year later, Leonard was still waiting to find out if *Tony* was on the schedule for the fall of '68, or, at the very least, slotted in as a January 1969 midseason replacement.

Contractually obligated and now cornered, NBC had no option left to them and had to make room for *Tony*. Something from their schedule would have to go. So the powers that be made a decision.

Star Trek, in its second season, was doing respectable business in its Friday night, 8:30 P.M. slot. Like *I Spy*, it was pulling in good numbers. Like *I Spy*, it was usually number two in its time period. Like *I Spy*, it was in a top ten demographics chart from A.C. Nielsen, this one involving teenagers. Unlike *I Spy*, it was not appreciated by its network and, therefore, could be sacrificed.

NBC started a rumor in the trades. *Star Trek*, the network claimed, was doing poorly in the ratings. It was reported then, and is still widely believed today, that *Star Trek*, a show that had nearly 20 million viewers each week, and was in the Nielsen Top Ten with viewers between the ages of 12 and 17, was a ratings failure.

But NBC didn't count on the wrath of the *Star Trek* fans, who were extremely loyal—and vocal.

Within weeks of the announcement of the cancellation of *Star Trek*, the NBC offices in New York were flooded with over one million letters. Protest marches were organized and carried out in Rockefeller Plaza, as well as NBC Burbank on the West Coast.

The network was overwhelmed, and shamed into reversing their decision. On March 1, 1968, NBC made an on-air announcement, following the broadcast of an episode of the science fiction series, declaring that *Star Trek* would remain on the schedule. The purpose of the televised statement was to make the letters stop. Immediately following this, the network received tens of thousands of letters thanking them for their decision.

One problem solved, for now. One problem remained. What to do with *Tony*?

In the February 10, 1968, issue of *TV Guide*, NBC indicated that a decision had yet to be made as to the renewal of *I Spy*. And no mention was made of a new series called *My Friend Tony*, either. The poker game had begun.

Meanwhile, at Paramount Studios, preproduction was underway for Leonard's hit series. *I Spy* was most certainly gearing up for its fourth year. *My Friend Tony* was in limbo.

Then, on March 3, 1968, it was announced that *I Spy* had been cancelled.

Sheldon Leonard remembered a stunned Bill Cosby calling him the day after the announcement was made. Cosby asked Leonard to tell him that it wasn't true. Leonard couldn't, nor could he share the whole story regarding the "cancellation."

What Leonard *did* tell Cosby was that he shouldn't be upset. Cosby could make far more money away from the series than he could on it. He had a contract with NBC to deliver more variety specials, and the network had already expressed interest in giving the comedian his own series once *I Spy* had run its course.

Cosby, however, didn't want *I Spy* to end. It was exhausting work. Often, with the inconsistency of the scripts, it was frustrating work. But Cosby also knew that it was important work. He was proud of what he had accomplished in the series, for himself, and for Blacks.

Cosby: "We had some new things in mind for the fourth year, and I'm sorry we didn't get a chance to do them. Our producers had opened their eyes and ears to us. We got Sheldon to agree to more love stories for me in the fourth season, also to do more scripts for Bob carrying a whole show by himself."[26]

This is the chronology of what happened between February 26, when new script assignments for *I Spy* were being recorded by the Writers Guild, and March 3, when the cancellation of the series was announced:

According to Sheldon Leonard, in his 1995 autobiography, he and he alone made the decision to end the series.

"As its third year came to a close," Leonard recalled, "Mort Werner and Herb Schlosser asked for a meeting with me to discuss the future of *I Spy*. They had a problem, which they dumped in my lap."

The problem, as Leonard went on to explain, had nothing to do with *I Spy*. It was the new series he was to produce that was in jeopardy.

"NBC was contractually obligated to put a new one-hour show on the air for me," Leonard explained. That show, of course, was *My Friend Tony*.

"The network claimed there was no room on the schedule. If I insisted that they honor their contractual commitment to *Tony*, *I Spy* would have to be dropped. They said it was up to me."

NBC was bluffing. There was no way they could see Leonard giving up a goose that was still laying golden eggs, and all for an ugly duckling like *My Friend Tony*.

But NBC made a serious mistake. They thought they understood how Sheldon Leonard's mind worked.

In Leonard's own words, "*Tony* was far from a sure thing." On the other hand, "*I Spy* was a pretty sure bet to continue for at least a couple of seasons."

But television is a complex business. And the movers and shakers within the TV industry are ego-driven people.

Leonard was feeling disappointed. He had promised Enzo Cerusico that he would have a series of his own, an American TV series, one to be presented by Sheldon Leonard.

Leonard wanted to recreate what he had done with *I Spy*; to break new ground; to do something different; and, perhaps most of all, to recapture the feeling of discovering new talent and guiding that new talent to stardom. He'd done that so many times before and the father figure in him was itching to feel like a proud dad once again.

On the other hand, there was *I Spy*. Leonard had already succeeded there. He had proven that he could do the impossible.

NBC had moved *I Spy* from its Wednesday night time slot, where it had dominated 10 P.M. The ratings, while still good, had been better before the move.

Friedkin and Fine, two of the Three F's, had walked away.

Fouad Said, a young man who had been like a son to Leonard, was also leaving home. He was going to start his own production company. The genius—who created the Cinemobile and made the road trips possible—would be gone.

Culp and Leonard had creative differences.

Cosby, the man Leonard called "son," was being wooed away by NBC. He had already made a variety special, and would do more, with a promise of a new series to follow. And yet no one, not Cosby, not NBC, had approached Leonard about producing these new shows.

And then there was an issue of money. Leonard's debt to the network, who was funding the loan for *I Spy*, was growing.

Leonard: "[*I Spy*] had been running a deficit with each episode and I was deeply in the red. I figured to recoup with syndication sales."[27]

But syndicated sales were way down the road. NBC's contract gave the network, not

Leonard, the right to decide how long *I Spy* would stay in production. And that meant, out of syndication. The agreement originally gave the network the option to keep the series for five years. Recently, as a consideration to loaning Leonard more money, that option period had been increased to seven years.

The earliest Leonard could now release the series into syndication would be September 1972, with NBC still in the middle, brokering the deals. That was, unless NBC allowed him an escape clause.

They had now done so. Like Friedkin and Fine, Leonard could bail out, but only if he chose to do so within a 72-hour period.

These were the issues on Leonard's mind during the few days he had to consider his options.

Earle Hagen: "Mort Werner was the guy on the phone that told him, 'You've got one hour [on their schedule] instead of two.' NBC did not give Sheldon a lot of time to make that decision."[28]

Leonard: "When Werner couldn't promise to return *I Spy* to its Wednesday time period, I opted to let it go, in favor of *My Friend Tony*."[29]

NBC was stunned. They had given Leonard a choice, never believing he would make the decision he did.

Culp and Cosby were stunned, as well. They had been told by Leonard that the network pulled the plug.

Ernest Frankel and Art Seid had been told by Leonard that the series was ending for another reason.

Frankel: "Sheldon said, 'Cosby is going to do something else for NBC. He won't be available for us, and that means we shut down.'"[30]

Many others in the *I Spy* family, the series writers and directors, included, thought that Leonard had run out of money and could borrow no more. They spoke of the "red ink" he was drowning in and, therefore, that was why he had to suddenly suspend production. This was what they had been lead to believe.

Hugo Friedhofer was under the impression that the real reason for the end was "on account of certain internal strife on the part of one of the principals in the cast."[31]

In other words, someone had given him the word that Culp was becoming more than difficult—possibly unreliable.

Calvin Brown was given another story entirely.

Brown: "In the end, it was scary on Sheldon's part. I think we had dropped down to number nine. When we got 'cancelled,' we all had tickets to Bangkok, Thailand, in our pockets. That was one of the next locales. But NBC would not guarantee the 26 shows for the season. They would only guarantee him 13. Sheldon said, 'No, I can't go over to Thailand and be over there and get cancelled.' He said he told NBC, 'You give me the 26 shows or nothing.' So it was nothing. He said to us, 'This is it, when we get done here, it's all through.' So I cried. I knew I would never find another job like that. It should never have ended when it did. It should have been going on for at least another five years."[32]

A few people from Leonard's inner circle of friends and business associates knew the real reason, including good friend Earle Hagen and Ruth Englehardt, Leonard's legal rep at William Morris. But, out of respect to Leonard, they kept silent.

It would take 27 years, until the release of his autobiography, before Leonard would make a definitive statement on the subject. It was a statement that had to do with betrayal. And the betrayal had been done by NBC.

The network had a contract with Leonard. He would have two hour-long series on television by 1968. He had not scrimped with *I Spy*. He had gone the extra mile over and over again with that show. And NBC tried to play him for a fool.

The last tie-in, Leonard rushes to sell raincoats in the middle of August 1968, before *I Spy* **leaves the network (© 3 F Prod.).**

Leonard: "The network had falsely claimed a shortage of time slots to make me forgo my contractual right to put a second hour on NBC. He [the NBC executive who was behind the deception] didn't think I'd give up *I Spy* in favor of *My Friend Tony*. So, *I Spy* came off the air and *Tony* went on."[33]

Once the decision was made, all that could be said, from the lips of Sheldon Leonard himself, was, "It was the end of a marvelous adventure."[34]

25

I Spy *Stripped*

How Networks Get Even

STEP ONE: RECOUP YOUR INVESTMENT

As the lender of Sheldon Leonard's *I Spy* loan, NBC was owed over eight million dollars.

The network's contracts with Leonard and Three F Productions guaranteed the repayment of that loan. Further, to insure satisfaction on the money due them, the network was allowed to be the direct broker on all domestic and foreign sales of the series.

Even before the plug had been pulled, NBC had started selling the rights for airing *I Spy* to numerous American TV markets, with no start date specified. The contracts merely stated that the stations would get the series when it became available.

Then, beginning in March 1968, the network's sales reps got busy. *I Spy* would be squeezed for every dollar they could get.

It's called "stripping." The requirements are the same now as they were then. One hundred plus episodes. It used to take a series three to four years of production to meet that number. Now it takes five.

One hundred plus episodes, running five nights a week, allows a show to go for five months before the episodes need to be shown again. If the series only made the minimum requirement of 100, then each episode would air three times a year, max, per market. And, for some series, primarily the ones that appeal to a young audience, viewers tend to be less discriminating over the redundancy of repeats.

Desi Arnaz, as well as being the innovator behind the "three camera technique" of shooting a situation comedy before a studio audience, was also the visionary behind the process of "stripping" a series in reruns. Arnaz reached into his own pocket and paid the difference between shooting a TV series live, with television cameras, and shooting it before an audience with film cameras, to be edited and aired at a later date.

To do it, Arnaz had to pay for the film cameras, for the film, for the processing, and for the film editing. In exchange, CBS gave him ownership of the syndication rights for the series. It didn't occur to CBS that the rerun ownership would be worth anything. Yet *I Love Lucy* fans wanted to see those episodes over and over again. And there were new *I Love Lucy* fans coming along all the time.

Several years later, CBS bought back the syndication rights for millions of dollars. And this was in the day when a million was considered a very big number.

It didn't take long for other series to follow suit and soon nearly every show on TV, drama, comedy, or otherwise, was being filmed, or at least taped.

The hope of every studio was that the series they made would last on the air for at least three years, giving them enough episodes to justify creating a rerun package.

The potential for making money through stripping was so great that some studios began

Into syndication, fall '68 (© 3 F Prod.).

releasing past episodes of long-running series even while new episodes were still being produced and aired by one of the three big networks.

This is commonplace today, but not when Universal thought of doing it with *Dragnet*. The series was continuing on NBC, in color, when the studio put together a sizable rerun package containing many of the 256 episodes that had been shot in black and white. That series of reruns was retitled *Badge 714*.

CBS followed Universal's lead and gave a new title to the half-hour long episodes of *Gunsmoke*, placing them into syndicated stripping while the hour-long version continued in prime time. The rerun package was called *Marshal Dillon*.

One hundred plus. That was the rule.

Then, in the fall of 1966, the rule was broken.

Two odd little sitcoms, *The Munsters* and *The Addams Family*, were cancelled by their networks. Both were popular shows and were expected to last longer. But, for whatever reason, CBS axed *The Munsters* just as ABC was cleaning house of *The Addams Family*.

Local TV stations across the country saw the potential of attracting young viewers in the afternoon, after school, and into the early evening with either of these shows.

What is interesting about these two series is that they lasted only two years on the networks. *The Addams Family* had 64 episodes made. *The Munsters* had 70.

In the world of stripping, that meant each episode would be shown up to four times in a year. It could hardly be expected that the shows could last long before burning out. One year later, by the fall of 1967, both series were still pulling in respectable numbers, and, therefore, still being stripped.

At the same time, *Gilligan's Island* ended its three-year run on CBS.

The series was extremely popular, always winning its time period for the network. But CBS president William S. Paley despised the show and ordered that it be removed from the schedule.

Local stations across the country were quick to snatch up the rights for their markets, expecting that the 98 filmed episodes would play well for a year, maybe two, maybe three.

Four decades later, those episodes are still playing.

In September 1968, the world of reruns went color.

Among the shows newly off the networks were *Batman*, *Run for Your Life*, and *I Spy*. This was the first time that series with episodes shot only in color were being offered as reruns. And, of these three, only *I Spy*, having been pulled from the network while still a hit, had the potential of making a big impact in syndication.

I Spy was booked into nearly every major U.S. market to play five nights a week. Most stations scheduled it for the 6 or 7 P.M. slot; but, many placed it into prime time, at either 8 or 9 P.M. The reruns were going head-to-head with the new shows on NBC, CBS and ABC.

RKO General, owner of several television stations across the nation, paid one million dollars for the right to air the series in the major markets of Los Angeles and New York. This was a staggering sum for only one year, but well worth it to RKO. The ratings were so impressive, five nights a week, that all the RKO stations, Los Angeles and New York included, renewed the deal for a second year and beyond.

I Spy was a syndicated hit. Only *Gilligan's Island* and *I Love Lucy* were booked in more markets.

By the fall of 1969, *I Spy* continued to look healthy in syndication, but it now had new competition for the coveted 6 and 7 P.M. weekday time slots. *Star Trek* had been cancelled by NBC.

Regardless, syndication sales remained strong and, by 1971, NBC had been repaid. The series was handed back to Leonard. By the end of that year, another million dollars had been made. The contractual split: Leonard made over $600,000; Freidkin and Fine, as limited partners, pocketed more than $250,000 between them; and Culp, with his 7.5%, saw a bonus check for over $100,000.

The partners in the series had waited four years for this day. There would be more money to come, but never in quite as generous proportions.

STEP TWO: NAIL THE BASTARD TO THE WALL

Years after "pulling the plug," Leonard himself admitted that he had stepped on some big toes at NBC when he decided to discontinue *I Spy* in favor of *My Friend, Tony*.

The network was contractually obligated to carry the new series—for 16 weeks.

My Friend Tony did not premiere in the fall of 1968 in *I Spy*'s time slot, as Leonard had believed it would. Instead, NBC pushed it back again, making it a midseason replacement entry. They also put it into their death slot: 10 P.M. Sunday nights. The show was given little, if any promotion.

Jerry Ludwig, whom Leonard brought over from *I Spy* to write for Tony, put it best: "The networks can't guarantee a success, but they sure *can* guarantee a failure."[1]

According to Ernest Frankel, the show's producer, NBC cancelled *Tony* within weeks of its much-delayed premiere, before a true sampling of the ratings could even be known.

Frankel: "The series did well. And the numbers were growing each week. But we got word that we would not be picked up, regardless."[2]

Playing out Leonard's contract, next on the chopping block was the 1969 comedy, *My World and Welcome to It*. The series was critically acclaimed. It won two Emmy Awards—Best Comedy Series on Television and Best Lead Actor in a Comedy Series for William Windom. But days before the Emmys aired in 1970, Leonard's *World* was cancelled.

The final contractual obligation NBC had with Leonard was a half-hour comedy, *From a Bird's Eye*. After numerous delays, in March of 1971, NBC tossed it out quietly and without publicity. Four months later it died.

NBC was done with Leonard.

The big toes Leonard had stepped on were doing some stepping of their own.

Leonard sidestepped NBC and knocked at ABC's door with a high-profile star, Shirley MacLaine, and her first venture in television, *Shirley's World*.

It premiered in the fall of 1971. It was gone by January of 1972.

That same January, Leonard's next project was another 30-minute comedy called *The Don Rickles Show*, this time on CBS. It died by May of that year.

NBC can't be blamed for the failure of Leonard's latest two series. But the peacock network *can* be credited with putting a sizable blemish on the producer's overall track record.

With *The Andy Griffith Show*, *The Dick Van Dyke Show*, *Gomer Pyle, U.S.M.C.*, and *I Spy*, alone, Leonard appeared invincible. But that all ended in 1968. From then on, and with a big head start from NBC, he had helmed five duds in a row. It didn't matter that one of those duds had been singled out by Leonard's peers as being the best comedy on TV. The bottom line was that five shows in a row had failed to last beyond a single season.

Four years after pulling the plug on *I Spy*, television pulled the plug on Leonard. His career as a TV series producer was over.

Aftermath

In three short years, *I Spy* had done more to change the face of television than any other series of its time.

It was no longer news if a series filmed segments outside of the United States, although few would attempt to do so, and, even then, only on rare occasion.

It was no longer uncommon to see smaller cameras, smaller lighting equipment, and smaller crews used for filming when on the road. And even Fouad Said's Cinemobile was for hire—and used in the making of other series and motion pictures.

It was no longer uncommon to see Black performers in staring roles on TV, or costarring with White actors.

It was no longer uncommon to see Blacks portraying police officers, detectives, attorneys, and doctors.

And it was no longer news that there was a new genre for TV and motion pictures. *Butch Cassidy and the Sundance Kid* would be the next to use it, to great success, in 1969.

I Spy had been, and, in reruns, would continue to be a hit.

It had also been the darling of the press, and a favorite of the critics.

Cleveland Amory, for the May 11, 1968, edition of *TV Guide*, wrote, "We have come to the conclusion that our 'Unaward' of the Year—familiarly known as the 'Enemy'—should go to NBC for its cancellation of *I Spy*. Not only has this show been—in acting, in dialog, and in scenery—the best one on the air for three years, it is still, for literally millions of people, their No. 1 favorite show."

TV Guide and its critics had loved *I Spy*. As stated before, no other entertainment series, in the entire history of the magazine, has received more coveted half-page Close Up listings than *I Spy* did.

It is unlikely that this record will ever be broken.

Stepping Through the Open Door

For the fall of 1968, Robert Hooks continued on *N.Y.P.D.*, as did Nichelle Nichols on *Star Trek*, Greg Morris on *Mission: Impossible*, Don Mitchell on *Ironside*, Hari Rhodes on *Daktari*, and Ivan Dixon on *Hogan's Heroes*.

And there were new faces of color popping up on TV screens across the country.

Gail Fisher was brought in to assist *Mannix*, a role for which she would win an Emmy. A Black family took up residence in *Peyton Place*. Don Matheson, along with Otis Young and Clarence Williams III would follow Cosby and Hooks' lead. They would be costars with White actors in prime-time network series. Matheson would costar with Gary Conway on *Land of the Giants*; Clarence William III shared the lead with Michael Cole and Peggy Lipton in *Mod Squad*. And Otis Young had equal status to Don Murray in *The Outcasts*.

The big news of the season, however, was that Diahann Carroll would be the star of her own series, *Julia*. For the first time since *Beulah* and *Amos & Andy*, a Black performer would take the lead in a weekly half-hour series.

In November, Lt. Uhura and Captain Kirk pressed lips together in an episode of *Star Trek* for television's first interracial kiss.

For the fall of 1969, Cosby returned in a new weekly series on NBC, Hari Rhodes was back to begin work as one of *The Protectors*, Terasa Graves joined the cast of *Laugh In*; Leslie Uggams was given her own variety series on CBS; and ABC put a pair of Black performers, Lloyd Hayes and Denise Nicholls, into the leading roles for *Room 222*.

For the fall of 1971 Lou Gossett was cast in *The Young Rebels* on ABC; Percy Rodriguez was put into *The Silent Force*; Judy Pace was on *The Young Lawyers*; and Rosey Grier was on *Make Room for Granddaddy*;

And the network tried out an all Black version of *Barefoot in the Park* with Scoey Mitchell, Tracy Reed, and Nipsy Russell.

On CBS, Hal Frederick was one of *The Interns*. And a new show about race relations had Mike Evans, Isabel Sanford, and Mel Stewart in the cast as Lionel, Louise and Henry Jefferson. They lived next door to the biggest bigot TV had ever seen: Archie Bunker. The show was *All in the Family*.

NBC had flipped over *The Flip Wilson Show*; Teresa Graves and John Amos went to work in *The Funny Side*; Rupert Crosse, alongside the former Maxwell Smart, Don Adams, was one of *The Partners*. And, not to be outdone by CBS, NBC came up with a Norman Lear show of their own, *Sanford & Son*, starring Redd Foxx and Desmond Wilson.

It truly was a different world. And *I Spy* had broken through only six years earlier.

Michael Zagor: "I remember coming off the show and thinking, 'What am I going to do?' It was just so cozy being there. There was something about the atmosphere in those offices, and in Sheldon, that would give you the permission to reach out a little bit further. We all felt we were doing something new and experimental."[3]

Jerry Ludwig: "We really were ahead of the game. We were just about neck to neck with *Guess Who's Coming to Dinner*, which was a similar kind of landmark. We were still pretty much in the civil rights dark ages—and these guys, Kelly and Scott, drank from the same water fountain."[4]

Steven Kandel: "It was like a vacation working on *I Spy*. It was a gift. To do a script for *I Spy* was a pleasure."[5]

Rick Mittleman: "I found *I Spy* easy to write for compared to other shows. The chemistry between the guys, the humor, for me was a cinch."[6]

Mark Rydell: "My experience with *I Spy* was sensational. I loved every minute of it."[7]

Richard Sarafian: "I can't tell you what a joy it was, and what an adventure it was. I just miss them all so much."[8]

Earle Hagen: "*I Spy* was back when the industry was exciting as hell. I think the thing that made it so enjoyable was that everyone was giving it their best shot. They knew the show was special."[9]

Ernest Frankel: "I'm just one producer who learned from *I Spy*. TV was never the same after that."[10]

Ron Jacobs: "Knowing that the show spawned other things, other shows, other movies, other careers, makes me feel that we'd done something that had never been done before, and we succeeded. Working with Sheldon—that was a plus. Working with Bob Culp and Bill Cosby—that was a plus and a half."[11]

Calvin Brown: "It was so great to work on it and to be a part of *I Spy*. There was nothing but good people on it, because all the bad people would only last a week. It was all about family. Right now, if I could put it—everything that was *I Spy*—in a ball and keep it, I'd do that."[12]

Anthony Friedkin: "My Dad would say that *I Spy* raised a consciousness about the civil rights issues. My Dad hated prejudice to his gut. He was proud that a Black man and a White man could room together on TV—and that it was okay."[13]

Gregory Friedkin: "Dad would point out that *Spy* was revolutionary. It was totally unique, exceptional, groundbreaking. It added meaning to our lives, not because it was a hit show—there were a lot of hit shows—but because of the nature of the show."[14]

Andrea Bershad: "I knew that my dad used the show as a vehicle to travel and continue his career at the same time. It was just a perfect mixture for him. He enjoyed it immensely."[15]

Sheldon Leonard: "*I Spy* was not merely a TV series. It was an adventure."[16]

Bill Cosby: "Everybody's always comparing me with Jackie Robinson. But the thing of it is, you don't want to look at the first Black doing a thing and say, 'Wow, boy!' It's the man who had the guts to give the break who really counts."[17]

Robert Culp: "*I Spy* to us was a living, breathing, beautiful woman, who we made love to every day—and it was great love and fun love, because we knew we were going somewhere. We were on the track and there's no way to stress that in words."[18]

Barry Oringer: "About the ad-libbing: tell Robert Culp I'm over it. He and Cosby *were* that show. What they did was terrific."[19]

Michael Zagor: "Robert Culp said I was his favorite writer on the show? I can't wait to go downstairs and tell my wife and grandchildren. My God, you just made my day."[20]

26

The First Reunion

Within five years of what appeared to be the end of *I Spy*, there would be a reunion, of a sort, on the big screen.

But not all would be invited to the party.

Much would happen in five years for the men who helped to change television.

Sheldon Leonard's fortunes have already been noted. Now for the rest.

David Friedkin & Mort Fine

David Friedkin made a complete recovery after his health setbacks. He and his partner recharged their creative batteries, then resumed work.

Universal turned Friedkin and Fine's attention back to television, as producers of the popular movies of the week. They would make two: *The Most Deadly Game* in 1970 and *River of Gold* in 1971.

Bearcats, a new series, followed in the fall of 1971. It starred Rod Taylor and Dennis Cole. It involved a pair of adventurers who traveled the globe. When described in that way, it sounded a bit like *I Spy*. It was sure to be a hit. It lasted three months.

In 1972, with no development deals in place, David Friedkin went to work as a director for *Hawaii Five-O*, *Ironside*, and *Kojak*. He would win a Directors Guild Award, his second, for one of his *Kojak* episodes. Mort Fine was busy writing scripts for *McCloud*, *Banacek*, and *Banyon*.

The team of Friedkin and Fine, for the time being, was on hold.

Robert Culp

In the fall of 1968, as *I Spy* was leaving NBC, the series was a hot property. As were its stars.

Robert Culp had blocked off the year for the shooting of the fourth season. Now the time had to be filled.

According to Joy Keller, Culp's secretary, when the series suddenly ended, Culp became "lost."

Keller: "He is a wonderful man. A perfect boss. He treated me as a friend, and he taught me a lot. I loved that show, and so did he. When it ended, something in him ended as well."[1]

Culp: "Anybody who comes off of a three year series that was dear to them — and *I Spy* was certainly dear to both Bill and me — and it's suddenly gone, just like overnight — it's a total surprise. Nobody, not even Bill and me, expected it. So it's just not logical to think that we had anything lined up to do. We didn't.

"Both of us were at loose ends. And then, all of a sudden, Dr. King gets killed.

"I called Bill on the phone, the instant I heard, and said 'What are you going to do?' He said, 'I'm going to Memphis to march with the Garbage Men.' I said, 'Not without me, you're not.' So we jumped on a plane together and went.

"We got there a little bit late because of airplane connections, and wound up at the very end of the line of marchers in Memphis, making our way into the town square. As we approached, we could hear both Sidney Poitier and Harry Belafonte's voices on loud speakers. But we couldn't get in. We couldn't get past the crowd. It was worse than shoulder to shoulder.

Top: Cosby and Culp, *Hickey & Boggs*, '72 (courtesy Robert Culp). *Bottom*: *Bob & Carol & Ted & Alice* (unknown, Robert Culp, Natalie Wood and Elliot Gould), 1969 (courtesy Robert Culp).

"Then we went on to Atlanta for the funeral. Bill and I had hung together the whole way. I wasn't saying much, I was pretty glum. Bill was cheering everybody up on the bus, making jokes, and just lightening it up, because everybody was suicidal. And on the bus is Aretha Franklin, sobbing. And Stevie Wonder was there. Bill told jokes, and Stevie was both laughing and crying.

"I got back to Los Angeles and I had nothing to do. When you come off that really hard road, where you put out all that energy, and then there's no place to put it, you just get self-destructive. So I threw myself into a cause.

"Jim Brown, the former football player, who had been on *I Spy*, introduced me to Jessie Jackson, a kid of 25 or so. Jackson had been extremely close to Dr. King and was running a thing called 'Operation Breadbasket.' It was the economic arm of King's church. There had been no national coverage on it, or on him. Nothing. But I was very impressed by Jackson—by what he had to say—by what he offered all of us in a time when our spirits were suddenly so low.

"I remember getting home from the meeting, and it was late, and France was asleep. So I quietly got into bed, and went to sleep. In the morning, I woke up and she was already up, down in the kitchen. I went down, and she had the TV on. She looked shocked. I saw on the TV that Bobby Kennedy had been killed—shot the night before, while I was at the meeting, and died later that night while I slept. And I just lost it. That was it. *I Spy*, Dr. King, Bobby Kennedy, all gone, all within a couple months. So I got myself a camera man and a sound man and some equipment, all out of my own pocket, and got on a plane and we went to Atlanta. For the next year, that's all I did—wrote, directed, filmed *Operation Breadbasket*."[2]

Culp's film would provide Jessie Jackson with his first national exposure, helping to launch his career as a social leader.

But Culp would later admit that this undertaking was a financial and professional mistake. His first step after leaving *I Spy* was a treacherous one, and it kept him away from acting and out of the eye of the mainstream public for nearly a year.

Operation Breadbasket was only 64 minutes in length—not long enough to be considered a feature film documentary. Furthermore, it was felt that the subject matter would not bring people together into movie houses across the country. So there were no takers.

Culp offered his film to TV. ABC acquired the broadcast rights, paying Culp 50 cents on the dollar for his investment.

The ABC in-house news department could not have made a documentary like *Operation Breadbasket*.

Culp: "No network newsman—and they were all White back then—could have gained the trust and been so welcomed into the Black community as I was. And that was a gift from *I Spy*."[3]

In July of 1969, on a Friday night at 10 P.M., Culp's documentary, now edited down to fit into a 60-minute slot, had its world premiere.

TV Guide threw a spotlight on *Operation Breadbasket* with a half-page Close Up listing, reading, in part, "Based in Chicago, Breadbasket is lining up jobs for thousands of Blacks across the Nation. With the boycott as one of its primary tactics, it's also trying to change the economic structure of the ghetto."

There were those who appreciated Culp for his efforts. On October 4, 1968, Culp was presented with the ADL—B'nai B'rith Human Relations Award—for his quiet and very private participation in human rights matters that only then were coming into light.

Culp's first turn as an actor after *I Spy* was for the big screen film, *Bob & Carol & Ted & Alice*.

When Paul Mazursky was first given the chance to direct his original screenplay, and the deal was being inked in the summer of 1968, Culp was still being seen every week on NBC.

Mazursky recalls *I Spy* as being "the big thing then." And Mazursky was in a good place to know. He had lost his job in television because of *I Spy*. Mazursky had been a writer on *The Danny Kaye Show*.

But Mazursky felt Culp would be ideal for his movie, saying: "He was so perfect, he used his own wardrobe. Moss Mabry, the costume [designer] went to his house and said, 'I don't have to buy anything for him. He's got more zippers than anyone.'"[4]

It is curious to watch *Bob & Carol & Ted & Alice* after viewing the episodes of *I Spy*. In many scenes, Culp appears as he had as Kelly Robinson. The trademark white jeans and white sneakers are still there. And so is the blonde sheepskin jacket he began wearing for the episodes filmed in chilly Spain in late 1966. Just as Kelly would, Culp comes off as being confident, in control, and on top of the world.

Yet Culp recalls this period as being one of the lowest in his life. Besides losing a series that he loved, and that he had sacrificed so much for, his new marriage to France Nuyen was faltering.

To distract himself, Culp had remained busy, writing, and pursuing work as a director. But this only added to his frustration, as he quickly discovered the meaning behind an industry term known as "development hell," where a proposed film project lingers indefinitely in limbo.

As 1969 closed, Culp accepted an acting job that would take him to where *I Spy* very nearly went—England.

For *Married Alive*, in a marketing triumph, Culp was cast opposite Diana Rigg. For what *TV Guide* called "a sophisticated suspense comedy with a twist," Emma Peel and Kelly Robinson, a pair of 1960s pop icons, would share the screen.

"Diana Rigg was wonderful," Culp recalled. "She knew it was a rough time for me, and she was very supportive."[5]

The title of the televised play carried some irony of its own: Culp truly was feeling buried alive in marriage.

It was announced in a celebrity magazine that Culp filed for divorce from France Nuyen on December 9, 1969, on the date of their second wedding anniversary.

By mid–1970, with his writing and directing projects still "in development," Culp needed to get back onto TV for a series of high-profile guest appearances.

The first was for the prestigious 90-minute NBC series, *The Name of the Game*. In a dispute with producers, series costar Tony Franciosa had been suspended by Universal, and Culp was quickly tapped to stand in for him, taking the lead in two episodes.

The pair of hour-and-a-half programs aired on October 2 and November 6, 1970. The first, "Cynthia Is Alive and Living in Avalon," like *Married Alive*, was a network ad-man's dream come true. Once again, for the second project in a row, Culp appeared opposite another familiar face from the 1960s TV spy game. This time it was Barbara Feldon, Agent 99 from *Get Smart*.

For the second installment, "Little Bear Died Running," Culp would work with an actress who would later become the fourth Mrs. Robert Culp. Her name was Sheila Sullivan.

The following year, Culp made two more high-profile television appearances. First up, "Death Lends a Hand," the first regular episode to be filmed for *Columbo*, now a series on NBC.

In December, he starred in a TV Movie of the Week entitled *See the Man Run*, a bizarre tale in the Hitchcock style.

Costarring with Culp were Angie Dickinson, Eddie Albert, and June Allyson.

In 1971, sandwiched in between Culp's television appearances, *Hannie Caulder* was released to the big screens. Culp did not direct the movie, as originally announced to the trades, but did costar opposite Raquel Welch in the violent Western shot in Spain.

The movie was reviewed in *Variety* on November, 11, 1971. The magazine found it to be a "rough-and-ready Western for popular tastes [with] Raquel Welch and Robert Culp [as] selling angles."

Hannie Cauler is, in fact, a very good movie. Welch surprises, and Culp delivers. Appearing in his first Western in eight years, since guest starring in 1964 episodes of *The Virginian* and *Gunsmoke*, Culp gets a chance to demonstrate his fast draw. The man who played Hoby Gibson on *Trackdown* always maintained that only one actor was faster at the quick draw than him—Sammy Davis Jr.

Culp did get his chance to direct for the big screen with his next project. The feature film was set for 1972, and it would allow him his first reunion with Bill Cosby.

Bill Cosby

As *I Spy* ended production, Bill Cosby was in position to continue to dominate on TV and in the record stores. He had his NBC deal for more variety shows, and then a TV series, just as quick as he could develop one and get it into production. Being freed from *I Spy* allowed him an early start.

Cosby, regretful that *I Spy* had folded, never had a chance to sit back and reflect on the loss.

The second variety special came first, on April 4, 1969.

In June, Cosby was there to see his first NBC solo venture win an Emmy for Outstanding Variety Special. It was the fourth year in a row that he would take home an Emmy. And he would be the only Black to do so that night, or on any of the previous nights during that four-year period.

Later in the month, Cosby's third special aired on NBC. This one was called *As I See It*, and had a more serious tone than the previous two, even dealing with race issues.

By midyear 1969, a biography on Cosby entitled *Cool Cos* had been published, and Cosby himself went on record for an extensive *Playboy* interview, reflecting now about his years on *I Spy*.

The Bill Cosby Show, the new series NBC had been pushing for, premiered in the fall of 1969, just 12 months after *I Spy* departed the network schedule.

For the new show, Cosby played Chet Kincaid, a Los Angeles high school physical-education instructor, coach, and occasional substitute teacher.

With this series, Cosby had found a way to remain an entertainer, and, at the same time, play at living the life he originally saw for himself—as a physical-education teacher and coach.

America wanted to love *The Bill Cosby Show*. The series did exceptionally well in the ratings, placing in the top ten of the Nielsens. By month two of the new season, the series hit its peak at number three. By the new year, it was still riding high at number four. By season's end, it was given an overall ranking by Nielsen of number 11. But, by the time that report was written, by the start of its second year, the show had already dropped out of the top 20.

Even before *The Bill Cosby Show* started to lose a portion of its audience, during that first year back on NBC, the network gave America a second dose of Cos, with a prime-time special based on characters from Cosby's comedy routines. The animated show was called *Fat Albert*.

At season's end, *The Bill Cosby Show* was nominated for an Emmy as Outstanding Comedy Series. Cosby was nominated for his work, as a lead actor in comedy, as well. Both he and his series, however, would lose the Emmy to Sheldon Leonard's ill-fated *My World and Welcome to It*, and its star, William Windom.

For its next season, *The Bill Cosby Show* would experience a much bigger slide in the ratings, and would be cancelled by the network.

Cosby's next endeavor was to return to serious acting. He would also wear the hat of a producer. Both goals were achieved at the start of 1972 with a TV movie for CBS entitled *To All My Friends on Shore*.

To play his wife, Cosby chose Gloria Foster, who had appeared in the title role of "Shana," the final episode of *I Spy*.

One month later, in March 1972, Cosby had his big screen premiere with a Western entitled *Man and Boy*. Like *To All My Friends*, he was the coproducer of this new project. With the film's release, Cosby found himself on the cover of *Ebony* magazine, for the second time in his life.

With *Man and Boy*, Cosby acted opposite Gloria Foster for the third time. Once again, she played his wife. Their performances together continued to be a success. The movies, however, were not.

Cosby needed a hit, and the big news inside the industry was the talk of a possible reunion of those two guys from *I Spy*. There was a script. There was a director. There was financing and a producer, too.

Fouad Said

After leaving *I Spy*, Fouad accepted a job as location manager on Woody Allen's 1969 film *Take the Money and Run*.

Allen had a modest budget for his first film as a director, but a desire to shoot in as many real locations as he possibly could. Fouad would enable him to do that.

Fouad also had a plan for the future. He was going to find a way around the union rules that dictated what he, as a member of the crew, could or could not do.

As a producer, he could oversee all aspects of the production of the motion picture. He could drive his Cinemobile onto the location, if he wanted, and offer advice as to how certain shots could be accomplished. He could use the equipment that he preferred—his beloved Arriflex camera and quartz lights. He could hire smaller crews and he could show those crews how they could accomplish his goals, with less gear, less men, less time, and less money.

Fouad was not going to allow Hollywood's union block to stop him.

His first film as a producer would be Culp's first film as a director. It would costar Culp and Cosby. Born out of the ashes of *I Spy*, it was to be called *Hickey & Boggs*.

The First Reunion

In early 1971, Warner Brothers approached Culp and Cosby with a movie project.

The story of *Hickey & Boggs* involved two down-and-out private eyes, struggling to make ends meet, who take on the minor assignment of locating a missing woman. As all good private eye flicks go, they are pulled into a web of murder, deceit, and money. In this case, the money involved the theft of $400,000 from a bank in Pittsburgh.

Culp agreed to do the movie, with one stipulation—he wanted to direct.

"They said no way," Culp recalled for a 1972 *Los Angeles Times* interview, "So I said, sell it to us then."

It was the decision of John Calley, Warner Brothers executive vice president in charge of production, that Culp not be given the directing assignment.

"I don't blame Warners for being reluctant," Culp said at the time. "John Calley told me that even if my credentials were in order, he couldn't go into [Warner Bros. board chairman] Ted Ashley's office and suggest an actor direct. Historically, their guts have been splattered all over the ceiling time after time by actors who want to direct. It has to do with business sense."[6]

Once having acquired the property from Warners Brothers, Culp spent six months "running and falling down" trying to get the money. Culp preferred not to act in the film, but couldn't raise the money without the guarantee of his own drawing power as a star.

Finally, after securing modest financial backing, and a distribution arrangement through United Artists, Culp prepared *Hickey & Boggs* for production.

Culp: "I rewrote this screenplay that Walter Hill, who was busy working for Peckinpah [writing "The Getaway"], should have been doing under my supervision. But I couldn't get him, because he was busy with Sam. So I had to go off into the mountain for two weeks and do this rewrite myself."[7]

And then Culp cut the shooting schedule, pushed the cast and crew to the breaking point, and brought in the film—originally budgeted for $2.4 million by Warners Brothers—ahead of schedule and under budget for only $1.1 million.

United Artists snuck the film out, between August and November 1972, playing only in a few cities at a time, with minimal promotion. UA felt the film would appeal to *I Spy* fans only, and that those fans would find the movie, with or without a big promotional push.

In October 1972, writer Martin Rips, in an article for the *Los Angeles Times*, wrote, "For a man whose principal vocation is the speaking of words, *Hickey & Boggs* is very much a visual film, with a strong sense of direction and purpose."

To achieve this, however, "Culp the director left close to 50 minutes on the cutting room floor, much of it pertaining to character development for Culp the actor."

The article further noted that Culp added a bit of painful realism to his character. In several chase sequences, Boggs is limping.

"Two weeks before shooting began," Culp told the *Times* writer, "I went in for a hernia operation. At one point in the Coliseum shoot-out, Boggs suddenly bends over and grips his side in agony. That was for real."

It was Culp's intent that Hickey and Boggs not resemble Robinson and Scott.

"This was a deliberate design to kill those characters," he admitted.

But the *Los Angeles Times* reported that many critical responses suggested that the fans were missing the camaraderie of Kelly and Scott.

Cosby: "We did exactly what we wanted to do, which, I guess, was wrong. What we should have done was make an *I Spy*. Make it lighter—with more joking between the two of us."[8]

Variety, in its August 1972 review of the movie, wrote, "Starting slow, plottage seldom rises above the confusing stage, but later action is sufficiently fast and violent to rate as okay melodrama."

The review continued to criticize that Culp and producer Fouad Said "should have paid more attention to the story line of the Walter Hill screenplay, which suffers through audience never being entirely certain as to the identity of some of the characters."

An example of this is how it was wildly believed by those who saw the movie that Culp's character, Frank Boggs, was gay. There were three reasons for this.

We never see the face, or even much of the body, of the prostitute that visits Boggs in his office. The careful camera angles raise suspicion.

When Boggs visits a strip club and watches a young girl peel her clothes off on stage, he barely has a reaction for her. Hickey even asks, in a disapproving tone, "Why do you come in here?" Boggs replies, "I like the music."

This exchange is better understood if it is known that the stripper is actually Edith Boggs, the former Mrs. Frank Boggs. The information is there, but it is provided in an extremely subtle manner, and therefore can be missed.

And, finally, the clincher, Hickey's wife, while arguing with her husband, refers to Boggs as "Your faggot partner."

Culp: "When I was rewriting the script, I got to that scene, and I wanted something powerful out of her mouth. And what's stronger than calling your husband's partner a fag? It's strong, it's why women do that, it's why Cary Grant said 'Every woman I was ever married to said I was gay.' Because it's a punch in the chops. But a lot of people who saw the movie misconstrued that."[9]

Cosby: "Yeah, well, that's in those days when women became very angry with men. And they would go to that. She was threatened by our relationship. Very much so."[10]

On the plus side, the reviewer for *Variety* admitted that Culp "tosses in plenty of strong production values" and "keeps his direction at a good pace after an overflow of un-relating early sequences."

It was also felt that "both Cosby and Culp give good accounts of themselves and are backed by a capable cast."

The cast indeed was impressive. Robert Mandan, recognizable to anyone who ever watched *Soap*, played the mob boss. Vincent Gardenia, a veteran character actor, played the head cop. His boss, from the D.A.'s office, was none other than James Woods, in a brief appearance. Also look for a very young Michael Moriarty as one of the hoods.

Leonard Maltin saw *Hickey & Boggs* as a "tough melodrama," and wrote, "Well made but extremely violent and downbeat: will come as a surprise to fans of the stars' tongue-in-cheek antics on their *I Spy* TV series."

For his October 1, 1972, review, Charles Chaplin of the *Los Angeles Times*, gave positive notice, writing: "What lifts *Hickey & Boggs* above the ordinary is the sardonic naturalism of the Culp and Cosby performances. They avoid the polished wisecracks or the easy cynicism of the customary private eyes, and project instead a kind of angry dismay at their lives and their world which is unusually persuasive. They come off as real men operating in a real world."

Regarding the caliber of the production, Champlin wrote, "Shot entirely on location in Los Angeles, *Hickey & Boggs* looks so real your eyes smart from the smog. The movie marks Fouad Said's debut as a producer and inevitably his Cinemobile got a good workout."

And, of the star/director, Champlin said, "Culp has brought off the difficult task of doubling as actor and director with remarkable assurance and control."

Good words from a seasoned film critic. But *Hickey & Boggs* did not do the business it was expected to, and, in an industry that doesn't always allow second chances, Robert Culp had his turn at bat and had failed to hit a home run.

The lingering sadness is that *Hickey & Boggs* is a good movie. Since it was directed by the writer of seven of the darkest episodes of the entire *I Spy* series, it should not come as a surprise that the tone of the movie is relentlessly somber.

Further, Culp has admitted that he was a fan of film noir, including the screen versions of Raymond Chandler's books. Chandler was known for creating mysteries that were highly intelligent and stylistic, but also extremely hard, often impossible to figure out. *Hickey & Boggs* was all of that.

There would be no sequel. And, sadly, this fine movie by Robert Culp would fade from view.

Regardless, *Hickey & Boggs* has its fans—one being Bill Cosby.

Cosby: "*Hickey & Boggs* has a cult following. It's a helluva' movie Bob directed—and what he did—*Oh, man*. Bob was wonderful in that."[11]

27

The Second Reunion

After *Hickey & Boggs*, it would take 15 years to bring Culp and Cosby together again. Much would happen in that time.

David Friedkin & Mort Fine

In the mid–1970s, the two former "show runners" of *I Spy* were hopping from series to series, hiring themselves out, separately, one as a writer, one as a director. They were expecting their next big success in TV, as a team, to be just around the corner.

It wasn't.

In March of 1976, Friedkin and Fine would briefly get one more series up and running. *Bert D'Angelo/Superstar* was for ABC. It was a cop show. It was a midseason replacement. It starred Paul Sorvino. It lasted a mere four-and-a-half months, and was gone by July.

Three months later, on October 15, 1976, David Friedkin died at the age of 64.

The man who had a hand in creating *I Spy*, who produced, as well as wrote, directed, and acted in the series, was gone.

Anthony Friedkin: "Both my Mom and my Dad smoked three packs a day. They loved to drink and talk about art and politics. They were the 'booze generation.' Dad hated any drug except alcohol. And from those years, when he was doing *I Spy*, I did see the side issues eat away at him: the pressure, the anxiety, the anger. The colon cancer had hit him hard. He had major surgery and then chemo. When he died, it was from lung cancer. Three packs a day, plus that pressure in your life—it's going to tag you."[1]

Gregory Friedkin: "My Dad had a love and a need—not selfish, not for himself—but a need to reach out to others to try and make the world a better place. My entire life, as I've worked in entertainment, I've had people come up to me and say, 'Your Dad was the nicest guy I've worked with. He was wonderful. He was generous. He was giving.'

"I know Dad was proud of *I Spy*. He knew he had helped to create a genre. Of all his work, all those scripts, all the directing, and the producing, he was most proud of three things: *The Price of Tomatoes*, *The Pawnbroker*, and *I Spy*. How do you top that?"[2]

Anthony Friedkin: "I'm thrilled that my father did *I Spy*. It was an incredible accomplishment."[3]

Mort Fine would continue on, alone. He wrote scripts for various network series, usually cop shows. He had enough friends in the industry and, with his impressive list of credits, work would still come his way. But the jobs he was offered no longer challenged or excited him.

Bernice Fine: "After a time, he retired from writing. He just didn't want the hassle anymore. From radio to TV to movies, they were never without work. But, of course, there's

Culp and Cosby on *The Tonight Show*, 1981 (courtesy NBC).

that bit about 'script writers being too old,' and Mort was starting to get that so he retired. We traveled a lot. And he had so much fun teaching overseas."[4]

Mort Fine's son, David: "He didn't like the class where you sit around and have students discuss other student's scripts. He was much more of a one-on-one guy. He was interested in hearing the voices of the characters."[5]

Bernice Fine: "Mort and Bill Froug were good friends. So, when Bill got a teaching post in Australia, he mentioned Mort, and Mort went. When Mort got a job in Denmark, he got Bill to go over, too. He really liked teaching—especially in Denmark. He went there twice a year, for four years."[6]

Marion Hargrove would remain a close friend until Fine's death from cancer on March 7, 1991. Fine telephoned Hargrove the night before he passed, to say that very soon he would be "one with the ages." Aching to make his friend smile, Hargrove responded that he thought Mort was a little young for the ages. It would be their last conversation.

Mort Fine was 74.

Bernice Fine: "After *The Pawnbroker*, *I Spy* was his favorite. Mort loved that show and the people, too."[7]

Fouad Said, a Farewell to Hollywood

Following *Hickey & Boggs*, Fouad Said produced a second film for release in 1972. *Across 110th Street* starred Anthony Quinn, Yaphet Kotto, and Tony Franciosa. Barry Shear was the director. The premise involved the New York City police racing the mob to catch three Blacks who, disguised as cops, stole $300,000 from a Mafia-controlled bank. Movie critic Leonard Maltin saw *Across 110th* as "exciting, well-paced, and extremely violent, with fine use of Harlem locations."

Like *Hickey & Boggs*, *Across 110th Street* had a modest budget. It needed to look bigger than it was. Anthony Quinn had arranged for the financing. Fouad, although new to the world of producing films, was the technical wizard who could pull off such an endeavor.

The Deadly Trackers came next in 1973. Richard Harris and Rod Taylor starred. Barry Shear again sat in the director's chair, taking over for Sam Fuller, who wrote the screenplay, then began the film, only to be removed. The Western involved Harris, as an Irish sheriff of a small Texas town, trailing bank robber Taylor and gang to Mexico to avenge the deaths of his wife and son. Leonard Maltin was less impressed with this outing, rating the entire endeavor as a "BOMB," and describing it as a "dreadful, violent Western."

In 1975, two years later, Fouad's fourth and final film as a producer was released. *Aloha, Bobby and Rose* starred Paul LeMat as an auto mechanic and Dianne Hull as his girlfriend, who are inadvertently drawn into crime, causing them to take it on the lam, with the law in hot pursuit. Again, a road show. Again, a perfect vehicle for Fouad. The movie received moderate to poor reviews, and did similar business.

And then Fouad walked away.

Richard Sarafian: "Lew Wasserman, chairman of the board of MCA, wanted to hire Fouad to design a Cinemobile for Universal. Foo said, 'Mr. Wasserman, I can't do that. But here are my plans. Build it yourself.' Taft Broadcasting ended up buying Cinemobile for 50 million dollars."[8]

On a visit to his family's home in Egypt, Fouad observed that there was a shortage of air-conditioned housing in the region. As inventive as always, Fouad was struck by an idea.

Andrea Bershad: "He took the money from Cinemobile and started building prefabricated housing for the oil workers in the Middle East. He's very rich now."[9]

The Leonards stayed in close touch with Fouad. Leonard's daughter recalls, "My dad always traveled with Fouad and they were really close. We last saw him in the mid-nineties when Fouad and his wife took all of us on a luxury cruise on their private yacht out of Sardinia. At that time we hooked up with Bill and Camille Cosby, who were in the South of France. It was really a very nice reunion of all those people who had worked together, and continued to have nice feelings for one another."[10]

The little Egyptian who proved to be a magician when it came to hiding his cameras and microphones is now rumored to be a billionaire.

Robert Culp

After completing the publicity circuit for *Hickey & Boggs*, Culp turned his attention back to his most recent writing project, a screenplay entitled *Under the Sun*. The script was finished and Culp was determined to use all his resources to get the project into production with himself as director.

Under the Sun would never see the light of day.

In the meantime, to stay busy and in the public eye, Culp, the actor, continued working.

He appeared twice more as a murderer in *Columbo*, tying with Jack Cassidy as the crafty lieutenant's most frequent adversary. The episodes, both clocking in at the length of a TV movie, were "The Most Crucial Game" and "Double Exposure."

Culp was also highly sought as a lead in the popular 1970s Movie of the Week (MOW).

In 1973, he made an offbeat psychological horror tale with Eli Wallach, entitled *A Cold Night's Death*. That same year, he played a father and husband, battling with out-of-control teens in an affluent Southern California community, in *Outrage*.

In 1974, Culp and Sheila Sullivan appeared together again, this time playing husband and wife in a big-event MOW, *Houston, We've Got a Problem*. The movie chronicles the events of the near disastrous Apollo 13 space mission.

And, by this time, Culp and Sullivan weren't just playing the part, they *were* husband and wife.

Culp had also appeared with Sullivan in a big screen offering, the steamy horror film *A Name for Evil*.

In a *Playboy* picture article, from March 1973, a reviewer wrote, "The best thing about *A Name for Evil*, a recently released film starring Robert Culp and Samantha Eggar, is its scenery," which included, "breath-taking mountain country and amply exposed anatomies."

In other worlds, nudity.

The *Playboy* writer went on to say, "The screenplay is so convoluted that it's unlikely to advance the careers of either Culp or Miss Eggar, who plays his screen wife, but it has already done something for a movie newcomer, co-star Sheila Sullivan: She's since become Mrs. Culp."

Both would also be exploited in the pages of that month's *Playboy*, fully naked.

For the 1973–74 TV season, Culp made four well-hyped appearances.

The first was for *Shaft*, a new television series, starring Richard Roundtree, based on his popular Black exploitation films of the same name. In the premiere episode, Culp, a long-time supporter and advocate of civil rights, lent his name to help launch this new series with a Black lead. He would play the heavy.

In the September 22, 1973, issue of *TV Guide*, Culp's appearance on *Shaft* was announced, along with a career update on the actor/writer/director. Culp told the magazine that he had been busy writing two projects, one which he was to direct in Spain, but it had fallen through. The second was a movie he was still hopeful for, and planned to direct in the coming year in the United States. He said he expected to continue to act, but would focus more on writing and directing.

Culp was not absent from the big screen in 1974. In the Disney-produced *The Castaway Cowboy*, he appeared with James Garner and Vera Miles.

Daily Variety gave *Castaway* a good notice, and wrote, "Miles is pleasantly effective in widow role and Culp is smooth as a tricky businessman who wants femme for his very own."

That same year, Culp would appear in a well-received MOW, *Strange Homecoming*. For this project, he took lead billing over Glen Campbell, and played a charismatic but psychopathic man, on the run, who returns home for a chance to lay low. With *Homecoming*, Culp was reteamed with two former *I Spy* writers, Eric Bercovici and Jerry Ludwig, who served here as writer/producers.

Ludwig recalls that the working title for that project was *Everybody Loves Uncle Jack*. Both he and Bercovici agree that it was a rip-off of Alfred Hitchcock's *Shadow of a Doubt*. In the movie, Culp plays Uncle Jack, a character very similar to the uncle Joseph Cotton played in the Hitchcock film. He is a thief who has turned to murder and is now seeking refuge. The twist here is that his brother, the man he is staying with, played by Campbell, is a cop.

Ludwig: "We wrote the thing for NBC, and the guy there had been so nice when we pitched the story. He knew it was inspired by *Shadow of a Doubt*.[11]

But later, when the script was turned in, Ludwig remembers the network man as saying, "Take out all the Freudian horseshit."

Ludwig: "It's brother against brother, that's the essence of the story, that's what it all comes down to. We said 'okay,' but, when we got done, we told him, 'We'd like to use Bob Culp to play Jack.' And he says 'Yeah, fine, he's good.' And we thought, Bob will bring all the craziness back in. And he was terrific.

"Bob Culp, for my money or anyone else's, can do anything in the world—except for one thing: he can never be ordinary. He just doesn't blend into a crowd like other people."[12]

Recalling the looping sessions for the film, Ludwig said, "The thing we didn't know, because we hadn't been involved with the postproduction of *I Spy*, is that Bob has these 'readings' that he does, these strange starts and stops. So when it came time to loop this stuff, we thought, 'Is he just going to stand there in the darkness with the headset on, and is he going to hate that asshole up on the screen and think, how can I do that?' But he *did* do it. Easily, bam, bam, bam. What a professional, that he could do it again. There's a lot of thought to what he does. He's a very prepared actor. And a pretty fair director, and quite a good writer, as well. You don't find someone who can hit with all three hands that often."[13]

Over the next few years, Culp would continue to try to hit with all three hands—and continue to break the rules of Hollywood, by appearing on the big screen while, at the same time, taking occasional work in television.

In 1975, Culp starred in a two-part episode for the popular and critically acclaimed series, *Police Story* on NBC. Next came the lead in yet another MOW, *A Cry for Help*. This time he played a cynical radio talk-show host who receives a suicide threat from a nameless young girl. As he becomes haunted by the call, he frantically tries to get his listeners to locate the girl before she can carry out her threat.

Later that year, Culp was back on the big screen for the heist-caper, *Inside Out*, starring Telly Savalas. Culp had the second spot, just above James Mason, and would play an ex-con recruited by Savalas to engineer the caper.

Inside Out offered fans of *I Spy* something they had seen little of since the demise of the series. Here, for the first time since his two appearances on *The Name of the Game*, Culp plays a character reminiscent of Kelly Robinson.

Sky Riders came next, released in 1976. Culp, lending support in this violent and graphically realistic action thriller, had third billing under James Coburn and Susannah York.

Less than a month later, at the start of June, Culp was back in the movie houses with second billing, under Bo Svenson, in the revenge actioner, *Breaking Point*.

A few weeks later, Culp showed up in another box office release, his third for the year, the Western-comedy, *The Great Scout and Cathouse Thursday*. This time he played a cad, with third billing under Lee Marvin and Oliver Reed.

Later in the year, Culp returned to TV once more for the lead in another big-event Movie of the Week—as big as they got in 1976. *Flood!* was produced by Irwin Allen, hot off his box office hits of *The Poseidon Adventure* and *The Towering Inferno*.

At a reported cost of $2.5 million, *Flood!*, according to network publicity, was the most expensive film ever made for television.

By 1977, Culp was still reluctant to consider returning to television in a weekly series. But television was more than happy to consider Culp.

The pilot would be called *Spectre*. The writer and producer was none other than Gene Roddenberry, the creator of *Star Trek*, another innovator from the 1960s who had been having trouble finding his next great project.

In the television movie, Culp plays a criminologist, who, along with his 'Doctor Watson,' an alcoholic played by an alcoholic Gig Young, is summoned to England to investigate a series of supernatural occurrences involving a suspicious, wealthy financier.

Spectre was aired as a Movie of the Week in May 1977, and may have had a shot at becoming a series, except for one small problem: No one had told Culp that this was a pilot.

The disappointment and the exhaustion that came from his experience with *I Spy* still sat heavy on Culp's shoulders. And he had not given up his dream to write and direct for the movies.

Next up, Culp acted in another Movie of the Week. This time, for the first time, he did not receive top billing. In *Cry for Justice*, a movie Culp doesn't even remember making, the actor would take the second lead, under Sharon Acker. Also in the cast were Larry Hagman, Diana Muldaur, and Dennis Weaver.

Back in the first position in 1978, Culp headed the cast of the TV movie, *Last of the Good Guys*. Once again, listed under Culp, was Larry Hagman.

In 1979, Culp lent his name and support to launch a spin-off of *Columbo*, this time dealing with the famous detective's never before seen wife. The title would be *Mrs. Columbo*. And, as he had done on three different occasions in the parent series, Culp plays a murderer. The twist, this time, is Culp's character would also get murdered, just as the crafty police detective's crafty wife closes in.

Also in '79, for *Goldengirl*, intended for the big screen, but dumped onto TV, Culp took third billing under James Coburn and Susan Anton.

During the decade of the 1970s, Culp clearly had not been idle. He had received top billing in several high profile Movie of the Weeks, and second or third billing in several big screen releases, as well as numerous more "special guest star" performances in prestigious prime-time series. And, during this time, he had directed a big screen release starring himself and Bill Cosby. Culp had good reason to believe his career was progressing nicely ... until one day when the words of a casual fan had a profound effect on the man who had found fame as Kelly Robinson over a decade earlier.

Culp: "After *I Spy*, sometime in the late '70s, something went wrong with my car and I took it into a service station up on Sunset at Doheny. I knew the guy there, and I said, 'Can you listen to my engine, there's something wrong.' And, without hesitation, he turned around and pointed to this guy that I didn't know. He was a 'grease monkey,' he was just a very gifted mechanic. And he said, 'Come ride around the block with Mr. Culp and see what's wrong with his car.' So he got in on the driver's side and he started to drive, and I sat beside him. And, while we're driving, out of nowhere, he says, 'If I live to be a hundred, I'll never understand why you didn't become a star.'

"The guy's statement went through me like a railroad spike. And I still remember it, all these years later. What he said wasn't a question, so I didn't answer him. What was there to say?"[14]

Culp suddenly realized that, even with the small features he had been making—four alone in 1976—and the Movie of the Weeks, and the killers he had been playing on *Columbo*, and *Mrs. Columbo*, and *Shaft*, he had been too absent from the public eye for too long. Movies like *Inside Out*, *Sky Riders*, *Breaking Point*, and *The Great Scout and Cathouse Thursday*, were not playing to big audiences. The visibility he had achieved with *I Spy* had faded from view. By refusing to do a series, in order to stay free to take writing and directing assignments that never seemed to materialize, Culp had jeopardized his celebrity status. And, by doing that, he had given up much of his Hollywood clout.

Culp relented. He was now ready to settle down into a show of his own.

His agent sent word out that Culp was willing to consider doing another series.

The first offer to come in was a surprising one.

Dallas had been on for three seasons. In the final episode filmed, J.R. had been shot by an unknown assailant. The world was suddenly struck with J.R. mania, and the burning question around water coolers in the work places of America was "Who shot J.R.?"

Larry Hagman, who had been playing the part of J.R., now wanted more money, and the actor had refused to report for work.

Frustrated by Hagman's demands, the producers offered the role to Culp. It would be explained in the series that J.R. had been shot in the face, and had undergone plastic surgery. He would now look different. He would look like Robert Culp instead of Larry Hagman. He would sound different too. And walk different. And act different. But America would understand—a near-death experience can have a profound effect on a man, and result in even more profound changes.

It could work.

Days before Culp was set to step before the cameras, a deal was finally worked out with Hagman. He would return to the role that had made him famous far beyond his 1960s fame as an astronaut with a genie.

Culp didn't waste any time. He accepted the next best offer that had come his way. He would costar in a new series for producer Stephen J. Cannell. It would be for ABC. It would be an action-comedy–science fiction called *The Greatest American Hero*.

William Katt was to star as Ralph Hinkley, a high school teacher who encounters extraterrestrial beings while on a field trip into the desert. The aliens present him with a red flying suit, which, when worn, gives him the ability to behave like a superhero. A high-strung FBI agent named Bill Maxwell finds out about Ralph's gift, and convinces him to use the suit to help fight crime.

Culp would play Maxwell.

With this series, Culp would also be given the opportunity to write and direct again.

Only one problem: The series was not a huge hit. It did well enough when it began, in a trial run as a midseason replacement, amusing enough viewers to get renewed for a second year. But ratings slipped in the second season, its first full year, and the pick up for a third season was late in coming. When the show was finally added back to the network schedule, the ratings had again dropped. *Greatest American Hero* was cancelled with some of its 13 final season episodes left unaired, including one written and directed by Culp. A total of 45 had been produced.

Even so, Culp had gained the attention of a new generation of TV viewers, many of whom had never even heard of Kelly Robinson. Culp was now Maxwell. Over the top. Funny.

This new Culp, the over-the-top-funny Culp, would also host *Saturday Night Live*.

Next up, Culp received second billing for playing a red herring, a suspected stalker and killer who turns out to really be one of the good guys, in *Killjoy*, a TV movie with a young Kim Bassinger.

In the mid- and late 1980s, Culp continued to work regularly, popping in and out of various network series as a guest star, and with prominent supporting roles in feature films.

Among his more interesting roles were two big screen appearances, first as a greedy politician in *Turk 182,* then a reporter, second in billing to Angie Dickinson, in *Big Bad Mama II.*

It had been a long time since *I Spy*.

But *I Spy* was about to come back and play a part in the actor/writer/director's life.

Bill Cosby

By 1972, Cosby had tried to make it on his own on television in a TV sitcom. It didn't click.

He had also returned to serious acting, with *To All My Friends on the Shore*, *Man and Boy*, and *Hickey & Boggs*. But few had noticed.

On TV, Cosby was still making money. He created and provided voices for a Saturday morning cartoon series entitled *Fat Albert and the Cosby Kids*.

In September of 1972, six months after *Man and Boy* failed to find an audience at the

27—The Second Reunion 395

Connie Selleca, William Katt and Robert Culp in *Greatest American Hero* (1982) (courtesy Image Entertainment).

box office, and as *Hickey & Boggs* was faltering, Cosby returned to prime-time television with a new venture, this time reprising the variety format that had brought him success with his NBC specials.

CBS was the taker. The hour-long series would be called *The New Bill Cosby Show*. It would get Cosby on the cover of *TV Guide* for a fifth time, the second time as a solo performer. But the series would fail, and was cancelled before the end of its first year, lasting on the air for only eight months.

Cosby was anxious to reclaim the success that was so suddenly eluding him. As 1974 came to a close, he would try for another chance on the big screen. This time he would focus on being funny. He had yet to do comedy for the movie houses.

In June 1974, Cosby's fortunes turned a sharp corner with *Uptown Saturday Night*, directed by and costarring Sidney Poitier.

The reviews were mixed, including *Variety*'s dismissal review of it as being "an uneven Black melodramatic comedy," that "too much of the time just lies there, impatiently waiting for more inventive comedy business and a zippier pace than the sober Poitier seems able to provide."

But the box office was good.

And Cosby received good notices. *Variety* wrote, "Cosby's prior film appearances have not capitalized on his richly amusing video-nitery personality, but his work here could be a real shot in the arm for a recently quiescent career."

A sequel was quickly arranged, and the appropriately titled *Let's Do It Again* found its way into movie houses in October 1975, on the same day that Culp's *Inside Out* opened.

While Culp's movie was ignored, Cosby's was an instant hit. And, this time, the reviews were better, including those from *Variety*. The trade magazine wrote, "The gang from *Uptown Saturday Night* encores successfully in *Let's Do It Again*, a funny, free-form farcical revue reminiscent in substance of classic Hal Roach comedy."

Complimenting Cosby, the paper noted that the comedian's "versatility herein seems as great as that of Peter Sellers."

Mother, Jugs and Speed, another comedy destined to do respectable business at the box office, came out the following year. For that movie, Cosby costarred with Raquel Welch, who had played opposite Robert Culp four years earlier in *Hannie Caulder*.

Variety was neutral in its review, neither praising the movie, nor attacking it. Leonard Maltin was more certain of his feelings concerning *Mother, Jugs and Speed*, declaring the movie to be a "hilarious Black comedy about a rundown ambulance service more interested in the number of patients serviced than their welfare."

The movie fared well.

Encouraged by his success on the big screen, Cosby tried his hand in another variety series, this time for ABC, this time called simply *Cos*. It was September of 1976. The series was off the schedule by November.

In 1977, Cosby returned to the big screen for yet another sequel to *Uptown Saturday Night*, the less-successful *A Piece of the Action*.

The reviews and the business were moderate.

In late 1977 Cosby went to work for Sheldon Leonard.

Catching Up with Sheldon Leonard

Three years after his luck had seemed to run out, Leonard attempted a return to weekly TV. It was in a role the former producer was familiar with, that of an actor.

The series was called *Big Eddie*. CBS gave it a try. Leonard starred, but did not produce. He played the title character, a reformed gambler who was trying his luck as the owner-promoter of New York's Big E Sports Arena.

Big Eddie was a big flop. It lasted on the air for three months.

For the next four years, Leonard made the rounds of TV panel shows and occasionally taking a guest spot on a sitcom.

During this time, Leonard also continued to try to get a project off the ground that would put him back into the producer's chair. One such project involved an unproduced *I Spy* script. It would have been a stand-out fourth season episode, had there been a fourth season.

Ron Jacobs: "Monica" was wonderful. Sheldon and I kept that script and tried to put it together as a little movie."[15]

The Jerry Ludwig script was a love story for Kelly, set in London, England. Leonard owned it. But, without the attachment of Robert Culp, there were no takers for "Monica."

Regardless, Leonard believed that *I Spy* was the most important series he had ever made. According to Earle Hagen, it was also the series Leonard was most proud of. *I Spy* was his greatest challenge as a producer, and the pinnacle of his success.

In the late 1970s, to no one's surprise, Leonard wanted to taste the glory of that ten-year-old series again. He first approached his friends and colleagues, former *I Spy* writers, Eric Bercovici and Jerry Ludwig.

Bercovici: "He basically pitched us *I Spy*. It was another buddy show. And I know Jerry and I thought it was sort of like *I Spy*. He wanted us to write it. And probably produce it. It was an awkward moment. We didn't know what to do with it."[16]

Bercovici and Ludwig turned the project down.

Ludwig: "I felt bad, because Sheldon had slipped into obscurity, and he was such a giant. He was a marvelous craftsman. I think *I Spy* was his favorite of them all."[17]

Bercovici: "But he didn't seem down on his luck. He was the usual Sheldon."[18]

And the usual Sheldon was determined. He was going to make this pilot, or some pilot, and it *would* bring back the *I Spy* formula, as well as the *I Spy* magic.

Top Secret would be the project.

Leonard connected with Cosby for the idea of a TV movie and possible series.

Top Secret would be Sheldon Leonard, Bill Cosby, location production, and a mix of humor and drama, all seamlessly woven within tales of espionage and intrigue.

In the tele-picture, which is mostly played straight, Cosby portrays a Military Intelligence agent who is sent to Italy to hunt for a shipment of nuclear material that was stolen from a U.S. base.

Cosby's wife in the movie is played by Gloria Foster, making her fourth appearance opposite the actor. His partner in espionage is a beautiful Black woman, well presented by Tracy Reed.

The location manager for the project was none other than Leon Chooluck.

Leonard would appear in the pilot himself, playing a cultured thug, a man of power and taste, capable of desperate behavior—not unlike Sorge, the character he brought to life in two episodes of *I Spy*.

But the pilot for *Top Secret* was stillborn when it aired in June of 1978.

The *I Spy* formula was incomplete—and it showed.

By the start of the 1980s, it appeared Leonard, as a producer, was down for the count.

Bill Cosby, King of Television

The 1980s were kinder to Bill Cosby.

The Cosby Show, not to be confused with *The Bill Cosby Show* from the late 1960s, or *The New Bill Cosby Show*, from the early 1970s, or *Cos*, from the late 1970s, was an immediate and major hit. For its first season, it placed at number three in the Nielsens. By year two, it was firmly planted at number one and would remain there for most of its eight-year run.

Also, for year one, it picked up the Emmy for Outstanding Comedy Series, as well as two more Emmy Awards for Outstanding Direction in a Comedy Series and Outstanding Writing in a Comedy Series.

Cosby himself lost out to Robert Guillaume of *Benson*.

It didn't matter. The series had a hell of a start.

For the new show, Cosby played Dr. Heathcliff Huxtable, an obstetrician who lives and maintains an office in a New York City brownstone. The gentle yet hip family comedy dealt primarily with that—the family.

By the second year, *The Cosby Show* had became so popular that it pulled NBC out of the ratings cellar and helped to place the network back in the top spot. And it did one other thing, it brought about a reunion with Robert Culp, the first of three to happen between 1987 and 1999.

The episode was entitled "Bald and Beautiful," and aired on NBC on April 9, 1987. For his appearance, Culp played an old friend of Cliff's, who drops in for a visit. In a wink to fans of *I Spy*, the character's name was Scott Kelly.

With *The Cosby Show*, Bill Cosby gained entertainment capital that far exceeded what he had experienced during his *I Spy* days. Now he was a producer as well as a star.

One of his projects would be a spin-off from *The Cosby Show*, a series called *A Different World*. NBC was happy to have a second series under the Cosby banner.

Two was a charm, but three might prove to be a crowd.

Culp: "You have no idea how many times Bill has tried to help me with projects. In '85 or '86, when his show was certified a hit—a smash number one—Bill called me on the phone and said, 'What do you want to do?' And I said, 'What do you mean?' And he said, 'I'm an eight-hundred pound gorilla, so what do you want to do?' And I said, 'Oh, you mean a series?'

"He tried to help me get on something I wanted to do that was an hour-long. And we danced around quite a while, but it never happened."[19]

Culp felt responsible. Perhaps his ideas for a series weren't good enough for NBC. Cosby would not let his friend believe this.

Culp: "Bill said, 'Sometimes I think that I hurt people that I'm trying to help—hurt them more than I can help them. Sometimes it gets to be a disservice to the project—not just you—but other people, as well. My efforts fail when it should, otherwise, be fine.'

"It's always bothered him. And he has tried to help me, many times, with many different projects. It's just the luck of the draw.

"I do know as a fact that [Brandon] Tartikoff [president of NBC's entertainment division] said, because there was *The Cosby Show*, and *A Different World*, that if he put one more show by Cosby on NBC, that NBC stand for the National Broadcasting Company of Cosby. They didn't want to give him that much power, because, at that point, Bill was talking about buying the network. And he was serious about it. I called him and asked him. And he said, 'That's serious money, you bet I'm serious.'"[20]

As it turned out, Cosby would pass on buying NBC. The network, instead, was sold to General Electric.

While on hiatus from his series, and away from NBC, Cosby was back in front of the cameras for a big screen feature entitled *Leonard Part 6*, with a second film, *Ghost Dad*, to begin production the following year with Sidney Poitier in the director's chair. Both were expected to do big business, for Columbia/Tri-Star and Universal, respectively. A third studio, Warner Brothers, wanted a piece of Bill Cosby for themselves and came to the television superstar with a proposal. They wanted Cosby to consider making a big screen version of *I Spy*.

I Spy: The Movie, *Written and Directed by Robert Culp*

That was how it would read.

Warner Brothers had acquired the rights for *I Spy* from Sheldon Leonard, who was now shut out by an industry he once dominated. Leonard relented and accepted an option offer on the title and concept of the series he had brought into the world. Warner Brothers wanted to bring it back as a feature film, but they didn't want him. It was all about Cosby. The studio was certain that their idea for a Cosby feature film would far surpass the other two studios' projects. And Cosby was interested, with one condition:

"If Warner Brothers want Culp and Cosby, they can have Culp and Cosby, but only if Culp directs and edits."[21]

That was the response Cosby gave, the words Culp vividly remembers reading in a trade magazine by Hollywood columnist Army Archerd. It was the first he had heard of it.

Culp: "They didn't want Culp, they wanted Cosby. But, when he made that statement to the press, he put *my* name first."[22]

Cosby made sure Warner Brothers understood, when it came to *I Spy*, it wasn't just about Cosby. It was Culp *and* Cosby, in that order, just as it had always been.

By stating that Culp would also edit, Cosby was telling Warner Brothers that Culp was going to have final cut, a commodity studios are very reluctant to give away to any director, especially a director not on their "A" list.

The idea of having Bill Cosby in 1989, at the peak of his television comeback, in a big screen version of the series that started it all for him, was too tempting for Warner Brothers to resist. They agreed to Cosby's terms. Robert Culp would costar in the movie with Cosby. He would direct and he would also write the screenplay.

Culp: "I dealt with two guys, Mark Canton and a guy who worked for him, Bill Gerber. Gerber was smart as hell. We never had a dispute, not on material, not on anything. I sold them my pitch on what to do with *I Spy*. To keep Cosby, Canton's job was to smile as white as he could and say 'Yeah.' And he did."[23]

So Culp went to work. His script, simply titled "*I Spy*," involved the reactivation of former agent Alexander Scott. Kelly is in trouble. He appears to be involved in covert operations for the other side. An order to terminate him may be put out if Scott isn't able to make contact and clear his former partner's name.

Scott, now a college professor, has been away from the spy game for 20 years. Moreover, he hasn't had contact with Kelly for nearly as long. The two men, who once appeared inseparable, *did* separate, but not under good terms. Kelly didn't appreciate Scott's desire to leave the service and end their partnership. And, as we all know, Kelly does not take rejection well.

Scott, not able to turn his back on his friend, resumes his espionage duties, finding his former partner and traveling with him to India in search of the answers that will expose the true traitor.

Along the way, we meet one other familiar face, Jimmy, their helpful, double-dealing supplier from Hong Kong. Jimmy, who was played by Japanese actor Mako, was first seen in the Culp written episode, "The Loser." Friedkin and Fine placed Jimmy in a second episode, "No Exchange on Damaged Merchandise."

In the 1989 screenplay, Jimmy plays a major role.

Another lead character is Genet, a lovely woman of 20, part Asian, part Caucasian. It will be discovered that she is Kelly's daughter—with Sam MacLean, the woman who left him in 1967 in the episode "Magic Mirror." Sam had been played in two episodes from the series by France Nuyen.

The antagonist in the story, the man behind the attempt to frame Kelly, is Cochran, a former company man who oversaw the training of Kelly and Scott.

While not as strong as some of Culp's other works for *I Spy*, the script is nonetheless an effective reteaming of Kelly and Scott, and would have pleased many fans from the original series.

But it did not please Warner Brothers.

Culp admits that he struggled with the script.

Culp: "I was trying to write this thing the same way I had written the best of my *I Spys*, by the seat of my pants. Well, this is not a one-hour episode, where, if you've got one good scene, you got it. This is a feature film. The rules are different."[24]

As Culp was attempting to find his way through the script, the time allotted for writing the first draft had ended.

A deadline is a word with an appropriate name and meaning. Miss it, and your career may very well be dead.

Culp turned in his first draft.

Culp: "I handed in something that wasn't ready."[25]

Believing it would take the studio time to tear apart the script, Culp flew to India to hook up with his son, Josh, who had been scouting locations.

Culp: "No sooner do I arrive there and Gerber calls to say, 'We've read the material and probably the best thing to do is to get on a plane and come home.' I asked him if he was ordering me to come back. He said 'no, it wasn't an order,' then he repeated that 'it would just be best' for me to do as he suggested."[26]

Culp knew what this meant. As a writer, he had failed to please Warner Brothers. The tone of Gerber's voice on the phone made that very clear. He was being called in on the carpet, and it would be a long journey home.

Culp: "So I got on a plane and came home. God, it was awful.

"It took me forever to finally solve the problem with the script. And, during all this, along comes the longest writers strike in the history of the business—eight months! It was a horrible hardship on everybody."[27]

The Warner heads who had given the project a green light were now having second thoughts.

Leonard Part 6, the first movie to put Bill Cosby in a lead in nearly 20 years, had been released, and it was not being well received by the critics, or the public, or even by Cosby himself.

The story, like the intended *I Spy* movie, had Cosby playing a former spy who comes out of retirement, this time to take on a rogue group that is knocking off the government's top-secret agents. According to film critic Leonard Maltin, "Even Cosby, who received story and producer credits with the film, warned audiences to stay away from this megabomb."

Tri-Star lost a bundle. Warner Brothers was worried.

When the writers strike finally ended, Culp was asked to bring in another writer to help him with the script.

Culp: "They left it up to me. I interviewed other writers, hired one, and then went to work on another version. The other guy would fail, then another would be hired, and he would fail. This went on for almost a year. I knew what to do with the script, I knew what the elements should be, but I couldn't line up my ducks. I couldn't get that one great idea that drives everything else. So I finally wound up with what would be the final draft—but that was too late."[28]

Culp sent in the script he felt would be good enough, and then waited for notes. They never came.

Culp: "No one wanted to talk to me at this point. But it was all my fault. I couldn't solve the problems, and I couldn't get anybody to tell me the one thing I needed to know—to keep it cheap. If anybody had said that, I would have said, 'Oh, you mean like the TV series. And I would have found a way to do it.

"I had a vision of enormous grandeur. I had a good enough story; some good scenes, maybe not great, but good solid stuff. And I had fascinating visuals. But I don't think that anyone at Warner Brothers ever read that final script. Everything was blocked. Nothing was going to happen. And I realized that this picture wasn't going to get made."[29]

As the Warner Brothers deal unraveled, Culp was carrying a great weight. It was his script, his budget, his vision, and it had taken longer than originally expected. He had let his friend and partner down.

But Bill Cosby stepped in to share the blame.

Culp: "Bill said to me, after it was all over and done with, 'It wasn't you. It wasn't your fault. It was my fault, because of those two pictures. They don't want to talk to either one of us anymore.'"[30]

The second picture Cosby referred to was *Ghost Dad*, the movie he was shooting as Culp was laboring on the *I Spy* script.

Culp: "*Ghost Dad* comes out and it tanks in exactly the same manner [as] *Leonard Part 6* did. Seriously tanks. Death, on the first weekend."[31]

That was Universal's problem. Warner Brothers made their decision. The *I Spy* movie was off.

28

The Third Reunion

In 1992, after eight seasons, many of which were spent at the top of the ratings, *The Cosby Show* left NBC. Still a major hit, and easily the most successful series of the previous decade, it ended by Cosby's own decision.

Cosby was aching to do something new, and something with more serious content.

At the time he left his successful comedy series, Cosby was quoted as saying that *I Spy* was the best and most important work of his life. He wanted to recapture that. And so, in 1993, a new project was put into development for NBC, a two-hour movie that could be spun off into a series—*The Cosby Mysteries*.

Cosby would play Gary Hanks, a criminologist with the New York Police Department, who retires after he wins a large sum of money in the state lottery. Often bored with early retirement, Hanks continues to dabble in the art of solving crimes, coming to the aid of Detective Adam Sully, a friend and former colleague.

The tone of the movie, and the proposed series, would be as *I Spy* was, a mix of comedy, drama, and intrigue.

The pilot was well received by the network and was given the green light to begin as a one-hour series in September 1994.

Meanwhile, the 1990s continued to provide work for Robert Culp, but more often than not, it was just that—merely work. Culp would pop up as a guest performer on various television series, like *Murder, She Wrote*, *Matlock* and *Dr. Quinn, Medicine Woman*.

Culp had recently turned 60, and the acting roles that challenged him artistically, or paid him handsomely, and the offers that gave him hope as a writer and director, were now eluding him.

As it had happened in the past, when a much younger but equally frustrated Robert Culp wrote a TV pilot called *Danny Doyle*, it would now be up to him to write a role for himself that would create the potential for a show business future.

There was only one place to go, and it was the same place that *Danny Doyle* had lead him nearly 30 years earlier: *I Spy*.

Culp: "Warren Littlefield, who was running NBC, got the idea of doing an *I Spy* reunion movie. He talked to Bill, and Bill mentioned it to me. I said, 'Hell, yes, let's get the rights from Sheldon.'"[1]

Culp remembered Cosby snickering, as he would in his comedy routines when imitating himself as a mischievous boy leading a younger brother named Russell into trouble with their humorless dad.

Culp: "Bill said, 'Go ahead. I'll back you up. Really.'

"I said, 'Come on, you can make the call.'

"He said, 'Nah, you do it.'

"So I went to Sheldon, to his house, and he walked me through the living room, and he said, 'You were married in that room.'

28—The Third Reunion

"I said, before he could even finish getting it out of his mouth, 'Don't remind me!'"[2]

It had been a long time since Culp had been a visitor in Leonard's home. That day in December 1967 was the last time. A lot of water had run under the bridge since then. Raging water.

Culp: "We sat outside and I said, 'This is what I want.' And he said, 'Let me think about it.' And the next thing I knew, he had gone to NBC."[3]

Leonard had been retired for over ten years, reluctantly. Culp, the man who, in 1964, had brought Leonard the first glimpse of an idea that inspired his greater vision for *I Spy*, had done it again. There was a bigger opportunity here. Not just for a one-shot TV reunion movie, but for a whole new series. A brand new *I Spy*.

Culp: "Bill said, 'You woke up a sleeping giant.' And that's exactly what happened."[4]

Leonard pitched his idea to NBC. Culp and Cosby would reprise their roles as Robinson and Scott. Leonard would produce. But there would be two new cast members, new blood to mix with the old: a daughter and a son. The reunion of an old generation would give birth to the future of a new one. The offspring would become the new team, one White, one Black. Period. One male, one female. Period. And, of course, there would be the expected sexual tension between them. In other words, conflict. Period.

Leonard understood the formula for success: Conflict, romance, humor, action, all staged in front of an international backdrop.

Littlefield didn't like it. *The Cosby Mysteries* was a go, so NBC had no use for a weekly dose of *I Spy*. It would have to remain a one-shot deal.

Leonard disagreed. He had taken *I Spy* away from NBC once before—and he would do it again.

The next thing Culp knew, Leonard had arranged a deal with CBS to back the project. It would air in the 1993–94 season as a big-event TV movie.

Culp: "Littlefield threw up a hell of a stink when NBC didn't get it.

"CBS then came to me. They wanted to see if I was going to do it. I said, 'Yes—as long as I get to write.'"[5]

Culp didn't trust anyone else to write for him and Cosby.

Culp: "CBS said okay. So I sat down and started to write. But Sheldon was writing behind me—with somebody else."[6]

Leonard was also determined. This movie would serve as a springboard to a new television series, and he was convinced that Culp was not the writer for the job.

In Leonard's mind, when it came to weekly television, writers write, directors direct, and actors act. Attempting to wear more than one hat at any one time was not conducive to a smooth-running operation.

That opinion had always been one of the main differences between Leonard and Culp. It was the greatest obstacle in their working together with any real harmony. They were from different schools of thought, different generations, and had different temperaments. Neither one had ever found the words to communicate with the other.

Even so, Culp believed it would be a fair competition to find the best material.

Culp: "I got a good amount to write this, almost a hundred G's, and the other guy got paid well, too. It was a contest, I thought. But I also knew it *wasn't* a contest, because I knew what Sheldon could do, or couldn't do. And I knew I'd beat him. I can't tell you how angry I was when I realized that what he had said to the network was, 'If you pick Culp's script over mine, I'll pull the plug.'"[7]

Leonard had the trump card: *I Spy* belonged to him. The irony, and the heartache, was that Culp had written an exceptional script, as good as the best he had ever produced for *I Spy*. It was also far superior than the script that came from Leonard.

Culp: "They picked Sheldon's. Nobody even read my script. It was a done deal. That was it. We were stuck with it."[8]

In *I Spy—The Movie*, as Culp named the project, the writer in him was at the top of his game.

The cleverness began on page one.

The script read:

"As we Fade Up to the Original Music Sting and Main Titles, as they first appeared in 1965 and in every rerun since ... Sheldon Leonard Presents ... *I Spy* ... Bill Cosby ... Robert Culp ... exactly the same..."[9]

But it wasn't exactly the same. Culp was now giving Cosby top billing. Yet he was the one who wrote "exactly the same," as if he hadn't seen what he had just done, as if it was merely a reflex to introduce his other self first.

The story opens with Gabe—the same Gabe we met in Culp's *Danny Doyle* pilot script, which was then rewritten into "The Tiger." He was Colonel Gabe Wise then, and he was still named that when Culp brought him back for "Magic Mirror," when Ken Tobey took over playing the part.

Now, in Culp's new script, someone is trying to kill Gabe—and, a short while later, also tries to take out Scott.

Scott, a widower and a college professor residing in Philadelphia, is nearly killed. He barely escapes. Next someone tries to eliminate Kelly, who now makes his living as a consultant in the designing of high-end security systems.

Gabe contacts Kelly and Scott, tying them all together by a three-way conference call. The two men have not talked since 1971 when Scott quit the service.

Gabe warns Kelly and Scott that they, as well as himself, have been placed on a hit list and that they need to converge in Washington, D.C. to watch one another's backs. Gabe also tells them there is a fourth name on the list. But Gabe is killed in a violent explosion before divulging who. The line goes dead.

Kelly hops on a plane for Washington. Scott borrows a car belonging to one of his two adult daughters. In an emotional scene, he reveals the truth about his past to his girls, a truth his departed wife never wanted them to know. He tells them to wait a couple of days and then report the car stolen.

The smart and fast-paced script glides along as Kelly lands in Washington, only to be met by agents of Military Intelligence. One is a fan, having viewed many training films featuring the legendary Kelly Robinson and Alexander Scott. He knows about all their cases, all the women, all the close calls, and even all the famous locked rooms.

This clever device allows a character within the story to see Kelly and Scott in much the same way the television viewing audience would, as celebrity icons from the 1960s.

But not all the "spooks" from the department feel the same way. Times have changed, and nobody trusts anybody else, especially these "two flower power rejects," as one cynical agent refers to them.

The reason for Gabe's death, and the attempts on Kelly and Scott's lives, is soon revealed. A former agent, Walter Bishop, who was presumed dead, is alive and threatening to talk about things best kept secret. Bishop was a player in a cover-up, code named "Iran-gate," and what he knows can topple some very powerful people in Washington. Bishop is an old-school agent, and was even the man who first brought Kelly and Scott together. He has now named them, as he had also named Gabe, as being the only ones he would trust enough to talk to. Thanks to his faith in Kelly and Scott, they are now "moving targets."

Kelly and Scott, along with the young agent/fan travel to Eastern Europe in search of

Bishop. They find him, along with his confederates, hiding out in an old castle—something right out of *Dracula*.

Once there, in an effort to rescue Bishop, they are double-crossed by their former colleague. Thinking Bishop is inside a dungeon cell, after hearing him call out, they enter, and then are imprisoned. You guessed it: in a locked room.

The dialogue written by Culp is priceless, beginning as Kelly and Scott helplessly watch as their captors slap mortar and bricks into place, swiftly walling up the cell, sealing them in forever. Scott speaks first:

"If you're going to sit there and pout, you can leave any time. I won't be offended."

"Just let me get one thing straight, Stanley," Kelly says, "He WAS here. You didn't make that up?"

"I didn't make it up," Scott answers. "He was here."

"Thank you."

"Unless we're both nuts," Scott finishes.

"No, that doesn't happen for another five or six minutes," Kelly adds.

Kelly becomes frustrated, remembering when his cell phone was taken from him before they entered into the room to meet with Bishop. Now he knows why. They were walking into a trap.

"I should have known when the guy took my telephone," Kelly says. "Didn't you think that was strange?"

"I should have known when my car blew up and all of a sudden we're running around like the last twenty-five years never happened. THAT was strange."

"Oh, it's all my fault for bringing a little excitement into your dull, boring life."

"Well, it was boring, but it wasn't OVER!"

"At least we're talking," Kelly says.

"We haven't talked yet," Scott answers back. "Gabe said we had to bury the hatchet, maybe he was right."

Kelly clears his throat. "You want to go first? Because ... I never really had a problem."

"NOW who's in denial?"

"Okay. Oh, boy. Okay. Well, let's see ... *You* quit *me*."

"I quit the SERVICE, Kel."

"Because I thought the War was okay, and you knew damn well it wasn't," Kelly says, referring to Vietnam. "You might have told me."

"I did! Repeatedly!"

"By the time I figured it out, you were long gone," Kelly says, "And, I was so embarrassed, I couldn't call you. Lap-dissolve twenty-five years!"

"There was more to it than that," Scott says, preparing to take a load of weight off Kelly's shoulders. "Why didn't *I* call YOU?"

Kelly doesn't know how to answer that, so Scott does it for him.

"We only fought one time. Once. Over nothing. Remember?"

"Hah!" Kelly responds, remembering. "Tokyo hotel room, oh yes."

The reference is to the brutal fight from "Tatia." Any fan of *I Spy* would know this. And the dialogue in this script proves that Robert Culp, as much as anyone else, was a fan.

The scene continues:

Scott says, "I couldn't stand up for a week. You said, 'What in the world happened?'"

"And you said, 'Nothing. That's the way brothers do it.'"

"You never had any, but I did," Scott adds, "And that's what happens. When you got mad at me, I got mad at YOU—for being mad at ME."

"Who's on first?" Kelly adds.

"What's on second?" Scott instantly responds. "Anyway, it was fifty-fifty."

And there was Culp's statement. It was 50/50. It was the way he went into *I Spy*, and the way he wanted to leave it.

Leonard remembered the episode "Tatia," too. He liked the fight in the Tokyo hotel room equally as much—but for different reasons. It gave the episode conflict, something his instincts always told him a TV show needed.

Leonard was right, conflict is an important element to any good drama, and even to any good comedy. His gut told him Kelly and Scott needed more of it, something he felt Culp and Cosby were taking away from the show by talking alike, acting alike, thinking alike.

Conflict. A difference in personalities. It worked in Leonard's other triumphs.

Sheriff Andy Taylor was certainly cooler headed than high-strung deputy Barney Fife; Hot-headed marine Sgt. Carter had plenty of opportunity to yell at his hillbilly recruit, Gomer Pyle; Buddy Sorrell certainly liked to sling bald jokes at Mel Cooley, and Mel would always respond by summing up his feelings for Buddy with a simple, "Yuck"; and Rob Petrie loved to throw darts at a picture of his boss, the egotistical Alan Brady.

By the numbers, by the rules, and it all worked beautifully.

But *I Spy* broke the rules and played by its own numbers.

Culp and Cosby liked the fight scene from "Tatia," not because it had conflict, but because it defined who they were—two brothers.

Now, a quarter of a century later, Robert Culp's script for the television reunion movie was a true love letter—not just to Cosby—but to the fans of the series—and to Sheldon Leonard. That one scene in the locked room, if nothing else, spoke directly about the stubbornness of two men who could let 25 years slip by without talking—and all because they were that close.

It might have helped if Leonard had read it.

It might have helped Culp to know he had read it.

If produced, this "lost episode" of *I Spy* would have been a remarkable achievement.

But, in the end, Cosby was the only one who did read it.

Leonard wouldn't. And Leonard made sure no one at CBS would either.

Culp: "Now Bill calls me from New York. He had read mine, and he had read Sheldon's. And that's when he says, 'Well, what do you want to do?' And I said, 'I don't know. I just don't know. I don't want to do *this*.'

"Now mind you, Bill is a billionaire at this point. A kid from the projects in Philadelphia. He's done all that. And I'm in trouble—because I'm seven years older and life's closing down. And this is a lot of money. So Bill says, 'Why don't you come back to New York. We'll have dinner and talk.'

"I know what he wanted me to do. He wanted me to turn it down. He never said so, but I'm positive that's what he wanted. But he also wanted to hear it from me. And I wanted so desperately to tell Sheldon to take a leap. But I couldn't do that. It was just too much money."[10]

Culp had another job offer at this time, a role in a major motion picture. He would play the president of the United States in *The Pelican Brief*, starring Julia Roberts and Denzel Washington. It was a good part, the best that had come his way in several years. But Culp needed more than one good job for 1993.

Culp: "I looked at Bill and said, 'If we can bring this off, it will be a huge year for me, better than any year in the last several, and there might be something really good to come out of it. Two high profile performances in a single year ain't bad for a senior citizen.'"[11]

Culp had chosen the words. A senior citizen. That much time had slipped by. And he knew that television and motion pictures were now obsessed with youth.

Culp: "I said, 'I don't think I can turn this down. I think I should do it.' And Bill said, 'Okay.'

"He wasn't going to say 'no' to Sheldon, and he wasn't going to say 'no' to me. He was stuck."[12]

Hilly Elkins, Culp's longtime friend and manager, echoes Culp's feelings on the subject. "Bill is a very loyal man. He never forgets. And he would never forget Bob."[13]

Just as Cosby would never forget Sheldon Leonard, he would never forget *I Spy*.

Culp: "Bill could survive it. He could survive anything. But he knew what the price of tomatoes was, and that we were taking a risk in regard to *I Spy*. This picture could have gone much further south than it did. If either one of us had given up for a second in the middle, the whole thing would have been an utter debacle."[14]

So Culp and Cosby began production, much as they had when they were making the series, looking for ways to add to the script, to discover what each individual scene "was about" and to find a way to realize the intent of the writer. And that meant ad-libbing.

Cast of *I Spy Returns* (1993)—Salli Richardson, Robert Culp, Bill Cosby and George Newbern (© 3 F Prod., courtesy Peter Rogers Organization).

I Spy Returns could have been titled *Sheldon Leonard Returns*, that's how much the project represented to him. And Leonard was willing to let this be his comeback project, or his swan song. Either way, it was going to be done on his terms.

Leonard's idea was to introduce a second generation of spies: Scott's daughter and Kelly's son.

CBS gave it a green light.

Leonard's second idea was to have an Oscar-winning screenwriter with a flair for bright dialogue, and an ability to handle the tough mix of comedy and action, do the script. He gave the young network development executives the name of the writer.

The red light went on. And then the former TV mogul was told: "No. He's not acceptable. He's not on our list of acceptable writers."[15]

Leonard suggested a second writer, and then a third. All were not on "the list."

Leonard's reaction was to tell the CBS execs, "Then I'm not on your list either."[16]

And then he walked.

It took a phone call from Bill Cosby to put the two parties back together again.

A compromise was made. A writer was hired.

After submitting the second draft, Leonard received a seven-page memo from CBS. The first two pages dealt with the philosophy of drama and the character relationship between Scott and Kelly.

According to Leonard, this portion of the communiqué began: "Our audience has considerable expectations of these men—Scott and Kelly were the first fully-grown, masculine team of their era. They created the modern Buddy Movie concept. They were funniest when the situation was bleakest. Use this irony more in our script. Let's not sell our guys short. They can be silly, over-concerned, even over-the-hill. But where is their genuine growth? Where is that moment between them? How has the world changed for them? There is no triumph, finally. No tragedy. No gain. No loss. No coming together, not in any meaningful sense."[17]

This came from the network. It had come first from Robert Culp in 1965.

Sheldon Leonard did not appreciate it—not in 1965, not in '66, not in '67. And he didn't appreciate it in 1993, either.

Leonard replied to the network notes by saying, "I did not understand what was meant by 'genuine growth.' What growth? Physical? Intellectual? Financial? Political? Who cares how the world has changed for them? And what is meant by 'no tragedy, no pain, no coming together?' In fact, 'What the hell does the whole paragraph mean?'"[18]

Once again, it came down to two opposing schools of thought. Many people prefer not to be challenged by the television they watch. Some of the most popular and classic shows of all time never took chances. They played it safe. And, on occasion, *I Spy* would be that show. Then there are others, like the executive at CBS who gave Leonard feedback on the script, and Culp and Cosby, who preferred stories and characters that made a statement. And often *I Spy* would be that show, too.

Leonard complained how another network note on his script read, "Though we seem to approach it, we never feel a sense of real danger, real jeopardy."[19]

The mogul responded, "The writer of the note either never saw any of the original *I Spy*s, or did not appreciate their scrupulously maintained tone. The series was basically tongue-in-cheek. My reply [to CBS] concluded, 'Though I have been assured by my associates that the network requests are usually negotiable, I must make it plain that, in defense of a valuable property, my position is not.'"[20]

Next Leonard recommended a director for the assignment. All of his suggestions were rejected, regardless of how talented the directors were, or how he felt they were right for the job.

Leonard: "No matter how they danced around the subject, it was clear that the directors I suggested were rejected by the network because they were too old."[21]

There was a time in Hollywood when most producers had grey hair, and they were free to hire whomever they wished. Leonard found out that that time had passed.

Leonard: "It is an inescapable fact that, for some years, all three networks have been obsessed with the pursuit of a young audience. To that end, they have been favoring youth over experience in the selection of writers, directors and other key personnel."[22]

Even in the area of casting, Leonard found obstacles at every turn with the network.

Leonard: "Take the matter of Baroodi, the heavy in our picture. There is a scene in which Scott and Kelly force Baroodi out into the crowded lobby of a Viennese hotel—naked! The actor I wanted for the part is talented, experienced AND fat. I cherished the idea of a naked fat man scrambling around a crowded hotel lobby! The network said no. We were already in production. Days went by as I wrestled with the network people. We got closer and closer to the time when I had to release Cosby. Finally, I said, 'The hell with it.' I settled for a talented THIN actor."[23]

Leonard's battles were not with the network alone. Culp and Cosby, although attempting to keep quiet, were unhappy with the material and the direction the project was taking.

Culp: "We liked those two kids in the movie, both me and Bill. They were good actors, and wonderful people. But it wasn't the way to go."[24]

Friedkin and Fine did not live to see *I Spy Returns*. But David Freidkin's son, Gregory, believes he knows what his father and his father's partner would have said about it.

Gregory Friedkin: "*I Spy* was a hit because it was buddy-buddy. Then, in the TV movie, you have a daughter. It can't be buddy-buddy that way. It was totally the opposite of what Culp and Cosby had created. They should have had two sons, or two daughters. Then it could really be buddy-buddy. The movie violated the basic premise of the show: Both of them were single men."[25]

The best moments in the reunion movie, in Culp's opinion, were the ones that he and Cosby invented, as their personalities blended once more before the cameras.

Culp: "When we enter the grounds of the mansion, and I start to climb the gate, Bill just lifts the latch and lets the gate swing open—with me still on it. That was one. And then there was the scene, after Scott is kicked in the groin, where Bill sits in a tub of ice and I say, 'Just what I need for a partner, a fat man in a bucket.' That was Bill's line. He gave that to me."[26]

But his fondest memory of the changes he and Cosby made to the script involve the end of the story.

Culp: "As it was, Sheldon stuck around, primarily because he didn't trust me—until the last 48 hours. That's when he split and went home. He wasn't feeling good. I went into Bill's hotel room the night before and said, 'Take a look at this, I've written a new scene to take the place of the one we're supposed to shoot tomorrow—that horrible, unplayable scene Sheldon had written. It's the last scene between you and me.'"[27]

Culp described the existing scene as a bit of sentimental fluff where he was to say "thank-you" to Bill over and over again.

Culp: "It was as if Sheldon was saying 'thank-you' to Bill, and he was rubbing my nose in that concept. Once I perceived that, whether it was conscious or not on Sheldon's part—and Sheldon didn't do very many things that weren't conscious—I said, 'I'm not doing it, no matter what.'"[28]

Culp admits that the scene he wrote was a takeoff of the final moments in *Gunga Din*, which he also shared with Cosby.

Culp: "I told him, 'That's perfectly legitimate, we've stolen from the best in the

Culp & Cosby, ad-libbing again, *I Spy Returns*, 1993 (© 3 F Prod., courtesy Peter Rogers Organization).

past, so why not now?' So he looks at it and I remember him saying, 'Yes, I'm ready to do this.'"[29]

By agreeing to do it, by saying he was "ready," Cosby knew what the ramifications would be. But he also knew the importance in doing what he and Culp were planning. *I Spy* was their child too.

Culp: "Bill said, 'I should tell you this, because I've already shot the last scene to the movie, and you weren't in it. In the scene, my wife says to me, 'Do you miss it?' And I say, 'No, not really.' Then, the moment she leaves the room, and leaves me alone, I say, 'I only miss him.' And that wasn't in the script."[30]

Cosby had rewritten the final scene in the movie, without Leonard knowing. And now Culp had rewritten the second to last scene, again without the consent or knowledge of the owner of *I Spy*.

Culp: "So we did it. We laid the scene I had written on the director in the morning, and he didn't say a word, because he hated the other scene, too. Whatever it was, was going to be an improvement."[31]

But it didn't go the way Culp had envisioned.

Culp: "The scene was predicated on my breaking down. And I never could do it. I talked to myself, worked myself into a situation where I had to deliver the goods, but it took so much out of me to do it, that I couldn't free up enough to go to where the actor needed to go. And I never could get it. My own scene, for Christ's sakes. It was there, but I couldn't uncork it. So what you get is less strong from Kelly than it was supposed to be. It doesn't matter. The point is made. It's just that I didn't break up the way that I wanted to. I wish I could have, because I knew I was never going to see him again."[32]

The movie had been improved. The final moments, along with bits and pieces of inspired humor and prime examples of the Culp/Cosby "blendship" along the way, make *I Spy Returns* a worthwhile final visit, even with its flaws.

Back in Los Angeles, Leonard viewed the footage from Vienna. He saw the changes. And then, the man who said of himself, "I was never known for diplomacy," wrote a letter to Robert Culp.

Culp: "We come back to the United States, and I get a letter from Sheldon. He unloaded this avalanche of anger on me for having ruined his piece. Sheldon said, 'You left me with no ending'—which *wasn't true*. It just plain wasn't true. We *gave* him an ending."[33]

But it was not the ending Leonard wanted. It didn't convey a personal message of love to Bill Cosby from Sheldon Leonard, nor did it leave an obvious door open for more appearances in the new series by Culp and Cosby, should the new series come about. In Leonard's script, Scott doesn't walk away. Instead, he signs on to work further with Kelly.

In Culp's version, Scott makes it clear he will never again return.

The fight continued as the movie shifted into the postproduction phase. Leonard wanted Earle Hagen to compose the score and conduct the orchestra, just as he had done for the original series. But CBS didn't want to pay for an orchestra. The music would have to be performed electronically.

Earle Hagen turned the job down.

Hagen: "When it came out, there was a review in *People* magazine and I remember the last line: 'There is a tinny synthesizer arrangement to Earle Hagen's once exciting theme.' Sheldon called and said, 'Did you see the review in *People?* You're probably going to take that as a compliment.' And I said, 'You bet your ass I am.'

"He had lost the one thing he had never wanted to give up, which was creative control. He was disappointed. But he had this tremendous desire to get back on the heat, because he had been quiet for a long time. At one point, he was the most successful director/producer in the business. Being out of action was hard for him. He gave up a lot to get back in. And the condition of his deal was, that if *I Spy Returns* was successful, it would be a series—the son of *I Spy*. He wanted that. He wanted to be back in action. I didn't."[34]

CBS postponed airing Sheldon's comeback vehicle. On November 12, 1993, for his *Dailey Variety* column, Army Archerd asked: "What happened to the two-hour CBS *I Spy Returns?* The Sheldon Leonard production was rushed into readiness for the end of August, as they were told the show would air in September. Nothing happened. Then it was skedded for November sweeps. And nothing happened. Word from CBS was that the show was 'a gem.' According to Leonard, they would be interested in 'Spy' sequels. So what's happening with CBS? Jeff Sagansky says the show will positively air in January. He tells me, 'It's a terrific picture and we hope they keep doing it for us—one a year."

CBS was putting on a good front.

I Spy Returns aired on CBS on Monday, January 31, 1994. While not as satisfying as the best of the 1960s series, or even the mere average, it does, at least, play better than the worst episodes from the original 82.

Even Sheldon Leonard admitted, "With all [the compromises], the picture came out well."[35]

Variety, February 3rd: "Look and feel of *I Spy Returns* is comfortable and appealing echo of original vintage comedy-action series, updated with some '90's technology and attitude. Plot's okay, but the main thrust is on relationships between the Robinsons and Scotts, in all possible combinations. Not surprisingly, Culp and Cosby take charge here, bantering seemingly improvised dialogue, like a loving but scrappy old married couple."

Chicago Tribune TV Week, January 30th: "*Lethal Weapon's* Mel Gibson and Danny Glover owe a lot of thanks to Robert Culp. Twenty-eight years ago, Culp elevated Bill Cosby to his partner in a new series called *I Spy*, and thus introduced racial balance to mainstream entertainment. (But) according to Culp, further *I Spy* movies are unlikely."

Culp: "It ended that way between me and Sheldon. Candace, my wife for the last 22 years, was always after me to try to make up with him. She'd say, 'You can't carry this shit around with you your entire life. It just doesn't make sense.' And I'd say, 'I would make up with him if I knew where to start.' I have as much respect and love, in my own way, for Sheldon as anyone else does. It's just that when he's impossible, he's *really impossible*. And why can't anyone get that, and stop playing lip-service to a lot of bullshit?!"[36]

And then, one day, two years after the filming of *I Spy Returns*, an opportunity to make up presented itself. There was a tribute dinner at the Directors Guild of America (DGA) for Leonard. Culp, a card-carrying member of the DGA, was on the invite list. More so, he would be one of the speakers.

Andrea Bershad: "My mother had a stroke in 1991, and my dad never really wanted to acknowledge that. She was badly brain-damaged. She was paralyzed on her left side, and she was incontinent. Her awareness was only what was right in front of her. But he made sure she went to every black-tie event that came along, because he didn't want to leave her alone. He was sure she might enjoy it.

"There was a wonderful Directors Guild tribute to him in September of '96. He was very sick at that time."[37]

For the evening, Culp prepared a series of humorous stories and jokes.

Culp: "In a way, it was like a roast. I got up and said, 'When I first met Sheldon Leonard, he was the single most powerful purveyor of television on the planet. At least, that's what he told me.'"[38]

Culp would also rib Leonard about the battle over the ad-libbing.

Hagen: "One of the last jokes Culp made was, 'Sheldon was never big on the way Bill and I ad-libbed, but, for three good years, it didn't keep him from laughing all the way to the bank.' Then he sat down. Carl Reiner stepped to the microphone next and he said to Culp, 'If you two had stuck to the scripts, Sheldon might have had *five* good years of laughing to the bank instead of only *three*!'"[39]

It was all in good fun. And, at this, Sheldon Leonard laughed.

Culp: "At some point, I had gone over to see him. He was sitting with Frankie, who was in a wheelchair because she had suffered a severe stroke a few years prior. I went there out of respect. And I was hoping, of course, that he would receive it as such. He looked at me across the table without saying anything, but with such hatred that I was just blown away by it. So I said a couple of things, as nicely as I could, and then retired. And then I just got in my car and went home. It's too bad that, after all the things we went through together, it had to end up that way."[40]

Ron Jacobs: "Bob was misreading Sheldon. I know, I was there. Concerning that reunion movie, Sheldon was not happy about them changing the ending. No question. But he didn't hold a grudge over it. When Sheldon was mad about something, everyone around him knew it. And, that business about the reunion movie, he was over it. But that evening at the DGA dinner—which was a great evening—was the beginning of the end. Sheldon could barely get up the stairs. He was in a lot of pain. If Bob Culp saw anything on Sheldon's face, it was an effort to mask the pain."[41]

Andrea Bershad: "It was the last night my dad ever went out. He had gotten a bacterial

Sheldon loves Frankie (courtesy Andrea Bershad).

infection. He had just been diagnosed with it. He was able to make his last outing to this show, and it was a beautiful tribute from a lot of people who had worked with him. But the infection killed him fast, in just four months."[42]

Sheldon Leonard died of that bacterial infection on January 11th, 1997. He was 89.

He left behind more hours of classic TV than perhaps any other producer in the history of television. He also left behind two children, grandchildren, and a loving wife.

Andrea Bershad: "My dad and mom met when they were teenagers, and they were married 65 years. They enjoyed one another for a very long time.

"He really was a trooper, and stepped right up to the plate, and did a beautiful job of caring for her at the end. My dad passed away in January, and mom passed away two-and-a-half years later. And she didn't even know he was dead."[43]

29

The Fourth Reunion

Culp & Cosby, Full Circle

The Cosby Mysteries lasted only one season on NBC, and was gone from the schedule by the fall of 1995.

One year later, Cosby was back on television, in his third weekly half-hour sitcom, but this time for CBS. The title was merely *Cosby*. The star would play Hilton Lucas, forced into retirement and now spending most of his time at home, to the distress of his wife.

Never as successful as his previous sitcom, the series had a respectable run of four years and brought forward a classic premise for a reunion episode between Cosby and Culp.

On September 29, 1999, for the fourth season opener, entitled "My Spy," we find out that Lucas is a big *I Spy* fan. As he falls asleep while watching a holiday marathon of the original series, he dreams that he himself is a spy, and he meets up with Kelly Robinson.

As the 1990s wound down, Cosby was pulling double shifts on CBS, continuing with *Cosby*, and hosting a second prime-time series, *Kids Say the Darndest Things*, a revival of the old Art Linkletter program which featured the velvet smooth host interacting with children who had plenty on their minds.

Culp, meanwhile, began a series of appearances on the new number-one rated comedy series, *Everybody Loves Raymond*, as Warren, Raymond's father-in-law. By 2005, as the series was ending its successful run, he had been featured in more than a dozen episodes.

In 2004, Cosby served as producer on a big screen production of *Fat Albert*.

Culp and Cosby are still active, 40 years after meeting, 40 years after creating the harmony that was, and is, *I Spy*.

And *I Spy* continues to pop up in their lives, sometimes in the most unlikely ways.

One day after giving his final interview for this book, in December 2004, Robert Culp and his wife Candace boarded a plane and flew to Hong Kong to visit their daughter Rachel. Culp hadn't been there since 1965.

A very proud Robert Culp said, "My daughter is over there. She is in the middle of a two-year contract teaching English at the University of China at Hong Kong. And she's doing just fine. She's just sold a couple of articles to be published there, so she's starting to kick in as a professional writer."[1]

A very proud Bill Cosby, Rachel's godfather, said, "The ending of the book is already written—that Bob's daughter, after graduating from Yale, winds up where we started, with a job in Hong Kong. Now that's full circle."[2]

Culp and Cosby team up for another reunion, 1999 (courtesy Robert Culp).

Epilogue

In the opening title sequence to *I Spy*, Kelly holds a cannonball-shaped bomb, then uses a Zippo to light the fuse. He tosses the explosive at the camera, the picture is replaced by a flash, and the episode begins with a big bang.

In 2002, Columbia-Tristar tossed a bomb at the camera, too. It was a big screen version of *I Spy*. It had big stars: Eddie Murphy and Owen Wilson. A big director: Betty Thomas. A big budget. A big action sequences. A big splash. And it was a big nothing.

It also had a character named Kelly Robinson, and another named Alex Scott. One was a spy, the other an athlete turned spy.

And that is where the similarities with the original *I Spy* end.

The plot has to do with the disappearance of the Switchblade, the latest prototype to the Stealth Fighter. Top spy Alex Scott, played by Wilson, is called into action. What he doesn't expect, and what he is mortified to learn, is that he is being teamed up with a cocky civilian, World Class Boxing Champion Kelly Robinson, played by Murphy.

Yes, the writers and director and producers of the movie, with a tagline that read, "Attitude meets espionage," decided to reverse the characters. Scott would be the White guy. Kelly would be the Black guy. And boxing would be Kelly's game, not tennis. These two would be reluctant partners. More so, one would be a pro, the other an amateur, creating an absolute imbalance between the two.

Jerry Ludwig: "I read the reviews, and I couldn't bring myself to go see the *I Spy* movie; but I thought, if you're starting off with the usual conflict between the two guys, and they'll gradually come to like each other, you're not doing *I Spy*. You're doing something else. You can call it whatever you want to, but you're misleading anybody who ever saw or heard of *I Spy*."[3]

Culp and Cosby didn't bother to see the movie, either. All they heard, all they read, and all their gut told them was that sitting through this version of *I Spy* would be unbearably painful.

Culp: "They didn't even come close to what we were doing. They didn't because they didn't want to. There was no friendship between these characters. There was no connection. There was no reason for them to be together. Therefore, there was no story. What is a story? It's about character. Not about who stole a prototype Stealth Fighter. Who cares? Nobody."[4]

Gregory Friedkin: "*I Spy*, the series, was intellectually high standard. It had a witticism about it, an intellectuality about it, and it reflected the times and the civil rights movement. *I Spy*, the movie, was dumb-down entertainment. The movie missed on all sides. There was no warmth between the two leads, no smart dialogue, nothing."[5]

The two original partners had protected *I Spy* for as long as they could.

In the end, for this big budget, big screen, big bomb, *I Spy* become a faint and distorted shadow of itself. It was part of what Leonard had always wanted: tongue-in-cheek action, exotic locales, and two guys assigned to work together who, in order to introduce conflict into the story, are worlds apart.

But, at its heart, *I Spy* had another element.

At times, behind closed doors, it could be a war zone.

But on the screen it became a lesson in harmony.

I Spy was the harmony between two characters, Kelly and Scott; between a White man and a Black man; between a television series and its audience.

Cosby and Culp in the eye of the hurricane, Venice 1966 (© 3 F Prod.).

Yes, it did create the buddy genre. It opened a door for Black performers on television. It broke free of the studio system, and reinvented the way and the means in which a television series could be produced.

It was all of that, and more.

It was Sheldon Leonard, David Friedkin and Mort Fine. It was Earle Hagen and Hugo Friedhoffer. It was Ronald Jacobs, Leon Choolock and Michael Fenton. It was Mark Rydell and Richard Sarafian. And it was Fleet Southcott and Fouad Said, and "Crazy" Fouad's Cinemobile.

It was also Robert Culp and Bill Cosby.

It was that 50/50 balance, something that had never been tried, something that had never been seen, not before, and not since.

I Spy changed lives. And it did it as sometimes only a TV show can.

It lived in its moment. And, for those of us who witnessed it, it lived in us as well.

It still does.

The title Leonard chose for the reunion movie Culp and Cosby made in 1993 was *I Spy Returns*. But that title was wrong. *I Spy*—and the magic it created—could not return.

It never went away.

Chapter Notes

Prologue

1. Robert Culp, interview with the author, 2004.

Chapter 1

1. Ed Goodgold, I Spy, *Robert Culp & Bill Cosby: TV's Swift and Swinging Spies*, New York: Grossett & Dunlap, 1967, p. 31.
2. Robert Culp, interview with the author, 2004.
3. *Ibid.*
4. *Ibid.*
5. *Ibid.*
6. *Ibid.*
7. *Ibid.*
8. *Ibid.*
9. *Ibid.*
10. *Ibid.*
11. *Ibid.*
12. *Ibid.*
13. *Ibid.*
14. *Ibid.*
15. *Ibid.*
16. *Ibid.*
17. *Ibid.*
18. *Ibid.*
19. *Ibid.*
20. *Ibid.*
21. *Ibid.*
22. *Ibid.*
23. Andrea Bershad, interview with the author, 2005.
24. *Ibid.*
25. Norman Brokaw, interview with the author, 2005.
26. Earle Hagen, interview with the author, 2004.
27. Bershad, interview.
28. *Ibid.*
29. *Ibid.*
30. Culp, interview, 2004.
31. *Ibid.*
32. *Ibid.*
33. Dave Kaufman, "Fine, Friedkin, Plot 'Spy' Spinoff," *Daily Variety*, February 22, 1965, p. 12.
34. Anthony Friedkin, interview with the author, 2005.
35. *Ibid.*
36. *Ibid.*
37. *Ibid.*
38. Bernice Fine, interview with the author, 2005.
39. *Ibid.*
40. Gregory Friedkin, interview with the author, 2005.
41. *Seattle Post-Intelligencer*, "How I Spy Was Born," September 26, 1965, p. 2.
42. Bernice Fine, interview.
43. Richard Sarafian, interview with the author, 2005.
44. Michael Zagor, interview with the author, 2004.
45. Barry Oringer, interview with the author, 2004.
46. Eric Bercovici, interview with the author, 2004.
47. Rick Mittleman, interview with the author, 2004.
48. Jerry Ludwig, interview with the author, 2004.
49. Sarafian, interview.
50. NBC Contract between Sheldon Leonard and Herbert Schlosser, NBC Archives, June 26, 1964.
51. Culp, interview, 2004.
52. *Ibid.*
53. Brokaw, interview.
54. Sheldon Leonard, *And the Show Goes On*, New York: Proscenium, 1994, p. 145.
55. *Playboy*, Bill Cosby interview, May 1969, p. 80.
56. Friedkin, interview.
57. *Playboy*, Cosby interview, p. 80.
58. Sarafian, interview.
59. *Playboy*, Cosby interview, p. 76.
60. *Ibid.*
61. Goodgold, *I Spy, Robert Culp & Bill Cosby*, p. 19.
62. Culp, interview, 2004.
63. *Ibid.*
64. *Ibid.*
65. *Ibid.*
66. *Playboy*, Cosby interview, p. 80.

Chapter 2

1. Sheldon Leonard, *And the Show Goes On*, New York: Proscenium, 1994, p. 153.
2. Earle Hagen, interview with the author, 2004.
3. Ron Jacobs, interview with the author, 2004.
4. Robert Culp, interview with the author, 2005.
5. Bill Cosby, interview with the author, 2005.
6. Robert Culp, interview, with the author, 2004.
7. *Ibid.*
8. Cosby, interview.
9. Culp, interview, 2005.
10. *Playboy*, Bill Cosby interview, May 1969, p. 80.
11. Cosby, interview.
12. Culp, interview, 2004.
13. Cosby, interview.
14. Culp, interview, 2004.
15. Cosby, interview.
16. Culp, interview, 2004.
17. *Ibid.*
18. Cosby, interview.
19. Culp, interview, 2004.
20. Hagen, interview.
21. Culp, interview, 2004.
22. *Ibid.*
23. *Ibid.*
24. *Ibid.*
25. *Ibid.*
26. *Ibid.*
27. *Ibid.*
28. *Ibid.*
29. *Ibid.*
30. *Ibid.*
31. *Ibid.*
32. Leonard, *And the Show Goes On*, p. 162.

33. Michael Preece, interview with the author, 2005.
34. *Ibid.*
35. Calvin Brown, interview with the author, 2005.
36. Culp, interview, 2004.
37. *Ibid.*
38. Hagen, interview.

Chapter 3

1. Robert Culp, interview with the author, 2004.
2. Bill Cosby, interview with the author, 2005.
3. Mark Rydell, interview with the author, 2005.
4. *Ibid.*
5. Culp, interview, 2004.
6. Robert Culp, *I Spy* DVD commentary, Image Entertainment, 2001.
7. Earle Hagen, interview with the author, 2004.
8. Culp, *I Spy* DVD.
9. Rydell, interview.
10. Martin Landau, interview with the author, 2005.
11. *Ibid.*
12. Rydell, interview.
13. Culp, interview, 2004.
14. *Ibid.*
15. Cosby, interview.
16. Culp, interview, 2004.
17. *Ibid.*
18. *Ibid.*
19. *Ibid.*
20. *Ibid.*
21. Rydell, interview.
22. *Ibid.*
23. *Ibid.*
24. Cosby, interview.
25. Michael Preece, interview with the author, 2005.
26. Culp, interview, 2004.
27. Rydell, interview.
28. Cosby, interview.
29. Culp, interview, 2004.
30. Ron Jacobs, interview with the author, 2005.
31. Preece, interview.
32. *Ibid.*

Chapter 4

1. Robert Culp, interview with the author, 2004.
2. *Ibid.*
3. Andrea Bershad, interview with the author, 2005.
4. Michael Preece, interview with the author, 2005.
5. *Ibid.*
6. Sheldon Leonard, *And the Show Goes On,* New York: Proscenium, 1994, p. 162.
7. Culp, interview, 2004.
8. Calvin Brown, interview with the author, 2005.
9. Culp, interview, 2004.
10. *Ibid.*
11. Leonard, *And the Show Goes On,* pp. 151–152.
12. Preece, interview.
13. Culp, interview, 2004.
14. *Ibid.*
15. *Ibid.*
16. *Ibid.*
17. *Ibid.*
18. Brown, interview.
19. *Ibid.*
20. *Ibid.*
21. *Ibid.*
22. *Ibid.*
23. Culp, interview, 2004.
24. *Ibid.*
25. *Ibid.*
26. *Ebony,* "'*I Spy*': Comedian Bill Cosby Is First Negro Co-Star in TV Network Series." September 1965, p. 66.
27. Stanley Karnow, "Bill Cosby: Variety Is the Life of Spies," *Saturday Evening Post,* September 25, 1965, p. 88.
28. *Ibid.*
29. *New York Journal American,* "*I Spy*" review, September 1965.

Chapter 5

1. Robert Culp, interview with the author, 2004.
2. Michael Preece, interview with the author, 2005.
3. Culp, interview, 2004.
4. *Ibid.*
5. Earle Hagen, interview with the author, 2004.
6. Culp, interview, 2004.
7. Bill Cosby, interview with the author, 2005.
8. Culp, interview, 2004.
9. *Ibid.*
10. *Ibid.*
11. *Ibid.*
12. *Ibid.*
13. *Ibid.*
14. *Ibid.*
15. Cosby, interview.
16. Preece, interview.
17. Culp, interview, 2004.
18. Robert Culp, *I Spy* DVD commentary, Image Entertainment, 2001.
19. Ron Jacobs, interview with the author, 2005.

Chapter 6

1. Richard Sarafian, interview with the author, 2005.
2. *Ibid.*
3. Michael Preece, interview with the author, 2005.
4. Bill Cosby, interview with the author, 2005.
5. Preece, interview.
6. Sarafian, interview.
7. Robert Culp, interview with the author, 2004.
8. Sarafian, interview.
9. *Ibid.*
10. Preece, interview.
11. Culp, interview, 2004.
12. Preece, interview.
13. Cosby, interview.
14. Culp, interview, 2004.
15. *Ibid.*
16. *Ibid.*
17. Andrea Bershad, interview with the author, 2005.
18. Robert Culp, *I Spy* DVD commentary, Image Entertainment, 2001.
19. *Ibid.*
20. *Ibid.*
21. Culp, interview, 2004.

Chapter 7

1. Eric Bercovici, interview with the author, 2004.
2. Bill Cosby, interview with the author, 2005.
3. Earle Hagen, interview with the author, 2004.
4. Cosby, interview.
5. Bercovici, interview.
6. Robert Culp, interview with the author, 2004.
7. Richard Sarafian, interview with the author, 2005.
8. Michael Preece, interview with the author, 2005.
9. Sarafian, interview.
10. *Ibid.*
11. Culp, interview, 2004.
12. *Ibid.*
13. Michael Zagor, interview with the author, 2004.
14. Culp, interview, 2004.
15. Zagor, interview.
16. *Ibid.*
17. Bercovici, interview.
18. Culp, interview, 2004.
19. *Ibid.*

20. Sarafian, interview.
21. *Ibid.*
22. Preece, interview.
23. Sarafian, interview.
24. Cosby, interview.
25. *Ibid.*
26. Calvin Brown, interview with the author, 2005.
27. Preece, interview.
28. Steven Kandel, interview with the author, 2005.

Chapter 8

1. Bill Cosby, interview with the author 2005.
2. Richard Sarafian, interview with the author, 2005.
3. Robert Culp, interview with the author, 2004.
4. *Ibid.*
5. *Ibid.*
6. *Ibid.*

Chapter 9

1. Gregory Friedkin, interview with the author, 2005.
2. Anthony Friedkin, interview with the author, 2005.
3. Bernice Fine, interview with the author, 2005.
4. *Ibid.*
5. Anthony Friedkin, interview.
6. Gregory Friedkin, interview.
7. Bernice Fine, interview.
8. Gregory Friedkin, interview.
9. Anthony Friedkin, interview.
10. Bernice Fine, interview.
11. Anthony Friedkin, interview.
12. Gregory Friedkin, interview.
13. Calvin Brown, interview with the author, 2005.
14. Steven Kandel, interview with the author, 2005.
15. Rick Mittleman, interview with the author, 2005.
16. Kandel, interview.
17. Barry Oringer, interview with the author, 2005.
18. Kandel, interview.
19. Oringer, interview.
20. Jerry Ludwig, interview with the author, 2005.
21. Oringer, interview.
22. Ludwig, interview.
23. Eric Bercovici, interview with the author, 2005.
24. *Ibid.*
25. Kandel, interview.
26. *Ibid.*
27. Robert Culp, interview with the author, 2004.
28. Bill Cosby, interview with the author, 2005.
29. Ron Jacobs, interview with the author, 2005.
30. Richard Sarafian, interview with the author, 2005.
31. *Ibid.*
32. Culp, interview, 2004.
33. Michael Preece, interview with the author, 2005.
34. Sarafian, interview.
35. Dick Hobson, "Little Fou's Big Revolution," *TV Guide,* March 23, 1968, p. 23.
36. *Ibid.*

Chapter 10

1. Calvin Brown, interview with the author, 2005.
2. Michael Zagor, interview with the author, 2005.
3. Richard Sarafian, interview with the author, 2005.
4. *Ibid.*
5. Zagor, interview.
6. Bill Cosby, interview with the author, 2005.
7. Sarafian, interview.
8. Michael Preece, interview with the author, 2005.
9. *Ibid.*
10. Cosby, interview.

Chapter 11

1. Robert Culp, interview with the author, 2004.
2. Ernest Frankel, interview with the author, 2005.
3. Culp, interview, 2004.
4. *Ibid.*
5. Robert Culp, interview with the author, 2005.
6. Culp, interview, 2004.
7. *Ibid.*
8. Robert Culp, *I Spy* DVD commentary, Image Entertainment, 2001.
9. Frankel, interview.
10. Sheldon Leonard, *And the Show Goes On,* New York: Proscenium, 1994, p. 171.
11. Culp, *I Spy* DVD.
12. Frankel, interview.
13. Leonard, *And the Show Goes On,* p. 171.
14. Culp, interview, 2004.
15. *Ibid.*
16. Barry Oringer, interview with the author, 2005.
17. Culp, interview, 2004.
18. Michael Preece, interview with the author, 2004.
19. *Ibid.*
20. Jerry Ludwig, interview with the author, 2005.
21. Michael Zagor, interview with the author, 2005.
22. *Ibid.*
23. Ludwig, interview.
24. Oringer, interview.
25. Preece, interview.
26. Richard Sarafian, interview with the author, 2005.
27. Steven Kandel, interview with the author, 2005.
28. Leonard, *And the Show Goes On,* p. 172.
29. Zagor, interview.
30. Ludwig, interview.
31. Eric Bercovici, interview with the author, 2005.
32. Oringer, interview.
33. Rick Mittleman, interview with the author, 2005.
34. Kandel, interview.
35. Preece, interview.
36. Culp, interview, 2004.
37. Cosby, interview.
38. Culp, interview, 2004.
39. Sarafian, interview.
40. *Ibid.*
41. Rick Logan, "The Oriental Girl Robert Culp Left his Wife For," *Screenland,* December 1966, p. 62.

Chapter 12

1. Steven Kandel, interview with the author, 2005.
2. Michael Preece, interview with the author, 2005.
3. *Ibid.*
4. Barry Oringer, interview with the author, 2005.
5. Preece, interview.
6. Robert Culp, interview with the author, 2004.
7. Alan Oppenheimer, interview with the author, 2005.
8. Robert Culp, *I Spy* DVD commentary, Image Entertainment, 2001.
9. *Ibid.*
10. Preece, interview.
11. Culp, interview, 2004.

12. *Ibid.*
13. *Ibid.*
14. Preece, interview.
15. Bill Cosby, interview with the author, 2005.
16. Oringer, interview.
17. *Ibid.*

Chapter 13

1. Robert Culp, interview with the author, 2004.
2. *Ibid.*
3. Robert Culp, *I Spy* DVD commentary, Image Entertainment, 2001.
4. *Ibid.*
5. Bill Adler, *The Cosby Wit: His Life in Humor,* New York: Carroll and Graff, 1986, p. 154.
6. Michael Preece, interview with the author, 2005.

Chapter 14

1. Robert Culp, interview with the author, 2004.
2. Robert Culp, *I Spy* DVD commentary, Image Entertainment, 2001.
3. Michael Preece, interview with the author, 2005.
4. Culp, interview, 2004.
5. *Ibid.*
6. *Ibid.*
7. Preece, interview.
8. Culp, interview, 2004.
9. Preece, interview.
10. Culp, interview, 2004.
11. Preece, interview.
12. Earle Hagen, interview with the author, 2004.
13. Culp, interview, 2004.
14. Bill Cosby, interview with the author, 2005.
15. Preece, interview.
16. *Ibid.*
17. Culp, interview, 2004.
18. *Ibid.*
19. Michael Zagor, interview with the author, 2005.
20. Salome Jens, interview with the author, 2005.
21. Culp, interview, 2004.
22. *Ibid.*
23. Preece, interview.
24. Rick Mittleman, interview with the author, 2005.
25. Preece, interview.
26. Alan Oppenheimer, interview with the author, 2005.
27. *Ibid.*
28. Preece, interview.
29. Barbara McNair, interview with the author, 2005.
30. Steven Kandel, interview with the author, 2005.
31. Preece, interview.
32. Cosby, interview.
33. *Ibid.*
34. Robert Culp, interview with the author, 2005.
35. Culp, interview, 2004.
36. McNair, interview.
37. Jerry Ludwig, interview with the author, 2005.
38. *Ibid.*
39. Cosby, interview.
40. Culp, interview, 2004.
41. Cosby, interview.

Chapter 15

1. Bill Cosby, "Why Did They Have To Split Us Up?" *Motion Picture Magazine,* January 1967.
2. Robert Culp, interview with the author, 2004.

Chapter 17

1. David Fine, interview with the author, 2005.
2. Sheldon Leonard, *And the Show Goes On,* New York: Proscenium, 1994, p. 180.
3. Bernice Fine, interview with the author, 2005.
4. Calvin Brown, interview with the author, 2005.
5. Leonard, *"And the Show Goes On,"* p. 185.
6. Brown, interview.
7. Richard Sarafian, interview with the author, 2005.

Chapter 18

1. Michael Preece, interview with the author, 2005.
2. Barry Oringer, interview with the author, 2004.
3. *Ibid.*
4. Michael Zagor, interview with the author, 2004.
5. Earle Hagen, interview with the author, 2004.
6. Jerry Ludwig, interview with the author, 2004.
7. Robert Culp, interview with the author, 2004.

Chapter 19

1. Steven Kandel, interview with the author, 2004.

Chapter 20

1. Michael Zagor, interview with the author, 2004.
2. Steven Kandel, interview with the author, 2004.
3. Michael Preece, interview with the author, 2005.
4. Ernest Frankel, interview with the author, 2004.
5. Jerry Ludwig, interview with the author, 2004.
6. *Ibid.*
7. Zagor, interview.
8. Preece, interview.
9. Richard Sarafian, interview with the author, 2005.
10. Mark Rydell, interview with the author, 2005.

Chapter 21

1. Anthony Friedkin, interview with the author, 2005.
2. Robert Culp, *I Spy* DVD commentary, Image Entertainment, 2001.
3. Steven Kandel, interview with the author, 2004.
4. Michael Preece, interview with the author, 2005.
5. Bill Cosby, interview with the author, 2005.

Chapter 22

1. Bill Cosby, interview with the author, 2005.
2. *Ibid.*
3. Sheldon Leonard, *And the Show Goes On,* New York: Proscenium, 1994, pp. 170–171.
4. Calvin Brown, interview with the author, 2005.
5. Michael Preece, interview with the author, 2005.
6. *Ibid.*
7. Earle Hagen, interview with the author, 2004.
8. Jerry Ludwig, interview with the author, 2004.
9. Cosby, interview.
10. *Ibid.*
11. *Ibid.*

Chapter 23

1. Joel Whitburn, *Top Pop Singles, 1955–2002,* Menomonee Falls, WI: Record Research, 2003.

2. Bill Cosby, interview with the author, 2005.

Chapter 24

1. Michael Preece, interview with the author, 2005.
2. Ernest Frankel, interview with the author, 2004.
3. Gregory Friedkin, interview with the author, 2005.
4. Ron Jacobs, interview with the author, 2005.
5. Robert Culp, interview with the author, 2004.
6. Frankel, interview.
7. Sheldon Leonard, *And the Show Goes On*, New York: Proscenium, 1994, pp. 172–173.
8. *Ibid.*
9. Bill Cosby, interview with the author, 2005.
10. Leonard, *And the Show Goes On*, pp. 172–173.
11. Mort Fine, UCLA Collection.
12. Frankel, interview.
13. Earle Hagen, interview with the author, 2004.
14. Frankel, interview.
15. *Ibid.*
16. *Ibid.*
17. Jerry Ludwig, interview with the author, 2004.
18. Steven Kandel, interview with the author, 2004.
19. *Ibid.*
20. *Ibid.*
21. Frankel, interview.
22. *Ibid.*
23. Culp, interview, 2004.
24. Leonard, *And the Show Goes On*, p. 197.
25. *Ibid.*
26. *Playboy*, Bill Cosby interview, May 1969, p. 82.
27. Leonard, *And the Show Goes On*, p. 198.
28. Hagen, interview.
29. Leonard, *And the Show Goes On*, p. 198.
30. Frankel, interview.
31. Linda Danly, *Hugo Friedhoffer: The Best Years of his Life,* Lanham, MD: Scarecrow Press, 1999, p. 143.
32. Calvin Brown, interview with the author, 2005.
33. Leonard, *And the Show Goes On*, p. 198.
34. *Ibid.*

Chapter 25

1. Jerry Ludwig, interview with the author, 2004.
2. Ernest Frankel, interview with the author, 2004.
3. Michael Zagor, interview with the author, 2004.
4. Ludwig, interview.
5. Steven Kandel, interview with the author, 2004.
6. Rick Mittleman, interview with the author, 2004.
7. Mark Rydell, interview with the author, 2005.
8. Richard Sarafian, interview with the author, 2005.
9. Earle Hagen, interview with the author, 2004.
10. Frankel, interview.
11. Ron Jacobs, interview with the author, 2005.
12. Calvin Brown, interview with the author, 2005.
13. Anthony Friedkin, interview with the author, 2005.
14. Gregory Friedkin, interview with the author, 2005.
15. Andrea Bershad, interview with the author, 2005.
16. *Ibid.*
17. Bill Cosby, interview with the author, 2005.
18. Robert Culp, interview with the author, 2004.
19. Barry Oringer, interview with the author, 2004.
20. Zagor, interview.

Chapter 26

1. Joy Keller, interview with the author, 2004.
2. Robert Culp, interview with the author, 2004.
3. *Ibid.*
4. Nancy Kapitanoff, "Under the Influence of Paul Mazursky's *Bob & Carol & Ted & Alice,*" DGA Archives, September 9, 2003.
5. Culp, interview, 2004.
6. Martin Rips, "Culp's Hickey Topples Hollywood's Occupational Class System," *Los Angeles Times*, October 5, 1972, Calendar section, p. 15.
7. Culp, interview, 2004.
8. Bill Cosby, interview with the author, 2005.
9. Robert Culp, interview with the author, 2005.
10. Cosby, interview.
11. *Ibid.*

Chapter 27

1. Anthony Friedkin, interview with the author, 2005.
2. Gregory Friedkin, interview with the author, 2005.
3. Anthony Friedkin, interview.
4. Bernice Fine, interview with the author, 2005.
5. David Fine, interview with the author, 2005.
6. Bernice Fine, interview.
7. *Ibid.*
8. Richard Sarafian, interview with the author, 2005.
9. Andrea Bershad, interview with the author, 2005.
10. *Ibid.*
11. Jerry Ludwig, interview with the author, 2004.
12. *Ibid.*
13. *Ibid.*
14. Robert Culp, interview with the author, 2005.
15. Ron Jacobs, interview with the author, 2005.
16. Eric Bercovici, interview with the author, 2004.
17. Ludwig, interview.
18. Bercovici, interview.
19. Robert Culp, interview with the author, 2004.
20. *Ibid.*
21. *Ibid.*
22. *Ibid.*
23. *Ibid.*
24. *Ibid.*
25. *Ibid.*
26. *Ibid.*
27. *Ibid.*
28. *Ibid.*
29. *Ibid.*
30. *Ibid.*
31. *Ibid.*

Chapter 28

1. Robert Culp, interview with the author, 2004.
2. *Ibid.*
3. *Ibid.*
4. *Ibid.*
5. *Ibid.*
6. *Ibid.*
7. *Ibid.*
8. *Ibid.*
9. Robert Culp, *I SPY: The Movie* screenplay, 1988.
10. *Ibid.*
11. *Ibid.*
12. *Ibid.*
13. Hillard Elkins, interview with the author, 2004.

14. Culp, *I SPY: The Movie.*
15. Sheldon Leonard, "Sheldon Leonard Is Mad as Hell . . . and It's the TV Network's Fault," *DGA News,* February/March, 1995, p. 15.
16. *Ibid.*
17. Leonard, "Sheldon Leonard Is Mad as Hell . . . ," p. 16.
18. *Ibid.*
19. *Ibid.*
20. *Ibid.*
21. *Ibid.*
22. *Ibid.*
23. *Ibid.*
24. Culp, interview, 2004.
25. Gregory Friedkin, interview with the author, 2005.
26. Culp, interview, 2004.
27. *Ibid.*
28. *Ibid.*
29. *Ibid.*
30. *Ibid.*
31. *Ibid.*
32. *Ibid.*
33. *Ibid.*
34. Earle Hagen, interview with the author, 2004.
35. Leonard, "Sheldon Leonard Is Mad as Hell . . . ," p. 16.
36. Culp, interview, 2004.
37. Andrea Bershad, interview with the author, 2005.
38. Culp, interview, 2004.
39. Hagen, interview.
40. Culp, interview, 2004.
41. Ron Jacobs, interview with the author, 2005.
42. Bershad, interview.
43. *Ibid.*

Chapter 29

1. Robert Culp, interview with the author, 2004.
2. Bill Cosby, interview with the author, 2005.
3. Jerry Ludwig, interview with the author, 2004.
4. Robert Culp, interview with the author, 2005.
5. Gregory Friedkin, interview with the author, 2005.

Bibliography

"Actor Robert Culp Gets Human Relations Award." *Los Feliz Hills News*, September 26, 1968.

Adams, Val. "'I Spy' with Negro Is Widely Booked." *New York Times*, September 10, 1965.

Adler, Bill. *The Cosby Wit: His Life in Humor*. New York: Carroll and Graff, 1986.

Amory, Cleveland. *TV Guide*. April 18, 1964, p. 14.

_____. *TV Guide*. October 9, 1965, p. 1.

_____. *TV Guide*. May 11, 1968, p. 42.

"As We See It." *TV Guide*, November 20, 1965.

Bercovici, Eric. Interview with Cushman, October 12, 2004.

Bershad, Andrea. Interview with Cushman and LaRosa, January 2005.

Bill Cosby interview. *Playboy*, May 1969, pp. 73–88.

"Bill Cosby's TV Special an Emmy Winner." *Jet*. June 26, 1969, p. 54.

"Bob Culp/France Nuyen: Even Society Couldn't Stop their Wedding." *Movie Life*, April 1968, pp. 20–12.

"Bob Culp, France Nuyen, Reaching for that Dream." *TV Picture Mirror*, May 1967.

"Bob Culp's Inter-Racial Marriage to France Nuyen." *TV Radio Mirror*, March 1968.

Brokaw, Norman. Interview with Cushman and LaRosa, March 2005.

Brooks, Tim, and Earle Marsh. *The Complete Directory to Prime Time Network TV Shows*. New York: Ballantine Books, 1988.

Brown, Calvin. Interview with Cushman and LaRosa, March 22, 2005.

Champlin, Charles. "From the People Who Brought You *I Spy*." *Los Angeles Times*, October 1, 1972, Calendar section, p. 3.

"Color Him Funny." *Newsweek*, January 31, 1966, p. 76.

"Cool Talk from a Hot Property." *Look*, May 30, 1967, pp. 21–22.

Cosby, Bill. "How I Became Seriously Serious." *TV Week, Citizen-News* (Glendale, CA), August 20, 1966, p. 22.

_____. Interview with Cushman and LaRosa, February 24, 2005.

_____. "Why Did They Have to Split Us Up?" *Motion Picture Magazine*, January 1967.

"Cosby in 'Spy' Puts NBC Dixie Affils on Spot." *Variety*, April 7, 1965.

Culp, Robert. *I Spy* DVD commentary. Image Entertainment, 2001.

_____. *I Spy: The Movie* screenplay, 1988.

_____. Interview with Cushman, April 3, 2005.

_____. Interview with Cushman and LaRosa, November 7 and 13, 2004.

_____. Interview with Cushman, November 17, December 4, 2004.

_____. *Television Chronicles #3, Interview: Robert Culp*. October 1995.

_____. "We're Brothers under the Skin." *Motion Picture Magazine*, February 1966, pp. 42, 84.

Danly, Linda. *Hugo Friedhoffer: The Best Years of his Life*. Lanham, MD: Scarecrow Press, 1999.

David, Peter. "The Letter that Broke Six Hearts," *TV Radio Mirror*, September 1966.

Denton, Gary. "Mr. & Mrs. Robert Culp's Beautiful Wedding." *TV Radio Mirror*, March 1968, pp. 30–33.

Doan, Richard K. "The Doan Report." *TV Guide*, December 3, 1966, p. A-1.

_____. "The Doan Report." *TV Guide*, February 10, 1968, p. A-1.

_____. "The Doan Report." *TV Guide*, March 2, 1968, p. A-1.

Donnelly, William. "'*I Spy*' Is an Oasis on TV Desert." *TV Week, Citizen-News*, February 4, 1966.

Du Brow, Rick. "Comedy Adds Appeal to the *I Spy* Twins." *UPI*, January 6, 1966.

Elkins, Hillard. Interview with Cushman and LaRosa, 2004.

Elliot, Andrea. "How Nancy Culp Faced the Grim Reality of a Wife All Alone!" *TV Radio Mirror*, May 1967 pp. 38, 63–64.

Engelhardt, Ruth. Interview with Cushman and LaRosa, 2004.

Fein, Phyllis. "How the Spies Make Love." *Inside Movie Magazine*, July 1966.

Fine, Bernice. Interview with Cushman and LaRosa, March 2005.

Fine, David. Interview with Cushman and LaRosa, March 2005.

Fine, Mort. UCLA Collection: various letters, reviews, clippings, interviews, press releases, ratings reports, censorship reports, contracts, scripts, interoffice memos, and fan mail.

Frankel, Ernest. Interview with Cushman and LaRosa, 2004.
Friedkin, Anthony. Interview with Cushman and LaRosa, April 2005.
Friedkin, Gregory. Interview with Cushman and LaRosa, April 2005.
Gardner, Paul. "Comic Turns Quips into Tuition." *New York Times,* June 25, 1962.
Goodgold, Ed. I Spy, *Robert Culp & Bill Cosby, TV's Swift and Swinging Spies.* New York: Grosset & Dunlap, 1967.
Goodwin, Fritz. "The Operation Was a Failure . . . But the Patient Survived." *TV Guide,* May 31, 1969, pp. 12–14.
Gray, Dick. "*I Spy.*" *Atlantic Journal,* July 10, 1965.
Grant, Hank. "*I Spy.*" *Hollywood Reporter,* October 29, 1965.
Gross, Ben. "*I Spy*" review. *New York Daily News,* September 16, 1965.
Hagen, Earle. Interview with Cushman and LaRosa, 2004.
Hannah, Marilyn. "Bob Culp—Absence Makes the Heart Ache." *TV Picture Life,* February 1966.
Hickey & Boggs review. *Variety,* August 30, 1972.
Hickey, Neil. "TV Teletype." *TV Guide,* October 30, 1965, p. 4.
Higgins, Charles. "Stars Support Breadbasket Self-Help Project." *Jet,* August 8, 1968, pp. 14–23.
Hobson, Dick. "He Bears Witness to His Beliefs." *TV Guide,* January 15, 1966, pp. 10–12.
_____. "Little Fou's Big Revolution." *TV Guide,* March 23, 1968, pp. 22–27.
_____. "The Ptomaine in Spain Came Mainly on the Plane." *TV Guide,* March 25, 1967, pp. 15–18.
Horne, Jim. "*I Spy*" review. Associated Press, September 1965.
"How Cool Can a Bride Groom Be? Plenty if He's Bob Culp." *Inside TV,* April 1968, pp. 27–31.
"How I Spy Was Born." *Seattle Post-Intelligencer,* September 26, 1965, p. 2.
Humphrey, Hal. "No Racial Issues for This Spy Team." *Los Angeles Times,* May 17, 1965.
"I Hate a Woman who Clings." *Photoplay,* December 1967, pp. 24–25.
IMDB.com. Internet Movie Data Base for film and television credits for directors, writers and actors.
"'*I Spy*' Clearance Grows in Dixie." *Variety,* October 1966.
"'*I Spy*': Comedian Bill Cosby Is First Negro Co-Star in TV Network Series." *Ebony,* September 1965, pp. 65–71.
"*I Spy.*" *Independent Star News* (Pasadena, CA), *TV Week,* February 6, 1966.
I Spy production files. Various correspondence, memos, scripts, script notes, NBC Broadcast Standards and Practices reports, ratings reports, budget statements, travel itineraries, Western Union telegrams, fan mail, press releases, licensing agreements, etc.
I Spy Returns review. *Variety,* February 3, 1994.

"*I Spy*" review. *Los Angeles Times,* September 16, 1965.
"*I Spy*" review. *Lutheran Monthly,* November 1966.
"*I Spy*" review. *New York Journal American,* September 1965.
I Spy review. *Variety,* September 16, 1965.
I Spy review. *Variety,* September 22, 1965.
"*I Spy* Star Brawl Denied." *The News, Mexico,* December 16, 1965.
"I'm Not a Wronged Wife: Mrs. Bob Culp's Own Story of the Divorce." *TV Picture Magazine,* March 1967.
Jacobs, Ronald. Interview with Cushman and LaRosa, March, 2004.
Jens, Salome. Interview with Cushman, April 2005.
Kandall, Steven. Interview with Cushman, October 15, 2004.
Kapitanoff, Nancy. "Under the Influence of Paul Mazursky's *Bob & Carol & Ted & Alice.*" DGA Archives, September 9, 2003.
Karnow, Stanley. "Bill Cosby: Variety Is the Life of Spies." *Saturday Evening Post,* September 25, 1965, pp. 86–88.
Kaufman, Dave. "Cosby Mad at Mad. Ave." *Daily Variety,* November 23, 1965, p. 12.
_____. "Fine, Friedkin Plot 'Spy' Spinoff." *Daily Variety,* February 22, 1966, p. 12.
Keller, Joy. Interview with Cushman and LaRosa, 2004.
Kreiling, Ernie. "*I Spy*" review. *TV Week, Citizen-News* (Hollywood, CA), December 26, 1965, p. 15.
Landau, Martin. Interview with Cushman and La Rosa, 2005.
Lechat, Fred. "My Unpredictable Buddy, Bob." *Movie Mirror,* May 1967, pp. 22, 56.
Leonard, Sheldon. *And the Show Goes On.* New York: Proscenium, 1994.
_____. "Having a Wonderful Time—Minus the Typhoons and Other Stalls in the Process." *TV Guide,* July 1965, pp. 6–8.
_____. "Sheldon Leonard Is Mad as Hell . . . and It's the TV Network's Fault." *DGA News,* February/March 1995, pp. 16–19.
"Let's Kill Karlovassi" review. *Variety,* September 13, 1967.
Location filming report. *TV Guide,* August 6, 1966.
Logan, Rick. "The Oriental Girl Robert Culp Left his Wife For." *Screenland,* December 1966, pp. 24, 60–62.
"Lori" review. *Variety,* September 23, 1966.
"The Love They Couldn't Hide Any More." *Photoplay,* January 1967, pp. 28, 74.
"Lovers who Mixed Race and Religion." *Silver Screen,* May 1968.
Ludwig, Jerry. Interview with Cushman, November 13, 2004.
Mahooney, John. "Let's Kill Karlovassi" review. *Hollywood Reporter,* September 13, 1967, p. 4.
Maltin, Leonard. *2001 Movie & Video Guide.* New York: New American Library, 2001.

McGregor, Don. "Robert Culp: Building a Career in the Hollywood Jungle." *StarLog*, February 1982.
McNair, Barbara. Interview with Cushman, April 2005.
Michael, Paul, and James Robert Parish. *The Emmy Awards*. New York: Crown.
Mills, Nancy. "*I Spy Returns*." *TV Week, Chicago Tribune*, January 30, 1994, p. 5.
Mittleman, Rick. Interview with Cushman, October 19, 2004.
NBC Contract between Sheldon Leonard and Herb Schlosser. NBC Archives, June 26, and July 22, 1964.
NBC Financial Report. *I Spy*. September 30, 1971.
NBC Interoffice Memos. October 13, 1964, November 6, 1964, November 2, 1964, January 2, 1965, February 4, 1965.
NBC Loan Agreement with Sheldon Leonard. April 22, 1966.
"New Cosby Contract with NBC." *TV Guide*, November 19, 1966.
Nielsen, A.C. Ratings reports. 1966 through 1967.
O'Brian, Jack. *I Spy* review. *New York Journal-American*, September 16, 1965.
_____. "Tatia" review. *New York Journal-American*, November 1965.
"Off the Record." *TV Guide*, March 26, 1966.
"Operation Breadbasket." Close Up. *TV Guide*, July 1968.
Oppenheimer, Alan. Interview with Cushman and LaRosa, May 2005.
Ornstein, Ben. *I Spy* review. *Hollywood Reporter*, September 16, 1965.
_____. "The War Lord" review. *Hollywood Reporter*, February 2, 1967.
Oringer, Barry. Interview with Cushman, 2004.
Preece, Michael. Interview with Cushman and LaRosa, 2005.
Rahn, Peter. "*I Spy*'s Winning Ways." *TV Digest, Globe-Democrat*, February 12, 1966, p. 10.
Ratings report. *Variety*, November 23, 1965.
Report on *I Spy* company missing in north Africa. *Variety*, April 27, 1967.
Report on Nielsen ratings. *TV Guide*, October 14, 1967.
Report on ratings. *TV Guide*, March 18, 1967.
Rips, Martin. "Culp's Hickey Topples Hollywood's Occupational Class System." *Los Angeles Times*, October 5, 1972, Calendar section, p. 15.
"Robert Culp, France Nuyen, Love Is a Many-Splendored Thing." *TV and Screen World*, April 1968.
Rydell, Mark. Interview with Cushman and LaRosa, April 2005.
Salerno, Al. *I Spy* review. *New York World-Telegram*, September 16, 1965.
Sarafian, Richard. Interview with Cushman and LaRosa, 2005.
"Sex and the Swinging Spy, Robert Culp: Caught in the Venus Fly Trap." *TV and Screen World*, March 1968, p. 14.
"So Coldly Sweet" review. *Hollywood Reporter*, September 16, 1966.
"So Coldly Sweet" review. *Variety*, September 21, 1966.
Stang, Joanna. "The Case of the Scholarly Spy." *New York Times*, October 7, 1965.
Sullivan, Jack T. "Casting of Negro Actors Shows TV Has Grown Up." *TV Magazine, Boston Sunday Herald*, October 23, 1966.
"Teletype." *TV Guide*, February 10, 1968.
"Teletype." *TV Guide*, February 25, 1967.
"Teletype." *TV Guide*, July 5, 1969.
"Teletype." *TV Guide*, March 3, 1968.
"The Tiger" review. *Variety*, January 7, 1966.
Tusher, William. "First After the Wedding Interview with Robert Culp." *Motion Picture Magazine*, March 1968.
TV ratings. *Variety*, September 17, 1965.
TV ratings. *Variety*, September 27, 1965.
USC Cinema-Television Library, Mort Fine Collection. Various correspondence, interoffice memos, script notes, etc.
"The War Lord" review. *Variety*, February 3, 1967.
Whitburn, Joel. *Top Pop Singles, 1955–2002*. Menomonee Falls, WI: Record Research, 2003.
"Who Watches Who." *TV Guide*, July 27, 1968.
"A Woman's Love Is Not Enough." *Photoscreen*, December 1966.
Zagor, Michael. Interview with Cushman, 2004.

Index

Abbott, John 104
Abbott and Costello 3
ABC (American Broadcasting Company) 19, 22, 37, 57, 110, 209, 229, 230, 257, 278, 292, 375–377, 381, 388, 394, 396
ABC Stage 67 162, 170, 173, 178, 180, 199, 201, 204–206, 209, 212, 217, 221, 229, 266
Academy Awards (aka Oscar) 60, 70, 167, 180, 226, 249, 261, 304, 331, 342, 350, 408
Academy of Television Arts and Sciences 317
Acapulco, as filming location 110, 115, 129, 139, 335–337, 350, 352, 353
ACE Awards (American Cinema Editors) 70
Acker, Susan 393
Across 110th Street 389, 390
Actors' Studio 69, 319
Adam-12 104, 323, 348
Adams, Don 261, 361, 377
The Addams Family 84, 257, 374, 375
Ad-libs 34, 49, 50, 53, 56, 59, 66, 72, 88, 91, 95, 97, 98, 115, 120, 123, 124, 126, 133, 136, 138, 141, 166, 167, 170, 173, 182, 183, 185, 186, 196, 201, 204, 211, 221, 229, 236, 246, 251, 257, 260, 286, 289, 291, 299, 302, 306, 307, 324, 327, 340, 348, 351, 352, 362–364, 407, 410, 412
Adventures in Paradise 53, 64, 94
The Adventures of Huckleberry Finn 94, 124
The Adventures of Johnny Fletcher 22
The Adventures of Rin Tin Tin 223
The Adventures of Superman 167
"Affair in T'Sien Cha" episode, *I Spy* 24, 31–34, 39, 49–50, 62, 182, 364
An Affair of the Skin 120
Aged-Old Friends 249
Ahn, Phillip 52, 57, 325
Al Capone 216
Albert, Eddie 383

Alexander, Paris 294
Alfred Hitchcock Presents 15, 23, 139, 197, 300
Ali, Muhammed (aka Cassius Clay) 55
All in a Night's Work 260
All in the Family 91, 139, 141, 249, 252, 377
All Quiet on the Western Front 103
All the Way Home 304
Allen, Irwin 135, 237, 392
Allen, P.S. 104, 105
Allen, Woody 60, 352, 384
Ally McBeal 142
Allyson, June 383
Aloha, Bobby and Rose 390
Alpert, Herb, and the Tijuana Brass 266
Altars of the World 104
"Always Say Goodbye" episode, *I Spy* 79, 98–100, 112, 183, 349
The Ambushers 278
The Amen Corner 261
American Cinematographers Union 157–159
"An American Empress" episode, *I Spy* 313, 319, 323–325
"An American Princess" script 313
Amin, Idi 108
Amory, Cleveland 18, 53, 84, 377
Amos, John 377
Amos Burke, Secret Agent (aka "Burke's Law") 57, 110, 163, 266, 367
Amos 'n Andy 19, 83, 224, 377
Anderson, Al 271
Anderson, Eddie "Rochester" 19
Anderson, Richard 180, 181
Andes, Keith 247, 300, 301
The Andy Griffith Show 17, 18, 34, 46, 51, 53, 58, 100, 163, 174, 180, 208, 210, 219, 223, 257, 260, 353, 367, 376
"Angel on My Shoulder" 300
Angely, Barbara 352
Anton, Susan 393
"Any Place I Hang Myself Is Home" episode, *I Spy* 313, 318–320, 355
The Apartment 167

Apocalypse Now 219
"Apollo" episode, *I Spy* 313, 327, 331–334
Apollo Theater, Harlem 219
Archerd, Army 399, 411
Ariza, Paco 287
Arkin, Alan 178
Arnaz, Desi 24, 50, 309, 373
Arnold, Jeanne 93, 94
Arsenic & Old Lace 240
"As I See It" (Bill Cosby special) 383
Ashby, Hal 252
Ashe-Culp, Nancy 11, 13, 74, 76, 77, 114, 117, 148, 149, 190, 225
Ashenden: The British Agent 7
Asher, Bill 16
Ashley, Ted 385
Askin, Leon 174
Assignment: Vienna 132
The Association 359
Aster, Fred 124
Athens, Greece, as filming location 280, 297, 300
Australia, as filming location 365, 366, 368
The Autobiography of Miss Jane Pitman 172
The Avengers 110, 151, 182, 294
Ayres, Lou 101, 103, 104

Babylon 5 165
Bacall, Lauren 22
The Bachelor and the Bobby Soxer 100
Bachelor Father 343, 353
Back Stairs at the White House 328
"Back to Crawford" episode, *Trackdown* 13, 14, 231
Backus, Jim 341, 342, 362, 363
A Bad Day at Black Rock 325
"Badge of Honor," pilot film, *Trackdown* 11, 231
Badge 714 374
Badolati, Mario 208, 210
Baines, Barbara 60
Bal, Jeanne 341, 343
"The Bald and Beautiful," episode *Cosby Show* 398
Ball, Lucille 24, 50, 310, 361
Ballinger, Bill 213, 216

429

Banacek 379
Banyon 379
Barefoot in the Park 377
Bang the Drum Slowly 249
Bangkok, Thailand, as filming location 368, 371
Barabbas 207
Baral, Eileen 231
Barbara McNair Show 258
Barret, Earl 98, 100, 124, 343, 344, 366
"The Barter" episode, *I Spy* 77, 104, 105
Bassinger, Kim 394
Batanides, Arthur 208, 210, 292, 304
Batman 70, 100, 120, 132, 163, 258, 283, 287, 375
Baum, Thomas 219
Bay, Don R. 230
Bearcats 379
Beatty, Warren 213, 252
"The Beautiful Children" episode, *I Spy* 293, 294, 297
A Beautiful Mind 180
Behind Closed Doors 9
Belafonte, Harry 380
Bellamy, Earl 219, 220, 223, 266, 283, 288, 290, 293, 300, 301, 303, 304, 315, 320, 323, 324, 329, 331, 334, 336, 337, 340–342, 346, 348–350, 352
Belson, Jerry 71, 72
Ben Casey 15, 54, 58, 60, 96, 129, 137, 142, 174, 181, 245, 249, 261, 309, 364
Ben-Hur 94
Benedict, Richard 135
Benkovsky, Colonel (recurring character) 200, 252–254
Bennett, Tony 164
Benny, Jack 19
Benson 398
Bercovici, Eric 23, 118, 120, 129, 131, 132, 157, 188, 259, 391, 397
Beregi, Oscar 181
Berghof, Herbert 10, 11
Bernstein, Jay
Berry, Gene 231
Bershad, Andrea 16, 17, 74, 116, 378, 390, 412, 414
Bert D'Angelo: Superstar 388
Bertoya, Paul 346
Bessie Loo Talent Agency 57
Best, James 167, 349
"Bet Me a Dollar" episode, *I Spy* 120–122, 183, 203, 349
"Better Never Than Late" script 366
Beulah 19, 219, 377
The Beverly Hillbillies 84
Bewitched 53, 237, 258, 287
"Beyond the Blues" 120
Big Bad Mama II 394
Big Eddie 254, 396

The Big Sky 223
The Big Sleep 261
The Big Valley 64, 290, 292, 294, 297, 333
Bikini Paradise 294
Bill, Tony 211–213
Bill Cosby Is a Very Funny Fellow, Right! 27, 266
The Bill Cosby Show 383, 384, 397
The Bill Dana Show 17
Bishop, Joey 249
Black, Walter 163, 165
"Black Coffee" 68
Black Gunn 261
Black Sunday 197
Blackman, Joan 105
"Blackout" episode, *I Spy* 200, 252–254
The Blacks 108
Bloch, Robert 39, 137, 139
Blue Dragons 64
Blue Hawaii 105, 139
Blyden, Larry 258
Bob & Carol & Ted & Alice 306, 380–382
Bob Hope's Chrysler Theater 120
Bob Newhart Show 347, 349
Bober-Leonard, Frances "Frankie" 16, 24, 113, 281, 312, 412–414
Bogart, Humphrey 22, 132, 261
Bogdanovich, Peter 240
Bold Venture 22, 132, 249, 252
Bonaduce, Joe 366, 367
Bonanza 15, 58, 142, 165, 174, 178, 180, 197, 205, 207, 231, 261, 353, 367
Bond, James 7, 9, 15, 19, 24, 29, 37–39, 44, 47, 49, 55, 99, 106, 110, 182, 184, 192, 271, 278, 298, 323, 328
Bondie, Ula 330
Bonnie & Clyde 170, 342
Boratto, Caterina 203
Borisoff, Norman, 205, 208, 210
Boskin, Jean 287
Bourdon Street Beat 328
Bowen, Roger 323
Bower, Antoinette 124
The Box Tops 359
The Boy in the Plastic Bubble 178
Boyett, William 104
Brando, Marlon 170, 252, 320
Brandt, Carl 320
Brazzou, Anna 294
Breaking Point 392, 393
Breck, Peter 292
Brennan, Walter 330
Bride of Frankenstein 240
"Bridge of Spies" episode, *I Spy* 189, 190, 192–197
Bridge on the River Kwai 162
Broadway Answers Selma 106

Brokaw, Norman 16, 25
Broken Arrow 240, 292
Bronco 122, 252
Brooks, George W. 93, 112, 142, 333
Brotherhood of the Bell 181
Brown, Calvin 45, 51, 75, 78, 79, 136, 155, 161, 281, 283, 371, 378
Brown, Jim 259–261, 381
Browning, Tod 94
Brubaker, Robert 104
Buchan, John 7
Buddy genre 3, 84, 188, 189, 195, 257, 408, 412
Bugliosi, Vincent 323
Bugsy 331
Bulgaria, as location 301
Bull, Richard 142
Bullitt 313
Bullock, Harvey 104, 105
Buono, Victor 119, 120
Burke, Walter 67
Burke's Law (aka "Amos Burke, Secret Agent") 57, 110, 163, 266, 367
Burma, as location 240
Burnett, Carol 292–294
Burr, Raymond 278
Burroughs, Edgar Rice 184
Burton, Norman 323
Burton, Richard 225
Butch Cassidy & the Sundance Kid 3, 188, 350, 376
Butler, Robert 139, 142, 190, 191, 200, 205, 208
"Butter Fingers" script 63
Bye Bye Birdie 199

Caan, James 71
Cabin in the Sky 94
Cagney & Lacey 323
Caine, Michael 139
Cain's Hundred 15
Calhoon, Richard H. 292, 319, 331, 342, 346
Calhoun, Rory 127–129
California, as filming location 168, 325, 334
"Call Monica" script 366, 397
Calley, John 385
Cambridge, Godfrey 105–108
Camelot 227
Campbell, Glen 391
Can-Can 207
Cannell, Stephen J. 394
Cannon 137, 355
Canton, Mark 399
Capitol Records 276
Caplan, Saul 353
Capote, Truman 212
Captain Fantasma 41
Captain Midnight 323
Carmel, Roger C. 48, 50, 77, 104, 105, 307–309
"Carmelita Is One of Us"

Index

episode, *I Spy* 334, 336, 343–346, 350
Carmichael, Hoagy 65
The Carol Burnett Show 292, 294, 297, 333, 359
Carr, Vikki 230
Carra, Rafaelia 203
Carroll, Diahann 351, 352, 377
Carroll, Elayne 9
"Carry Me Back to Old T'Sing-Tao" episode, *I Spy* 50–54, 148, 213
Carry On movie series 366
Carson, Johnny 3, 27, 231, 237
Carter, Linda 323
Casablanca, as location 248, 293
"Casanova from Canarsie" episode, *I Spy* 249–252, 255
Cash McCall 165
Casino Royale 7, 278
Cassidy, David 237
Cassidy, Jack 235–237, 390
Cassidy, Shaun 237
Cassidy, Ted 328
The Castaway Cowboy 391
Catacombs, Guadalajara, Mexico, as filming location 343, 345
CBS (Columbia Broadcasting System) 12, 19, 20, 22, 37, 57, 73, 81, 110, 131, 165, 182, 219, 224, 229, 230, 257, 266, 292, 297, 328, 329, 359, 373–377, 384, 395, 396, 403, 406, 408, 411, 415
Censorship 49, 66, 71, 108, 176–178, 180, 198, 212, 230, 239, 257, 338, 348, 352
Cerusico, Enzo 203, 368, 370
Chamberlain, Richard 104
Chambers, John 226, 241
Chandler, Raymond 387
Chaplin, Charles 386
Chapman, Leigh 366, 367
Charade 352
Charlie Chan film series 65, 325, 353
Charlie's Angels 333
Chavez, Jose 349, 350
Checker, Chubby 65
Cheers 60
Cheyenne 122
"Child Out of Time" episode, *I Spy* 228–231
Chimes of Midnight 227
China, as filming location 279, 310, 311, 314, 332, 334
"The Choice" script 366
Choolyck, Leon 73, 112, 226, 242, 281–283, 287, 310–312, 397, 418
Christie, Agatha 255
"Chrysanthemum" episode, *I Spy* 62, 63, 70, 198
CIA (Central Intelligence Agency) 63, 269, 318, 323

Cimarron City 322
Cinderella Liberty 71
Cinemobile 43, 159, 370, 376, 384, 386, 390, 418
Citizen Kane 318
Civil Rights movement 82, 83, 380, 381
Clark, Dane 22, 130, 132, 340
Clash of Night 247
Clavell, Shelby, recurring character 123, 124
Cleave, Van 294
Clement, Homer 114
Cleopatra 60, 174
Clerk, Clive 165
Climax 22, 96, 367
Cloak & Dagger 126
Coburn, James 67, 151, 278, 328, 392, 393
Coit Tower, San Francisco, as filming location 318, 319
Colasanto, Nick 60
A Cold Night's Death 390
Cole, Dennis 379
Cole, Michael 377
Cole, Nat King 81, 82, 83
Colgate Theater 16
Colt .45 322
Columbia-TriStar 416
Columbo 72, 142, 231, 237, 254, 317, 382, 390, 393
Combat! 15, 18, 94, 137, 234, 301
Come September 221
Condon, Richard 7
Coney Island 129
Confidential Agent 205
Connell, Richard 351
Connors, Mike 335
"The Conquest of Maude Murdock" episode, *I Spy* 60, 124–126, 148, 167, 183, 184, 359
Conrad, Michael 53, 179
Constantine, Michael 165, 200
Converse, Frank 364, 365
Conway, Gary 377
Conway, Russ Gabriel "Gabe," recurring character 234, 284, 286, 287, 291, 315–319, 341, 342, 351–353
Cook, Elisha 216
Cool Cos 383
Cooper, Hal 249, 250, 252
"Cops and Robbers" episode, *I Spy* 258–261, 316
Corman, Roger 105, 197
"The Corpus Earthling" episode *Outer Limits* 247
Cos 396, 397
Cosby 415
Cosby, Anna 256
Cosby, Bill 1, 3–5, 25–40, 42–50, 53, 55, 56, 59–61, 64, 66, 67, 69–72, 74–76, 78, 79, 81–85, 87–89, 91–93, 95, 97, 98, 101, 103, 106, 108, 111, 113–115,

118–120, 123, 126, 133, 134, 136, 138–141, 143–155, 158, 161, 163, 166, 168–174, 176, 177, 179, 181–183, 185–189, 194, 196, 197, 201, 202, 204, 209, 211–222, 224–231, 234, 236, 238, 239, 242, 246, 247, 251, 253, 254, 256, 257, 259–268, 272, 273, 275, 278–281, 283, 285, 286, 289, 291, 298, 299, 302–307, 312, 316, 320, 324, 327, 328, 330, 331, 334–337, 339–345, 348, 351–353, 355–359, 361–365, 367–372, 374, 377, 378, 380, 381, 383–390, 393, 394–403, 406–412, 415–418
Cosby, Camille 25, 27, 34, 35, 74, 75, 149, 189, 281, 288, 345, 390
Cosby, Erikka 34, 35, 227
Cosby, William H. 26
The Cosby Mysteries 403, 415
The Cosby Show 163, 261, 397, 398, 402
Cosbyisms 66, 88
Cotton Comes to Harlem 108
"Court of the Lion" episode, *I Spy* 37, 73, 77, 105–109, 121, 150, 241
The Courtship of Eddie's Father 221
The Cowboys 71
Cox, Wally 249–251, 255
C.P.O. Sharkey 257
Crawford, Oliver 307, 309
Crenna, Richard 4
Crete, Greece, as filming location 282
Crimes and Misdemeanors 60
Croccolo, Carlo 197
Crosby, Bing 290
Crosse, Rupert 261, 377
"Crusade to Limbo" episode, *I Spy* 113, 123, 132–135, 348
A Cry for Help 392
Cry for Justice 393
"Cry Me a River" 98
Culp, Candace 412, 415
Culp, Jason 256
Culp, Josh 400
Culp, Rachel 415
Culp, Robert 1, 4, 5, 9–16, 18–20, 22, 25, 27–34, 36–40, 42–47, 49, 50, 53–56, 58–61, 63, 64, 66–70, 72, 74–77, 79–84, 87–89, 91–103, 105–109, 111, 113–118, 120–124, 126, 128, 129, 131–134, 136–138, 140, 141, 143–152, 154, 155, 157, 158, 160, 166, 167, 170–177, 179, 182–191, 193, 194, 196, 197, 198, 202–204, 206–209, 211–216, 218–222, 225–227, 229–234, 236–247, 249, 251, 253, 254, 256, 257, 260–268, 272,

273, 275, 277, 279, 281, 283, 285, 286, 289, 291, 294, 298, 299, 302–307, 309, 312, 313, 316, 320, 324, 325, 327–332, 334–341, 343–345, 348–353, 356–358, 361–365, 367, 368, 370–372, 374, 375, 378–412, 415–418
"A Cup of Kindness" episode, *I Spy* 46, 54, 60–62, 71, 83, 100, 121, 130, 148, 167, 183, 184, 295, 296
Curtis, Tony 23

Daktari 9, 174, 224, 278, 377
Dales, Arthur 58, 60, 346, 349
Dali, Salvador 154
Dallas 393
Dana, Mark 124
Dane, Lawrence 253
Danger Man (aka "Secret Agent") 7, 8, 9, 73, 110, 151, 182, 197, 244, 366
Daniel Boone 122, 200, 231
"Danny Doyle" script 16, 19, 37, 101, 402, 404
The Danny Kaye Show 4, 57, 162, 164, 170, 173, 178, 180, 199, 201, 204, 206, 209, 212, 214, 217, 221, 230, 237, 244, 260, 266
"Danny Was a Million Laughs" episode, *I Spy* 45, 58–60, 126, 137, 349
The Dark Past 231
Darling 242
Davis, Miles 172
Davis, Sammy, Jr. 13, 15, 16, 83, 144, 249, 383
Davis Cup 48
Day, Doris 202
"A Day Called 4 Jaguar" episode, *I Spy* 126–129, 183
The Day the Earth Stood Still 300
"The Day They Gave the Bride Away" script 366
Days of Our Life 165
Dead Men Don't Wear Plaid 208
The Deadly Trackers 390
The Dean Martin Show 165, 260, 266, 359
Dear Phoebe 249
Death Valley Days 129
Dee, Sandra 214
"The Defector" script 334
The Defenders 54, 137
Deighton, Len 7
De Havilland, Olivia 206
Dekker, Albert 355
Delos, Greece, as filming location 282, 300
Del Rio, Dolores 122–124, 364
DeMille, Cecille B. 174
"The Demon with a Glass Hand" episode *Outer Limits* 15
Denning, Richard 317
Dennis, Robert C. 98, 100, 124, 343, 344, 366
Denoff, Sam 359
Denver, Bob 171
Der, Rickey 55, 58
Desilu Playhouse 24, 50
Desilu Studios 16, 18, 24, 25, 34, 44, 46, 49, 50, 51, 58, 105, 112, 116, 156, 158, 191, 219, 228, 234, 238, 242, 256, 307, 310
Desperate Hours 259, 325
Destination Tokyo 261
Detroit 9000 328
De Vega, Joe 139
Devon, Laura 77, 90, 92
Diamonds Are Forever 7, 323
The Dick Powell Theater 15
The Dick Van Dyke Show 17, 25, 46, 53, 72, 139, 142, 163, 174, 208, 252, 257, 355, 359, 366, 376
Dickinson, Angie 383
Die Hard 2 271
"Die Spy," episode, *Get Smart* 357
A Different World 398
Directors Guild of America Award (DGA) 22, 23, 412
The Dirty Dozen 260
The Division 142, 394
Dixon, Ivan 24, 54, 56, 57, 278, 377
Doan, Richard K. 224
Dr. Death: Seeker of Souls 100
Dr. Kildare 94, 103, 104, 172, 213, 261, 317
Dr. No 7, 9, 38
Dr. Quinn, Medicine Woman 402
Dr. Who 244, 294
Don Rickles Show 257, 376
Donat, Peter 350
Donat, Richard 350
Donnelly, William 103
Donner, Richard 331
Donovan's Reef 178
The Doomsday Flight 180
"Double Eagle" script 54
Douglas, Kirk 165, 230
Downy, California, as filming location 332
Dracula 405
Dragnet 12, 15, 18, 70, 132, 167, 219, 231, 303, 323, 374
"Dragon's Teeth" episode 64–67, 71, 89, 130, 139, 331
Drasin, Robert 305
Drucker, Mort 277
Drug Theme 68
Du Brow, Rick 103
Duff, Howard 113, 114, 133, 134, 348

Duggan, Andrew 325, 327, 328
The Dukes of Hazzard 167
Duncan, Troy, recurring character 300
Duryea, Dan 323
Duryea, Peter 323

East Side/West Side 19, 57, 81, 120, 234
Eastwood, Clint 342
The Ed Sullivan Show 27
Ed Wood 60
EDDIE Award (American Cinema Editors) 150, 208
Edge of Night 258
Edwards, Blake 213
Eggar, Samantha 391
Eight Is Enough 178
Eisenhower, Dwight D. 328
Elkins, Hilliard "Hilly" 10, 11, 13–15, 106, 407
Elliot, Ross 350
Ellison, Harlan 15
Emergency! 98
Emmy Awards 3–5, 22, 39, 54, 60, 61, 62, 70, 120, 125, 126, 148, 149, 174, 178, 183, 189, 197, 201, 218–220, 223, 234, 241, 249, 254, 261, 266, 287, 299, 332, 333, 360, 361, 376, 377, 383, 384, 398
"The Enchanted Cottage" 117, 232
The Enemy Below 72
Engelhardt, Ruth 262, 371
England, as location 365–368, 397
"Epitaph for a Spy" episode, *Climax* 22
Esformes, Nate 346
Espionage 9
Evans, Linda 292
Evans, Maurice 280, 281, 284, 286, 287
Evans, Mike 377
Evening in Byzantium 64
Everybody Loves Raymond 415

Falcon Crest 172
Falk, Peter 23, 231
Fame 328
Fame Is the Name of the Game 207
Famous Locked Room 62, 69, 167, 173, 221, 234, 251, 286, 289, 291, 301, 324, 344, 354
Fanny 297
Fantasy Island 234, 352
Fat Albert 384, 415
"Fat Albert and the Cosby Kids" 394
Fat Jones Stables 11, 12
"Father Abraham" episode, *I Spy* 190, 210–213
Faulkner, Mike 65, 139
The FBI 181, 258

Index

Feldon, Barbara 382
Fell, Norman 292
Felony Squad 134, 346
Felton, Norman 15, 20, 29
Fennelly, Vincent 12, 13, 14
Fenton, Mike, *I Spy* series casting director 200, 287, 289, 290, 330, 418
Ferry to Hong Kong 260
"A Few Miles West of Nowhere" episode, *I Spy* 312, 313, 325–328
Fiedler, John 349
Field, Sally 137
Film Score Monthly Silver Age Classics 276
Fine, Bernice 22, 23, 154, 281, 388
Fine, David 279, 388
Fine, Mort 4, 20–25, 27, 28, 31, 33, 34, 39, 40, 46, 48, 49, 51, 54, 60, 62, 64, 69, 72, 88, 94–96, 99, 112, 116, 120–122, 124, 128, 129, 132, 134, 135, 144, 148, 152, 155, 156, 160–162, 171, 178, 182–186, 190, 196, 200, 203, 213, 216, 228, 235–238, 241, 242, 252, 259, 279–281, 294, 296, 297, 299, 300, 307, 312, 313, 317, 319, 321, 329, 336, 338, 340, 341, 346, 347, 351, 361–366, 370, 371, 375, 379, 388, 389, 399, 418
Fisher, Gail 377
Fisher, Steve 39
Fitzgerald, Nancy 322
Five Fingers 9
Flaming Star 237
Fleming, Ian 7, 15, 19, 29, 39
Flint, Shelby 300
The Flip Wilson Show 377
Flipper 216, 305
Flood! 392
Florence, Italy, as filming location 190, 191, 205, 206–209
Florida, as filming location 304
Flower Drum Song 62, 98
The Flying Doctor 317
Flying Down to Rio 124
The Flying Nun 137, 172, 346
Flynn, Joe 18, 19
Foch, Nina 230, 231
Fonda, Henry 71
Fonda, Jane 15
Fong, Benson 325
For Love or Money 165
For Your Eyes Only 7
Forbidden Planet 89
Ford, John 333
Foreign Correspondent 346
Forest, Michael 105
Forever, Darling 50
Fort San Diego, Mexico, as filming location 349
The Fortune Cookie 333
48 Hours 3, 188

Forty Pounds of Trouble 174
Foster, Alan 286, 287
Foster, Gloria 354, 384, 397
The Fountain of Youth 50
Four Star Studios 11
The Fox 71
Fox, Bernard 53
Foxx, Redd 377
Francin, Victor 204, 205
Franciosa, Tony 382, 389
Franco, Francisco 232
"Frank Sinatra Goes USO" script 255
Frankel, Ernest 183, 185, 301, 303, 304, 314, 322, 331, 332, 349, 362, 364–367, 371, 376, 378
Frankenheimer, John 247
Frankenstein 240
Franklin, Aretha 381
Frank's Place 261
FranShel 24
Fraser, Tony 341, 342
Frawley, James 142
Freaks 94
Frederick, Hal 377
Freinberg, Ronald 219
French, Leigh 322
The French Connection 342
Friedhofer, Hugo 100, 122, 200, 255, 371, 418
Friedkin, Anthony 20, 22, 154, 155, 336, 378, 388
Friedkin, David 4, 20–25, 27, 28, 31, 33, 34, 39, 40, 46, 48, 49, 51, 54, 60–62, 64, 69, 72, 86, 88, 89, 91–96, 98–100, 104, 109, 112, 113, 116, 120–122, 124, 128, 129, 132, 134, 135, 148, 152, 154–156, 160–162, 173, 182–186, 190, 200, 213, 216, 228, 230, 231, 235–238, 241, 244, 246, 252, 254, 255, 259, 279, 294, 296–300, 307, 312, 313, 317, 319, 321, 336, 337, 338, 340–342, 346, 347, 351, 361–366, 370, 371, 375, 379, 388, 399, 409, 418
Friedkin, Gregory 22, 25, 152, 154, 155, 256, 362, 378, 388, 409, 417
"Friends & Nabors" 199
Fritch, Bob 219
From a Bird's Eye 376
From Russia with Love 7, 9, 38, 298
Frontier 20, 22
Froug, Bill 389
The Fugitive 4, 18, 54, 129, 141, 143, 174, 181, 230, 292, 318, 335
Fulton, Robert 323
Funeral in Berlin 7
The Funny Side 377

Gabriel's Fire 219
Galindo, Pepito Hector 122

Game of Death 351
Garbo, Greta 103
Gardenia, Vincent 249, 386
Garland, Richard 92
Garner, James 165, 391
Gast, Harold 39, 135, 137
Gazarra, Ben 335
Geer, Will 329–331
Geisha Boy 201
Geller, Bruce, producer, *Mission: Impossible* 362
General Electric Theater 16
Gerber, Bill 399, 400
Get Smart 62, 100, 110, 143, 151, 160, 182, 257, 307, 353, 357, 382
"Get Thee to a Nunnery" episode, *I Spy* 247–249
The Getaway 385
The Ghost and Mrs. Muir 167
Ghost Dad 398, 401
Gibson, Mel 412
Gielgud, John 178
"A Gift to Alexander" episode, *I Spy* 190, 197–200
Gilligan's Island 84, 165, 213, 223, 257, 342, 375
Gillis, Jackson 165, 167, 315, 317
Gilman, Hoby 12
Gleason, Jackie 213
Glover, Danny 412
Go, Man, Go 132
"God Bless the Child" 92
Goff, Ivan, producer, *Mannix* 362
Golden Boy 20
Golden Globe Awards 60, 104, 150, 266
Goldeneye estate 7
Goldengirl 393
Goldfinger 7, 38, 39, 55, 57, 220
"Goldswinger" script 99
Golonka, Arlene 353
Gomer Pyle, U.S.M.C. 17, 58, 78, 84, 139, 174, 178, 199, 210, 257, 376
Gomez, Marie 346
Gone with the Wind 124
Gonzales-Gonzales, Pedro 126
Good Times 139
Goodbye Mr. Chips 350
Goodgold, Ed 262
Gossett, Lou 377
Gould, Elliot 380
Grable, Betty 129
Gracia, Sancho 245
The Graduate 292
Grant, Cary 240, 261, 352, 386
Grant, Hank 59, 60
Grant, Lee 178
The Grapes of Wrath 20
Graves, Terasa 377
Gray, Dick 81
The Great Scout and Cathouse Thursday 392, 393

Greatest American Hero 219, 331, 394
Greece, as filming location 189, 278, 279, 281–283, 285, 293, 297, 298, 300–302, 304, 307, 312
Greek Islands, as filming location 295, 296, 300, 304, 306
Green Acres 214
Green Hornet 49
Greene, Graham 7
Greenstreet, Sidney 65, 67
Gregory, Dick 82
Grey, Virginia 234
Grier, Rosey 377
Gries, Tom 231–235
Griffith, Andy 256
Guadalajara, Mexico, as filming location 336, 338, 343–346, 362, 363
Guanajauto, Mexico, as filming location 336, 340, 343
Guess Who's Coming to Dinner 261, 378
Guhl, Robert 361
Guillaume, Robert 398
Gulf-Western Corporation 310
"The Gunfighter" script 15
Gunga Din 409
Guns of the Magnificent Seven 181
Guns of Will Sonnet 330
Gunsmoke 15, 20, 22, 32, 34, 54, 89, 104, 122, 139, 210, 229, 258, 261, 322, 328, 374, 383
Gwyynne, Fred 328

Hackman, Gene 341–343, 362, 363
Hagen, Earle 16, 17, 29, 34, 38, 46, 47, 58, 63, 91, 100, 119, 120, 197, 202, 234, 238, 275, 276, 297–300, 320–332, 345, 352, 360, 361, 364, 371, 378, 397, 411, 418
Hagen, Uta 10, 11
Hagman, Larry 393, 394
Haight-Ashbury district, San Francisco, as filming location 320
Halop, Florence 355
Hamlet 287
Hampton, Orville 366
Handle with Care 22
The Hanged Man 15
Hannah and Her Sisters 351
Hannie Caulder 383, 396
Hanson Dam, California, as filming location 288
"Happy Birthday, Everybody" episode, *I Spy* 336, 337, 340–343, 354, 363
Happy Days 72, 180
Harbor Master "Spymaster" weather coats 372
The Harder They Fall 216

Hargrove, Marion 163, 165, 203, 247, 248, 284, 288, 304, 313, 366, 389
Harlem Globetrotters 132
Harris, Richard 227, 390
Harris, Stacy 131, 132
Harry's Girls 258
Hart, Stan 277
Hart to Hart 333, 352
Have Gun—Will Travel 167
Hawaii Five-O 135, 137, 213, 219, 231, 258, 317, 325, 379
Hawaiian Eye 89, 122, 252
Hawks, Howard 261
Hayes, Lloyd 377
He & She 237
He Who Gets Slapped 11
Hearts of Darkness 128
Heatherton, Joey 191, 206–210
Hedison, David 9
Hefferman, Dick 296
Hell and High Water 205
Helter Skelter 234, 323
Hepburn, Audrey 174
Herbert Berghof Acting Studio 10
Heston, Charlton 234
Hey, Landlord 108
Hickey, Neil 110
Hickey & Boggs 249, 380, 384–390, 394, 395
The High Chaparral 135, 139, 346
Hill, Marianna 258
Hill, Walter 385
Hill Street Blues 53, 179
Hillaire, Marcel 64
Hitchcock, Alfred 7, 50, 60, 201, 255, 279, 297, 307, 346, 382, 391
Hobson, Dick 250
Hoffman, Charles 39
Hogan's Heroes 53, 57, 105, 143, 174, 200, 224, 258, 278, 377
Holden, William 20, 231
Hollywood Palace 214
Hollywood Squares 251
Home Testing Institute 143, 224, 266
"Home to Judgment" episode, *I Spy* 313, 319, 328–331, 350, 361
Homer 306
Hondo 100, 346
Honeybaby, Honeybaby 120
Hong Kong, as filming location 25, 29, 30, 32–34, 41–46, 48, 51, 54, 58, 60, 64, 67, 71, 74, 81, 84, 97, 100, 125, 227, 242, 250, 271, 281, 415
"The Honorable Assassins" episode, *I Spy* 288–290
Hooks, Robert 278, 377
Hoover Dam, Nevada, as filming location 160, 161

Hope, Bob 3, 148, 170, 221, 288, 290
Horne, John 53
Horne, Lena 83
Hot Rods to Hell 346
Hot Summer Nights 22
House of 1000 Corpses 172
The Hound of the Baskervilles 366
Houston, We've Got a Problem 391
How the Grinch Stole Christmas 180, 240
Howard, Ronnie 179, 180
Hudis, Norman 366
Hudson, Rock 162, 247
Hull, Dianne 390
Humphrey, Hal 82
Humphrey, Hubert 348
Hungry I comedy club 25
Hurricane 290
Huston, John 209
Hyland, Diana 175, 177, 178
Hyndra, Greece, as location 282

"I Am the Greatest" script 55
"I Lost It in Tangiers" script 366
I Love Lucy 50, 373, 375
I Never Sang for My Father 342
I Spy (the motion picture, 2002) 416
I Spy Gold Key Comic 1 271
I Spy Gold Key Comic 2 271
I Spy Gold Key Comic 3: "A Deadly Friend" 272–274
I Spy Gold Key Comic 4: "Duet For Danger" 272
I Spy Gold Key Comic 5: "The Maximum Guerrilla" 274
I Spy Gold Key Comic 6: "Live Bait" 274
I Spy Ideal Toys Board Game 274, 275
I Spy Ideal Toys Card Game 274, 275
I Spy Ideal Toys Gun & Holster Set 274
I Spy: The Motion Picture, unproduced 399
I Spy: The Movie, unproduced 404
I Spy: Music from the Television Series 275
I Spy Novelette 1 269
I Spy Novelette 2: "Masterstroke" 269
I Spy Novelette 3: "Superkill" 269
I Spy Novelette 4: "Wipeout" 270
I Spy Novelette 5: "Countertrap" 270
I Spy Novelette 6: "Doomdate" 270
I Spy Novelette 7: "Death-Twist" 270, 271

"One Thousand Fine" episode, *I Spy* 129–132, 340
Opatashu, David 217, 219
Operation Breadbasket 381
Oppenheimer, Alan 200, 252–254
Orchard, John 50
Oringer, Barry 23, 156, 157, 186–188, 197, 198, 219–221, 252, 254, 290–292, 352, 366, 378
Ornstein, Bill 56
Our Man Flint 151
Our Miss Brooks 139
The Outcasts 377
The Outer Limits 15, 50, 57, 60, 89, 100, 141, 174, 247
Outrage 94, 261, 390
The Owl and the Pussycat 120

Paar, Jack 25, 204
Pace, Judy 377
Pace, Tom 301
Pacific Ocean Park, Santa Monica, as filming location 180
Page, Geraldine 212
Paley, William S. 375
Palm Springs, California, as filming location 157, 159, 172, 173, 175, 281
The Paper Chase 255
Paradise Cove, California, as filming location 22, 107, 108, 213
Paramount Pictures 310, 313, 320, 323, 327, 337, 352, 366, 369
Parker, Cecil 244
Parker, Ed 108
The Partners 261, 377
Passport to Danger 9
"Patrol" episode, *Frontier* 22
Paulson, Albert 70
The Pawnbroker 23, 184, 388, 389
Pay or Die 254
Peabody Award 50
Pearl Harbor 108
Peck, Gregory 23
Peckinpah, Sam 14, 15, 46, 79, 114, 137, 144, 184, 185, 329, 330, 385
The Pelican Brief 406
Peninsula Hotel, Hong Kong 33, 34, 45, 53, 58
Penn, Christopher 72
Penn, Leo 46, 54, 58, 60, 62, 64, 66, 70, 71, 72, 247
Penn, Michael 72
Penn, Sean 72
Pentagon 71, 97, 100, 160, 163, 249
Pentagon Confidential 9
Perkins, Anthony 221
Perry Mason 57, 180, 231, 240, 292, 304
Persky, Bill 359

Persoff, Nehemiah 214, 216, 290
Peter Gunn 47, 290
Peters, Brock 24
Peyton Place 105, 132, 178, 258, 377
Philadelphia, Pennsylvania, as location 258, 262
The Phillip Morris Playhouse on Broadway 9
Phillips, Barney 303
Phillips, Lee 172, 174
"Philotimo" episode, *I Spy* 292, 301–304
Pickett, Bobby "Boris" 240
A Piece of the Action 396
Pine, Les and Tina 288, 290
The Pink Panther 62
"Pinwheel" episode, *I Spy* 337, 352, 353, 355
The Pit and the Pendulum 197
"A Place for the Devil" script 366
Placios, Bergonia 137
Planet of the Apes 242, 287
Playhouse 90 231
"Pluck Went the Strings of My Heart" script 366
Poitier, Sidney 24, 253, 254, 258, 380, 396
Police Academy 210
Police Story 392
Pollard, Michael J. 170, 171, 172
The Ponder Heart 331
The Poseidon Adventure 305, 392
Powell, Dick 11, 12, 15, 78, 185
The Practice 261
Preece, Michael 44, 45, 69, 72, 75, 76, 91, 107, 113, 114, 122, 133, 138, 159, 180, 181, 186–188, 195, 198, 206, 213, 227, 233, 234, 236, 249, 250, 254, 256, 288, 303, 317, 322, 329, 336, 345, 362
Prescription: Murder 231
The President's Analyst 67, 108, 278
Presidio, California, as filming location 313
Presley, Elvis 105, 237
"The Price of Tomatoes" episode, *Dick Powell Presents* 23, 388
The Prisoner 182
Private Hell 36 134
Producers Guild of America Award (PGA; aka Screen Producers Guild) 23, 150
The Protectors 174, 377
The Proud and the Profane 170
Pryor, Richard 25, 255
Psycho 50, 139
P.T. 109 15

A Question of Adultery 98
The Quiet American 7
Quinn, Anthony 207, 389, 390

Race issues in television 3, 4, 19, 20, 24, 38, 40, 55–57, 66, 69, 70, 81, 82, 83, 84, 143, 188, 189, 195, 217, 221, 224, 257, 278, 377, 381, 383
The Raiders 15
A Raisin in the Sun 120
Ralston, Gilbert 64, 67, 86, 89
Randell, Sue 72
Ratings 57, 83, 143, 162, 164, 170, 173, 178, 180, 199, 204, 206, 209, 212, 214, 217, 221, 224, 229, 237, 244, 260, 266, 292, 294, 297, 332, 359
Rawhide 15, 92, 165, 172
Rayboud, Harry 139
Reagan, Ronald 129
The Real McCoys 17, 46
Rear Window 201
Red River 261
"Red Sash of Courage" episode, *I Spy* 307–309
The Red Skelton Show 37
Redmond, Marge 172
Reed, Donna 86
Reed, Oliver 392
Reed, Tracy 377
Reeves, George 340
Reeves, Steve 203
Reiner, Carl 16, 19, 25, 208, 412
Reiner, Rob 25
Reisner, Allen 94, 96, 98, 100, 104, 105
The Reivers 71, 261, 329
Remington Steele 174
Rennie, Michael 298, 300
Rentzel, Lance 210
Return of the Vampire 231
"Return to Glory" episode, *I Spy* 122–124, 138
Revenge 265
Reviews 56, 57, 59, 60, 84, 92, 98, 124, 129, 134, 161, 171, 177, 237, 240, 248, 296, 325
Rey, Alejandro 137
Reynolds, Debbie 162
Rhino! 15
Rhodes, Hari 172, 174, 224, 278, 377
Rhodes Scholar 48
Rhue, Madlyn 86, 88, 89
Rich, John 137–139
Rich, Ron 333
Richard II 287
Richards, Beah 261
Richards, Louise 71, 72
Richards, Paul 340
Richardson, Salli 407
Richmond, Mark 15
Rickles, Don 255–257
Rigg, Diana 382
The Right Hand of the Devil 41
Rio Conchos 260
Riot 261
Rips, Martin 385
River of Gold 379

197, 202, 232, 281, 334–337, 339, 340, 343, 347, 348, 349, 356, 363
Mexico City, as filming location 122, 123, 132, 133, 336, 346, 347
MGM (Metro-Goldwyn-Mayer) 18, 23, 29, 203, 234
Miami Vice 3, 188
Midler, Bette 71
Miles, Vera 49, 50, 391
Military Intelligence (Army and Navy) 19, 20, 63, 269, 313, 320, 397
Miller, Denny 319, 320
Miller, John 271
Mission: Impossible 59, 60, 132, 163, 184, 208, 219, 224, 231, 271, 278, 333, 359, 361, 366, 377
"The Mission Is the Mission" script 366
Mr. and Mrs. North 317
Mr. Lucky 213, 290
Mr. Novak 343
Mr. Peepers 249, 251
Mr. Wonderful 13
Mitchell, Don 278, 377
Mitchell, Gordon 203
Mitchell, Scoey 377
Mittleman, Rick 23, 156, 172, 174, 188, 249, 250, 252, 366, 378
Mod Squad 377
Molin, Bud 50, 58, 70, 109, 142, 150, 208
Moll, Elick 306, 307, 313, 323, 325
Mona McCluskey 320
The Monkees 62, 142, 266, 346, 359
Monkey Hustle 328
Monroe, Marilyn 209, 249
"The Monster Mash" 240
Montaigne, Lawrence 142
Montalban, Ricardo 232, 234
Montgomery, George 127–129
Moonlighting 355
Moonraker 7, 328
Moonstruck 249
Moore, Bob 58, 179
Moriarty, Michael 386
Mork & Mindy 331
Morocco, as filming location 157, 248, 278, 279, 281, 284, 288, 291, 366
Morris, Greg 24, 76, 163, 278, 377
Morrison, Richard 231
Morrow, Vic 18
The Most Dangerous Game 351
The Most Deadly Game 379
Mother, Jugs and Speed 396
The Mothers-in-Laws 309
Motion Picture Magazine 33
Move Over, Darling 202

Moving On 364
Mrs. Columbo 393
Muldaur, Diana 317, 318, 393
Mullen, Barbara 300, 301
The Mummy 240
The Munsters 84, 172, 223, 257, 328, 374, 375
Murder, She Wrote 89, 105, 402
Murders' Row 64
Murphy, Eddie 416
Murphy, Mary 320
Murphy Brown 254
Murray, Don 377
Museum of Television 16
The Music Man 165
My Bodyguard 213
My Favorite Martian 17
My Friend Flicka 219
My Friend Tony (aka "My Pal Tony") 368–372, 375, 376
"My Mother the Spy" episode, *I Spy* 60, 135–137
My Six Loves 162
My Three Sons 94, 165
My World and Welcome to It 252, 294, 376, 384
Mykonos, Greece, as filming location 296, 300
Mystic River 72

Nabors, Jim 199
The Naked City 50, 67, 134, 141, 249, 290
A Name for Evil 391
Name of the Game 382, 392
"The Name of the Game" episode, *I Spy* 334, 337, 350–352
The Nanny and the Professor 231
NBC (National Broadcasting Company) 3, 4, 15, 18–20, 22, 24, 29, 30, 34, 36, 37, 38, 39, 112, 114, 115, 116, 143, 144, 150, 154, 157, 164, 165, 185, 200, 211, 219, 224, 229, 230, 250, 251, 254, 257, 258, 262, 277, 278, 279, 282, 283, 293, 311, 343, 359, 364, 368–377, 379, 382, 383, 391, 392, 395, 398, 402, 403, 415; affiliates 3, 81, 83, 144; scheduling 49, 53, 55, 58, 83, 110, 164, 166, 173, 176, 189, 204, 220, 265, 266, 286, 288, 292, 294, 295, 301, 305, 317, 319, 324, 346, 348, 357; standards and practices 49, 66, 129, 176, 180, 196, 198, 201, 212, 230, 239, 257, 338, 340, 348, 352
Nelson, Harriet 86
"Never My Love" 359
Never So Few 100
The New Bill Cosby Show 395, 397
New Ontani Hotel, Japan 75, 77, 99, 364
Newbern, George 407

Newmar, Julie 70
Newton, Wayne 212
Nicholls, Denise 377
Nichols, Nichelle 224, 278, 377
Nielsen, A.C. 57, 110, 143, 162, 164, 170, 171, 173, 178, 180, 184, 199, 201, 206, 209, 212, 214, 217, 221, 229, 230, 237, 244, 260, 266, 292, 297, 332, 359, 369, 383, 397
Nieto, Jose Pepe 245
Night Court 355
Night Gallery 105
"Night Is Coming" script 366
"Night Train to Madrid" episode, *I Spy* 254–258, 328
Niven, David 278
"No Exchange of Damaged Merchandise" episode, *I Spy* 71, 72, 97, 130, 399
"Nobody Dies on Delos" script 301
Nolan, Jeanette 60, 125, 126, 148
Nolan, Lloyd 351, 352
North by Northwest 60
Novello, Jay 89, 200
"Now You See Her, Now You Don't" episode, *I Spy* 300, 331, 325
The Nurses 137
Nuyen, France 79, 80, 99, 100, 101, 103, 114, 115, 117, 190, 191, 225–227, 232–234, 324, 325, 337, 356, 357, 364, 381, 382, 399
Nyby, Christian 258, 261, 283, 284, 288, 289, 295, 297, 306, 307, 318, 329, 334, 337, 338, 343, 344, 346, 352, 353, 355
N.Y.P.D. 224, 278, 377

Oates, Warren 13
Oberon, Merle 178
Obie Awards 11, 108
O'Brian, Jack 56, 92
Ocean's Eleven 319
O'Conner, Donald 199
O'Connor, Carroll 140, 141
Octopussy 7
The Odd Couple 72, 252, 349
The Odyssey 306
"Oedipus at Colonus" episode, *I Spy* 284–288, 292, 295, 296, 304, 355
The Old Man and the Sea 112
Oliver, Susan 130, 132
"Oliver's Twist" script 313, 321
On Golden Pond 71
On Her Majesty's Secret Service 7
One-Eyed Jacks 100, 170
100 Rifles 261
One Life to Live 297
"One of Our Bombs Is Missing" episode, *I Spy* 191, 219–223, 266

257, 259, 262, 275, 280–283, 286, 287, 288, 294, 296, 298, 299, 304–306, 310–313, 322, 329–332, 335, 345, 346, 351, 353, 355, 356, 362–373, 376, 378, 379, 384, 390, 396, 397, 399, 402, 403, 406, 407, 409–414, 417, 418
Leonard Part 6 398, 400, 401
Lethal Weapon 3, 188
Let's Do It Again 396
"Let's Kill Karlovassi" episode, *I Spy* 295–297, 355
Let's Scare Jessica to Death 254
Lewin, Robert 89, 92, 93, 353–355
Lewis, Bob 210
Lewis, Jerry 201, 244
Lewis, Roger 39
Liberace 230
Lifeboat 297
Lina B. (ocean liner) 282, 283
Linde, Jed 129
Linkletter, Art 415
Linville, Joanne 65, 66
Lipton, Peggy 377
"Lisa" episode, *I Spy* 165–168, 292, 317, 349
"Little Boy Lost" episode, *I Spy* 179–181, 189
"Little Ole Man" 359
Littlefield, Warren 402, 403
Live and Let Die 7
Location production/travel 18, 19, 31–34, 41–46, 64, 73, 74, 75, 76, 77, 107, 110–116, 157–159, 189–191, 206, 225–227, 242, 279, 280–283, 286, 287, 310–314, 334–336, 345, 346, 363
London, Julie 97, 98, 123
The Lone Ranger 223
Long, Richard 292
Long Hot Summer 297
Loo, Richard 57, 77
Look, We've Come Through 254
Lord, Jack 180, 234
Loren, Sophia 23
The Loretta Young Show 50
"Lori" episode, *I Spy* 160–163, 184
Los Angeles, California, as filming location 157, 288, 313, 331, 332
"The Loser" episode, *I Spy* 37, 40, 67, 68, 69, 70, 71, 148, 150, 160, 167, 169, 184, 399
Lost in Space 64, 84, 131, 135, 139, 167, 172, 213, 251, 328
"The Lotus Eater" episode, *I Spy* 301, 306, 307, 313, 349, 355
Love & Marriage 343
Love Boat 297
Love on a Rooftop 252
Love with the Proper Stranger 208

Lucas, John Meredyth 39
"Lucy in London" 165
The Lucy-Desi Comedy Hour 134
Ludwig, Jerry 23, 132, 156, 157, 186–188, 258–256, 300, 325, 326, 327, 350, 351, 366, 376, 378, 391, 392, 397, 416
Lugosi, Bella 60
Lupino, Ida 134

Mabry, Moss 382
Macauley, Charles 231
Macbeth 60, 287
MacGyver 174, 252
MacLachlan, Janet 298, 300
MacLaine, Shirley 167, 376
MacLean, Sam-Than, recurring character 79, 100, 101, 231–233, 399
MAD Magazine satire 268, 276, 277
Madrid, Spain, as location 228, 232, 235, 237, 254
"The Magic Mirror" episode, *I Spy* 103, 226, 231–234, 236, 287, 323, 399, 404
Magnum P.I. 72
Mahooney, John 296
Main, Laurie 200
"Mainly on the Plains" episode, *I Spy* 237–240, 262
Majors, Lee 292
Make Room for Daddy (aka "The Danny Thomas Show") 16, 17, 355
Make Room for Granddaddy 377
The Making of Star Trek 262
Mako 70, 72, 108, 399
Malibu, California, as filming location 179
The Maltese Falcon 65, 216
Maltin, Leonard 386, 390, 400
Man and Boy 354, 384, 394
Man Called X 9
The Man from U.N.C.L.E. (aka "Solo") 4, 15, 20, 29, 31, 37, 73, 84, 110, 132, 135, 137, 143, 151, 167, 182, 195, 197, 202, 205, 237, 246, 254, 258, 305, 307
Man of La Mancha 300
The Man Who Knew Too Much 279
The Man Who Loved Cat Dancing 331
The Man with the Golden Gun 7
The Manchurian Candidate 7, 139
Mancini, Henry 47, 63
Mandan, Robert 386
Mann, Larry D. 258
Mannix 60, 105, 181, 333, 335, 377
Mantee, Paul 323

The Many Loves of Dobie Gillis 171
The Marcuseo 137
Marks, Arthur 325, 328
Marly, Florence 100
Marrakech, Morocco, as filming location 279, 281, 283, 284, 287, 288, 290, 292
"Married Alive" 382
Marsh, Jean 242–244
Marsh, Tiger Joe 57, 62
Marshal Dillon 374
Marshall, Garry 71, 72
Marshall, Joan 22, 252
Marshall, Sarah 181
Martin, Dean 151, 210, 249, 266, 278
Martin, Dewey 222, 223
Martin, Quinn 181, 318
Martin, Steve 172
Marvin, Lee 392
Marx, Groucho 126
Mary Hartman, Mary Hartman 247
Mary Poppins 167
The Mary Tyler Moore Show 72, 252
Mase, Marino 353
*M*A*S*H* 50, 136, 252, 323
The Mask of Fu Manchu 240
Mason, James 162, 392
Mason, Marilyn 94
Mather, Berkely 293, 294, 304, 305
Matheson, Don 377
Matlock 72, 402
The Matrix 354
The Matrix: Reloaded 354
Maugham, W. Somerset 7
Mauro, David 222
Maverick 94, 122, 252
Mayama, Miki 108
Mayberry R.F.D. 17, 179, 353
Mazursky, Paul 382
McCallum, David 4
McCarthy, Joseph 309
McCloud 64, 379
McGoohan, Patrick 8, 73, 182, 197, 255
McHale's Navy 18, 37
McIntire, John 126
McNair, Barbara 255–258
McQueen, Steve 13, 14, 71, 208, 213, 261, 313
"The Medarra Block" episode, *I Spy* 290–292, 297, 304
Medea 354
Medina, Hazel 261
Megna, John 302–304
Merkel, Una 329–331
Merlin, Barbara 247–249
Merlin, Milton 247–249
The Merv Griffin Show 70
Mexico, as filming location 75, 79, 110–116, 118, 120, 121, 124, 126–129, 135, 137, 161, 182,

Index

I Spy: Original Television Soundtrack 276
I Spy Returns 407–412, 418
I Spy: Robert Culp & Bill Cosby TV's Swift and Swinging Spies 265
I Spy Whitman Hardback: "Mission from Moscow" 271, 272
I Started Out as a Child 36, 266
I Vampiri 41
The Ice Follies 174
Ice Station Zebra 261
Idaho, as location 319, 328
In Like Flint 278, 328
In the Heat of the Night 258
In White America 354
Ingram, Rex 93, 94
Inside Out 392, 393, 396
The Interns 377
The Invaders 100, 181, 367
The Investigators 320
The Invisible Man 9
The Ipcress Files 7, 139
Ironside 278, 377, 379
The Islanders 53
It Happened in Athens 294
It Takes a Thief 163, 205, 213, 366
It! The Terror from Beyond Space 137
Italy, as filming location 157, 183, 189, 190, 197, 202, 206, 219, 227, 281, 368
"It's All Done with Mirrors" episode, *I Spy* 112, 139–143, 218, 234, 319, 323
It's Only Money 244
Izu Peninsula, Japan, as location 73

J. Edgar Hoover 328
The Jack Benny Show 19
Jack the Ripper 54
Jackie Gleason Show/The Honeymooners 165, 170, 178, 199, 202, 205, 207, 214, 221, 260, 333
Jackson, Jessie 381
Jacobs, Arthur 242
Jacobs, Ron 30, 31, 67, 70, 109, 157, 158, 378, 397, 412, 418
Janitzio Island, Mexico, as filming location 336, 338
Jansen, David 4, 335
Japan, as filming location 71, 72, 73, 74, 75, 76, 77, 86, 89, 93, 94, 96, 98, 99, 104, 105, 106, 121, 271, 281
The Jeffersons 139
Jens, Salome 245–247
Jensen, Roy 142, 323
The Jerk 208
The Jim Backus Show 342
Jimmy, recurring character 70, 72, 399

The Joey Bishop Show 17
Johnny Belinda 104
Johnny Quest 165
Johnny Stool Pigeon 134
Johnson, Harald 45, 91
Johnson, Lyndon B. 348
Jones, Shirley 236, 237
Jory, Victor 124
Journey into Fear 124
The Joy Luck Club 325
Judd for the Defense 137
Judging Amy 142
Julia 351, 355, 377
Juilliard University 20, 68
Jungle Princess 290

Kadison, Ellis 366, 367
Kandel, Steven 137, 139, 141, 155–157, 175, 187, 188, 192, 195, 210, 254, 256, 313, 320, 321, 323, 336, 366, 367, 378
Karina, Anna 198–200
Karloff, Boris 227, 238–240, 300
Karnow, Stanley 83
Karp, David 39, 51, 53, 54
Kasznar, Kurt 237
Katt, William 394, 395
Kaufman, Dave
Kaye, Danny 3, 4, 148, 230
Keith, Brandon 271
Keller, Joy 367, 379
Kellerman, Sally 135, 136, 137
Kelly's Heroes 141
Kennedy, John F. 15, 122, 204, 249
Kennedy, Robert 249, 381
Kentucky Jones 58
Kenyon, Sandy 252
Kid Galahad 105
Kids Say the Darndest Things 415
Kiel, Richard 328
The Killers 355
Killer's Kiss 134
Killjoy 394
King, Alan 178
King, Reverend Dr. Martin Luther, Jr. 82, 380, 381
King Hedley II 219
The Kiss 103
Kitt, Eartha 67, 68, 70, 148, 160
Kjellin, Alf 190, 192, 195–197, 200, 203, 213, 216, 228, 240, 247, 252, 254
Knots Landing 325
Knotts, Don 256
Koenig, Walter 165
Kojak 355, 379
Kolima, Lee 62, 100
Koller, Ernie 271
Korvin, Charles 178, 179
Kotto, Yaphet 389
Kovacs, Nancy 333
Kreiling, Ernie 84
Kruger, Kurt 72

Krumholz, Chester 179, 181
Kruschen, Jack 167, 290, 292
Kubrick, Stanley 134
Kuluva, Will 252
Kung Fu 325
Kyoto, Japan, as filming location 86, 96

The Lady Vanishes 255, 300, 325
Lake Arrowhead, California, as filming location 313, 315, 317, 327
Lake Mead, California, as filming location 163
Lake Patzcuaro, Mexico, as filming location 336, 338
Lakso, Edward J. 39, 62, 64
Lambert, Paul 231
Lamour, Dorothy 123, 288–290
Lampert, Zohra 254
Lancer 328
Land of the Giants 135, 237, 377
Landau, Martin 59, 60
Laramie 323
Laredo 67, 367
Las Brisas resort, Mexico, as filming location 110, 111, 112, 119, 131, 141, 336, 349
Las Vegas, Nevada, as filming location 143, 157, 159, 160, 161, 163, 173, 281, 291
Lassie 16, 92, 261
Last of the Good Guys 393
The Last Sunset 162
Laugh-In (aka "Rowan & Martin's Laugh In") 249, 357, 377
Laurel, Stan, and Hardy, Oliver 363
Laverne & Shirley 72
Law & Order 142
Lawford, Peter 227, 247–249, 313
"Laya" episode, *I Spy* 297–300, 331, 332, 353, 361
Leader, Tony 210, 213
Lear, Norman 156, 247, 377
Leave It to Beaver 72, 223
LeCarre, John 7, 194
Lee, Gypsy Rose 22
Lee, Peggy 212, 223
LeMat, Paul 390
Lemmon, Jack 144, 167, 333
Leonard, Sheldon 4, 16–20, 22, 24, 25, 28–34, 36–44, 46–48, 50, 54, 58–60, 62, 64, 66, 67, 71, 73, 74, 76, 77, 79–81, 91, 96, 98, 102, 103, 106, 110, 112–118, 124, 129, 137, 139, 143, 147, 150, 151, 154, 156–158, 163, 164, 169, 174, 177, 179, 183–187, 189, 190, 200, 202, 208, 210, 218, 223, 226, 230, 241, 250, 252, 254, 256,

RKO General 375
RKO Studios 24
The Road to Hong Kong 290
The Road to Morocco 288
The Road to Singapore 290
Roberts, Julia 406
Robertson, Cliff 15, 217
Robertson, Dale 320
Robinson, Jackie 83, 135, 378
Robinson, John 12, 14
Robinson Crusoe on Mars 323
Rock, Chris 25
Rockadyne Jet Propulsion facility, California, as filming location 314, 332
Rocky and Bullwinkle 128
Roddenberry, Gene 60, 392
Rodriguez, Percy 377
Rogers, Ginger 124
Roman, Letricia 250
Roman, Ruth 295, 297
Roman Holiday 174
Romancing the Stone 350
Rome, Italy, as filming location 190, 200, 203, 206, 210, 211, 213, 216, 217, 219
"Rome Take Away Three" episode, *I Spy* 190, 213–216, 222, 290
Romero, Cesar 9
Room 222 377
"A Room with a Rack" episode, *I Spy* 72, 244–247, 297, 300
Roots 174
The Rose 71
Rosemary's Baby 287
Rosenberg, Sy 22
"Rotten Town" script 325
Roundtree, Richard 391
Route 66 18, 96, 135, 234
Rowan, Dan 249
Rowan, Mary 249
Roxanne 172
Roy, Ben H. 163
The Roy Rogers Show 261
Run, Buddy, Run 70
Run for Your Life 257, 335, 351, 375
Russell, Nipsy 377
The Russians Are Coming, the Russians Are Coming 16, 172
Rydell, Mark 46, 51, 54, 58, 59, 60, 64, 66, 67, 68, 69, 70, 288, 329, 330, 378, 418

Saboteur 346
Sahara 72
Said, Fouad 41, 42, 43, 46, 59, 113, 114, 157–159, 242, 243, 246, 283, 284, 297, 335, 346, 348, 370, 376, 384–386, 389, 390, 418
The Saint 210, 244, 307, 366
St. Elsewhere 325
St. Jacques, Raymond 172
Salerno, Al 56

Salmi, Albert 93, 94
San Francisco, California, as filming location 288, 313, 316, 318–321, 323, 324
San Pedro, California, as filming location 165
The Sand Pebbles 70
Sands, Diana 119, 120
Sanford, Isabel 377
Sanford & Son 139, 377
"Santa Baby" 70
Santa Barbara 325
Santa Monica, California, as filming location 179
Saperstein, Abe 132
Sarafian, Richard 23, 24, 26, 110, 113, 114, 120–122, 124, 126, 128, 133, 148, 158, 165, 168, 170, 172, 174, 187, 190, 195, 283, 288, 328–331, 348, 378, 390, 418
Saturday Night Live 394
Saunders, Mary Jane 139
Savalas Telly 392
Scandinavia, as filming location 365
The Scarlet Pimpernel 7
Schlosser, Herb 18, 370
Scott, George C. 20
Scott, Pippa 333
Screen Actors Guild 57
Sea Hunt 104, 305
Seal, Judith 200
The Searchers 333
Seconds 247
Secret Agent (aka "Danger Man") 7, 8, 9, 73, 110, 151, 182, 197, 244, 366
See Here, Private Hargrove! 165
See the Man Run 382
Seid, Art 240, 255, 301, 304, 319, 322, 331, 341, 342, 346, 349, 350, 363–367, 371
Selleca, Connie 395
Seller, Peter 63, 396
Seminole Uprising 223
Senensky, Ralph 315, 318
Serato, Massimo 205
Sergeants 3 319
Serling, Rod 180
Seurat, Pilar 52, 53, 79
"The Seventh Captain" episode, *I Spy* 294, 304, 305, 350
The Seventh Samurai 106
77 Sunset Strip 64, 89, 120, 122, 251, 252, 258
Seville, Spain, as location 237, 252
Shadow of a Doubt 391
Shaft 391, 393
Shampoo 213, 252
"Shana" episode, *I Spy* 92, 336, 337, 353–355
Shannon, John 338
Shapiro, Marty 156
"The Shark Affair" episode, *The Man from U.N.C.L.E.* 29, 30

Shatner, William 100
Shaw, Rita 167
Shaw, Run Run 32, 41
"She Sleeps, My Lady Sleeps" script 288, 313, 366
Shear, Barry 389, 390
Sheiner, David 53, 213
Sheldon, Jack 68, 70
"Sheldon's Folly" 3, 29
Sherman, Allan 27
Shigeta, James 98
Ship of Fools 187
Shirley's World 376
Shogun 132
Shore, Dinah 129
A Shot in the Dark 62
The Silencers 151
Silent Force 377
Silva, Henry 319
Silver, Roy 26
Silver Streak 255
"Silver Throat" 359
Silvera, Frank 134, 135
Simon & Simon 174
Sinatra, Frank 207, 249, 255, 319
Sitting Bull 320
The Six Million Dollar Man 181
Sky Riders 392, 393
Slattery's People 4, 129
Slaughter 261
Slaughter's Big Rip-Off 261
Slezak, Erika 297
Slezak, Walter 295–297
Sloan, Everett 10
Smith, Kent 100
Smith, John 322, 323
The Smothers Brothers Comedy Hour 322, 359
"So Coldly Sweet" episode, *I Spy* 175–179, 184, 210
"So Long Patrick Henry" episode, *I Spy* 37, 39, 43, 44, 54–58, 60, 62, 68, 77, 83, 116, 148, 172, 184
Soap 386
Soldier in the Rain 213
Son of Frankenstein 240
"Sophia" episode, *I Spy* 190, 200–203
Sorel, Louise 307, 308
Sorge, recurring character 96–98, 306, 307, 397
Sorvino, Paul 388
The Sound of Music 208
"The Sound of One Hand Clapping" episode, *Ben Casey* 245
Sounds Like 266
South Pacific 100
Southcott, Fleet 34, 136, 159, 352, 418
Soviet Union, as filming location 271, 279, 310–312, 314, 332, 334, 347
Spain, as filming location 117, 189, 225, 226, 228, 231, 232,

237, 242–244, 246, 247, 249, 252, 281
Spain, Fay 139
"Sparrowhawk" episode, *I Spy* 163–165, 200
Spartacus 231
Spectre 392
Spies, Adrian 39
Splendor in the Grass 254
Spock, Dr. Benjamin 343
Spradlin, G.D. 219
"The Spy Business" episode, *I Spy* 334, 336, 338–340, 355
Spy genre 7, 8, 9, 15, 19, 20, 39, 73, 110
The Spy Who Came In from the Cold 7
The Spy Who Loved Me 7, 328
Stang, Joanne 84, 227
Stanwyck, Barbara 292
Star Search 9
Star Trek 54, 60, 64, 67, 72, 89, 96, 105, 108, 124, 132, 137, 139, 142, 163, 165, 171, 181, 213, 219, 224, 231, 234, 247, 252, 258, 262, 278, 300, 304, 307, 308, 317, 318, 323, 325, 333, 343, 349, 359, 369, 375, 377, 392
Star Trek: Deep Space 9 247
Star Trek: The Next Generation 355
Star Trek II: The Wrath of Khan 89, 234
Starsky & Hutch 3, 188, 210, 333, 352
Stedes, Paul 305
Steele, Barbara 193, 195, 197
Steiger, Rod 23
Stevens, Connie 304
Stevens, Warren 89
Stewert, Mel 377
The Sting 213
Stone, Harold J. 294, 303, 305
Stone, Leonard 327, 328
Stoney Burke 234
Storm, Debbi 326
The Story of Gilbert & Sullivan 287
Strader, Paul 155
Strange Homecoming 132, 391
Strange Lovers 41
Streets of San Francisco 165
Stromstedt, Ulla 215
Strong, Michael 258
Studio One 179
"Suitable for Framing" episode, *I Spy* 60, 334, 336, 346–349
Sullivan, Barry 9
Sullivan, Jack T. 224
Sullivan, Sheila 382, 391
Summer and Smoke 331
Summers, Eleanor 304
Sunday in New York 15
Surfside 6 89, 252
Suskind, David 224

Svenson, Bo 392
S.W.A.T. 165
Sweat box 43
"The Swinger" script and episode, *Cain's Hundred* 15, 16
Swingin' Affair 231
Swofford, Ken 328
"The Sword of God" script 284
Syracuse University 185

T & L Productions (Thomas-Leonard) 17, 18, 24, 30, 58
"Tag, You're It" episode, *I Spy* 313, 320–323
Tak, Kwan 62
Take the Money and Run 384
Takei, George 96, 105
Tales of Wells Fargo 139
Tammi Tell Me True 214
Targets 240
Tartikoff, Brandon 398
Tarzan 58, 133
Tarzan the Ape Man 319, 320
Tarzan's Savage Fury 179
"Tatia" episode, *I Spy* 77, 89–93, 112, 184, 196, 298, 354, 355, 405, 406
Taxco, Mexico, as filming location 138
Taylor, Elizabeth 225
Taylor, Rod 15, 379, 390
Telefon 271
Temple of the Moon Pyramids, Mexico, as filming location 113, 133, 348
Temple University 26, 27, 71, 95, 246
Tennis bum 48
Terry and the Pirates 79, 101, 102, 309
The Texan 129
Texas Rangers 12, 230
Thailand, as filming location 365, 368, 371
Than, Joseph 306, 307, 313, 323, 325
"There Was a Little Girl" episode, *I Spy* 137–139
They Call Me Mr. Tibbs 208
The Thin Man 249
The Third Man 240, 300
The 39 Steps 7, 346
"39 Ways to Go" script 210
"This Guy Smith" episode, *I Spy* 312, 313, 315–318, 324
Thomas, Betty 416
Thomas, Danny 16, 17, 18, 24, 50, 164
Thompson, Marshall 9
Thorsten, Erik 71
Three F Productions (aka Triple F Productions) 24, 27, 155, 211, 282, 310, 321, 368, 373
"Three Hours on a Sunday Night" episode, *I Spy* 75, 96–98, 307

3 Nuts in Search of a Bolt 41
The Three Stooges 240
The Three Stooges Academy of Murder and Mayhem 48, 163, 176, 346
Three's Company 292
Thriller 139, 240
Throne, Malachi 163
Thunderball 7, 110, 304, 305
Tick, Tick, Tick 261
Tiger, John 63, 269–271
Tiger Balm Gardens, Hong Kong, as filming location 32, 33, 48, 50
"The Tiger" episode, *I Spy* 37, 76, 79, 80, 100–105, 115, 116, 130, 231, 404
"Tigers of Heaven" episode, *I Spy* 94–96, 121
"Time of the Knife" episode, *I Spy* 67, 86–89, 130, 184, 193, 200
The Time Tunnel 137
Tinker, Tailor, Soldier Spy 7, 194
The Titan: Story of Michelangelo 208
To All My Friends on the Shore 354, 384, 394
To Catch a Thief 352
"To Florence with Love" episode, *I Spy* 191, 205–210, 292
To Have and Have Not 65, 261
To Kill a Mockingbird 304
To Russell, My Brother, Whom I Slept With 357
"To Sir, with Love" 359
Tobey, Ken 234, 284, 286, 287, 291, 303, 317, 319, 337, 342, 351–353, 404
Tobin, Dan 100, 349
Tokyo, Japan as filming location 75, 98
Tom Corbett, Space Cadet 349
"Tonia" episode, *I Spy* 190, 216–219, 298
The Tonight Show, Starring Johnny Carson 3, 25, 27, 237
Tony Awards 120, 219, 254, 261, 297, 331
Top Secret 354, 397
Torme, Regina 350
Tors, Ivan 305
Touch of Evil 23
Towering Inferno 392
Trackdown 12, 13, 14, 18, 75, 103, 132, 147, 167, 221, 231, 294, 353, 383
Travolta, John 178
Treasure of Sierra Madre 115, 330
"Trial by Treehouse" episode, *I Spy* 57, 163, 168, 169–172, 216, 349
Triple F Productions (aka Three

F Productions) 24, 27, 155, 211, 282, 310, 321, 368, 373
"The Trouble with Temple" episode, *I Spy* 235–237, 240
Troup, Bobby 98
Tsu, Irene 62
Tucker 60
Tuley, Jack 132, 135
Turk 182 394
"Turkish Delight" episode, *I Spy* 118–120, 132
"Turnabout for Traitors" episode, *I Spy* 334, 336, 349, 350
TV Guide Close Up Listing 70, 92, 98, 124, 134, 202, 237, 240, 243, 247, 248, 325, 340, 377, 381
TV Guide covers 145, 250, 262, 263, 348, 356, 358
TVQ 143, 224, 266, 359
12 O'Clock High 64, 92, 318
The Twilight Zone 57, 89, 94, 142, 167, 181, 244, 294, 328
Twilight's Last Gleaming 271
Two Mules for Sister Sara 350
Typhoon 290
Tyson, Cicely 20, 54, 57, 168, 172

UCLA (University of California at Los Angeles) 23
Underdog 251
Uggams, Leslie 217–219, 377
Ulysses 230
"Under the Sun" script 390
Under the Yum Yum Tree 62
Unforgiven 342
United Artists 385
U.S. House of Representatives, Committee on Un-American Activities 179, 331
U.S. Steel Hour 106
The Untouchables 15, 24, 54, 137, 181, 246, 252
Upstairs, Downstairs 244
"Uptight, Everything's Alright" 359
Uptown Saturday Night 396

Van Dreelan, John 88, 89
Van Dyke, Dick 199
Van Patton, Dick 178
Vanishing Act 331
Vaughn, Robert 29
"Vendetta" episode, *I Spy* 190, 203–205
Venice, Italy, as location 183, 190, 192–194, 197, 198, 272, 417
Ventura, Vivian 307
Victory at Entebbe 106
Vienna, Austria, as location 411
Vietnam, as location 100, 103
Village Inn, Lake Arrowhead, as location 317
Violence on television 194, 195, 214, 215

Virgin Sacrifice 41
The Virginian 15, 22, 137, 172, 213, 249, 328, 333, 350, 383
"The Voice in the Wind" 300, 332
Voskavek, George 340
Voyage to the Bottom of the Sea 9, 58, 84, 137, 142, 162, 199, 305

Wager, Walter 271
Waggoner, M.J. 313, 320, 321
Wagner, Robert 163
Wagon Train 15, 50, 167, 223, 231, 320
Wallach, Eli 390
Walters, Ethel 219
The Waltons 331
Wanted: Dead or Alive 13, 14
War & Remembrance 197
War of the Worlds 350
"The Warlord" episode, *I Spy* 157, 190, 226, 240–244, 266
Warner Brothers Records 28, 36, 85. 151, 153, 224, 265, 275
Warner Brothers Studios 122, 252, 384, 385, 398–401
Washington, Denzel 406
Washington, D.C., as location 100, 160, 321
"The Waste" episode *Rifleman* 14
Waterhole #3 141
Watermelon Man 106
Wayne, Carol 235–237
Wayne, John 71, 178, 195
Weaver, Dennis 58, 393
Webb, Jack 12, 18, 70, 98, 132, 219, 231, 323, 348
Webb, Richard 323
Webber, Peggy 231
"Weight of the World" episode, *I Spy* 92–94, 352, 353, 355
Welch, Raquel 383, 396
Welles, Orson 50, 60, 70, 124, 227, 318, 350
Wendkos, Paul 86, 89, 93, 96, 100, 110, 113, 118, 124, 126, 129, 144, 160, 161, 163, 175, 179, 181, 288
Werner, Mort 18, 370, 371
West Side Story 139
Western Heritage Award 213
The Westerner 14, 184, 185
What Ever Happened to Baby Jane? 120
Whelan, Ron 67
"Where Is Diablo?" script 64
Where Love Has Gone 208
Where's Poppa 208
The Whirlybirds 234
White Christmas 180, 294
White jeans 91, 97, 166
Whitfield, Stephen 262
Whitmore, James 368
Why Is There Air? 84, 85, 266

Wickes, Mary 355
Wilcoxon, Henry 174
Wild and Wonderful 64
The Wild Bunch 350, 355
The Wild Ones 320
The Wild Wild West 62, 71, 100, 110, 120, 135, 137, 139, 141, 167, 182, 249, 307, 328, 333, 346, 367
Wilde, Oscar 173
Will Penny 234
"Will the Real Good Guys Please Stand Up" episode, *I Spy* 172–174, 252
Williams, Clarence, III 377
Williams, Diahn 258, 328
William Morris Agency 10, 16, 25, 260, 262, 304, 371
Willis, Austin 213
Wilson, Desmond 377
Wilson, Nancy 160, 161, 163
Wilson, Owen 416
Windom, William 384
Woman of the Year 100
Wonder, Stevie 359, 381
Wonderfulness 53, 62, 66, 74, 88, 151, 153, 266, 275
Wood, Ed 348
Wood, Natalie 208, 380
Woods, James 386
World of Giants 9
World of Suzie Wong 79, 100
Wrangell, Basil 94, 142, 220, 252
Writers Guild of America Award (WGA) 23, 294, 366, 370
The Wrong Man 50, 216
Wyatt Earp 132, 350

The X-Files 350

York, Suzanne 392
You Are There! 240
You Bet Your Life 126
You Only Live Twice 7, 278
Young, Gig 392
Young, Otis 377
Young Dr. Malone 178
Young Frankenstein 181
The Young Lawyers 377
The Young Lions 100
The Young Rebels 377
Your Hit Parade 213
Yung, Victor Sen 353

Zacharias, Ellis (rear admiral) 9
Zagor, Michael 23, 126–129, 156, 168, 169, 170, 187, 188, 216, 218, 244, 245, 246, 247, 258, 259, 295, 296, 300, 313, 318, 319, 329, 338, 366, 378
Zane Grey Theatre 11, 78
Zarkas (recurring character) 294, 301–305
Zorro 179